Victorian Poets
After 1850

Dictionary of Literary Biography

Manufactured by Edwards Brothers, Inc.
Ann Arbor, Michigan
Printed in the United States of America

Copyright © 1985
GALE RESEARCH COMPANY

Library of Congress Cataloging in Publication Data
Main entry under title:

Victorian poets after 1850.

(Dictionary of literary biography; v. 35)
"A Bruccoli Clark book."
Includes index.
1. English poetry—19th century—History and criti-
cism. 2. English poetry—19th century—Bio-biblio-
graphy. 3. Poets, English—19th century—Biography
—Dictionaries. I. Fredeman, William E. (William Evan),
1928-   . II. Nadel, Ira Bruce. III. Series.
PR591.V5   1984   821'.8'09   84-21119
ISBN 0-8103-1713-3

Dictionary of Literary Biography • Volume Thirty-five

Victorian Poets
After 1850

Edited by
William E. Fredeman
University of British Columbia
and
Ira B. Nadel
University of British Columbia

A Bruccoli Clark Book
Gale Research Company • Book Tower • Detroit, Michigan 48226

For Luke and Ryan

Contents

Contents

Plan of the Series

. . . Almost the most prodigious asset of a country, and perhaps its most precious possession, is its native literary product—when that product is fine and noble and enduring.

Mark Twain*

The advisory board, the editors, and the publisher of the *Dictionary of Literary Biography* are joined in endorsing Mark Twain's declaration. The literature of a nation provides an inexhaustible resource of permanent worth. It is our expectation that this endeavor will make literature and its creators better understood and more accessible to students and the literate public, while satisfying the standards of teachers and scholars.

To meet these requirements, *literary biography* has been construed in terms of the author's achievement. The most important thing about a writer is his writing. Accordingly, the entries in *DLB* are career biographies, tracing the development of the author's canon and the evolution of his reputation.

The publication plan for *DLB* resulted from two years of preparation. The project was proposed to Bruccoli Clark by Frederick G. Ruffner, president of the Gale Research Company, in November 1975. After specimen entries were prepared and typeset, an advisory board was formed to refine the entry format and develop the series rationale. In meetings held during 1976, the publisher, series editors, and advisory board approved the scheme for a comprehensive biographical dictionary of persons who contributed to North American literature. Editorial work on the first volume began in January 1977, and it was published in 1978.

In order to make *DLB* more than a reference tool and to compile volumes that individually have claim to status as literary history, it was decided to organize volumes by topic or period or genre. Each of these freestanding volumes provides a biographical-bibliographical guide and overview for a particular area of literature. We are convinced that this organization—as opposed to a single alphabet method—constitutes a valuable innovation in the presentation of reference material. The volume plan necessarily requires many decisions for the placement and treatment of authors who might

properly be included in two or three volumes. In some instances a major figure will be included in separate volumes, but with different entries emphasizing the aspect of his career appropriate to each volume. Ernest Hemingway, for example, is represented in *American Writers in Paris, 1920-1939* by an entry focusing on his expatriate apprenticeship; he is also in *American Novelists, 1910-1945* with an entry surveying his entire career. Each volume includes a cumulative index of subject authors. The final *DLB* volume will be a comprehensive index to the entire series.

With volume ten in 1982 it was decided to enlarge the scope of *DLB* beyond the literature of the United States. By the end of 1983 twelve volumes treating British literature had been published, and volumes for Commonwealth and Modern European literature were in progress. The series has been further augmented by the *DLB Yearbooks* (since 1981) which update published entries and add new entries to keep the *DLB* current with contemporary activity. There have also been occasional *DLB Documentary Series* volumes which provide biographical and critical background source materials for figures whose work is judged to have particular interest for students. One of these companion volumes is entirely devoted to Tennessee Williams.

The purpose of *DLB* is not only to provide reliable information in a convenient format but also to place the figures in the larger perspective of literary history and to offer appraisals of their accomplishments by qualified scholars.

We define literature as the *intellectual commerce of a nation*: not merely as belles lettres, but as that ample and complex process by which ideas are generated, shaped, and transmitted. *DLB* entries are not limited to "creative writers" but extend to other figures who in this time and in this way influenced the mind of a people. Thus the series encompasses historians, journalists, publishers, and screenwriters. By this means readers of *DLB* may be aided to perceive literature not as cult scripture in the keeping of cultural high priests, but as at the center of a nation's life.

DLB includes the major writers appropriate to each volume and those standing in the ranks immediately behind them. Scholarly and critical counsel has been sought in deciding which minor figures to include and how full their entries should be.

*From an unpublished section of Mark Twain's autobiography, copyright © by the Mark Twain Company.

Wherever possible, useful references will be made to figures who do not warrant separate entries.

Each *DLB* volume has a volume editor responsible for planning the volume, selecting the figures for inclusion, and assigning the entries. Volume editors are also responsible for preparing, where appropriate, appendices surveying the major periodicals and literary and intellectual movements for their volumes, as well as lists of further readings. Work on the series as a whole is coordinated at the Bruccoli Clark editorial center in Columbia, South Carolina, where the editorial staff is responsible for the accuracy of the published volumes.

One feature that distinguishes *DLB* is the illustration policy—its concern with the iconography of literature. Just as an author is influenced by his surroundings, so is the reader's understanding of the author enhanced by a knowledge of his environment. Therefore *DLB* volumes include not only drawings, paintings, and photographs of authors, often depicting them at various stages in their careers, but also illustrations of their families and places where they lived. Title pages are regularly reproduced in facsimile along with dust jackets for modern authors. The dust jackets are a special fea-

ture of *DLB* because they often document better than anything else the way in which an author's work was launched in its own time. Specimens of the writers' manuscripts are included when feasible.

A supplement to *DLB*—tentatively titled *A Guide, Chronology, and Glossary for American Literature*—will outline the history of literature in North America and trace the influences that shaped it. This volume will provide a framework for the study of American literature by means of chronological tables, literary affiliation charts, glossarial entries, and concise surveys of the major movements. It has been planned to stand on its own as a vade mecum, providing a ready-reference guide to the study of American literature as well as a companion to the *DLB* volumes for American literature.

Samuel Johnson rightly decreed that "The chief glory of every people arises from its authors." The purpose of the *Dictionary of Literary Biography* is to compile literary history in the surest way available to us—by accurate and comprehensive treatment of the lives and work of those who contributed to it.

The *DLB* Advisory Board

Foreword

Victorian Poets After 1850, the sequel to *Victorian Poets Before 1850 (DLB 32)*, contains forty-one entries beginning with William Allingham and ending with Thomas Woolner. Eight of the figures are of major importance and receive extended treatment: Gerard Manley Hopkins, George Meredith, William Morris, Coventry Patmore, Christina Rossetti, Dante Gabriel Rossetti, A. C. Swinburne, and James Thomson (B. V.).

The volume also includes two appendices that deal with topics related to the poetry of the late Victorian era. Appendix I contains five essays by poets and critics of the period on late Victorian aesthetic concerns. In Appendix II readers will find a series of documents that outline the issues and reactions to what generally became known as the Pre-Raphaelite controversy, which arose during the 1870s when the Pre-Raphaelite Brotherhood came under violent attack for threatening the conventions and conservatism of Victorian poetry. This material complements the individual biographical entries found in the volume on such figures as Christina Rossetti, Dante Gabriel Rossetti, A. C. Swinburne, and William Morris.

The rationale for the division of 1850 recognizes the viability of what Carl Dawson terms the Victorian noon, in his book of the same name, as a transition between early and late Victorian poetry. While any date would inevitably be arbitrary, a genuine case can be made for 1850 on several different grounds: the death of the Romantic poet laureate, Wordsworth, and the publication of his *Prelude;* the appointment of Tennyson as the Victorian poet laureate and the publication of his *In Memoriam.* The year 1850 has always been regarded as Tennyson's annus mirabilis, but because it forces immediate comparisons between the two poets and their two major works, it is perhaps of even greater importance to the history of Victorian poetry. The year, however, hardly marks the end or even the beginning of an era—Wordsworth had long been a living anachronism, a fact to which in some ways *The Prelude* is a literary testament; and Tennyson's personal triumphs in 1850 only climaxed the new career he had launched after the "Ten Years' Silence" with the publication of *Poems* in 1842.

The two laureates' works are striking examples of Romantic and Victorian poetic sensibilities. Notwithstanding the obvious similarities in *The Prelude* and *In Memoriam* as poetic autobiographies—Rossetti's term *autopsychologies* might be more apt—the works are inherently different. Not only do they proceed from different world views but their respective personae speak for two generations that have little in common, intellectually or spiritually. *The Prelude* is essentially a personal and highly subjective document, archetypically romantic in its treatment of the "growth of a poet's mind." In some ways equally subjective, anchored as it is in personal grief and loss, *In Memoriam* manages to transcend the personality of the narrator and to generalize the experience of the poet into a universal grief, tempered by hope. The narrational "I" in *The Prelude* is always Wordsworth; in *In Memoriam*, Tennyson said, "I is not always the author speaking of himself, but the voice of the human race speaking through him." In this elementary distinction lies one of the major contrasts between the poetry of the Romantics and the Victorians.

The year 1850 marked not only the appearance of Wordsworth's *The Prelude* and Tennyson's *In Memoriam:* the Pre-Raphaelite Brotherhood began their short-lived periodical the *Germ,* while Dickens started *Household Words;* Leigh Hunt published his *Autobiography;* Rossetti published "The Blessed Damozel"; Sir Robert Peel died and Prince Albert planned the Great Exhibition, which opened in May of the following year. It was unquestionably a time of change, but the innovations in form, departures in theme, and originality of subject matter expressed by Victorian poetry after 1850 marked not so much a break with its antecedents as it did an extension of the form, quality, and imagination that the preceding generation of Victorian poets initiated.

Thus, 1850 does provide a convenient transition between early and late Victorian poetry. The editors have imposed broad guidelines to assist in assigning individual poets to one volume or the other, and these have had the fortunate result of roughly equalizing the contents of the two volumes, both in terms of the number of poets and the major poets of the period, though the three giants—Browning, Tennyson, and Arnold—all appear in the first volume. Obviously, the poetic careers of many poets, including Browning, Tennyson, and Arnold, extend well beyond 1850; but the division into two volumes at 1850 does provide some insight into the scope and the chronological development of Victorian poetry.

—William E. Fredeman
Ira B. Nadel

Acknowledgments

This book was produced by BC Research. Karen L. Rood is senior editor for the *Dictionary of Literary Biography* series. Margaret A. Van Antwerp was the in-house editor.

Art supervisor is Claudia Ericson. Copyediting supervisor is Joycelyn R. Smith. Typesetting supervisor is Laura Ingram. The production staff includes Mary Betts, Rowena Betts, Kimberly Casey, Patricia Coate, Kathleen M. Flanagan, Joyce Fowler, Judith K. Ingle, Vickie Lowers, Judith McCray, and Jane McPherson. Jean W. Ross is permissions editor. Joseph Caldwell, photography editor, did photographic copy work for the volume.

Walter W. Ross did the library research with the assistance of the staff at the Thomas Cooper Library of the University of South Carolina: Lynn Barron, Daniel Boice, Sue Collins, Michael Freeman, Gary Geer, Alexander M. Gilchrist, David L. Haggard, Jens Holley, David Lincove, Marcia Martin, Roger Mortimer, Jean Rhyne, Karen Rissling, Paula Swope, and Ellen Tillet.

Victorian Poets
After 1850

Dictionary of Literary Biography

William Allingham
(19 March 1824-18 November 1889)

Bernard R. Kogan
University of Illinois at Chicago

SELECTED BOOKS: *Poems* (London: Chapman & Hall, 1850; enlarged, Boston: Ticknor & Fields, 1861);

Day and Night Songs (London: Routledge, 1854); revised and enlarged as *The Music-Master, a Love Story. And Two Series of Day and Night Songs* (London & New York: Routledge, 1855); rearranged and enlarged again as *Day and Night Songs* (London: Philip, 1884);

Peace and War (London: Routledge, 1854);

Laurence Bloomfield in Ireland. A Modern Poem (London & Cambridge: Macmillan, 1864); republished with preface added as *Laurence Bloomfield in Ireland; or, The New Landlord* (London: Macmillan, 1869); republished as *Laurence Bloomfield; or, Rich and Poor in Ireland* (London: Reeves & Turner, 1890);

Fifty Modern Poems (London: Bell & Daldy, 1865);

Rambles, as Patricius Walker (London: Longmans, Green, 1873);

Songs, Ballads and Stories (London: Bell, 1877);

Evil May-Day, Etc. (London: Stott, 1882);

Ashby Manor: A Play in Two Acts (London: Stott, 1883);

Blackberries Picked Off Many Bushes (London: Philip, 1884); revised as *Blackberries* (London: Reeves & Turner, 1890);

Irish Songs and Poems (London: Reeves & Turner, 1887);

Rhymes for the Young Folk (London & New York: Cassell, 1887); republished as *Robin Redbreast, and Other Verses* (New York: Macmillan, 1930);

Flower Pieces and Other Poems (London: Reeves & Turner, 1888);

Life and Phantasy (London: Reeves & Turner, 1889);

Thought and Word and Ashby Manor, A Play in Two Acts

William Allingham

(London: Reeves & Turner, 1890);

Varieties in Prose, 3 volumes (London & New York: Longmans, Green, 1893);

William Allingham: A Diary, edited by Helen Allingham and D. Radford (London: Macmillan, 1907);

By the Way: Verses, Fragments, and Notes, edited by Helen Allingham (London & New York: Longmans, Green, 1912).

OTHER: *The Poetical Works of Edgar Allan Poe,* introduction by Allingham (London: Low, 1858);

Nightingale Valley, a collection, including a great number of the choicest lyrics and short poems in the English language, edited by Allingham as Giraldus (London: Bell & Daldy, 1860);

The Ballad Book. A Selection of the Choicest British Ballads, edited with a preface by Allingham (London & Cambridge: Macmillan, 1864);

The Poetical Works of Thomas Campbell, edited by the Rev. W. A. Hill, introduction by Allingham (London: G. Bell & Sons, 1875).

William Allingham is best known today for a few poems in anthologies, of which "The Maids of Elfin-Mere," "The Fairies," and "The Winding Banks of Erne" are the three most frequently republished. Among students of English literature, however, he is remembered as the author of a significant body of short lyrics, especially those evocative of his native Ireland; a confidant and memorialist of Victorian literary greats—Carlyle, Tennyson, Browning, and D. G. Rossetti, among many others; and a major influence on Yeats and other twentieth-century Irish poets.

Allingham was descended from Protestant Englishmen who had immigrated to Ireland from Hampshire in Elizabethan times. He was born in the town of Ballyshannon, by the river Erne, in county Donegal, on 19 March 1824, the eldest son of William and Elizabeth Crawford Allingham. His formal education ended by the time he was fourteen, and for the next eight years he worked in the Ballyshannon bank, of which his father was manager. On his own after working hours, he spent time reading widely in the classics and in English literature, mastering French and German, and writing poetry. In 1846, he left the bank and entered the national excise service, working for the next twenty-four years as a customs officer in various cities in Ireland and England. He made his first trip to England in 1843 and afterward visited at least once a year until 1863, when he settled there permanently.

Allingham's first literary association was with Leigh Hunt, poet, critic, editor, and friend of Shelley, Keats, and Byron. After an extended correspondence with Hunt, the young poet met him in London in 1847. Through Hunt and, a few years later, Coventry Patmore, Allingham was introduced to Tennyson and other prominent writers and launched on a literary career. As a mark of his admiration for Allingham's first published volume, *Poems* (1850), Tennyson invited him to his home in 1851 and read aloud a few of the works that he had found particularly impressive. The friendship, which on Allingham's part amounted almost to idolatry, grew stronger with time, enduring until Allingham's death, thirty-eight years later.

Poems contains a selection of the poet's favorite themes and forms. Most of the 114 poems are relatively short and either entirely lyric or a fusion of lyric and narrative. Some, such as "The Goblin Child of Ballyshannon" and "The Maidens of the Mere" (the original title of "The Maids of Elfin-Mere"), derive from Irish folkloristic fantasy. Six brief lyrics are identified by a common rubric, "Aeolian Harp." One, "The Fairies" (subtitled "A Nursery Song"), has been republished many times and set to music more than once. In many ways, "The Fairies" represents that phase of Allingham's poetry which has found widest acceptance, and its opening lines—in the poem as revised by Allingham for *Irish Songs and Poems* (1887)—are familiar:

> Up the airy mountain,
>   Down the rushy glen,
> We daren't go a-hunting
>   For fear of little men;
> Wee folk, good folk,
>   Trooping all together;
> Green jacket, red cap,
>   And white owl's feather!

Poems such as "The Crucible" and "In Highgate Cemetery" sound an elegiac note that persists in later volumes. In "Justice for Ireland," a polemic, Allingham speaks out against the traditional view of the Irishman as "blundering or roguish." He urges less provincialism in Ireland, fewer "oddities and rags" and "party-words and flags," and in their place "more of human-nature" and marching "under something greater." He beseeches priests, "both Protestant and Roman," to "anger no man," reminding them that "All love is of celestial birth,/ All hatred, of infernal." He berates "empty agitators" and, anticipating the book-length *Laurence Bloomfield,* he urges Irish landlords to treat their tenants with understanding and respect.

In the longest poem of the book, "The Music-Master," a work that would be republished in extensively revised versions, Allingham tells the sad tale of Claude (whose name was later changed to

Dante Gabriel Rossetti's illustration for "The Maids of Elfin-Mere" in Allingham's The Music-Master, a Love Story. And Two Series of Day and Night Songs *(1855)*

Gerald White), who falls in love with his young pupil, Milly. Forced to leave her for a five-year spell, he returns to find her dead and buried. After learning of Milly's last days and of her love for him, Claude departs for America, bereft, to live out his life in mournful seclusion.

In 1854, Allingham published a volume of *Day and Night Songs,* short, somewhat melancholy lyrics. In later editions, these poems appeared with "The Music-Master" and other previously published works—"Robin Redbreast," "Four Ducks on a Pond," and "The Lover and Birds" are three memorable ones—and in definitive form in the 1888 *Flower Pieces and Other Poems.*

Allingham's longest single poem, the one that he undoubtedly considered his major production,

appeared originally in *Fraser's Magazine* in 1862 and 1863. In its final published form, as *Laurence Bloomfield; or, Rich and Poor in Ireland* (1890), this novel in pentameter couplets fills a 152-page book, with notes, an index, chapter summaries, a preface detailing the history of the poem and its background, and a dedication to the Irish poet Samuel Ferguson, Allingham's distinguished contemporary. Claiming for his poem "truth of detail" and impartiality, the poet relates the story of young Bloomfield, twenty-six, Irish-born and English-bred, who comes into possession of an estate in the town of Lisnamoy, a rural district of Ireland. Landlordism is very much the issue of the book. Bloomfield's fellow owners are unresponsive to the needs of their tenants. With a Carlylian sense of noblesse oblige, Bloomfield feels he must exert all his efforts to bring about better relations between owners and tenants. Pigot, the land-agent, ruthlessly evicts rent-delinquents from their homes and is eventually murdered, but Bloomfield and his wife Lady Jane continue to bestow their benevolence upon the village. Their show of love, Allingham wants us to know, is the saving remedy, the hope that may operate to make of Ireland "a noble place."

Allingham's *Fifty Modern Poems* of 1865 is another collection of short lyric fantasies and narratives. Among these is "Abbey Asaroe," a poem in heptameter couplets describing the mournful ruins of an ancient Cistercian religious house by a picturesque waterfall and recalling its founders. "The Lepracaun, or Fairy Shoemaker" is a children's song. "The Abbot of Innisfallen" is a "Killarney legend" recounting the singular experience of Abbot Cormac, who leaves his abbey for a stroll, and on his return, finds that two hundred years have elapsed. A longer poem is "George Levison; or, The Schoolfellows," a dramatic monologue in blank verse telling the sad story of the speaker's former schoolmate, of whom much was expected but who failed to live up to his promise. This poem was a favorite of Dickens's and appeared originally in his periodical, *Household Words,* in 1857. But the most notable poem in this volume is "The Winding Banks of Erne: or, The Emigrant's Adieu to Ballyshannon" (subtitled "A Local Ballad"). First published in book form in the United States in the 1861 revised and enlarged edition of *Poems,* in its final revision in *Irish Songs and Poems,* with "Ballyshannon" changed to the more authentic "Belashanny," the work is a poignant, if occasionally sentimental, evocation of the expatriate's longing for his homeland. As such, it has become one of the two or three poems most often identified with Allingham during the course

Cover designed by Dante Gabriel Rossetti for the 1884 edition of Allingham's second poetry volume

of his career and to this day. The poem begins:

> Adieu to Belashanny! where I was bred and born;
> Go where I may, I'll think of you, as sure as night and morn.
> The kindly spot, the friendly town, where every one is known,
> And not a face in all the place but partly seems my own;
> There's not a house or window, there's not a field or hill,
> But, east or west, in foreign lands, I'll recollect them still.
> I leave my warm heart with you, tho' my back I'm forced to turn—
> Adieu to Belashanny, and the winding banks of Erne!

In 1870, Allingham retired from the customs service to act as subeditor of *Fraser's Magazine* under the celebrated historian James Anthony Froude. He continued in that capacity until 1874, when he succeeded Froude as editor. On 22 August 1874, he married Helen Paterson, who would eventually distinguish herself as a watercolorist and book illustrator. Twenty-four years younger than the poet, Mrs. Allingham lived until 28 September 1926, having survived her husband by thirty-seven years.

In addition to bearing their three children—Gerald Carlyle (born 8 November 1875), Eva Margaret (born 21 February 1877), and Henry William (born 11 May 1882)—she edited or coedited several posthumously published volumes of his prose and verse, including his *Diary* (1907). In 1879, Allingham resigned his editorship at *Fraser's* and for the remaining decade of his life devoted his energies exclusively to writing.

One of his first volumes published after leaving *Fraser's* was *Evil May-Day, Etc.* (1882), a slim book of one hundred pages containing fifty-three poems. Aside from the title work, which is long and philosophical, most of the poems are short lyrics. "The First English Poet" is a celebration of Caedmon, and "Three Sisters" is the original version of a brief elegy commemorating the Brontës. "News from Pannonia" is a dramatic interlude set in Rome in 180 A.D. involving two citizens who discuss the death of Marcus Aurelius. "No Funeral Gloom," a brief elegiac stanza, seems to be Allingham's most personal lyric statement. According to Helen Allingham's account in an editorial note to the *Diary*, the last line of this poem was among the dying poet's final words to her:

> No funeral gloom, my dears, when I am gone,
> Corpse-gazing, tears, black raiment, graveyard grimness;
> Think of me as withdrawn into the dimness,
> Yours still, you mine; remember all the best
> Of our past moments, and forget the rest;
>   And so, to where I wait, come gently on.

The title poem, more than seven hundred lines of blank verse cast into three parts, is a working out of religious doubt. The speaker first poses the dreadful possibility that there is no God. But his doubt is resolved by an essentially deistic response: God exists in nature, and one must avoid putting one's trust in words, science, or terrestrial wisdom.

Blackberries Picked Off Many Bushes, published in 1884, contains the least characteristic of Allingham's poems. Many of them are short, epigrammatic, and untitled snippets. Many reflect homely wisdom on religion, marriage, true love, science, politics, British imperialism, critics and criticism, writers and writing. A deistic note is sounded again, censuring both Darwinian scientific skepticism and traditional ecclesiastical orthodoxy. Though Allingham can write that "Man's only true delight/Flows from the infinite," he can also chide the church: "Clergy to guide poor us are given;/We

Helen Paterson Allingham's portrait of her husband, painted two years after their marriage in 1874 (National Portrait Gallery)

shall have need of none in Heaven./A life relieved from clergymen—/O yes, we shall be happy then!" While he attacks earthbound science—"The eyes of Modern Science do not grow/In the head, but hind-parts, and still gaze below"—he also gives the back of his hand to "primitive Christians": "'An infidel!' you shout. I have, 'tis true,/But very little faith, sweet Sir, in you." To England, growing in imperial might, he throws out admonitory advice: "England! leave Asia, Africa, alone,/And mind this little country of thine own." And for his Irish countrymen he expresses a bemused sympathy: "An Englishman has a country/A Scotchman has two;/An Irishman has none at all,/And doesn't know what to do."

The *Irish Songs and Poems* volume of 1887 consists primarily of Allingham's final revisions of previously published poems, with musical settings for nine of them. Allingham's note to "The Girl's Lamentation" recalls that he first heard this song sung by a peasant boy in Ballyshannon and later recast it, a practice which he had pursued with several of his Irish poems based on local or national legends. (In 1864 Allingham had been awarded a Civil List pension of sixty pounds, increased to one

hundred pounds in 1887, for thus contributing to the perpetuation of Irish folk culture.) In "The Girl's Lamentation" the tale is of a maiden who is betrayed by her lover, bears his child, and is subsequently abandoned and disgraced. "Kate O'Belashanny," a bittersweet tribute to a proud and beautiful girl, is one of the poems with a musical setting.

The frontispiece to *Flower Pieces and Other Poems* (1888) is an 1855 woodcut by D. G. Rossetti illustrating "The Maids of Elfin-Mere." The book is dedicated to Rossetti, "whose early friendship brightened many days of my life, and whom I never can forget." Rossetti and Allingham were close friends during the flush years of the Pre-Raphaelite Brotherhood. P. R. Brethren Rossetti, Thomas Woolner, and Edward Millais saw in Allingham's Irish songs and legends the kind of poetry that the Brotherhood cherished. Though he was never a member of the P. R. B., he filled the role of sometime Irish auxiliary. *Flower Pieces and Other Poems* contains mostly revisions of earlier poems. "The Wondrous Well" is a curiously enigmatic poem concerning four pilgrims who die searching vainly for a miraculous well, while "Shepherds who by the mountain dwell,/Dip their pitchers in that Well." "The Faithless Knight" tells of an abandoned girl and her inconstant lover. "Squire Curtis" is a ballad of the ghost of a murdered wife haunting her husband-murderer and causing him to confess his crime. "The Dirty Old Man," published originally in Dickens's *Household Words* and another favorite of his, is a balladlike rendering of the true story of Nathaniel Bentley, known inelegantly as Dirty Dick, and of his hardware shop, called The Dirty Warehouse. Conceivably, as Allingham remarks in a note, the eccentric Bentley might have given Dickens the idea for Miss Havisham in *Great Expectations*.

Life and Phantasy (1889) includes definitive revisions of "George Levison" and "Three Sisters," among other reworkings of poems. Two short lyrics, one dealing with Goethe and the other with Wordsworth, appear in a section labeled "Places." In this section, too, is "Stratford-on-Avon," a dialogue between two contemporaries of Shakespeare; their Warwickshire dialect, Allingham tells us in a note, was authenticated by no less an expert than George Eliot. A group of poems under the heading of "Natural Miracle" tells of life's disappointments and bittersweet pleasures. The poems in "Shadowings" reflect doubts and misgivings about life in general.

Beginning in 1887 with *Irish Songs and Poems*, Reeves and Turner published a six-volume edition of Allingham's works. The last of these volumes, containing *Thought and Word and Ashby Manor, A Play in Two Acts,* was published posthumously in 1890. *Ashby Manor* (first published in 1883) has to do with the conflict between Cavaliers and Roundheads in the middle of the seventeenth century. Despite a few excellent moments, it is an unimpressive work; it is no surprise that it was never produced. The poems in the volume are somber and in the grim philosophical mode. Under the heading of "Graves and Urns," the poet repeats "No Funeral Gloom," "In Highgate Cemetery," "Urn Burial," and "The Funeral." In anticipation of his cremation he includes "A Poet's Epitaph": "Body to purifying flame,/Soul to the Great Deep whence it came,/Leaving a song on earth below,/An urn of ashes white as snow." Allingham died in London on 18 November 1889. Estranged from his native Donegal for a quarter of a century, the exile returned at the last to be buried in the Ballyshannon churchyard.

In its obituary notice of 21 November the *London Times* identified Allingham as "an agreeable poet." Such uncontested faint praise seems to have become the poet's posthumous lot. "Agreeable" enough he was, in person (subdued and somewhat self-effacing) and in his writings, but any more significant estimate of his life and work is a matter of real dispute. The principal matters at issue are his poetic accomplishment and his authenticity as an Irishman. As for the first, the critical consensus has been that Allingham did not wish to, or could not, fulfill the promise of a considerable lyrical gift. Even Yeats, one of his greatest admirers, faults him for spending so much time on incessant revision of works, for lacking the discipline to vault into the sphere of the major poets. Says Yeats: "He was the poet of little things and little moments. . . . The charm of his work is everywhere the charm of stray moments and detached scenes that have moved him. . . . Exquisite in short lyrics, this method of his was quite inadequate to keep the interest alive through a long poem. *Laurence Bloomfield,* for all its stray felicities, is dull, and 'The Music-Master' and 'The Lady of the Sea' are tame and uninventive. He saw neither the great unities of God or of man, of his own spiritual life, or of the life of the nation about him. . . ."

One can hardly disagree with Yeats's judgment. The case of *Laurence Bloomfield* is especially ironic. Allingham was proud of Turgenev's praise of the poem—"I never understood Ireland before," the Russian is reported to have said after reading it. But though others, including George Eliot, praised it too, *Laurence Bloomfield* failed to win

popularity in the poet's lifetime and is now almost completely neglected, and understandably so. Also, as Yeats suggests in connection with "Evil May-Day," though Allingham as a philosopher is mildly attractive (he abhors cant, he stands out against ostentation and hypocrisy in religion, he is intellectually honest and clear-headed), he is ultimately unimpressive in his verse.

The second point of dispute has to do with Allingham's claim to being an Irish poet. Though born and raised in Ireland, he was not of ancient Celtic stock, was neither Catholic nor conservative in politics, and did spend the last twenty-five years of his life in England. To many Irishmen of his day and afterward, therefore, he was, to a degree, a deserter, just as he proved to be an exotic to his British friends. In 1970, in *The Concise Cambridge History of English Literature,* Allingham is identified as "not really an Irish poet. His literary affinities were with the English Pre-Raphaelites, and he had no marked feeling for Irish thought and speech." Actually, both before and after his self-exile, he retained a keen interest in his Irish heritage and in the plight of Ireland centering about the land question; and he conducted elaborate researches into ancient Irish balladry.

But when all is finally said, Allingham deserves to be read as the writer that he elected to be, not as the one that he might have been. His fragile lyric achievement survived him and may yet retain for him a minute but secure place in English literature. Yeats was ever fond of a brief verse in which Allingham offers his poetic apologia. One may observe that for all his insufficiencies, he lived up to this credo as he conceived of it:

A wild west Coast, a little Town,
Where little Folk go up and down,
Tides flow, and winds blow:
Night and Tempest and the Sea,
Human Will and Human Fate:
What is little, what is great?
Howsoe'er the answer be,
Let me sing of what I know.

References:

Alfred Perceval Graves, *Irish Literary and Musical Studies* (London: Mathews, 1913; republished, Freeport, N.Y.: Books for Libraries Press, 1967), pp. 70-100;

Lionel Johnson, "William Allingham," in *A Treasury of Irish Poetry in the English Tongue,* edited by Stopford A. Brooke and T. W. Rolleston (New York: Macmillan, 1932), pp. 364-367;

Alan Warner, *William Allingham* (Lewisburg, Pa.: Bucknell University Press, 1975);

Warner, *William Allingham: An Introduction* (Dublin: Dolmen Press, 1971);

William Butler Yeats, "William Allingham," in *The Poets and the Poetry of the Nineteenth Century,* volume 5, edited by Alfred H. Miles (London: Routledge, 1905), pp. 241-244.

Edwin Arnold
(10 June 1832-24 March 1904)

Bernard R. Kogan
University of Illinois at Chicago

SELECTED BOOKS: *The Feast of Belshazzar: A Prize Poem* (Oxford: Macpherson, 1852; New York, 1868);

Poems, Narrative and Lyrical (Oxford: Macpherson, 1853);

Griselda, a Tragedy, and Other Poems (London: Bogue, 1856);

The Wreck of the Northern Belle: A Poem (Hastings: Bacon, 1857);

Education in India (London: Bell & Daldy, 1860);

The Marquis of Dalhousie's Administration of British India, 2 volumes (London: Saunders, Otley, 1862-1865);

The Poets of Greece (London & New York: Cassell, Petter & Galpin, 1869);

A Simple Transliteral Grammar of the Turkish Language with Dialogues and Vocabulary (London: Trübner, 1877);

The Light of Asia; or, the Great Renunciation—Mahâbhinishkramana; Being the Life and Teaching of Gautama, Prince of India and Founder of Buddhism (as Told in Verse by an Indian Buddhist) (London: Trübner, 1879; Boston: Roberts Brothers, 1880);

Poems (Boston: Roberts Brothers, 1880);

Indian Poetry (London: Trübner, 1881; New York: Dutton, 1881);

Pearls of the Faith, or Islam's Rosary; Being the Ninety-Nine Beautiful Names of Allah (Asmâ-el-husmâ) With Comments in Verse from Various Oriental Sources as Made by an Indian Mussulman (London: Trübner, 1883; Boston: Roberts Brothers, 1883);

The Secret of Death, With Some Collected Poems (London: Trübner, 1885; Boston: Roberts, 1885);

Edwin Arnold Birthday Book, Compiled From the Works of Edwin Arnold, With New and Additional Poems Written Expressly Therefor, edited by Katherine

Edwin Arnold

Lilian Arnold and Constance Arnold (Boston: D. Lothrop, 1885);

India Revisited (London: Trübner, 1886; Boston: Roberts Brothers, 1886);

Death—and Afterwards (London: Trübner, 1887);

Lotus and Jewel, Containing "In an Indian Temple," "A

Casket of Gems," with Other Poems (London: Trübner, 1887);

Poems, National and Non-Oriental, With Some New Pieces (London: Trübner, 1888);

With Sa'di in the Garden, or the Book of Love; Being the "Ishk" or Third Chapter of the "Bostân" of the Persian Poet Sa'di—Embodied in a Dialogue Held in the Garden of the Taj Mahal, at Agra (London: Trübner, 1888; Boston: Roberts Brothers, 1888);

In My Lady's Praise; Being Poems, Old and New, Written to the Honour of Fanny, Lady Arnold, and Now Collected for Her Memory (London: Trübner, 1889);

The Light of the World; or, The Great Consummation (London: Longmans, Green, 1891; New York: Funk & Wagnalls, 1891);

Japonica (New York: Scribners, 1891; London: Osgood, McIlvaine, 1892);

Seas and Lands (New York: Longmans, Green, 1891);

Potiphar's Wife and Other Poems (London: Longmans, Green, 1892; New York: Scribners, 1892);

Adzuma; or, The Japanese Wife. A Play in Four Acts (London & New York: Longmans, Green, 1893);

Wandering Words (London & New York: Longmans, Green, 1894);

The Tenth Muse and Other Poems (London: Longmans, Green, 1895);

Victoria, Queen and Empress: The Sixty Years (London & New York: Longmans, Green, 1896);

The Queen's Justice: A True Story of Indian Village Life (London: Burleigh, 1899);

The Voyage of Ithobal: A Poem (London: Murray, 1901; New York: Dillingham, 1901).

Collection: *Sir Edwin Arnold's Poetical Works*, 8 volumes (London: Kegan Paul, Trench, Trübner, 1891-1909).

TRANSLATION: *The Gulistan; Being the Rose-Garden of Shaikh Sa'di. The First Four "Babs," or "Gateways,"* translated in prose and verse by Arnold (New York & London: Harper, 1899).

The reputation of Sir Edwin Arnold is today in almost total eclipse; but in his adult lifetime, during the last five decades of the nineteenth century, he enjoyed great popularity as an influential London journalist and a best-selling poet of the Orient. One of his long narrative poems, "The Light of Asia," achieved astounding commercial success in England and America and, in translation, throughout the world. Little read now, Arnold's books deserve

serious study if only to discover why and how such phenomenally popular literary works failed to survive even a modest test of time.

Edwin Arnold was born on 10 June 1832, in Gravesend, near London, the son of Robert Coles Arnold, a Sussex magistrate. He attended King's School in Rochester, King's College in London, and, as a scholarship student, University College, Oxford. Arnold's career at University College was brilliant. He earned a B.A. degree with honors in 1854 and an M.A. two years later. In 1852 he won the Newdigate Prize in poetry for *The Feast of Belshazzar*; the following year, when he was twenty-one, his first book of verse, *Poems, Narrative and Lyrical*, was published.

Poems, Narrative and Lyrical prefigures the course of Arnold's literary career. The narratives are more numerous and more impressive than the lyrics, and Arnold in time won fame as a writer of narrative verse. Also, the verses draw upon the esoteric, the pleasantly melancholic, the lushly descriptive and decorative, the ancient past, eastern and classical learning and legend—all of which became staples of Arnold's writings.

The volume includes *The Feast of Belshazzar* (first published separately after Arnold won the Newdigate Prize), with a synopsis of Daniel as an epigraph. That Arnold, who eventually became best known as an Orientalist, should begin his career with such a poem is altogether appropriate. In 274 lines of pentameter couplets, he recounts the familiar tale of the handwriting on the wall, Daniel's interpretation of it, and Belshazzar's speedy demise. The bare narrative is expanded principally by decorative detail, as in the following passage describing King Belshazzar's palace:

> By court and terrace, minaret and dome,
> Euphrates, rushing from his mountain home,
> Rested his rage, and curbed his crested pride
> To belt that palace with his bluest tide;
> Broad-fronted bulls with chiselled feathers barred
> In silent vigil keeping watch and ward,
> Giants of granite wrought by cunning hand
> Guard in the gate and frown upon the land.

Biblical themes are worked out in two other poems: "Hagar in the Wilderness" and "The Egyptian Princess." Greek subjects are treated in "Iphigenia," a subdued lyrical portrait, and "Academe." "Alley" suggests the contemporary record of crime and family disturbances as reported in the London newspapers. "The Marriage" is a balladlike story of a rejected suitor who kills both bride and groom at their wedding ceremony. "The Angel's Blossom" is a verse paraphrase of a Hans Christian Andersen tale.

In 1854 Arnold married Katharine Elizabeth Biddulph. After leaving Oxford, he taught for two years as a master at King Edward's School, in Birmingham. In 1856, he accepted the position of principal of the government Deccan College at Poona, in the state of Bombay, India. At the same time, he became a fellow of Bombay University, and for the extent of his six-year stay in India, he studied Sanskrit, Persian, Arabic, and Turkish.

As a consequence of his wife's illness (Katharine Arnold died in 1864) and the death of their young child, Arnold left India in 1861 to pursue a new career in England. He applied for a position with the London *Daily Telegraph* and was accepted. Thereafter, until his semiretirement in 1888, he served as news-, editorial-, and leader-writer, subeditor, and editor of the *Telegraph.*

Arnold won a reputation as a distinguished journalist during the course of his twenty-eight years at the newspaper. Like Trollope and Matthew Arnold, he composed most of his literary works in his spare hours, while pursuing an active and demanding career. In *The Tenth Muse and Other Poems,* (1895), published after Arnold left the *Telegraph,* the title poem exalts the journalistic profession as the province of "Ephemera," the newest of the Muses, "Our Lady of the Lamp,/Whom we, of many a camp,/Serve daily—for her work's sake—and obey;/. . . ./Nor ever once ashamed/So we be named/Press-men; Slaves of the Lamp; Servants of Light."

But his experience in India had made a lasting impression on him. Having mastered some of the principal Eastern languages and absorbed a vast amount of Indian literature, religion, and philosophy, Arnold wrote voluminously on Indian themes and spectacularly on the life and teachings of Buddha. The popular success of *The Light of Asia; or, the Great Renunciation,* first published in 1879, was phenomenal. By the time of Arnold's death, this romantic rendering of the experiences and ideas of Siddârtha Gautama, later to become the Buddha, had gone through sixty editions in England and eighty in the United States. In addition, it had been translated into several foreign languages.

A brief verse preface to *The Light of Asia* represents the work as "The Scripture of the Saviour of the World,/Lord Buddha—Prince Siddârtha styled on earth—/In Earth and Heavens and Hells Incomparable,/All-honoured, Wisest, Best, most Pitiful;/The Teacher of Nirvâna and the Law." In eight "books" of blank verse, Arnold spells out the story of the Prince Siddârtha: his miraculous birth; his youth, sybaritic young manhood, and marriage; his taking on the ascetic life and his assumption of the enlightened state of the Buddha; and his return to the world to teach his lessons. A passage in book two describing Prince Siddârtha's palace, Vishramvan, recalls the luxuriant lines of *The Feast of Belshazzar:*

THE TENTH MUSE

AND OTHER POEMS

BY

SIR EDWIN ARNOLD, M.A., K.C.I.E., C.S.I.
AUTHOR OF
"THE LIGHT OF ASIA," "THE LIGHT OF THE WORLD,"
ETC.

LONDON
LONGMANS, GREEN, AND CO.
AND NEW YORK
1895

All rights reserved

Title page for Arnold's volume published soon after his retirement as editor of the London Daily Telegraph *(courtesy of Thomas Cooper Library, University of South Carolina). The title poem exalts the journalistic profession as the province of the tenth Muse, Ephemera.*

> Midway in those wide palace-grounds there rose
> A verdant hill whose base Rohini bathed,
> Murmuring adown from Himalay's broad feet,
> To bear its tribute into Gunga's waves.
> Southward a growth of tamarind-trees and sâl,
> Thick set with pale sky-coloured ganthi flowers,
> Shut out the world, save if the city's hum
> Came on the wind no harsher than when bees
> Hum out of sight in thickets.

With the publication of *The Light of Asia* Arnold became known as a writer of "Oriental" poems. His later works included many such poems, original verses with an Oriental flavor, as well as translations or translations combined with paraphrases of such classics as the Indian epic poem the *Mahâbhârata* and the works of the thirteenth-century Persian poet Sa'di. *The Light of Asia* and the other Eastern works enjoyed an enthusiastic public response and a favorable reception from some established critics. Oliver Wendell Holmes, for one, wrote of the epic of Buddha: "It is a work of great beauty. It tells a story of intense interest, which never flags for a moment; its descriptions are drawn by the hand of a master with the eye of a poet and the familiarity of an expert with the objects described; its tone is so lofty that there is nothing with which to compare it but the New Testament; it is full of variety, now picturesque, now pathetic, now rising into the noblest realms of thought and aspiration; it finds language penetrating, fluent, elevated, impassioned, musical always, to clothe its varied thoughts and sentiments."

However, a substantial body of criticism was distinctly negative. Several critics, including William Cleaver Wilkinson, attacked the poem on both literary and moral-religious grounds. Few were as harsh as Wilkinson, but his book-length examination, *Edwin Arnold as Poetizer and as Paganizer* (1884), written from an admittedly partisan Christian position, represented the views of many who refused to be won over by the incantatory verses. Wilkinson takes to task both Arnold and his hordes of admirers. "To admire," he writes, "is delightful. To admire wisely is well. But to admire unwisely is not well, however delightful. Those who admire Mr. Edwin Arnold's poetry, admire unwisely." The major fault of *The Light of Asia* in Wilkinson's view is simply that it is bad poetry. "The true way to treat 'The Light of Asia' is to laugh at it. That is, when you treat it on the ground of literary merit alone. On that ground, 'The Light of Asia' is, for the most part, just a broad joke from beginning to end. Regarding it as literature you may simply grin at it, and do so with perfect complacency of conscience." More significant, however, Wilkinson faults the poem for its bad history and theology. Very simply, Arnold misrepresented Buddhism, superimposed upon it the tenets and consolations of Christianity and thus ensnared vast numbers of Christian readers who have been put in danger of being driven away from their ancient faith into the arms of a not altogether wholesome pagan one. Arnold, Wilkinson believed, supplanted the Christian deity with a

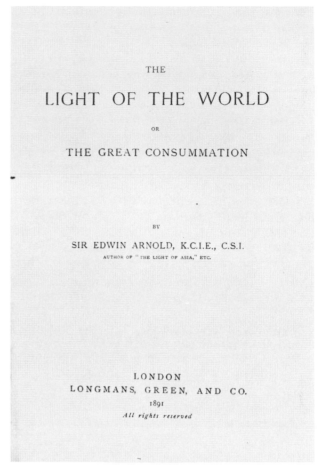

THE

LIGHT OF THE WORLD

OR

THE GREAT CONSUMMATION

BY

SIR EDWIN ARNOLD, K.C.I.E., C.S.I.
AUTHOR OF "THE LIGHT OF ASIA," ETC.

LONDON
LONGMANS, GREEN, AND CO.
1891
All rights reserved

Title page for Arnold's blank-verse Christian "epic" tracing the life of Jesus (courtesy of Thomas Cooper Library, University of South Carolina)

pagan one, whom he represented as "the Lord" who has shown the world the way to Nirvâna and spiritual contentment. *The Light of Asia,* to a Christian reader at least, is a pernicious book.

As if in response to the attacks by Wilkinson and others, Arnold in 1891 published *The Light of the World; or, The Great Consummation,* which presumably brought Jesus of Nazareth and Christianity into a position of parity with Siddârtha Gautama and Buddhism. Arnold's Christian "epic" is a paraphrase of selected portions of the New Testament. After a "Proeme" and the prefatory "At Bethlehem" in pentameter couplets recounting the birth of Jesus, Arnold traces, in blank verse, the course of Jesus' life through to the last of eight "books," "The Great Consummation." The end of the poem, like the conclusion of the Buddha epic, is cast in rhyming lines and printed in all caps. Again following the earlier poem, Arnold presents the account of the "consummation" as it is told to an Indian devotee. It is Mary Magdalen who tells of Jesus' last words on the cross; and it is the Indian who likens Jesus' teaching to Buddha's. Despite his noblest intentions, in *The Light of the World* Arnold failed to mitigate the negative feelings generated by the earlier *Light of Asia,* and the Christian epic achieved only a moderate success.

In response to the reiterated charge that he wrote only Oriental poems, in 1888 Arnold produced his volume of *Poems, National and Non-Oriental.* Few of the eighty-six poems in this collection are impressive. In addition to verses written for particular national occasions—"To H.R.H. The Princess of Wales," "The First Distribution of the Victoria Cross," "On the Death of the Princess Alice"—Arnold included a quiet narrative-lyric, "She and He," that by general agreement has been placed at the top of his poetic achievement precisely because it avoids the gratuitously florid and lush.

Arnold spent the years from his retirement from the *Telegraph* to his death on 24 March 1904 basking in the public acclaim he had achieved, producing new books, sailing on his yacht, traveling widely—to America (a lecture tour in 1891), Japan, and other foreign lands. In 1889 another volume of his non-Oriental poems entitled *In My Lady's Praise* appeared. The principal works assembled here were written in 1870 but included in this collection dedicated to the memory of Lady Arnold, his recently deceased second wife, the former Fannie Maria Adelaide Channing of Boston. Arnold wrote imaginatively of Japan in the four-act drama *Adzuma; or, The Japanese Wife,* published in 1893 (his third wife, whom he married in 1897 and who survived him, was Tama Kura Kawa, of Sendai, Japan), and in the form of travel literature in *Seas and Lands* (1891) and other books.

Though beset by infirmities in his last years—partial paralysis and near blindness, among them—Arnold pursued life with vigor. The honors bestowed upon him were too numerous to be listed after his name on the title pages of the eight-volume set of his poetical works. He was made a Companion of the Star of India (C.S.I.) in 1877, on the occasion of the proclamation of Queen Victoria as Empress of India. In 1888, as Knight Commander of the Order of the Indian Empire (K.C.I.E.), he became Sir Edwin Arnold. He was also an officer of the Order of the White Elephant of Siam, a member of the Third Class of the Imperial Order of the Medjidie, a Fellow of the Royal Asiatic and Royal Geographical Societies, and an honorary member of the Société de Géographie of Marseilles.

In a long obituary essay the *London Times* summed up Arnold's journalistic and literary careers, acknowledging his "astonishing fertility of language, luxuriant wealth of imagery, the faculty of becoming acquainted with men of eminence in every walk of life. . . ." He was a poet with "a subject of his own on which most of his countrymen and countrywomen were sadly ignorant, and of which they were quite willing to learn so much as could be presented to them in an attractive form." Arnold's subject—India and Buddhism as delineated in *The Light of Asia*—"appealed to many at once by its strangeness and its familiarity, presenting, as it did, the moral doctrines its readers had been used to all their lives in a new and unexpected setting. The verse flows easily and is rich and luscious with oriental imagery; the thought never rises into heights where it is hard to follow, and is constantly saved from being too obviously commonplace by the novelty of the scenes and characters that are the vehicle of its expression. . . ." But, the *Times* concluded, "The qualities which won instant fame for the author are not the qualities of which great poetry is made."

However unfavorable such a conclusion may sound, it nevertheless has the ring of truth. Arnold's career does seem to have consisted of a triumph of mere industry and imagination. For all of his vast output, he comes close to being a one-poem poet; and the merits of that one poem, despite its sensational popularity, remain questionable. An attractive man he undoubtedly was—there is ample testimony to his vivacity and good nature, his literary and oratorical fluency and phenomenal memory. But beyond these personal dimensions, there is left only a little worth remembering. The vast body of his journalistic writing is ephemeral almost by definition. *The Light of Asia* remains in print through the good offices of occult theosophical societies, but it is not very widely read. Arnold maintains a small place in the history of English literature by the measure of a short paragraph or a sizeable footnote, a situation that is all the more ironic for his light having once burned so brightly.

References:

Mackenzie Bell, "Sir Edwin Arnold," in *The Poets and the Poetry of the Nineteenth Century,* volume 5, edited by Alfred H. Miles (London: Routledge, 1905), pp. 573-578;

William Cleaver Wilkinson, *Edwin Arnold as Poetizer and as Paganizer* (New York & London: Funk & Wagnalls, 1884).

Alfred Austin
(30 May 1835-2 June 1913)

Norman Page
University of Alberta

SELECTED BOOKS: *Randolph: A Poem in Two Cantos* (London: Saunders & Otley, 1855); revised as *Leszko the Bastard: A Tale of Polish Grief* (London: Chapman & Hall, 1877);

Five Years of It, 2 volumes (London: J. F. Hope, 1858);

The Season: A Satire (London: Hardwicke, 1861; revised, London: Manwaring, 1861; revised again, London: Hotten, 1869);

The Human Tragedy: A Poem (London: Hardwicke, 1862; revised, Edinburgh & London: Blackwood, 1876; revised again, London: Macmillan, 1889);

An Artist's Proof: A Novel, 3 volumes (London: Tinsley, 1864);

Won by a Head: A Novel, 3 volumes (London: Chapman & Hall, 1866);

A Vindication of Lord Byron (London: Chapman & Hall, 1869);

The Poetry of the Period (London: Bentley, 1870);

The Golden Age: A Satire in Verse (London: Chapman & Hall, 1871);

Interludes (Edinburgh & London: Blackwood, 1872);

Madonna's Child (Edinburgh: Blackwood, 1872);

Rome or Death! (London: Blackwood, 1873);

The Tower of Babel: A Poetical Drama (Edinburgh: Blackwood, 1874);

Savonarola: A Tragedy (London: Macmillan, 1881);

Soliloquies in Song (London: Macmillan, 1882);

At the Gate of the Convent and Other Poems (London: Macmillan, 1885);

Prince Lucifer (London: Macmillan, 1887; enlarged, London & New York: Macmillan, 1887);

Love's Widowhood and Other Poems (London: Macmillan, 1889);

Lyrical Poems (London & New York: Macmillan, 1891);

Narrative Poems (London & New York: Macmillan, 1891);

Fortunatus the Pessimist: A Dramatic Poem (London & New York: Macmillan, 1892);

The Garden that I Love (London & New York: Macmillan, 1894);

In Veronica's Garden (London & New York: Macmillan, 1895);

Alfred Austin in 1900, from a miniature by W. T. Scott Barber

England's Darling (New York & London: Macmillan, 1896); republished as *Alfred the Great: England's Darling* (London: Macmillan, 1901);

The Conversion of Winckelmann, and Other Poems (London: Macmillan, 1897);

Victoria: June 20 1837-June 20 1897 (London: Macmillan, 1897);

Lamia's Winter-Quarters (London: Macmillan, 1898);

Songs of England (London: Macmillan, 1898; enlarged, London: Macmillan, 1900);

Spring and Autumn in Ireland (Edinburgh & London: Blackwood, 1900);

Polyphemus (London: Heinemann, 1901);

Victoria the Wise (London: Eyre & Spottiswoode, 1901);

Haunts of Ancient Peace (New York & London: Macmillan, 1902; London: A. & C. Black, 1902);

A Tale of True Love and Other Poems (New York & London: Harper, 1902);

Flodden Field: A Tragedy (New York & London: Harper, 1903; London: Macmillan, 1903);

A Lesson in Harmony (New York: French, 1904);

The Poet's Diary (London: Macmillan, 1904);

The Door of Humility: A Poem (London & New York: Macmillan, 1906);

The Garden that I Love, second series (London: Macmillan, 1907);

Sacred and Profane Love and Other Poems (London: Macmillan, 1908);

The Bridling of Pegasus: Prose Papers on Poetry (London: Macmillan, 1910);

The Autobiography of Alfred Austin, Poet Laureate, 1835-1910, 2 volumes (London: Macmillan, 1911).

OTHER: *An Eighteenth Century Anthology,* edited by Austin (London: Blackie, 1904).

Alfred Austin was a prolific author who produced more than twenty volumes of verse during the period 1854-1908. He was also a novelist, critic, and political journalist. He was an editor of the *National Review* (1883-1895) and succeeded Alfred, Lord Tennyson as poet laureate in 1896.

Born in Leeds of Roman Catholic parents, Joseph and Mary Austin, Austin was educated at Stoneyhurst College and Oscott College, University of London, which awarded him a B.A. in 1853. Austin trained as a lawyer but embarked on a literary career in 1858. He had already published *Randolph: A Poem in Two Cantos* (1855), and in 1858 a novel, *Five Years of It,* appeared. Although his first works were not well received, he continued to publish regularly during the next fifty years. As a political journalist, he was for thirty years (1866-1896) leader-writer for the *London Standard,* specializing in foreign affairs.

Austin's verse, though influenced by Scott and Byron, quickly became a byword for pretentious emptiness. His Byronic satire *The Season* (1861) led Browning to describe Austin in his *Pacchiarotto* (1876) as "Banjo-Byron that twangs the strumstrum there." Austin attempted the narrative, dramatic, and epic forms without any real gift for such large-scale undertakings; and, with a stock of ideas that were merely commonplace, aspired to handle grandiose philosophical themes. Swinburne called him "broken-winded Austin," and a modern critic, B. Ifor Evans, has dismissed his poetry as "a bleak example of ambition without accompanying powers." His novels are weak in narrative power

and overloaded with platitudinous moralizing. As a critic, he attacked the alleged triviality of much contemporary verse, proclaiming the narrative and dramatic forms to be the highest kinds of poetry and Shakespeare and Milton as the masters worthy of imitation by modern poets. Austin's attacks in *The Poetry of the Period* (published in *Temple Bar* in 1869 and in book form in 1870) on such figures as Tennyson, Browning, Whitman, and Swinburne only rendered him ridiculous. His prose work *The Garden that I Love* (first series, 1894; second series, 1907) was very popular for its account in diary form of the English countryside.

It was probably his journalistic services to the Conservative Party rather than his standing as a poet that led to Austin's becoming poet laureate—an appointment that helped bring the laureateship into disrepute. Succeeding Tennyson in that capacity, he has been compared to "a dwarf straddling in the trappings of a giant." The appointment was promptly ridiculed in a *Punch* cartoon, "Alfred the Little" (the title alludes satirically to *England's Darling,* Austin's 1896 play about Alfred the Great), and he continued to be a favorite target of that journal. "Ode," his first effort as

Cartoon from Punch *ridiculing Austin's appointment as poet laureate in 1896*

laureate, was a jingoistic poem on the Jameson Raid that embarrassed the government and was typical of the fervent patriotic vein in his verse. It has been said that "few, if any, eminent Victorians can have aroused among their more intelligent contemporaries such universal ridicule and such intense dislike" as Austin, who "became the butt of every late Victorian wit, in conversation or print." When he died, the *Athenaeum* announced that the laureateship, "virtually vacant since the death of Tennyson, became actually so on Monday by the death . . . of Mr. Alfred Austin"—an epitaph that is brutal but not unfair.

Reference:

Norton B. Crowell, *Alfred Austin, Victorian* (Albuquerque: University of New Mexico Press, 1953).

T. E. Brown
(5 May 1830-29 October 1897)

Richard Tobias
University of Pittsburgh

BOOKS: *Fo'c's'le Yarns, Including Betsy Lee, and Other Poems* (London: Macmillan, 1881);

The Doctor and Other Poems (London: Sonnenschein, Lowrey, 1887);

The Manx Witch and Other Poems (London & New York: Macmillan, 1889);

Old John and Other Poems (London: Macmillan, 1893).

Collection: *The Collected Poems of T. E. Brown,* edited by H. F. Brown, H. G. Dakyns, and W. E. Henley (London & New York: Macmillan, 1900); republished as *Poems of T. E. Brown,* with an introductory memoir by Sir Arthur Quiller-Couch, 2 volumes (Liverpool: University Press, 1952).

Thomas Edward Brown is the national poet of the Isle of Man, an island in the Irish Sea. Like other nineteenth-century writers influenced by Wordsworth, Brown sought to write "in the language really used by men." Eighty percent of Brown's poetry is written in the English dialect spoken by the modern Manx. Brown hoped, according to the dedication of his first collection of Manx narratives in 1881, "To unlock the treasures of the Island heart." In his 1887 dedication to *The Doctor and Other Poems,* he promised to fix Manx life upon the page,

> That so the coming age,
>   Lost in the empire's mass,
> . . . . .here

> May see, as in a glass,
>   What they held dear.

Brown's narrative gift and fine sense of character sustain tales with superlative energy. His poems have the character of nineteenth-century photographs—solid and determined. They also have Brown's antic humor and a clear sense of the tragedy of Romantic Celtism. As Matthew Arnold has it, "For ages and ages the world has been constantly slipping, ever more and more, out of the Celt's grasp. 'They went forth to the war,' Ossian says most truly, *'but they always fell.'* " In Brown's Manx poems an ethnic minority desperately attempts to preserve its native magic in opposition to modern conventionality, conformity, and efficient dullness. In this battle the Manx again fall, but in Brown's poems we glimpse them just before their defeat.

T. E. Brown was born the son of Robert Brown, a priest in the Manx Church, and Dorothy Thomson Brown. In 1825 his father had a book of poems published in London, but all the poems use the English language as approved by Dr. Johnson's dictionary. When Robert Brown sent a copy to Wordsworth, the Lake Poet praised "My Native Land," a poem in which the father lamented, "No minstrel of immortal fame/Has yet among thy sons been found." His own son became that minstrel. T. E. Brown was the fifth of his seven progeny, all left helpless in 1845 when the father died. With no provision to maintain them, Dorothy Brown and

T. E. Brown

the children became wards of the Manx Church. From that church in 1849 T. E. Brown obtained funds to attend Christ Church, Oxford, as a servitor, a role which gave him residence and tuition but made him a menial in the college. When he became a fellow at Oriel in 1854, Brown had to be shown the university as if he were a visitor. During his undergraduate years as servitor, Brown lived quietly at the back of Christ Church, sat in special seats during divine service, ate before the others, and studied so single-mindedly that he graduated in 1853 with a double first.

Brown planned to return to the Isle of Man to become a priest in the Manx Church, but at the university he came into contact with the Oxford Movement, the effort by John Henry Newman and others to instill a more rigorous sacramentalism into the English church. The Manx, heavily influenced by Charles Wesley in the eighteenth century, eyed such newfangled notions suspiciously. In an application letter to a Manx clergyman, Brown argued that his Oxford experience made him highly qualified to meet modern challenges to the church, but the Manx Church never ordained Brown. Bishop Wilberforce made Brown a deacon at Oxford, but

he was not priested until 1885, when he became curate of a worker parish in Bristol.

With his church career blocked, Brown stood for and won the fellowship at Oriel, but he resigned after two years to become vice-principal of King William's College on the Isle of Man. In 1857 he married his cousin Amelia Stowell, with whom he had three daughters and two sons. In 1861, the Crypt School, Gloucester, chose him as headmaster; among his students was the poet W. E. Henley. Brown proved an unsatisfactory head, and so he accepted a role as master on the modern side at Clifton College, near Bristol, a secondary school where he taught until retirement in 1892.

While a student at Oxford Brown wrote verse. He won no prizes at Oxford, and he seems to have abandoned poetry until 1868, the year he produced "Christ Church Servitors in 1852," an essay published in *Macmillan's Magazine* describing the terrible social burden that Oxford imposed on servitors. The Oxford experience confirmed his alienation, but the essay liberated his creative powers. In an 1870 letter John Addington Symonds reports Brown reciting Manx stories, and in 1871 Brown had printed at a newspaper office in Cockermouth (Wordsworth's birthplace in Cumberland) a long narrative poem entitled "Betsy Lee." In 1873, a truncated version appeared in *Macmillan's,* and in 1881, the Macmillan firm published a collection of four of these tales, all of which had previously appeared in private editions: "Betsy Lee," "Christmas Rose," "Captain Tom and Captain Hugh," and "Tommy Big-Eyes." Fortunately a few copies of the private editions survive so that we can know how severely the poems were mangled for the 1881 publication.

In each story, Tom Baynes, a Manx sailor aboard a sailing ship, not only tells the stories but also participates in the action. He is Betsy Lee's disappointed lover in the first poem; in the second he helps Parson Gale to raise Gale's two sons and a girl rescued from a shipwreck. The boys fall desperately in love with the girl. In "Captain Tom and Captain Hugh," Baynes tries to avert tragedy when the children of two brother sea captains fall in love. Baynes swims out to sea to rescue an eloping Manx girl in "Tommy Big-Eyes."

When Macmillan published the trade edition of the first four poems, the editors asked Brown to cut his expletives, reduce his framing device, and tame his physical descriptions. In "Tommy Big-Eyes," the role of a Methodist preacher is drastically reduced. All subsequent printings follow the Mac-

joyed himself as a licensed critic of Manx life and manners. Even through the reporter's notes, a more lively Brown emerges than in the official volume of letters.

The *Memorial Volume* of 1930 has also a "Memoir" signed by Sir Arthur Quiller-Couch. The same memoir is reprinted in the 1952 Liverpool University Press edition of Brown's *Poems.* In the 1930 volume, an introductory note thanks William Radcliffe for gathering the materials for the memoir. In May 1930 a Manx newspaper published William Radcliffe's biography. The text is nearly the same as that in the *Memorial Volume.* Quiller-Couch only edited Radcliffe's material. Further, the Manx newspaper prints a paragraph thanking Brown's three daughters for their help. The Memoir published in 1930 and 1952 presents a clerical English poet who occasionally indulged himself in Manx high jinks. To the memorialist, the Manx poems are an aberration.

Brown sometimes thought of himself as a Manx Burns, and the comparison has merit. Brown, like Burns, articulates the national soul of his people, and Manx throughout the world recite Brown's verses to preserve their racial identity. Brown, however, was not strongly Manx (both parents had Scots ancestors), nor was he the natural product of an indigenous culture as Burns was. Brown also might be compared to the Dorset poet, William Barnes, but Brown has greater artistic skill and control. Brown has more muscle and energy than the American dialect poets Oliver Wendell Holmes or James Whitcomb Riley, and he has an unexpected and surprising mate in the black poet Paul Laurence Dunbar, a writer whose dialect verse also preserves cultural patterns and meaning. Like Thomas Hardy's characters, Brown's men and women bear a heavy curse of life, and Brown uses unusual and inventive stanzaic forms, just as Hardy does. Tom Baynes reminds us of Joseph Conrad's Marlow, but Baynes is much more innocent, ingenuous, and plain, and he is not telling his story to explore or explain his own character. Celticism is as much a worry and a refuge in Brown as it is in the early W. B. Yeats, and occasionally Brown uses an image or a turn of phrase that recalls Yeats's early poems.

Brown, however, is a comic poet, and thus he is suspect. Readers fear the comic poet is laughing at them or that he lacks "high seriousness." The dialect poet eternally sets himself at odds with readers of standard English, but Brown could no more be translated into standard English than Burns or

Hugh MacDiarmid. Brown demands that his reader enter the Manx world by means of Manx words and objects.

Ostensibly the Isle of Man is independent within the United Kingdom. It has its own church and its own parliament, the Tynwald; it issues stamps and money; it has its own legal and taxation systems. Ordinary acts of the English parliament do not apply to Man. Its independence, however, is a patriotic and legal fiction. For practical purposes, the Isle of Man is much like any other English county, "Lost in the empire's mass," except that the empire is now Western Europe. The truly independent Manx live only in Brown's poems. In his poems tolerant and sympathetic readers will find the charm of different worlds and values. Brown's art captured the Manx world of the 1830s and 1840s before tourists, industry, and alienation arrived. His art holds, as if in amber, the treasures of a lost island world, a world that new readers may find as dear as the Manx do.

Letters:

Letters of Thomas Edward Brown, edited by Sidney T. Irwin (2 volumes, New York: E. P. Dutton/ Westminster: Constable, 1900; 1 volume, Liverpool: University Press, 1952).

Bibliographies:

William Cubbon, comp., *Thomas Edward Brown; the Manx Poet (1830-1897), A Bibliography* (Douglas: Manx Museum and Ancient Monuments Trustees, 1934);

Simon Nowell-Smith, "Some Uncollected Authors XXXIII: Thomas Edward Brown, 1830-1897," *Book Collector,* 11 (1962): 338-344.

References:

F. S. Boas, "T. E. Brown," in *The Eighteen Eighties,* edited by Walter de la Mare (Cambridge: Cambridge University Press, 1930), pp. 44-68;

M. R. Ridley, "A Forgotten Poet," in his *Second Thoughts* (London: Dent, 1965), pp. 133-145;

Selwyn G. Simpson, *Thomas Edward Brown: the Manx Poet: An Appreciation* (London: Walter Scott Publishing, 1906);

Thomas Edward Brown: A Memorial Volume. 1830-1930 (Cambridge: Isle of Man Centenary Committee, 1930);

Richard Tobias, *T. E. Brown* (Boston: Twayne, 1978);

Cornelius Weygandt, *The Time of Tennyson: English Victorian Poetry as It Affected America* (New York & London: Appleton-Century, 1936; republished, Port Washington, N.Y.: Kennikat Press, 1968).

Papers:
The Manx Museum and National Trust Library, Douglas, Isle of Man, contains a rich collection of materials by and about Brown, including cuttings from Manx newspapers.

Robert Buchanan
(18 August 1841-10 June 1901)

Christopher D. Murray
University of Regina

See also the Buchanan entry in *DLB 18, Victorian Novelists After 1885*.

BOOKS: *Poems and Love Lyrics* (Glasgow: Murray/ Edinburgh, Sutherland & Knox/London: Hall, Virtue, 1858);

Mary, and Other Poems, as the Author of *Lyrics* (Glasgow: Murray/Edinburgh: Paton & Ritchie/ London: Hall, Virtue, 1859);

Storm-Beaten: or, Christmas Eve at the "Old Anchor" Inn, by Buchanan and Charles Gibbon (London: Ward & Lock, 1862);

Undertones (London: Chatto & Windus, 1863; revised and enlarged, London: Strahan, 1865);

Idyls and Legends of Inverburn (London: Strahan, 1865);

London Poems (London: Strahan, 1866);

Ballad Stories of the Affections: From the Scandinavian (London: Routledge, 1866; New York: Scribners, Welford, 1869);

North Coast and Other Poems (London: Routledge, 1868);

David Gray and other Essays, Chiefly on Poetry (London: Low & Marston, 1868);

The Book of Orm: A Prelude to the Epic (London: Strahan, 1870);

Napoleon Fallen: A Lyrical Drama (London: Strahan, 1870);

The Drama of Kings (London: Strahan, 1871);

The Land of Lorne (2 volumes, London: Chapman & Hall, 1871; 1 volume, New York: Felt, 1871);

The Fleshly School of Poetry and other Phenomena of the Day (London: Strahan, 1872; New York: Boni & Liveright, 1926);

Saint Abe and His Seven Wives: A Tale of Salt Lake City, anonymous (London: Strahan, 1872; New

Robert Buchanan

York: Routledge, 1872);

White Rose and Red: A Love Story, as the Author of *St. Abe* (London: Strahan, 1873; Boston: Osgood, 1873);

Master-spirits (London: King, 1873);

The Shadow of the Sword (3 volumes, London: Bentley, 1876; 1 volume, New York: Appleton, 1877);

Balder the Beautiful: A Song of Divine Death (London: Mullan, 1877);

A Child of Nature: A Romance (3 volumes, London: Bentley, 1881; 1 volume, New York: Harper, 1881);

God and the Man (3 volumes, London: Chatto & Windus, 1881; 1 volume, New York: Munro, 1881);

Foxglove Manor: A Novel, 3 volumes (London: Chatto & Windus, 1881);

The Martyrdom of Madeline: A Novel (3 volumes, London: Chatto & Windus, 1882; 1 volume, New York: Munro, 1882);

Ballads of Life, Love and Humour (London: Chatto & Windus, 1882);

Love Me Forever: A Romance (New York: Munro, 1882; London: Chatto & Windus, 1883);

Annan Water: A Romance (3 volumes, London: Chatto & Windus, 1883; 1 volume, New York: Munro, 1884);

A Poet's Sketch-Book: Selections from the Prose Writings of Robert Buchanan (London: Chatto & Windus, 1883);

The New Abelard: A Romance (New York: Lovell, 1883; 3 volumes, London: Chatto & Windus, 1884);

The Master of the Mine: A Novel (2 volumes, London: Bentley, 1885; 1 volume, New York: Munro, 1885);

Matt: A Story of a Caravan (London: Chatto & Windus, 1885); republished as *Matt: A Tale of a Caravan* (New York: Appleton, 1885);

Stormy Waters: A Story of To-day (3 volumes, London: Maxwell, 1885; 1 volume, New York: Munro, 1888);

The Earthquake; or, Six Days and a Sabbath (London: Chatto & Windus, 1885);

That Winter Night; or, Love's Victory (Bristol: Arrowsmith, 1886; New York: Harper, 1886);

A Look Round Literature (London: Ward & Downey, 1887);

The City of Dream: An Epic Poem (London: Chatto & Windus, 1888);

The Heir of Linne: A Novel (2 volumes, London: Chatto & Windus, 1888; 1 volume, New York: Munro, 1888);

On Descending into Hell: A Letter Addressed to the Right Hon. Henry Matthews, Q.C., Home Secretary, Concerning the Proposed Suppression of Literature (London: Redway, 1889);

The Moment After: A Tale of the Unseen (London: Heinemann, 1890; New York: Lovell, 1891);

Come, Live with Me and Be My Love: A Novel (2 volumes, New York: Lovell, 1891; 1 volume, London: Heinemann, 1892);

The Coming Terror and Other Essays and Letters (London: Heinemann, 1891; New York: United States Book Company, 1891);

The Wedding Ring: A Tale of To-Day (New York: Cassell, 1891);

The Outcast: A Rhyme for the Time (London: Chatto & Windus, 1891);

The Piper of Hamelin: A Fantastic Opera in Two Acts (London: Heinemann, 1893);

The Wandering Jew: A Christmas Carol (London: Chatto & Windus, 1893);

Woman and the Man: A Story, 2 volumes (London: Chatto & Windus, 1893);

Red and White Heather: North Country Tales and Ballads (London: Chatto & Windus, 1894);

Rachel Dene: A Tale of the Deepdale Mills (2 volumes, London: Chatto & Windus, 1894; 1 volume, New York: Neely, 1894);

Lady Kilpatrick: A Novel (London: Chatto & Windus, 1895; New York: Rand, McNally, 1897);

The Charlatan, by Buchanan and Henry Murray (London: Chatto & Windus, 1895; New York: Neely, 1895);

Diana's Hunting: A Novel (London: Unwin, 1895; New York: Stokes, 1895);

A Marriage by Capture: A Romance of To-day (London: Unwin, 1896; Philadelphia: Lippincott, 1896);

Effie Hetherington: A Novel (London: Unwin, 1896; Boston: Roberts, 1896);

Is Barabbas a Necessity? (London: Buchanan, 1896);

The Devil's Case: A Bank Holiday Interlude (London: Buchanan, 1896);

The Ballad of Mary the Mother: A Christmas Carol (London: Buchanan, 1897);

Father Anthony: A Romance of To-day (London: Long, 1898; New York: Dillingham, 1900);

The Rev. Annabel Lee (London: Pearson, 1898);

The New Rome: Poems and Ballads of Our Empire (London: Scott, 1898);

Andromeda: An Idyll of the Great River (London: Chatto & Windus, 1900; Philadelphia: Lippincott, 1901);

The Voice of "The Hooligan": A Discussion of Kiplingism, by Buchanan and Sir Walter Besant (New York: Tucker, 1900);

Sweet Nancy: A Comedy in Three Acts (London: French, 1914).

Collections: *Poetical Works,* 3 volumes (London: King, 1874; Boston: Osgood, 1874);

Selected Poems (London: Chatto & Windus, 1882);

The Complete Poetical Works of Robert Buchanan, 2 volumes (London: Chatto & Windus, 1901).

SELECTED PLAYS: *The Shadow of the Sword,* London, Olympic Theatre, 8 April 1882;

Stormbeaten, London, Adelphi Theatre, 14 March 1883; New York, Union Square Theatre, 26 November 1883;

Bachelors, London, Theatre Royal, 1 September 1884;

Alone in London, by Buchanan and Harriett Jay, Philadelphia, Chestnut Street Theatre, 30 March 1885; London, Olympic, 2 November 1885; New York, Niblo's, 9 November 1885;

Sophia, London, Vaudeville, 12 April 1886; New York, Wallack's Theatre, 4 November 1886;

Joseph's Sweetheart, London, Vaudeville Theatre, 8 March 1888;

Roger la Honte, or A Man's Shadow, London, Theatre Royal, Haymarket, 12 September 1889; New York, Niblo's Theatre, 8 October 1889;

Clarissa, London, Vaudeville Theatre, 6 February 1890;

The English Rose, by Buchanan and George R. Sims, London, Adelphi Theatre, 2 August 1890; New York, Proctor's Theatre, 9 March 1892;

The Sixth Commandment, London, Shaftesbury Theatre, 8 October 1890;

The Trumpet Call, by Buchanan and Sims, London, Adelphi Theatre, 1 August 1891.

OTHER: *The Life and Adventures of J. J. Audubon,* edited by Buchanan (London: Low & Marston, 1868; New York: Putnam's, 1869).

SELECTED PERIODICAL PUBLICATIONS: "Poems and Ballads by Algernon Charles Swinburne," *Athenaeum,* no. 2033 (4 August 1866): 137-138;

"The Session of the Poets," *Spectator,* 39 (15 September 1866): 1028;

"Walt Whitman," *Broadway,* 1 (1867-1868): 188-195;

"The Ring and The Book by Robert Browning," *Athenaeum,* no. 2148 (26 December 1868): 875-876; no. 2160 (20 March 1869): 339-340;

"The Fleshly School of Poetry: Mr. D. G. Rossetti," as Thomas Maitland, *Contemporary Review,* 18 (October 1871): 334-350.

Robert Buchanan is now remembered neither as a poet nor as a novelist, only as the attacker of D. G. Rossetti and A. C. Swinburne. His biographers have argued, as he did, with some justice, that his literary eclipse was due to the fact that most late nineteenth-century arbiters of literary taste were sympathetic to Rossetti, and hence his work never received objective appraisal. In many ways, however, Buchanan was his own worst enemy, and he was certainly too careless of his talents, and thus with his reputation, to enjoy the sympathy of those, including Robert Browning and R. H. Hutton, who admired him and encouraged him at the beginning of his career but were profoundly disappointed by his shifts to earn money later.

Robert Owen, pioneer of British socialism, gave away the bride at the wedding of Robert Buchanan, Sr., and Mary Williams, daughter of a well-known radical solicitor from Stoke-on-Trent; and it was, as he put it, in the "odor of infidelity" that young Robert grew up, first in London and later in Glasgow, where his father owned and edited several socialist newspapers until his bankruptcy in 1859. Robert Buchanan had a varied educational experience, being expelled from a private boys' school at Rothesay, and spending two years at the University of Glasgow, where he became a close friend of David Gray. Like Gray, Buchanan aspired to be a poet and published verses in the local papers. Like Gray, he wrote to leading men of letters for advice and an assessment of his chances; to one such inquiry G. H. Lewes, who had fostered George Eliot's talent, responded with encouragement. In May 1860, Gray and Buchanan made their way to London. Buchanan, who was used to normal middle-class comforts, found the subsequent privations particularly galling. He survived by writing a weekly political column for an Ayr newspaper, by acting, and by accepting any literary work, however humble, that came his way. Within a year he was publishing verse and essays in minor periodicals such as *Temple Bar* and the *Welcome Guest*; in 1861, he married sixteen-year-old Mary Jay. He established friendships with Lewes and George Eliot, and, through them, with Robert Browning, Dinah Maria Mulock, Bryan Waller Procter, Hepworth Dixon, and Thomas Love Peacock. *Undertones* (1863), Buchanan's "first" book of poetry (there were actually two earlier verse publications) was composed, in Buchanan's words, under Peacock's "watchful eye," and Buchanan's memoirs of life at Lower Halliford in *A Look Round Literature* (1887) remain invaluable to Peacock's biographers.

Much influenced by Keats, Tennyson, and Browning, *Undertones* is a series of dramatic monologues uttered by the gods and goddesses and heroes and heroines of Greece and Rome. Highly praised by Hutton and Lewes, among others, it remains an impressive achievement. Buchanan, how-ever (and his subsequent clashes with Swinburne certainly fostered this attitude), tended to under-value his gift for music and image; for him, he once wrote to Browning, it was ever "Truth first; after-wards, if possible, Beauty."

Undertones opened many doors for Buchanan. Had he been careful of his resources, financial hardship need no longer have threatened him. Ed-ward Moxon offered him Keats and Longfellow to edit; Sampson Low had him prepare a life of J. J. Audubon the ornithologist (which survives yet in the Everyman edition). Buchanan extensively re-vised *Undertones* for republication in 1865; *Idyls and Legends of Inverburn,* containing dramatic mono-logues of humble Scots people close to Buchanan's experience and expressing his true interests, was republished that same year. In 1866, after return-ing from Denmark where he had covered Bis-marck's invasion of Schleswig-Holstein as a war cor-respondent and had met Hans Christian Andersen in Copenhagen, he touched the high-water mark of his poetic achievement with *London Poems,* an at-tempt to articulate the tragedies of the slum-dwellers of the metropolis, an attempt at realism in stark contrast to his early, and to much other con-temporary, verse.

Thus Buchanan's severe review of Swin-burne's *Poems and Ballads,* published in August 1866, was by no means inconsistent with his aes-thetics. He was incensed at Swinburne's choice of subjects and with his provocative treatment of them. In September 1866, eliciting the epithet "clever" from another of his targets, Matthew Arnold, he published "The Session of the Poets" in which Swinburne's notorious alcoholism was first bruited. Swinburne answered Buchanan and other critics provocatively in *Notes on Poems and Reviews,* and William Michael Rossetti quite uncharacteristically called Buchanan a "poor and pretentious poetaster" in his defense of Swinburne; thus the Fleshly Con-troversy began.

Frenetically busy throughout this period, Buchanan translated, with some skill, Scandinavian ballads for George Routledge, who also paid him £400 (a very large sum) for *North Coast and Other Poems* (1868), which despite impressive illustrations by G. J. Pinwell and A. B. Houghton was a financial failure. Buchanan inflicted the first serious damage to his reputation by publishing the very uneven *David Gray and other Essays* (1868). In it he called Thomas Carlyle "a humbug and a ranter" and in an angry reply to a review in the *Spectator* called Mat-thew Arnold "a trifler." Buchanan's quick success

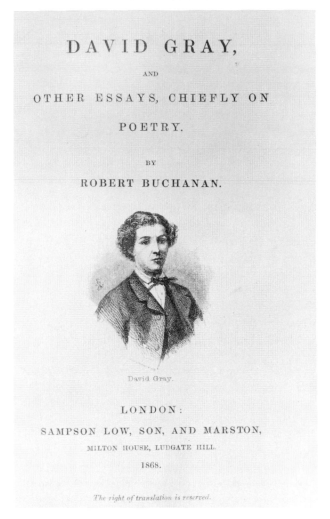

Title page for Buchanan's first volume of criticism. Reviewers reacted favorably to the title piece, in which Buchanan praised the work of his good friend David Gray, but many were offended by his querulous attitude toward others, including Thomas Carlyle, Matthew Arnold, and Sir Walter Scott.

fostered his tendencies to conceit and belligerence. His heroes he praised, however, and he rounded out this active phase with admiring reviews of Robert Browning's *The Ring and the Book* in the *Athenaeum* and of the first British edition of Walt Whitman's poems in *Broadway.*

Buchanan suffered some kind of nervous breakdown after his father's death in 1866. Thoroughly aware of the danger of prostituting his talents and considering London with its myriad temptations to represent such a danger, he moved first to Sussex, where he met Roden Noel, who remained a close friend, and then on to Oban in Argyllshire to a life as literary recluse and yachtsman. In 1870 he published *The Book of Orm* in which he turned away from dramatizing the lives of the humble and tried to express his own convictions (he had recently become a Christian) about the nature of the universe. Mystical and vatic, containing verse of much power, such as "The Vision of the Man Accurst" and the sonnets inspired by the desolate mountainscape surrounding Loch Corruisk on Skye, *The Book of Orm* was neither a critical nor popular success.

Knowing that Buchanan considered him responsible for Swinburne's social and literary excesses, D. G. Rossetti orchestrated the response to his *Poems,* published in 1870, with the avowed purpose of stifling Buchanan. Not knowing this and not reading *Poems* until a year after publication, Buchanan wrote the notorious notice published pseudonymously in the *Contemporary Review* (October 1871). Provoked by the reaction of the Rossetti circle as expressed in articles for *Academy* (15 October 1871) and *Athenaeum* (9 December 1871) by the influential critic Sidney Colvin, Buchanan expanded his review for publication in May 1872 as *The Fleshly School of Poetry and other Phenomena of the Day.* Evidently with the intention of doing for Rossetti and Swinburne what W. E. Aytoun had done for the Spasmodics seventeen years earlier, Buchanan not only engaged in self-parody in the first chapter so that he might make subtle, but not actionable, references to Swinburne's dipsomania and Rossetti's adulterous liaison with Jane Burden Morris, but then proceeded (so Rossetti, his brother, and Joseph Knight believed—in all probability, quite correctly) to review the pamphlet severely on the front page of the *Echo* newspaper (18 May). When the *Saturday Review* (2 June), which Colvin had promised would be sympathetic to Rossetti, castigated Buchanan as expected but then turned on Rossetti, Rossetti became convinced that a conspiracy had formed to hound him out of the society of decent men and attempted to take his life. No one familiar with the facts could forgive Buchanan his conduct. Lewes and George Eliot snubbed him in Regent's Park. Swinburne savaged him in *Under the Microscope* (1872) and in his introduction to *The Works of George Chapman: Poems and Minor Translations* (1875); and when the *London Examiner* published Swinburne's "The Devil's Due" (December 1875), Buchanan sued its proprietor for £5,000, but winning £150 damages and losing more goodwill in the process, he began to relish the role of maverick.

At the very height of the Fleshly Controversy, and not, as he and his biographer Harriett Jay claimed, a result of the animosity it caused, Buchanan decided to publish anonymously a satire of

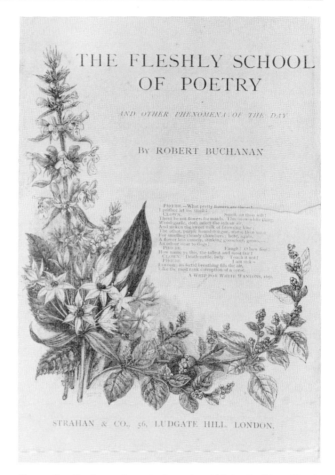

Cover for Buchanan's notorious pamphlet attacking Dante Gabriel Rossetti as the leader of a "fleshly school of verse-writers" and "public offenders . . . diligently spreading the seeds of disease. . . ."

Mormon polygamy in December 1872. *Saint Abe and His Seven Wives* was instantly popular and soon ran into several editions, strengthening Buchanan's suspicion that many reviewers tended to judge books by who their authors were rather than by literary merit. Buchanan's deft and humorous handling of matters sexual (if not his clumsy attempts at Western U.S. vernacular, which at the time at least were sufficiently authentic for most reviewers to consider the author American) continues to impress. A year later "The Author of St. Abe" produced *White Rose and Red,* containing remarkable verse and adumbrating a philosophy (not unlike that of D. H. Lawrence) in which sexual love holds the promise of self-realization, of becoming in Buchanan's words "a soul."

Buchanan did not publicly acknowledge authorship of the two works until years later. He wished his name to be associated with more serious verse and continued in the mystical vein with *Balder the Beautiful* (1877), in which he eloquently voiced his perdurable conviction that only human love, the supreme human beauty, can conquer death.

On returning to London in 1878, Buchanan began a new weekly political and literary journal, *Light.* Browning refused to submit verses, and thus to break a lifelong practice of never offering work for journal publication, but Trollope, Thomas Hardy, and R. D. Blackmore published fiction in *Light;* as happened so often with his enterprises, however, Buchanan's enthusiasm waned and within six months the journal ceased.

In 1881 Andrew Chatto (through having acquired Henry King's stock) became, to Swinburne's intense chagrin, Buchanan's publisher. The relationship was uneasy: Chatto really wanted access to Buchanan's potentially lucrative fiction; Buchanan hoped that a new publisher with fresh ideas would regain him the audience for his verse he had lost. Of bibliographic interest is the *Selected Poems*

(1882), in which Buchanan carefully revised his best work; unfortunately, the revisions were not incorporated into the hastily produced *Poetical Works* (1874) which, unchanged, became the first volume of the posthumous *Complete Poetical Works* (1901).

In 1884 and 1885 Buchanan and his sister-in-law, adopted daughter, and subsequent biographer, Harriett Jay, visited the United States. In Camden, New Jersey, they met Walt Whitman, on whose behalf Buchanan had been active for seventeen years; in Philadelphia Buchanan produced the melodrama *Alone in London.* Written in collaboration with Harriett Jay, it was the most lucrative work he ever wrote, yet one of which he was heartily ashamed. It was subsequently produced in London and New York and was revived many times in England. While in New York Buchanan was offered the editorship of the *North American Review,* but, unwell, he returned to London in the summer of 1885.

There followed frenetic activity in the theater,

Photo. Barraud, London

Truly yours
Robert Buchanan

THE

COMPLETE POETICAL WORKS

OF

ROBERT   BUCHANAN

IN TWO VOLUMES—VOL. II.

WITH   A   PORTRAIT

LONDON
CHATTO & WINDUS
1901

Frontispiece and title page from the posthumously published collection which, despite its title, omits several of Buchanan's early poems

Buchanan's tombstone at the unveiling ceremony in Falkirk Cemetery

with play after play dashed off almost at a sitting, never carefully revised, all aiming for a smash. He came close with several, Beerbohm Tree starring in *Roger la Honte, or A Man's Shadow* (1889), and *Sophia* (1886), an adaptation of Henry Fielding's *Tom Jones,* running 500 nights. In 1888 he found time to complete his last ambitious poem, *The City of Dream,* a Bunyanesque tour of man's creeds notable for much good poetry, of which the sensual evocation of Greek myth is particularly impressive.

Throughout this period Buchanan engaged in public debate on a variety of issues in the daily press; on blood-sports, vivisection, and the rights of women, Buchanan's arguments read well today. In 1890, to no apparent good effect, he spoke up on Irish nationalist leader Charles Parnell's behalf, and in 1895 his was a lone voice asking for humane treatment and a fair trial for Oscar Wilde. In 1891, more conscious than ever of his own isolation if not ostracism, he published *The Outcast;* a highly readable indictment of his times in Byronic measure with Byronic hero, it earned the admiration of Richard Le Gallienne and Israel Zangwill among the rising generation of litterateurs. Two years later appeared *The Wandering Jew,* another outspoken poem, in which Christ is arraigned for all the evils perpetrated by man in his name; it became the

occasion for another press debate summarized in the *London Daily Chronicle* headline "Is Christianity Played Out?"

Buchanan's fragile financial world toppled in 1894, when his theatrical speculation failed and bankruptcy proceedings began. In the same month his mother died, his constant inspiration and by all accounts a remarkable woman. He struggled on, trying to earn enough to give his beloved Harriett financial independence, but he suffered a stroke in October 1900 and, never regaining consciousness, died the following June.

Robert Buchanan's garish bohemianism was ill-suited to the received Victorian ideal of right conduct for a serious poet. Undignified imbroglios in the press, frequent appearances in the courts (he sued Lillie Langtry for breach of contract because she failed to include one of his plays in her 1889 American tour) culminating in his bankruptcy, a well-known love of horseracing, crude melodramas bearing his name running at the Adelphi or touring the country—all bespoke the fact that Buchanan, abrasive and arrogant, had sold his poetic birthright for a mess of pottage. Buchanan received due warning of the reputation he had earned when at a Royal Academy dinner, on hearing W. E. H. Lecky praise *The City of Dream,* Browning asked a neighbor,

"Of whom is he speaking? Of Buchanan the writer of plays?" The question was understood by those who heard it, and heard it repeated, to imply ironical contempt. Buchanan was jealous of his poetic reputation, but not jealous enough; he wrote too much verse of uneven quality and rarely took the pains necessary to produce poetry, yet a judicious selection of his work would give him a place that even his most unsympathetic contemporaries would have accorded him, but which is not his yet.

References:

Harriett Jay, *Robert Buchanan: Some Account of his Life, his Life's Work and his Literary Friendships* (London: Unwin, 1903);

John Cassidy, *Robert W. Buchanan* (New York: Twayne, 1973).

C. S. Calverley
(22 December 1831-17 February 1884)

Patrick Scott
University of South Carolina

BOOKS: *Parthenonis Ruinae: Carmen Latinum. . .* , as Charles S. Blayds (Oxford: J. Vincent, 1851);

Verses and Translations (Cambridge: Deighton, Bell/London: Bell & Daldy, 1862);

Fly Leaves (Cambridge: Deighton, Bell, 1872; New York: Holt & Williams, 1872; enlarged, New York: Holt & Williams, 1872);

Literary Remains (London: Bell/Cambridge: Deighton, Bell, 1885);

The English Poems of Charles Stuart Calverley, edited by Hilda D. Spear (Leicester: Leicester University Press, 1974; New York: Humanities Press, 1974).

Collections: *Works,* 4 volumes (London: Bell, 1883-1885);

The Complete Works of C. S. Calverley (London: Bell, 1901).

TRANSLATIONS: *Translations into English and Latin* (Cambridge: Deighton, Bell/London: Bell & Daldy, 1866);

Theocritus Translated into English Verse (Cambridge: Deighton, Bell, 1869);

The Hymnary: A Book of Church Song (London: Novello, 1872)—includes translations by Calverley;

The Eclogues of Vergil, Translated into English Verse, edited by Moses Hadas (New York: A. Colish, 1960).

Charles Stuart Calverley is one of the best-known, and one of the best, practitioners of the Victorian art of light verse. He wrote almost no obviously serious poetry but instead applied his virtuosity as a verse craftsman to classical translation, to lighthearted humorous writing, and to incisive parodies of such famous contemporaries as Browning, Tennyson, and D. G. Rossetti. He is an outstanding parodist in that he moves beyond the broad mockery of earlier parodists to a much more pointed and subtle imitative mockery of style and meter, and in this he set the pattern for such later Victorian parodists as J. K. Stephen. Calverley's verse also has a historical significance, beyond the specialized tradition of parody, because its formalism is a symptom of the increasing reservations many educated later Victorians felt about the innovative stylistic individuality of the great early Victorian poets.

Calverley was born Charles Stuart Blayds, the son of a country clergyman, in Worcestershire in 1831, and he spent his early childhood in the village of South Stoke, near Bath. Educated at first privately, then briefly at the brand-new Marlborough College and from 1846 at Harrow, he was a clever if indolent schoolboy, already excelling in the much-prized art of Latin verse composition. In 1850, he went up to Balliol College, Oxford, and gained a scholarship but quickly made a reputation for good-humored yet "perpetual warfare with constituted authority"; for instance, once when showing visitors around the college, he pointed out a window with "That is the Master's room" and then threw a stone crashing through the glass, so that, when the occupant looked out to find the thrower, he could go smoothly on, "And that is the Master." On the

flights of stairs, over walls or streams, through tree forks, and, on one occasion, clean over a cart-horse in a Cambridge street (ostensibly to avoid the effort of walking round it). In general, however, he led at Cambridge a much more circumspect life than he had at Oxford, and he amassed many classical honors—including the Craven Scholarship, the Member's Prize for Latin Prose, and medals for both Latin and Greek verse. He gained a first class in the Classical Tripos in 1856 and was elected a fellow of his college in 1858.

It was during the next few years, when he was a Cambridge don, that he first made his reputation as a verse humorist. He had already, in 1857, produced a witty mock-examination paper devoted to Dickens's *Pickwick Papers* ("1. Mention any occasions on which it is specified that the Fat Boy was *not* asleep. . . . 4. Who little thinks that in which pocket, of what garment, in where, he has left what, entreating him to return to whom, with how many what, and how big?"). In 1862, he published his first full-scale volume, *Verses and Translations.* It was put out by a Cambridge publisher, and some of the light verse in it is specifically local in its allusions. For instance, the "Ode to Tobacco" concludes with a tribute to Bacon, the Cambridge tobacconist (and a bronze tablet with Calverley's poem now graces the Bacon shop). "*Hic Vir, Hic Est*" is about a Cambridge graduate revisiting his university, seeing the new undergraduate generation ("those noblest of their species/Called emphatically *men*"), and remembering the wide-eyed eagerness of his own first arrival:

> Once, an unassuming Freshman,
>   Through these wilds I wandered on,
> Seeing in each house a College,
>   Under every cap a Don:
> Each perambulating infant
>   Had a magic in its squall,
> For my eager eye detected
>   Senior Wranglers in them all.

(*Senior Wrangler* is the Cambridge term for a first-class mathematician, but the wit surely lies less in the local knowingness than in the way Calverley has made the innocent active verb *to perambulate* appear to derive by back-formation from that most passive of vehicles, the perambulator.)

Other poems, less narrowly Cantabrigian in subject, nonetheless grew out of his life and friendships there. His medievalizing treatment of a cabmen's strike recalls not only the contemporary Pre-Raphaelite interest in medieval ballad forms

proofs of his poem *Parthenonis Ruinae,* which won him the Chancellor's Prize for Latin Verse and was published as a pamphlet (1851), he described himself rather cheekily, but not surprisingly, as "*e Coll. Balliol prope ejectus*" ("nearly expelled"). After only two years, in 1852 (perhaps significantly, the same year in which his reverend father changed the family name from Blayds to Calverley), he abandoned Oxford for a new start at Christ's College, Cambridge. Here, too, authority was sometimes the butt of his wit; once, leading a boisterous crowd of students who had stolen a local inn sign, he responded to the challenge of a college Fellow with the scriptural warning, "A wicked and adulterous generation seeketh after a sign." One further detail of his school and college days is suggestive, because it indicates something of his character and so of his approach to the challenge of verse-making: his favorite physical exercise was one that involved neither long training nor team competition but instead combined spontaneity, display, and individual bravado—it was challenge-jumping, down long

but also Calverley's college friendship with the medieval scholar W. W. Skeat:

It was a railway passenger
    And he lept out jauntilie.
"Now up and bear, thou stout portér,
    My two chattéls to me."

Many of the broader topics of Calverley's affectionate-satirical poems in his first volume—the enthusiasm of young love, the innocent absurdity of adolescent social pretension, mock-serious valentine sentiments, the pleasures of tobacco and beer—seem to fit the youthful, male, upper-class ethos of the mid-Victorian university; but Calverley's tone and perspective came because he himself was now thirty-odd, no longer an undergraduate of twenty, and so he could use the knowing elegance of his verse not merely to savor or to elegize the undergraduate ethos but also to "place" it. His "A, B, C" on formal summer balls, for instance, strikes a characteristic note of distanced, and slightly supercilious, amusement:

A is an Angel of blushing eighteen:
B is the Ball where the Angel was seen:
C is her Chaperon, who cheated at cards:
D is the Deuxtemps, with Frank of the Guards:
. . . .
S is the Supper, where all went in pairs:
T is the Twaddle they talked on the stairs:
. . . .
Y is a Yawning fit caused by the Ball:
Z stands for Zero, or nothing at all.

Even the most famous poem of the volume, the ode to "Beer," is mock-heroic in the grandeur with which it so appreciatively lists all the most famous mid-Victorian breweries:

O Beer! O Hodgson, Guinness, Allsop, Bass!
    Names that should be on every infant's tongue!
Shall days and months and years and centuries pass,
    And still your merits be unrecked, unsung?

The style and the deflationary neatness of some of the rhyming in this poem undermine, or at least diminish, the tongue-in-cheek claim that the verses make for their subject's universal significance ("The heart which Grief hath cankered / Hath one unfailing remedy—the Tankard"); even when writing of beer, Calverley's effect rests on the style, not just on the jocularly collegiate subject matter. *Verses and Translations* includes a few verse puzzles in

"charade" form (a stanza of clues for each syllable of a mystery word and then one for the whole word), but most of the poems rely less on wordplay, or on the puns that had fascinated such earlier Victorian verse humorists as Thomas Hood, than on a relaxed and amused manipulation of verse styles that implies the author's social and aesthetic independence. The only parody in this first volume, a wickedly accurate mockery of M. F. Tupper's best-selling *Proverbial Philosophy,* shows how clearly Calverley's aesthetic disdain for Tupper's quasi-scriptural verse is linked to an upper-class social disdain for Tupper's middle-class moralizing. Some of Calverley's lines are very broad attacks indeed on Tupper's stuffiness ("Study first Propriety: for she is indeed the Pole-Star"), but some sections hit off his poetical absurdity much more subtly:

Art thou beautiful, O my daughter, as the budding
    rose of April?
Art all thy motions music, and is poetry throned in
    thine eye?
Then hearken unto me; and I will make the bud a fair
    flower,
I will plant it upon the bank of Elegance, and water it
    with the water of Cologne;
And in the season it shall "come out," yea bloom. . . .

This parody of Tupper points to the direction Calverley would take in his later verse.

In 1863, shortly after the publication of *Verses and Translations,* he left Cambridge, entering the Inner Temple in London to study law, and in the same year he married his cousin Ellen Calverley; they had one daughter, who died young, and two sons. Calverley was called to the bar in 1865 and apparently enjoyed his new career, but it was soon to be cut short. In the winter of 1866, he tripped while ice-skating near his father-in-law's Yorkshire seat and sustained a severe concussion, which, remaining too long undiagnosed, led to continuing pain and eventually forced him to abandon his profession.

Calverley did, however, continue his writing, at least for a few more years. During the 1860s, he had contributed light verse and parodies to several periodicals, including the new humor magazines, *Aunt Judy's* and *Fun.* More seriously, he had continued to publish translations from the classics into English, including Homer, Virgil, and Horace (1866) and Theocritus (1869), and translations of such English authors as Milton and Tennyson into Latin; he had even translated Robert Burns's "John Anderson, My Jo" from Scots into Greek. He made, too, a series of translations of medieval Latin hymns for a new church hymnary. His parody of Sir Theodore Martin's very loose and colloquial translation of Horace (included in Calverley's posthumously published *Literary Remains,* 1885) shows his high standards of accuracy for translation, and an article he contributed to the *London Student* in 1868 (also in the *Remains*) shows how closely he had studied current theories of translation technique. The aim of most mid-Victorian translators was to render not merely the meaning of their original but also its style and meter, rather like an affectionate parody. Calverley accepted this aim but argued for the translator's freedom in handling the details of such a rendering; good verse, he wrote, is like "a rose or vine" trained on the trellis of the original metrical pattern, but trained naturally, "so that, while it adheres firmly, it is still left to follow its own devices and form its own pattern over the laths."

Few of Calverley's translations in fact show the freedom and playfulness of tone and meter that distinguish his lighter verse, but there are close links between these two sides of his verse-making talent. Both required an imaginative sympathy with some original on the part of the writer, and both emphasized the formal and stylistic aspects of poetry. It may be that Calverley's liking for translation indicates a radical poetic inhibition, that he could only indulge his talent when he was working on safely impersonal and public material. Neither translation nor parody, however, is merely imitative or impersonal; rather, they both involve the evaluative re-creation of their poetic originals, the one for praise, the other for criticism, and there is, therefore, a positive connection between Calverley's two kinds of verse-writing in that both require a lively, critically alert mind at work behind the apparent impersonality.

Calverley's second volume of poetry, and the one which gave him more than a Cambridge reputation, was *Fly Leaves,* published in 1872. Again, many of the poems were light verse, good-tempered and poised, though now their topics were less Cambridge than London life. "Arcades Ambo" (a burlesque of Matthew Arnold's style) describes the impressive Beadle of the Burlington Arcade; "Precious Stones" mocks the adulation given to titled high society; "Play" focuses, rather less tolerantly, on the disruptions small children bring to an urban neighborhood; and "Lines on Hearing the Organ" is about the barrel-organ men who haunted the London streets:

> Grinder, who serenely grindest,

> At my door the Hundredth Psalm,
> Till thou ultimately findest
> Pence in thy unwashen palm.

The tone of the poems shows a change, too. Though a few of the poems are still mere jeux d'esprit (as in "Under the Trees," where Calverley produces over fifty rhymes for the word trees in just forty-three lines), in most the tone seems mellower, mixing irony with a gentler, more humane sympathy. For instance, "On the Beach" is the monologue of a private tutor who buys himself a cheap love-locket and creates an entirely imaginary girl friend, simply to solace his loneliness. "On the Brink" explores the ambivalence of a middle-aged bachelor, about to propose to a young widow but drawing back when she speaks roughly to her child. Both these poems have stock humorous situations, but both treat these situations with considerable delicacy. A third poem, "Peace," shows an understated irony of insight rare in Victorian poetry; it describes a "worn-out City clerk" on his first seaside vacation, contrasting in his mind the happy shore scene with the clash of the noisy German bands outside his suburban London home:

> And at the thought
> He laughed again, and softly drew
> That *Morning Herald* that he'd brought
> Forth from his breast, and read it through.

But it is the literary parodies in *Fly Leaves* that have attracted most readers. As in the earlier Tupper parody, Calverley gently exaggerates the style of each original and so makes the reader critically aware of its idiosyncrasies. He picked on the incantatory refrain of some of D. G. Rossetti's and William Morris's Pre-Raphaelite ballads, for instance, and made the device absurd by using in his parody the constant refrain, *"Butter and eggs and a pound of cheese."* As Hilda Spear has pointed out, his "Lovers, and a Reflection" hits off the popular Victorian poetess Jean Ingelow by picking on the empty prettiness of her vocabulary:

> In moss-prankt dells which the sunbeams flatter
> (And heaven it knoweth what that may mean;
> Meaning, however, is no great matter)
> Where woods are atremble, with rifts atween.

It is notable that "Wanderers," the parody of Tennyson, is based on one of the laureate's English idylls, "The Brook" from his 1842 *Poems,* in which the style is most mannered, and not on the more serious or disciplined Tennyson, whom Calverley greatly admired (and translated). The most famous parody in the volume, that of Browning's *The Ring and the Book,* uses, as Spear has shown, a pastiche of borrowed words and phrases, drawn from all twelve books of the original poem. Under the unflattering title "The Cock and the Bull," Calverley hits off many of the oddities of Browning's "grotesque" style—the ellisions, omissions, slang, jargon, ostentatious learning, the mid-sentence side-trip into self-explanation, the splutter of specificity—as in this passage, in which the poet is simply going out of his house:

I shoved the timber ope wi' my omoplat;
And *in vestibulo,* i' the lobby to-wit,
(Iacobi Facciolati's rendering, sir,)
Donned galligaskins, antigropeloes,
And so forth; and, complete with hat and gloves,
One on and one a-dangle i' my hand,
And ombrifuge (Lord, love you), case of rain,
I flopped forth, 'sbuddikins! on my own ten toes.

Calverley's point was how much of Browning's poem rested simply on an idiosyncratic mannerism: "You see the trick on't though, and can yourself/ Continue the discourse *ad libitum.*" The demand that Calverley implies here, for more stable and central standards of poetic taste, parallels the reaction against stylistic idiosyncrasy in Matthew Arnold's critical writings and seems to be a concern of Calverley's generation, as well as a result of their members' common classicism.

After 1872 Calverley wrote comparatively little. His health further deteriorated, and the few poems that he did publish (for example, in *Scribner's Monthly* and in *Punch*), while still technically accomplished, seem trivial and jokey beside his earlier work. Only the extended horror-piece, "The Poet and the Fly" (in *Aunt Judy's* in 1880), still retains interest as an influence on the contemporary British playwright Tom Stoppard's radio play, *Artist Descending a Staircase.* All these later humorous poems were collected in *Literary Remains.* Among the later "serious" writing, completed only a month before his death (and also in *Remains*), is an ingenious translation of a medieval Latin hymn on the Day of Judgment, in which Calverley has reproduced in English the meter and alphabetical format of the original with a different letter of the Roman alphabet beginning each alternate line; even his religious verse had taken on the character of a word game. After prolonged suffering from a degenera-

Title page for the posthumously published volume which, in Walter J. Sendall's words, contains "all that remains of interest from Calverley's pen, not included in the works already published under his name"

tive kidney disorder, Bright's Disease, Calverley died in 1884 and was buried at Folkstone.

Calverley's career as a light-verse writer started in mainly local, collegiate humor, but, in the words of Walter Sendall, his first biographer, the "boyish glee" soon became an "elvish mockery." Though in real life he had to face both bereavement and illness, in his poetry he seems free of those deeper problems that his older poetic contemporaries were confronting; in Sir John Seeley's words, "it was his lot to saunter along the highroad of life, where the cases do not arise which call for such powers as his." Because of his metrical skill and broadening human and literary interests after he left Cambridge, he developed into a distinctive, if unusually downbeat, countervoice to the ambitious importance of major Victorian poetry. His modern reputation rests almost exclusively on his literary parodies, but his work as a whole remains a readable corrective to any easy generalization about the poetry of his period.

References:

Percy L. Babington, *Browning and Calverley; or, Poem and Parody, an Elucidation* (London: Castle, 1925);

Herbert H. Huxley, "The *Carmen Saeculare* of C. S. Calverley," *Leeds Philosophical Society Proceedings* (1950): 472-481;

Richard B. Ince, *Calverley and Some Cambridge Wits of the Nineteenth Century* (London: Richards & Toulmin, 1929);

Hilda D. King, "A Descriptive Catalogue of the Calverley Material in Toronto University Library," *Notes and Queries,* new series 1 (1954): 450-453; 536-539;

George Kitchin, *A Survey of Burlesque and Parody in English* (Edinburgh: Oliver & Boyd, 1931): 298-304;

Max H. Massey, "Charles Stuart Calverley, Poet and Parodist," Ph.D. dissertation, University of California, Davis, 1973;

Anthony W. Preston, "Calverley of Cambridge," *Queen's Quarterly,* 54 (1947): 47-60;

Walter J. Sendall, "Memoir," in *Literary Remains of Charles Stuart Calverley* (London: Bell, 1885): 1-116;

Hilda D. Spear (*née* King), "Calverley and Jean Ingelow," *Notes and Queries,* 197 (August 1952): 385-386;

Spear, Introduction to Calverley's *The English Poems* (Leicester: Leicester University Press, 1974): 9-14;

Walter Whyte, "C. S. Calverley," in *Poets and Poetry of the Nineteenth Century,* volume 9, edited by Alfred H. Miles (London: Hutchinson, 1894), pp. 433-442.

Papers:

A few of Calverley's manuscripts are in London, at the British Library and with the publisher Novello and Company; the manuscript of "Three Charades" is at the University of Illinois, Urbana; but the major collection is in Toronto at the Toronto University Library.

Mortimer Collins
(29 June 1827-28 July 1876)

Norman Page
University of Alberta

See also the Collins entry in *DLB 21, Victorian Novelists Before 1885.*

BOOKS: *Idyls and Rhymes* (Dublin: McGlashan, 1855);

Summer Songs (London: Saunders & Otley, 1860);

Who Is the Heir? A Novel, 3 volumes (London: Maxwell, 1865);

Sweet Anne Page, 3 volumes (London: Hurst & Blackett, 1868);

The Ivory Gate, 2 volumes (London: Hurst & Blackett, 1869);

A Letter to the Right Honourable Benjamin Disraeli MP (London: Hotten, 1869);

The Vivian Romance (3 volumes, London: Hurst & Blackett, 1870; 1 volume, New York: Harper, 1870);

Marquis and Merchant (3 volumes, London: Hurst & Blackett, 1871; 1 volume, New York: Appleton, 1871);

The Inn of Strange Meetings and Other Poems (London: King, 1871);

The Secret of Long Life (London: King, 1871);

The British Birds: A Communication from the Ghost of

Aristophanes (London: The Publishing Co., 1872);

The Princess Clarice: A Story of 1871, 2 volumes (London: King, 1872);

Two Plunges for a Pearl (3 volumes,(London: Tinsley, 1872; 1 volume, New York: Appleton, 1872);

Squire Silchester's Whim, 3 volumes (London: King, 1873);

Miranda: A Midsummer Madness, 3 volumes (London: King, 1873);

Mr. Carington: A Tale of Love and Constancy, as Robert Turner Cotton, 3 volumes (London: King 1873);

Transmigration, 3 volumes (London: Hurst & Blackett, 1874);

Frances, 3 volumes (London: Hurst & Blackett, 1874);

Sweet and Twenty, 3 volumes (London: Hurst & Blackett, 1875);

Blacksmith and Scholar and From Midnight to Midnight, 3 volumes (London: Hurst & Blackett, 1876);

A Fight with Fortune, 3 volumes (London: Hurst & Blackett, 1876);

You Play Me False: A Novel, by Collins and Frances Collins, 3 volumes (London: Bentley, 1878);

The Village Comedy, by Collins and Frances Collins, 3 volumes (London: Hurst & Blackett, 1878);

Pen Sketches from a Vanished Hand, from the Papers of the Late Mortimer Collins, edited by Tom Taylor, with notes by the editor and Mrs. Mortimer Collins, 2 volumes (London: Bentley, 1879);

Thoughts in My Garden, edited by Edmund Yates, with notes by the editor and Mrs. Mortimer Collins, 2 volumes (London: Bentley, 1880);

Attic Salt: or, Epigrammatic Sayings in Prose and Verse, edited by Frank Kerslake (London: Robson, 1880);

Selections from the Poetical Works, edited by F. P. Cotton (London: Bentley, 1886).

Mortimer Collins, the only child of Francis Collins, whose *Spiritual Songs* appeared in 1824, was a prolific novelist and journalist who began his literary career by writing poetry and continued to do so for some twenty years. His career illustrates the pressures upon the Victorian man of letters to produce at great speed a succession of works in the most popular genres. When he died, the *Athenaeum* remarked in an obituary (5 August 1876) that he had "succumbed, at a comparatively early age, to the severe toil that a life devoted to authorship and the struggle to gain a livelihood by the pen entail."

Mortimer Collins

Edward James Mortimer Collins was born in Plymouth and educated at private schools. He entered the teaching profession but resigned his position in 1856 in order to devote himself to writing. His first poems had appeared in the "Poet's Corner" of Bristol newspapers, and in 1855 he had his first volume, *Idyls and Rhymes*, published. Later he was active as a journalist, as the editor of various provincial papers, and as a novelist. His unconventionality of dress and manners earned him the nickname of King of the Bohemians, but his outlook was fundamentally conservative and religious, and he was fond of English country life. From 1862 until his death he lived at Knowl Hill in Berkshire.

Collins's specialty was light verse or *vers de société*, witty, polished, and metrically skillful. During the 1860s he contributed to a short-lived periodical, the *Owl*, and it was in this journal that "Ad Chloen, M.A.," which has been described as the most brilliant of his short poems, appeared. It was republished in his volume *The Inn of Strange Meetings and Other Poems* (1871), which was favorably reviewed by the *Athenaeum* (11 November 1871), where he is described as a "thoroughly successful" humorous poet in the manner of W. M. Praed and praised for the "good-humoured banter which is the special characteristic of his verse." The title poem of the volume, a long piece in ottava rima, recounts a fanciful narrative. During the last two years of his life Collins frequently contributed poems to *Punch.* The existence of two posthumously published volumes suggests that his work was not quickly forgotten: in 1880 appeared *Attic Salt,* a collection of epigrams in prose and verse from Collins's works, edited by Frank Kerslake; and in 1886 F. P. Cotton edited selections from Collins's poems. In the *Cambridge History of English Literature,* George Saintsbury singles out two poems by Collins for special mention: "To F. C." as an example of his love poetry, and "The British Birds" as illustrating his "brilliant satiric verse." Collins's clever parodies of

Swinburne, Tennyson, and Browning have not lost their point and find a well-deserved place in Dwight Macdonald's anthology *Parodies* (London: Faber, 1961) and other collections.

The urbanity of Collins's light verse no doubt owed much to his fondness for classical literature. His literary friendships included Richard Hengist Horne, Frederick Locker-Lampson, and R. D. Blackmore. He married Susannah Crump (neé Hubbard) about 1849 and, after her death in 1867, in the following year married Frances Cotton, who was a collaborator in some of his later novels.

Letters:

Mortimer Collins: his Letters and Friendships, With Some Account of his Life, edited by Frances Collins (London: Low, 1877).

William Johnson Cory
(9 January 1823-11 June 1892)

' Tirthankar Bose
University of British Columbia

BOOKS: *Ionica,* anonymous (London: Smith, Elder, 1858);
Eton Reform (London: Longmans, 1861);
Nuces (Eton: Privately printed, 1869);
Early Modern Europe (Cambridge: E. Johnson, 1869);
Lucretilis (Eton: Privately printed, 1870);
Iophon (London: Rivingtons, 1873);
Ionica II, anonymous (Cambridge: Privately printed, 1877);
A Guide to Modern English History, 2 volumes (London: Kegan Paul, 1880, 1882);
Ionica, revised and enlarged edition (London: Allen, 1891)—includes *Ionica, Ionica II,* and twenty additional poems, omitting five poems from the previous volumes;
Ionica, enlarged edition (London: Allen, 1905)—includes the five poems omitted from the 1891 edition and one additional poem.

OTHER: "On the Education of the Reasoning Faculties," in *Essays on a Liberal Education,* edited by F. W. Farrar (London: Macmillan, 1867).

William Cory, born William Johnson, left behind him a modest literary corpus but a vast reputation as poet, teacher, and scholar. Because of his single-minded devotion to pedagogy, Cory is known as the singer of the transmuting power of a great school over youth at the threshold of life. Yet within his admittedly narrow ambit, Cory goes beyond the celebration of school life, for he directs a vigorous yet graceful imagination to the perennial theme of defining the value of human existence in terms of unaffected human relationships.

Cory was born on 9 January 1823, the younger son of Charles and Theresa Furse Johnson of Torrington in Devonshire. In 1832 he was elected king's scholar to Eton, where he capped a brilliant career by winning the Newcastle scholarship in 1841. On 23 February 1842 he was elected to a scholarship at King's College, Cambridge, where he distinguished himself both by his classical scholarship and by his deep interest in contemporary history and social issues. Brought up as a Tory, at Cambridge he became a wholehearted Whig, although this conversion to liberalism could not soften his violent antipathy toward the Catholic church.

In 1843 Cory won the chancellor's medal for an English poem on Plato and the Camden medal for a Latin poem on Archimedes. Having won the Craven scholarship in 1844, he succeeded to a fellowship at his college in 1845, the year in which he graduated B.A. Soon after graduation, in September 1845, he was appointed an assistant master at Eton. He had had some notion of taking Anglican Orders or perhaps studying for the bar but found the prospect of teaching far more attractive.

The incisive intellect and forceful character that had marked Cory's career at Cambridge made him a figure both of awe and admiration at Eton, especially because his highly original views lent him an air of eccentricity. Sensitive and gifted students found him an attractive guide through the maze of scholarship as well as through the emotional crises of youth. His greatest ambition, as he said in a letter, was to turn out of his pupil room "one brave soldier, or one wise historian, or one generous legislator, or one patient missionary." This dream was fulfilled in Cory's lifetime; several of his students went on to become some of England's most eminent men. Lord Rosebery, one of Cory's favorite pupils, entered the Gladstone cabinet of 1886 as secretary of state for foreign affairs, a post that Cory valued above most other ministries. Also among his students were the famous Lyttleton brothers, one of whom later became headmaster of Eton. On such students Cory expended limitless affection and labor.

To the less gifted student—which meant the average Eton boy—Cory was a comparatively distant though no less conscientious mentor. His teaching went above the heads of ordinary students, but his direct nature, his insistence on approaching the pupil with love rather than the rod made him a popular master, affectionately known as Billy Johnson. Among his peers his formidable scholarship and proven value as the molder of brilliant young minds earned him universal respect. Not a disciplinarian in the ordinary sense, Cory achieved order in the classroom and outside it by his cutting though good-natured wit. He would, for instance, bark at the latecomer stealthily creeping into the room, "Well, you have pretty much established *your* insignificance!" Of a bearded colleague, much despised, Cory said, "Formerly wise men kept beards; now others do so."

For Cory, Eton was more than a living; it was his life. He could not do enough for the school. He would buy scientific apparatus for the students. He was the first to institute prizes for athletic competitions between school houses. More important, he took the leading part in establishing programs in

William Johnson Cory

science and mathematics, bestowing a generous exhibition fund of £400 and adding to the bequest frequently. He strongly believed in the pedagogic value of Greek and Latin verse composition, at which he had himself excelled as a student. To give substance to his theory, he prepared thorough exercises in verse composition which the school continued to use well into the twentieth century.

That Cory's poetic talents went beyond mere pedagogic expertise was proved in 1858 with the appearance of *Ionica*. The much delayed sequel to this volume was *Ionica II* (1877), a collection of twenty-five new poems. Still later, in 1891, Cory produced another edition of *Ionica*, which contained all but five of the poems in the previous volumes and twenty new ones. The corpus of Cory's English verses is small, but his poetic endeavor was not limited to English. Indeed, it is arguable that Cory's greater distinction as a poet lies in the Latin verses he composed as school exercises. Published in 1870 under the title *Lucretilis*, the volume drew high praise from such Latinists as Cory's contemporary H. A. J. Munro and the twentieth-century scholar John Sparrow. *Lucretilis* had been preceded by a manual of Latin prose composition, *Nuces*

(1869), and was succeeded by a companion volume of original Greek verse, *Iophon* (1873).

The originality of these works, both as literature and as teaching tools, explains the recognition Cory enjoyed in the world of letters. He was often called to Cambridge, where he still held his fellowship at King's, to examine the moral science tripos. In 1860 he came close to being offered the chair in modern history at King's as a nominee of the prime minister, Lord Palmerston, and was passed over only because of the prince consort's insistent support of another scholar. A second attempt, in 1869, to have Cory elected to the same chair also failed. These unsuccessful attempts were hardly disappointments, or at least not conspicuously so, for Cory gave priority to Eton and to the teaching of the young. To the philosophy of education he applied an innovative intellect, as evidenced by his essay "On the Education of the Reasoning Faculties," collected in *Essays on a Liberal Education*, edited by F. W. Farrar (1867).

Despite his receptive intellect and liberal sympathies, Cory was surprisingly rigid in his religious views and ingenuous in his patriotic fervor. His poems in praise of English arms ("War Music") and the English Queen ("A Queen's Visit") are saved— barely—from fatuousness only by their brevity. His fascination with things military was also one of his many eccentricities. The story is told of Cory rushing down the stairs from his pupil room whenever soldiers marched through Eton High Street and snapping at the boys crowding behind him, "Brats, the British army!"

For such quirks of character as much as for his influence, Cory became an institution around whom legends grew thick. One story, a true one, was that he could—and would—recite the details of every recent campaign to the last field order and every naval battle to the disposition of the last ship. Another, an apocryphal but not unlikely tale, was that Cory, a phenomenally shortsighted man, once chased a black hen down Eton High Street, mistaking it for his hat—which was on his head all the time. He was loved for the care he took to entertain students, giving lavish teas and suppers and "water parties" or excursions on the river. One such trip is remembered in Cory's poem "Below Boulter's Lock," according to Reginald Brett, Viscount Esher, in his *Ionicus*. It is not surprising that Cory's influence should have been "impossible to exaggerate," as Oscar Browning put it in *Memories of Sixty Years* (1910), endowed as it was with "an evanescent individuality."

Ironically, it was his total devotion to his stu-dents that dealt him the one harsh blow of his life. Not all parents approved of the delight he took in the company of his charges, a pleasure he always expressed openly in conversation and in letters. It seems, by the account of Henry S. Salt in *Memories of Bygone Eton* (1928), that in 1872 "an indiscreet letter" to a pupil was brought to the notice of the headmaster. Cory resigned and left Eton overnight. Earlier he had rented from his brother an estate at Halsdon near Torrington, and now this became his home. Soon he resigned his fellowship at King's and marked the beginning of a new life by changing his name from Johnson to Cory.

Though he had as many friends as ever, Cory found his suddenly inactive life oppressive. He also suffered from a heart ailment. In 1878 he went to Madeira for his health, where he met a previous acquaintance, Rosa Caroline Guille, daughter of George de Cartaret Guille, rector of Little Torrington. In August of that year Cory married Rosa. Eccentric as ever, Cory refused to let his wife be addressed as Mrs. Cory and insisted on *Madame*. When their son was born in July 1879, Cory chose the name Andrew for him because there never had been a pope of that name.

Cory enjoyed Madeira but could not put his mind to any sustained activity. He finished his two-volume *Guide to Modern English History* (1880, 1882), begun some years earlier to help teach history to a

Portrait of Cory by Charles Furse

Japanese student. Completing the work was an amazing feat in view of the paucity of reference material in Madeira, but the book turned out to be too full of Cory's highly idiosyncratic interpretation of events to be of scholarly value. His eccentricity extended to other writings. In *Ionica II* he carefully excised all punctuation marks, substituting spaces to denote pauses.

In September 1882 Cory returned to England with his family and settled in a house in Pilgrim's Lane, Hampstead. For the next ten years he led an uneventful life, attended by his devoted wife and equally solicitous former students. On 11 June 1892 he died of his old heart ailment; on 16 June he was buried at Hampstead.

Cory's poetical output was scanty and never commanded a wide readership. His only English work, *Ionica,* is too full of classical allusions to have appealed to readers outside his relatively narrow cultural universe. In this slim volume Cory speaks from a direct engagement with the life he knew best, the brief but thrilling life of young minds and hearts opening to the complexities of the world. The central experience that captures Cory's imagination is that of the primacy of unconditional human relationships, of which the most compelling expression occurs in Cory's best-known poem, "Mimnermus at Church":

> You say there is no substance here,
> One great reality above:
> Back from that void I shrink in fear,
> And child-like hide myself in love:
> Show me what angels feel. Till then,
> I cling, a mere weak man, to men.

It is the need for "This warm kind world" of "Mimnermus at Church" that lends poignancy to—and perhaps inspires—Cory's treatment of youth and of school life. It is not the Wordsworthian joy in boyhood that Cory celebrates; rather he thirsts for the emotional nourishment that an engagement with youth may afford. Understandably, this theme is usually set in the context of the school life that he knew so well, as we see in "Academus," "School Fencibles," "Lacordaire at Oxford," "A Retrospect of School Life," and "An Epoch in a Sweet Life." But Cory's intellectual vigor is too great for his feelings to trap his imagination into Kiplingesque paeans of the *Stalky and Co.* (1899) brand. Even within their restricted sphere Cory's poems go far toward stating the universals in man's search for order and permanence.

Occasionally, as in "A Dirge," Cory lapses into

a mannered picturesqueness derived from Tennyson, whom he greatly admired:

> Glide we by, with prow and oar:
> Ripple shadows off the wave,
> And reflected on the shore,
> Haply play about the grave.
> Folds of summer-light enclose
> All that once was Anteros.

But even here or in "Moon-set" an eye for sharp details and an ear for soft cadences ensure elegance. Moreover, an imagination disciplined by the direct vision of Greek and Latin poetry shields Cory from maudlin sentimentalism. His imagery is concrete, often pregnant with a personal understanding of nature, and always phrased felicitously, as the progress of the following stanza from "Mortem, quae violat suavia, pellit amor" to its last line demonstrates:

> The plunging rocks, whose ravenous throats
> The sea in wrath and mockery fills,
> The smoke, that up the valley floats,
> The girlhood of the growing hills.

The symmetry of perception and statement evident in Cory's poetry is on too small a scale to make his contribution to his age a major one, but it reveals a poetic spirit surely aligned with the well-wrought sensibility of Victorian England.

Both as a poet and as a man Cory was modest in his ambitions. He recognized all too clearly his own limitations and the limitations of human joys, those "blossoms rained from windy trees" ("A Separation"). The lines that continue the metaphor best provide Cory's epitaph:

> So let that garden bloom; and I,
> Content with one such flower, will die.

Letters and Journals:
Extracts from the Letters and Journals, selected and arranged by Francis Warre Cornish (Oxford: Privately printed, 1897).

Bibliography:
John Carter, *A Hand-List of the Printed Works of William Johnson, Transactions of the Cambridge Bibliographical Society,* no. 1 (1949-1953): 69-87.

Biography:
Faith Compton Mackenzie, *William Cory, A Biography* (London: Constable, 1950).

References:

Reginald [Brett], Viscount Esher, *Ionicus* (Garden City: Doubleday, Page, 1924);

Oscar Browning, *Memories of Sixty Years* (London & New York: John Lane, 1910);

John Carter, "A Great Eton Master," *Times Literary Supplement,* 2 June 1950, p. 340;

Christopher Hollis, *Eton* (London: Hollis & Carter, 1960), pp. 276-282;

F. J. Lelievre, *Cory's Lucretilis* (Cambridge: Rampant Lions Press, 1964);

Geoffrey Madan, "William Cory," *Cornhill Maga-zine,* 65 (August 1928): 207-213;

Sir Henry Newbolt, "Ionicus," in his *The Island Race* (London: Elkin Mathews, 1898);

Henry S. Salt, "William Johnson (Cory)," in his *Memories of Bygone Eton* (London: Hutchinson, 1928), pp. 112-122;

"William Cory," *Bookman,* 2 (August 1892): 147-149; republished as "The Author of *Ionica*," in W. R. Nicoll and T. J. Wise, *Literary Anecdotes of the Nineteenth Century* (London: Hodder & Stoughton, 1896).

Dinah Maria Craik

(20 April 1826-12 October 1887)

Mabel L. Colbeck
University of British Columbia
and
Tirthankar Bose
University of British Columbia

SELECTED BOOKS: *The Ogilvies: A Novel,* 3 volumes (London: Chapman & Hall, 1849; New York: Harper, 1850);

Cola Monti: or The Story of a Genius (London: Hall, 1849);

Olive, 3 volumes (London: Chapman & Hall, 1850);

The Head of the Family (1 volume, New York: Harper, 1851; 3 volumes, London: Chapman & Hall, 1852);

Alice Learmont: A Fairy Tale (London: Chapman & Hall, 1852; Boston: Mayhew & Baker, 1859);

Bread Upon the Waters: A Governess's Life (London: Governesses' Benevolent Institution, 1852);

Avillion and Other Tales (3 volumes, London: Smith & Elder, 1853; 1 volume, New York: Harper, 1854);

Agatha's Husband: A Novel (3 volumes, London: Chapman & Hall, 1853; 1 volume, New York: Harper, 1853);

A Hero: Philip's Book (London: Addey, 1853);

John Halifax, Gentleman (3 volumes, London: Hurst & Blackett, 1856; 1 volume, New York: Harper, 1856);

Nothing New: Tales (London: Hurst & Blackett, 1857; New York: Harper, 1857);

A Woman's Thoughts About Women (London: Hurst & Blackett, 1858; New York: Rudd & Carleton, 1858);

A Life for Life (3 volumes, London: Hurst & Blackett, 1859; 1 volume, New York: Harper, 1859);

Poems (London: Hurst & Blackett, 1859; Boston: Ticknor & Fields, 1860);

Romantic Tales (London: Smith, Elder, 1859);

Domestic Stories (London: Smith, Elder, 1859);

Our Year: A Child's Book in Prose and Verse (Cambridge: Macmillan, 1860; New York: Harper, 1860);

Studies From Life (London: Hurst & Blackett, 1861; New York: Harper, 1861);

Mistress and Maid (2 volumes, London: Hurst & Blackett, 1863; 1 volume, New York: Harper, 1863);

The Fairy Book (London: Macmillan, 1863; New York: Harper, 1870);

Christian's Mistake (London: Hurst & Blackett, 1865; New York: Harper, 1865);

A New Year's Gift for Sick Children (Edinburgh: Edmonston & Douglas, 1865);

A Noble Life (2 volumes, London: Hurst & Blackett, 1866; 1 volume, New York: Harper, 1866);

Two Marriages (2 volumes, London: Hurst & Black-
    ett, 1867; 1 volume, New York: Harper,
    1867);
The Woman's Kingdom (1 volume, New York:
    Harper, 1868; 3 volumes, London: Hurst &
    Blackett, 1869);
A Brave Lady (3 volumes, London: Hurst & Blackett,
    1870; 1 volume, New York: Harper, 1870);
The Unkind Word and Other Stories (2 volumes, Lon-
    don: Hurst & Blackett, 1870; 1 volume, New
    York: Harper, 1870);
Fair France: Impressions of a Traveller (London: Hurst
    & Blackett, 1871; New York: Harper, 1871);
Little Sunshine's Holiday (London: Low, 1871; New
    York: Harper, 1871);
Hannah (London: Hurst & Blackett, 1872; New
    York: Harper, 1872);
The Adventures of a Brownie as Told to My Child (Lon-
    don: Low, Marston, Low & Searle, 1872; New
    York: Harper, 1872);
My Mother and I (London: Isbister, 1874; New York:
    Harper, 1874);
Songs of Our Youth (London: Daldy, Isbister, 1875;
    New York: Harper, 1875);
Sermons Out of Church (London: Daldy, Isbister,
    1875; New York: Harper, 1875);
The Little Lame Prince (London: Daldy, Isbister,
    1875; New York: Harper, 187?);
Will Denbigh, Nobleman (Boston: Roberts Brothers,
    1877);
Young Mrs. Jardine (3 volumes, London: Hurst &
    Blackett, 1879; 1 volume, New York: Harper,
    1880);
Thirty Years: Being Poems New and Old (London:
    Macmillan, 1880; Boston: Houghton Mifflin,
    1881); republished as *Poems* (London: Mac-
    millan, 1888);
Children's Poetry (London: Macmillan, 1881);
His Little Mother and Other Tales (London: Hurst &
    Blackett, 1881; New York: Harper, 1881);
Plain Speaking (London: Hurst & Blackett, 1882;
    New York: Harper, 1882);
An Unsentimental Journey Through Cornwall (London:
    Macmillan, 1884);
Miss Tommy: A Medieval Romance (London: Macmil-
    lan, 1884; New York: Munro, 1884);
About Money and Other Things (London: Macmillan,
    1886; New York: Harper, 1887);
King Arthur—Not a Love Story (London: Macmillan,
    1886; New York: Harper, 1886);
Work for Idle Hands (London: Spottiswoode, 1886);
An Unknown Country (London: Macmillan, 1887;
    New York: Harper, 1887);

Dinah Maria Craik

Concerning Men and Other Papers (London: Macmil-
    lan, 1888).

OTHER: François Guizot, *M. de Barante, A Memoir*,
    translated by Craik (London: Macmillan,
    1867);
Is It True? Tales Curious and Wonderful, edited by
    Craik (London: Low, 1872).

Dinah Maria Craik, born Mulock, was a
novelist who occasionally expressed herself in verse.
Somewhat lacking in imaginative perception of experience and overburdened with presumed lofti-
ness of sentiment, her poetry is mainly distinguished by careful and coherent structure.
    One of three children, Craik was born on 20
April 1826 at Stoke-on-Trent in Staffordshire. Her
father, Thomas Mulock, was a clergyman and a man
of some learning with a strong taste for literature.
Her mother, Dinah Mulock, kept a small school.
From her earliest days Craik was exposed to a great
respect for literature and religion. Not surprisingly,
she grew up to be a literary personality as well as an

earnest churchwoman with a warm admiration for the Baptist way of life as one that embodied a simple and ideal Christianity.

Craik was not only a precocious poet (she wrote her first poem, "The Party of Cats," when she was ten) she was also a precocious scholar. By the time she was thirteen she was proficient enough in Latin to teach it at her mother's school. Her first published poem, on the birth of the Princess Royal, appeared in the *Staffordshire Advertiser* when she was sixteen. It was to the benefit of Craik and her family that these qualities were manifested early, since her father had little or no idea how to provide the necessities of life. Craik was only twenty when, in 1846, despairing at her father's neglect of his family, she took her invalid mother and two small brothers to

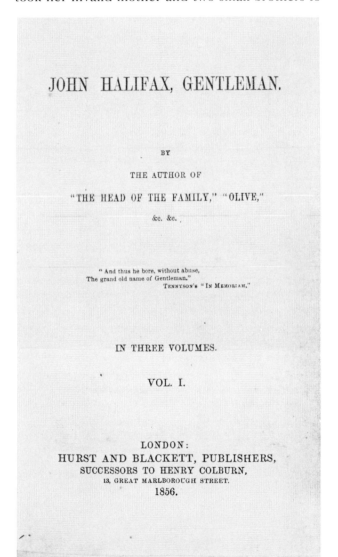

JOHN HALIFAX, GENTLEMAN.

BY

THE AUTHOR OF

"THE HEAD OF THE FAMILY," "OLIVE,"

&c. &c.

" And thus he bore, without abuse,
The grand old name of Gentleman."
                    TENNYSON'S "IN MEMORIAM."

IN THREE VOLUMES.

VOL. I.

LONDON:
HURST AND BLACKETT, PUBLISHERS,
SUCCESSORS TO HENRY COLBURN,
13, GREAT MARLBOROUGH STREET.
1856.

Title page for Craik's best-known novel (courtesy of Thomas Cooper Library, University of South Carolina)

Craik at Lineacre Grange, 1858

London, where she proposed to support them by her literary efforts. The struggles of the early years to earn a living were severe but not protracted. She was fortunate in receiving encouragement from her friends, among whom were Alexander Macmillan, the publisher; Charles Mudie, the founder of Mudie's Library; and Mrs. Oliphant, already an established author. Another friend, Camilla Toulmin, introduced her to John Westland Marston, with whose family Craik formed a lifelong attachment. Her poems, articles, and short stories, in the beginning addressed chiefly to the young, began to appear in a variety of popular magazines, including *Good Words, Littell's Living Age, La Belle France, Macmillan's Magazine,* and *Once a Week.* She took a cottage in Hampstead, where she lived for several years with her family.

With a modest reputation established as a short-story writer, Craik began to work on novels, which were all well remunerated. *The Ogilvies* appeared in 1849, the first of over a score of lengthy novels dealing with the issues of everyday life. The best of her novels is *John Halifax, Gentleman* (1856), which presents an idealistic picture of middle-class English life against a realistic background. In a

Engraved frontispiece and title page for Craik's first poetry collection (courtesy of Thomas Cooper Library, University of South Carolina)

sympathetic, perceptive sketch of her life for the *Dictionary of National Biography,* Richard Garnett describes Craik as a novelist: "She was not a genius, and she does not express the ideals and aspirations of women of exceptional genius: but the tender and philanthropic, and at the same time energetic and practical, womanhood of ordinary life, has never had a more sufficient representative." Generally speaking, in her fiction Craik's chief interest is in presenting the upright, resolute yet sensitive individual in a setting deliberately rendered ordinary.

In 1864 Craik was awarded a civil list pension of £60 annually. A year later she married George Lillie Craik, a partner in the publishing firm of Macmillan and a nephew of the well-known critic and historian of the same name. The Craiks lived at Shortlands, near Bromley. Mrs. Craik spent a great deal of her time and money in arranging recrea-

tional activities for working women, with whom she felt a genuine bond. As there was no child of the marriage, the Craiks adopted a baby girl from a parish workhouse in 1869, an act of considerable social courage in the context of current prejudices.

Although Craik made fiction her province, she by no means gave up poetry. In 1859 her *Poems* appeared, collecting many pieces which had already been published in periodicals. But she was not a prolific poet, and her next volume of poetry, *Songs of Our Youth,* was not published until 1875. In 1880 the two volumes were combined in *Thirty Years: Being Poems New and Old.* This collection was republished as *Poems* in 1888, soon after her death. In 1881 she produced a collection of poems for young readers under the title *Children's Poetry.*

Craik's poems are primarily concerned with the immutability of true love. Constancy is seen as both an emotional value and a moral one which necessarily admits the reality of loss and death. In "Lettice," for instance, "our sister Lettice" is untroubled by warnings regarding her man's dour nature, for, "A true heart's safe, both in smile or frown." Similarly, she is unperturbed by the thought of his frail health, for,

> If death should enter, smite to the centre
> Our poor home palace, all crumbling down,
> He cannot fright us, nor disunite us,
> Life bears LOVE'S cross, death brings LOVE'S
> crown.

The same attitude informs "Semper Fidelis" which contemplates "the dust of broken idols" (one of Craik's rare striking phrases) only to reiterate the permanence of true love which endures

> By a man's will—"See, I hold thee: mine thou art,
> and mine shalt be."
> By a woman's patience—"Sooner doubt I my own soul
> than thee."

A different kind of love, but no less ardent, inspired Craik's best-known poem, "Philip My King," addressed to her godson Philip Bourke Marston, the poet. The syrupy adoration Craik offers in the poem suggests both an acute need for love and a deep capacity for it, not surprising qualities in a childless woman who had in her works identified the family as the proper arena of a worthwhile life. In this poem, as in all others by Craik, her lack of an original response to experience and of imaginative phrasing is partly offset by an undeniable competence in creating clear and simple patterns of statement and rhythm. This ability was responsible for her success in ballads and songs. The ballad "In Swanage Bay," a simple and touching narrative, was immensely popular as a recitation piece. Several of Craik's poems were set to music and are still sung today, most notably her version of the Christmas carol "God rest ye, merry gentlemen." A hundred years after she wrote it, the nostalgic Scottish song "Rothesay Bay" can still be heard, although her authorship of the lyrics is unacknowledged even in recordings. A remarkable feature of this song is Craik's skill with folk dialect, also demonstrated in her novels.

In her personal life Craik was admired by all who knew her as a compassionate and upright woman who was proud of her identity as a profes-

The Corner House, Shortlands, Kent, designed for Craik by William Morris and built with the proceeds from John Halifax, Gentleman. *Craik lived at the Corner House from 1869 until her death in 1887.*

sional. She reportedly put the suave Oscar Wilde to some discomfiture when she suggested that the title of a journal he was proposing to edit for Macmillan be changed from *Lady's World* to *Woman's World.* One of her closest friends was the French historian François Guizot, whose *M. de Barante, A Memoir* she translated into English in 1867. One of her interests was travel, and she wrote successful travel books on France, Cornwall, and Ireland. Another activity, writing for children, was a lifelong pleasure for her. On the more solemn side, Craik could not refrain from drawing morals for everyday use and wrote several didactic essays, such as "A Woman's Thoughts about Women," in which she reinforces the Victorian image of the woman as the angel in the house. It should be remembered that she herself successfully fulfilled the role she saw for women by taking care of her family.

A highly energetic professional author, Craik worked ceaselessly to the end of her life. She was making plans for the wedding of her adopted daughter, Dorothy, when, on 12 October 1887, she suddenly died of a heart attack.

Commenting on the range of Craik's poetry, Richard Garnett essentially repeats his judgment on her novels: "They are a woman's poems, tender, domestic, and sometimes enthusiastic, always genuine song, and the product of real feeling." Her own expectation from poetry seems to have been modest. In *John Halifax, Gentleman* she writes: "I do like poetry to be intelligible. A poet should see things more widely, and express them more vividly, than ordinary folk." Her own poetry is eminently intelligible, but whether she sees things more widely and expresses them more vividly than ordinary folk is open to question.

Reference:

Sally Mitchell, *Dinah Mulock Craik* (Boston: Twayne, 1983).

Papers:

Some of Craik's correspondence is in the Berg Collection at the New York Public Library. The Morris L. Parrish Collection at Princeton University Library has manuscripts and letters by Craik.

Lord De Tabley
(John Byrne Leicester Warren)

(26 April 1835-22 November 1895)

Richard Eaton
West Virginia University

SELECTED BOOKS: *Poems,* as George F. Preston (London: Kent, 1859);

Ballads and Metrical Sketches, as George F. Preston (London: Kent, 1860);

The Threshold of Atrides, as George F. Preston (London: Kent, 1861);

Glimpses of Antiquity, as George F. Preston (London: Kent, 1862);

Praeterita, as William Lancaster (London & Cambridge: Macmillan, 1863);

An Essay on Greek Federal Coinage, as J. Leicester Warren (London, 1863);

On Some Coins of Lycia Under the Rhodian Domination, and of the Lycian League, as J. Leicester Warren (London, 1863);

The Copper Coinage of the Achaean League (London, 1864);

Eclogues and Monodramas, as William Lancaster (London: Privately printed, 1864);

Studies in Verse, as William Lancaster (London: Privately printed, 1865);

Philoctetes: A Metrical Drama, as M. A. (London: Bennett, 1866);

Orestes: A Metrical Drama, as W. P. Lancaster (London: Bennett, 1867);

A Screw Loose: A Novel, as W. P. Lancaster (London: Bentley, 1868);

Ropes of Sand: A Novel, as W. P. Lancaster (London: Bentley, 1869);

Rehearsals: A Book of Verses, as J. Leicester Warren (London: Strahan, 1870);

Hence These Tears, anonymous (London: Bentley, 1872);

Searching the Net: A Book of Verses, as J. Leicester

Warren De Tabley

Warren (London: Strahan, 1873);

Notes on a Projected Cheshire Flora, as J. Leicester Warren (London: Privately printed, 1873);

The Soldier of Fortune: A Tragedy [in verse], as J. Leicester Warren (London: Smith, 1876);

Salvia Richmond, anonymous (London: Bentley, 1878);

A Guide to the Study of Book Plates, (ex-libris), as J. Leicester Warren (London: Pearson, 1880);

Poems, Dramatic and Lyrical, as Lord De Tabley (London: Elkin Mathews & John Lane/New York: Macmillan, 1893);

Poems, Dramatic and Lyrical, Second Series, as Lord De Tabley (London: Lane, 1895);

The Flora of Cheshire, as Lord De Tabley, edited by Spencer Moore (London: Longmans, Green, 1899);

Orpheus in Thrace and Other Poems, as Lord De Tabley, edited by Eleanor, Lady Leighton-Warren

(London: Smith, Elder, 1901);

The Collected Poems, as Lord De Tabley (London: Chapman & Hall, 1903);

Select Poems of Lord De Tabley, edited by John Drinkwater (London: Milford, 1924).

Lord De Tabley was a classicist, numismatist, bibliophile, and botanist of distinction, whose poetry, though never widely read, was held in high regard by his fellow poets.

Born at Tabley House, near Knutsford, Cheshire, John Byrne Leicester Warren (his name till he succeeded to the peerage) was the eldest son to survive infancy of George Fleming Leicester (later Warren), the second Lord De Tabley. The first thirteen years of his life were spent mostly with his mother, Catharina Barbara (née de Salis-Soglio), Lady De Tabley, at home or abroad—in Germany and Italy—where an early interest in antiquities was cultivated in him by his godfather, Lord Zouche. His education was at his father's school and college, Eton, which he entered in 1848, and Christ Church, Oxford, where he matriculated on 20 October 1852. He graduated from Christ Church with a B.A., with a second-class in history and classics in 1859, and with an M.A. in 1860.

After a brief spell in the embassy at Constantinople, he returned to England and was called to the bar from Lincoln's Inn. As the law, however, offered him no real prospects for success, he returned to Cheshire, where he resided for the next ten years. During this period of rustication, De Tabley engaged in the study of numismatics, producing several monographs on the subject within a short period (1863 and 1864) and began the intense examination of local botany that resulted in his valuable work *The Flora of Cheshire,* posthumously published in 1899. He also served as an officer in the Cheshire Yeomanry and, in 1868, attempted, but failed, to win a seat in parliament as a liberal (his father at that time was consistently voting liberal in the House of Lords).

Upon the remarriage of his father in 1871 (his mother died in 1869), De Tabley left Cheshire to make his residence in London. However, rarely at ease in populous centers, he spent much time during his later years at Bournemouth, Poole, or Ryde, in the Isle of Wight. His interest in bibliophily resulted, in 1880, in the publication of *A Guide to the Study of Book Plates,* a work which became standard on the subject. In 1883 he became a fellow of the Society of Antiquaries. The death of his father in 1887 brought him, at the age of fifty-two, to the peerage, and the new Lord De Tabley was faced with the position's concomitant business and legislative obligations. Public life, however, was not congenial to his personality or habits (he made only one speech in the House of Lords and, though he was a liberal, did not vote on the Home Rule Bill of 1893), and he soon retired to the Tabley House. In 1895 he died in the Isle of Wight and was buried at Little Peover, Cheshire. He was sixty years old and had never married.

If not actually reclusive, De Tabley was of a retiring disposition. Much of his youth had been spent in the company of his mother, a noticeably sensitive and melancholy woman. His most intimate friend at Oxford, George Fortescue, died in an accident in 1859. (De Tabley may have borrowed Fortescue's first name for the nom de plume he used on his first four publications; the first of these, *Poems*, 1859, was rumored—though the rumor has been rejected by A. H. Miles—to have been the joint effort of De Tabley and Fortescue.) Though he attempted to pursue an active life between 1860 and 1868, he seemed dogged by failure. His inclinations were toward the studious; his friends—Richard Le Gallienne, Theodore Watts-Dunton, Richard Garnett, Edmund Gosse—were men of letters. These friendships, along with his personal loss and general lack of success, possibly helped to encourage that side of him devoted to the close observation of nature, to scholarship, and to writing.

De Tabley's involvement in these activities was considerable and productive: from 1859 to 1870 he produced at least fifteen published works—eight volumes of verse, two metrical dramas, two novels, and several monographs on early Greek and Byzantine coins. During the 1870s, the decade after his mother's death, De Tabley's poetic activity slackened—one verse tragedy, two books of poetry—though in other ways his industry continued in force—two novels, several articles in the *Journal of Botany,* and a privately printed prospectus for what was to be the labor of a lifetime, *The Flora of Cheshire.* His study of book plates appeared in 1880, and then nothing for thirteen years when, after a flurry of interest in his poetry generated by the appearance in 1891 of some of his poems in A. H. Miles's *Poets and Poetry of the Nineteenth Century,* De Tabley was induced to bring out what became the highly successful *Poems, Dramatic and Lyrical* (1893). The volume went through three editions. In 1895 *Poems, Dramatic and Lyrical, Second Series* appeared.

De Tabley is most often remembered for his poetry, despite his erratic publishing history. Extremely productive from 1859 to 1873, he bent before the discouragement of poor public response by

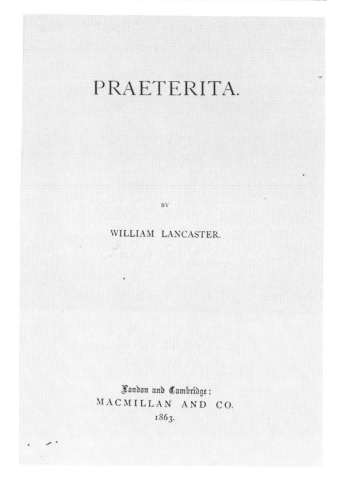

PRAETERITA.

BY

WILLIAM LANCASTER.

London and Cambridge:
MACMILLAN AND CO.
1863.

Title page for the first of De Tabley's three poetry collections published under the pseudonym William Lancaster (courtesy of Thomas Cooper Library, University of South Carolina)

publishing no poetry for twenty years. The burst of interest in his work after Miles's 1891 anthology came too late to inspire much new activity—though the collections of 1893 and 1895 included some verse written after 1873. By dubbing him a "new" poet on the scene, Miles placed him inappropriately among those who were not his contemporaries: his proper place was with his own contemporary A. C. Swinburne, or with Alfred Tennyson and Robert Browning (all three of whom held him in high esteem among modern poets), not with the poets of the fin de siècle.

De Tabley attempted a wide range of verse forms and, though his writing is of uneven quality, he frequently exhibited a real metrical skill. For instance, the ten stanzas of his "An Ode" show a complex arrangement of rhymes and meters brought together without any sense of forced artifice. There is the occasional strained rhythm

("Who stung me redly first, and, when blood dried"—from "Jael"—is inept as a pentameter) or faulty accentuation ("Writhing its wings, as eagle Prómethéan"—in "The Windmill"). And despite the fine imagery of his "Daffodils," it is impossible to avoid unfortunate comparison with Wordsworth on the same subject. But such problems are not excessive, and at times De Tabley rises to Browningesque heights, as in the ending of "The Knight in the Wood":

> You saw the place was deadly; that damned pair,
> The wretched rider and the hide-bound steed,
> Feared to advance, feared to return—that's all!

or in the beginning of "Jael":

> So then their hymn of victory is done.
> Thank God for that. Home are the soldiers gone.

In terms of his themes De Tabley is in the main

Bookplate designed for De Tabley by William Bell Scott

current of mid-nineteenth-century English poetry. "Phaethon" and "Echoes of Hellas" reflect his frustration with the materialism of the age. The metrical drama *Orestes* (1867) might be described as a retelling in ancient Greek setting of the *Hamlet* story, following Goethe's interpretation of the prince. "A Daughter of Circe" (in *Orpheus in Thrace,* 1901), is a classical version of Keats's "La Belle Dame sans Merci." The ebb of faith and indifference of fate in the verse drama *Philoctetes* (1866) recalls, from a Victorian point of view, the fatalism of the Greek tragic spirit.

Interestingly, De Tabley did not often draw on materials from his own past, although much in his environment and his background was the stuff of romance. Descended in the male line from the Byrne family that had received an Irish baronetcy in 1671 (De Tabley was the seventh baronet) and its peerage in 1826, representing as heir general two distinguished west country families (the Leicesters, who had possessed the lands of Tabley since the time of Henry III, and the Warrens of Poynton),

---

P O E M S
DRAMATIC AND
LYRICAL : By
LORD DE TABLEY

SECOND SERIES

LONDON: JOHN LANE, *at the Sign*
of the BODLEY HEAD *in Vigo Street*
NEW YORK: MACMILLAN *and* COMPANY

M DCCC XCV

Title page for the last volume by De Tabley published during his lifetime (courtesy of Thomas Cooper Library, University of South Carolina)

grandson through his mother of a count of the Holy Roman Empire (who could quarter the arms of three great medieval families and was heir general of Sir Francis Drake), De Tabley was, in a sense, heir to the ages. From his youth he moved within an interlocking kinship of the leading county families of the west of England; eventually owner of a 500-year-old house on a 6,000-acre estate, son of a father who was a lord in waiting, a treasurer of the Royal Household, and a privy councillor, De Tabley certainly possessed all the ingredients necessary to inspire dishes of rare pleasure for the readers of an age so enthusiastic about the medievalism of Tennyson and William Morris and the ceremonial of the Queen-Empress Victoria. But with few exceptions De Tabley's muse was either classical or biblical. His achievements were based more on his studies, his classical learning (Watts-Dunton called him "the most learned of English poets"), than on the surrounding natural or social world.

What kept reappearing in De Tabley's poetry—as manifest in his choice of classical and biblical subjects—was his fatalism, a very Victorian sense of forces and inevitabilities that operated on man but were beyond his control. To one critic (George Saintsbury), the word that struck the keynote of De Tabley's poetry was *inevitability;* to another (Gordon Pitts), it was *frustration.* These qualities are different sides of the same coin (cause and effect). To the first critic, De Tabley's work passed all tests except that of facing the issue of inevitability, meeting it head on, and coping with it. To the second, De Tabley was the explorer of frustration—displacing it, examining it in different settings, and doing so successfully, but feeling no obligation to resolve emotional quandaries. These two responses, the first published nearly thirty years and the second more than sixty years after De Tabley's death, show him as a poet who remained capable of finding a generous and appreciative, if temperate, audience.

References:

George Edward Cockayne, "De Tabley, Barony," in his *The Complete Peerage* (London: St. Catherine Press, 1916);

Sir Mountstuart Grant Duff, "A Biographical Notice of the Author," in De Tabley's *The Flora of Cheshire,* edited by Spencer Moore (London: Longmans, Green, 1899);

Sir Edmund Gosse, "Lord De Tabley," *Contemporary Review,* 69 (January 1895): 84-99;

Gordon Pitts, "Lord de Tabley: Poet of Frustration," *West Virginia University Philological Papers,* 14 (1963): 57-73;

Pitts, "The Poetry of John Byrne Leicester Warren, Lord De Tabley, Exclusive of the Dramas," Ph.D. dissertation, University of Pennsylvania, 1956;

Gardner B. Taplin, "The Life, Works, and Literary Reputation of Lord de Tabley," Ph.D. dissertation, Harvard University, 1942;

Theodore Watts-Dunton, "Lord de Tabley," *Athenaeum,* no. 3553 (30 November 1895): 755-756.

Aubrey de Vere
(10 January 1814-21 January 1902)

Lawrence Poston
University of Illinois at Chicago

SELECTED BOOKS: *The Waldenses; or, The Fall of Rora: A Lyrical Sketch. With Other Poems* (Oxford: Parker, 1842);

The Search after Proserpine, Recollections of Greece, and Other Poems (Oxford: Parker, 1843);

English Misrule and Irish Misdeeds: Four Letters from Ireland, Addressed to an English Member of Parliament (London: Murray, 1848);

Picturesque Sketches of Greece and Turkey, 2 volumes (London: Bentley, 1850);

Poems (London: Burns & Lambert, 1855);

May Carols (London: Longman, Brown, Green, Longmans & Roberts, 1857; enlarged, London: T. Richardson/New York: H. H. Richardson, 1870; enlarged again, London: Burns & Oates, 1881; enlarged again, London & New York: Macmillan, 1897);

The Sisters, Inisfail, and Other Poems (London:

Longman, Green, Longman & Roberts/
Dublin: McGlashan & Gill, 1861);

Ireland's Church Question: Five Essays (London:
Longmans, Green, Reader & Dyer, 1868);

Irish Odes and Other Poems (New York: Catholic Publication Society, 1869);

The Legends of St. Patrick (London: King, 1872);

Alexander the Great (London: King, 1874);

St. Thomas of Canterbury (London: King, 1876);

*Antar and Zara: An Eastern Romance. Inisfail and Other
Poems, Meditative and Lyrical* (London: King,
1877);

Legends of the Saxon Saints (London: Kegan Paul,
1879);

Constitutional and Unconstitutional Political Action
(Limerick: McKern, 1881);

*The Foray of Queen Maeve and Other Legends of Ire-
land's Heroic Age* (London: Kegan Paul,
Trench, 1882);

Ireland and Proportional Representation (Dublin:
Hodges, Figgis, 1885);

Legends and Records of the Church and the Empire
(London: Kegan Paul, Trench, 1887);

Essays, Chiefly on Poetry, 2 volumes (London & New
York: Macmillan, 1887);

*St. Peter's Chains, or, Rome and the Italian Revolution: A
Series of Sonnets* (London: Burns & Oates,
1888);

Essays, Chiefly Literary and Ethical, 2 volumes (London & New York: Macmillan, 1889);

Religious Problems of the Nineteenth Century: Essays,
edited by J. G. Wenham (London: St. Anselm's
Society, 1893);

Mediaeval Records and Sonnets (London: Macmillan,
1893);

Recollections of Aubrey de Vere (New York & London:
Arnold, 1897).

Collection: *The Poetical Works of Aubrey de Vere* (volumes 1-3, London: Kegan Paul, Trench,
1884; volumes 4-6, London & New York:
Macmillan, 1897, 1898).

OTHER: Edward O'Brien, *The Lawyer, His Charac-
ter and Rule of Holy Life, after the Manner of
George Herbert's Country Parson*, edited by de
Vere (London: Pickering, 1842);

Heroines of Charity, edited by de Vere (London:
Burns & Lambert, 1854);

*Select Specimens of English Poets, with Biographical
Notices*, edited by de Vere (London: Burns &
Lambert, 1858);

Sir Aubrey de Vere, *Sonnets: A New Edition*, edited
by de Vere (London: Pickering, 1875);

Proteus and Amadeus: A Correspondence, edited by de

De Vere at age twenty

Vere (London: Kegan Paul, 1878);

*The Household Poetry Book: An Anthology of English-
Speaking Poets from Chaucer to Faber*, edited by
de Vere (London: Burns & Oates, 1893);

"The Reception of the Early Poems [of Tennyson],"
in [Hallam Tennyson], *Alfred Lord Tennyson: A
Memoir by His Son*, volume 1 (London: Macmillan, 1897), pp. 501-511.

SELECTED PERIODICAL PUBLICATIONS:
"Tennyson's Princess," *Edinburgh Review*, 90
(October 1849): 388-433;

"Hartley Coleridge," *Edinburgh Review*, 94 (July
1851): 64-97;

"Longfellow," *Fraser's Magazine*, 47 (April 1853):
367-382;

"Longfellow's Works," *Dublin Review*, 34 (June
1853): 359-407;

"The Song of Roland," *Edinburgh Review*, 153 (April
1881): 190-199;

"Odes and Epodes of Horace," *Edinburgh Review*,
190 (July 1899): 119-146.

Aubrey Thomas de Vere's claim to importance in the literary history of Victorian England
rests on two principal accomplishments: his career

Aubrey de Vere

not to narrate it." Dedicated to Tennyson, the poem does vaguely suggest Tennyson's *Maud* in its technique of focusing on moments of emotion rather than employing continuous narrative, but there are two speakers, not one, and each speaks in a different, recurrent verse form. Of more interest are the two dramas, which were obviously to some extent intended to be juxtaposed. In *Alexander the Great* the hero is undone by his pride, claiming as he does the privileges of a god. The empire he labors to construct is a false, perverted anticipation of the true empire of the Church which St. Thomas defends. Only Arsinoe, the daughter of Darius, imagines a Lord of Love who testifies to patience, triumph over death, and ultimate peace. De Vere's version of Thomas à Becket's story in *St. Thomas of Canterbury* is somewhat less interesting thematically but more varied in its array of characters. The central scene between Becket and Henry II (Act IV, scene vi) has genuine dramatic momentum, and the

contrast between worldly, self-seeking clerics and the heroic Becket or the gentle, mystical Herbert of Bosham is clearly etched. One may regret that de Vere did not turn earlier to the verse drama as a medium for his ideas; the form itself forces him to find ways of dramatizing opposing views, and it is that element of conflict which is generally missing from the narrative poems.

De Vere's last years were spent primarily in editing his earlier prose and finishing his *Recollections* (1897). He died unmarried in 1902 at Curragh Chase, and was buried in Askeaton churchyard. His was a life of singularly even tenor devoted to his friends, his poetry, and Irish welfare. In a letter of 1851, Sara Coleridge described those traits which endeared him to others throughout his life: "I have lived among poets a great deal, and have known greater and better poets, . . . but a more *entire poet* . . . in his whole mind and temperament, I never knew or met with. He is most amiable, uniting a feminine gentleness and compassionateness with the most perfect manliness, both negative and positive. He is all simplicity—yet so graceful and gracious! . . . sportive and jestful, yet with a depth of seriousness in his nature ever present." De Vere's *Recollections* give little idea of the man. When he died, Francis Thompson hailed him as the last link with Wordsworth, one who never departed from his discipleship and who lived long enough to see Wordsworthianism go into eclipse and re-emerge more modestly in the younger poet William Watson. De Vere is of interest now as chief among a group of poets—Frederick William Faber, Henry Taylor, Hartley Coleridge, R. C. Trench—who represent a minority tradition in Victorian poetry. It is a group, deeply conservative in its use of poetic language, whose achievements are outweighed by more daring spirits, such as Alfred, Lord Tennyson and Robert Browning, or, in the devotional vein, Gerard Manley Hopkins and Christina Rossetti, but also one resistant as a matter of principle to A. C. Swinburne and the poetic currents he represented. De Vere's letters to Father Matthew Russell in 1882 show his horror at Swinburne's *Tristram of Lyonesse;* he wrote that the poem "seems written to invest the most undisguised sensuality with poetic interest. He has put his hand to a great chivalrous theme only to dirty it. Byron was never half as deliberately, and elaborately, immoral." De Vere is scrupulously moral but at times, particularly in his retelling of Irish and medieval Continental stories, quite dull. Again, it was his fellow poet Thompson who unerringly pinpointed "the defect which [de Vere] shared with all Wordsworthian poets and Wordsworth himself; he was hopelessly prolix, quite unaware when he was not inspired, and left his true poetry to welter amidst masses of dignifiedly prosaic verse." An adroit anthologist could do much to retrieve de Vere's reputation and secure readers to recognize his very real merits.

Letters:
[Matthew Russell, ed.] "Unpublished Letters of Aubrey de Vere," *Irish Monthly,* 39 (August 1911): 421-429; 39 (September 1911): 506-510; 39 (October 1911): 557-566; 40 (January 1912): 35-41; 40 (February 1912): 100-106; [continued by J. F. X. O'Brien] 42 (November 1914): 620-628; 43 (April 1915): 215-223.

Bibliography:
Paul A. Winckler and William V. Stone, "Aubrey Thomas de Vere, 1814-1902: A Bibliography," *Victorian Newsletter,* no. 10 (Autumn 1956).

References:
Calvert Alexander, S. J., *The Catholic Literary Revival: Three Phases in Its Development from 1845 to the Present* (Milwaukee: Bruce, 1935), pp. 37-46;
Katherine Brégy, "Aubrey de Vere and His Prose Work," *Catholic World,* 86 (October 1907): 1-17;
Brégy, "The Poetry of Aubrey de Vere," *Catholic World,* 84 (March 1907): 788-801;
Andrew J. George, "Aubrey de Vere," *Atlantic Monthly,* 89 (June 1902): 829-835;
[R. H. Hutton] "The Poetical Works of Aubrey de Vere," *Spectator,* 57 (25 October 1884): 1407-1409;
Th. A. Pijpers, *Aubrey de Vere as a Man of Letters* (Nijmegen-Utrecht, Netherlands: Dekker & Van de Vegt, 1941);
Lawrence Poston, "Wordsworth among the Victorians: The Case of Sir Henry Taylor," *Studies in Romanticism,* 17 (Summer 1978): 293-305;
S. M. Paraclita Reilly, C. S. J., *Aubrey de Vere: Victorian Observer* (Lincoln: University of Nebraska Press, 1953);
[Hallam Tennyson] *Alfred Lord Tennyson: A Memoir by His Son,* 2 volumes (London: Macmillan, 1897), volume 1, pp. 207-211, 287-294, 378-379; volume 2, pp. 190-191;
Francis Thompson, "Aubrey de Vere," *Academy,* 62 (25 January 1902): 93-94;
Wilfrid Ward, *Aubrey de Vere: A Memoir Based on His Unpublished Diaries and Correspondence* (London: Longmans, Green, 1904).

Austin Dobson
(18 January 1840-2 September 1921)

Michael Darling
Vanier College

SELECTED BOOKS: *Vignettes in Rhyme* (London: King, 1873; revised, London: King, 1874);
The Civil Service Handbook of English Literature (London: Lockwood, 1874; revised and enlarged, London: Lockwood, 1880);
Proverbs in Porcelain and Other Verses (London: King, 1877; enlarged, London: Kegan Paul, 1878);
Hogarth (London: Low, Marston, Searle & Rivington, 1879); enlarged as *William Hogarth* (London: Low, Marston, Searle & Rivington, 1891; enlarged again, London: Kegan Paul, Trench, Trübner, 1898);
Vignettes in Rhyme and Other Verses (New York: Holt, 1880); revised as *Old-World Idylls* (London: Kegan Paul, Trench, 1883);
Fielding (London: Macmillan, 1883; New York: Harper, 1883);
Thomas Bewick and His Pupils (London: Chatto & Windus, 1884; Boston: Osgood, 1884);
At the Sign of the Lyre (New York: Holt, 1885; London: Kegan Paul, Trench, 1885—omits thirteen poems; London: Kegan Paul, Trench, 1889—with additions and omissions);
Richard Steele (London: Longmans, Green, 1886);
Life of Oliver Goldsmith (London: Scott, 1888);
Poems on Several Occasions, 2 volumes (New York:

Austin Dobson, circa 1910

Dodd, Mead, 1889; revised and enlarged, London: Kegan Paul, Trench, Trübner, 1895);

The Sun Dial: A Poem (New York: Dodd, Mead, 1890);

Four Frenchwomen (London: Chatto & Windus, 1890; New York: Dodd, Mead, 1890);

Horace Walpole: A Memoir (London: Osgood, McIlvaine, 1890; New York: Dodd, Mead, 1890);

Eighteenth Century Vignettes, first series (London: Chatto & Windus, 1892; New York: Dodd, Mead, 1892; revised and enlarged, London: Chatto & Windus, 1897);

The Ballad of Beau Brocade and Other Poems of the XVIIITH Century (London: Kegan Paul, Trench, Trübner, 1892);

Eighteenth Century Vignettes, second series (London: Chatto & Windus, 1894; New York: Dodd, Mead, 1894);

The Story of Rosina and Other Verses (London: Kegan Paul, Trench, Trübner, 1895; New York: Dodd, Mead, 1895);

Eighteenth Century Vignettes, third series (London: Chatto & Windus, 1896; New York: Dodd, Mead, 1896);

Collected Poems (London: Kegan Paul, Trench, Trübner, 1897; enlarged, London: Kegan Paul, Trench, Trübner, 1902; enlarged again, London: Kegan Paul, Trench, Trübner, 1909; enlarged again, London: Kegan Paul, Trench, Trübner, 1913);

Fanny Burney (London & New York: Macmillan, 1903);

De Libris: Prose and Verse (London: Macmillan, 1908; New York: Macmillan, 1908; enlarged, London: Macmillan, 1911);

Old Kensington Palace and Other Papers (London: Chatto & Windus, 1910; New York: Stokes, 1910);

At Prior Park and Other Papers (London: Chatto & Windus, 1912; New York: Stokes, 1912);

Rosalba's Journal and Other Papers (London: Chatto & Windus, 1915);

Later Essays 1917-1920 (London & New York: Oxford University Press, 1921).

Collection: *The Complete Poetical Works of Austin Dobson* (London & New York: Oxford University Press, 1923).

OTHER: *A Bookman's Budget,* compiled with contributions by Dobson (London & New York: Oxford University Press, 1917).

The late-nineteenth-century vogue for light verse, especially in forms borrowed from the French, is well illustrated by the poetry of Austin Dobson, whose craftsmanship and formal elegance give permanence to a body of poetry that is unremarkable for the profundity of its themes. Perhaps best remembered now for his biographical scholarship, Dobson was in his own time a widely known and admired poet both in England and America, and many of his books were published in multiple editions, testifying to the popularity of verse whose nostalgia for the eighteenth century offered a secure haven removed from the daily vicissitudes of Victorian life.

Born at Plymouth, England, on 18 January 1840, Henry Austin Dobson was the son of George Clarisse Dobson, a civil engineer, and Augusta Harris Dobson. He was educated at Beaumaris Grammar School, at a Coventry private school, and at the gymnase in Strasbourg. At the age of sixteen, he returned to London as a clerk in the Board of Trade, where he was to remain for the next forty-five years, eventually becoming principal of his de-

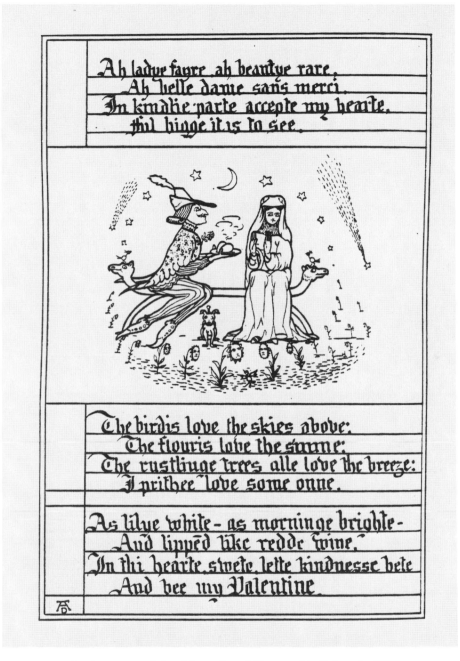

Valentine composed, hand-lettered, and illustrated by Dobson in 1865

partment. In every way, Dobson was a respectable Victorian. He was married at the age of twenty-eight to Frances Mary Beardmore, fathered ten children, and lived quietly at Ealing, devoting his spare time to the composition of poetry and to research in the literature of the eighteenth century. As his close friend and colleague Edmund Gosse remarked, "No writer of equal distinction can ever have exceeded Austin Dobson in the absence of saliency in the personal details of his life."

After an abortive attempt to develop his talents as a painter, Dobson turned to verse, and his first poem, "A City Flower," was published in *Temple Bar* in 1864. In 1865 and 1866 he contributed a series of poems to the *Englishwoman's Domestic Magazine*. From 1868 on his special talent for light verse found an avid supporter in Anthony Trollope, in whose *St. Paul's* magazine appeared several of Dobson's poems, including some of his most popular works—"Une Marquise," "A Dead Letter,"

London Dec. 10. 1860.

My dear Fanny Catherine Lise,

I am obliged to write all your three names because it is such a very long while since I wrote to you that I cannot tell which of them you like to be called by. I suppose Mamma has told you that I am coming down to see you after Christmas Day & to stay a week, which you know is seven whole days. I want you to write if you can and tell me what you would like me to bring out of the fine shops I pass every day — Would you like a book of Fairy Tales about the little wee men & women who sleep all day in the bells of the flowers and at night dance polkas and waltzes like Jimmy does you know — all in the moon-light — You need not look out of window

what do you do with yourself all day? I sit all day in a large room with a great inkbottle and many pens and write in a great book. My Master is a tall man with a great beard like that Agrippa in Willy's book. He does not pinch me tho', but I think he would like to put me into his inkstand [little bottle] sometimes — only I am too large, and his bottle is not so large as Agrippa's. In the evening when you are in bed I draw pictures, or else I take my gun and go and play at soldiers. My gun is very large, and I look like this:

Sometimes I read fairy-tales do you know, last Saturday I had a friend to tea and we read oh! such funny fairy Tales. That reminds me that it will be soon Christmas Day when there are lots of fairies about — Mind you are very good — and be sure

might to try and see them, because it is too cold now and they would get pains in their backs and arms and legs, like poor old Granny has. Or about the poor man who had such a large long, heavy nose that he could not walk without having two strong men to carry it, like this:

He has got his pocket-handkerchief in his hand. It is very large you see — but when he had a cold, he took out [wore out] forty every day — or more than you and Willy and Papa and Mamma, and Baker have got all together. Or would you like a little tea-set or a dinner set or any thing else — You will have a long time to think about it — but mind you can only have one of these things — Will you ask Willy what he would like — and tell me.

Before you eat your plum-pudding that little Tom Thumb isn't hidden somewhere in it because if you bite him in two pieces he will die.

Please give my love to Mamma and Papa & all the rest and Believe me

     My dear little sister.

       Your affecte Brother

         Austin Dobson.

An early letter from Dobson to his sister (Austin Dobson: Some Notes by Alban Dobson, *1928*)

"Avice," "The Story of Rosina," "The Drama of the
Doctor's Window," and "A Gentleman of the Old
School." The tone and atmosphere of a typical Dobson lyric—its sensory evocation of the past through
nostalgic reminiscence bordering on sentimentality
and its uncritical irony provoking smiles but never
laughter—are perfectly conveyed in the opening
lines of "A Dead Letter":

> I drew it from its china tomb;—
>   It came out feebly scented
> With some thin ghost of past perfume
>   That dust and days had lent it.
>
> An old, old letter,—folded still!
>   To read with due composure,
> I sought the sun-lit window-sill,
>   Above the grey enclosure,
>
> That glimmering in the sultry haze,
>   Faint-flowered, dimly shaded,
> Slumbered like Goldsmith's Madam Blaize,
>   Bedizened and brocaded.

The contemplative atmosphere of eighteenth-century pastoral is conveyed in "A Gentleman of the Old School" (sometimes thought to be a
portrait of Dobson himself), with its allusions to Sir
Joshua Reynolds and Robert Blair's poem *The Grave*
(1743). The poem was successful enough to prompt
a sequel—"A Gentlewoman of the Old School"—in
which the lady's taste for "finest tea (she called it
'tay'),/And ratafia" and "ballads set/By Arne or
Jackson" testify to the author's familiarity with the
Georgian era.

In some of his early poems there is also a
distinct Pre-Raphaelite flavor. Dobson was an admirer of D. G. Rossetti and William Morris, though
he disliked the work of A. C. Swinburne, undoubtedly on moral rather than aesthetic grounds. The
Pre-Raphaelite influence is especially marked in the
medieval settings of Dobson's "André le Chapelain"
and "The Dying of Tanneguy du Bois." These
poems, however, are less successful than his
"eighteenth-century" verse in giving a sense of life
in the time and place they describe.

In his first volume, *Vignettes in Rhyme* (1873),
Dobson collected most of the poems that had appeared in periodicals, dedicating the work to Trollope. Although the book was a great critical and
popular success, he realized that he could not long
sustain his readers' interest in his subject matter
without some variation in form. There was no
shortage of competition in the magazines churning
out sentimental light verse in ballad stanza. Break-

*Dobson's wife, Frances Mary Beardmore Dobson, whom he
married in 1868*

ing free of the mold in which his early work had cast
him, Dobson hit upon the use of medieval French
forms, including the triolet, the ballade, and the
rondeau, which he had read about in Théodore de
Banville's *Petite Traité de poésie française,* published in
1872. In an earlier book entitled *Odes funambulesques*
(1858), Banville had experimented with these
forms, and his work was just becoming known in
England. Dobson was one of the first Victorians to
fully explore the potential of French forms in his
poetry, and many of his experiments remain the
finest of their kind in the English language. His first
published collection of triolets appeared in the
Graphic in May 1874. The triolet, a delicate eight-
line poem rhyming ABaAabAB (the capital letters
indicate repetition of entire lines), demands a deft
turn in the middle to lend subtle irony to the final
echo of the opening lines. Dobson does just this in
"A Kiss," perhaps the best-known example of an
English triolet:

> Rose kissed me to-day.
>   Will she kiss me to-morrow?

Let it be as it may,
Rose kissed me to-day,
But the pleasure gives way
  To a savour of sorrow; —
Rose kissed me to-day, —
  Will she kiss me to-morrow?

He followed his triolets with the publication of several rondeaux in the *Spectator* and *Examiner* and included many of these "French" poems in his next book, *Proverbs in Porcelain* (1877). This volume is noteworthy for another of its author's specialties — the poem in dialogue. Frequently set in the boudoirs and gardens of pre-Revolutionary French châteaux, these poems, as Dobson notes in the prologue to *Proverbs in Porcelain,* assume "A common taste for old costume, —/Old pictures, —books." "The Ballad à-la-Mode" and "The Secrets of the Heart" are typical in their almost feminine sensibility, delighting in the same kind of glittering and insubstantial world that Alexander Pope had immortalized in *The Rape of the Lock* (1712).

Dobson's verses in the French forms found great favor with the public, and he joined an increasing number of poets — Robert Bridges, W. E. Henley, Andrew Lang — who were successfully exploiting Banville's rediscovery. Dobson continued to perfect the ballade, his best work in this form being "On a Fan that Belonged to the Marquise de Pompadour," first published in 1878. Several critics have suggested that this is Dobson's masterpiece, with its finely ironic envoi:

Where are the secrets it knew?
  Weavings of plot and of plan?
  —But where is the Pompadour, too?
This was the Pompadour's *Fan!*

W. E. Henley acknowledged Dobson's mastery, crediting him with writing the three best ballades in English — "The Ballad of Prose and Rhyme," "The Ballad of Imitation," and "A Ballad to Queen Elizabeth." But despite his evident success, Dobson did not persist with his experiments, and, in fact, less than a third of his poems are written in French forms. The public began to lose interest in them toward the end of the century, and writers such as Robert Louis Stevenson, who had dabbled with villanelles and rondeaux, came to denounce them as trivial and affected.

Dobson ceased to develop as a poet after 1880. His next book, *Old-World Idylls,* published in 1883, consists mostly of poems from the earlier volumes, with some revisions. By the time his fourth collec-

tion, *At the Sign of the Lyre,* appeared two years later, he was almost wholly occupied by his eighteenth-century studies, and though he continued to produce poems well into the twentieth century, the bulk of his later work consists of occasional verse and dedications to his friends. He also embellished his collections of essays with prologues in verse. An example is the prologue to *A Bookman's Budget;* a brief extract suffices to indicate to what extent Dobson's poetic efforts had declined into banality by 1917:

Good-bye, my Book. To other eyes
  With equal mind, I now address you,
Since in Dame Fortune's lap it lies
  Either to ban you or to bless you.

Though a brief comment here cannot do justice to Dobson's scholarship, it should be said that his lives of Henry Fielding, Oliver Goldsmith, Horace Walpole, and others are by no means the work of a dilettante. His biographies are, for their time, models of scrupulous accuracy, and yet they are characterized by an enchantment with the past that rarely animates the modern scholarly biography. His better essays, such as those in the three series of *Eighteenth Century Vignettes* (1892, 1894, 1896), are similar to the best of his poems in their wholehearted devotion to recapturing the essence of the era they celebrate.

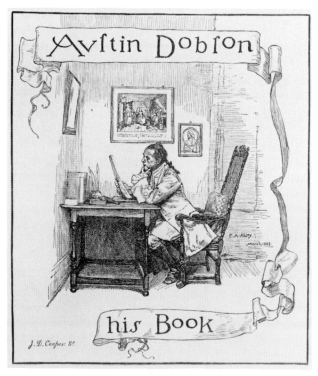

Bookplate by Edwin A. Abbey

In his later years, Dobson won many honors. He was made a fellow of the Royal Society of Literature, awarded an honorary LL.D. by the University of Edinburgh, and named an honorary member of the Author's Club of New York. With advancing age, his health declined, and he was troubled by failing eyesight and rheumatoid arthritis. He suffered a severely debilitating heart attack in June 1921, and died at Ealing on 2 September of that year.

In assessing Dobson's contribution to Victorian poetry, some literary historians have identified him as a practitioner of *vers de société* and compared his work to that of his friend Frederick Locker-Lampson. Though Dobson himself classified poems such as his "The Screen in the Lumber Room" and "Growing Gray" as *vers de société,* these lyrics, like the greater part of his work, are more humorous than witty, more gently ironic than satirical, and characterized by a quality of sentiment that is, if seldom maudlin or cloying, nonetheless foreign to the hard-edged brilliance of, say, Matthew Prior, W. M. Praed, or Locker-Lampson. Though unambitious and unspectacular, his verse will continue to be read by those who delight in formal perfection and who do not disdain the wistful nostalgia it evokes.

Bibliographies:

F. E. Murray, *A Bibliography of Austin Dobson* (Derby: Murray, 1900);

Alban Dobson, *A Bibliography of the First Editions of Published and Privately Printed Books and Pam-*
phlets by Austin Dobson (London: First Edition Club, 1925);

Dobson, *Catalogues of the Collection of the Works of Austin Dobson, 1840-1921* (London: University of London Library, 1960).

References:

Alban Dobson, *Austin Dobson: Some Notes* (London: Oxford University Press, 1928);

Herbert C. Lipscomb, "Horace and the Poetry of Austin Dobson," *American Journal of Philology,* 50, no. 197 (1929): 1-20;

Brander Matthews, "Two Latter-Day Lyrists," in his *Pen and Ink,* revised edition (New York: Scribners, 1902), pp. 121-165;

James Keith Robinson, "Austin Dobson and the Rondeliers," *Modern Language Quarterly,* 14 (March 1953): 31-42;

Arthur Symons, "Austin Dobson," in his *Studies in Prose and Verse* (London: Dent, 1904), pp. 224-229;

A. W., "Austin Dobson: 1840-1921: A Poet of Two Worlds," *Times Literary Supplement,* 13 January 1940, p. 22;

Cornelius Weygandt, "Austin Dobson, Augustan," in his *Tuesdays at Ten* (Philadelphia: University of Pennsylvania Press, 1928), pp. 232-239.

Papers:

The Austin Dobson Collection at the University of London includes books, manuscripts, notebooks, reviews, and correspondence.

Edward Dowden
(13 May 1843-4 April 1913)

Richard Eaton
West Virginia University

SELECTED BOOKS: *Shakspere: A Critical Study of His Mind and Art* (London: King, 1875; New York: Harper, 1880);

Poems (London: King, 1876; enlarged, London & Toronto: Dent, 1914);

Shakspere (London: Macmillan, 1877; New York: Appleton, 1878);

Studies in Literature 1789-1877 (London: Kegan Paul, 1878);

Southey (London: Macmillan, 1879; New York: Harper, 1880);

Spenser the Poet and Teacher, volume 1 of *The Complete Works of Edmund Spenser,* edited by A. B. Grosart (London & Aylesbury: Privately printed, 1882);

The Life of Percy Bysshe Shelley, 2 volumes (London: Kegan Paul, Trench, 1886; Philadelphia: Lippincott, 1892);

Transcripts and Studies (London: Kegan Paul,
    Trench, Trübner, 1887);
New Studies in Literature (London: Kegan Paul,
    Trench, Trübner, 1895; Boston: Houghton
    Mifflin, 1895);
The French Revolution and English Literature (London:
    Kegan Paul, 1897; New York: Scribners,
    1897);
A History of French Literature (New York: Appleton,
    1897; London: Heinemann, 1899);
Puritan and Anglican: Studies in Literature (London:
    Kegan Paul, Trench, Trübner, 1900; New
    York: Holt, 1900);
Robert Browning (London: Dent / New York: Dutton,
    1904); republished as *The Life of Robert
    Browning* (London & Toronto: Dent / New
    York: Dutton, 1915);
Michel de Montaigne (Philadelphia & London: Lip-
    pincott, 1905);
Essays Modern and Elizabethan (London: Dent, 1910;
    New York: Dutton, 1910);
A Woman's Reliquary (Dublin: Privately printed,
    1913; London: Dent, 1914).

Edward Dowden was a poet, scholar, and critic
who directed his major attention to the professional
study of English letters. Because English literature
was a new field of academic investigation, he always
had to contend with the fact that it lacked the reputation that mathematics and classics had. He
brought stature to his discipline by applying to it the
spirit and some of the tools of more traditional
studies (careful editing, scrupulous handling of
materials), as well as by his graceful writing style and
immense industry.

Born at Cork in 1843, Dowden was the fourth
son of John Wheeler Dowden and his wife Alicia
Bennett. The Dowdens were a family of English and
Scottish origin that had been settled in Ireland for
two hundred years. His immediate forebears, Protestant and, in culture and tradition, English, were of
the affluent merchant middle class, with connections in the academic and ecclesiastical world (Dowden's brother John became bishop of Edinburgh;
his cousin and college tutor was George Salmon, the
mathematician and divine who subsequently became provost at Trinity College, Dublin; George
Cresley Perry, the church historian, was a distant
connection). Dowden attended Queens College in
Cork, and then Trinity College, Dublin, where he
won the Wray Prize in metaphysical studies, a first-
class moderatorship in logic and ethics, and the vice
chancellor's prize in English verse and prose composition. In 1863 he took his B.A. After graduation,

Edward Dowden

rather than taking orders (he had doubts about the
genuineness of the Bible), he studied toward the
M.A., which was conferred in 1867. In 1866 Dowden took up the post of professor of English literature at Alexandra College, a women's college in
Dublin. That same year he married Mary Clerke, by
whom he had three children. In 1867 he was appointed to the newly founded chair of English literature at Trinity College, a post he retained till his
death. Sometime before 1872 he met Elizabeth
Dickinson, the daughter of John West, dean of St.
Patrick's Cathedral, Dublin. She became a friend,
correspondent, and adviser in literary matters. In
1895, three years after Mary Clerke's death, Dickinson became Dowden's second wife.

Though Dowden traveled widely (including
two journeys to America) and lectured away from
Dublin frequently—at Oxford in 1889 (the Taylor-
ian lectures), at Cambridge between 1892 and 1896
(the Clark lectures), and at Princeton in 1896—his
home was always Dublin, and for many years it
served as a center for literary discussion and en-

couragement. A college friend of John Butler
Yeats, for a short while he had an avuncular relationship with his friend's son William Butler
Yeats. Indeed, the young William Butler Yeats described Dowden as "wise in his encouragement,
never overpraising, and never unsympathetic"; his
house was "orderly" and "prosperous," "where all
was in good taste, where poetry was rightly valued,"
a home that "made Dublin tolerable for a while."
E. J. Gwynn, a friend and colleague in Dowden's
later years, found Dowden "tolerant, undogmatic,
deeply serious" though incapable of "sophisticating
moral issues," and "leaning towards skepticism."
But whereas Gwynn thought Dowden "peremptory
in matters of conduct," Yeats, seeing him as "for
perhaps a couple of years . . . an image of romance,"
imagined Dowden's having "a past worthy of that
dark, romantic face . . . and believed that he had
loved unhappily and illicitly." The relationship with
Yeats was later to cool, partly, no doubt, because of
Dowden's lack of sympathy with Irish nationalism
and with what he viewed as a concomitant literary
provincialism.

Dowden's most important work came early in
his career—with his first book, *Shakspere: A Critical
Study of His Mind and Art* (1875). Despite the reverses
of over a century of scholarship and criticism (led by
Lytton Strachey's attack on Dowden in 1904), Dowden's study has survived. It was immediately successful and continued to be so, going through sixteen English editions during the forty-three years
after its publication. Because of *Shakspere* Dowden
was linked with A. C. Swinburne and Andrew Cecil
Bradley as one of the three major Shakespeareans
of the Victorian era. His was the first effort to try to
take the measure of Shakespeare's personality from
the plays and poems. Reacting to the popular view
of Shakespeare as (in the words of T. J. B. Spencer)
the "keen young man of humble rank who got on"
and the contrary view of Taine that Shakespeare
was driven by almost overpowering passions, Dowden presented a Shakespeare poised between the
demands of practicality and passion. As Arthur M.
Eastman summarizes in *A Short History of Shakespearean Criticism* (1968), Dowden's Shakespeare,
though not didactic (generally "without an ethical
tendency"), reflected a clear "ethical effect": a
"stern and persistent resolution." Though Dowden's book is now thought of as "tentative, inconsistent, and ultimately, not unified," to quote
Eastman, it did provide a point of departure for
such critics as Sidney Lanier, Swinburne, Frank
Harris, Ernest Jones, Middleton Murry, George
Bernard Shaw, Caroline Spurgeon, Wyndham

Lewis, G. Wilson Knight, and D. A. Traversi.

Dowden had long hoped to become a poet and
toward that end produced a volume of verse—
Poems—in 1876. But the needs of a growing family
pulled him back to his academic labors. His efforts
at verse, however, did have admirers; a second edition of *Poems* appeared in 1877, and another volume, *A Woman's Reliquary*, was published posthumously in 1913 (both volumes were republished as
edited by his widow, in 1914). Though John Butler
Yeats was impatient with Dowden for not pursuing
poetry, there are few subsequent readers who
would share Yeats's enthusiasm. The influence of
Wordsworth (an early enthusiasm of Dowden's) is
apparent in the poetry, and William Butler Yeats
noted a Swinburnian rhetoric in Dowden's verse.
Dowden's five monologues spoken by classical
Greek women, collectively titled "The Heroines,"
are more specifically reminiscent of Tennyson (in
their romantic imagery) and Browning (in their
psychological concerns); the monologue by Helen
may have influenced Yeats's "Leda and the Swan."

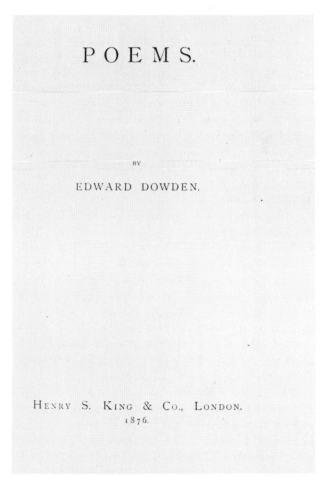

POEMS.

BY

EDWARD DOWDEN.

HENRY S. KING & CO., LONDON.
1876.

*Title page for Dowden's first volume of verse (courtesy of Thomas
Cooper Library, University of South Carolina)*

W. H. Auden saw fit to include "In the Cathedral Close" in his *Nineteenth-Century British Minor Poets* (1965). Alfred H. Miles selected some fourteen of Dowden's poems, among them "Andromeda" (from "The Heroines") and "In the Cathedral Close," for inclusion in his anthology *Robert Bridges and Contemporary Poets* (1892), one of the volumes of Miles's *The Poets and Poetry of the Nineteenth Century*. However, the promise shown early in Dowden's verse never developed. He was an echo of other poets. Whatever the passions that generated his desire to compose, they were so tightly reined that what in other, more successful poets might have been thought of as control or classical equilibrium between emotion and expression emerged, in Dowden, as placidity.

In 1877 Dowden produced his primer, *Shakspere*. Aimed at a nonacademic audience, it gained him wide popularity. However, its oversimplified periodization of Shakespeare's career has tended to detract from Dowden's critical standing. The volume has attained a dubious immortality in Buck Mulligan's ironic paraphrase of its first sentence in James Joyce's *Ulysses*.

Dowden's most ambitious work was his two-volume *Life of Percy Bysshe Shelley* (1886). Though Dowden showed little sympathy for his subject and was compelled, in his research, to juggle the opposing interests of Shelley's two families by his wives Harriet Westbrook and Mary Godwin, Dowden's *Shelley* is, in the words of a recent critic, a work of "impressive scholarship, dignity and magnitude." Dowden's biography dominated Shelley studies for half a century, till it was supplanted by Newman Ivey White's *Shelley* in 1940.

Dowden's work on the impact of the French Revolution on English literature (from his Princeton lectures of 1896) and his *Robert Browning* (1904), though dated in their scholarship, still repay readers' efforts. *The French Revolution and English Literature* (1897), a forceful beginning to the serious study of the relationship between France and the pre-Romantics, is lively in its characterizations and rich in biographical detail. His criticism of Browning is sensible, and his remarks on Browning's relation to the English novel are especially insightful.

In sum, then, it is Dowden's scholarly and critical work that rates most attention. In these his activity was enormous. His editions of Edward Trelawny's *Recollections of the Last Days of Shelley and Byron* (1906) and Thomas Jefferson Hogg's *Life of Percy Bysshe Shelley* (1906) are still standard. He collected in five books his essays and lectures on Transcendentalism, the relationship between science and

Drawing of Dowden by John Butler Yeats (Anderson Galleries, sale 1783, 10-12 December 1923)

literature, Arnold, Richard Baxter, Robert Bridges, Thomas Browne, Browning, Bunyan, Samuel Butler, Carlyle, Coleridge, Cowper, Donne, George Eliot, Goethe, Heine, Herbert, Richard Hooker, Hugo, Ibsen, Landor, Marlowe, Meredith, Milton, Pater, Shakespeare, Shelley, Spenser, Jeremy Taylor, Tennyson, Henry Vaughan, Whitman (of whom he was an early supporter and with whom he corresponded), and Wordsworth. In book-length studies he examined Montaigne, Southey, and Spenser. His editions of writers' works are too numerous to list; W. J. Craig's edition of Shakespeare's *Works,* containing Dowden's introductory studies of the plays, was republished by the Oxford University Press as recently as 1962.

Always uncomfortable with traditional religious forms (though not outspoken on the matter, as became the brother of a bishop), Dowden was from early life a transcendentalist; ethical concerns were important to him, as was manifest in his earliest choices of writers to study. His subjects tended to be moralists and, indeed, as with Whitman, even prophets. As a transcendentalist, Dowden sought in his examination of literature to find some single principle dominating the temperament of the writers—an aim inspired, possibly, by Emerson's *Representative Men* and Carlyle's *Heroes and Hero-Worship.* Though now much of Dowden's work is dated, and some simply no longer fashionable, at least ten of his books have been republished in the last twenty years, while *Shakspere: A Critical Study of His Mind and Art* has had influence in Shakespearean studies longer than the work of anybody but Bradley.

Letters:

Letters of Edward Dowden and His Correspondents, edited by Elizabeth D. and Hilda M. Dowden (London: Dent, 1914; New York: Dutton, 1914);

Fragments from Old Letters, E. D. to E. D. W., 1869-1892, edited by Elizabeth D. Dowden (London: Dent, 1914; New York: Dutton, 1914);

Letters About Shelley, Interchanged by Three Friends—Edward Dowden, Richard Garnett, and W. Michael Rossetti, edited by R. S. Garnett (Lon-

don & New York: Hodder & Stoughton, 1917).

References:

Louise S. Boas, "Edward Dowden, the Esdailes, and the Shelleys," *N and Q,* new series 12 (May 1965): 163-166, and 12 (June 1965): 227-231;

Arthur M. Eastman, *A Short History of Shakespearean Criticism* (New York: Random House, 1968), pp. 139-151;

Kathryn R. Ludwigson, *Edward Dowden* (New York: Twayne, 1973);

F. S. L. Lyons, "Yeats and Victorian Ireland," in *Yeats Sligo and Ireland,* edited by A. Norman Jeffares (Totowa, N.J.: Barnes & Noble, 1980), pp. 115-138;

Aron Y. Stavisky, *Shakespeare and the Victorians: Roots of Modern Criticism* (Norman: University of Oklahoma Press, 1969), pp. 69-79;

William Butler Yeats, *The Autobiography of William Butler Yeats* (New York: Macmillan, 1971), pp. 56-59, 64, 158, 191, 354.

Papers:

Manuscripts, letters, and diaries by Dowden are in the Trinity College archives, Dublin.

George Eliot
(Mary Ann Evans)

(22 November 1819-22 December 1880)

Rowland L. Collins
University of Rochester

See also the Eliot entry in *DLB 21, Victorian Novelists Before 1885.*

BOOKS: *Scenes of Clerical Life* (2 volumes, Edinburgh & London: Blackwood, 1858; 1 volume, New York: Harper, 1858);

Adam Bede (3 volumes, Edinburgh & London: Blackwood, 1859; 1 volume, New York: Harper, 1859);

The Mill on the Floss (3 volumes, Edinburgh & London: Blackwood, 1860; 1 volume, New York: Harper, 1860);

Silas Marner: The Weaver of Raveloe (Edinburgh &

London: Blackwood, 1861; New York: Harper, 1861);

Romola (3 volumes, London: Smith, Elder, 1863; 1 volume, New York: Harper, 1863);

Felix Holt, The Radical (3 volumes, Edinburgh & London: Blackwood, 1866; 1 volume, New York: Harper, 1866);

The Spanish Gypsy: A Poem (Edinburgh & London: Blackwood, 1868; Boston: Ticknor & Fields, 1868);

How Lisa Loved the King (Boston: Fields, Osgood, 1869);

Middlemarch: A Study of Provincial Life (8 parts, Edin-

*George Eliot. Chalk-drawing by Frederick Burton, 1865
(National Portrait Gallery).*

burgh & London: Blackwood, 1871-1872; 2
volumes, New York: Harper, 1872-1873);

The Legend of Jubal and Other Poems (Edinburgh &
London: Blackwood, 1874; Boston: Osgood,
1874);

Daniel Deronda (8 parts, Edinburgh & London:
Blackwood, 1876; 2 volumes, New York:
Harper, 1876);

Impressions of Theophrastus Such (Edinburgh & London: Blackwood, 1879; New York: Harper,
1879);

Essays and Leaves from a Note-Book, edited by C. L.
Lewes (Edinburgh & London: Blackwood,
1884; New York: Harper, 1884);

Quarry for Middlemarch, edited by Anna T. Kitchel
(Berkeley: University of California Press,
1950);

Essays of George Eliot, edited by Thomas Pinney (New
York: Columbia University Press, 1963; London: Routledge & Kegan Paul, 1963);

*Some George Eliot Notebooks: An Edition of the Carl H.
Pforzheimer Library's George Eliot Holograph
Notebooks, Mss. 707, 708, 709, 710, 711* [the

Daniel Deronda notebooks], edited by William
Baker (Salzburg: Universität Salzburg, 1976);

George Eliot's Middlemarch Notebooks: A Transcription,
edited by John Clark Pratt and Victor A.
Neufeldt (Berkeley: University of California
Press, 1979);

*A Writer's Notebook, 1854-1879, and Uncollected Writ-
ings,* edited by Joseph Wiesenfarth (Charlottesville: University of Virginia Press, 1981).

Collection: *The Works of George Eliot,* Cabinet Edition, 24 volumes (Edinburgh & London:
Blackwood, 1878-1885).

TRANSLATIONS: David Friedrich Strauss, *The
Life of Jesus, Critically Examined,* translated
from the fourth German edition, 3 volumes
(London: Chapman, 1846);

Ludwig Feuerbach, *The Essence of Christianity,*
translated as Marian Evans from the second
German edition, *Chapman's Quarterly Series,* no.
6 (London: Chapman, 1854).

SELECTED PERIODICAL PUBLICATIONS:
" 'Knowing That Shortly I Must Put Off This
Tabernacle,' " *Christian Observer* (January
1840): 38;

"Scenes of Clerical Life," *Blackwood's Edinburgh
Magazine,* 81-82 (January-November 1857):
1-22, 153-172, 319-334, 416-434, 521-539,
685-702; 55-76, 189-206, 329-344, 457-473,
519-541;

"The Lifted Veil," *Blackwood's Edinburgh Magazine,*
86 (July 1859): 24-28;

"Romola," *Cornhill Magazine,* 6-8 (July 1862-August
1863): 1-43, 145-186, 289-318, 433-470, 577-
604, 721-757; 1-30, 145-171, 281-309, 417-
440, 553-576, 681-705; 1-34, 129-153;

"Brother Jacob," *Cornhill Magazine,* 10 (July 1864):
1-32;

"Address to Working Men, by Felix Holt,"
Blackwood's Edinburgh Magazine, 103 (January
1868): 1-11;

"How Lisa Loved the King," *Blackwood's Edinburgh
Magazine,* 105 (May 1869): 513-528;

"Agatha," *Atlantic Monthly,* 24 (August 1869): 199-
207;

"The Legend of Jubal," *Macmillan's Magazine,* 22
(May 1870): 1-18; *Atlantic Monthly,* 25 (May
1870): 589-604;

"Armgart," *Macmillan's Magazine,* 24 (July 1871):
161-187;

"A College Breakfast Party," *Macmillan's Magazine,*
38 (July 1878): 161-179.

Griff House, Arbury, childhood home of Mary Ann Evans

George Eliot is widely recognized as one of the most important writers of the nineteenth century; yet, more often than not, her two volumes of poetry are ignored in modern critical assessments. Like so many of her contemporaries, she tried to make significant literary contributions in more than one genre; her poems—both narrative and lyric—deal, however, with some of the same themes which inform her novels and her short stories. Her poems are much less accomplished than her prose fiction—only one poem, "O May I Join the Choir Invisible," has achieved any lasting fame—but they do stand as an informative window to her life as a writer and as an important gloss on aspects of her better-known work.

George Eliot was born Mary Ann Evans in rural Warwickshire, near Arbury Hall on the estate of Sir Francis Newdigate, for whom her father, Robert Evans, was agent. Her mother, Christiana Pearson, was Evans's second wife, and Mary Ann was their youngest child. She had two full siblings, Christiana and Isaac, as well as a half sister and a half brother from Evans's first marriage. The social assumptions of the Evans family did not deviate from those of the world around them. Unques-

tioning adherence to orthodox Christianity was the normal pattern of life. So, also, was a general acceptance of the prevailing social order, and at least a modest respect for education and learning. Eliot's formal education consisted of early training at Miss Lathom's school in nearby Attleborough, several more years at Mrs. Wallington's Boarding School in Nuneaton, and at the Misses Franklins' school in Coventry. She was well educated, unusually so for a woman at that time. Eliot's mother died after a lengthy illness when her younger daughter was only sixteen. A year or so later, Eliot's sister married, and, thus, at seventeen, Eliot became the mistress of Griff, the agent's house where the Evanses had lived. She rallied to the task of keeping her father's house with a remarkable sense of duty and dedication.

The influence of her Evangelical teachers had its immediate fruit in Eliot's first publication, a poem published in the *Christian Observer* in January 1840. The title, " 'Knowing That Shortly I Must Put Off This Tabernacle,' " suggests that the speaker is aged and ready to die; each of the three-line stanzas has the refrain *"Farewell!,"* a solemn leave-taking of earth's best joys. Eliot was only twenty, but she was a

*Marian Evans. Watercolor sketch by Caroline Bray, 1842
(National Portrait Gallery).*

to question the historical foundations of Christianity so much that she thought she must not only abandon her faith but also stop attending church services. This public change in her behavior led to strenuous conflict with her father and to their separation for five or six weeks. A reconciliation brought her back to her father and to church attendance but not to active faith. Morality had become for Eliot the highest duty, and it was no longer derived from Christianity.

Charles Hennell's marriage in 1843 to Elizabeth Rebecca ("Rufa") Brabant, daughter of a diligent but unproductive scholar, opened several other new intellectual doors for Eliot. Hennell had been asked to translate D. F. Strauss's monumental work, *Das Leben Jesu* (1835), into English. He declined and so did his sister, Sara; Rufa started the task but ultimately turned it over to Eliot, who devoted two and a half years to its completion. Her translation of this exhaustive Germanic examination of the historic Jesus was published in the late spring of 1846 and still is the standard English version of this seminal work. Eliot, whose name did not appear on the edition, was paid £20 for her work.

Eliot dedicated the next few years almost wholly to caring for her father. He died in late May 1849 and left his daughter £100 in cash and the income on £2,000 for life. While this legacy did not make her financially independent, it did give her a degree of freedom, at least for a time. Within a week of her father's burial, Eliot left with the Brays on a trip to the Continent. She stayed on in Geneva for some time, returning to England in March of the following year, and then went to stay with the Brays again near Coventry.

In October 1850 London publisher John Chapman visited the Brays and renewed his acquaintance with Eliot, whom he had met first in 1846 when he had published her translation of Strauss. In the course of subsequent visits to Coventry, he engaged her to write a review essay for the *Westminster Review*. When she delivered it in November, Eliot stayed as a paying guest at his house at 142 Strand. This visit led to an association with Chapman and his family which proved both rewarding and distressing. Eliot, who had by now begun to use the name Marian instead of the traditional form Mary Ann, was excited by her entrée to the London literary world and decided to try to earn her living by her pen. Conflicts with Mrs. Chapman and with Chapman's mistress, Elizabeth Tilley, however, caused Eliot to return to Coventry in March 1851. Later that year, Chapman prepared to buy the *Westminster Review*, but he knew he had little

decidedly humorless young lady, and this pompous lyric probably reflects her intellect accurately at that time.

In 1841 Robert Evans turned over Griff to Isaac; he and his youngest daughter moved nearer Coventry to a handsome house known as Bird Grove at Foleshill. The new location brought Eliot into contact with a group of active philosophical thinkers, and her passionate commitment to Christianity began to find new directions. Her closest friends soon were Caroline and Charles Bray. Although he was a well-to-do ribbon manufacturer, his chief interest was philosophical inquiry, and he was the author of *The Philosophy of Necessity* (1841), an inquiry into the workings of natural law. Caroline Bray's brother and sister, Charles and Sara Hennell, also became friends of Eliot. Charles had written *An Inquiry Concerning the Origin of Christianity,* which was published in 1838. Here he examined the life of Jesus as a piece of Hebrew history, devoid of theological import. By early 1842 Eliot had come

London publisher John Chapman, whose professional relationship with Eliot began in 1846 (photo by Meisenbach)

hope of success without the dedicated and learned services of Marian Evans. He managed to patch things up with his wife and his mistress sufficiently, and Eliot returned to London in late September as assistant editor. Eliot edited ten numbers of the *Review* and contributed to it regularly. In the course of her association with the journal, she met many literary figures of England and America, most important of whom for her future life were Herbert Spencer, the author of *Social Statics* (1851), and George Henry Lewes, the drama critic and founder of the *Leader*.

In 1851 Eliot also began work on a second major translation from German, Ludwig Feuerbach's *Das Wesen des Christenthums (The Essence of Christianity)*, which Chapman published in June 1854. Her own name, Marian Evans, appeared on the title page of this book and on no other in her career. Feuerbach's ideas about the origin of Christian faith in the social imagination formed, for Eliot,

an interesting extension from Strauss and an important connection with Spencer's sociology and with the moral code of positivism. Little more than a week after the publication of the Feuerbach translation, Eliot took one of the most important steps in her life. She left London with George Henry Lewes, and they established their union, which they considered and called marriage. Their union, which lasted until Lewes's death twenty-four years later in 1878, was a brave one because it flew directly in the face of social convention. Lewes had been married for thirteen years to Agnes Jervis, and they had four sons; after eight years of marriage, however, Agnes had borne a fifth son by their married friend Thornton Leigh Hunt. Lewes forgave her and allowed the child to bear his name. Because of this generosity, Lewes had no legal grounds for divorce when Agnes and Thornton continued their adulterous relationship. The marriage of Agnes and Lewes was now one in name only, but in Agnes's hands it served to give the name Lewes to all four of her children by Hunt. Society could not accommodate these unusual and tragic circumstances sufficiently to accept the union of Eliot and Lewes. Saddest for Eliot was the great disapproval of her family; her beloved brother, Isaac, broke communication completely.

The happiness of Eliot and Lewes's life together is nowhere more evident, however, than in Eliot's development as one of the great novelists of her age. The couple spent the first years of their marriage in Germany; he was working on *The Life and Works of Goethe* (1855); she, on a translation of Spinoza's *Ethics* (never published) and on several reviews. After their return to England in March 1855, she continued her work of translating and reviewing until she began to respond, in the summer of 1856, to Lewes's repeated encouragement that she write fiction. Her first response was a manuscript entitled "The Sad Fortunes of the Reverend Amos Barton," which she developed into her first piece of narrative. It was combined with two other stories, "Mr Gilfil's Love-Story" and "Janet's Repentance," to form "Scenes of Clerical Life," published in *Blackwood's Edinburgh Magazine* in 1857 and the next year in book form. It was for this first fictional publication that she adopted the pseudonym George Eliot, which is the name used on all of her works from then on.

Although she started her career as a novelist at a later age than many other writers, she wasted no time. Within a year she had published a full-length novel, *Adam Bede,* and another story, "The Lifted Veil," and by 1860 the strongly autobiographical

The Mill on the Floss was also in print. In 1861 the now-classic *Silas Marner: The Weaver of Raveloe* appeared. Her fourth novel in as many years, "Romola," began serial publication in the *Cornhill Magazine* in July 1862 and concluded in August 1863. Until this time all her fiction had been published by William Blackwood of Edinburgh; an unusually handsome offer, however, led her to change publishers, and *Romola,* a historical novel set in Renaissance Italy, was published by Smith, Elder and Company. Her union with Smith, Elder was short-lived, however; after the publication of the short story "Brother Jacob" in 1859, Eliot returned to Blackwood, who remained her British publisher for the rest of her life.

In 1864 Eliot had first had the idea of writing a major poem on the conflicts in a woman's life when she must choose between great duty and the prospect of a happy marriage. She thought then that a suitable historic moment for this human choice would be the struggle among the Moors, the Spanish establishment, and the gypsies; renunciation of happy marriage would be required by the claims of the heroine's gypsy race. It was to be a verse drama, but she did not produce it easily. Lewes actually took the unfinished manuscript away from her in 1865. About this time, she wrote a short blank-verse narrative, "A Minor Prophet," which she seems to have been able to complete with less difficulty. The subject was Elias Baptist Butterworth, a millenarian who receives a few jabs from his creator. The notion that the past shapes the present is prominent in Eliot's exposition; she says, "Our finest hope is finest memory" and reminds us that no revolution is possible on earth without the slow workings of history. In 1866 she wrote a poem of six stanzas, "Two Lovers," which chronicles the romance of the subjects as they go from youth to old age, rejoicing in the happy and healthy life they have because their past has been simple and good. Her concluding ejaculation underlines a familiar sentiment, "O memories!/O past that is!" The year 1867 marks the composition of the only one of Eliot's poems which has enjoyed any lasting recognition. "O May I Join the Choir Invisible" takes its title from its first line; in its forty-three lines of blank verse, Eliot states a creed of meliorism. The only afterlife one can have comes from participation in the growing group of men and women who make the world a better place to live—better in human terms, individually and collectively.

Perhaps because she had completed these three short poems, Eliot was able to return to her long Spanish poem with greater success. A trip to

Eliot's "husband," George Henry Lewes. Drawing by Rudolph Lehmann, 1867 (British Museum).

Spain in the winter of 1867 also contributed to her renewed interest. She abandoned the idea of a drama and turned to blank-verse narrative. The chief character, Fedalma, adopted daughter of a Spanish duchess, approaches a joyful marriage to the duchess's son. Just before this marriage she is summoned by her natural father, Zarca, a gypsy leader, to join him in restoring their people to a better life. After much struggle, she renounces her joy and supports his cause. Her fiancé, Don Silva, responds by renouncing his Christian knighthood, and, for the love of Fedalma, he becomes a gypsy. The gypsies and the Moors collaborate in deadly conflict with the Christians; Silva is torn and attacks Zarca in revenge for the deaths of his Christian friends and relatives. Both Silva and Fedalma must seek their futures separately, renouncing love for racial loyalty.

Eliot had real problems writing *The Spanish Gypsy,* finally published in 1868, and the earnestness of the ideology she sought to express added great weight and great length to the narrative. While she made an effort to vary the pace of the blank verse by including songs at several points, the narrative fails at times to maintain a steady and lively interest. Nevertheless, when the book was published it was widely reviewed and fairly well received, especially in America. The reviewer for the *Spectator* found it "much the greatest poem on any wide scope . . . which has ever proceeded from a woman." Henry James, writing for the *North American Review,* praised the characters but, while he thought them "marvellously well *understood,*" he recognized that they still had "an indefinably factitious air." *The Spanish Gypsy* was, for him, "an admirable study of character" and a "noble literary performance," but it was not a "great drama" and, alas, "not a genuine poem." Matthew Browne, after much detailed praise in the *Contemporary Review,* still felt "compelled to say the bird-note is missing." One steady pattern in reviews of this poem was praise for Eliot as a novelist. Statements on her greatness as a literary figure could wax all the more laudatory in the face of her lesser accomplishment with narrative poetry.

Eliot never again attempted a book-length poem, but after *The Spanish Gypsy* she did continue to write shorter narrative poems and some lyrics. In January 1869, she completed "Agatha," a dramatic blank-verse narrative which tells the story of a poor, elderly maiden and her two maiden cousins, who work unassumingly for the good of their mountain village. A little more than two weeks later, she finished another narrative, "How Lisa Loved the King," derived from Boccaccio. This story, cast in heroic couplets, tells of the physical decline of a maiden because of her unrequited love for her king. Her desperate parents are relieved when the king, hearing through a singer of the maiden's desperation, visits her and, with the cooperation of his queen, chastely restores the girl to health. "How Lisa Loved the King" was published in *Blackwood's Edinburgh Magazine* in May and shortly thereafter in book form in Boston; it was the second of Eliot's mature poems to see print. "Agatha" was not far behind, appearing in the *Atlantic Monthly* in August.

In 1869 George Eliot was also working on what was to be her masterpiece, *Middlemarch: A Study of Provincial Life.* The imaginative return to her Midlands past probably also stimulated her work on a sequence of eleven sonnets which she called "Brother and Sister." These sentimental poems are built on happy memories of her early years with her brother, Isaac, and revel in her "present past," her "root of piety." Later that same year she wrote a long blank-verse poem, "The Legend of Jubal," based on the story of the sons and grandsons of Cain given in Genesis but building on Jubal's accomplishments in the arts and on Cain's growth in his sense of God as the central aspect of the world. "The Legend of Jubal" was published simultaneously in Great Britain (in *Macmillan's Magazine*) and in America (in the *Atlantic Monthly*) in May 1870.

As she continued work on *Middlemarch* in 1870, Eliot wrote "Armgart," a verse drama in five scenes which concerns a famous singer (for whom the poem is named) who loses her voice. Although Armgart has been surrounded by relatives and friends who have sacrificed to make her artistic life viable, she finds it difficult to understand human intercourse or art when she is not at the center of the activity. The poem was published in *Macmillan's Magazine* in July 1871.

The publication, in parts, of *Middlemarch* began in late 1871 and continued well into 1872. In 1873 Eliot wrote "Stradivarius," a poem in blank verse on the artistic motives of the great violin maker, and "Arion," a poem of sixteen rhyming four-line stanzas on the mythic poet-singer. In both she is concerned with music and with the dedication of men to art as an activity of unfathomable human worth.

In 1874 Eliot gathered her mature published poems, except *The Spanish Gypsy,* and added six others ("A Minor Prophet," "Brother and Sister," "Stradivarius," "Two Lovers," "Arion," and "O May I Join the Choir Invisible") for publication under the title *The Legend of Jubal and Other Poems.* William Blackwood, while admiring her work, wrote to ask if she had "any lighter pieces" which she might have composed before she came to her "sense of what a great author should do for mankind"; she had none. As it stands, *The Legend of Jubal and Other Poems* has a remarkable emphasis on music, one of Eliot's great passions. Well over half the poems have musical themes. Although the volume was less widely reviewed than *The Spanish Gypsy,* Henry James again commented on Eliot's work in the *North American Review.* Though he found this book "an unmistakable manifestation" of Eliot's genius, it was "a narrow manifestation." Of all the poems James preferred "Brother and Sister," but the reason for his preference seems largely to have been the relationship between this sonnet sequence and *The Mill on the Floss.* James's detailed notice of seven of the ten poems, however, led him to some unusual generalizations about George Eliot's oeuvre as a whole. She impressed him "as a spirit mysteriously perverted from her natural temper," as a writer

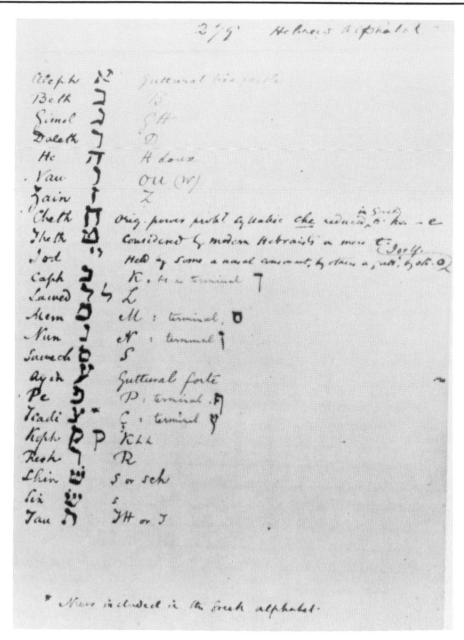

The Hebrew alphabet as recorded by Eliot in her notebook (Beinecke Rare Book and Manuscript Library, Yale University)

with "magnificent gifts" who fell "upon a critical age and felt its contagion and dominion. If . . . she had been borne by the mighty general current in the direction of passionate faith, . . . she would have achieved something incalculably great."

In 1874, after publication of *The Legend of Jubal,* Eliot wrote a long blank-verse narrative of witty conversation among students with names drawn from *Hamlet.* They attempt to settle the chief problems of the universe in a convivial corner of a place that seems like Cambridge. She called this poem "A College Breakfast Party" and published it

four years later in *Macmillan's Magazine.*

After 1874 Eliot returned to prose fiction and concentrated on the narratives which were to become *Daniel Deronda,* published in parts in 1876. She wrote no more poems, and the group of ten or so still-unpublished poems which she left in manuscript at her death appear to have been written in the late 1860s. The complete canon of George Eliot's poetry also includes three undated poems ("Self and Life," "Sweet Evenings Come and Go," and "The Death of Moses"), published posthumously as part of the collected edition of her works, and many of the epigraphs which head chapters in *Middlemarch* and *Daniel Deronda*. The authorship of all the epigraphs has not yet been established, but most of the unsigned ones are now accepted as Eliot's own compositions.

In late 1878, Eliot endured her worst loss, the death of George Henry Lewes, her "husband" of nearly a quarter-century. Not until the new year did she begin to recover. In the spring of 1879, she published a collection of essays and comments as *Impressions of Theophrastus Such* and resumed active life. She had become increasingly dependent on her young friend John Walter Cross, and they shocked their friends when they were married on 6 May 1880. Eliot was sixty; Cross, forty. After a wedding trip to the Continent, they settled in Chelsea. Their new house had been decorated, arranged, and occupied less than three weeks when George Eliot took sick and died on Wednesday evening, 22 December 1880. She was buried in Highgate Cemetery, near the grave of Lewes, and her brother, Isaac Evans (who had reestablished communication only after her marriage to Cross), joined Charles Lee Lewes (Lewes's only surviving son), Cross, and a crowd of mourners to bid her farewell.

Letters:

John W. Cross, ed., *George Eliot's Life as Related in Her Letters and Journals,* 3 volumes (Edinburgh & London: Blackwood, 1885);

Gordon S. Haight, ed., *The George Eliot Letters,* 9 volumes (New Haven: Yale University Press, 1954-1955; 1978).

Bibliography:

David Leon Higdon, "A Bibliography of George Eliot Criticism, 1971-1977," *Bulletin of Bibliography,* 37 (April-June 1980): 90-103.

Biography:

Gordon S. Haight, *George Eliot: A Biography* (Oxford: Clarendon Press, 1968).

References:

Gordon S. Haight, ed., *A Century of George Eliot Criticism* (Boston: Houghton Mifflin, 1965);

David L. Higdon, "George Eliot and the Art of the Epigraph," *Nineteenth-Century Fiction,* 25 (September 1970): 127-151;

Bernard J. Paris, "George Eliot's Unpublished Poetry," *Studies in Philology,* 56 (July 1959): 539-558;

A. E. S. Viner, *George Eliot* (Edinburgh: Oliver & Boyd, 1971);

Martha S. Vogeler, "The Choir Invisible: The Poetics of Humanistic Piety," in *George Eliot: A Centenary Tribute,* edited by Gordon Haight and Rosemary T. Van Arsdel (London: Macmillan, 1982), pp. 64-81.

Papers:

The major collection of George Eliot's manuscripts is at the British Library. The Beinecke Rare Book and Manuscript Library, Yale University, has an important collection of letters. Other collections are at the New York Public Library, the Pforzheimer, the Folger Shakespeare Library, and the Princeton University Library.

Sebastian Evans
(2 March 1830-19 December 1909)

Alan Hertz
Jesus College, Cambridge

SELECTED BOOKS: *Sonnets on the Death of the Duke of Wellington* (Cambridge: Macmillan, 1852);
Brother Fabian's Manuscript, and Other Poems (London: Macmillan, 1865);
In the Studio: A Decade of Poems (London: Macmillan, 1875);
In Quest of the Holy Graal: An Introduction to the Study of the Legend (London: Dent, 1898).

OTHER: *Shakespeare: A Cantata,* words by Evans, in *Our Shakespeare Club* (Birmingham?: Privately printed, 1864);
The Upper Ten, translated and adapted by Sebastian and Frank Evans from E. Pailleron's play *Le Monde ou l'on s'ennuie* (London: Low, 1891); republished as *Lady Chillingham's House-Party* (London: Dent, 1901);
Leo of Assisi, St. Francis of Assisi, The Mirror of Perfection, translated by Evans (London: Nutt, 1898);
The High History of the Holy Graal, translated by Evans (London: Dent, 1898);
Geoffrey of Monmouth, translated by Evans (London: Dent, 1904).

Sebastian Evans was born on 2 March 1830 in Market Bosworth, Leicestershire, the youngest son of Arthur and Anne Dickinson Evans. Evans's father, an Anglican clergyman, master of the local grammar school, and prolific writer of prose and poetry, educated his children himself and communicated his energy and taste for the arts to more than one. John Evans became an eminent geologist, archaeologist, and numismatist, served as president of many scientific societies, and was eventually knighted. Anne Evans, long an invalid, wrote poetry and music; a volume of her works was published posthumously in 1880, with a memoir by Anne Ritchie, Thackeray's daughter.

In 1849 Sebastian Evans won a scholarship to Emmanuel College, Cambridge, where he took his B.A. in 1853. He earned an M.A. in 1857, the year of his marriage to Elizabeth Goldney. One of the anecdotes included by Mrs. Ritchie in the memoir accompanying Anne Evans's *Poetry and Music*

epitomizes the exuberant humor typical of Evans's personality and poetry: "On one occasion, while still at college, Mr. Sebastian Evans thought himself ill-used by his family, who had not written to him as regularly as they were used to do. He sent home a letter full of extraordinary news: described himself as married, with a resident mother-in-law; as having given up his college career to turn coal-merchant in the neighbourhood of Cambridge; and also inclosed a little bunch of hair off a paint-brush as a specimen of his bride's locks." His sister replied with a mock-Chaucerian ballad.

Like many of his Cambridge contemporaries, Evans found his way to the Macmillans' bookshop on Trinity Street. In retrospect, he saw his friendship with Alexander Macmillan as the great educational experience of his undergraduate years, compensation for the stimulation lacking in the normal routines of his college life: "Once in the year we were invited to 'take wine' with the Master, between 'hall' ending at five and 'chapel' beginning at six, and once in every term with the tutor; and these functions afforded our sole opportunities of what was called 'social intercourse' with those dignitaries. . . . For some of us this sort of go-as-you-please independence was probably wholesomer and more stimulating than the stricter restraint of the contemporary system at Oxford, but it left everything to be desired in the way of intellectual training and equipment for the battle of life."

Evans emphasized Macmillan's influence on the religious beliefs of undergraduates, but he was himself never attracted to the theology of F. D. Maurice which Macmillan so eagerly proselytized. He had already developed the idiosyncratic combination of dogmatic scepticism and antipapal bigotry that remained his creed all his life. Macmillan was later to refuse a book of his poems as too aggressively un-Christian; it is a measure of Evans's affection for his publisher that it never appeared under a rival imprint.

Although Evans resented the neglect of his supposed teachers, he knew how to occupy himself profitably. The Macmillans published his *Sonnets on the Death of the Duke of Wellington* (1852) while he was

The Last Shot of Robin Hood, *one of Evans's stained glass windows displayed at the International Exhibition of 1862*

still an undergraduate, and free copies coaxed complimentary responses from Sir James Stephen and Alfred, Lord Tennyson. Evans also·began the study of medieval literature and art that remained a lifelong interest. By the time he left Cambridge to study law at Lincoln's Inn, he had a growing reputation as both poet and artist.

In 1855, Evans abandoned his legal studies to become secretary of the Indian Reform Association, and in 1857 he joined Chance Brothers, a glassworks near Birmingham, as manager of the art department. In the same year he married Elizabeth Goldney, a London banker's daughter. During the next ten years he designed stained-glass windows,

some of which were displayed at the International Exhibition of 1862. He also exhibited paintings at the Royal Academy, became one of Macmillan's favorite illustrators, and was increasingly active in local Conservative politics.

Brother Fabian's Manuscript, and Other Poems, perhaps his best volume of verse, appeared in 1865. The title sequence occupies half the book. Evans first tells "How the Abbey of Saint Werewulf juxta Slingsby Came by Brother Fabian's Manuscript." Title, subject, and dense blank verse show the extent of Evans's debt to Robert Browning; but, if anything, he is more explicit than his mentor about the corruption of the monastic system. His prioress has had a child by the abbot, and all his clergy connive at producing false miracles, relics, and conversions and live as superstitious, ignorant, cunning parasites on the secular world. The poem shows Evans's verbal facility, sense of the ridiculous, and eccentric learning to advantage:

> Well, down steps Randal to the pool, when, lo,
> Just as he pinned his gudgeon on the hook,
> A herd of fat geese from the garage-yard gate
> Marched cackling through the meadow.
>   Quick as thought,
> Randal was in among them, gripped the neck
> Of him who gabbled loudest, held him tight,
> Bore him, a fluttering prisoner to the pool,
> Made fast his line,—the gudgeon on the hook,
> About the fowl's left leg and let him swim.
> Dame Juliana Berners, by the way,
> Had taught this double treatment in her tract
> Then lately printed with new-fangled types
> By Caxton at Saint Alban's, which discourse
> Being sent, a gift from Sopwell to my Dame,
> Was read to Randal through by Margery,
> Not without profit,—as the gander felt.

The "manuscript" itself is less satisfactory, its medievalism being derived almost entirely from Keats and Coleridge.

The second half of the volume contains poems on contemporary topics. Several are occasional, including those commemorating the arrival of Princess Alexandra and Garibaldi's visit, eulogizing Garibaldi's cohort Camillo di Cavour and Thackeray at length. In the rest Evans shows himself a capable craftsman, but he is irritatingly imitative in his diction and choice of subjects. The same criticism applies to *In the Studio* (1875), which contains Browningesque artists' monologues and Tennysonian narratives of the Round Table. It also contains Evans's translations of Jeande Gerson, the first of the renderings of medieval literature which were to be his main literary efforts thereafter.

In 1867 Evans was appointed editor of the *Birmingham Daily Gazette.* He unsuccessfully contested Birmingham for the Tories in the election of the next year and took his LL.D. from Cambridge. In 1870 he resumed his legal studies and was called to the bar in 1873. A successful practice on the Oxford circuit did not keep him from journalism, however; in 1878 he founded the *People,* a weekly which he edited for three years.

Evans and his son Frank collaborated on *The Upper Ten,* a translation and adaptation of a French farce, in 1891; it was later republished as *Lady Chillingham's House-Party* (1901). In 1898 he produced his contributions to the study of the Grail legend: a translation of *The High History of the Holy Graal,* which was republished in 1969, and *In Quest of the Holy Graal,* in which he argued that the romance allegorized the events leading up to the Albigensian Crusade. In the same year, his translation of Leo of Assisi's *St. Francis of Assisi, The Mirror of Perfection* appeared. His last major work, a translation of Geoffrey of Monmouth's twelfth-century history of the kings of Britain, was published six years later; it was republished with alterations in 1963. Sebastian Evans died on 19 December 1909.

Violet Fane
(Mary Montgomerie Lamb Singleton Currie, Lady Currie)

(24 February 1843-13 October 1905)

Dorothea Mosley Thompson
Carnegie-Mellon University

SELECTED BOOKS: *From Dawn to Noon Poems* (London: Longmans, Green, 1872; New York: Carleton, 1880);

Denzil Place: A Story In Verse (London: Chapman & Hall, 1875); republished as *Constance's Fate: A Story of Denzil Place* (New York: Carleton, 1876);

The Queen of the Fairies (A Village Story) and Other Poems (London: Chapman & Hall, 1876);

Anthony Babington: A Drama (London: Chapman & Hall, 1877);

Sophy; or The Adventures of a Savage, 3 volumes (London: Hurst & Blackett, 1881);

Thro' Love and War, 3 volumes (London: Hurst & Blackett, 1886);

The Story of Helen Davenant, 3 volumes (London: Chapman & Hall, 1889);

Autumn Songs (London: Chapman & Hall, 1889);

Under Cross and Crescent Poems (London: Nimmo, 1896);

Betwixt Two Seas: Poems and Ballads (London: Nimmo, 1900);

Two Moods of a Man, With Other Papers and Short Stories (London: Nimmo, 1901).

Collection: *Collected Verses* (London: Smith, Elder, 1880).

TRANSLATION: *Memoirs of Marguerite de Valois, Queen of Navarre,* translated by Fane (London: Nimmo/New York: Scribners, 1892).

SELECTED PERIODICAL PUBLICATIONS: "Two Moods of a Man," as Mary Montgomerie Singleton, *Nineteenth Century,* 31 (February 1892): 208-223;

"The Way of Dreams," as Mary Montgomerie Currie, *Nineteenth Century,* 53 (June 1903): 950-967;

"The Feast of Kebobs: A Reminiscence," as Mary Montgomerie Currie, *Blackwood's Edinburgh Magazine,* 175 (April 1904): 459-482;

"Concerning Some of the 'Enfants Trouvés' of Literature," as Mary Montgomerie Currie,

Violet Fane

Nineteenth Century, 56 (July 1904): 126-141;

"Are Remarkable People Remarkable Looking?," as Mary Montgomerie Currie, *Nineteenth Century,* 56 (October 1904): 622-642;

"From the Toll-Bar of the Galata Bridge," as Mary Montgomerie Currie, *Nineteenth Century,* 57 (February 1905): 307-323.

Lady Currie, who wrote under the pen name of Violet Fane, was a much admired, well-known poet of the last quarter of the nineteenth century. Like many of the minor poets of Victorian England, Lady Currie was born to privilege and social rank. That she drew on her social connections does not detract from the fact that she was serious about the craft which she pursued throughout her life and continued to grow in her ability to write. At the beginning of her career, writing under the pen name of Violet Fane, she attempted to convey her sentiments about love and nature in Romantic poetry. But her best writing appears in the essays that she wrote under her own name, beginning in 1892. In one of these late essays, "Are Remarkable People Remarkable Looking?" (1904), Lady Currie reveals that she took her pen name Violet Fane from Benjamin Disraeli's novel *Vivian Grey* (1826): "Lord Beaconsfield had spoken of me as his 'god-daughter' because I had selected Violet Fane as a nom de plume, the name of the heroine of one of his early novels."

Born at Beauport, Sussex, on 24 February 1843, Mary Montgomerie Lamb was the eldest daughter of Charles J. M. Lamb and Anna Charlotte Gray and could claim kinship with the witty and eccentric John, Earl of Rochester, as well as with other authors of aristocratic lineage. Little is known of her early life other than that she loved nature and gardening.

In the late essay "The Feast of Kebobs" (1904), she describes her family's move to London when she was eleven or twelve because her father's blindness required better medical care. In "The Feast of Kebobs" the gaiety and pleasure that the British upper class derived from their social connections are vividly portrayed by Lady Currie. She tells how a chance meeting with his former Turkish donkey driver inspired her father to join the Turks in preparing a feast in order to demonstrate to British friends how real kebobs should taste. Days of preparation gave way to a joyous fancy-dress party.

On 27 February 1864 Lady Currie married her first husband, Henry S. Singleton, an Irish landowner with whom she had four children, two sons and two daughters. She was well known in London society as a great beauty and a witty conversationalist. A sense of her power in that society can be obtained from W. H. Mallock's *The New Republic* (1877), which he dedicated "To 'Violet Fane' authoress of 'Anthony Babington' 'The Queen of the Fairies,' etc. . . ." A roman à clef, Mallock's work portrays a country house party attended by famous cultural, political, and intellectual figures of the day. That Mallock placed Lady Currie, called Mrs. Sinclair in the novel, in the company of more important writers such as Thomas Huxley, Benjamin Jowett, Matthew Arnold, and John Ruskin can be attributed only to his deep affection for her. She is portrayed as being quintessentially feminine, witty, and somewhat sly in conversational manner. One character in the novel tells another that "That . . . is

Mrs. Sinclair, who has published a volume of poems, and is a sort of fashionable London Sappho."

A year after the death of her first husband in 1893, she married Sir Philip Henry Currie, who was ambassador to Constantinople from 1843 to 1898 and then ambassador to Rome from 1898 to 1903. The Curries then retired to Hawley, Hampshire. Lady Currie died of heart failure while visiting at the Grand Hotel, Harrogate, on 13 October 1905.

According to reviewers, Lady Currie's poetry was much admired by upper-class women as well as by milliners' apprentices and ballet girls. Reviewers also described her poetry as drawing-room verse, referring to its moderate picturesqueness and delicate fancy to convey their lukewarm approval of the slim volumes of verses that she produced at regular intervals.

From Dawn to Noon (1872), Lady Currie's first volume, exemplifies all the characteristics of her collections of short poems. Major themes are love or absence of love, longing, sorrow or regret, and, predictably, the main focus is on deep emotional feelings. "For ever and for ever," one of the poems from this collection, was set to music by Paolo Tosti and became one of the hit songs of the Victorian era. In another poem, "Lines," Currie tells her readers that she has been scolded for her melancholy by those who say she is too young to have such a sorrowful attitude toward the world.

Denzil Place (1875), her second book, was republished as *Constance's Fate: A Story of Denzil Place*. Here, Lady Currie's skillful use of rhyme enhances what would otherwise be a trite story. Constance, the young wife of an old squire, and Denzil, the neighboring young squire, inadvertently fall in love with each other. Banishment from England, separation, reunion, and the conventional accidental death of the old squire finally lead to the marriage of the two lovers. Lady Currie's talent for projecting passion clothed in delicate thoughts is undoubtedly her forte. Two impassioned lines on the beauty of married love exemplify much of her writing. "But let me glory in the unknown joy / Of some such days and nights before I die."

The Queen of the Fairies (1876), a more sentimental story written, like *Denzil Place,* in blank verse, does not rise to the level of its predecessor, possibly because the author is less emotionally involved with her subject. *The Queen of the Fairies* is the story of pure, sweet Nelly, who had been wronged by a handsome captain who goes off to war. Nelly leaves the baby born of her union with the captain with the young curate who has always loved her, since her only professional option is a career on the stage. In the end she perishes tragically in a theater fire.

Anthony Babington (1877), a drama in verse, is based on events surrounding the plot by the Catholic Babington and others to assassinate Queen Elizabeth I and install Mary Queen of Scots in her place. A curious intermingling of verse and prose creates the verve and movement which maintain interest in this dated story of religious zeal and high treason.

In *Autumn Songs* (1889), published when Lady Currie was forty-six, the poet summons up an aura of nostalgia with themes of regret, loss, and aging love. Many of these poems contain trite themes of the period. Titles such as "A Homeless Love" and "A Widow Knitting by an Empty Cradle" indicate a lack of originality and good judgment, yet many poems represent genuine emotion and feeling and hold some appeal for the modern reader. "In Memoriam," one of the volume's most successful poems, is a sonnet in which the speaker considers the flight of time: "We are survivors: from the echoing street/One more familiar footstep dies away into eternal silence."

Lady Currie's interest in historical subjects led to her literal translation of the *Memoirs of Marguerite de Valois, Queen of Navarre,* published in 1892. She states in her fifty-nine-page introduction that she found Queen Marguerite of interest because of the queen's reputation as a villainess of low morals; Lady Currie sought evidence of compensating qualities in Marguerite's autobiography and concluded that the work seemed to have been written by a prude.

In addition to producing slim volumes of poetry, a translation of a historical work, and a verse drama, Lady Currie published three novels —*Sophy* (1881), *Thro' Love and War* (1886), and *The Story of Helen Davenant* (1889)—that were mildly successful. At least one critic of the times, Alexander H. Japp, found her novels to be "exceptionally attractive by their fresh views of life and careful delineation of character."

The reviewers of Lady Currie's poetry indicated that much of what she wrote might better have been communicated in some form of prose; and indeed, toward the end of her life, Lady Currie did write essays on various subjects. "Two Moods of a Man," published in 1892, is a satirical sketch on the theme of modern man's wife-hunting customs. A faintly feminist attitude emerges from her cynical characterization of men who worm their way out of emotional entanglements when they are tired of them. Lady Currie's slightly malicious discussion of the work of several unidentified young poets in "Concerning Some of the 'Enfants Trouvés' of Literature" conveys her own assumptions of expertise as a poet. She insists that more important for a good poem than beautiful words is the "human sympathy" of the poet. It is evident that Lady Currie considers her poems to contain both the beautiful words and the human sympathy that the poets whom she criticized lack.

Because her work accurately portrays the mood of late nineteenth-century aristocratic life, it is of interest to modern readers who wish to learn more about the times. When Lady Currie died in 1905 obituaries in the *London Times* and the *Illustrated London News* recognized her achievement as a "minor poet" and as an essayist best remembered for her clear, intelligent observations of her society.

Dora Greenwell
(6 December 1821-29 March 1882)

Tirthankar Bose
University of British Columbia

SELECTED BOOKS: *Poems* (London: Pickering, 1848);

Stories that Might be True, With Other Poems (London: Pickering, 1850);

A Present Heaven. Letters to a Friend (Edinburgh, 1855); republished as *The Covenant of Life and Peace* (London & Edinburgh, 1867);

The Patience of Hope (Edinburgh, 1860; Boston: Ticknor & Fields, 1862);

Poems (Edinburgh: Strahan, 1861; enlarged, London: Strahan, 1867);

Two Friends (London: Strahan, 1862; Boston: Ticknor & Fields, 1863);

Home Thoughts and Home Scenes, by Greenwell and others (London: Routledge, Warne & Routledge, 1865; Boston: Tilton, 1865);

Essays (London & New York: Strahan, 1866);

Lacordaire (Edinburgh: Edmonston & Douglas, 1867);

Carmina Crucis (London: Bell & Daldy/Boston: Roberts Brothers, 1869);

Colloquia Crucis: A Sequel to Two Friends (London: Strahan, 1871);

John Woolman: A Biographical Sketch (London: Kitto, 1871);

Songs of Salvation (London: Strahan, 1873);

The Soul's Legend (London: Strahan, 1873);

Liber Humanitatis (London: Daldy, Isbister, 1875);

Camera Obscura (London: Daldy, Isbister, 1876);

A Basket of Summer Fruit (London & Edinburgh, 1877).

OTHER: George MacDonald, *The Wow o'Rivven: or The Idiot's Home,* edited by Greenwell (London: Strahan, 1868);

C. Bowles, *Harmless Johnny: or The Poor Outcast of Reason,* edited by Greenwell (London: Strahan, 1868).

SELECTED PERIODICAL PUBLICATIONS: "Our Single Women," *North British Review,* 36 (February 1862): 62-87;

"On the Education of the Imbecile," *North British Review,* new series 10 (September 1868): 73-100;

"The East African Slave Trade," *Contemporary Review,* 22 (1873): 138-164.

Dora Greenwell's poetry reflects a cultivated intellect and a sensitive heart but an inadequate imagination. Although marked by the loftiest philosophical ideals and the deepest human sympathy, Greenwell's poems lack the originality of perception that might have won for her the unconditional title of poet rather than the dubious distinction of woman poet.

Greenwell was born on 6 December 1821 at Greenwell Ford, the family home since the time of Henry VIII, in the county of Durham. Her father, William Thomas Greenwell, was the deputy-lieutenant of Durham county and a much-respected magistrate, and her mother, Dorothy Smales, was the daughter of a well-known lawyer of Durham. Greenwell had two brothers, William and Alan.

At Greenwell Ford Dora led an idyllic life in beautiful surroundings. The charm and peace of the garden and nearby woods appear again and again in her works. Her education, conducted entirely at home, was evidently very full, for her writings show from the beginning her knowledge of Latin, modern European languages, and the social thought of her time. At an early age she began to write poems on a wide variety of subjects drawn from nature, religion, and everyday experience. Her poetic idols were Alfred Tennyson and Elizabeth Barrett Browning. Even when quite young, she was known for her lively conversation and quick sympathy for the poor and the backward, and these qualities gained her the many friendships she enjoyed throughout her life.

Unfortunately, Greenwell's blissful existence at Greenwell Ford was terminated in 1847, when her father lost the estate through financial misjudgment. This catastrophe, coupled with Greenwell's poor health, very likely brought out her mystical-religious tastes, although religion evidently ran strong in the family, for both her brothers became ministers of the church.

It was to Ovington Rectory, Northumberland, the home of her brother William, that Greenwell went with her parents after the loss of Greenwell Ford. The family lived with William from 1848 to 1850. Soon after moving there Greenwell collected her poems to make them ready for publication. *Poems,* her first appearance in print, was published in 1848 by William Pickering of London.

The themes that run through the fifty-five poems in the volume are the passage of time and youth, human suffering, death, and the love for Christ that enables mankind to bear all sorrows. In "The Dream of a Poet's Youth," a twenty-page monologue, and in "The Old Family," Greenwell speaks of lost joys and the inescapable mutability of all things, but she does so in a voice of gentle regret rather than of despair. Her relative equanimity is explained by her attitude to death and loss in such poems as "The Song of Death," "The Dying Child," and "Songs of Farewell: Death," in which the perception of suffering and death is lightened by the faith that

> He taketh to his Garner-house the things that ripened be;
> He gathereth his store from Earth, all silently —
> And he will gather me, my friends,
> He will gather me!

In almost all her poems Greenwell is keenly aware of nature, which is always a source of peace and happiness, as in "The Silent Grave-stone" and "The Last Wish," reflecting no doubt Greenwell's memories of the home of her youth.

Greenwell had a special concern for the disadvantaged, which she expressed in such poems as "The Deformed Child" and "The Blind School." In these verses her responses are again tethered to the central idea of a life made ultimately sweet by God's purpose. Her religious preoccupation is evident also in poems inspired by Goethe, Johann Ludwig Uhland, and Hans Christian Andersen, with whose works she was obviously familiar.

While Greenwell reveals a mind finely tuned to emotional experience in her evocation of nature and her reflections on life and death, she gives no proof of originality either of thought or expression. Cluttering her verses with tired phrases such as "Time's measured sands" or "the hidden pearls of Truth," she trundles out trite statements as profound, heart-wringing insights, as in "The Irish Emigrant's Song":

> my little Kathleen sat by me, her hand within my own,

> And wept to think that I should go so far away alone.

or,

> And should I be, through all my life, a care unto my friends;
> Yet Father says, there are *worse* cares than God Almighty sends!

in "The Deformed Child."

Greenwell's *Poems* did not achieve spectacular success, but the volume received enough appreciation to encourage publisher William Pickering to bring out in 1850 a second book entitled *Stories that Might be True, With Other Poems.* This volume contains nothing to distinguish it from the earlier one. A typical poem is "Childhood," which presents the characteristic mélange of nostalgia for past joys, sadness at the mutability of life, and the faith that "Each promise earth hath broken/Shall yet be kept in Heaven."

In 1850 Greenwell and her parents left Ovington and stayed briefly at several other places before going to live with Alan Greenwell in his parish of Golbourne in Lancashire. The most notable of these brief visits was to Edinburgh, where Greenwell became a close friend of the Constable family, who owned the publishing house of that name. Through them the poet came to know many literary figures. At Golbourne, where the family lived from 1850 to 1854, Greenwell threw herself with energy and compassion into charitable work in the parish. Her parents too increasingly became her charge, especially her father, whose health was failing fast. He died sometime in the early 1850s.

In 1854 Alan Greenwell had to move from Golbourne for reasons of health, and his mother and sister were forced again to move. They went to live in Durham, which became their home for the next eighteen years, from 1854 to 1872. These years were filled with social and literary activity for Greenwell. Her concern for the disadvantaged focused on the mentally handicapped, for whose well-being and instruction she worked indefatigably, as did her brothers. Intellectually, the Durham years were Greenwell's most active period. A full view of her literary and other interests is afforded by her long correspondence with the Reverend William Knight, professor of moral philosophy at the University of St. Andrews and editor of Wordsworth. The correspondence, included in William Dorling's *Memoirs of Dora Greenwell* (1885), shows an impressively wide and critical knowledge of the scriptures, ethics, and social thought. Her comments on Mill, Voltaire, Comte, and other philosophers are both well informed and acute, though always colored by her intensely Christian views.

Among Greenwell's close friends were Jean Ingelow and Christina Rossetti. A correspondent to the *Athenaeum* (9 August 1897) recounts an amusing exchange regarding a proposed needlework contest among the three women (in which Christina Rossetti had too much good sense to participate). Greenwell and Christina Rossetti probably met for the first time at Newcastle-on-Tyne in the house of William Bell Scott. Their mutual regard is recorded in the poems they addressed to each other, "Autumn Violets" by Rossetti and "To Christina Rossetti" by Greenwell.

A prolific writer on a wide range of subjects, Greenwell wrote both prose and verse. Two prose works that explore the Christian life are *The Patience of Hope* (1860) and *Two Friends* (1862). Another work, an 1867 biography of Dominican monk Jean Baptiste Henri Lacordaire, has a religious theme, but its chief interest lies in Greenwell's ability to penetrate the character of a complex and brilliant personality and set it against a lucidly delineated cultural background. She also contributed essays, mainly on social themes, to journals. In the essays she not only shows a clear understanding of social issues but also leavens serious questions with a gentle irony. For instance, in "Our Single Women," published in *North British Review*, she speaks of "the gentle, dove-like Old Maid of modern fiction, of smooth, braided, silvery hair, and soft speech and eye, generally, it may be remarked, dressed in grey, who is supposed to have some tender secret buried in her heart, some letter or lock of hair shut within a secret drawer, but who, ever serene and cheerful, flits in and out between the scenes, listening, consoling, cheering, at all times ready to take up a little of existence at second-hand." One poem of the Durham period deals with the shameful exploitation of child laborers in agriculture known as gang-children. The poem, quoted in part by Dorling with no mention of where it appeared, is a spirited response to a politician's advocacy of the practice. One of Greenwell's most important works, an essay entitled "On the Education of the Imbecile," was also written in Durham.

While at Durham, Greenwell had two volumes published, in 1861 and 1867; the 1867 *Poems* is essentially an enlarged edition of its predecessor. The poems added to the 1867 edition are not appreciably different from the earlier ones either in

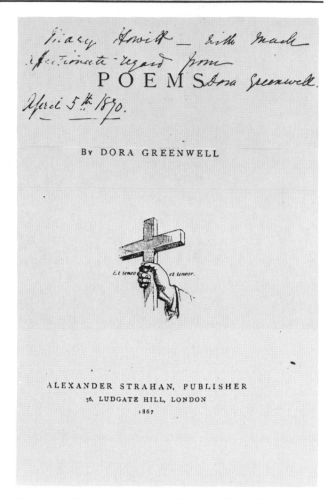

Inscribed title page from the enlarged edition of Greenwell's second volume of verse published during the years she lived at Durham (courtesy of Thomas Cooper Library, University of South Carolina)

theme or technique and least of all in attitude. Greenwell still reflects on the insubstantiality of worldly existence ("Consolation," 1867) and limps on with clichés, as in "Christina" (1861):

> I have been
> Saved as by fire,—a brand plucked from the burning

or "One Flower" (1867):

> The sweet Rose as I passed
> Blushed to its core, its last
> Warm tear the Lily shed,
> The Violet hid its head.

Yet Greenwell could occasionally step beyond the confines of sentiment and philosophy, as in the

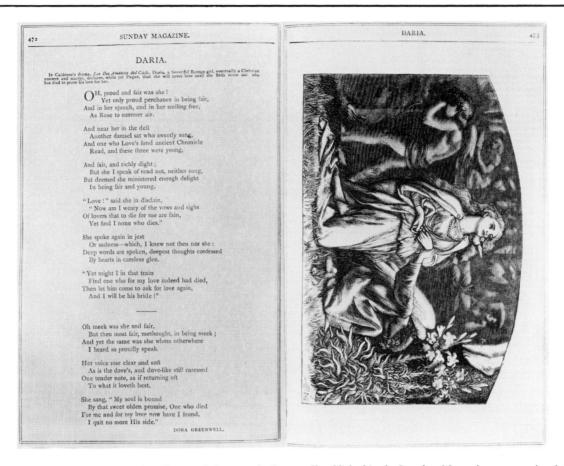

Pre-Raphaelite painter Arthur Hughes illustrated this poem by Greenwell published in the Sunday Magazine, *new series, 1 (1872).*

sharply sarcastic "The Saturday Review." In the main, however, she had little ability to lend immediacy to the reconstruction of experience or concept, but on rare occasion she could produce a striking phrase or image, as here in "To an Early Friend" (1867):

> the sunshine fell
> Betwixt the boughs, and on our faces laid
> A loving finger, marking, where it strayed,
> A Dial for the hours.

Greenwell's closest personal attachment was to her mother. When the old lady died, Greenwell decided to leave Durham. She stayed briefly at Torquay and longer at Clifton, where her brother Alan lived. In 1874 she moved to London, where she lived until 1881. There she was received into literary circles warmly and had frequent visits from old friends such as Tom Taylor, Alfred Hunt, and their wives, and William Bell Scott. It is not unlikely that she was a Quaker, for in 1871 she produced a bio-

graphical account of John Woolman, a distinguished member of the Society of Friends. She also continued to interest herself in the welfare of the poor and the oppressed. She was an outspoken antivivisectionist and a strong supporter of women's voting rights, although declining health limited her public activity in support of such causes to voicing her opinions in print. A striking essay is her attack on slavery, "The East African Slave Trade," published in 1873 in the *Contemporary Review.*

Greenwell's failing health severely restricted her movements, and in 1881 an accident so disabled her that she was obliged to take up residence with her brother Alan at Clifton, where she died on 29 March 1882. She was buried in Arno's Vale cemetery in Bristol.

Dora Greenwell was better at exercising the intellect than the imagination. Very likely she herself realized the limitation this propensity for the intellectual imposed on her poetic endeavors, for she once told a visitor, "One word would alone tell my story—inadequacy." Yet she was not embittered by this self-awareness, for she saw herself as an evolving being who could rejoice in the process of life; toward the end of her life, she once buried her face in the leaves of a window-box plant and whispered, "The only joy is growth."

References:

Henry Bett, *Dora Greenwell* (London: Epworth, 1950);

William Dorling, *Memoirs of Dora Greenwell* (London: Clarke, 1885).

Gerard Manley Hopkins

Jerome Bump
University of Texas at Austin

BIRTH: Stratford, Essex, 28 July 1844 to Manley and Kate Hopkins.

EDUCATION: B.A., Balliol College, Oxford, 1867.

DEATH: Dublin, 8 June 1889.

SELECTED BOOKS: *Poems of Gerard Manley Hopkins,* edited by Robert Bridges (London: Milford, 1918); enlarged, edited by Bridges and Charles Williams (London: Oxford University Press, 1930); enlarged again, edited by W. H. Gardner (London & New York: Oxford University Press, 1948); revised, edited by Gardner (London & New York: Oxford University Press, 1956); enlarged again, edited by Gardner and N. H. MacKenzie (London & New York: Oxford University Press, 1967); corrected, edited by Gardner and MacKenzie (London & New York: Oxford University Press, 1970);

The Notebooks and Papers of Gerard Manley Hopkins, edited by Humphry House (London & New York: Oxford University Press, 1937); enlarged as *The Journals and Papers of Gerard Manley Hopkins,* edited by House and Graham Storey (London & New York: Oxford University Press, 1959);

The Sermons and Devotional Writings of Gerard Manley Hopkins, edited by Christopher Devlin (London & New York: Oxford University Press, 1959).

SELECTED PERIODICAL PUBLICATIONS: "Winter with the Gulf Stream," *Once a Week,* 8 (February 1863): 210;

Gerard Manley Hopkins

"Barnfloor and Winepress," *Union Review,* 3 (1865): 579-580.

Gerard Manley Hopkins is one of the three or four greatest poets of the Victorian era. He is regarded by different readers as the greatest Victorian poet of religion, of nature, or of melancholy. However, because his style was so radically different from that of his contemporaries, his best poems

Dandelion, Hemlock, and Ivy, *an early sketch by Hopkins showing the influence of Maria Smith Giberne's teaching (courtesy of the Society of Jesus)*

were not accepted for publication during his lifetime, and his achievement was not fully recognized until after World War I.

Hopkins's idiosyncratic creativity was the result of interactions with others, beginning with the members of his family. Hopkins's extended family constituted a social environment that made the commitment of an eldest son to religion, language, and art not only possible but also highly probable. His mother, Kate Smith Hopkins (1821-1900), was a devout High Church Anglican who brought up her children to be religious. Hopkins read from the New Testament daily at school to fulfill a promise he made to her. The daughter of a London physician, she was better educated than most Victorian women and particularly fond of music and of reading, especially German philosophy and literature, the novels of Dickens, and eventually her eldest son's poetry.

Her sister Maria Smith Giberne taught Hopkins to sketch. The drawings originally executed as headings on letters from her home, Blunt House,

Croydon, to Hopkins's mother and father reveal the kind of precise, detailed drawing that Hopkins was taught. The influence of Maria Smith Giberne on her nephew can be seen by comparing these letter headings with Hopkins's sketch, *Dandelion, Hemlock, and Ivy,* which he made at Blunt House. Hopkins's interest in the visual arts was also sustained by his maternal uncle, Edward Smith, who began as a lawyer but soon made painting his profession; by Richard James Lane, his maternal great-uncle, an engraver and lithographer who frequently exhibited at the Royal Academy; and by Lane's daughters, Clara and Eliza (or Emily), who exhibited at the Society of Female Artists and elsewhere. Another maternal uncle, John Simm Smith, Jr., reinforced the religious tradition which Hopkins's mother passed on to him; Smith was churchwarden at St. Peter's, Croydon.

These artistic and religious traditions were also supported by Hopkins's paternal relations. His aunt Anne Eleanor Hopkins tutored her nephew in sketching, painting, and music. His uncle Thomas

Marsland Hopkins was perpetual curate at St. Saviour's, Paddington, and coauthor with Hopkins's father of the 1849 volume, *Pietas Metrica Or, Nature Suggestive of God and Godliness,* "by the Brothers Theophilus and Theophylact." He was married to Katherine Beechey, who, with her cousin Catherine Lloyd, maintained close contacts with the High Church Tractarian movement which deeply affected Hopkins at Oxford. Her sister, Frances Ann Beechey, was a good painter, famous in North America for her documentary paintings of the Canadian voyageurs. In 1865 she was in London, where Hopkins met her, and after 1870 she exhibited at the Royal Academy. Charles Gordon Hopkins, Hopkins's uncle, developed the family interest in languages as well as religion. He moved to Hawaii, where he learned Hawaiian and helped establish an Anglican bishopric in Honolulu. In 1856 he helped Manley Hopkins, the poet's father, become consul-general for Hawaii in London.

Manley Hopkins was the founder of a marine insurance firm. It is no accident that shipwreck, one of the firm's primary concerns, was the subject of Hopkins's most ambitious poem, *The Wreck of the Deutschland* (1875). Nor can the emphasis on religion in that poem be attributed solely to the mother's influence. Manley Hopkins was a devout High Church Anglican who taught Sunday School at St. John's in Hampstead, where he was churchwarden. He loved music and literature, passing on his fondness for puns and wordplay to his sons Gerard and Lionel and his love for poetry to Gerard especially. His publications include *A Philosopher's Stone and Other Poems* (1843), *Pietas Metrica* (1849), and *Spicelegium Poeticum, A Gathering of Verses by Manley Hopkins* (1892). He also reviewed poetry for the *London Times* and wrote one novel and an essay on Longfellow, which were never published.

This concern for art, language, and religion in Hopkins's extended family had a direct effect on the Hopkins children. Hopkins's sister Milicent (1849-1946) was originally interested in music but eventually became an "out-sister" of All Saints' Home, an Anglican sisterhood founded in London in 1851. She took the sister's habit in 1878. Hopkins's sister Kate (1856-1933) shared her brother's love of languages, humor, and sketching. She helped Robert Bridges publish the first edition of Hopkins's poems. Hopkins's youngest sister, Grace (1857-1945), set some of his poems to music and composed accompaniments for Hopkins's melodies for poems by Richard Watson Dixon and Robert Bridges.

Hopkins's brother Lionel (1854-1952) sus-

tained the family interest in languages. He was top of the senior division of Modern School at Winchester, with a reputation for thoughtful and thorough work in French and German. He became a world-famous expert on archaic and colloquial Chinese. He loved puns, jokes, parodies, and all kinds of wordplay as much as his father and his brother Gerard. Hopkins's brother Arthur (1847-1930) continued the family interest in the visual arts. He was an excellent sketcher and became a professional illustrator and artist. He illustrated Thomas Hardy's *Return of the Native* in 1878, was a member of the Royal Watercolour Society, and exhibited at the Royal Academy. The youngest brother, Everard (1860-1928), followed in Arthur's footsteps. He too became a professional illustrator and cartoonist for newspapers and periodicals, and he exhibited his watercolors and pastels in London. Both Everard and Arthur were regular contributors to *Punch* and shared Hopkins's admiration for the paintings of John Everett Millais.

The relationship between Hopkins and his father reveals important early instances of creative collaboration and competition within the family. Hopkins copied eleven of the poems from his father's volume *A Philosopher's Stone* into his Oxford notebooks. In those poems his father expressed a Keatsian dismay over science's threat to a magical or imaginative response to nature. Manley Hopkins's desire to preserve a Wordsworthian love of nature in his children is evident in his "To a Beautiful Child":

> . . . *thy* book
> Is cliff, and wood, and foaming waterfall;
> Thy playmates—the wild sheep and birds
>   that call
> Hoarse to the storm;—thy sport is with the
>   storm
> To wrestle;—and thy piety to stand
> Musing on things create, and their Creator's
>   hand!

This was a remarkably prophetic poem for Manley Hopkins's first "beautiful child," Gerard, born only a year after this poem was published. The phrase "And birds that call/Hoarse to the storm," invites comparison with the son's images of the windhover rebuffing the big wind in "The Windhover" (1877) and with the image of the great stormfowl at the conclusion of "Henry Purcell" (1879). The father's prophecy, "thy sport is with the storm/To wrestle" is fulfilled in Gerard's *The Wreck of the Deutschland* and "The Loss of the *Eurydice*" (1878). These two shipwreck poems, replete with spiritual instruction for those in doubt and danger, were the son's poetic and religious counterparts to his father's 1873 volume, *The Port of Refuge, or advice and instructions to the Master-Mariner in situations of doubt, difficulty, and danger.*

Gerard's response to nature was also influenced by a poem such as "A Bird Singing in a Narrow Street," one of the eleven poems from *The Philosopher's Stone* he copied into his notebook. This theme of the bird confined recurs most obviously in Gerard's "The Caged Skylark" (1877) but may be detected even in comments on the imprisoning narrowness of urban civilization in his letters. In addition, the son answered the father's representation of a bird filling the "throbbing air" with sound and "making our bosoms to thy cadence thrill" in "The Nightingale" (1866):

> For he began at once and shook
> My head to hear. He might have strung
> A row of ripples in the brook,
>   So forcibly he sung,
> The mist upon the leaves have strewed,
> And danced the balls of dew that stood
> In acres all above the wood.

This particular motif of the singing bird appears again in Gerard's "Spring" (1877): "and thrush/ Through the echoing timber does so rinse and wring/ The ear, it strikes like lightnings to hear him sing." The father's attempt to represent what it is like to live in a bird's environment, moreover, to experience daily the "fields, the open sky,/ The rising sun, the moon's pale majesty;/ The leafy bower, where the airy nest is hung" was also one of the inspirations of the son's lengthy account of a lark's gliding beneath clouds, its aerial view of the fields below, and its proximity to a rainbow in "Il Mystico" (1862), as well as the son's attempt to enter into a lark's existence and express its essence mimically in "The Woodlark" (1876). A related motif, Manley's feeling for clouds, evident in his poem "Clouds," encouraged his son's representation of them in "Hurrahing in Harvest" (1877) and "That Nature is a Heraclitean Fire" (1888).

Competition and collaboration between father and son continued even long after Hopkins left home to take his place in the world. In 1879, for instance, Gerard Manley Hopkins wrote to Bridges, "I enclose some lines by my father called forth by the proposal to fell the trees in Well Walk (where Keats and other interesting people lived) and printed in some local paper." Two months later

Hopkins composed "Binsey Poplars" to commemorate the felling of a grove of trees near Oxford. Clearly, competition with his father was an important creative stimulus.

In addition to specific inspirations such as these, the father communicated to his son a sense of nature as a book written by God which leads its readers to a thoughtful contemplation of Him, a theme particularly evident in Manley and Thomas Marsland Hopkins's book of poems, *Pietas Metrica.* Consequently, Gerard went on to write poems which were some of the best expressions not only of the Romantic approach to nature but also the older tradition of explicitly religious nature poetry.

Pietas Metrica was devoted explicitly to that marriage of nature and religion which became characteristic of Gerard's poetry. This book is also valuable as a model of the norm of contemporary religious nature poetry which Hopkins was trying both to sustain and surpass. The aims of the authors of *Pietas Metrica* became Hopkins's own. As noted in the preface, "It was the design of the writers of this volume to blend together two of Man's best things, Religion and Poetry. They aimed at binding with another tie the feeling of piety with external nature and our daily thoughts. The books of Nature and Revelation have been laid side by side and read together."

The most joyous synchronic reading of the Bible and the Book of Nature was the hymn of creation, a traditional genre inspired by Psalm 148 to which such poems of Gerard's as "God's Grandeur" (1877), "Pied Beauty" (1877), "Hurrahing in Harvest," and "Easter" (1866) belong. A line such as "Flowers do ope their heavenward eyes" in Hopkins's "Easter," for instance, would normally be ascribed to the influence of George Herbert, but the representation of a flower "breathing up to heaven/ The incense of her prayer" like a "natural altar" in "The Fraxinella" in *Pietas Metrica* reveals that it is just as appropriate to look to contemporary poetry for a context for Hopkins's poems as it is to look back to Metaphysical poets such as Herbert. Indeed, in some cases it may be more appropriate to seek contemporary models. Though Herbert's "The Flower" is a famous example of a flower straining toward heaven, he employs no satellite imagery of opening eyes; indeed he only twice uses the word *ope* in all of his poems, neither time referring to flowers, and he never uses the adjective *heavenward.*

The personification of Earth in Hopkins's "Easter"—"Earth throws Winter's robes away,/ Decks herself for Easter Day"—also recalls the personification of Nature in "Catholic Truth" from *Pietas Metrica*. A reader of Hopkins's poetry familiar with contemporary creation hymns such as "Catholic Truth" would also expect the song rhythm which Hopkins employs in the third stanza of "Easter," because in this genre nature, rather than mankind, is usually represented as more faithfully singing God's praise:

> Gather gladness from the skies;
> Take a lesson from the ground;
> Flowers do ope their heavenward eyes
> And a Spring-time joy have found;
> Earth throws Winter's robes away,
> Decks herself for Easter Day.

Ultimately, mankind joins in the song in related hymns in this genre, including Christina Rossetti's "And there was no more Sea," in which all possible voices are united "In oneness of contentment offering praise." Hence Hopkins extends the rhythm to include man in the fourth stanza of "Easter":

> Beauty now for ashes wear,
> Perfumes for the garb of woe.
> Chaplets for dishevelled hair,
> Dances for sad footsteps slow;
> Open wide your hearts that they
> Let in joy this Easter Day.

Although man and nature are ultimately bound by love in one hymn of creation, contemporary readers of poems such as "Easter" know that nature is traditionally represented not only as more consistently heeding the commandment to song which concludes Hopkins's "Easter" but also as best fulfilling the demand of his first stanza for a plenitude of offerings:

> Break the box and shed the nard;
> Stop not now to count the cost;
> Hither bring pearl, opal, sard;
> Reck not what the poor have lost;
> Upon Christ throw all away:
> Know ye, this is Easter Day.

"Where are the Nine?" in *Pietas Metrica* develops this concept of nature's unstinted offering and points the traditional contrast between man and nature implicit in the first stanza of "Easter": "And is it so that Nature stints her praise,/With niggard thanks makes offering to her God?" The answer of Hopkins's father and uncle is clear:

> No, Nature is not backward, she declares

> Each blessing as it comes, and owns her Lord,
> She is no miser of her thanks, she spares
> No praise, due to Heaven, beloved adored.

Hopkins agreed with his father and uncle that man seemed "backward" in comparison with nature, especially in "God's Grandeur," "Spring," "In the Valley of the Elwy" (1877), "The Sea and the Skylark" (1877), "Binsey Poplars," "Duns Scotus's Oxford" (1879), and "Ribblesdale" (1882). Hopkins also discovered to his despair the truth of the final complaint of "Where are the Nine?":

> Alas for man! day after day may rise,
> Night may shade his thankless head,
> He sees no God in the bright, morning skies
> He sings no praises from his guarded bed.

This apparent disappearance of God from nature in the nineteenth century inspired some of the didacticism which pervades Hopkins's later nature poetry. Unlike the Romantics, many Victorians thought of nature as another Book of Revelation to be used for the same practical ends as the Bible: to inculcate lessons in the religious life. As the statement in the Hopkins brothers' preface about placing the books of Nature and Revelation side by side suggests, *Pietas Metrica* is an excellent illustration of this tradition. While the Wordsworthian influence in the volume is occasionally implicit in poems such as "Love," the sermonical aim is almost always explicit, as in the title "Autumnal Lessons."

Flowers were especially popular for purposes of instruction, their function in Hopkins's "Easter." The flowers in "Catholic Truth," for example, are "All telling the same truth; their simple creed," and the author of "The Fraxinella" sighs, with the exclamation mark so characteristic of Hopkins, "Ah! could our hearts/Read thoughtful lessons from thy modest leaves." When we place Hopkins's nature poetry in this tradition we not only perceive the contemporary precedents for the homilies which conclude so many of his nature poems, we also begin to discern some of the distinguishing features of his didacticism. Hopkins's commands strike us as more direct and imperative, and we discover that his religious poetry was unusually proselytical before he became a Catholic and long before he became a Jesuit.

Nature poetry was not the only area in which father and son were rivals. Romantic love of childhood as well as nature is evident in Manley Hopkins's "To a Beautiful Child" and "The Nursery Window," and this theme of childhood innocence is also stressed by his son in "Spring," "The Handsome Heart" (1879), and "The Bugler's First Communion" (1879). The father also composed straightforward religious poems such as his long poem on John the Baptist in *A Philosopher's Stone,* and the son soon surpassed his father in this category as well. Gerard's many poems about martyrs recall his father's preoccupation with physical suffering in poems such as "The Grave-Digger" and "The Child's Dream" from *A Philosopher's Stone.*

The son's melancholy, evident in poems such as the undated "Spring and Death," "Spring and Fall" (1880), and "The Leaden Echo" (1882), can also be traced to poems such as his father's sonnet "All things grow old—grow old, decay and change" and "A Philosopher's Stone," which warns that "The withered crown will soon slide down / A skull all bleached and blent" and concludes in that didactic mode typical of several of his son's religious poems:

> "The Alchymists rare, are they who prepare
>   For death ere life be done;
> And by study hard WITHIN THE CHURCHYARD
>   IS FOUND THE PHILOSOPHER'S STONE."

Gerard also wrote a poem about an alchemist, "The Alchemist in the City," but the poem of his which captures this didactic tone best is perhaps *The Wreck of the Deutschland,* especially the eleventh stanza:

> 'Some find me a sword; some
>   The flange and the rail; flame,
> Fang, or flood' goes Death on drum,
>   And storms bugle his fame.
> But we dream we are rooted in earth—Dust!
> Flesh falls within sight of us, we, though our
>   flower the same,
>   Wave with the meadow, forget that there must
> The sour scythe cringe, and the blear share come.

The son clearly surpassed the father in many ways. For instance, the son resisted the temptation to become morbid better than the father's example might lead one to expect. Compare Gerard Manley Hopkins's version of an attempted rescue with the account in the *London Times,* one of the sources he used for *The Wreck of the Deutschland.* According to the *Times,* "One brave sailor, who was safe in the rigging went down to try to save a child or woman who was drowning on deck. He was secured by a rope to the rigging, but a wave dashed him against the bulwark, and when daylight dawned his headless body, detained by the rope, was swinging to and fro with the waves." Hopkins wrote:

> One stirred from the rigging to save
>   The wild woman-kind below,
> With a rope's end round the man, handy and
>   brave—
>   He was pitched to his death at a blow,
> For all his dreadnought breast and braids of thew:
> They could tell him for hours, dandled the to and fro
>   Through the cobbled foam-fleece.

Hopkins transformed the prose into song, but he deleted the morbid details of the decapitation.

It was no doubt partly to escape contemplation of such details connected with his marine-insurance business that Manley Hopkins cultivated a Wordsworthian love of nature. The example of Wordsworth's youth in nature and the contrasting example of Coleridge's youth in the city, "Debarr'd from Nature's living images, / Compelled to be a life unto itself" (*The Prelude* VI: 313-314), encouraged Manley Hopkins to live in Hampstead rather than in London proper where he worked. He moved his family to Hampstead in 1852, and Gerard and his brother Cyril (1846-1932), who later rejoined his father's firm, were sent to live with relatives in the Hainault Forest, where they spent the summer exploring and studying nature. When he returned to his family, Gerard found himself living near groves of lime and elm, many fine views, the garden where Keats composed his "Ode to a Nightingale" under a mulberry tree and the Heath celebrated in painting after painting by Constable. Hopkins obviously enjoyed living there: Cyril recalls that he was a fearless climber of trees, especially the lofty elm which stood in their garden.

At the age of ten, Hopkins left the garden and his family home for Robert Cholmondley's boarding school at Highgate, a northern height of London less populous and more forested than Hampstead. Like Hampstead, it commanded a good view of the surrounding area and was associated with the memories of such artists as Marvell, Lamb, Keats, and De Quincey; the tomb, even the coffin, of Coleridge could be seen in Highgate when Hopkins was there. One of Hopkins's friends at Highgate was Coleridge's grandson E. H. Coleridge, who became a biographer of Byron and named one of his sons after his friend Hopkins. While at Highgate Hopkins composed "The Escorial" (1860), his earliest poem extant. The description of the destruction of the Escorial by the sweeping rain and sobbing wind recalls Byron, but the allusions to Raphael, Titian, Velásquez, Rubens, and Claude, as well as to various styles of architecture, reveal Hopkins's desire to unite in some way his love of the visual arts and his love of poetry.

The sketches of Bavarian peasants Hopkins produced when his father took him to southern Germany in 1860 reveal his growing interest in being a painter as well as a poet. The only drawing manual in the Hopkins family library, as far as is known, was John Eagles's *The Sketcher* (1856). Rev. Eagles, who was Manley Hopkins's maternal uncle, recommends the classical idealism of Gaspard Poussin and an elegant, expressive mode of pastoral. However, the fourth volume of John Ruskin's *Modern Painters* was published the same year as *The Sketcher*, and it promulgated important modifications of Eagles's ideal of amateur drawing. Ruskin's emphasis on objective, detailed representation of nature soon became evident in the sketches of Hopkins and other members of his family.

Hopkins's Ruskinese sketches are significant because although Hopkins is remembered as a poet, he wanted to be a painter, deciding against it finally because he thought it was too "passionate" an exercise for one with a religious vocation. Nevertheless,

even after he became a Jesuit he continued to cultivate an acquaintance with the visual arts through drawing and attendance at exhibitions, and this lifelong attraction to the visual arts affected the verbal art for which he is remembered. In his early poetry and in his journals wordpainting is pervasive, and there is a recurrent Keatsian straining after the stasis of the plastic arts.

Hopkins's finely detailed black-and-white sketches were primarily important to him as special exercises of the mind, the eye, and the hand which could alter the sketcher's consciousness of the outside world. The typical Hopkins drawing is what Ruskin called the "outline drawing"; as Ruskin put it, "without any wash of colour, such an outline is the most valuable of all means for obtaining such memoranda of any scene as may explain to another person, or record for yourself, what is most important in its features." Many such practical purposes for drawing were advanced by Ruskin, but his ultimate purpose was to unite science, art, and religion. As Humphry House put it, "Because the Romantic tradition said that Nature was somehow the source of important spiritual experience, and because the

Manor Farm, Shanklin, *one of Hopkins's Ruskinesque sketches showing an obsession for minute detail (courtesy of the Society of Jesus and the Humanities Research Center, University of Texas at Austin)*

Hopkins's May 12 n.r. Oxford *(courtesy of the Society of Jesus
and the Humanities Research Center, University
of Texas at Austin)*

habit of mind of the following generation (with an empiric scientific philosophy) was to dwell lovingly on factual detail, a suspicion came about that perhaps the cause of the spiritual experience lay in detail."

This is part of the motivation for the obsession with minute detail seen in Hopkins's *Manor Farm, Shanklin Sept. 21, 1863* and in his *May 12 n. r. Oxford.* According to Ruskin, those who sketched in this way possessed the further advantage of cultivating certain special powers of the eye and the mind: "By drawing they actually obtained a power of the eye and a power of the mind wholly different from that known to any other discipline, and which could only be known by the experienced student—he only could know how the eye gained physical power by the attention to details, and that was one reason why delicate drawings had, above all others, been most prized; and that nicety of study made the eye see

things and causes which it could not otherwise trace." *Manor Farm* uses fairly heavy shading but combines it with fine detail for a more delicate effect. An effect of lighter delicacy is achieved in *May 12 n. r. Oxford,* a sketch of a convolvulus, by restricting the heavy shading to the shadows and by using fairly delicate gradations.

The powers of the mind which such study granted included the cultivation of patience, discipline, earnestness, and a love of work for its own sake, but perhaps the most important power developed was the ability to concentrate. Ruskin stressed the importance of concentration to perceptions of the unity of things: "No human capacity ever yet saw the whole of a thing; but we may see more and more of it the longer we look." By concentrating on the whole of a thing Hopkins was able to discover the "inscape," the distinctively unifying pattern of, say, "a white shire of cloud. I looked long up at it till the tall height and the beauty of the scaping—regularly curled knots springing up if I remember from fine stems, like foliage on wood or stone—had strongly grown on me. . . . Unless you refresh the mind from time to time you cannot always remember or believe how deep the inscape in things is. . . . if you look well at big pack-clouds overhead you will soon find a strong large quaining and squaring in them which makes each pack impressive and whole." By concentrating in this way also on the formal aspects of running water he was able to discover some of the deeper, recurrent formations of "scaping" even in a tumultuous river: "by watching hard the banks began to sail upstream, the scaping unfolded." This kind of concentration was clearly aided by drawing exercises such as *July 18. At the Baths of Rosenlaui.*

A search for recurring regularity and distinctively unifying forms was one of the primary motivations of an outline drawing of a tree such as *June 26, '68.* Many of Hopkins's sketches of trees seem to be attempts to discover what Ruskin called the "fountain-like impulse" of trees in which "each terminates all its minor branches at its outer extremity, so as to form a great outer curve, whose character and proportion are peculiar for each species"; ultimately both Ruskin and Hopkins were seeking "organic unity; the law, whether of radiation or parallelism, or concurrent action, which rules the masses of herbs and trees."

One of Hopkins's journal entries makes this motivation clear and serves as an effective summary of his typically Victorian union of science and aesthetics: "Oaks: the organization of this tree is difficult. Speaking generally no doubt the deter-

June 26, '68, *one of Hopkins's attempts to discover what Ruskin called the "fountain-like impulse" of trees (courtesy of the Society of Jesus)*

July 18. At the Baths of Rosenlaui, *drawn by Hopkins in 1868 (courtesy of the Society of Jesus and the Humanities Research Center, University of Texas at Austin)*

mining planes are concentric, a system of brief contiguous and continuous tangents, whereas those of the cedar would roughly be called horizontals and those of the beech radiating but modified by droop and by a screw-set towards jutting points. But beyond this since the normal growth of the boughs is radiating and the leaves grow some way in there is of course a system of spoke-wise clubs of greensleeve-pieces. . . . I have seen also the pieces in profile with chiselled outlines, the blocks thus made detached and lessening towards the end. . . . Oaks differ much, and much turns on the broadness of the leaves, the narrower giving the crisped and starring and Catherine-wheel forms, the broader the flat-pieced or shard-covered ones, in which it is possible to see composition in dips etc on wider bases than the single knot or cluster." Hopkins discovered that his genius lay in such translations of visual perceptions into words.

His drawings were often remarkably similar to the early sketches of his brother Arthur, although Arthur's drawings are often more fully detailed and unified. Hence it is difficult to accept the belief of critics that Gerard had more talent than his brother. On the contrary, the differences between Gerard's sketches and Arthur's suggest a need to revise the accepted opinion that Gerard could have been a professional painter if he had wanted to. Rather, it would appear that just as Lope de Vega's success in Spanish drama induced Cervantes to develop an alternative genre, Arthur Hopkins's superior sketching abilities encouraged his older brother to concentrate his energies on literary and religious creativity instead.

This sibling rivalry between Hopkins and his brother Arthur reveals how crucial adaptive compromise can be in the development of a genius's creative potential. Although some of Hopkins's drawings suggest that he could have achieved more detail if he had tried, it is apparent that, while he shared the motivations of his family for drawing, he soon developed specific aims and interests which often differed significantly from theirs. His letter of 10 July 1863 to his friend A. W. M. Baillie confirms that he had developed special interests and did not find any member of his own family a congenial thinker in these matters: "I venture to hope you will approve of some of the sketches in a Ruskinese point of view:—if you do not, who will, my sole congenial thinker on art?"

Some of the differences between Hopkins's aims and those of his brother Arthur are most obvious in the results of their sketching from the cliff in Freshwater Bay on the Isle of Wight in 1863. Arthur, focusing on an unusual bridgelike rock formation in the sea, produced a memorable subject for a picturesque travel record: *Arched Rock. Freshwater Bay. (from the cliff) July 23. 1863.* Gerard, on the other hand, tried to reproduce the pattern made by the waves below and wrote: "Note: The curves of the returning wave overlap, the angular space between is smooth but covered with a network of foam. The advancing wave, already broken, and now only a mass of foam, upon the point of encountering the reflux of the former. Study from the cliff above. Freshwater Gate. July 23." Gerard's aims clearly diverged from Arthur's in at least two important ways: he became more interested in drawing as a means of visual research and more willing to supplement this visual art with verbal art.

In addition, these two sketches illustrate the meaning of "inscape," that conundrum of Hopkins's readers. A common misconception of the word is that it signifies simply a love of the unique particular, the unusual feature, the singular appearance, but that meaning fits *Arched Rock* better than it does Gerard's note on waves. Gerard lost interest in what was merely unique; as in the wave study he usually sought the distinctively unifying design, the "returning" or recurrent pattern, the internal "network" of structural relationships which clearly and unmistakably integrates or *scapes* an object or set of objects and thus reveals the presence of integrating laws throughout nature and a divine unifying force or "stress" in this world. The suggestion of metaphysical significance is obvious in an 1874 note by Hopkins on waves: "The laps of running foam striking the sea-wall double on themselves and return in nearly the same order and shape in which they came. This is mechanical reflection and is the same as optical: indeed all nature is mechanical, but then it is not seen that mechanics contain that which is beyond mechanics."

Arthur was also fascinated by waves and produced some excellent sketches of them, especially *1st September, '75, Breaking Waves, Whitby,* and *Study of the back of a breaking wave seen from above and behind. Whitby. 30 Aug. '75.* These sketches are clearly superior to any of Gerard's drawings of waves in detail, finish, delicacy of shading, and illusion of motion. Likewise, Arthur's *Study of 'The Armed Knight', a reef at the Land's End. 4 Sept. '79* easily surpasses Gerard's 1863 sketches of rock formations, both in truth of detail and aesthetic development, and his *At Whitnash. Warwickshire 8 Sept. '77* reproduces more subtle and delicate effects of light and shade than Gerard achieved in his studies of groups of trees.

1863 study by Hopkins of wave patterns along the coast of the Isle of Wight (courtesy of the Society of Jesus)

Gerard did not even try to sketch the majesty and sublimity of an ocean wave as Arthur did, however. Characteristically, in his *Study from the cliff above* Gerard conveyed the motion of the waves with words. Phrases such as "the advancing wave already broken, and now only a mass of foam" supply a scenario, a succession of events in time to complement the spatial representation. Eagles recommended not only sea-pieces such as this but also shipwrecks, and eventually this advice, along with similar recommendations from Ruskin, and the family preoccupation with danger at sea due to the father's insurance business inspired Gerard's attempt to represent a shipwreck. Besides his father's publication of *Port of Refuge* another factor that motivated Gerard may well have been Arthur's wave studies of 30 August and 1 September 1875.

Only a few months after Arthur executed these studies, Gerard began his own response to the sea in the genre which was to make him famous: not painting, but poetry. If he had insisted on competing directly with his brother, he might well have gone on to become a draughtsman less well known than Arthur. However, his response to the sea, *The Wreck of the Deutschland,* was in some ways an even better fulfillment of the suggestion of his great-uncle, John Eagles, that those who appreciate the sublime acquire "greater notions of the power and majesty of Him who maketh the clouds his chariot, and walketh upon the wings of the wind."

It has been argued that the visual image, the painter's vision, is predominant in Hopkins's journal, but the essence of his creativity was verbal rather than visual, as this description of a glacier reveals: "There are round one of the heights of the Jungfrau two ends or falls of a glacier. If you took the skin of a white tiger or the deep fell of some other animal and swung it tossing high in the air and then cast it out before you it would fall and so clasp and lap round anything in this way just as this glacier does and the fleece would part in the same rifts: you must suppose a lazuli under-flix to appear. The spraying out of one end I tried to catch but it would have taken hours: it is this which first made me think of a tiger-skin, and it ends in tongues and points like the tail and claws: indeed the ends of the glaciers are knotted or knuckled like talons." Hopkins had tried to "catch" the spraying out of one end of the glacier in three sketches inscribed *July 15, '68; July 15;* and *July 15, Little Scheidegg,* but he realized that he had relatively little talent for sketching. He could have "taken hours" and persisted, but instead he let his visual impression stimulate his linguistic creativity, specifically his ex-

traordinary capacity for metaphor. His frustration in one genre only stimulated him to be creative in another.

A similar shift from the visual to the verbal is suggested by his "A Vision of the Mermaids" (1862), a pen-and-ink drawing followed by a poem, both apparently inspired by the poetic vision of the mermaids in *The Sketcher.* Eagles's comment, "How difficult it would be, by any sketch, to convey the subject!," explains why Hopkins followed his drawing with words such as the following:

> Plum-purple was the west; but spikes of light
> Spear'd open lustrous gashes, crimson-white;
> (Where the eye fix'd, fled the encrimsoning spot,
> And gathering, floated where the gaze was not;)
> And thro' their parting lids there came and went
> Keen glimpses of the inner firmament:
> Fair beds they seem'd of water-lily flakes
> Clustering entrancingly in beryl lakes.

This kind of poetic diction reflects the influence of one of Hopkins's teachers at Highgate, Richard Watson Dixon. Dixon had been involved in the vanguard of much that seemed exciting in the art of the time. Dante Gabriel Rossetti had taught him painting and had praised his poems. Dixon's *Christ's Company and Other Poems* (1861) featured Rossetti's decorative, sensuous beauty and remote dream worlds and a typically Victorian love of wordpainting.

Yet Dixon's title emphasizes the fact that his longer poems are High Church hagiographical verses and the Incarnation is a pervasive theme in the poems in this volume. Dixon had been attracted to the Oxford Pre-Raphaelites who followed Rossetti because of their Ruskinese stress on Christian art and because of the original pietism of the group itself. Almost every member of the group had initially intended to take Holy Orders, but most of them were deflected from their purpose by their desire to be artists. Dixon also at one point had given up his religious commitment to become a Pre-Raphaelite painter, but, unlike other members of the group, Dixon finally did take Holy Orders. He thus became an important model for Hopkins of the possibility of combining poetic and religious vocations.

Hopkins praised and respected Dixon's poetry and even copied out favorite stanzas when he entered the Jesuit novitiate. The affinities between Dixon's poems and Hopkins's early poetry are evident when we compare the descriptions of the sunsets in "The Sicilian Vespers," Dixon's boyhood prize poem, and in "A Vision of the Mermaids,"

A Vision of the Mermaids *(1862), pen-and-ink heading by Hopkins for his poem of the same title (courtesy of the Society of Jesus)*

thought by some to be one of Hopkins's best poems at Highgate. Both teacher and student focus on an isle breaking the sunset's tide of light; and both reveal a preference for iambic pentameter couplets and the adjectival compounds, long sentences, and colorful pictorial images characteristic of Victorian wordpainting.

In short, Dixon introduced Hopkins to "the school of Keats" in Victorian poetry. As Hopkins recalled, Dixon would "praise Keats by the hour." The result is obvious in "A Vision of the Mermaids," which reproduces the archaic diction, literary and mythological allusiveness, precious neologisms, luxurious sensuality, subjective dreaminess, and amoral, otherworldly aestheticism of Keats's early poems. Hopkins's comments about Keats's choice of subjects apply to his own poem as well: "His contemporaries . . . still concerned themselves with great causes [such] as liberty and religion, but he lived in mythology and fairyland the life of a dreamer." The mermaids' song of "piteous siren

sweetness" in Hopkins's poem, the Keatsian temptation for him and the other Victorian poets, was to live alone in a world of private visions where the reality of the impersonal world might be freely altered to fit personal desire.

Yet Hopkins could resist the temptation even in his early poetry. Again what he said about Keats applies as well to his own early poems: "even when he is misconstructing one can remark certain instinctive turns of construction in his style, shewing his latent power." The most significant "instinctive turn" in Hopkins's early poetry occurs in "Il Mystico" (1862), in which older, more traditional religious ideals replace his Keatsian dream visions. "Il Mystico" anticipates that general move that Hopkins, like Tennyson, made from the imitation of Keats to a more explicitly Christian Romanticism, a conversion which enabled him to fulfill his own prophecy for Keats: "what he did not want to live by would have asserted itself presently and perhaps have been as much more powerful than that of his contemporaries as his sensibility or impressionableness, by which he did not want to live, was keener and richer than theirs."

"Il Mystico" contains another "instinctive turn." The poem begins as an imitation of Milton's "Il Penseroso," but its development embodies in embryo the general movement in Hopkins's early art from representations of ideal worlds to representations of this world which culminated in his famous 1877 poems on nature. His initial attempt to attain a spiritual vision in "Il Mystico" is fragmented until the speaker finds that his best expression of his aspiration for some other, more perfect realm is an objective correlative in nature, the ascent of the lark, which translates that desire into action.

Hopkins cultivated this "instinctive turn" and the result was his first published poem, "Winter with the Gulf Stream," which appeared in the popular periodical *Once a Week* on 14 February 1863, when Hopkins was only eighteen years old. This poem reveals the beginning of Hopkins's movement away from a pseudo-Keatsian dreamy subjectivity toward imitation of those traits of Keats's most valuable to Hopkins at this stage of his development: mastery of objective correlatives and evocative natural detail. Rather than being introduced to the speaker, as we are in "A Vision of the Mermaids," we are introduced to the object. The poem begins not with "Rowing, *I* reached a rock," but with "The boughs, the boughs"; the "I" is not introduced until six stanzas later. The objects to which we are initially introduced are, moreover, more closely observed than those of his earlier poems. We are not shown general features of a landscape from a distance but an immediate foreground of branches and vines—"Frost furred our ivies are and rough/With bills of rime the brambles shew." Instead of masses of trees we are shown their leaves hissing and scuttling along the ground and the clammy coats of foliage they become when the rain-blasts are unbound.

Hopkins eventually began to be critical of mere love of detail, however—"that kind of thought which runs upon the concrete and the particular, which disintegrates and drops toward atomism in some shape or other," he wrote in his journal—and he became increasingly aware of the importance of religion as the ultimate source of unity.

His religious consciousness increased dramatically when he entered Oxford, the city of spires. From April of 1863, when he first arrived with some of his journals, drawings, and early

Keatsian poems in hand, until June of 1867 when he graduated, Hopkins felt the charm of Oxford, "steeped in sentiment as she lies," as Matthew Arnold had said, "spreading her gardens to the moonlight and whispering from her towers the last enchantments of the Middle Ages." Here he became more fully aware of the religious implications of the medievalism of Ruskin, Dixon, and the Pre-Raphaelites. Inspired also by Christina Rossetti, the Catholic doctrine of the Real Presence of God in the Eucharist, and by the Victorian preoccupation with the fifteenth-century Italian religious reformer Girolamo Savonarola, he soon embraced Ruskin's definition of "Medievalism" as a "confession of Christ" opposed to both "Classicalism" ("Pagan Faith") and "Modernism" (the "denial of Christ").

At Oxford Hopkins's consciousness of competition with contemporaries increased, apparently partly as a result of the tradition of oral contests which persisted at Oxford and also because of Hopkins's decision to focus on classical studies which tended to be highly agonistic and rhetorically oriented. At Highgate Hopkins was encouraged to begin his literary career as a student of Keats by his teacher Dixon, who also showed Hopkins how to resist Keats's dominance, partly by sublimating it in devotional poetry. While the initiation and direction of Hopkins's creativity in the relationship with Dixon was positive, Hopkins's relationship with a more famous teacher at Oxford, Walter Pater, was fiercely dialectical, with Hopkins defining his position in opposition to Pater's. Yet there was also a curious symbiotic quality in their relationship; they remained friends and shared related interests in Dante, Savonarola, medievalism, and the Pre-Raphaelites.

Among the Pre-Raphaelites the most important figure for Hopkins was Christina Rossetti. She benefited from the emphasis on the feminine in the Pre-Raphaelite focus on Marian figures such as Dante's Beatrice. When Hopkins met her in 1864 he met an icon, the model for the Virgin in the paintings of her brother Dante Gabriel Rossetti. She influenced Hopkins more than any other contemporary at this point in his career and was particularly important in Hopkins's replacement of Keats with Dante as the dominant paradigm in his poetic imagination.

Christina Rossetti became for Hopkins the embodiment of the medievalism of the Pre-Raphaelites, the Oxford Movement, and Victorian religious poetry generally. In the 1860s Hopkins was profoundly influenced by her example and succeeded, unbeknownst to her and to the critics of his time, in becoming a rival far greater than any of her contemporaries.

Their rivalry began with Hopkins's response to her poem "The Convent Threshold." Geoffrey Hartman was clearly on the right track when he suggested in the introduction to *Hopkins: A Collection of Critical Essays* (1966) that "Hopkins seems to develop his lyric structures out of the Pre-Raphaelite dream vision. In his early 'A Vision of the Mermaids' and 'St. Dorothea' he may be struggling with such poems as Christina Rossetti's 'Convent Threshold' and Dante Gabriel Rossetti's 'The Blessed Damozel,' poems in which the poet stands at a lower level than the vision, or is irrevocably, pathetically distanced." Such poems were the essence of medievalism in poetry according to William Morris, who felt that Keats's "La Belle Dame Sans Merci" was the germ from which all Pre-Raphaelite poetry sprang. Standing beyond Keats, however, the primary source was Dante, as Christina Rossetti made clear.

She clearly alludes to Beatrice's appeal to Dante in "The Convent Threshold":

I choose the stairs that mount above,
Stair after golden skyward stair,
. . . .
Lo, stairs are meant to lift us higher:
Mount with me, mount the kindled stair.
    Your eyes look earthward, mine look up.
. . . .
How should I rest in Paradise,
Or sit on steps of heaven alone?
. . . .
Oh save me from a pang in heaven,
By all the gifts we took and gave,
Repent, repent, and be forgiven.

Hopkins read this appeal at a crucial moment in his career, when he was actually considering renouncing his own powerful attraction to this world for a life beyond the cloister threshold. He translated portions of Rossetti's poem into Latin elegiacs and devoted much of his poetic creativity in 1864 to his own response to it, which he called at first "A Voice from the World" (later "Beyond the Cloister") and subtitled "An Answer to Miss Rossetti's *Convent Threshold*." The surviving fragments express the speaker's sense of spiritual inferiority and his admiration for the decision of Christina Rossetti's heroine to join the convent. Hopkins's first title identifies his persona as the one whose eyes "look earthward," but he is willing to lift up his gaze:

At last I hear the voice well known;
. . . .
You see but with a holier mind—
You hear and, alter'd, do not hear
Being a stoled apparel'd star.

. . . .
Teach me the paces that you went
I can send up an Esau's cry;
Tune it to words of good intent.
This ice, this lead, this steel, this stone,
This heart is warm to you alone;
Make it to God. I am not spent
. . . .
Steel may be melted and rock rent.
Penance shall clothe me to the bone.
Teach me the way: I will repent.

Hopkins was clearly oriented to the Pre-Raphaelite dream vision in which the poet is represented on a lower plane than the vision. By taking the part of Rossetti's heroine's earthly lover in his poem, moreover, Hopkins invites a comparison between his persona and Christina's erstwhile lover, James Collinson, who also became a follower of the Pre-Raphaelites and convert to Catholicism and, for a while, a Jesuit. Eventually, by converting to Catholicism himself and joining the Society of Jesus, Hopkins exchanged the inferior position articulated in "A Voice from the World" for a superior one, superior at least in the sense that Christina Rossetti apparently felt that her sister Maria, who actually did cross the convent threshold and become a religious, had achieved a higher stage of religious development than she herself did.

Both Hopkins and Christina Rossetti believed that religion was more important than art. The outline of Hopkins's career follows that of Christina Rossetti's: an outwardly drab, plodding life of submission quietly bursting into splendor in holiness and poetry. Both felt that religious inspiration was more important than artistic inspiration. Whenever religious renunciation and self-expression were felt to be at odds, as they often were, self-expression had to be sacrificed. Poetry had to be subordinated to religion.

No doubt partly as a result of this attitude, both Hopkins and Rossetti were subject to intermittent creativity. Both thought of poetry as a gift which could not be summoned at will, and each turned to prose between bursts of poetic inspiration. In fact each went through a stage of about seven years in which writing prose almost entirely replaced composing poetry. Hopkins's prose period stretched from 1868 to 1875, when his literary

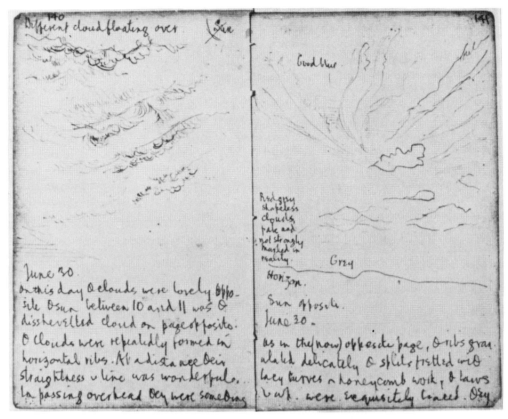

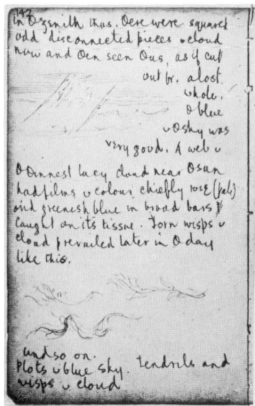

Pages from Hopkins's diary for 1864 (courtesy of the Society of Jesus)

energies were devoted primarily to his journal. In addition to passing through periods of writing prose, both poets concluded their literary careers with devotional commentaries: in Hopkins's case, his unfinished "Commentary on the Spiritual Exercises of St. Ignatius."

The attitudes of Christina Rossetti and Hopkins toward art and religion have destined them to share much the same fate at the hands of twentieth-century readers: criticism for deliberately narrowing their subjects to a range too limited for modern palates, for expressing religious convictions with which it is now difficult to sympathize, for allowing religion to take precedence over poetry, or for actually impairing the creative gift itself. On the other hand, both are often praised by twentieth-century readers for the same feature: the expression of counterpoised forces generating dramatic tensions.

One of the most dramatic tensions was that between their attraction to this world and their determination to transcend it. Like Hopkins, Christina Rossetti often reveals a Keatsian attraction to the life of sensations, especially to nature. Hopkins's wide variety of responses to nature, especially in the 1860s and 1880s, ranging from strong attraction to its beauty to belief that this beauty must be denied on religious grounds, is congruent with the range of Christina Rossetti's responses. Ultimately, however, she believed that God was not in nature but above and therefore that one must ascend the heavenly stair invoked in "The Convent Threshold," "A Shadow of Dorothea," and other poems. Hopkins's version of the legend of Saint Dorothea, "For a Picture of St. Dorothea" (1864), and his "Heaven-Haven" reveal a similar transition from the natural to the supernatural in his early poetry.

Hopkins's "For a Picture of St. Dorothea" originated in that section of his journal devoted primarily to the representation of nature. However, the flowers in his poem are not rooted in the earth but in legend. Hopkins's aim was not truth to nature primarily in this poem but the revival of medieval legend by defamiliarizing it, putting it in a new context and thereby restoring its original impact in the service of religion.

In "Heaven-Haven" Hopkins again responded to the transcendental, otherworldly aspiration so evident in the Dorothea legend and in Christina Rossetti's "A Shadow of Dorothea." As "Heaven-Haven" suggests, Hopkins's sense of the unreliability and instability of this world led him to a desire to transcend this world in order to discover some other, better world less subject to the triumph of time. Of the two paths to holiness, the outward or the inward—contemplation of God's presence in this world or contemplation of His presence within the self—by far the most common is the one Christina Rossetti usually followed: withdrawal from the external world in order to plumb the secret depths of one's own soul. Hopkins is perhaps more famous for his 1877 nature sonnets which focus on God in nature, but his sonnets of desolation of the 1880s turn inward, returning to the impulse already apparent in "Heaven-Haven," subtitled "A Nun Takes the Veil":

> I have desired to go
>   Where springs not fail,
> To fields where flies no sharp and sided hail
>   And a few lilies blow.
>
> And I have asked to be
>   Where no storms come,
> Where the green swell is in the havens dumb,
>   And out of the swing of the sea.

Hopkins's "A Soliloquy of One of the Spies Left in the Wilderness" (1864) is also a response to the recurrent call of desert Christianity. It appears to be based directly on one of the biblical interpretations of the great reformer Savonarola, the famous burner of profane art in Renaissance Italy. As Hopkins commented in a letter, Savonarola was "the only person in history (except perhaps Origen) about whom" he had "real feeling," because for Hopkins Savonarola was "the prophet of Christian art." Savonarola's example reinforced Christina Rossetti's and at first encouraged Hopkins to move beyond not only his Greek studies but also the imitation of nature that had characterized his early art. Ultimately, Savonarola's example inspired Hopkins to give up nature, beauty, and art altogether.

The sequence of events is clear. On 18 January 1866 Hopkins composed his most ascetic poem, "The Habit of Perfection." On 23 January he included poetry in the list of things to be given up for Lent. In July he decided to become a Catholic, and he traveled to Birmingham in September to consult the leader of the Oxford converts, John Henry Newman. Newman received him into the Church in October. On 5 May 1868 Hopkins firmly "resolved to be a religious." Less than a week later, apparently still inspired by Savonarola, he made a bonfire of his poems and gave up poetry almost entirely for seven years. Finally, in the fall of 1868 Hopkins joined a "serged fellowship" like Savonarola's and like the one he admired in "Eastern Communion" (1865), a commitment foreshadowed by the emphasis on vows of silence and poverty in "The Habit of Perfection."

Hopkins had been attracted to asceticism since childhood. At Highgate, for instance, he argued that nearly everyone consumed more liquids than the body needed, and, to prove it, he wagered that he could go without liquids for at least a week. He persisted until his tongue was black and he collapsed at drill. He won not only his wager but also the undying enmity of the headmaster Dr. John Bradley Dyne. On another occasion, he abstained from salt for a week. His continuing insistence on extremes of self-denial later in life struck some of his fellow Jesuits as more appropriate to a Victorian Puritan than to a Catholic.

Thus it is important to realize that he converted to Catholicism not to be more ascetic, for asceticism was as Protestant as it was Catholic, but to be able to embrace the Catholic doctrine of the Real Presence. This explanation was not enough to satisfy his family, however. Hopkins's letter informing them of his conversion came as a great shock. He wrote to Newman: "I have been up at Oxford just long enough to have heard fr. my father and mother in return for my letter announcing my conversion. Their answers are terrible: I cannot read them twice." Meanwhile, Manley Hopkins was writing to Gerard's Anglican confessor, H. P. Liddon: "The blow is so deadly and great that we have not yet recovered from the first shock of it. We had observed a growing love for asceticism and high ritual, and/ . . . we believed he had lately resolved on taking orders in the English Church . . . . save him from throwing a pure life and a somewhat unusual intellect away in the cold limbo which Rome assigns to her English converts. The deepness of our distress, the shattering of our hopes and the foreseen estrangement which must happen, are my excuse for writing to you so freely." After receiving Liddon's reply, Manley Hopkins wrote to Liddon again, accusing Gerard of speaking "with perfect coldness of any possible estrangement from us, who have loved him with an unchanging love. His mother's heart is almost broken by this, and by his desertion from our Church, her belief in, and devotion to, which are woven in with her very being." Manley used similar terms in his letter to Gerard: "The manner in which you seem to repel and throw us off cuts us to the heart . . . . O Gerard my darling boy are you indeed gone from me?"

As these words suggest, when Hopkins converted to Catholicism he felt he had actually forfeited his rightful place in the family home; he did not even know if his father would let him in the house again. A letter from Hopkins reveals that his father consented to his presence there on one condition: "You are so kind as not to forbid me your house, to which I have no claim, on condition, if I understand, that I promise not to try to convert my brothers and sisters." This was not an easy condition for him to accept, however; "Before I can promise this I must get permission, wh. I have no doubt will be given. Of course this promise will not apply after they come of age. Whether after my reception you will still speak as you do now I cannot tell." Despite these differences Hopkins did spend his Christmas holidays with his family in 1866 and 1867, but what his father called "the foreseen estrangement which must happen" necessarily increased when Hopkins began his novitiate in the Society of Jesus at Manresa House, Roehampton, in September 1868 and later moved to St. Mary's Hall, Stonyhurst, for his philosophical studies in 1870. He spent Christmas away from his family from 1868 to 1871. He returned to the family hearth for the holiday in subsequent years, but in 1885 his Dublin poems still testify to the lonely isolation and anticipation of death characteristic of many Victorian orphans:

> To seem the stranger lies my lot, my life
> Among strangers. Father and mother dear,
> Brothers and sisters are in Christ not near
> . . . .
> I am in Ireland now; now I am at a third
> Remove. Not but in all removes I can
> Kind love both give and get.

When, aged only forty-four, he was finally close to the farthest remove, death, another reconciliation was attempted, but it was too late. His was a painful and poignant tragedy all too typical of Victorian families.

His father had written "by study hard WITHIN THE CHURCHYARD/IS FOUND THE PHILOSOPHER'S STONE." Ironically, it was by following this advice that father and son became estranged. The son did study hard within the churchyard, and he found that the Catholic concept of the Real Presence was his philosopher's stone. The Catholic doctrine of Transubstantiation became for him the mystical catalyst which could transmute into gold, redeem, and regenerate all that is base—what Hopkins called "the triviality of this life," "the *sordidness* of things." Contrary to his father's assertions, this was not a last-minute discovery. As early as June of 1864 Hopkins wrote to E. H. Coleridge: "The great aid to belief and object of belief is the doctrine of the Real Presence in the Blessed Sacrament of the Altar. Religion without that is sombre, dangerous, illogical, with that it is—not to speak of its grand consistency and certainty—loveable. Hold that and you will gain all Catholic truth." Ironically, as we have seen, "Catholic Truth" was the title of one of the poems in *Pietas Metrica*.

The next month Hopkins wrote to Baillie, "I have written three religious poems which however you would not at all enter into, they being of a very Catholic character." The first of these poems was apparently "Barnfloor and Winepress," published the next year in the *Union Review*. This poem adumbrates the poetic as well as religious importance of Hopkins's belief in the Real Presence of God in the Eucharist, the "Half-Way House" of God in this world as Hopkins called the sacrament in a poem of that name in 1864. "Barnfloor and Winepress" in some respects foreshadows the poetry of nature Hopkins was to compose in the late 1870s.

Though primarily a celebration of the Real Presence, this poem reveals how Hopkins could in his imagination extend the idea of the mystical Body of Christ in the communion bread and wine to the rest of nature. In this poem the wheat and grapes are not mere raw materials for Transubstantiation but are represented metaphorically as if they were already participating in the Being of God. One of the attractions of the doctrine of the Real Presence for Hopkins was that it was, as depicted in "Barnfloor and Winepress," the central instance of a metaphor participating in the reality it represents, an archetype for a sacramental poetry of nature.

This potential for a new sacramental poetry was first realized by Hopkins in *The Wreck of the Deutschland*. Hopkins recalled that when he read about the wreck of the German ship *Deutschland* off the coast of England it "made a deep impression on me, more than any other wreck or accident I ever read of," a statement made all the more impressive when we consider the number of shipwrecks he must have discussed with his father. Hopkins wrote about this particular disaster at the suggestion of Fr. James Jones, Rector of St. Beuno's College, where Hopkins studied theology from 1874 to 1877. Hopkins recalled that "What I had written I burnt before I became a Jesuit and resolved to write no more, as not belonging to my profession, unless it were by the wish of my superiors; so for seven years I wrote nothing but two or three little presentation pieces which occasion called for [presumably 'Rosa Mystica' and 'Ad Mariam']. But when in the winter of '75 the Deutschland was wrecked in the mouth of

the Thames and five Franciscan nuns, exiles from Germany by the Falck Laws, aboard of her were drowned I was affected by the account and happening to say so to my rector he said that he wished someone would write a poem on the subject. On this hint I set to work and, though my hand was out at first, produced one. I had long had haunting my ear the echo of a new rhythm which now I realized on paper."

The result is an ode of thirty-five eight-line stanzas, divided into two parts. The first part, consisting of ten stanzas, is autobiographical, recalling how God touched the speaker in his own life. The second begins with seven stanzas dramatizing newspaper accounts of the wreck. Then fourteen stanzas narrow the focus to a single passenger, the tallest of the five nuns who drowned. She was heard to call on Christ before her death. The last four stanzas address God directly and culminate in a call for the conversion of England.

The Wreck of the Deutschland became the occasion for Hopkins's incarnation as a poet in his own right. He broke with the Keatsian wordpainting style with which he began, replacing his initial prolixity, stasis, and lack of construction with a concise, dramatic unity. He rejected his original attraction to Keats's sensual aestheticism for a clearly moral, indeed a didactic, rhetoric. He saw nature not only as a pleasant spectacle as Keats had; he also confronted its seemingly infinite destructiveness as few before or after him have done. In this shipwreck he perceived the possibility of a theodicy, a vindication of God's justice which would counter the growing sense of the disappearance of God among the Victorians. For Hopkins, therefore, seeing more clearly than ever before the proselytic possibilities of art, his rector's suggestion that someone write a poem about the wreck became the theological sanction he needed to begin reconciling his religious and poetic vocations.

Nevertheless, although *The Wreck of the Deutschland* was a great breakthrough to the vision of God immanent in nature and thus to the sacramentalism that was to be the basis of the great nature poems of the following years, when Hopkins sent the poem to his friend Robert Bridges, Bridges refused to reread it despite Hopkins's pleas. The poem was also rejected by the Jesuit magazine the *Month*, primarily because of its new "sprung" rhythm, and many subsequent readers have had difficulty with it as well.

Hopkins's readers have more easily understood the sonnets he wrote about the landscape he actually saw around him near St. Beuno's College,

Wales. It was in an earlier poem, "Half-Way House," that Hopkins most clearly recorded his need to approach God in this world: "I must o'ertake Thee at once and under heaven/If I shall overtake Thee at last above." As "The Windhover," "God's Grandeur," and Hopkins's other sonnets of 1877 reveal, Hopkins found such a halfway house not only in the communion bread and wine but also in the Vale of Clwyd and the rest of the countryside around St. Beuno's. Wales clearly provided the occasion for his greatest experience of nature, as it had for Wordsworth (on Mt. Snowdon and near Tintern Abbey), John Dyer (on Grongar Hill), and Henry Vaughan.

Some of the most luminous symbols of the presence of God in Hopkins's Welsh poems are the sunrises and the "sea-sunsets which give such splendour to the vale of Clwyd," as Wordsworth put it in the preface to his own *Descriptive Sketches*. Such sights were prized and distilled in Hopkins's nature poetry in his imagery of sunlight which "sidled like dewdrops, like dandled diamonds" ("The furl of fresh-leaved dogrose down," 1879). Everything from ploughed furrows to clouds to their reflections in pools is shining and gleaming. Even night reveals a world of strangely translucent moonshine or of stars that gleam like "bright boroughs" or "diamond delves" or "quickgold" in gray lawns; all of nature was perceived as a "piece-bright paling" that was Christ's "home" ("The Starlight Night," 1877).

Hopkins's most famous Welsh sonnet, "The Windhover," reveals that for him this Book of Nature, like the Bible, demanded a moral application to the self. Hopkins wrote in his notes on St. Ignatius: "This world is word, expression, news of God"; "it is a book he has written. . . . a poem of beauty: what is it about? His praise, the reverence due to him, the way to serve him. . . . Do I then do it? Never mind others now nor the race of man: DO I DO IT?" One of Hopkins's attempts to answer that question is "The Windhover."

The initial "I" focuses attention on the speaker, but the explicit application of the lesson of the Book of Nature to him does not begin until the line "My heart in hiding/stirred for a bird" at the conclusion of the octet. One biographical interpretation of this line is that he was hiding from fulfilling his ambitions to be a great painter and poet. Instead of ostentatiously pursuing fame in that way, wearing his heart on his sleeve, he had chosen to be the "hidden man of the heart" (1 Peter 3:4), quietly pursuing the imitation of Christ. As Hopkins put it, Christ's "hidden life at Nazareth is the great help to

faith for us who must live more or less an obscure, constrained, and unsuccessful life."

Hopkins did live such a life, but the windhover reminded him of Jesus' great achievements after Nazareth. The windhover "stirred" his desire to become a great knight of faith, one of those who imitate not only the constraint but also the "achieve of, the mastery of" this great chevalier. The "ecstasy" of the windhover recalls Hopkins's initial desire in "Il Mystico" to be lifted up on "Spirit's wings" so "that I may drink that ecstasy/Which to pure souls alone may be." Ultimately, Hopkins became aware that he had been hiding from the emotional risks of total commitment to becoming a "pure" soul. The phrase "hiding" thus suggests not only hiding from the world or from worldly ambition but also hiding from God.

The words "here/Buckle" which open the sestet mean "here in my heart," therefore, as well as here in the bird and here in Jesus. Hopkins's heart-in-hiding, Christ's prey, sensed Him diving down to seize it for his own. Just as the bird buckled its wings together and thereby buckled its "brute beauty" and "valour" and capacity to "act," so the speaker responds by buckling together all his considerable talents and renewing his commitment to the imitation of Christ in order to buckle down, buckle to, in serious preparation for the combat, the grappling, the buckling with the enemy. As Paul said, "Put on the whole armour of God, that ye may be able to stand against the wiles of the Devil."

Hopkins wrote "The Windhover" only a few months before his ordination as a Jesuit priest, the ultimate commitment to sacrifice his worldly ambitions. Just as Jesus' paradoxical triumph was his buckling under, his apparent collapse, so Hopkins felt that the knight of faith must be prepared for the same buckling under or collapse of his pride, for a life of "sheer plod" and "blue-bleak" self-sacrifice, if need be. Nevertheless, the imagery of "The Windhover" promises that the knight of faith will have a fire break from his heart then — galled, gashed, and crucified in imitation of Christ. The fire will be "a billion times told lovelier" than that of his "heart in hiding," and far more "dangerous," both to his old self (for the fire is all-consuming) and to his enemy, Evil.

In Hopkins's case, the fire also became far more "dangerous" to his worldly poetic ambitions. Among other things, "The Windhover" represents Hopkins's Pegasus, the flying steed of classical myth. The collapse of his old poetic self is implied in the imagery, for Bellerophon was thrown off Pegasus because of his pride. Fearing his pride in

mination of *acedia* according to John Chrysostom and others. Despair in turn often leads to the death wish, as implied in the conclusion of Hopkins's "No worst," in his "The Times are nightfall," and in his lament in "To seem the stranger": "Not but in all removes I can/Kind love both give and get."

However, the conclusion of Hopkins's "I wake and feel"—"The lost are like this, and their scourge to be/As I am mine, their sweating selves; but worse"—is an allusion to Dante which clearly distinguishes the speaker of Hopkins's terrible sonnets from the damned who are continually referred to in the *Inferno* as "the lost" and the "sorrowful" who have lost all hope, even hope of death. Like Dante, Hopkins faced the "lost" and that which was most like them in his own soul, but his speaker also remains separated from the lost in that he is a living soul still addressing God in his prayers, still purging himself of his sins, and still living by hope in grace.

The ultimate context of Hopkins's purgation, therefore, as of Dante's, was the Bible. One of the biblical incidents echoed in the imagery and phraseology of "No worst," for instance, is that of Jesus' exorcism of the demons of Gadara. Like the imagery of Dante's *Purgatorio,* this exorcism imagery obviously provides a significant counterpoint of meaning. The suggestion is that the speaker is attempting to herd and huddle all the demons of ennui together in one category, "world-sorrow," and "heave" them out of himself. Hopkins's sonnets of desolation are especially suited to this cathartic, purging function because they are prayers as well as poems. Like Jesus' cry on the cross, Hopkins's sonnets of desolation are addressed to God and are themselves consolations.

Eventually, Hopkins, like Dante, was granted a glimpse of Paradise. Hopkins's sonnet of 1888, "That Nature is a Heraclitean Fire and of the comfort of the Resurrection," is apparently a direct reply to "No worst, there is none": the question in the earlier poem, "Comforter, where, where is your comforting?," is answered in the title of the later poem. *Acedia* has been conquered: "Enough! the Resurrection,/A heart's clarion! Away grief's gasping, joyless days, dejection." As Dante put it, "The inborn and perpetual thirst for the godlike kingdom bore us away. . . . It seemed to me that a cloud covered us, shining, dense, solid and smooth; like a diamond smit by the sun." Hopkins concludes this poem with similar imagery: "I am all at once what Christ is, since he was what I am, and/This Jack, joke, poor potsherd, patch, matchwood, immortal diamond,/Is immortal diamond."

Letters:

Further Letters of Gerard Manley Hopkins, edited by Claude Colleer Abbott (London: Oxford University Press, 1938; revised and enlarged, London: Oxford University Press, 1955);

The Letters of Gerard Manley Hopkins to Robert Bridges, edited by Abbott (London: Oxford University Press, 1955);

Correspondence of Gerard Manley Hopkins and Richard Watson Dixon, edited by Abbott (London: Oxford University Press, 1955).

Bibliography:

Tom Dunne, *Gerard Manley Hopkins, A Comprehensive Bibliography* (Oxford: Clarendon Press, 1969).

Biographies:

G. F. Lahey, *Gerard Manley Hopkins* (London: Oxford University Press, 1930);

Eleanor Ruggles, *Gerard Manley Hopkins: A Life* (New York: Norton, 1944);

Alfred Thomas, *Hopkins the Jesuit: The Years of Training* (London: Oxford University Press, 1969);

Paddy Kitchen, *Gerard Manley Hopkins* (New York: Atheneum, 1979).

References:

Bernard Bergonzi, *Gerard Manley Hopkins* (New York: Macmillan, 1977);

Jerome Bump, *Gerard Manley Hopkins* (Boston: G. K. Hall, 1982);

Robert J. Dilligan and Todd K. Bender, *A Concordance to the English Poetry of Gerard Manley Hopkins* (Madison: University of Wisconsin Press, 1970);

W. H. Gardner, *Gerard Manley Hopkins (1844-1889), A Study of Poetic Idiosyncrasy in Relation to Poetic Tradition*, 2 volumes (London: Secker & Warburg, 1944, 1949);

Gerard Manley Hopkins, by the Kenyon Critics (New York: New Directions, 1945);

Geoffrey H. Hartman, ed., *Hopkins: A Collection of Critical Essays* (Englewood Cliffs: Prentice-Hall, 1966);

Alan Heuser, *The Shaping Vision of Gerard Manley Hopkins* (London: Oxford University Press, 1958);

Wendell Stacy Johnson, *Gerard Manley Hopkins, the Poet as Victorian* (Ithaca: Cornell University Press, 1968);

Norman MacKenzie, *A Reader's Guide to Gerard*

Manley Hopkins (Ithaca: Cornell University Press, 1981);

Paul L. Mariani, *A Commentary on the Complete Poems of Gerard Manley Hopkins* (Ithaca: Cornell University Press, 1970);

J. Hillis Miller, "Gerard Manley Hopkins," in his *The Disappearance of God: Five Nineteenth-Century Writers* (Cambridge: Harvard University Press, 1963);

John Pick, *Gerard Manley Hopkins: Priest and Poet* (London: Oxford University Press, 1942);

Alison G. Sulloway, *Gerard Manley Hopkins and the Victorian Temper* (London: Routledge, 1972);

R. K. R. Thornton, ed., *All My Eyes See: The Visual World of Gerard Manley Hopkins* (Sunderland: Coelfrith Press, 1975).

Papers:

The most extensive collections of Hopkins's papers are at the Bodleian Library and Campion Hall, Oxford, and the Humanities Research Center of the University of Texas at Austin.

Jean Ingelow
(17 March 1820-20 July 1897)

Bruce A. Castner
University of South Carolina

SELECTED BOOKS: *A Rhyming Chronicle of Incidents and Feelings,* anonymous, edited by Edward Harston (London: Longman, Brown, Green & Longmans, 1850);

Allerton and Dreux; Or, The War of Opinion, anonymous, 2 volumes (London: Wertheim, 1851);

Tales of Orris (Bath: Binns & Goodwin/London: Marlborough, 1860); abridged as *Stories Told to a Child* (London: Strahan, 1865; Boston: Roberts Brothers, 1866);

Poems (London: Longman, Green, Longman, Roberts & Green, 1863; Boston: Roberts Brothers, 1863);

Studies for Stories, anonymous (2 volumes, London: Strahan, 1864; 1 volume, Boston: Roberts Brothers, 1865);

Home Thoughts and Home Scenes, by Ingelow and others (London: Routledge, Warne & Routledge, 1865; Boston: Tilton, 1865);

A Story of Doom, and Other Poems (London: Longmans, Green, 1867; Boston: Roberts Brothers, 1867);

A Sister's Bye-Hours, anonymous (London: Strahan, 1868; Boston: Roberts Brothers, 1868);

Mopsa the Fairy (London: Longmans, Green, 1869; Boston: Roberts Brothers, 1869);

The Little Wonder-Horn (London: King, 1872);

Off the Skelligs (4 volumes, London: King, 1872; 1 volume, Boston: Roberts Brothers, 1872);

Jean Ingelow

Poems, first and second series, 2 volumes (London: Longmans, 1874, 1877);

Fated to be Free (3 volumes, London: Tinsley Brothers, 1875; 1 volume, Boston: Roberts Brothers, 1875);

The Shepherd Lady, and Other Poems (Boston: Roberts Brothers, 1876);

One Hundred Holy Songs, Carols, and Sacred Ballads (London: Longmans, Green, 1878);

Sarah de Berenger (1 volume, London: Low, Marston, 1879; Boston: Roberts Brothers, 1879; 3 volumes, London: Sampson, Low, Marston, Searle & Rivington, 1880);

Don John (3 volumes, London: Low, Marston, Searle & Rivington, 1881; 1 volume, Boston: Roberts Brothers, 1881);

Poems, third series (London: Longmans, Green, 1885); republished as *Poems of the Old Days and the New* (Boston: Roberts Brothers, 1885);

John Jerome (London: Low, Marston, Searle & Rivington, 1886; Boston: Roberts Brothers, 1886);

Very Young and Quite Another Story (London: Longmans, Green, 1890);

A Motto Changed (New York: Harper, 1894).

Minor poets who can shed important light on their more famous contemporaries are often overlooked by nineteenth-century scholars. Jean Ingelow is one such minor Victorian poet who has been all but forgotten by modern critics, yet her contemporary popular appeal rivaled Alfred, Lord Tennyson's. Her popularity, her acquaintance with the major writers and artists of both England and America (including Tennyson, Christina Rossetti, and Henry Wadsworth Longfellow), and her prolific output make Ingelow a worthy subject of investigation.

Jean Ingelow was born on 17 March 1820 in the small seaport of Boston, Lincolnshire. Her father, William Ingelow, was at the time a successful banker, and her mother, Jean Kilgour, was descended from a Scottish Aberdeenshire family. Jean, the first-born of ten children (the youngest was born when Jean was twenty), grew into her teens at Boston. When she and her sisters and brothers were not being tutored at home, she spent time becoming familiar with the river that flowed past the family's first house and with the ships, sailors, and docks. Because of an opportunity for financial gain, the Ingelows moved to Ipswich, on the river Orwell, in 1834. Here, Jean Ingelow had a bedroom of her own, a rarity for a teenage girl in a growing family. Her early interest in writing was

first manifested on the backs of her room's white window shutters, where she wrote verses when her mother, who thought poetry a frivolous pursuit, denied her writing paper. The discovery of Ingelow's verses by her mother led to a relaxation of the stricture against writing and encouraged the future poetess. In the early 1840s, Ingelow was introduced to Edward Harston, a curate whose interest in literature provided a strong impetus to her literary career. He encouraged her poetic writings and even suggested topics and themes. His continued enthusiasm was such that when the Ingelows moved to London in 1850, Ingelow was on the verge of having her first book published.

Ingelow's major themes, concerns, and techniques remained consistent throughout her career. The dominant thematic concern of her poetry is love in all its phases—lost love, newfound love, troubled love, earthly love, and religious love. Coupled with her themes of love are very detailed yet simple descriptions of nature, particularly of rivers, the sea, birds, and the fen. Sincere religious beliefs and the concept of family are often combined with love in her lyrical poems. Her language is usually clear and simple, and frequently she uses dialogue to create tension in her poetry. Ingelow's characters often become self-absorbed in life's common elements.

The year the Ingelows moved to London, 1850, was an exciting one in literary circles. Elizabeth Barrett Browning's volume of *Poems* including "Sonnets from the Portuguese" was published; Tennyson's new work *In Memoriam* appeared, and he was named poet laureate. It is little wonder that Ingelow's small volume of verse *A Rhyming Chronicle of Incidents and Feelings* was ignored. Critics were too busy to notice her anonymous volume of sentimental verse which was indistinguishable from so many other attempts by young female poets. However, an advance copy had been sent to her fellow Lincolnshire author Tennyson, who commented in a letter to Ingelow's cousin Barbara Holloway, "Your Cousin must be worth knowing; there are some very charming things in her book." Tennyson does find fault with Ingelow's cockneyisms and rhymes but excuses them because of her youth. He added: "If the book were not so good I should not care for these specks, but the critics will pounce upon them, and excite a prejudice. I declare that I should like to know her." However, it was not until 1863, after her successful *Poems* had been published, that Tennyson finally met Ingelow.

By the time of their meeting, Ingelow had

produced a two-volume novel, *Allerton and Dreux* (1851), and had published at her own expense *Tales of Orris* (1860), a collection of children's short stories originally written for the *Youth Magazine.* In 1860 Ingelow joined the Portfolio Society. Her first poem written for the group was "Persephone," which was read in 1862. It received high praise. In June 1863 *Poems,* Ingelow's most critically acclaimed volume of verse, appeared. It went through thirty editions. Maureen Peters reports from publisher's records that Ingelow made £327:3:2d within the first three months of the initial printing, and it has been estimated that some 200,000 of Ingelow's books were sold in the United States. The most important poem in the 1863 volume is "Divided," in which Ingelow's major theme of love and her descriptions of the fen and river can be clearly seen. Two lovers, holding hands, begin to walk westward on either side of a small creek. As the creek grows into a stream and finally a river, symbolizing life's relentless journey and the unknown events which interfere with personal desires, the lovers are forced to separate. A pessimistic attitude is avoided at the conclusion of the poem by the sure knowledge that thoughts of love help relieve the pain of physical separation:

> And yet I know past all doubting, truly—
> And knowledge greater than grief can dim—
> I know, as he loved, he will love me duly—
> Yea, better—e'en better than I love him.
>
> And as I walk by the vast calm river,
> The awful river so dread to see,
> I say, "Thy breadth and thy depth forever
> Are bridged by his thoughts that cross to me."

Another well-known poem in the collection is "The High Tide on the Coast of Lincolnshire (1571)." This ballad describes a devastating flood and the drowning of a young woman. The interesting point of this poem is that the loss of the girl is greater for the woman's mother-in-law, who is the speaker in the poem, than for the woman's husband. Again, the theme of love and descriptions of the river dominate. Other significant poems in the 1863 volume are "Honours," part one and part two, which suggest that doubt can be overcome by hard work, sincere friendships, and an appreciation of the beauty in nature; *"Requiescat in Pace,"* which shows how accepting the premise that all things must die can bring peace to both the departed and the bereaved; "Supper at the Mill," a slice-of-life poem which incorporates examples of peasant songs; and "Songs of Seven," a seven-part journey through the

stages in a woman's life. The critical response to *Poems* ranged from the effusiveness of the *Athenaeum* reviewer who saw in Ingelow "the power to fill common earthly facts with heavenly fire; a power to gladden wisely and to sadden nobly; to shake the heart, and bring that mist of tears into the eyes through which the spirit may catch its loftiest light," to the more perceptive and cautious appraisal of the *London Times* critic who recognized that Ingelow's poetry was "full of feeling and bright with suggestions," but found her style vague and wordy; she was only "a child of promise—of great promise certainly, but still only of the future."

Ingelow's second collection of children's stories, *Studies for Stories,* appeared in 1864. And in 1865, Ingelow met her female contemporary and future friend, Christina Rossetti. A new volume of poetry, *A Story of Doom, and Other Poems,* appeared in 1867. The title poem in this volume takes for its topic the story of Noah and the Flood. Included are Noah's building of the ark, his warnings to unrepentant sinners, the love story of Noah's youngest son, and the loading of the ark. The poem ends with a multiple-meaning line, perhaps one of Ingelow's best, "The door is shut." The closed door suggests safety to Noah's party but the denial of salvation to mankind. Although "A Story of Doom" is decidedly inferior to *Paradise Lost,* Milton's influence is evident in Ingelow's portrayal of both Noah's side and Satan's side of the events leading up to the Flood. Her Satan, who is as deceitful and masterful as Milton's, can be seen in this passage preparing to journey to earth:

> "Whereas I surely rule the world,
> Behooves that ye prepare for me a path,
> And that I, putting of my pains aside,
> Go stir rebellion in the mighty hearts
> O' the giants; for He loveth them, and looks
> Full oft complacent on their glorious strength.
> He willeth that they yield, that He may spare;
> But, by the blackness of my loathed den,
> I say they shall not, no, they shall not yield."

In "The Dreams That Came True," Ingelow uses a technique similar to that of Charles Dickens in "A Christmas Carol." A wealthy uncaring country justice dreams of his poor tenants and resolves to better their living conditions in the morning. The emotions of guilt and remorse are fully examined, but the poem suffers from a wordiness that is evident in other poems, such as "Laurance." This story of thwarted but finally rewarded love drags on interminably. The conventional Victorian moral mes-

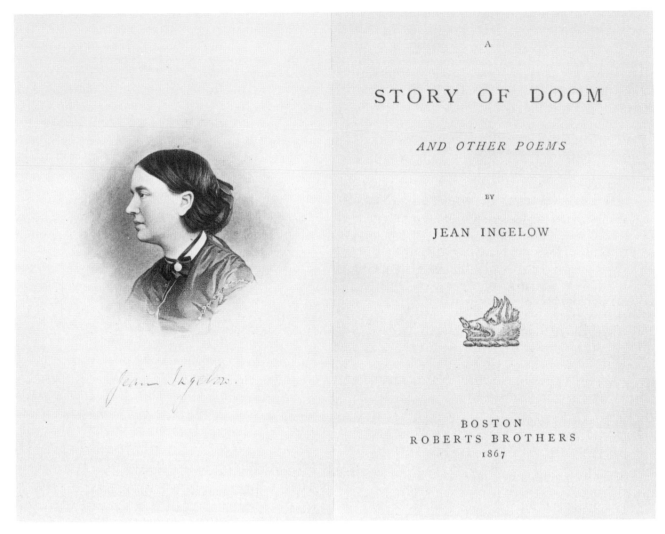

Frontispiece and title page for the first American edition of Ingelow's collection that includes the Miltonic poem "A Story of Doom," based upon the biblical narrative of Noah and the Flood

sage is quite obvious. The most imaginative poem in *A Story of Doom* is "Gladys and Her Island." Gladys, a solitary, lonely teacher, gets an unexpected holiday and visits the seashore. She imagines an island paradise and meets various spirits, characters, and gods connected with poetry and myth. The universal lesson she learns is that "it is well/For us to be as happy as we can!" The seashore again provides the setting for "Winstanley," in which a determined man builds a lighthouse, only to lose his life in it during a violent storm. Even though Ingelow uses some imagination in portraying her favorite themes of religious and personal love and family relationships and her favorite settings of the seashore and rivers, the poetry in the 1867 volume is often vague, wordy, and unsatisfying. The poems are longer than earlier ones but not significantly better.

Ingelow's most famous children's story, *Mopsa the Fairy,* appeared in 1869, and her largely autobiographical four-volume novel, *Off the Skelligs,* was published in 1872. *Poems,* second series, was issued in 1874. There are many sonnets in this volume, including "Work," which argues that work is its own reward since death prevents the worker from viewing the results of his efforts. The best lyrical poem in the volume is "The Long White Seam." The action of a voyaging sailor heading home to his betrothed who is sewing the long white seam on her wedding gown uses again the theme of love, the setting of the sea, and a favorite Ingelow character—the sailor. The long, two-part work "The Two Margarets" is the most depressing poetry in this volume. Lost love provides the impetus for many tears of pathos.

In 1876, the year after her novel *Fated to be Free* appeared, Roberts Brothers of Boston published *The Shepherd Lady, and Other Poems,* which is basically a collection of the poems in *Mopsa the Fairy.* The verses are mainly childlike and contain many songs; however, a few poems, such as "Failure" and "Above the Clouds," are written on a level far above a child's comprehension. They are for the adult reader. The most memorable poem is "At Once Again," in which the love between the children of two neighbors helps solve the feud between them over the rights to a stream adjoining their properties.

Two more novels—*Sarah de Berenger* (1879) and *Don John* (1881)—appeared before Ingelow's next verse publication. In 1885, *Poems,* third series, was published. (A different title was used in America.) Three noteworthy poems are "Rosamund," which demonstrates that love can even con-

quer political enemies as an English girl marries, with her father's blessing, a Spanish sea captain; "Echo and the Ferry," a delightful example of Ingelow's ability to capture childish song and fancy in echoing phrases; and "Perdita," an example of how Ingelow uses Victorian morality to paint a portrait of a fallen woman whose consolations are a trust in God and a personal "I am what I am" philosophy. The critical reception of Ingelow's *Poems,* third series, can be best summed up by the *Academy's* obituary notice on the poet several years later: "Of her quick and keen popularity there has been some failure, no doubt, in later days." Apparently, however, when Tennyson died in 1892, Ingelow was considered for the position of poet laureate, though she did not get it.

The constant in Ingelow's lengthy poetic career is that she never changed. She used the same style and the same themes over and over. Unlike her friend Tennyson, who moved toward a socially oriented poetry, Ingelow remained stagnant. Since

Publisher's advertisements for American editions of Ingelow's books

there is no standard critical biography, the reasons for her stagnation can only be guessed at from the two chronological accounts of her life, the anonymous *Some Recollections of Jean Ingelow* (1901) and Maureen Peters's *Jean Ingelow: Victorian Poetess* (1972).

The element in Ingelow's life that most suggests a reason for her not desiring to confront the public issues of the age is her life-style — more specifically her total involvement with her family. She never married; instead, she chose to live at home and help care for her many brothers and sisters, and later she provided a home for her ailing mother. Insulated in her home environment, she relied on personal episodes of her own or of her friends to form the basis of her poetry, which remained domestic, romantic, and religious.

In her poetry she was not trying to find answers to the problems of the age, as other poets were, since she felt she had the answers in her traditional Victorian ideals, which included the primacy of the family and God. Her poetry, so quickly popular on both sides of the Atlantic, was not a message; it was an expression of belief. She did not consider herself a prophet, but rather a Victorian lady who wrote poetry about love, nature, religion, and the family. She was confident that her beliefs would get her and her readers through the coming years.

The dominant impression Jean Ingelow gives is one of contentment. As she says in "Gladys and Her Island":

Hence we may learn, you poets, that of all
We should be most content. The earth is given
To us: we reign by virtue of a sense
Which lets us hear the rhythm of that old verse.
The ring of that old tune whereto she spins.
Humanity is given to us: we reign
By virtue of a sense, which lets us in
To know its troubles ere they have been told,
And to take them home and lull them into rest
With mournfullest music. Time is given to us,—
Time past, time future. . . .

Unfortunately, Ingelow did not receive time future. Her choice not to pursue poetic themes outside of herself cost her lasting popular and critical acclaim. Naomi Lewis says, "In poetry, Jean Ingelow seems all too often on the edge of writing something better, but she always halts at the frontier." Denied the status of a great poet, Jean Ingelow can, at the very least, illuminate new avenues of investigation concerning the "important" poets of the Victorian age.

References:

Lafcadio Hearn, *Appreciations of Poetry,* edited by John Erskine (London: Heinemann, 1916), pp. 334-348;

Naomi Lewis, "A Lost Pre-Raphaelite," *Times Literary Supplement,* 8 December 1972, pp. 1487-1488;

Maureen Peters, *Jean Ingelow: Victorian Poetess* (Ipswich, U.K.: Boydell Press, 1972);

Some Recollections of Jean Ingelow (London: Gardner, Darton, 1901; republished, Port Washington, N.Y.: Kennikat Press, 1972).

Frederick Locker-Lampson
(29 May 1821-30 May 1895)

Norman Page
University of Alberta

SELECTED BOOKS: *London Lyrics* (London: Chapman & Hall, 1857; final revision, London: King, 1876);

My Confidences: An Autobiographical Sketch Addressed to My Descendants, edited by Augustine Birrell (London: Smith, Elder, 1896; New York: Scribners, 1896).

OTHER: *Lyra Elegantiarum: A Collection of Some of the Best Specimens of Vers de Société and Vers d' Occasion in the English Language by Deceased Authors,* edited by Locker-Lampson (London: Moxon, 1867; revised, London: Moxon, 1867);

Patchwork, edited with contributions by Locker-

Frederick Locker-Lampson (National Portrait Gallery)

Lampson (London: Privately printed, 1879).

Frederick Locker-Lampson (as he is usually called), poet, anthologist, and bibliophile, was a prominent member of fashionable literary society in London during the second half of the nineteenth century. Among his acquaintances were Dickens, Thackeray, Tennyson, Trollope, George Eliot, and many others; and his name appears in numerous memoirs of the period. Although his output was small, he was well known as a writer of light verse.

Frederick Locker, second son of Edward and Eleanor Locker, was born at Greenwich, where his father was one of the administrators at the Naval Hospital. After an undistinguished school career at Clapham and elsewhere, he became a civil-service clerk, and it is said that he began to compose light verse in order to relieve the monotony of office life. In 1850 he married Lady Charlotte Bruce, daughter of the Earl of Elgin (who brought the Elgin Marbles to England) and a favorite of Queen Victoria. The Lockers' daughter Eleanor married first Lionel Tennyson, younger son of the poet, and

subsequently Augustine Birrell, author and statesman. Locker suffered from ill health and soon after his marriage retired from civil service. Locker moved in fashionable literary and political circles and began to acquire a reputation for his *vers de société*—elegant, urbane, technically accomplished light verse in the tradition of Thomas Hood and W. M. Praed.

His collection *London Lyrics* first appeared as a slim volume in 1857 and was republished many times; new poems were added to successive editions, and the poet's final revision appeared in 1876. Typical titles are: "Piccadilly," "The Pilgrims of Pall Mall," "On an Old Muff," and "The Old Government Clerk." A selection from his poems was published in 1865 in Edward Moxon's Miniature Poets series.

In 1867 Locker produced a popular anthology of *vers de société* and *vers d'occasion* under the title *Lyra Elegantiarum*. The first edition was quickly withdrawn from circulation on account of an infringement of copyright: forty poems by Walter Savage

Drawing of Locker in 1872, two years before he married Hannah Lampson and added her last name to his

Landor had been included without the permission of Landor's executor, John Forster. A revised edition followed in the same year. Reviewing a revised and enlarged edition of this book that appeared in 1891, A. C. Swinburne wrote that "there is no better or complete anthology than this in the language: I doubt indeed if there be any so good and so complete." (The review was included under the title "Social Verse" in Swinburne's *Studies in Prose and Poetry,* 1894.) Another anthology, *Patchwork,* consisting mainly of prose extracts, appeared in 1879. The autobiography *My Confidences* was published posthumously in 1896.

Locker's wife died in 1872, and in 1874 he married Hannah Lampson, by whom he had four children. In 1885 he adopted her name in addition to his own. In his later years Locker lived at Rowfant in Sussex and became well known as a collector of rare books, especially Shakespearean quartos. A catalogue of his library was published in 1886. Even after his death, his work and personality were not forgotten: an edition of *London Lyrics,* with an introduction by Austin Dobson, appeared in 1904, and a short memoir by his son-in-law Augustine Birrell in 1920.

Reference:

Augustine Birrell, *Frederick Locker-Lampson: A Character Sketch* (New York: Scribners, 1920).

Philip Bourke Marston
(13 August 1850-13 February 1887)

Lori Duin Kelly
Carroll College

BOOKS: *Song-Tide, and Other Poems* (London: Ellis & Green, 1871); enlarged as *Song-Tide, Poems and Lyrics of Love's Joy and Sorrow,* edited by William Sharp (London: Scott, 1888);
All in All: Poems and Sonnets (London: Chatto & Windus, 1875);
Wind-Voices (London: Stock, 1883; Boston: Roberts Brothers, 1883?);
For a Song's Sake, and Other Stories, edited by Sharp (London: Scott, 1887; Boston: Roberts Brothers, 1887);
Garden Secrets, edited by Louise Chandler Moulton (Boston: Roberts Brothers, 1887);
A Last Harvest: Lyrics and Sonnets from the Book of Love (London: Mathews, 1891).
Collection: *The Collected Poems of Philip Bourke Marston,* edited by Moulton (London: Ward & Lock, 1892; Boston: Roberts Brothers, 1892).

Though little known today, Philip Bourke Marston was in his own time an enormously popular poet both in England and in America. An intimate friend of Dante Gabriel Rossetti and A. C. Swinburne, Marston was a prolific writer who had three collections of poetry published in his brief lifetime and contributed numerous short stories and re-

views to *Scribner's,* the *Athenaeum,* and other magazines of the day.

For the poet Philip Bourke Marston, life, both literally and figuratively, was dark. An accidental blow in childhood severely damaged his vision, and this handicap, coupled with the losses of several family members and close friends over a twelve-year period, haunted him and led one critic to comment that " 'I believe in death' seems to be the first article in the poet's gloomy creed."

Marston's early years held little hint of his subsequent sorrows. The only son of affectionate and indulgent parents and the brother of self-sacrificing and adoring sisters, he enjoyed a youth and adolescence rich with joy and promise. He was the lineal descendant of the Elizabethan playwright John Marston, and the godchild of poets Philip James Bailey, author of *Festus,* and Dinah Maria Mulock Craik. His father, John Westland Marston, was a popular dramatist and poetry critic for the *Athenaeum,* and the family home near Regent's Park, London, was often a gathering place for such literary luminaries as Robert Browning, William Makepeace Thackeray, Charles Dickens, Dante Gabriel Rossetti, and A. C. Swinburne.

Marston's own literary skills began to be evi-

Philip Bourke Marston

dent when he was very young. By the time he was out of pinafores, he had dictated to his mother a three-volume novel. By the time he was fifteen, he had written some first-rate poems, several of which were later included in his first volume of poetry. In 1871, this first collection of poems, *Song-Tide, and Other Poems,* appeared and was well received, earning for Marston, in the words of a reviewer in the *London Examiner,* "an equal place alongside Swinburne, Morris, and Rossetti." But shortly after the appearance of this volume, the "unhappy fate," as Marston called it, began to plague his life. In 1870 Marston's mother died, and the poet felt as if his world "had gone to pieces." His sorrow was alleviated somewhat by his devotion to his fiancée, Mary Nesbit, but in November of 1871, shortly after the publication of his first volume of poetry, she died of consumption. In 1874, Marston's beloved friend, the writer Oliver Madox Brown, died of blood poisoning. Fast on the heels of this tragedy were still more losses—the death of his sister and amanuensis Cicely in 1878, of his sister Eleanor in 1879 and her husband Arthur O'Shaughnessy in 1881, and finally of his friends and literary models, Rossetti and James Thomson, both in 1882.

In light of these events in his life it is significant

that Marston produced anything at all, but the output of these years is considerable. During this period he produced two more collections of poems, *All in All* (1875) and *Wind-Voices* (1883). Between the appearances of these volumes, Marston enjoyed some celebrity as a writer of novels and short stories, which were published in *Scribner's* and other British and American magazines. Marston died on 13 February 1887 of brain fever at the age of thirty-six. After his death, two collections of poems, *Garden Secrets* (1887) and *A Last Harvest* (1891), appeared, as well as a collection of his fiction, *For a Song's Sake, and Other Stories* (1887).

Perhaps the word that most accurately describes Marston's poetry is "competent." While he shows mastery over the forms and techniques of the poet's craft, his range is not wide and there is a certain predictable monotony to much of his work. Too often his verses reflect the gloomy side of his personality, and instead of sounding solemn notes on life, love, and death, his verses are more often in a minor key of pathetic yearning but touching sincerity.

The sonnets in *Song-Tide,* for example, while they show exceptional promise for a youth of twenty, deal repetitiously and in an undistinguished way with a single theme—the heart's passionate attachment to love without hope. The poems in *All in All* are likewise monotonous. There Marston sings but a single song with few variations—the heart, temporarily satisfied when it achieves union with its beloved, plummets into the depths of despair when the beloved dies.

Indeed, the distinguishing feature of Marston's poetry is its tone of unalleviated gloom, for in poems on love and death Marston's single preoccupation is with the swift and certain end to both. Because of his own skepticism about the existence of an afterlife—on his deathbed Marston requested a burial without religious services and in unconsecrated ground—his poems in memory of dead friends hold out no promise of comfort or reunion. Unlike his friend Alfred, Lord Tennyson, Marston was incapable of reaching the resignation and acceptance of an *In Memoriam.*

Though sonnets were his forte, Marston showed considerable proficiency with other poetic forms. The dramatic monologue "A Christmas Vigil" in *Song-Tide,* told from the point of view of a woman who is first abandoned by and then reunited with her dying lover, is very moving. The same is true of "Uncompleted Lives" and "Nightshade," two poems of lost love in *Wind-Voices.* Marston also

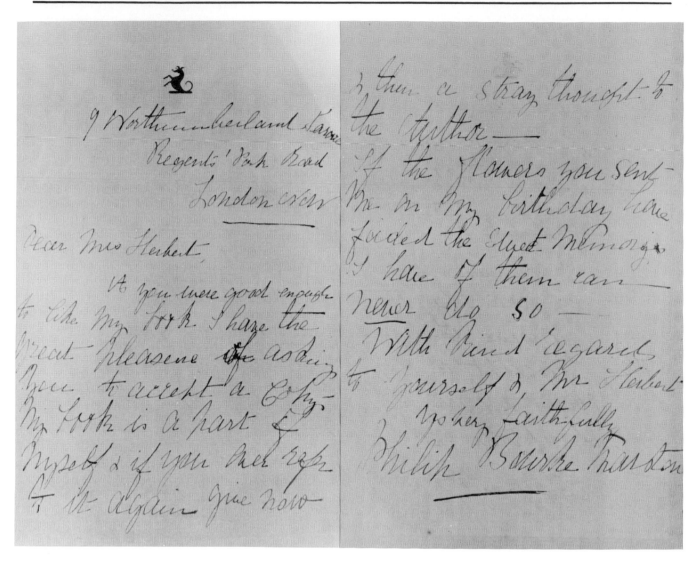

Letter from Marston to one of his admirers

showed aptitude for writing ballads. "A Ballad of Brave Women" in *Wind-Voices,* based on an actual event—two women's rescue of two men whose lifeboat had overturned off the coast of Swansea on 27 January 1883—is full of excitement and high drama. The humorous "Ballad of Monk Julius" in that same volume deals with a monk's futile efforts to forbear temptations of the flesh and shows a playful side to Marston's personality.

Marston is at his best, however, in his poems about nature. Seemingly, it was only in these that Marston could free himself from the gloomy preoccupations of his own sad life. While death robbed him of love, of hope, of family and friends, the flowers endured. His verses such as "The Rose and

the Wind" in *Song-Tide,* the sheaf of poems called "New Garden Secrets" in *Wind-Voices,* and the poems in the published collection *A Last Harvest* that tell, as Marston put it, "what the flowers said to me" deal with the imagined thoughts of blossoms and have the charm and simplicity of Elizabethan lyrics. Though his poems on a violet's thoughts on the loss of her sister to an early frost, a rose's terrifying dream of the devastation in the garden with the coming of winter, or the speculation of roses and lilies on the fate of a gathered flower echo the sentiments and themes of so many of his sonnets, namely, the brevity and frailness of earthly existence, his method of using the flower's point of view gave Marston a much-needed distance from the subject of death and rescued these poems from the melancholy that too often characterizes his poems on this topic.

Another significant feature of Marston's poetry is his imagery. Though he was nearly blind from the age of three, Marston's poems are not lacking in visual images, though these are rather conventional ones—the gray skies, the teary face of his beloved, a red rose. More original and noteworthy are his images of scents and sounds. With the wind he seemed to enjoy a particular empathy, and his descriptions of its moods and voices provide some exquisite moments in his poetry.

About Marston's fiction, the less said the better. The tales which comprise the collection *For a Song's Sake* are, as Marston characterized them, little more than "pot-boilers." Yet these stories which deal with such sensationalistic themes as madness, blighted love, miraculous rescues, and premature burials apparently enjoyed favorable reception in popular magazines of the day. More important, they provided Marston with a steady source of in-

come that freed him to concentrate on his poetry.

In fairness to Marston, it must be noted that though his range was limited, his talent was a very real one. The same events that darkened his life and limited the scope of his verse also enriched some of his poems and lent them a pathos and a heartfelt sadness that can be touching in the extreme. The musical quality of his verses is also distinguished. And while he never rose to the stature of his hero and great friend Rossetti, he did earn for himself a fond place in the hearts of English and American audiences alike as the "Blind Poet."

References:

Louise Chandler Moulton, Biographical sketch of Marston, in *The Collected Poems of Philip Bourke Marston* (Boston: Roberts Brothers, 1892);

Charles Churchill Osborne, *Philip Bourke Marston* (London: Times Book Club, 1926);

William Sharp, Memoir in Marston's *For a Song's Sake, and Other Stories* (Boston: Roberts Brothers, 1887).

Theo Marzials
(20 December 1850-2 February 1920)

John F. Stasny
West Virginia University

SELECTED BOOKS: *Passionate Dowsabella, a Pastoral* (London: Privately printed, 1872);

The Gallery of Pigeons and Other Poems (London: King, 1873);

Esmerelda: An opera in four acts, libretto by Marzials and Alberto Randegger, music by A. Goring Thomas (London: Miles, 1883?; New York: Rullman, 1900).

OTHER: *A Book of Old Songs, newly arranged and with accompaniments by Theo Marzials, set to pictures by Walter Crane, engraved in colours by Edmund Evans* (London: Routledge, 1881).

Theophile-Jules-Henri Marzials, or as he himself abridged it, Theo Marzials, published one volume of poetry when he was a young man; achieved a reputation during his early maturity as a composer and singer of popular songs; collaborated as a li-

brettist on *Esmerelda,* an opera based on Victor Hugo's *Notre Dame de Paris* and produced at the Drury Lane Theatre in March 1883; had in the 1890s two poems published in the *Yellow Book,* a quarterly devoted to Decadent literature and art; and then lingered on for two decades before dying and passing into apparent oblivion. John M. Munro, who edited a selection of Marzials's poems in 1974, establishes no claim that Marzials has been unjustly neglected and deserves rehabilitation, but Munro does provide, through the poems and in his introduction, access to one of those illuminating minor figures who add dimension to literary history. Marzials had associations with Dante Gabriel Rossetti and A. C. Swinburne. At least one of his poems was praised by Gerard Manley Hopkins, whose own lyrical experimentations find some curious analogues in Marzials. Marzials, especially through his use of the devices, themes, and intricate

Theo Marzials

In 1870 Theo Marzials became a junior assistant in the librarian's office of the British Museum, a contemporary there of Coventry Patmore, John Payne, Arthur O'Shaughnessy, and Edmund Gosse—"a nest of singing birds," as Gosse later recalled. Marzials remained at the British Museum until his retirement, with a pension of £38 a year, in 1882—a retirement dictated perhaps by ill health but possibly also motivated by the fact that he had by this time an estimated annual income of £1000 from his musical compositions and his recitals which exploited his fine baritone voice. Altogether Marzials published more than eighty musical pieces, among them the popular ballad "Twickenham Ferry" (1878) and musical settings of Christina Rossetti's "Birthday" lyric and of Swinburne's poem "Ask Nothing More of Me, Sweet"; the last became one of the most popular ballads of the 1880s. It was during this period that Marzials frequented Rossetti's house and established an intimate, probably homosexual, relationship with Edmund Gosse.

Marzials's retirement years are obscure. He

forms of Old French poetry, is one more example of nineteenth-century aestheticism.

Information on the life and family background of Theo Marzials can be briefly given. The family was Venetian in origin. Both his grandfather and father were prominent Protestant clergymen in France and Belgium. The father, Antoine-Theophile Marzials, published in 1835 a volume of translations, *Sermons choises de J. Wesley;* he traveled in 1839 to London to attend the centenary of Methodism and while there married Mary Ann Jackson, the daughter of the president of the Wesleyan Conference. In 1857 Antoine-Theophile was appointed pastor of the French Protestant Church of London, a post he held until 1877. Theo was the second son and youngest of five children. His mother edited a volume of *Gems of English Poetry from Chaucer to the Present Times* (1867). His sister, Elizabeth-Marianne, published a small volume of *Poems* (1864). The first son, Francois-Thomas or Frank, became in 1898 accountant general of the army and in 1904 was knighted Sir Frank T. Marzials. Frank was also a prolific author: a poet, essayist, and biographer. He was the family prop who bore the burdens of the debts, first of his improvident and ineffectual father and then of his profligate brother.

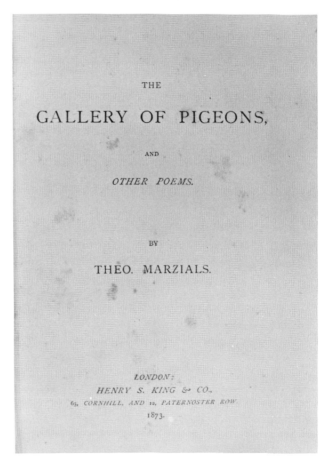

THE

GALLERY OF PIGEONS,

AND

OTHER POEMS.

BY

THEO. MARZIALS.

LONDON:
HENRY S. KING & CO.,
65, CORNHILL, AND 12, PATERNOSTER ROW.
1873.

Title page for Marzial's only volume of poetry (courtesy of Thomas Cooper Library, University of South Carolina)

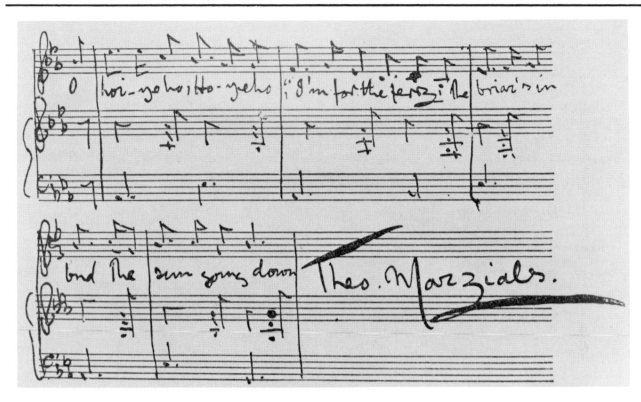

Excerpt from the score of Marzials's 1878 ballad "Twickenham Ferry" (Harper's New Monthly Magazine, *May 1880*)

spent much time during the ten years after leaving the British Museum in Italy and Paris. He became addicted to chloral, and there were reports of physical and mental collapse, a tragic end to his career, and even premature death. Briefly, in the 1890s he was "rediscovered" by Henry Harland, editor of the *Yellow Book,* but after 1899 Marzials published no more songs. His last two decades he spent in Devonshire, first with his sister and then as an eccentric recluse, charming his neighbors, until almost the very end, with his magnificent singing voice.

Marzials published his first poem, the privately printed *Passionate Dowsabella, a Pastoral,* in 1872. It was included the next year in Marzials's *The Gallery of Pigeons,* a collection of poems—the only volume of poetry Marzials published. One must assume that a lack of encouragement discouraged the aspiring young poet. Marzials had sent Dante Gabriel Rossetti a copy of his poems and received a letter from him which praised *Passionate Dowsabella* for being "something truly pastoral in a strange new way" but which criticized it for "the jarring points remaining in it" and for being "disjointed" and "a great deal inconceivably forced or neglected." Of the long poem in *The Gallery of Pigeons* Rossetti wrote that it "labours perhaps more under a throng

of (pardon again) puerile perversities in diction than any piece in the volume." Perhaps Rossetti had in mind such lines as these describing the flight of the pigeons:

> Then swirl and swoop, and far and free,
> And over the bean-slope, black and brown,
> . . . .
> Wave to the wenches, that yawn at the well
> And wring up above them their smocks and socks,
> And clash their pails and pannikins, Ho!
> And titter and splash, and splatter and splutter,
> Then flying a-thwart them, flaunt, in a flutter,
> Oho! hyüeèps, hyüeèps, Oho!
> Zounds! and Zephyr! and how they go!

Rossetti did express admiration for several more conventional short poems, including "And I was a full-leav'd, full-bough'd tree," "I dream'd I was in Sicily," and the "Aubade," one of the traditional forms inspired by Marzials's enthusiasm for medieval Provencal poetry and its nineteenth-century French imitators, to one of whom, Théodore Aubanel, Marzials dedicated his volume. Marzials complained that Rossetti misunderstood him. He wrote to William Bell Scott: "Rossetti does not seem to see (by what he picks out) what I am driving at; he praises my *imitations* and not the *me* in the book."

Gerard Manley Hopkins, praising Marzials's "Rondel" as "very graceful"with "an art and finish rare in English verse," shared the preference for the imitations; he disparaged "A Tragedy," a fifty-two-line Wertherian, suicidal monologue which begins

> Death!
> Plop.
> The barges down in the river flop.
> Flop, plop,
> Above, beneath.

Such a poem—a bizarre failure—was apparently part of Marzials's misunderstood "me"—an apprentice poet haunted by fresh sound patterns achieved through onomatopoeia and alliteration. "The Trout" has almost the effect of a Hopkinsian rough draft in such lines as "Where shimmers the sun in the hazes a-shimmer,/The shimmer of river, oh! river a-shimmer." Perhaps had Marzials pursued, with encouragement, his original "me," he might have matured into a significant artist. As it is, "he is," as Munro concludes, "interesting rather than significant, a literary curiosity, perhaps, rather than a neglected genius."

Reference:

John M. Munro, Introduction to *Selected Poems of Theo. Marzials* (Beirut, Lebanon: American University of Beirut, 1974).

George Meredith

Carol L. Bernstein
Bryn Mawr College

See also the Meredith entry in *DLB 18, Victorian Novelists After 1885.*

BIRTH: Portsmouth, Hampshire, 12 February 1828, to Augustus and Jane Eliza Macnamara Meredith.

MARRIAGES: 9 August 1849 to Mary Ellen Peacock Nicolls; child: Arthur Gryffydh. 20 September 1864 to Marie Vulliamy; children: William Maxse, Marie Eveleen.

AWARDS AND HONORS: Presidency of the Society of Authors, 1892; vice-presidency of the London Library, 1902; Order of Merit, 1905; Gold Medal of the Royal Society of Literature, 1905.

DEATH: Dorking, Surrey, 18 May 1909.

BOOKS: *Poems* (London: Parker, 1851; New York: Scribners, 1898);

The Shaving of Shagpat: An Arabian Entertainment (London: Chapman & Hall, 1856; Boston: Roberts Brothers, 1887);

Farina: A Legend of Cologne (London: Smith, Elder, 1857);

The Ordeal of Richard Feverel: A History of Father and Son (3 volumes, London: Chapman & Hall, 1859; 1 volume, Boston: Roberts Brothers, 1887);

Evan Harrington; or, He Would Be a Gentleman (New York: Harper, 1860; 3 volumes, London: Bradbury & Evans, 1861);

Modern Love and Poems of the English Roadside, with Poems and Ballads (London: Chapman & Hall, 1862); edited by E. Cavazza (Portland, Maine: Mosher, 1891);

Emilia in England, 3 volumes (London: Chapman & Hall, 1864); republished as *Sandra Belloni* (London: Chapman & Hall, 1886; Boston: Roberts Brothers, 1887);

Rhoda Fleming: A Story (3 volumes, London: Tinsley, 1865; 1 volume, Boston: Roberts Brothers, 1886);

Vittoria, 3 volumes (London: Chapman & Hall, 1866; Boston: Roberts Brothers, 1888);

The Adventures of Harry Richmond (3 volumes, London: Smith, Elder, 1871; 1 volume, Boston:

George Meredith, circa 1888 (photo by Thomson)

Roberts Brothers, 1887);

Beauchamp's Career (3 volumes, London: Chapman & Hall, 1876; 1 volume, Boston: Roberts Brothers, 1887);

The House on the Beach: A Realistic Tale (New York: Harper, 1877);

The Egoist: A Comedy in Narrative, 3 volumes (London: Kegan Paul, 1879; New York: Harper, 1879);

The Tragic Comedians: A Study in a Well-Known Story (2 volumes, London: Chapman & Hall, 1880; 1 volume, New York: Munro, 1881);

Poems and Lyrics of the Joy of Earth (London: Macmillan, 1883; Boston: Roberts Brothers, 1883);

Diana of the Crossways (3 volumes, London: Chapman & Hall, 1885; 1 volume, New York: Munro, 1885);

Ballads and Poems of Tragic Life (London: Macmillan, 1887; Boston: Roberts Brothers, 1887);

A Reading of Earth (London: Macmillan, 1888; Boston: Roberts Brothers, 1888);

Jump-to-Glory Jane (London: Privately printed, 1889; London: Swan Sonnenschein, 1892);

The Case of General Ople and Lady Camper (New York: Lovell, 1890);

The Tale of Chloe: An Episode in the History of Beau Beamish (New York: Lovell, 1890);

One of Our Conquerors (3 volumes, London: Chapman & Hall, 1891; 1 volume, Boston: Roberts Brothers, 1891);

Poems: The Empty Purse, with Odes to the Comic Spirit, to Youth in Memory and Verses (London: Macmillan, 1892; Boston: Roberts Brothers, 1892);

The Tale of Chloe; The House on the Beach; The Case of General Ople and Lady Camper (London: Ward, Lock & Bowden, 1894);

Lord Ormont and His Aminta: A Novel (3 volumes, London: Chapman & Hall, 1894; 1 volume, New York: Scribners, 1894);

The Amazing Marriage, 2 volumes (London: Constable, 1895; New York: Scribners, 1895);

An Essay on Comedy and the Uses of the Comic Spirit (London: Constable, 1897; New York: Scribners, 1897);

Selected Poems (London: Constable, 1897; New York: Scribners, 1897);

The Nature Poems (London: Constable, 1898);

Odes in Contribution to the Song of French History (London: Constable, 1898; New York: Scribners, 1898);

The Story of Bhanavar the Beautiful (London: Constable, 1900);

A Reading of Life, with Other Poems (London: Constable, 1901; New York: Scribners, 1901);

Last Poems (London: Constable, 1909; New York: Scribners, 1909);

Chillianwallah (New York: Marion Press, 1909);

Love in the Valley, and Two Songs: Spring and Autumn (Chicago: Seymour, 1909);

Poems Written in Early Youth, Poems from "Modern Love," and Scattered Poems (London: Constable, 1909; New York: Scribners, 1909);

Celt and Saxon (London: Constable, 1910; New York: Scribners, 1910).

Collections: *The Works of George Meredith,* De Luxe Edition, 39 volumes (London: Constable, 1896-1912); Library Edition, 18 volumes (London: Constable, 1897-1910); Boxhill Edition, 17 volumes (New York: Scribners, 1897-1919); Memorial Edition, 27 volumes (London: Constable, 1909-1911; New York: Scribners, 1909-1911);

The Poetical Works of George Meredith, edited by G. M. Trevelyan (London: Constable, 1912);

The Poems of George Meredith, edited by Phyllis B. Bartlett, 2 volumes (New Haven & London: Yale University Press, 1978).

It is difficult to define George Meredith's place among the major Victorian poets, in part because of his many claims to distinction. He is at once impresario and sage, prophet and man of the world. He is better known for his novels, although his poetry was at least as, if not more, important in his own eyes. The novels draw freely upon the resources of poetry—their style, for example, is often highly allusive and metaphorical. Meredith's poems, moreover, present in condensed and figurative form many of the concerns of the novels, among them a thematics of self and the place of self in society and nature, as well as a redefinition of narrative forms. But the poems are no mere gloss upon the novels. Their presentation of versions of the self, given to concealment, fictionalizing, and multiplicity; of landscape as a condition for self-discovery; and of a consequent profound and sophisticated consciousness of self and nature would alone stake out major territory in nineteenth-century poetry. Of importance too is Meredith's development of the mythmaking processes that stem from his Romantic precursors, as well as his exploration of forms of narrative that tend to question established genres and conventions. Like his contemporaries Robert Browning, Gerard Manley Hopkins, and A. C. Swinburne, Meredith viewed the language of poetry as a field for experiment. The style of the poems only proclaims its artifice: Meredith is a conjurer with words, a juggler with syntax. The norms of language seem to exist for him primarily as points of departure. Meredith's stylistic idiosyncrasies puzzled some readers and alienated others: it is only recently that critics have begun to give Meredith's poems the appreciative reading they deserve.

When Meredith published his first volume, *Poems,* in 1851—at his own expense—he seemed to be declaring his allegiance to the Romantic tradition but not in any specific way. His early life in Portsmouth yields little information for the biographer of the poet. The years (1842-1844) Meredith spent at Neuwied on the Rhine, at a school run by the Moravian Brothers, shed more light on his work. The school's liberal and humane cast of thought was important, as was Meredith's first direct contact with the Continental culture and landscape that were to figure so significantly in his writing. Significant also are the three years, 1846-1849, which Meredith spent articled to solicitor Richard Charnock. Contact with the literary circle to which Charnock belonged encouraged the nascent poet. Shared philological interests, poems, and articles gathered and circulated in the manuscript journal "The Monthly Observer": these are the somewhat sparse beginnings of Meredith's poetic career.

Like those of many first books, the early poems matter less for their accomplishment than for their promise. From the beginning Meredith was trying out new stanzaic forms; one of the more successful experiments was the first version of "Love in the Valley," one of his masterpieces. The coming to consciousness of oneself and one's desires in a pastoral setting that is at once innocent and erotic anticipates the great Meredithian thematics of self-realization in nature. "South-West Wind in the Woodland" is Meredith's first attempt to make myths out of a dynamic natural force. If the proliferation of similes tends to break the focus (the wind, compared successively to rider, meteor, foam, sail, and breaking heart, retains scant integrity as a mythic figure), nevertheless the sheer energy of the massed verbs, the rush of simile, and the emphasis on natural process point to a conception of nature that challenges the imagination.

The poems on more conventional mythic subjects—"Daphne" and "The Rape of Aurora," for example—are less problematic in their treatment of myth, but they are also less imaginatively daring. All these poems, however, reveal how much those early years were the seed-time for Meredith's poetry. The metaphorical use of color appears, albeit in a negative aspect, in the adjective "hueless" in "Requiem"; the word was to recur later in "Time and Sentiment" (1870) and "The Hueless Love" (1901). The gold-eyed serpent of *Modern Love* (1862) is anticipated in this volume. The "Hymn to Colour" of 1888 is the culmination of a line of thought begun early: "colour" is a central term of value in a universe that is understood first through perceptual means. In a broader way, the metaphor of the marriage of heaven and earth, as well as the insistence upon nature's implacable laws, appears in the early poems. The "Pastorals" and the "Pictures of the Rhine" offer more literal representations of natural scenes. "London by Lamplight" is an early meditation on a social theme—here, the evils of prostitution. But like the young Wordsworth, Meredith views society through the glasses of romance, distancing himself from it through literary language.

Meredith did not see publication of a second book of poetry until 1862. There is evidence of his continued poetic activity during the 1850s, though

The Death of Chatterton, *oil painting for which Henry Wallis used the twenty-eight-year-old Meredith as his model (Tate Gallery, London). In 1858, two years after completion of the canvas, Wallis eloped with Meredith's first wife, Mary Ellen Peacock Nicolls.*

some of it—notably a volume of "British Songs"—was abortive. Other poems were published in periodicals. There is certainly little direct indication that what many consider to be his most impressive work, *Modern Love,* would be the major fruit of that decade. Perhaps that is why one looks to Meredith's life for an originating impulse. In 1849, Meredith had married Mary Ellen Peacock Nicolls, the widow of a naval officer and the daughter of Thomas Love Peacock. After a time, the marriage began to show signs of strain: both partners were strong-minded, sensitive, and overly intense. Moreover, Meredith's literary activity was not financially rewarding; the couple had to live first with and later near Peacock. The combined pressures of poverty and personality conflicts led to a deepening rift between them. Mary Ellen Meredith's elopement with the painter Henry Wallis in 1858 effectively marked the end of the marriage. Meredith saw no more of his wife, who died in 1861.

Meredith's first marriage has always been of special interest to readers because of its connection with *Modern Love,* which was published in *Modern Love and Poems of the English Roadside, with Poems and Ballads* in 1862. The sequence of fifty sonnets traces the story of a failed marriage: husband and wife, both high-strung, realize that the love between them has fallen away from the ideal union of earlier days; the tension between them increases, although they play the surface game of being in love, of "Hiding the Skeleton." The wife takes a lover, and, subsequently, the husband seeks distraction with another woman. A brief attempt at reconciliation fails, and the wife commits suicide. Although the biographical origin is undeniable—with all its transpositions, the pattern of guilt, sorrow, and humiliation is recognizable—one should also take into account formal sources: the Victorian interest in the segmented long poem, the conventions of the sonnet sequence, the interest in developing new

Meredith and his son Arthur, circa 1862. Arthur Gryffydh Meredith was born in 1853 to Meredith and Mary Ellen Peacock Nicolls.

types of narrative form. There are literary as well as biographical sources for the plot. Thus, the grounds for *Modern Love*'s continuing appeal may be, in the end, formal rather than biographical.

Modern Love belongs to a group of major nineteenth-century long poems with lyric bases. Among these poems we may include Alfred, Lord Tennyson's *In Memoriam* and *Maud,* Coventry Patmore's *The Angel in the House,* and D. G. Rossetti's *The House of Life* (the last is also a sonnet sequence). Although *Modern Love*'s poems employ an unusual sixteen-line variant of the sonnet form, they nevertheless warrant the designation sonnet sequence. (At the end of Sonnet XXX the husband writes, "Lady, this is my sonnet to your eyes.") Such a variation is fitting for a sequence which sets itself at odds with tradition in so many ways. Modern love, tense and disillusioned, contrasts sharply with the romantic, idealizing love of Renaissance sequences, as well as with the paeans to domestic love

of contemporary long poems. The frank acknowledgement of sexual tensions in *Modern Love* did, in fact, shock many of the first reviewers. But Meredith's questioning of fictional conventions is at least as important as the challenge to societal norms. The frequent shifts in perspective as well as the diverse symbolic frameworks employed militate against the comfort of any single view of the fates of *Modern Love*'s husband and wife. Neither the conventions of pastoral—high or low—nor those of the French novel will suffice; even the plot of medieval romance offers no analogies: the husband becomes aware of love only as he leaves the Temple of Love. The uncomprehending though benign eyes of society see the husband and wife as devoted lovers in Sonnet XXIII; a more ironic social viewpoint diminishes the husband into an easily controlled "diminutive philosopher" (XXXI). The husband and wife are, in effect, "helplessly afloat" on the "lightless seas" of modern experience, and the fifty sonnets present their story from the perspectives of conflicting literary conventions.

In light of these different fictions about marriage, it is not surprising that the husband, who appears now as first- and now as third-person narrator, finds his own selfhood precarious. At times cuckold, at times man of the world, the husband envisages himself also as both fairy prince and Satanic lover. With so many competing roles, consciousness itself must face recurring threats of discontinuity. When marriage is a symbol of contract and order, then the failure of marriage must introduce chaos into the very centers of self. Those different images of self, like the varying plot conventions and like the recurring symbolic motifs (snakes and poison, Eve and Cleopatra, eating and drinking are only a few), mark the self's striving for continuity and understanding. Meredith's drawing upon several fictions and his suggestion that one's present emotions are capable of altering one's view of the past may stem from his new sense of the role of narrative. One employs fictions to arrive at the truth, in part because truth itself is so elusive. The demands of representation—when a marriage is so complex, communication so oblique, events so ambiguous—would require multiple and sometimes broken narrative lines. As each fiction or symbol offers an interpretive entrée to the poem, together they suggest that a central theme of *Modern Love* is coming to terms with the fictive and social conventions of marriage and selfhood.

Toward the end of *Modern Love,* when husband and wife move toward their last brief reconciliation, nature provides the symbolic context. In early sonnets of the sequence, nature is often psychologically distanced or personified (" 'I play for Seasons; not Eternities!'/Says Nature, laughing on her way" in Sonnet XIII). But in Sonnet XLVII, "We saw the swallows gathering in the sky," husband and wife share a moment of natural communion:

> We had not to look back on summer joys,
> Or forward to a summer of bright dye:
> But in the largeness of the evening earth
> Our spirits grew as we went side by side.
> The hour became her husband and my bride.

Free of fictions, the soul finds its true extension and continuity—"Where I have seen across the twilight wave/The swan sail with her young beneath her wings." But that moment cannot last; the wife, misconstruing the husband's sentiments and acting out of misguided generosity, takes poison and dies. Thus, at the end *Modern Love* poises natural order against natural chaos: "In tragic hints here see what evermore/Moves dark as yonder midnight ocean's

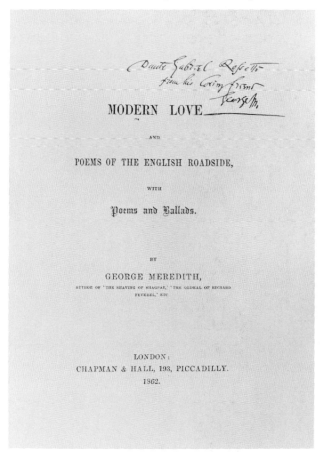

*Inscription to Dante Gabriel Rossetti in Meredith's
second volume of poetry*

force. . . ." Later poems explore more fully this precarious balance; one can find in *Modern Love,* with its limning of plots spun by the passions and its intimations of the tragic complexities of human desire, a dark ground. Meredith's move toward nature in later works was no escape, however; it was, rather, a quest for a more inclusive vision than the world of tangled human actions could offer.

The cast of homespun speakers in the poems of the English roadside—the other major group in the 1862 volume—are more prone to accept, or to question more gently, the ironies of fate. Thus Juggling Jerry dies, ceding the stage to God, the great juggler; the old Chartist and the Beggar live at the fringes of respectability, mildly upholding their patriotism and common sense. Although the poems are sometimes compared to Browning's, the resemblance is a general one: it lies in Meredith's use of colloquialism and, more important, in his speakers' obsessive urges to utter monologues. Meredith's speakers, however, are very different from the sophisticated characters of Browning's poems.

The poems of the English roadside reveal Meredith's ear for speech patterns and his growth away from the conventional diction of his earlier poems. What emerges from the 1862 volume is a sense of Meredith's versatility, witnessed by *Modern Love,* the roadside poems, a few sonnets and ballads, several lyrics in different forms, and the ambitious "Ode to the Spirit of Earth in Autumn." The ode is important less for its attempt at the sublime mode than for its lexicon of Meredithian themes and images; the value placed upon color as a sign of vitality; the personified southwester; the mythmaking nocturnal consciousness; the mingling of the spheres of earth, sea, and heaven; earth's laughter; and the invocation to nature: "Great Mother Nature! teach me, like thee,/To kiss the season and shun regrets."

For the two decades following publication of *Modern Love and Poems of the English Roadside,* Meredith's only published poems appeared in periodicals. In 1864 he married Marie Vulliamy, a member of an Anglo-French family that had lived in England for several generations. The 1860s and 1870s saw the publication of several major novels, culminating in *The Egoist* (1879). In 1860, Meredith became a reader for the publishing firm of Chapman and Hall, a position he held until 1894. That Meredith devoted his major authorial efforts to prose should not imply that he held poetry in any less esteem. But even in 1883, when he was a recognized novelist, admired by many aspiring writers, he had to pay for the publication of his own poetry.

recurs in the poems of the 1880s, is a sign of that presiding Spirit.

The title of the 1883 volume, *Poems and Lyrics of the Joy of Earth,* seems to distinguish Meredith's poetic concerns from the dominant political and social issues of the novels of the 1860s and 1870s. Yet certain images in the novels—the Alpine vision at the end of *The Egoist,* the description of dawn coming over the Alps in *Beauchamp's Career* (1876), the Rhineland passages of *The Adventures of Harry Richmond* (1871)—appear in the poetry as well. The Alpine vision symbolizes a triumph of the spirit over fleshly concerns in both poetry and prose. Landscape closer to home was also a source of natural imagery. In January 1868 Meredith moved to Flint Cottage, near Box Hill and the village of Dorking. This was to be his home for the rest of his life. The Surrey countryside was surely a source of inspiration; in fact, Norbury Park, near Mickleham—Marie Vulliamy's home, not far from Dorking—is the model for "The Woods of Westermain."

"The Woods of Westermain" sets the tone for the collection. The first lines—"Enter these enchanted woods,/You who dare"—are, on one level, a challenge to the reader. For Meredith's nature is discontinuous with the real world, much as Patterne Hall (of *The Egoist*) is sealed off from the hurly-burly of contemporary society. Although the woods "Are as others to behold," their space is self-enclosed, and they lack a clear visual plan. The price of entrance is fearlessness, a certain assurance of self that will allow an imaginative leap into that enchanted domain. Nature's gifts are bountiful, but they are available only to those willing to respond to nature from out of their own endowment of vision, imagination, and language. Thus "The Woods of Westermain" is a guided tour through an uncharted woods. It is an invitation to "read" ever more deeply, in effect, to interpret. The domain of the woods is the domain of life, history, love—and the hidden quest of the poem is to find the meanings and interrelationships of the three. Those meanings lie, however, not so much in a set of dicta as in a mode of vision, one "nourished . . . by light" and informed by love. Although Meredith was no friend to egoism (it is "the scaly Dragon-fowl" in this poem), the ideal perceiver is clearly an integrated self, one capable of enhancing and even transforming the natural scene into something more than nature, into a theater of the mind. Egoism, in this ideal world, is simply tamed and put to use. The spectres of discontinuity, so pressing in *Modern Love,* have not vanished, however. The self that

Marie Vulliamy, Meredith's second wife. Portrait by Frederick Sandys, 1864.

In one way, Meredith's mythmaking transcended generic bounds. His best-known mythic figure, the Comic Spirit, appears in three different works. It presides over the actions of *The Egoist.* Two years before that novel appeared, Meredith used the figure in a lecture on "The Idea of Comedy and the Uses of the Comic Spirit," which, after publication in 1897 as *An Essay on Comedy,* gradually became a major theoretical text. One of the lecture's tenets is that true comedy can appear only in a civilized nation and that civilization can flower only when men and women are equals. Conversely, the Comic Spirit can further the civilizing process. The product of comedy is laughter, "impersonal" and "thoughtful." The Comic Spirit thrives in a social context: human folly provides its sustenance, though the truly percipient can benefit from its laughter. The poetic counterpart to the lecture/essay, the "Ode to the Comic Spirit," was not written until 1892. But the motif of a healthy and restorative laughter, which

1866 letter from Meredith to A. C. Swinburne mentioning Meredith's Vittoria, *Swinburne's* Poems and Ballads, *and the poetry of Robert Buchanan (Maurice Buxton Forman,* A Bibliography of the Writings in Prose and Verse of George Meredith, *1922)*

succumbs to fear has only partial vision in Westermain: "All the eyeballs under hoods/Shroud you in their glare." The conditional mode, which holds the possibilities of selfhood for good or ill in precarious balance, runs through the poems of the 1880s.

The woods of Westermain are a repository of myth and legend, which are never entirely separate from a humanizing consciousness. Nature, on the other hand, is a powerful source of myth. In some poems, Meredith elaborates upon received myths. Thus, in "Day of the Daughter of Hades," Skiágeneia, the daughter of Pluto and Proserpine, slips from the chariot that has brought her mother from Hades to a meeting on earth with Demeter. Skiágeneia, whose name means "shadow-born," spends a day on earth in the company of the youth Callistes. The plot is minimal; rather, the actions are generic: running, climbing, singing. Skiágeneia's day involves coming out of the shadows to a full consciousness of earth's gifts—light, color, landscape, the basic grains and oils—and then learning of heroic human actions through the song of Callistes. Skiágeneia's song informs Pluto of her presence on earth, and he comes, thunderingly, to reclaim her. Callistes is left to sing of that day: he has been touched with wonder about unearthly things, about the spectres which exist beyond human events; his experience of earth's plenitude is matched by one of loss. The natural phenomena of light, storm, and shadow have their counterparts in the poem's dramatis personae; but whether one views the events as primarily human or mythic, they achieve their fullest significance in consciousness and in song. Callistes is the figure (perhaps a surrogate for the artist) who endows the day's events with narrative coherence, who ensures, through the repetition of his song, that narrative's enduring presence. Memory provides the matter for narrative and song.

That memory should be so crucial to the making of poetry is a theme Meredith returns to later in "The South-Wester" (1888):

> We could believe
> A life in orb and brook and tree
> And cloud: and still holds Memory
> A morning in the eyes of eve.

As in so many of Meredith's poems, time follows a natural cycle in "Day of the Daughter of Hades" and "The South-Wester": the progression from dawn to evening provides the temporal frame. In these poems the frame is sequential; curiously, in Meredith's great poem of the 1883 volume, "Love in

the Valley," it is not. Although several stanzas image seasons or times of day, sequence is displaced by the perceptions, desires, and fantasies of the speaker. His beloved is placed in an almost dazzling variety of natural contexts ("Heartless she is as the shadow in the meadows/Flying to the hills on a blue and breezy noon"). Whatever the lover perceives in nature seems to remind him of her existence:

> Darker grows the valley, more and more forgetting:
>   So were it with me if forgetting could be willed.
> Tell the grassy hollow that holds the bubbling well-spring;
>   Tell it to forget the source that keeps it filled.

Natural scene, beloved, speaker: each seems to enhance the others. If a passing shadow on the meadow is the proper simile for the maiden's heartlessness, it is her "beauty that makes holy/Earth and air." Further, love's natural morality transcends the world of gossips who count faults and mothers who seek to have their daughters married.

The intensity of "Love in the Valley" is due in part to its unusual eight-line stanzaic form, with alternating rhymed and unrhymed lines. Although the meter is initially dactylic, the placing of stresses frequently varies. This poem is one of Meredith's most successful metrical achievements; other *Poems and Lyrics of the Joy of Earth* are also noteworthy, among them "Earth and Man," with its quatrains of varying line lengths. Meredith was aware that he was departing from the iambic pentameter norm in English verse when he employed a mixture of seven- or eight-syllable lines, sometimes with an irregular rhyme pattern. The source for this variation might have been Milton's *Comus* or the *Walpurgisnacht* scene in Goethe's *Faust,* but it is equally effective for the rapid movement of "The Woods of Westermain," and later, for the strong beats of "The Nuptials of Attila" and the more meditative "A Faith on Trial."

Meredith's fourth collection, *Ballads and Poems of Tragic Life* (1887), places the materials of legend in societal and psychological perspectives. "The Song of Theodolinda" explores the psychology of religious fanaticism. "A Preaching from a Spanish Ballad" casts a cold eye on the double standard of marital fidelity whereby a faithless husband can justly condemn a faithless wife. "Archduchess Anne" recounts the aftermath of an extramarital affair between Anne and Count Louis. Count Louis marries, leads a rebellion against Anne, and is caught by the wiles of Kraken, Anne's minister. Moved by the pleadings of Louis's wife, Anne writes to Kraken recommending mercy; but he interprets this to mean only that Louis should undergo a merciful death and executes the count. The real subjects of the narrative are Anne's feelings, her indirect and ambiguous communication of those feelings, and the tensions of love and politics.

"The Nuptials of Attila" is one of the most powerful poems in the collection. The plot concerns Attila's determination to marry—against the wishes of his men, who are bent on further conquest. The marriage is celebrated, although the bride's silence is ominous; the next day, Attila is found dead, his bride crouching in a corner, apparently mad. The identity of the murderer remains a mystery, and the leaderless armies break up. The dispersal of the armies is likened to natural turbulence, to the breaking up of the ice on the frozen Danube. The thematic linking of natural and social chaos, which appeared earlier in *Modern Love,* develops here in a legendary context. At the same time, "The Nuptials of Attila" points, like *Modern Love,* to the mystery and uncontrollability of human emotion which can abrogate all signs of mutuality and contract. The poem's narrative lines develop obliquely. The narrator seems at times to be one of Attila's men and thus to play a choric role, but at other times he seems impersonal and distanced from the action. The thematic point is complex: it has to do with the inexplicability of certain actions, with questions about what the mind can know and what it must always perceive as indeterminate. From a more general perspective, the poem makes a statement about the inadequacies of conventional narrative to communicate human events. The reader should not construe this statement as a despairing one, however; Meredith embeds the action in subtleties and speculations of consciousness in order to juxtapose the distant with the contemporary, the mysterious event with the attempt to understand it. This poem, which derives its fable from a more primitive period of society, casts that fable into a sophisticated narrative that anticipates modern ways of delineating subjectivity.

Although the characters are among the more distanced of Meredith's subjects, the *Ballads and Poems of Tragic Life* are a reminder of the dark ground that is always part of Meredith's poetic universe. Meredith's fifth poetry collection, *A Reading of Earth,* published in 1888, turns away from legend and back to the natural world. Its essential, recurring subject is the dialectic between nature and consciousness. Consciousness appears in several versions of the self: in addition to the dramatis personae, there are the first-person speakers of the

lyrics; a group of semi-personifications that hover between natural image and mythic figure; fully mythopoeic creations; and worldly figures. These diverse figures appear in the poems of the 1880s and in several later lyrics, including "Night of Frost in May" (1892) and "Wind on the Lyre" (1892).

In Meredith's verse the self is sometimes suppressed or concealed. The poems often look outward toward natural enchantments—the "Classic splendours, knightly dyes" of Westermain or the "wild-cherry in bloom" which "struck as the birth of Light" in "A Faith on Trial"—even when the real subject is the coming to full consciousness of self. The personal pronoun may appear belatedly; in "Night of Frost in May," the word *my* appears first in line 47. Or consciousness may appear indirectly, as in the similes where mind is by implication the maker of those similes. (In "The South-Wester," woodland and sun become "as harp and harper"). The implicit imperative is for the self to acknowledge the gifts of perception; the difficulties of this enterprise are apparent in the conditional statements which end such poems as "The Thrush in February" ("For love we Earth, then serve we all") or "The South-Wester" ("we could believe").

Meredith admitted explicitly the importance of such writers as Shakespeare and Goethe ("Dirge in Woods," 1870, is apparently an imitation of Goethe's "Wanderers Nachtlied"); he was less candid about the influence of his nineteenth-century precursors and contemporaries. His literary friendships (rather briefly in the 1860s with Swinburne and Rossetti and with such men of letters as Leslie Stephen and John Morley) point to spiritual affinities rather than to an agreement on the practical details of poetic craftsmanship. Meredith wrote satiric poems on Byron, and his letters include Matthew Arnold and caustic observations about Tennyson. One letter expresses his admiration for Shelley, and there is in fact good reason to surmise that Meredith was indebted to the Romantics even if he was less overtly concerned with self-consciousness. What he did share with such poets as Wordsworth, Shelley, and Keats was the problem of entering into a relationship with the natural world. To grasp the import of Meredith's "greeting" of nature (not unlike Keats's greeting of the spirit with the object), one must understand what was entailed in the conception of nature as "other," as ostensibly indifferent to man. Meredith's poetry is dedicated to the project of asserting man's potential relation to Nature. She is more than the Wordsworthian foster mother who leads him to comprehend the strength of his own imagination. Although she is a source of

joy and even consolation, she is also a stern precep-
tress: she is more articulate, the literal ground and
personified speaker of the very words one needs to
interpret her. Thus a rift between self and
nature—a rift which threatens one's very capacity
to live in the world—may be healed by an act of
interpretation.

The Romantics had, in the form of the
"greater romantic lyric," set forth one procedure
for reestablishing a dialogue between man and nature. The poet's response to the natural world is
mediated by an inner meditation which, coming
between his initial and final perceptions of nature,
allows that final perception to signify a unity of self
and world. Meredith, however, shifts the terms.
Memory and imagination, freed of one kind of
doubt about self-consciousness, must nevertheless
contend with an obstructive egoism. As a result,
nature tends to play a more active role, equally
evident in the minutely observed detail ("a bud in
jewelled grasp was nipped" by frost) as in the massive personification. The overt terms for self may be
elided, but they are not excluded from all this
natural activity. Moreover, spiritual agons may be
projected onto the field of nature: thus, the quasi-
allegorical "cavern-cowl[ed]" dragons of self are
pitted against the wise gnomes who inhabit earth's
deepest mines ("The Woods of Westermain").

Readers of Meredith's poems have often
found a didactic strain in them; early readers in
particular regarded him as a philosopher as well as a
poet. It is possible to discern a positive response to
Darwinism in Meredith's belief that in the whole
man blood, brain, and spirit combine to further
growth: this is evolution transposed to the individual. The passions (blood) would be guided by
intellect (brain) and both would be informed or
even graced (in a secular way) by spirit. Man must
expend a conscious effort in his self-development;
on the other hand, a love of earth, properly directed, will elicit an answering strength:

> Love born of knowledge, love that gains
> Vitality as Earth it mates,
> The meaning of the Pleasures, Pains,
> The Life, the Death, illuminates.
>
> For love we Earth, then serve we all;
> Her mystic secret then is ours. . . .
> "The Thrush in February"

The Meredith who once defended the difficulty of his style on the grounds that "thought is

tough" would surely have wanted his poems to be
regarded as thought-full. But the didactic quality is
never as bare as the philosophic approach might
lead one to believe. The mentors in Meredith's
poetry are personifications who emerge from
natural events—from the day of the southwester,
or the encounter with the white cherry tree, or the
song of the nightingale on a frosty May night. The
perception of such figures is so intense ("The magic
swung my universe") that it becomes a form of imaginative dialogue. It is the experience of interpretation, the drama of a consciousness-in-nature, even
when that consciousness hides itself, that deter-
mines the thought of the poems of the 1880s. In
"Night of Frost in May," the late frost and the song
of the nightingale create a natural magic so intense
that the speaker has an epiphany: self-realization is
achieved through a perceptual experience. "The
South-Wester" makes a day's storm into the point of
departure for a myth about "The union of our earth
and skies," which is "renewed" both in the storm
and in the mind of the poet. In this poem, in "Night
of Frost in May," and in the more allegorical "Hymn
to Colour," natural events become meaningful as
they are perceived, remembered, and recreated in
poetry. Poetic creation, then, depends upon the
imaginative perception which grasps a shape or
"plot" in natural events. The tripartite unity of
mind, earth, and sky which those events bespeak
enables both the creative process and a self-
realization in which the self is purged of egoism to
come into being. The poems convey this less
through doctrinal statement than through the narrative shapes of the myths, which begin with description and end with assertions of union like that
in "The South-Wester": "melting," the heaven's
dream-messenger Iris "passed into the mind."

Such melting and such magic suggest that experience in nature is poised on the threshold of the
more-than-natural. Here the distinctiveness of
Meredith's style becomes crucial. There are words
of natural enchantment: on the "plumed and ar-
moured" night of frost in May (the image is visually,
conceptually, and imaginatively precise), "Then was
the lyre of earth beheld,/Then heard by me." We
find in Meredith's diction a stress on the qualitative
aspects of objects, as well as words such as "luminous" and "aery" which endow those objects with
value. Adjectives used as nouns ("our inmost,"
"their inner sweetest") as well as nouns used as adjectives jostle grammatical expectations and challenge readers to recognize their appropriateness.
"Our inmost," for example, represents an ideal

First page of the manuscript for one of the poems collected in Meredith's The Empty Purse, *1892 (Maurice Buxton Forman,*
A Bibliography of the Writings in Prose and Verse of George Meredith, *1922)*

which has no material analogue; it is that toward which consciousness strives and that which the unseen lark's song represents.

Despite the admiration that he earned, Meredith's literary success was never a popular one. Thus it is not surprising that he had to pay for the publication of all three volumes of poetry that appeared during the 1880s. His rewards were intangible and often qualified. There were fierce partisans among his readers; many reviewers, however, commented on the difficulties of Meredith's style. Perhaps that is why he did not send out *A Reading of Earth* for review.

The most severe trial of those years, however, came from the death of Marie Meredith in 1885. The evidence indicates that Meredith's second marriage was reasonably happy. His wife's illness was a lingering one, and from the strain of those days there emerged "A Faith on Trial" (included in *A Reading of Earth*)—what is, in effect, an elegy written in anticipation of death. Like so many nineteenth-century poems, it modifies the genre to which it belongs. The setting is pastoral, but the only allusion to the shepherd's task appears in Earth's metaphorical guidance. Nor are there deities. Nature, rather than anything beyond, gives, sympathizes, and controls; Earth alone is the catalyst for a spiritual rebirth. The frame, like that of so many of Meredith's poems, is a casual walk. To his darkness of spirit, the apparition of the cherry tree in bloom "struck as the birth of Light." The speaker's epiphany is marked by Meredith's characteristic proliferation of metaphor, whereby an awareness of earth's "mythy" meanings (to use Wallace Stevens's word), joined with memory, reshapes his perception of his world. The forces of death are overcome by a renewed dialogue with earth.

The pace of Meredith's novel writing slowed during his later years, although for some time his poetic output was steady. He produced three major volumes: *Poems: The Empty Purse, with Odes to the Comic Spirit, to Youth in Memory and Verses* (1892), *Odes in Contribution to the Song of French History* (1898), and *A Reading of Life* (1901). (*Last Poems* was published posthumously in 1909.) Readers found the poems of those later years increasingly difficult. The stylistic traits seem more pronounced: the subject-verb inversions, the ellipses, the dense, exuberant metaphors. In Meredith's later poems the dialogue with earth gives way to the single strong voice or to the speaker of epigrams. The writings often display an austere beauty; at the very least, they remind us of how much variety he was still capable.

Many of the poems aim high. The "Ode to the Comic Spirit" completes the triptych on that Meredithian deity first presented in the lecture of 1877. In the "Ode" Lucian's legend of Momus the jester, whose expulsion from Olympus deprived the gods of his satiric spirit, receives some elaboration. Earth and heaven suffer from the loss of his corrective spirit; the distortions they undergo can be relieved only by a return to the direct vision of the Comic Spirit. The message of the poem is clear enough, despite the difficult language in which it is embedded: the attainment of right vision is no easy accomplishment.

The theme of age runs through the later poems, although it appears in masked and impersonal ways. Only in certain brief lyrics, including "Song in the Songless" (1900), does the first person appear:

> They have no song, the sedges dry,
>   And still they sing.
> It is within my breast they sing,
>   As I pass by.
> Within my breast they touch a string,
>   They wake a sigh.
> There is but sound of sedges dry;
>   In me they sing.

This is Meredith's version of the autumnal stubble-fields of Keats's "To Autumn"; despite nature's waning, a persistent spirit carries the song. The "Ode to Youth in Memory" offers the consolations of memory for the loss of "days/Of radiant orb and daring gaze."

In the later poems there is often a pronounced distancing of the natural world. In "The Empty Purse," the dream of nature's fair season gives way to austerities of purse and age, expressed in images that are severe. Meredith's persona—often a sage—is tough in mind and style, as "The Sage Enamoured and the Honest Lady," another poem in the 1892 volume, reminds us. But the enchanted woods are by no means avoided, and the late poems are still peopled with mythic figures. Sometimes the allegorizing is more explicit: "Forest History" presents a narrative of man's life in nature and society, history and romance into a pattern of life. "The Night-Walk" opens in the mode of the earlier poems:

> Awakes for me and leaps from shroud
> All radiantly the moon's own night
> Of folded showers in streamer cloud.

"Meredith Destroying Literary Form," cartoon by E. T. Reed in
Punch, *28 July 1894*

But the night sky, a "parliament of chats," and "the moss-root smell where beeches grew"—all the objects which feed the discourse of the speaker and his companion—are part of a tale of life, of experience viewed from the perspective of age, which remembers the anticipations of youth. The consciousness of time, the poignant awareness that what was once "untold" can now only be a tale, heightens the speaker's own awareness of himself as poet. Artistic awareness, then, may come as a result of experiential or sensory loss.

Despite his activities as a newspaper correspondent in 1866 and despite the political concerns of the novels, few of Meredith's poems before the late period focus on public events. The notable exception is "France, December 1870," written in response to the Franco-Prussian War. Here Meredith's Continental affinities and his anguish over the clash of two cultures which he loved and admired found poetic form. The poem was published first in the *Fortnightly Review* in 1870 and then collected in *Ballads and Poems of Tragic Life* in 1887.

In the late 1880s and after, Meredith's interests and his personal associations turned more and more to public affairs. He wrote three additional poems on France, "The Revolution," "Napoleon," and "Alsace-Lorraine," which, with "France, December 1870," were published in 1898 as *Odes in Contribution to the Song of French History.* The French Revolution and the Napoleonic Wars had been a source of material for English poets, including Coleridge, Wordsworth, and Swinburne, throughout the nineteenth century; that interest was to culminate in Thomas Hardy's *The Dynasts* (1903-1908).

The *Odes* are a reading of a historical process, which Meredith saw as an aggregate of self-willed acts—those of Napoleon in particular. History for Meredith forms a pattern with natural cycles, and this new pattern is evident in two tendencies in the poetry. First, poetry can both create (or reconstruct) and convey a vision of natural order, even when the imagination is distanced by memory or conjecture from its natural sources. Second, there is the darker vision in Meredith's poetry, whereby chaos threatens to subvert the order of nature. Afer *Modern Love*, that vision reappears with some strength in *Ballads and Poems of Tragic Life*. The tangle of human affairs, including misconstrued intentions and ironic or belated acts, justifies the term "tragic life." The ending of "Periander," in which the tyrant pardons and sends for his exiled son, only to have the son's dead body delivered by islanders who are fearful of Periander's influence, is exemplary. The exile of Periander's son

> . . . had resemblance to a death: and on,
> Against a coast where sapphire shattered white,
> The seasons rolled like troops of billows blown
> To spraymist. The prince gazed on capping night.

That tide, which represents the forces of both passion and chaos, enters the world of history in the *Odes*. The destructive forces that sweep over France during the Revolution, and later during the Napoleonic and Franco-Prussian Wars, are likened to a tide that obliterates the structured French landscape, where the land is "Furrowed to likeness of the dim grey main/Behind the black obliterating cyclone." But the image of the tide implies that the waters can recede, that there can be a resurgence of the French spirit. If the demonic energies of Napoleon incur ruinous storms (he is comparable to Pluto in "Day of the Daughter of Hades"), the mediating figure of France can help to restore earth's bounty. France is a complex personification, humanized and connected with history on the one hand, but a

Napoleon

I.

Cannon his name,
Cannon his voice, he came.
Who heard of him heard shaken hills,
An earth at quake, to quiet stamped;
Who looked on him beheld the will of wills,
The driver of wild flocks where lions ramped.

Manuscript pages from two of the four poems collected in Meredith's Odes in Contribution to the Song of French History, *1898*
(Anderson Galleries, sale 1794, 14-16 January 1924)

Alsace-Lorraine.

I.

The sister Hours in circles linked,
Daughters of men, of men the mates,
Are gone on flow with this day that winked,
With the night that spanned at golden gates.
Mothers, they leave us, quickening seed;
They bear us grain or flower or weed,
As we have sown; is nought extinct
For them we fill to be our Fates.
Life of the breath is but the loan;
Passing swells what we have sown.

natural phenomenon and akin to earth on the other.

In the style of the *Odes* it is easy to find Meredith's idiosyncrasies writ large: the loose and reconstructive syntax, the emphasis on the single word used as metaphor, the somewhat unusual choice of words to suggest the value of action, energy, natural life. Images of natural energy — fountains and springs of fire, the song of birds — come to symbolize imaginative insight. But if the *Odes* demand an elevated style, elevation is not achieved through mere accumulation of metaphors. As one reviewer put it (*Literature,* 26 November 1898), Meredith's *Odes* were an "unbridled revel of words," a "persistent pursuing of a fanciful thought through the tangled underwood of a too luxuriant diction." Few readers, if any, saw how these poems may be linked to the corpus of his poetry.

From a modern critical perspective Meredith's style seems more powerful than it did to contemporary reviewers, who seem to have been losing patience with a late-century aesthetic — founded on artifice rather than on nature or simplicity. Meredith's "ear for the sweep and texture of harmonies," wrote Arthur Symons in *Athenaeum* (20 July 1901), "for the building up of rhythmical structure, is not seconded by an ear for the delicacies of sound in words or in tunes." But these faults, Symons notes, are comparable to those of Lizst and Berlioz. And as those composers required a modern sensibility to be appreciated more fully, so may Meredith be more fully understood in an age more atuned to dissonance, less prone to condemn as obscure that which is not immediately understood.

In Meredith's later years he was admired, even to excess, by younger writers, among them Robert Louis Stevenson. When the time of robust walks across the nearby countryside in the company of such figures as Leslie Stephen had passed and Meredith was limited more and more by an encroaching paralysis, there were still the ceremonial visits to Flint Cottage, and Meredith continued to have his share of formal public recognition. When he died, on 18 May 1909, he was still one of England's leading men of letters. But as stylistic norms changed, fewer novelists attempted to learn from the metaphorical brilliance of his prose style. It is still more difficult to find poetic successors. Meredith's affinities with his contemporaries are often more theoretical than practical — which may be a sign of how difficult it has been to find simple, inclusive categories for Victorian poetry. The significance of Meredith's poetry lies, rather, in its defiance of what he perceived as the conventions of his day (Meredith scorned what he termed the "satin lengths" of Tennyson's work), in its attempt to expand the domain of poetic language and to make vision survive the constrictions of doctrine. Thus, he experimented ceaselessly — "Change, the strongest son of Life," weds the Spirit — and used uncommon meters that moved hurriedly toward new poetic scenarios. No stranger to a vision of the contingent and the formless, but equally aware of earth's glories, Meredith's poetry asserts that imagination may break through what he describes as the "chrysalis" of the senses to find a new continuity between nature and self.

Letters:
The Letters of George Meredith, edited by C. L. Cline, 3 volumes (Oxford: Clarendon Press, 1970).

Bibliographies:
Maurice Buxton Forman, *A Bibliography of the Writings in Prose and Verse of George Meredith* (Edinburgh: Bibliographical Society, 1922);
Forman, *Meredithiana, Being a Supplement to the Bibliography of Meredith* (Edinburgh: Bibliographical Society, 1924);
H. Lewis Sawin, "George Meredith: A Bibliography of Meredithiana, 1920-1953," *Bulletin of Bibliography,* 21 (September-December 1955): 186-191, 215, 216;
Michael Collie, *George Meredith: A Bibliography* (Toronto & Buffalo: University of Toronto Press, 1974).

Biography:
Lionel Stevenson, *The Ordeal of George Meredith* (New York: Scribners, 1953).

References:
Carol L. Bernstein, *Precarious Enchantment: A Reading of Meredith's Poetry* (Washington, D.C.: Catholic University of America Press, 1979);
Oliver Elton, *A Survey of English Literature 1830-1880,* 2 volumes (London: Arnold, 1932);
Norman Friedman, "The Jangled Harp: Symbolic Structure in 'Modern Love,'" *Modern Language Quarterly,* 18 (March 1957): 9-26;
Arline Golden, "'The Game of Sentiment': Tradition and Innovation in Meredith's 'Modern Love,'" *Journal of English Literary History,* 40 (Summer 1973): 264-284;
Graham Hough, Introduction to *Selected Poems of*

George Meredith (London: Oxford University Press, 1962);

Norman Kelvin, *A Troubled Eden: Nature and Society in the Works of George Meredith* (Stanford: Stanford University Press, 1961);

Barbara Fass Leavy, "The Romanticism of Meredith's 'Love in the Valley,'" *Studies in Romanticism,* 18 (Spring 1979): 99-114;

John Lucas, "Meredith as a Poet," in *Meredith Now,* edited by Ian Fletcher (London: Routledge & Kegan Paul, 1971), pp. 14-33;

Dorothy Mermin, "Poetry as Fiction: Meredith's *Modern Love," Journal of English Literary History,* 43 (Spring 1976): 100-119;

G. M. Trevelyan, *The Poetry and Philosophy of George Meredith* (New York: Scribners, 1906);

Ioan Williams, ed., *Meredith: The Critical Heritage* (London: Routledge & Kegan Paul, 1971);

Elizabeth Cox Wright, "The Significance of the Image Patterns in Meredith's *Modern Love," Victorian Newsletter,* no. 13 (Spring 1958): 1-9.

Papers:

Meredith's papers are in the Altschul Collection at the Beinecke Rare Book and Manuscript Library, Yale University; the Berg Collection at the New York Public Library; and the Henry E. Huntington Library, San Marino, California.

Lewis Morris
(23 January 1833-12 November 1907)

Cheryl S. Conover
West Virginia University

SELECTED BOOKS: *Songs of Two Worlds,* anonymous (London: King, 1871);

Songs of Two Worlds (Second Series), anonymous (London: King, 1874);

Songs of Two Worlds (Third Series), anonymous (London: King, 1875);

The Epic of Hades (Book 2, London: King, 1876; Philadelphia: Lippincott, 1876; Books 1, 3, London: King, 1877; Boston: Roberts Brothers, 1879);

Gwen: A Drama in Monologue in Six Acts (London: C. Kegan Paul, 1879);

The Ode of Life (London: C. Kegan Paul, 1880; Boston: Roberts Brothers, 1880);

Songs Unsung (London: Kegan Paul, Trench, 1883; Boston: Roberts Brothers, 1884);

Gycia: A Tragedy in Five Acts (London: Kegan Paul, Trench, 1886);

Songs of Britain (London: Kegan Paul, Trench, 1887);

Odatis: An Old Love-tale (London: Heldesheimer & Faulkner, 1888);

A Vision of Saints (London: Kegan Paul, Trench, Trübner, 1890);

Love and Sleep and Other Poems (London: Faulkner/New York: Cassell, 1893);

Ode on the Marriage of H. R. H. the Duke of York and H. S. H. Princess Victoria Mary of Teck, July 6th, *1893* (London: Kegan Paul, Trench, Trübner, 1893);

Songs Without Notes (London: Kegan Paul, Trench, Trübner, 1894; New York: Scribners, 1894);

Idylls and Lyrics (London: Kegan Paul, Trench, Trübner, 1896);

The Diamond Jubilee: An Ode (London: Kegan Paul, 1897);

Harvest-Tide (London: Kegan Paul, Trench, Trübner, 1901; New York: Crowell, 1901);

The New Rambler: From Desk to Platform (London, New York & Bombay: Longmans, Green, 1905).

Collection: *Poems,* by Sir Lewis Morris (London: Routledge/New York: Dutton, 1904).

Great-grandson of the Welsh poet Lewis Morris, Sir Lewis Morris was esteemed by middle-class Victorian readers as one of the outstanding poets of his age. At the time of his death, he was considered the chief literary figure of Wales; his most famous book, *The Epic of Hades,* went through forty-five editions in his lifetime. But public acceptance is not always an indication of literary quality, for the buying public desired sentimentality, optimism, and simplistic versification, characteristics which permeated Morris's verse. Although he was strongly influenced by Alfred, Lord Tennyson, his technically perfect verses were often uninspired, sometimes to the point of mediocrity, and totally lacked Tennysonian spark.

Morris was born in Carmarthen, Wales, January 1833, the son of Lewis Morris, a solicitor, and Sophia Hughes Morris. He attended Queen Elizabeth's grammar school, Carmarthen, and Cowbridge and Sherborne schools. In 1856 he completed his B.A. at Jesus College, Oxford; he was awarded his M.A. in 1858, along with the chancellor's prize for the English essay "The Greatness and Decline of Venice." He was called to the bar in 1861 and practiced law as a conveyancer for twenty years. Politically a liberal, he favored social reform, home rule, and higher education for women; however, his numerous attempts to obtain a seat in Parliament failed. In 1878 Morris became interested in his Welsh heritage and particularly in the educational system of Wales. He served on a government-appointed committee commissioned to examine the state of higher education in Wales and eventually participated in the establishment of the University of Wales in 1893. He was named to the Queen's Privy Council in 1895 and subsequently received a literary knighthood, but the honor he most desired—the poet laureateship, left vacant after Tennyson's death—was never awarded to him. That his contemporaries considered him a likely candidate for the position is some indication of his popularity with the Victorian reading public; according to the *Athenaeum*, it was his liberal politics, not his poetry, that prevented Morris from being named poet laureate. Morris was shy, a quality sometimes mistaken for aloofness, and an unskilled public speaker. Although he married Florence Pollard in 1868, the marriage was not made public until 1902. He died 12 November 1907, at his home, Penbryn, in Carmarthen, bequeathing his personal library and manuscripts, which he felt would grow in value, to the University of Wales at Aberystwyth. His wife and three children survived him.

Morris greatly admired Tennyson, visiting him often in the years before Tennyson's death. Tennyson's poetry not only furnished him with ideas for his own poems but also provided models for his poetic forms. Morris's first book of poetry, *Songs of Two Worlds,* published anonymously in 1871, showed, along with Tennysonian characteristics, the obvious influence of George Herbert and Henry Vaughan. The popularity of the placid, optimistic lyrics encouraged Morris to publish, again anonymously, two more series of *Songs,* in 1874 and 1875, although the final poem in the third series, "To My Motherland," hinted at the writer's

Lewis Morris

identity. The saccharine quality of these early lyrics can best be illustrated by the following few lines from "Ode on a Fair Spring Morning" from the 1874 series:

> The birds awake which slumbered all night long,
> And with a gush of song,
> First doubting of their strain, then full and wide
> Raise their fresh hymns thro' all the country side;
> Already, above the dewy clover,
> The soaring lark begins to hover
> Over his mate's low nest:
> And soon, from childhood's early rest
> In hall and cottage, to the casement rise
> The little ones with their fresh morning eyes.
> And gaze on the old Earth, which still grows new,
> And see the tranquil heaven's unclouded blue.

The public accepted Morris's poetry as a welcome relief from the exotic mood and elaborate phrasing of much late-nineteenth-century verse.

In 1876 Morris published book two of what was to become his best-known and most rousing poem, *The Epic of Hades.* Books one and three followed in 1877, establishing Morris's reputation as a writer with mass appeal. The poem, possibly inspired by Tennyson's "A Dream of Fair Women," helped (in the words of one of Morris's contemporaries) "to make the literature of Greece a living reality for unlearned readers." The structure of the *Epic* is simple: as the poet travels through Tartarus, Hades, and Olympus, he meets different figures from Greek mythology, including Helen, Phaedra, Clytemnestra, Actaeon, and Psyche, who recite their stories to him in blank verse monologues. Although the blank verse form of the *Epic* helped obscure some of the poetic weaknesses which lowered Morris's lyrics into mediocrity, even the verse form cannot hide the triteness of Aphrodite's "The burning South, the icy North, the old/And immemorial East, the unbounded West." Morris's didacticism, willingly accepted by his Victorian audience, is also uncomfortably obtrusive to modern readers; Aphrodite's self-righteous "Shame is for wrong, and not for innocence" and Marsyas's "Godlike 'tis/To fail upon the icy ledge, and fall/Where other footsteps dare not" seem a bit ponderous, but it was partially for this moral frame that *The Epic of Hades* was admired. The contemporary press, even the *Saturday Review* which had attacked Morris earlier, praised *The Epic of Hades,* calling it "one of the most considerable and original feats of recent English poetry," "thoughtful and scholarly," "a poem of permanent power and charm," possessing a "noble" tone with portions that "are excessively beautiful." Over 50,000 copies of the complete *Epic* were sold in Morris's lifetime, confirming him as the poet of the middle class.

None of Morris's later works enjoyed the success of *The Epic of Hades. Gwen: A Drama in Monologue in Six Acts* appeared in 1879; the play, loosely similar in form to Tennyson's *Maud,* concerns the tragedy of a secret marriage. *The Ode of Life* (1880) and *Songs Unsung* (1883), the first of Morris's volumes to bear his name, are collections of uninspired lyrics. For example, in a section of *The Ode of Life* called "The Ode of Perfect Years," Morris extols the virtues of labor:

> Toil is the law of life, and its best fruit;
> This from the uncaring brute
> Divides:
> . . . .
> Toil is the mother of wealth,
> The nurse of health;
> Toil 'tis that gives the zest
> To well-earned rest.
> . . . .

> Oh, labour truly blest!
> Thou rulest all the race;
> . . . .
> Where most thou art,
> Man rises upward to a loftier height,
> And views the earth and heaven with clearer sight,
> And holds a cleaner heart.

Perhaps more than any other selection, this praise of labor not only clarifies Morris's appeal to the practical middle class but also firmly binds him in time and sentiment with Thomas Carlyle and John Ruskin. *A Vision of Saints* (1890) was meant to be the Christian counterpart of *The Epic of Hades,* with such Christian characters as St. Christopher, Elizabeth Fry, St. Perpetua, George Herbert, and Father Damien replacing the mythological pagans. The biographical monologues are weakly Miltonic rather than Tennysonian in vocabulary and syntax, and, according to B. Ifor Evans, "to consider this volume is one way of instructing oneself to think well of *The Epic of Hades.*" The last new work produced by Morris was a volume of autobiographical essays, *The New Rambler: From Desk to Platform,* published in 1905. In the essays he discusses his poetical philosophy and responds to charges leveled by some of his harshest critics. He also addresses the problem of Welsh education, one of his main interests in his later years.

In general, Morris's contemporaries were kind in their criticism of his poetry; what a current reader sees as major flaws in Morris's poetry—his didactic tone, simplistic thoughts, and facile versification—the average Victorian journalist praised. For example, in 1877, the *Scotsman* said of Morris's *The Epic of Hades:* "you have poetry which pleases you as you read, which shocks no sensibility, never wearies you, and often raises you into a serener atmosphere. . . . It will be surprising if the reader does not come to the conclusion that the author is a poet of very high order." The 1911 edition of *Encyclopaedia Britannica* says that Morris's poetry revealed his "genial optimism and evident sincerity," while the *Dictionary of National Biography,* admitting that his poetry lacked "subtlety," calls Morris a writer who expressed "simple truths in simple language" and whose poetry "exerted a wide moral influence." The writer of Morris's obituary for the *Athenaeum* was more critical, declaring that Morris's poetry had "no special distinction" about it and that Morris had "nothing new or disturbing to say." In short, his poetry "lacked personality," and this overwhelming blandness was what made his poetry suitable for all; he offended very few—except the literary. The critics recognized the debt

Morris owed to Tennyson, some hinting that perhaps Morris depended too heavily on his poetic idol; as one commentator remarked, "His later work follows too closely upon the influence of Tennyson, from which he is never altogether free." Most agreed with Sir Grant Duff, who wrote in his 1902 *Anthology of Victorian Poetry* that "Sir Lewis Morris will be long remembered." But Hugh Walker, in *The Literature of the Victorian Era* (1910), recognized that Morris's facility for writing verses on demand was a detriment: "He certainly cheapened the Muse," wrote Walker, and "it is probable that Lewis Morris's reputation will fade before many years have passed." He also recognized that Morris's audience consisted mainly of "those who prefer verse which makes no great demands upon thought."

Current criticism of Lewis Morris is nonexistent. The most recent critical comments of any length on Morris are by B. Ifor Evans in his book *English Poetry in the Later Nineteenth Century*, first published in 1933. In the two paragraphs he devotes to Morris he observes that "nowhere can the demand for Tennyson-made-easy be more readily perceived" than in Morris's poetry; Morris "chose themes which a great poet might have found strenuous and . . . he never has the imagination to dominate them." In Morris's favor, Evans admits that Morris "seldom descends to bathos and never to grossness" and that he "is frequently close to poetry in imagery and phrasing." The dearth of modern criticism indicates that Morris, possibly a legend in his own time, has been forgotten in ours.

References:

B. Ifor Evans, *English Poetry in the Later Nineteenth Century*, revised edition (New York: Barnes & Noble, 1966), pp. 329-330;

Hugh Walker, *The Literature of the Victorian Era* (Cambridge: University Press, 1910), pp. 571-573.

William Morris

K. L. Goodwin
University of Queensland

See also the Morris entry in *DLB 18, Victorian Novelists After 1885.*

BIRTH: Walthamstow, Essex, 24 March 1834, to William and Emma Shelton Morris.

EDUCATION: B.A., Exeter College, Oxford, 1856; M.A., 1875.

AWARDS AND HONORS: Honorary fellowship, Exeter College, Oxford, 1882.

MARRIAGE: 26 April 1859 to Jane Burden; children: Jane Alice (Jenny), Mary (May).

DEATH: Hammersmith, Middlesex, 3 October 1896.

BOOKS: *The Defence of Guenevere and Other Poems* (London: Bell & Daldy, 1858; Boston: Roberts Brothers, 1875);

The Life and Death of Jason: A Poem (London: Bell & Daldy, 1867; Boston: Roberts Brothers, 1867);

The Earthly Paradise: A Poem, 3 volumes (London: Ellis, 1868-1870; Boston: Roberts Brothers, 1868-1870);

The Lovers of Gudrun: A Poem (Boston: Roberts Brothers, 1870);

Love Is Enough; or The Freeing of Pharamond: A Morality (London: Ellis & White, 1873; Boston: Roberts Brothers, 1873);

The Story of Sigurd the Volsung and the Fall of the Niblungs (London: Ellis & White, 1876; Boston: Roberts Brothers, 1876);

Hopes and Fears for Art: Five Lectures Delivered in Birmingham, London, and Nottingham 1878-81 (London: Ellis & White, 1882; Boston: Roberts Brothers, 1882);

A Summary of the Principles of Socialism Written for the Democratic Federation, by Morris and H. M. Hyndman (London: Modern Press, 1884);

Textile Fabrics: A Lecture (London: Clowes, 1884);

Art and Socialism: A Lecture; and Watchman, What of

the Night? The Aims and Ideals of the English Socialists of Today (London: Reeves, 1884);

Chants for Socialists: No. 1. The Day is Coming (London: Reeves, 1884);

The Voice of Toil, All for the Cause: Two Chants for Socialists (London: Justice Office, 1884);

The God of the Poor (London: Justice Office, 1884);

Chants for Socialists (London: Socialist League Office, 1885; New York: New Horizon Press, 1935);

The Manifesto of the Socialist League (London: Socialist League Office, 1885);

The Socialist League: Constitution and Rules Adopted at the General Conference (London: Socialist League Office, 1885);

Address to Trades' Unions (The Socialist Platform—No. 1) (London: Socialist League Office, 1885);

Useful Work v. Useless Toil (The Socialist Platform—No. 2) (London: Socialist League Office, 1885);

For Whom Shall We Vote? Addressed to the Working-Men Electors of Great Britain (London: Commonweal Office, 1885);

What Socialists Want (London: Hammersmith Branch of the Socialist League, 1885);

The Labour Question from the Socialist Standpoint (Claims of Labour Lectures—No. 5) (Edinburgh: Co-operative Printing Co., 1886);

A Short Account of the Commune of Paris (The Socialist Platform—No. 4) (London: Socialist League Office, 1886);

The Pilgrims of Hope: A Poem in Thirteen Books (London: Buxton Forman, 1886; Portland, Maine: Mosher, 1901);

The Aims of Art (London: Commonweal Office, 1887);

The Tables Turned; or, Nupkins Awakened: A Socialist Interlude (play) (London: Commonweal Office, 1887);

True and False Society (London: Socialist League Office, 1888);

Signs of Change: Seven Lectures Delivered on Various Occasions (London: Reeves & Turner, 1888; New York: Longmans, Green, 1896);

A Dream of John Ball and A King's Lesson (London: Reeves & Turner, 1888; East Aurora, N.Y.: Roycroft, 1898);

A Tale of the House of the Wolfings and All the Kindreds of the Mark (London: Reeves & Turner, 1889; Boston: Roberts Brothers, 1890);

The Roots of the Mountains Wherein is Told Somewhat of the Lives of the Men of Burgdale, Their Friends, Their Neighbours, Their Foemen, and Their Fellows in Arms (London: Reeves & Turner, 1890;

William Morris (Radio Times Hulton Picture Library)

New York: Longmans, Green, 1896);

Monopoly; or, How Labour is Robbed (The Socialist Platform—No. 7) (London: Commonweal Office, 1890);

News from Nowhere; or, An Epoch of Rest: Being Some Chapters from a Utopian Romance (Boston: Roberts Brothers, 1890; London: Reeves & Turner, 1891);

Statement of Principles of the Hammersmith Socialist Society, anonymous (Hammersmith: Hammersmith Socialist Society, 1890);

The Story of the Glittering Plain Which Has Been also Called the Land of Living Men or the Acre of the Undying (Hammersmith: Kelmscott Press, 1891; London: Reeves & Turner, 1891; Boston: Roberts Brothers, 1891);

Poems by the Way (Hammersmith: Kelmscott Press, 1891; Boston: Roberts Brothers, 1892);

Address on the Collection of Paintings of the English Pre-Raphaelite School (Birmingham: Osborne, 1891);

Under an Elm-Tree; or, Thoughts in the Country-side (Aberdeen: Leatham, 1891; Portland, Maine: Mosher, 1912);

Manifesto of English Socialists, anonymous, by Morris,

Hyndman, and G. B. Shaw (London: Twentieth Century Press, 1893);

The Reward of Labour: A Dialogue (London: Hayman, Christy & Lilly, 1893);

Concerning Westminster Abbey, anonymous (London: Women's Printing Society, 1893);

Socialism: Its Growth and Outcome, by Morris and E. B. Bax (London: Sonnenschein, 1893; New York: Scribners, 1893);

Help for the Miners: The Deeper Meaning of the Struggle (London: Baines & Searsrook, 1893);

Gothic Architecture: A Lecture for the Arts and Crafts Exhibition Society (Hammersmith: Kelmscott Press, 1893);

The Wood beyond the World (Hammersmith: Kelmscott Press, 1894; London: Lawrence & Bullen, 1895; Boston: Roberts House, 1895);

The Why I Ams: Why I Am a Communist, with L.S. Bevington's Why I am an Expropriationist (London: Liberty Press, 1894);

Child Christopher and Goldilind the Fair (2 volumes, Hammersmith: Kelmscott Press, 1895; 1 volume, Portland, Maine: Mosher, 1900);

Gossip about an Old House on the Upper Thames (Birmingham: Birmingham Guild of Handicraft, 1895; Flushing, N.Y.: Hill, 1901);

The Well at the World's End: A Tale (Hammersmith: Kelmscott Press, 1896; 2 volumes, London: Longmans, Green, 1896);

Of the External Coverings of Roofs, anonymous (London: Society for the Protection of Ancient Buildings, 1896);

How I Became a Socialist (London: Twentieth Century Press, 1896);

Some German Woodcuts of the Fifteenth Century, edited by S. C. Cockerell (Hammersmith: Kelmscott Press, 1897);

The Water of the Wondrous Isles (Hammersmith: Kelmscott Press, 1897; London: Longmans, Green, 1897);

The Sundering Flood (Hammersmith: Kelmscott Press, 1897; London: Longmans, Green, 1898);

A Note by William Morris on His Aims in Founding the Kelmscott Press, Together with a Short Description of the Press by S. C. Cockerell and an Annotated List of the Books Printed Thereat (Hammersmith: Kelmscott Press, 1898);

Address Delivered at the Distribution of Prizes to Students of the Birmingham Municipal School of Art on 21 February 1894 (London: Longmans, Green, 1898);

Art and the Beauty of the Earth (London: Longmans, Green, 1899);

Some Hints on Pattern-Designing (London: Longmans, Green, 1899);

Architecture and History, and Westminster Abbey (London: Longmans, Green, 1900);

Art and Its Producers, and the Arts and Crafts of Today (London: Longmans, Green, 1901);

Architecture, Industry, and Wealth: Collected Papers (London: Longmans, Green, 1902);

Communism (Fabian Tract No. 113) (London: Fabian Society, 1903);

The Unpublished Lectures of William Morris, edited by Eugene D. LeMire (Detroit: Wayne State University Press, 1969);

Icelandic Journals of William Morris (Fontwell: Centaur Press, 1969);

A Book of Verse: A Facsimile of the Manuscript Written in 1870 (London: Scolar Press, 1980);

Socialist Diary, edited by Florence Boos (Iowa City: Windhover Press, 1981);

The Novel on Blue Paper, edited by Penelope Fitzgerald (London: Journeyman Press, 1982); *Dickens Studies Annual: Essays on Victorian Fiction,* volume 10, edited by Michael Timko, Fred Kaplan, and Edward Guiliano (New York: AMS Press, 1982), pp. 153-220;

The Juvenilia of William Morris, edited by Boos (New York: William Morris Society, 1983).

Collections: *The Collected Works of William Morris,* edited by May Morris, 24 volumes (London & New York: Longmans, Green, 1910-1915; New York: Russell & Russell, 1966);

William Morris: Artist, Writer, Socialist, edited by May Morris, 2 volumes (Oxford: Blackwell, 1936; New York: Russell & Russell, 1966).

TRANSLATIONS: *The Story of Grettir the Strong,* translated by Morris and Eiríkr Magnússon (London: Ellis, 1869; New York: Longmans, Green, 1901);

Völsunga Saga: The Story of the Volsungs and Niblungs, translated by Morris and Magnússon (London: Ellis, 1870; New York: Longmans, Green, 1901);

Three Northern Love Stories, and Other Tales, translated by Morris and Magnússon (London: Ellis & White, 1875; New York: Longmans, Green, 1901);

The Aeneids of Vergil Done into English Verse (Boston: Roberts Brothers, 1875; London: Ellis & White, 1876);

The Odyssey of Homer Done into English Verse (London: Reeves & Turner, 1887; New York: Longmans, Green, 1897);

The Saga Library, translated by Morris and Magnús-

son, 6 volumes (London: Quaritch, 1891-
1905);

The Tale of Beowulf, translated from Old English by
Morris and A. J. Wyatt (Hammersmith:
Kelmscott Press, 1895);

Old French Romances (London: Allen, 1896; New
York: Scribners, 1896);

The Story of Kormak, the Son of Ogmund, translated by
Morris and Magnússon (London: William
Morris Society, 1970).

Much praised in his own lifetime for the
"sweetness" of his lyrics, compared to Chaucer as a
narrative poet, and seriously considered as a successor to Tennyson in the laureateship, William Morris
has subsequently often been disparaged for writing
poetry which, in Henry James's words, evokes a
world where the reader has "neither to choose, to
criticize, nor to believe, but simply to feel, to look,
and to listen." Morris's evocation of a sturdy and
practical medieval world functions, however, as a
criticism of his own time and an expression of hope
for radical change to produce a nonbourgeois, non-
capitalist world in the future. In addition, his poetry
has historical interest within the Pre-Raphaelite
movement, for Morris's first book, *The Defence of
Guenevere,* was published a dozen years before
Dante Gabriel Rossetti's first volume of verse, *Poems*
(1870). Morris's versification is also of substantial
historical interest, for he develops the irregular,
lightened rhythms of the Spasmodics in both octosyllabic and decasyllabic couplets, experiments
with alliterative measure in *Love Is Enough* and his
translation of *Beowulf,* and creates an original form
of hexameter in *Sigurd the Volsung.*

Important as it is, Morris's poetry was only one
of many artistic activities in an industrious and
restless life that sought through unremitting work
to fend off boredom and the pain, disappointment,
and deprivation of an unsatisfactory emotional life.
He himself said that "If a chap can't compose an
epic poem while he's weaving tapestry, he had better shut up, he'll never do any good at all"; poetic
inspiration, he commented, is "sheer nonsense . . . it
is a mere matter of craftsmanship." Largely
through his activities in the decorators' and designers' firm of Morris, Marshall, Faulkner & Co.
(founded in 1861 and reconstituted as Morris & Co.
in 1875) he played a major part in the revolution of
English taste in the second half of the nineteenth
century. He and his associates (notably Edward
Burne-Jones, Dante Gabriel Rossetti, Philip Webb,
Ford Madox Brown, and later John Henry Dearle)
designed furniture, wallpaper, painted tiles, stained

glass, printed cottons, woven hangings, embroidery, tapestry, carpets, and interior decoration;
Morris himself also made notable contributions to
calligraphy and to the design of typefaces and
printed books. He was a political activist who for the
last decade of his life was, largely because of a heavy
lecture and public-speaking program, one of the
best-known British advocates of communism.
During the same period he turned to the writing of
prose romances which, set in preindustrial society,
explore the possibilities of establishing a morally
defensible society and satisfying personal relationships.

Morris grew up in a family of nine children,
though it was only with his two elder sisters, and
especially with the eldest child, Emma, that he established a close relationship. The family lived in
comfortable circumstances on the edge of Epping
Forest, in which the boy Morris, wearing a toy suit of
armor, used to ride his pony. This idyllic tract of
hornbeam forest appears frequently in his poetry.
Although he was not taught to write until he was
ten, he and his sisters never remembered a time
when he could not read. He had read all of Sir
Walter Scott's novels by the time he was seven and
moved on to the works of Frederick Marryat, E. W.
Lane's translation of *The Arabian Nights,* and Clara
Reeve's *The Old English Baron* (which in its use of
dreams and its situation of two friends in love with
the same woman underlies much of Morris's own
verse and prose).

At Marlborough College (1848-1851), where
he was known as Crab, Morris became a good antiquarian. Wandering often through Savernake
Forest, Pewsey Vale, and the Wiltshire downs, he
took careful note of the British and Roman remains
and especially of the many Gothic buildings.

He went up to Exeter College, Oxford, at the
beginning of 1853, at a time when his family lived in
Water House, Walthamstow (now the William Morris Gallery). At Oxford he met his lifelong friend
and artistic associate, Edward Burne-Jones, and
through him some of Burne-Jones's friends from
King Edward's School, Birmingham, including
Charles Faulkner, Richard Watson (later Canon)
Dixon, Cormell Price, and William Fulford. His
father had died in 1847, and at the age of twenty-
one Morris was due to receive an income of some
£900 per annum. He thought of using it to establish
with his friends a monastic "Brotherhood" devoted
to prayer and the production of religious art. He
intended to take holy orders, but even when that
ambition was set aside in his last year at the university he clung to the notion of some kind of sec-

ularized artistic brotherhood. His establishment and conduct of Morris & Co. and of the Kelmscott Press; his plans to collaborate with Burne-Jones in producing beautiful illustrated books of his own poetry; the theme of his longest poem, *The Earthly Paradise;* and even his hopes for the Socialist organizations he helped to found can be traced back to this early ideal.

Morris's university friends (who called him Topsy or Top because of his mass of dark curly hair) were taken by surprise when in the winter of 1854-1855 he began to read them his poetry. Unknown to them he had been writing for at least a year. He destroyed most of these early works, though a few were preserved by his favorite sister, Emma, and printed in *William Morris: Artist, Writer, Socialist* (1936), edited by Morris's daughter May. They contain faults of rhythm, rhyme, and diction—faults that Morris never managed to eradicate entirely even in his mature poems—but they also display many of his virtues: quick strokes of emblematic scenery, accumulating atmosphere (achieved largely through the use of repeated motifs), and the balladist's art of letting out the story in controlled leaps. Love is rarely triumphant: it is more often interrupted, marred, or ended by violence, ignominy, or death. The scene of two friends in love with the same beautiful woman, resulting in the thwarting of the protagonist's love, is so pervasive that a biographical origin has been suggested: shock, grief, and a sense of betrayal at the betrothal and marriage of his sister Emma to the Reverend Joseph Oldham in 1850. She had been the recipient of Morris's confidences, his playmate, and his devoted correspondent when he was away at school. May Morris has drawn attention to the profound loneliness that she detected in her father's personality and in his writings from beginning to end.

On a vacation tour of northern France with Burne-Jones and Fulford in 1855, Morris relinquished the intention of taking orders and, inspired by French Gothic, decided to become an architect. At the beginning of 1856 he entered articles with George Edmund Street, a prominent Gothic Revival architect. In Street's Oxford office he met another lifelong friend, the senior clerk Philip Webb, who later designed Morris's Red House and was a partner in Morris, Marshall, Faulkner & Co. During this year Morris and his friends produced twelve monthly numbers of the *Oxford and Cambridge Magazine.* Morris edited the first number and bore the financial losses of the enterprise. In the magazine he had five poems, eight prose tales, an article on Amiens cathedral, a review of Robert Browning's *Men and Women,* and a joint article with Burne-Jones on "Ruskin and the *Quarterly.*"

When Street's office moved to London, Morris took rooms with Burne-Jones and, under the influence of Rossetti, decided to abandon architecture for painting as a career. From November 1856 till Morris's marriage in 1859, he and Burne-Jones shared a studio and residence at 17 Red Lion Square, Holborn. Morris wrote, drew, painted, carved in wood, and tried manuscript illumination. In the last three months of 1857 he worked with Rossetti, Burne-Jones, Arthur Hughes, John Hungerford Pollen, Val Prinsep, and Spencer Stanhope on Rossetti's project to decorate the walls and roof of Benjamin Woodward's new Oxford Union Society debating hall. The subjects of the tempera paintings on the ten wall bays were Arthurian. Morris chose the subject of a rejected lover, "How Sir Palomydes loved La Belle Iseult with exceeding great love out of measure, and how she loved not him again but Sir Tristram." He also designed and in large measure executed the decoration of the roof (which was painted again by him to a new design in 1875).

While in Oxford he met, through Rossetti, the strikingly handsome seventeen-year-old Jane Burden, who posed in costume for several of the painters and became Morris's wife in 1859. Perhaps two of the thirty poems in *The Defence of Guenevere and Other Poems,* published (at Morris's expense) in March 1858, were inspired by her: "Praise of My Lady" and "Summer Dawn." They treat her as a divine object of supplication. Four of the poems, including the title poem, are derived from Morris's reading of Sir Thomas Malory's *Morte d'Arthur;* seven, including "Sir Peter Harpdon's End" and "The Haystack in the Floods," are set in fourteenth-century France and owe their inspiration to the *Chronicles* of Jean Froissart; another nine, including "A Good Knight in Prison" and "Riding Together," are also medieval, but not specific in period or inspiration; and eight, including "Rapunzel," are set in a nightmarish faery world. Twenty-five years later Morris called these early poems "exceedingly young also and very medieval." Like John Ruskin (a major influence on his artistic and political thinking) and G. E. Street, Morris reserved his greatest admiration for the art and architecture of the thirteenth century. Even Red House, planned during a visit to northern France with Webb and Burne-Jones in 1858, was conceived in thirteenth-century style. When it was built in 1860 at Bexleyheath, Kent, some ten miles from London, its steeply pitched roofs, gabled entrance porches, and

Jane Burden Morris, 1865, posed by Dante Gabriel Rossetti. Rossetti introduced Burden and Morris, who married in 1859. By the late 1860s Jane Morris had become the most important influence on Rossetti's emotional life.

stone seats followed Ruskin's prescriptions on domestic Gothic in *Lectures on Architecture and Painting* (1854), and its unrelieved use of red brick without stucco seemed quite startling.

The difficulty of furnishing Red House adequately provided a major impetus to the establishment of the firm of Morris, Marshall, Faulkner & Co. in 1861. The partners were Morris, Rossetti, Burne-Jones, Ford Madox Brown, Webb, Faulkner, and Peter Paul Marshall. Deeply resented at first by established professional firms, it announced itself as ready to execute wall decoration, architectural carving, stained glass, metal work, jewelry, furniture, embroidery, and household articles. The firm's success at the International Exhibition, South Kensington, in 1862, led to a constant stream of contracts for stained glass in churches. Morris designed in all mediums himself and with Webb supervised all the orders. He was, in fact, closely involved with the varied work of the firm for the rest of his life. In 1865, finding that severe illness prevented his driving to and from Bexleyheath each day, he reluctantly gave up Red House and

settled over the firm's workshops at 26 Queen Square, Bloomsbury.

Rossetti used to speak of a "blue closet" at Queen Square "entirely crammed with Morris's poetry from floor to ceiling." After a lull in 1859-1860, his production continued to be prodigious. At one time he intended to write a complete Arthurian cycle, combining the Arthurian poems of the first volume with some others written at the same time but not published. This project was, however, abandoned, perhaps because of the success of Alfred, Lord Tennyson's *Idylls of the King,* the first volume of which appeared in 1859. Another abandoned project of 1857 and 1858 was "Scenes from the Fall of Troy," a dramatic series in blank verse. It is a medievalized story sympathetic to the Trojans, with many vivid painterly descriptions of scenes and Morris's characteristic juxtaposition of love and violence. But the series also marks the beginning of a sense of despair at the futility of life that was to color most of Morris's subsequent work.

About 1861 Morris turned back energetically to poetry. For the next eight or nine years he was occupied with *The Earthly Paradise,* the longest poem in the English language. The plan remained the same over the period, though the contents were subject to change and rearrangement. "Certain gentlemen and mariners of Norway" set out at the time of the Black Death to find the Earthly Paradise. After many years of traveling they come as old men to "some Western land" where they are well received by the Greek-speaking residents. There they and the inhabitants alternate in telling each other stories over a twelve-month period. Twice a month they meet, once to hear a tale from the inhabitants' storehouse of Byzantine Greek tales, once to hear a story from the Wanderers' fund of medieval stories. And to introduce each month there is a song lyric, often incorporating, as J. W. Mackail, Morris's biographer, said, "an autobiography so delicate and so outspoken that it must needs be left to speak for itself." The reference is to the fact that over the period of publication of *The Earthly Paradise* (1868-1870) it became clear to Morris and all his friends that his wife and Rossetti were deeply in love.

Apart from the verses for the months, the stories themselves are largely about the search for love. The presiding goddesses are Artemis and Aphrodite, who are time and time again glimpsed by characters, consulted by them, worshiped, or listened to for advice. The conduct of the tales is languid and dreamlike, owing more to Chaucer's dream narratives (particularly *The Legend of Good Women*) than to the *Canterbury Tales,* which *The Earthly Paradise* resembles only in framework.

The story intended as the first of the classical tales told by the Elders of the land was *The Life and Death of Jason.* In length, however, it outgrew its place and was published separately, at Morris's expense, in June 1867. The *London Sunday Times* reviewer, Joseph Knight, expressed some surprise at the marked change of mood from Morris's first volume: "So completely has the fame of Mr. Morris been associated with Gothic art that it is not without a twinge of pain we see him desert it for Classic." As with much of the classical material in *The Earthly Paradise,* one of the main sources was Lemprière's *Classical Dictionary,* though Morris departed from this and other sources he used in having the heroes escape from the avenging Aeetes across central Europe up one of the Black Sea rivers then overland to one of the Baltic rivers. This route, along which they encounter primitive tribes, is in a sense a presage of his later interest in the Germanic tribes depicted in the prose romances *A Tale of the House of the Wolfings* (1889) and *The Roots of the Mountains* (1890). The characterization of Medea is also

noteworthy. Some deep-seated quality in Morris caused him almost always to sympathize with his female characters, ill-treated, traduced, or wounded as they often are, and to develop them more than the male ones. He was much more attracted to Medea as, in May Morris's words, a "woman weak in the very strength of her love" than to the "rather second-rate" hero.

The Life and Death of Jason introduces in Morris's work the sense of life as an endlessly repeated pattern. Fate imposes a pattern on human life that reduces the importance of individual differences, actions, and inspirations. That pattern repeats itself inexorably and endlessly. It is partially concealed, too complicated to be comprehended by the people it affects; its slight variations overthrow expectations and defy prediction. Happiness will assuredly be followed by misery, which one fears, and in misery one may hope for happiness. The sense of inevitable repetition has its visual analogue in a structural device that Morris began to use in his flat-pattern designing at the end of the 1860s: the serpentine line or curve of contraflexure.

In his own day *The Earthly Paradise* was easily the most popular of Morris's works. It was a favorite for reading aloud, perhaps because its uniformity

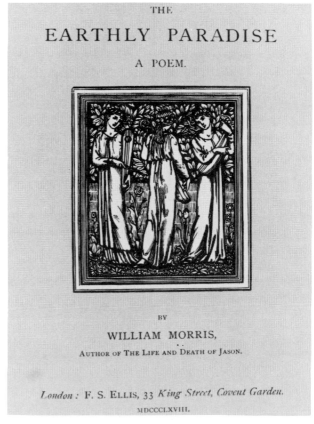

Title page with Morris's engraving Three Musicians

of sentiment allowed other activities to be undertaken simultaneously. Despite its great length of 42,000 lines (after several complete or partially complete tales had been discarded from the framework), it has only one mood, one theme, one pervasive set of sentiments, one group of ideas. Sorrow in life and in the contemplation of death is its theme, melancholy its characteristic mood. Morris's characters yearn for peace and stillness, as do his figures in stained glass or other decoration. They are isolated and lonely creatures.

Morris discarded one prologue for *The Earthly Paradise* written in jaunty octosyllabic quatrains more like his early verse. Its replacement was in languid decasyllabic couplets. In addition to the first prologue, other stories in *The Earthly Paradise* written during the first half of the 1860s were *Cupid and Psyche, The Lady of the Land, The Land East of the Sun and West of the Moon, The Son of Croesus, The Doom of King Acrisius, The Proud King, The Watching of the Falcon, The Hill of Venus,* and *The Writing on the Image,* all apparently done before *The Life and Death of Jason.* Of the later stories, the most admired was *The Lovers of Gudrun,* derived from Morris's study of the Icelandic sagas under the guidance of Eiríkr Magnússon at the end of the 1860s.

Every story in *The Earthly Paradise* concerns the search for the conditions that make life happy. In the early ones, dismay is often expressed at the thought that even the happiest human condition must be vitiated by the fearful certainty of approaching death or at least change toward unhappiness. By the end of the sequence of poems, these factors, though not denied, have been mitigated by stoic and epicurean considerations. Change and development have been accepted as inevitable, and the mere fact of acceptance has made them seem somehow more manageable. Human restlessness, dissatisfaction, and desire for knowledge and experience (even when forbidden) have been recognized as unavoidable causes of change, and solace has been sought in the process of search and discovery itself as an alternative to the unattainable desire for eternal happy changelessness. If there is a measure of permanence available, it is to be found through art rather than through deeds.

The alternation of states of happiness and sorrow in the tales, the pattern of life that swings from one to the other in a constant wave motion and the endless repetition of this pattern until it is cut short in individual lives by death, applies in the stories to groups of characters as well as individuals. The major characters are happy together and sorrowful together: their individual patterns run in sym-

pathetic phase with one other. Morris accomplishes the balance in part by underplaying the villains. Villainy in a narrative implies causation and often motivation, but Morris was not interested in either. His heroes and heroines meet their disasters less through the operation of baleful human activity than through that of mindless fate; changes from fortune to misfortune are generally inexplicable and unpredictable. There are villains in some of the stories—Samuel in *The Man Born to be King,* the foster parents in *The Fostering of Aslaug,* and Sthenoboea in *Bellerophon at Argos,* for instance—but their part is usually of minor and local importance (that is, they are powerless to prevent the fated outcome of the narrative), and they are generally people who are incapable of joy themselves and hence are outside the operation of the wave-pattern of emotion.

Some of the later stories—those written at the time of Rossetti's infatuation with Jane Morris—have touches of eroticism previously absent. Whereas reviewers had praised *The Life and Death of Jason* for its delicate transformation of the myth to make it suitable for the entire household, a few murmurs were raised about *The Lady of the Land, Ogier the Dane,* and *The Lovers of Gudrun.* Morris has much to say about the state of mind and feeling when a character is in love: the emphasis is not on scene, incident, or novelty, but on the commonality of mood. It is, indeed, the concentration on mood and emotion that can make *The Earthly Paradise,* especially the later tales, seem enervated and lax. Even Morris himself said that, with the exception of *The Lovers of Gudrun,* the later tales were "all too long and flabby."

At the same time he was finishing *The Earthly Paradise,* Morris was beginning the Icelandic studies that were to introduce him to a new and disturbing ethos and set of moral principles. As he came to think of publishing translations of the sagas, he settled into a sequence of work where Magnússon wrote a rough literal translation which Morris then turned into prose of biblical cadence and Saxon diction. The first saga they worked on together was *The Eyrbyggia Saga,* which Morris wrote out in a calligraphic hand and presented to Georgiana Burne-Jones in 1872. (He had become very close to the wife of his best friend during the period of Jane's dalliance with Rossetti and Edward Burne-Jones's affair with Marie Zambaco. His affection was expressed in some unpublished poems as well as in the gift of beautiful calligraphic manuscripts.) The first saga to be published was, however, *The Saga of Gunnlaug the Wormtongue,* which appeared in

" That spring was she just come to her full height,
Low-bosomed yet she was, and slim and light,
Yet scarce might she grow fairer from that day :
Gold were the locks wherewith the wind did play,
Finer than silk, waved softly like the sea
After a three days' calm, and to her knee
Wellnigh they reached : fair were the white hands laid
Upon the door-posts where the dragons played."

Morris's frontispiece for The Lovers of Gudrun, *an excerpt from* The Earthly Paradise *published in Boston, 1870*

the *Fortnightly Review* in January 1869; the major work at this time was Morris and Magnússon's translation *The Story of the Volsungs and Niblungs,* published in book form the following year.

In company with Magnússon, Faulkner, and W. H. Evans, Morris made a journey through Iceland in 1871. This, with a second visit made in 1873, when he saw more of the interior, provided material for some of Morris's later poetry. On each visit he kept a journal, both of which were included by May Morris in the *Collected Works* (1910-1915).

Before the first visit he had begun a prose novel of current life in England (published in 1982 as *The Novel on Blue Paper*), but he found it uncongenial and laid it aside. On his return from the first visit to Iceland he began another long poem, *Love Is Enough* (1873), written, like *The Earthly Paradise,* according to a formula. This poem, Morris's only venture into what Rossetti called "a sort of masque," gave him a great deal of trouble. Its construction is disconcertingly complex; its versification is experimental; it attracted few reviews and their authors felt bound to express puzzlement. In the 1880s Morris explicitly rejected the thesis stated in the title. Morris had intended that both *The Earthly Paradise* and *Love Is Enough* be illustrated with

LOVE AND DEATH

IN the white-flowered hawthorn brake
Love be merry for my sake;
Twine the blossoms in my hair
Kiss me where I am most fair
Kiss me, sweet, for who knoweth
What thing cometh after death!

NAY thy garlanded gold hair
Hides thee where thou art most fair,
Hides the rose-tinged hills of snow—
O my love I hold thee now!
Kiss me, sweet, for who knoweth
What thing cometh after death!

SHALL we weep for a dead day
Or set sorrow in our way?
Hidden in my golden hair
Wilt thou weep that the days wear?
Kiss me, sweet, for who knoweth
What thing cometh after death!

From A Book of Verse, *written, illuminated, and bound by Morris for Georgiana Burne-Jones in 1870*

woodcuts by Burne-Jones. In both cases the scheme was too costly (at a time when the dividend on Morris's inherited shares in Devon Great Consols was petering out).

The central story of *Love Is Enough* concerns a king, Pharamond, who is engaged on an all-absorbing and ultimately successful quest to find love. The play about him is enclosed within a series of inductions and postludes; it is virtually a play within a play within a play, and there are in addition two chorus figures, the Music and Love. The tableau of Pharamond's life is performed before a newly married emperor and empress, who spend the time before the play begins in observing and commenting on the real-life love of the player-king and player-maiden. Meanwhile the emperor and empress are observed by two "peasant-folk," Giles and Joan, who, having come to see the pageantry, interpret the life of the rulers in terms of their own love-relationship.

The subtitle, *The Freeing of Pharamond,* refers to the purification of Pharamond's spirit of all mundane concerns, a freeing from despair, hopelessness, and unalleviated depression. Indeed, as the central play proceeds—that is, as it becomes more distant from the domesticity of Giles and Joan and the worldly pomp and tribulation of the emperor and empress—it becomes less and less about carnal love. The quest becomes not so much one for satisfaction in human love as one for the inner life, the Romantic life of the spirit that may be pursued to the exclusion of worldly concerns. In this sense Love is not only enough; it is the whole of the self as well. In this sense, too, Morris was later to regard Love as not enough: he came to think that work for social justice was too important to be set aside for the life of the spirit.

Unlike all Morris's earlier poems, *Love Is Enough* completely suppresses scenes of violence and aggression. As a result, the plot is somewhat flaccid and limp. It is a very static poem, with the language constantly drawing attention to itself. Balanced lines, half-lines, and phrases; repeated words; alliteration; and end-stopped feminine line-endings are constantly recurring features. Each of the levels of the work has a different metrical form allotted to it. The result is that, although something of a metrical tour de force, the poem has never excited great enthusiasm.

Its subject and timing have, however, excited biographical speculation. Pharamond sets out from his kingdom leaving it in charge of the Constable. When he returns he finds that the Constable has usurped it. He considers the prospect of fighting

for it, but decides that his newfound self-realization is more precious than the retrieval of an ungrateful kingdom. Biographically interpreted, the kingdom is Jane Morris, the Constable Rossetti, Pharamond Morris, and the journey the first visit to Iceland. This theory is given some support by the fact that just before he set out for Iceland Morris took a joint tenancy with Rossetti of Kelmscott Manor, an early-seventeenth-century house some thirty miles upstream from Oxford. Jane and Rossetti moved in while Morris was away. The poem was begun shortly after his return.

The joint tenancy with Rossetti was terminated in 1874. Later the same year, Morris put pressure on the partners of Morris, Marshall, Faulkner & Co. to recognize the fact that the conduct of the business was now entirely his. They were paid for their designs, but in Morris's view, considering the minute capital they had invested, they did nothing to merit a share in the profits. With some acrimony, the firm was reconstituted as Morris & Co. Madox Brown, Rossetti, and Marshall insisted on being paid £1000 compensation each for their loss of profits. From this time until his involvement in Socialism in the 1880s Morris put much effort and time into trying to make the business profitable. In 1873 he had designed the firm's first chintz, "Tulip and Willow," though he was so dissatisfied with its printing by a commercial firm that he did not release it until he had the equipment, many years later, to print it himself.

He continued to work on Icelandic translations, working with Magnússon to bring out *Three Northern Love Stories* in 1875, and on calligraphic manuscripts. His ambition to produce a folio vellum manuscript of the *Aeneid* caused him to set about a complete translation from the Latin. It was published in October 1875 as *The Aeneids of Vergil Done into English Verse.*

His last major original poem was *The Story of Sigurd the Volsung and the Fall of the Niblungs,* published in November 1876. In it he returns to his favorite situation of two men in love with the same woman. (In this case there are also two women in love with the same man.) It marks a return to his poetry of violence intertwined with love, the love itself being of a wide variety of kinds. It is a poem that in many ways foreshadows future directions in Morris's life and work. It identifies the personal happiness of the hero, Sigurd, with the triumph of right and the success of his enemies with the victory of wrong. It uses apocalyptic prophecies similar to those of *Love Is Enough* to look forward to a time when right will finally vanquish wrong. Whereas in

The families of Morris and Edward Burne-Jones at Burne-Jones's home, The Grange, Fulham. Back row: Burne-Jones's father, Edward Richard Jones; Margaret Burne-Jones; Burne Jones; May Morris; Morris. Front row: Philip Burne-Jones; Georgiana Burne-Jones; Jane Morris; Jenny Morris.

The Earthly Paradise the failure of the Wanderers to achieve their goal had been accepted as final, here the fall in the fortunes of the hero is counterbalanced by the belief that a new order will succeed one day.

The thirteenth-century author of the *Völsunga Saga* had imposed substantial order and coherence on his disparate materials. He had provided a degree of chronological order and of motivation for the separate stories used as sources. Morris, working in the epic rather than the saga genre, imposed further order. He divided the work into four books, "Sigmund," "Regin," "Brynhild," and "Gudrun," beginning the story with King Volsung, the grandfather of Sigurd, and ending with the disasters of Gudrun's marriage to King Atli after the death of Sigurd. He omitted some, but possibly not enough, of the tangential material. In the first book the theme is conflict between instinctive, dynastic loyalty to one's brethren and the formal loyalty acquired due to an oath voluntarily taken or to a husband willingly married. The second book shows Sigurd increasing in knowledge and strength and successfully undertaking the quest to recover the treasure of Andvari the Elf. He slays the dragon Fafnir and plights his troth to the warrior-maiden, Brynhild. With considerable rearrangement of the order of the saga, Morris opens his third book in a new setting, the Burg of the Niblungs. Sigurd arrives and, through witchcraft, falls in love with Gudrun and marries her. Further witchcraft causes him to woo Brynhild on behalf of Gunnar, his brother-in-law. When Brynhild discovers the deception she arranges that the Niblungs will kill Sigurd. So the man who brought fame to the Niblungs is killed by them at the instigation of the woman he loves. She acts partly to spite Sigurd's wife, who had boasted of her marital bliss. Both women are grief-stricken. Gudrun flees into the wilderness and Brynhild kills herself.

In book four, Gudrun first uses her new husband, King Atli, to avenge herself on her brothers for killing Sigurd, then kills Atli and flings herself into the sea. At the end, Morris summarizes his view of the events: Sigurd's battles have been against "the foes of God"; his first encounter with Brynhild is the wakening of Love; the destruction and confusion that result from his marriage to Gudrun are caused by "the broken troth" to Brynhild; and the whole story represents a movement from delight in heroic achievement to a sense of inexorable doom. Death comes violently in this poem, but it is no longer feared as in the early poems and *The Earthly Paradise*. Here there is no attempt to escape from the common lot by seeking a new land or a new life. Instead, the characters press on to accept their doom. It is a stoic acceptance of fate or prophecy, not positive decision, that gets them into adventures. Honor is of more consequence than death, and death may even be welcomed as a release. This is, as Carlyle said of Scandinavian paganism, "the creed of our fathers; the men whose blood still runs in our veins, whom doubtless we still resemble in so many ways."

In many respects, Morris's narrative powers are shown here at their highest point of development. He has supplied motivation and consistency to the chroniclelike characters and plot. He outlines many times situations full of the seeds of passion and drama, but, unlike Browning, he was not interested in the subtle building up of character, nor was he concerned with using a character as a mouthpiece for ideas, as Matthew Arnold did in *Empedocles on Etna*. For Morris, the story, the doom-dictated action, was all important.

The hexameters are different from anything previously found in English prosody. The line is divided into two sections, each with three strong beats, by a heavy caesura; the number and placement of unaccented syllables are not fixed, so that there is a mixture of duple and triple rhythms, with triple predominating in the first half, duple in the second. The first half almost always ends with a weak beat, the second carries a couplet rhyme. As a result of this differentiation, the first half, with its leisurely, galloping movement, tends to be used for providing information, description, or names; the second half, with its more insistent beat, for concise summaries, alternative possibilities, additional details, consequences, results, interpretations, or swift action. It is a meter Morris used also in the occasional verse of *A Tale of the House of the Wolfings* (1889), in some sections of *The Pilgrims of Hope* (1886), and (in a slightly more regular version) in the Socialist poem "The Day is Coming," published in *Chants for Socialists* (1884).

Morris's last volume of poetry, a collection of shorter works, was *Poems by the Way*, published in

Morris in 1880

1891 as the second book from the Kelmscott Press, the handpress established by him for producing limited editions of fine printing. The fifty-five poems date from 1861 to 1891. They include several from the period of composition of *The Earthly Paradise* (including one or two incorporated in it); some translations from Icelandic and Danish and other original poems based on similar material; some poems, such as "Hope Dieth: Love Liveth," clearly addressed to Georgiana Burne-Jones and commenting on their hopeless love for each other; verses written for paintings and decorative objects such as painted tiles, tapestries, and embroideries; six Socialist songs; the melancholy Socialist verse-novel *The Pilgrims of Hope;* and a few ballads.

In the period between *The Story of Sigurd* and *Poems by the Way,* Morris's life had been full of strenuous activity. While composing *Sigurd* he had been learning the craft of dyeing, particularly the difficult and almost defunct indigo-vat process, and experimenting with other vegetable dyes that had almost entirely been driven out of use in England by the anilines. In the later 1870s, he put his knowledge to use in the production of textiles. His most notable new ventures were in carpet weaving and the revival of the high-warp loom for tapestry. Morris was now able to dye wool, cotton, and silk for such textiles. The expansion of the work of the firm into these areas resulted in a move of the workshops to Merton Abbey, to the west of London, in 1881. A showroom had been opened at 449 Oxford Street in 1877, so the Queen Square premises, the home of the firm for its first twenty years, were no longer needed. Morris's family had been driven from Queen Square some years before because of the need to expand the workshops there. Since late 1872 they had lived at Horrington House, Turnham Green. At the end of 1878 they moved about a mile to the riverbank, to Morris's last home, the Retreat (renamed Kelmscott House), on the Upper Mall at Hammersmith, a house now owned by the William Morris Society. In the coach house and stables were installed carpet looms, later used for the famous Hammersmith carpets.

In the later 1870s Morris was also becoming interested in political and social activity. In 1876, following a long letter to the *London Daily News* deploring British support for Turkish interests in the Balkans, he became an office-bearer of the newly formed Eastern Question Association, dedicated to the prevention of war with Russia. In 1877 a letter to the *Athenaeum* on the destruction of medieval buildings in the name of restoration suggested the establishment of a society "to keep a watch on old monuments." The suggestion resulted in the Society for the Protection of Ancient Buildings, which Morris usually referred to as the Anti-Scrape. In 1879 he became treasurer of the National Liberal League, a confederation of radical workers' societies. In January 1883, disgusted at the timidity of liberal policies and now counting himself a Socialist, he joined the Democratic Federation (later the Social Democratic Federation). He believed, like Ruskin, that art could not flourish in an unjust society and that the dehumanization of life attendant on the industrialization of society could only be corrected by a thoroughgoing revolution. Morris gave much of his time to speaking both at indoor meetings and in the streets, to writing, and to supporting the Federation's journal, *Justice*. In 1884, through distrust of H. M. Hyndman, the founder of the Federation, and jealousy at Hyndman's attempts to incorporate all socialist associations in Britain, a breakaway organization was formed, with Morris reluctantly in the forefront. It was the Socialist League, and Morris started a new paper as its organ, the *Commonweal*. When the Socialist League dwindled in numbers and fell into the hands of Anarchists in 1890, Morris withdrew

and set up the independent Hammersmith Socialist Society, which met twice a week at Kelmscott House.

Morris's full-blooded Socialist activities saw him twice arrested. In 1885 he was charged with disorderly conduct and striking a policeman during the trial of eight men who had been arrested at a street meeting. The magistrate discharged him. In the following year he was fined one shilling on a charge of obstructing the highway by refusing to stop addressing a street meeting. The confrontation in Trafalgar Square between demonstrators and combined forces of police and soldiers on Bloody Sunday, 13 November 1887, and episodes in subsequent years when strikers were fired on by soldiers, together with the internal strife of the Socialist organizations, convinced Morris that the forces of government were still too strong for a successful revolution to occur. He came to think that the most immediate, if transient, need was a strong Socialist party in Parliament, though his declining health in the 1890s and his own distaste for politics prevented his taking any active part in its establishment.

The first few years of his intense Socialist activity had left him very little time for writing imaginative literature. He did, however, write several songs for singing at Socialist gatherings and the loosely constructed verse-novel *The Pilgrims of Hope,* which first appeared in serial form in the *Com-*

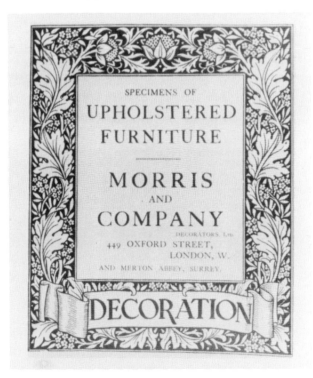

Cover for a catalogue circulated by Morris's firm in the 1880s

of his house which was new and goodly
sniffing the sweet scent of the morning. he
was clad in a goodly long gown of grey
with silver meet for the summer tide - for little
he wrought with his hands and much
with his tongue he was a man of 40 summers
black bearded and ruddy and his name was
Clement Chapman When he saw Ralph he
smiled kindly, and came and held his stirrup
and said welcome lord! art thou come to
eat and drink and give a message in a poor
pedlar's house. Yea said Ralph smiling (for
he was hungry: I will eat & drink with thee
and kiss my gossip
and go my way. And he got off his horse &
the Carle led him into his house And if it
were goodly without within it was better
For there was a fair chamber panelled
with carven work well wrought, and a cupboard
of no sorry vessels of silver, and the chairs & stools
as fair as might be, no Kings might be better
and the windows were glazed and there were
flowers & & posies in them and
the bed was hung with goodly webs from
over sea such as the Soldan loveth Also
whereas his ware bowers were hard by the chamber

Manuscript page from the first draft of Morris's 1896 romance The Well at the World's End *(H. Buxton Forman,* The Books of William Morris Described, with Some Account of His Doings in Literature and in the Allied Crafts, *1897)*

monweal. *The Pilgrims of Hope* concerns two lovers who travel from the country to London. Attending a Radical meeting addressed by a figure identifiable as Morris himself—"grizzled," "thickset and short, and dressed in shabby blue"—the young man, Richard, is converted to communism. His street preaching results in dismissal from his work as a joiner, but he continues to denounce imperialist wars and to praise the Paris Commune. Saved from wretched unemployment by a new friend, Arthur, Richard finds that his wife has transferred her affections to the friend. He receives this news without rancor. The three of them go to help the revolution in Paris. There Arthur and the woman are killed by "the brutal war-machine"; Richard returns sadly to England, his personal tragedy damping his radical fire. The characters are purposely flat—the woman, for instance, is never even named—so that they may be spokesmen for Morris's political and social doctrines. Those doctrines made it no longer possible for him to express in his poetry the notion that life oscillated inexorably from happiness to misery. Now he had to express the hope of the inevitability of social happiness for the masses.

Toward the end of the 1880s his literary productivity gathered pace again. In 1886 and 1887 he translated the *Odyssey* into *Sigurd* hexameters, a competent and accurate piece of work but loose and wavering in effect. The historical romance *A Dream of John Ball* appeared in 1888, accompanied by another very brief example of the same genre, *A King's Lesson*. They were followed in the next year by the first of his long prose romances, *A Tale of the House of the Wolfings*, which goes farther back for its setting than the Icelandic sagas, being concerned with the warfare between the Germanic tribes and the imperial Romans. The best of these dream or quest romances is probably *The Well at the World's End* (1896), a relaxed joyous quest for the abundant life symbolized by the well. Morris had contributed prose romances to the *Oxford and Cambridge Magazine* very early in his literary career, so in a sense he was returning to his literary origins. If a single major influence can be detected it is probably Grimm's *Teutonic Romances*, always one of his "Bibles" according to May Morris. The late prose romances have been repopularized in large part through their influence on such writers as Charles Williams, C. S. Lewis, and J. R. R. Tolkien.

News from Nowhere, the utopian pastoral romance published first in the *Commonweal* and then in book form in 1890, is a dream of a Communist England, with parliament abolished and self-sufficient communities enjoying useful work in the making of beautiful things, something like an unviolent version of the communal Wolfing society. But it has come about only through bitter warfare. The struggle is, however, in the past, and the dreamer experiences an idyllic voyage upriver to Kelmscott Manor.

Morris's last major artistic venture was the establishment of his own press at Hammersmith, made possible in part by the saving of some £500 per annum with which he had previously supported the Socialist League and the *Commonweal*. He designed for the Kelmscott Press three fonts of type (Golden, based on the Venetian style of Nicholas Jenson; Troy, A Germanic gothicized type; and Chaucer, a small version of Troy) together with a prolific series of borders and ornamental capitals. The first volume published was one of his own romances, *The Story of the Glittering Plain* (1891), the most sumptuous the edition of Chaucer (1896) with woodcuts by Burne-Jones. In all, fifty-three books were issued, constituting a major contribution to the history of type and page design.

Morris was also an avid and expert collector of medieval manuscripts and early printed books. Although he was apparently short of ready money and sold some books and most of his manuscripts about 1880, he became an active buyer again in 1890. At his death his library included the late-twelfth-century Huntingfield Psalter, the late-thirteenth-century "Windmill" Psalter, and the early-fourteenth-century Tiptoft Missal.

He continued to accept lecturing engagements until shortly before his death. In addition to his Socialist lectures, he gave many lectures on the arts and crafts, associating the production of the best specimens (as did Ruskin) with the quality of life of a society. The Arts and Crafts Society and the Art Workers' Guild were founded on principles derived largely from his lectures and from the works of Ruskin.

His many activities caused his health to decline steadily from 1891 on. He suffered from nervous prostration, sleeplessness, and diabetes. A sea voyage to Norway in 1896 was a burden rather than a refreshment, and he died at Kelmscott House, Hammersmith, on 3 October that year. The burial took place in the churchyard at Kelmscott three days later.

Morris's ability in so many fields and in particular his superlative ability as a designer of flat patterns tends to overshadow his poetic achievements. In his own lifetime he was sometimes dismissed as a "poetic upholsterer" and his poems were compared to his wallpapers—though, as G. K.

Page from the Kelmscott Press edition of The Works of Geoffrey Chaucer, *with woodcuts by Burne-Jones*

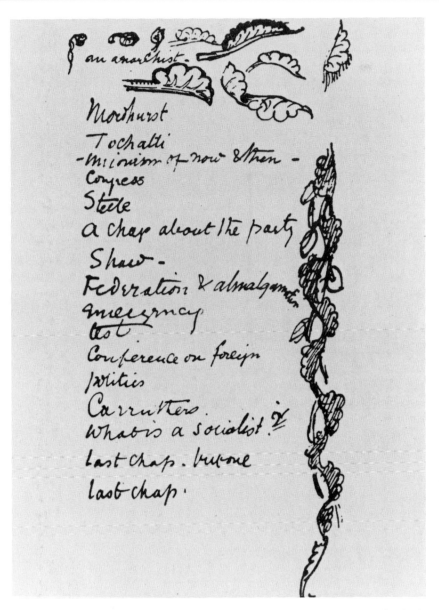

Morris's notes for his last public lecture, "Our Socialist Party," delivered to the Hammersmith Socialist Society on 5 January 1896
(Ian Bradley, William Morris and His World, *1978)*

Chesterton subsequently pointed out, often the wallpapers were so magnificent that the intended sneer turned into a compliment. The revival of critical interest in the poetry stems from the publication of E. P. Thompson's political and literary biography, *William Morris: Romantic to Revolutionary* (1955). Morris's work has come to seem much more integrated. The quest for the dream-mistress, a theme of his work from the beginning, is not mere escapism, but a literary analogue of his later struggle for a just society. The passionate condemnation of false standards in art is, as with Ruskin, tantamount to a criticism of the society that tolerates such standards. All Morris's life and work can be seen as a vigorous struggle toward a utopian stillness, unalloyed by sorrow and death. What once seemed like escapism is now seen as a practical and dedicated social endeavor toward the establishment of a just society. It was the unaffected wholeheartedness of Morris that caused Ruskin to say, "Morris is beaten gold." Wilfrid Scawen Blunt, who had become Jane Morris's lover in the late 1880s, wrote in his diary at Morris's death: "He is the most wonderful man I have known."

Letters:

The Letters of William Morris to His Family and Friends, edited by Philip Henderson (London: Longmans, Green, 1950);

The Collected Letters of William Morris, edited by Norman Kelvin, volume 1, 1848-1880 (Princeton: Princeton University Press, 1984).

Bibliographies:

H. Buxton Forman, *The Books of William Morris Described, with Some Account of His Doings in Literature and in the Allied Crafts* (London: Hollings, 1897; Chicago: Way & Williams, 1897);

Temple Scott [J. H. Isaacs], *A Bibliography of the Works of William Morris* (London: Bell, 1897);

William E. Fredeman, "William Morris & His Circle: A Selective Bibliography of Publications," *Journal of the William Morris Society,* 1 (Summer 1964): 23-33; 2 (Spring 1966): 13-26;

Fredeman, *Pre-Raphaelitism: A Bibliocritical Study* (Cambridge: Harvard University Press, 1965; London: Oxford University Press, 1965);

K. L. Goodwin, *A Preliminary Handlist of Manuscripts and Documents of William Morris* (London: William Morris Society, 1984).

Biographies:

J. W. Mackail, *The Life of William Morris,* 2 volumes (London & New York: Longmans, Green, 1898);

E. P. Thompson, *William Morris: Romantic to Revolutionary* (London: Lawrence & Wishart, 1955; New York: Monthly Review Press, 1961; new edition, London: Merlin Press, 1977; New York: Pantheon, 1977);

Philip Henderson, *William Morris: His Life, Work and Friends* (London: Thames & Hudson, 1967; New York: McGraw-Hill, 1967);

Jack Lindsay, *William Morris: His Life and Work* (London: Constable, 1975).

References:

R. Page Arnot, *William Morris, the Man and the Myth* (London: Lawrence & Wishart, 1964);

G. B. J. [Georgiana Burne-Jones], *Memorials of Edward Burne-Jones,* 2 volumes (London: Macmillan, 1904);

Blue Calhoun, *The Pastoral Vision of William Morris: The Earthly Paradise* (Athens: University of Georgia Press, 1975);

Gerald H. Crow, *William Morris, Designer,* special issue, *Studio* (Winter 1934);

A. R. Dufty, Introduction to *William Morris: The Story of Cupid and Psyche, with Illustrations by Edward Burne-Jones,* 2 volumes (London: Clover Hill Editions, 1974);

Joseph R. Dunlap, *The Book That Never Was: William Morris, Edward Burne-Jones and "The Earthly Paradise"* (New York: Oriole Editions, 1971);

Peter Faulkner, *Against the Age: An Introduction to William Morris* (London: Allen & Unwin, 1980);

Faulkner, ed., *William Morris: The Critical Heritage* (London & Boston: Routledge & Kegan Paul, 1973);

Delbert R. Gardner, *An "Idle Singer" and His Audience: A Study of William Morris's Poetic Reputation in England, 1858-1900* (The Hague & Paris: Mouton, 1975);

K. L. Goodwin, "Unpublished Lyrics of William Morris," *Yearbook of English Studies,* 5 (1975): 190-206;

Frederick Kirchhoff, *William Morris* (Boston: Twayne, 1979);

Jessie Kocmanová, *The Poetic Maturing of William Morris from "The Earthly Paradise" to "The Pilgrims of Hope"* (Prague: Státní Pedagogické Nakladatelství, 1964);

Paul Meier, *La Pensee utopique de William Morris* (Paris: Editions Sociales, 1972); translated by Frank Gubb as *William Morris: The Marxist Dreamer,* 2 volumes (Hassocks, Sussex: Harvester Press, 1978; Atlantic Highlands, N.J.: Humanities Press, 1978);

Paul Needham, ed., *William Morris and the Art of the Book* (New York: Pierpont Morgan Library, 1976; London: Oxford University Press, 1976);

Charlotte H. Oberg, *A Pagan Prophet: William Morris* (Charlottesville: University Press of Virginia, 1978);

A. Charles Sewter, *The Stained Glass of William Morris and His Circle,* 2 volumes (New Haven & London: Yale University Press for the Paul Mellon Centre for Studies in British Art, 1974, 1975);

Carole Silver, *The Romance of William Morris* (Athens: Ohio University Press, 1982);

H. Halliday Sparling, *The Kelmscott Press and William Morris, Master-Craftsman* (London: Macmillan, 1924);

Paul Thompson, *The Work of William Morris* (London: Heinemann, 1967; New York: Viking, 1967);

Aymer Vallance, *The Art of William Morris: A Record* (London: Bell, 1897);

Victorian Poetry, special issue on Morris, edited by William E. Fredeman, 13 (Fall-Winter 1975);

Raymond Watkinson, *William Morris as Designer*

(London: Studio Vista, 1967; New York: Reinhold, 1967);

William Morris Society (Kew, Surrey), *Journal* (1961-   ); *Transactions* (1960-   ).

Papers:

The great bulk of Morris's literary and political manuscripts, with many letters, is in the British Library, London. Other important holdings are at the Victoria and Albert Museum, London; the William Morris Gallery, Walthamstow; the Birmingham City Museum and Art Gallery; the Fitzwilliam Museum, Cambridge; the Bodleian Library, Oxford; and the International Institute of Social History, Amsterdam. In the United States the major repositories are the Humanities Research Center of the University of Texas, Austin, and the Henry E. Huntington Library, San Marino, California; other important holdings are at the Pierpont Morgan Library, New York; the Beinecke Rare Book and Manuscript Library, Yale University; the William R. Perkins Library, Duke University; and the Sanford and Helen Berger Collection, Carmel, California.

Arthur Joseph Munby

(19 August 1828-29 January 1910)

Alan Hertz
Jesus College, Cambridge

BOOKS: *Benoni: Poems* (London: Ollivier, 1852);
Verses New and Old (London: Bell & Daldy, 1865);
A Memorial of Joseph Munby, of Clifton Holme, near York (London: Privately printed, 1875);
Dorothy: A Country Story, anonymous (London: Kegan Paul, 1880; Boston: Roberts Brothers, 1882);
Vulgar Verses, as Jones Brown (London: Reeves & Turner, 1891);
Vestigia Retrorsum (London: Eden, Remington, 1891);
Susan: A Poem of Degrees, anonymous (London: Reeves & Turner, 1893);
Ann Morgan's Love: A Pedestrian Poem (London: Reeves & Turner, 1896);
Poems: Chiefly Lyric and Elegiac (London: Kegan Paul, 1901);
Relicta: Verses (London: Dobell, 1909).

OTHER: *Faithful Servants: Being Epitaphs and Obituaries Recording Their Names and Services,* edited by Munby (London: Reeves & Turner, 1891).

Arthur Joseph Munby, born near York on 19 August 1828, was the oldest child of Joseph Munby, a prominent local solicitor and philanthropist, and Caroline Forth Munby. Munby attended St. Peter's School, York, before entering Trinity College,

Arthur Joseph Munby, circa 1860

Page from Munby's diary entry for 25 June 1870 (courtesy of the Master and Fellows of Trinity College, Cambridge)

Cambridge, in 1846. He received his B.A. in 1851, having written most of his first volume of poetry, *Benoni* (1852), while still an undergraduate. Following his father's wishes, he entered Lincoln's Inn and was called to the bar despite a distaste for the legal profession. Until 1860, when he obtained a clerkship with the Ecclesiastical Commission, Munby earned little money or recognition from law or literature and was supported by his parents.

During these years, however, the events had occurred which were to shape his life. In 1854, he met Hannah Cullwick, the maid-of-all-work with whom he maintained a chaste romance until their clandestine marriage in 1873. Five years later he had his first modest literary success when his elegiac

verses won third prize in a Burns centenary competition. Most important, he began his diary in 1859.

For the next forty years, Munby seemed merely a minor civil servant: a charming, somewhat indolent bachelor with classical tastes and poetic pretensions, moderate in his Liberal politics and tolerant, if devout, in his Anglicanism. His journal gives an exhaustive account of such a life and includes descriptions and anecdotes about most contemporary artistic and literary celebrities. Much is said about the Mauriceans and the Working Men's College, where Munby taught Latin; much about the Pre-Raphaelites and their allies. There are also surprises, including Scottish physicist James Clerk

Maxwell's views on natural selection and a portrait of Thackeray's home life by his daughter.

The diary also complements formal newspaper accounts of great public occasions, including Garibaldi's visit to London in 1864, as well as great public disasters, such as the Cotton Famine, recalled in this entry for 15 July of that year:

Walking through S. James's Park about 4 p. m., I found the open spaces of sward on either side the path thickly dotted over with strange dark objects. They were human beings; ragged men & ragged women; lying prone & motionless, not as those who lie down for rest & enjoyment, but as creatures worn out and listless.... I looked and looked; it was Dante and Virgil gazing on the damned; and still they did not move. The men were more or less tattered, but their dress was working dress, & so did not seem out of place. But the girls were clothed in what had once been finery: filthy draggled muslins; thin remnants of gay shawls, all rent and gaping; crushed and greasy bonnets of fashionable shape, with sprigs of torn flow-

Munby in 1873 with Ellen Grounds, a collier at Rose Bridge Pits, Wigan (courtesy of the Master and Fellows of Trinity College, Cambridge)

ers, bits of faded velvet, hanging from them. Their hands and faces were dirty & weather-stained; and they lay . . . sprawling about the grass in attitudes ungainly, and unfeminine, and bestial: one flat on her face, another curled up like a dog with her head between her knees; another with her knees bent under her, and her cheek on the ground, and her arms spread out stiff and awkward, on either side of her. Every pose expressed an absolute degradation and despair: and the silence & deadness of the prostrate crowd was appalling.

Hannah Cullwick, one year before her secret marriage to Munby in 1873 (courtesy of the Master and Fellows of Trinity College, Cambridge)

Munby's fascination with this scene was characteristic, for working women were the great intellectual interest and, personified by Hannah, the great passion of his life. The diary reveals a side

Munby's drawing of bait girls climbing Brail Head, Filey, from his diary, 15 October 1868 (courtesy of the Master and Fellows of Trinity College, Cambridge)

of him unknown to his family and most of his fashionable friends. Not only did he chronicle his courtship and marriage; he also persuaded Hannah to keep a journal herself and even to compose several bits of autobiography. Together they left a record of a servant's life more authentic, more detailed, more eloquent in its way than Samuel Richardson's *Pamela* or George Moore's *Esther Waters*. In addition, Munby appointed himself the student and champion of the female manual laborer.

He traveled the country sketching, photographing, and interviewing ploughgirls and pitgirls, milkmaids and fisherwomen, female sailors and acrobats, women succeeding in the most bizarre and seemingly masculine occupations. Lovingly, he catalogued details of dress and working conditions, physical skills, strength, and appearance. The twenty-four fathoms of rope—"my gift and Molly's treasure"—by which the bait girls of Filey descended the Yorkshire cliffs to reach their work symbolize the undemonstrative aid he gave such women all his life. His attitudes were often shockingly modern; in private and in public, he protested against "humanitarian" legislation and "feminist" social pressures that enforced a dainty pretense of physical incapacity on what was often the stronger sex.

Munby's poetry was not popular in his lifetime and now seems remarkable more for variety than quality. He wrote lyrics in the inflated diction of mid-Victorian magazine verse, then parodied them in the manner of C. S. Calverley. His semi-autobiographical romances, all telling of a gentleman's love for a servant, complement Coventry Patmore's ethereal feminism (*Susan*, 1893, perhaps the best of them, might be subtitled "The Angel in the Kitchen") but are no more likely to find readers today than they were in Munby's time. Munby's lyrics could have been written, and written better, by several contemporaries; his narrative poems are immediately recognizable but are repetitive and often tiresomely self-absorbed. His most attractive work is perhaps the gallery of Yorkshire personalities in *Vulgar Verses* (1891). "Eawr Liz" is typical in its sensitivity to class prejudice and its eccentric attitude to feminine charms. Here are the opening stanzas:

> If Ah was lahk them graadely gells
>   Eawr Jemmy gans te see,
> 'At maks a peep-shaw o' theirsels,
>   He'd maybe think o' me.
>
> Bud wat, thah knaws Ah's nowt o' t' soort;
>   Ah's nobbut wat Ah is;
> An' them 'at thinks te mak ma' spoort,
>   Tha ca'n ma' Boompin Liz.
>
> Aye, an' it favvers ma', doos t' naam!
>   Ah likes it, ony waa:
> For why, it's nowther sin nor shaam
>   Te worrk an' nut te plaa.
>
> Ah niver reckon'd te be nesh —
>   Ah niver wanted teah;
> Ah'd liefer leeak as stoot an' fresh
>   An' boompin as Ah deah.

After 1860, Munby's life remained outwardly undisturbed. He worked for the Ecclesiastical Commission until 1889, advancing steadily in salary and responsibility. His relationship with Hannah became increasingly intense, as did his interest in working women. Munby never told his parents about Hannah and was himself reluctant to marry.

Photograph of Munby used as the frontispiece for his 1891 poetry collection Vestigia Retrorsum

She continued to work in London and Margate and lost more than one position because of her "follower." Intelligent, sensitive, and compulsively self-abnegating, she refused to attempt less menial service: drudgery was her chosen profession. Even after their marriage, she wanted only to be her husband's slave, calling him "Massa" and blacking her face to prove her affection. By her choice, he introduced her to few of his friends and, in public, still lived as a bachelor. Most visitors to his chambers knew Hannah only as the housekeeper, and she may never even have visited the house in Surrey he bought in 1878.

In the 1880s, Hannah's health deteriorated, and Munby bought her a cottage in her native Shropshire village. He remained in the South, however, and she occasionally reentered service, perhaps out of boredom. But despite their physical estrangement, they maintained an extraordinary emotional intimacy, and Hannah dominates Munby's later poetry to the point of obsession. She died in 1909, he a year later, their secret unknown to his large family and immense circle of acquaintances. His will had not been revised after her death and, to the joy of the tabloids, revealed all. In accordance with its provisions, the boxes containing the diary and other documents remained unopened until 1950. The voluminous and invaluable contents are now in the library of Trinity College, Cambridge: in 1972 Derek Hudson prepared an excellent selection with connecting biographical narrative.

Reference:
Derek Hudson, ed., *Munby, Man of Two Worlds: The*

Life and Diaries of Arthur J. Munby, 1828-1910 (London: Murray, 1972).

Papers:
The Munby Papers are at Trinity College, Cambridge. There are letters and manuscripts at the Working Men's College, the University of London Library, the libraries of Yale University and the University of Illinois, and the British Library. York City Library has a collection of Munby family papers.

Roden Noel
(27 August 1834-26 May 1894)

William B. Thesing
University of South Carolina

BOOKS: *Behind the Veil and Other Poems* (London & Cambridge: Macmillan, 1863);

Beatrice and Other Poems (London: Macmillan, 1868);

The Red Flag and Other Poems (London: Strahan, 1872);

Livingstone in Africa (London: Low, Marston, Low & Searle, 1874);

The House of Ravensburg: A Drama (London: Daldy, Isbister, 1877);

A Little Child's Monument (London: Kegan Paul, 1881);

A Philosophy of Immortality (London: Harrison, 1882);

Songs of the Heights and Deeps (London: Stock, 1885);

Essays on Poetry and Poets (London: Kegan Paul, Trench, 1886);

A Modern Faust and Other Poems (London: Kegan Paul, Trench, 1888);

Life of Lord Byron (London: Scott, 1890);

Poor People's Christmas (London: Mathews, 1890);

Poems of the Hon. Roden Noel: A Selection, edited by Robert Buchanan (London & New York: Scott, 1892);

My Sea and Other Poems, edited by Stanley Addleshaw (London: Mathews/Chicago: Way & Williams, 1896);

Selected Poems from the Works of the Hon. Roden Noel, edited by Percy Addleshaw (London: Mathews, 1897).

Collection: *The Collected Poems of Roden Noel* (London: Kegan Paul, Trench, Trübner, 1902).

Roden Noel, English poet, critic, biographer, philosopher, humanitarian, and travel writer, was the youngest son of Charles Noel, Lord Barham, who became the first Earl of Gainsborough (second creation), and Lady Frances (Jocelyn) Noel, the daughter of the third Earl of Roden. At age twelve he was enrolled at Harrow; at fourteen, he went to Hindon in Wiltshire to study under the Reverend Charles Harbin, a private tutor. During his five-year residence in Hindon, he developed a strong interest in philosophy. At the age of twenty, he entered Trinity College, Cambridge, with the intention of studying for clerical duties.

During his college years, Noel made many trips with his parents to Italy, Germany, and France. In 1858 he graduated with the master's degree. After graduation he traveled alone for two years in the Mid-east, including Egypt, Nubia, Palestine, Palmyra, Lebanon, Greece, and Turkey. From these travel experiences he derived the subjects of such poems as "Mencheres: A Vision of Old Egypt" and "Palmyra"; he also developed religious scruples which caused him to reject a vocation in the Church.

During his travels he became seriously ill with sunstroke and was transported in a felucca to Beirut. Madame de Broë, the wife of the Swiss director

Photogravure by Annan & Sons, Glasgow. From a Photograph by H.S. Mendelssohn, London.

of the Ottoman Bank in Beirut, cared for him in their private home. This prominent couple's eldest daughter, Alice de Broë, became Noel's wife on 21 March 1863. Their marriage produced three children: a daughter, Frances, and two sons, Conrad and Eric. Eric died at the age of five, and his tragic loss was commemorated in Noel's most popular volume of verse, *A Little Child's Monument* (1881).

In 1863 and 1864 Noel attempted unsuccessfully to work in business in Beirut. As Percy Addleshaw explains in his introduction to Noel's *Selected Poems* (1897), "As a business man he was ludicrously incapable, lacking both the training and qualifications that command success." Fortunately, Noel's mother was lady-in-waiting to Queen Victoria, and through his mother's influence, he was chosen to serve as groom of Privy Chamber to the queen. He served from 1867 to 1871, when he resigned the position because of his increasing preoccupation with the sufferings of the poor and his

attraction to socialistic ideas. Although Noel traveled to France, Germany, and Italy often, he spent most of his life in England, residing many years in London. His last years were spent at Brighton until he set out once again for the Continent—this time to visit a sister-in-law. He died suddenly on 26 May 1894 of heart seizure in the railway station at Mainz, Germany. He was buried in the English Cemetery there, and the inscription on his grave reads "Roden Noel, Poet."

In terms of personality, Noel's friends picture him as low-keyed in manner but, in the words of Dr. Henry Sidgwick, intensely sensitive "to all things beautiful in Nature and all things noble and pathetic in human life." Some sketches stress that he was capable of a quick and penetrating wit. Percy Addleshaw reports: "Though his writings are surprisingly destitute of humour, his talk was sparkling enough, and he could tell an anecdote with real dramatic effect. As a reader, too, he had a strange power over his hearers." During his formative years, Noel spent carefree days in impressive natural settings at Barham Court, Kent, at Exton Park, Rutlandshire, and at Tollymore Park, the Irish estate of his grandfather Lord Roden. Nature's most rugged scenes—the sea and the mountains—attracted him especially. He was always a fine swimmer, and he climbed mountains as a member of the English Alpine Club. His sense of social justice grew increasingly stronger after 1870. As a member of the Society for the Protection of Children, he transformed an inherent sympathy for the suffering victims of industrialism into specific activities for reform. As Emily Hickey writes in "Roden Noel, Poet" (1922), "Aristocrat by birth and breeding, he was democrat by principle, based on strong conviction and spiritual sympathy, however the clash of the dual strain might make itself felt." Along these same lines, in a "Notice" for *The Collected Poems* (1902) J. Addington Symonds calls him "an impassioned singer, a philosopher of marked originality, a tender-hearted Christian, and a democrat in the noblest sense of that term." His philosophy and faith, however, passed through a series of restless developments—from boyhood Calvinism to agnosticism, from an enticing pantheism to a measure of conventional Christianity after the death of his youngest son. In both his quest for spiritual truth and for social justice, Noel was an idealist; the motto of his house which he had printed on custom stationery was "Tout bien ou rien." In fact, the "real events" of Noel's life, as Percy Addleshaw points out, "were his gradual changes of opinion on religious and socialistic questions, his literary work, and the weaning of himself from prejudices, the inevitable outcome of his aristocratic training and position. . . . His writings were in great part a commentary on his own life."

Noel's first volume, *Behind the Veil and Other Poems* (1863), begins with a long title poem which is divided into a prologue and two parts. Part one is entitled "The Order of the Unseen"; part two is designated "Progress of Divine Order in the World" and further subdivided into four books: "This Present World," "Broken Lights," "Progress," and "The Future." The development of the poem is abstract and idealistic as the poet seeks glimpses of the unseen divine order and proceeds to speculate upon the progress of that force in the world. Book four of part two is interesting in its description of an ideal city of harmony and peace. Several other poems in the volume, including "A City Boy" and "The Idiot Children," foreshadow the poet's later interests in children and suffering in the city.

Soon after the volume was published, however, Noel came to consider it a great embarrassment, and he took deliberate steps to suppress it. His sister, Lady Victoria Buxton, honored his request that the volume not be included in *The Collected Poems* (1902). The poet himself was the volume's harshest critic. Of his initial poetic effort, he later wrote: "I forbade it to be advertised and *I wanted it forgotten*. It is so very crude in style. . . . It realises your sculptor, who had no power of expression for his idea! Before this, I wrote very fluent poetry by the yard, but with no ideas in it. Then I fell back on deep thought and study of prose; and when I tried to embody this in poetry, I made this fiasco of a book."

The volume shows the religious influence of his Calvinist upbringing, the philosophical influence of Swedenborg, and the poetic influence of Shelley. The book demonstrates also the positive influence that the Mid-eastern landscape had on Noel's poetic temperament. J. A. Symonds, for example, agrees that the volume is "immature and incoherent," but he is at least partially impressed by the fact that it exhibits "an extraordinary wealth of loaded luminous description, an Oriental luxuriance and vividness of colouring, a jungle of speculations, ideas, emotions, steeped in philosophical mysticism, and glowing with rich sensuous imagery."

In the title poem of the *Beatrice* volume (1868), Noel presents a series of narrative episodes which depict a young couple's romantic plight. The hero Clement lives in a lowly villa but comes from noble stock. His desire for "venturesome experience afar" leads him to strange and remote lands—and into contact with two wily and beautiful but treacherous women. After a time he finds true love and happiness with the heroine Beatrice, "a simple country girl." They pass two idyllic years together until a villainous French duke lures the innocent lass onto his yacht, takes her to Corsica, and holds her hostage in his castle. When Clement finally encounters the duke in a melodramatic scene on "an abyss," he unmercifully stones him to death. Although Beatrice is rescued, she dies in the felucca en route to the paradisal villa she was to share with Clement in southern Italy. The remainder of the poem is important for its Romantic conventions: the hero has endless debates with his soul, examining his heroic actions through "a mental lens"; he seeks solitude on sublime mountaintops; he mingles his lost lady's remains with the organic greenness of nature; and he relives memories and even posits a spiritualism whereby her individual personality will endure eternally. After communing with her soul, he joins a local revolution "Among a noble people who uprose/To free themselves from tyranny or die." After his heroic death, his "heart" is laid beside Beatrice's "meek" one in the garden. Besides these stock Romantic devices, Noel also first employed in this poem some of his later poetic trademarks: dialogue and the device of eavesdropping, or the lone, tormented speaker overheard.

Contemporary critics used general terms to describe the title poem as "a story of power and beauty"; however, they had more specific praise for such shorter poems in the volume as "Ganymede," "Pan," and "Summer Clouds and a Swan." When it first appeared, Sainte-Beuve called "Ganymede" a minor masterpiece; in 1892 Robert Buchanan found it to be "frankly and fearlessly pagan— interpenetrated . . . with the joy and glory of mere life, with that living beauty which is primitive and instinctive." Indeed, the poem's world is that of a sensuous classical idyll:

> Azure the heaven, with rare a feathery cloud;
> Azure the sea, far-scintillating light,
> Soft, rich, like velvet yielding to the eye;
> Horizons haunted with soft dreamlike sails.

"Pan" is a philosophical poem on the transmigration of souls and the higher pantheism; the *Athenaeum* reviewer called it "a sort of grandiose pantheistic hymn to Nature" in blank verse. Other lyrics in the volume present imaginative word-pictures of the beauty to be found in either simple or sublime natural landscapes.

During the period from 1867 to 1873 Noel took himself very seriously as a young poet. On the back page of a presentation copy of *Beatrice* he wrote: "I am very anxious the book should succeed, as I have devoted myself with no common love to poetry." In 1871 he wrote to Walt Whitman, whose poetry and democratic sympathies he admired. Although Whitman sent a photograph, he did not comment on Noel's work.

The years between 1867 and 1871, when Noel served in Queen Victoria's household, were financially secure but politically unsettling to him. He became increasingly concerned with the contrasts of England's social fabric that he observed on London's streets. He leaned more and more toward equalitarian and even socialist teachings until he finally felt compelled to resign his position in the royal household because of these newly formed political opinions.

Contemporary social and political issues—such as poverty versus wealth and the Franco-Prussian War—provide the material for the poetry in his third volume, *The Red Flag and Other Poems* (1872). An ambivalent attitude that is inspired by concern but incited by fear can be seen in the eight-line poem "To the Queen": the poet addresses her majesty as "Dear lady of our loyal hearts" but feels compelled to warn her that "There is a canker in the social core." Compassion and alarm also provide the underlying structure of the volume's long title poem. The *British Quarterly Review* was especially impressed by the poet's new voice and subject matter: " 'The Red Flag' is a terrible and thunderous poem. There are fine sympathies with the sorrows of London life and wonderful knowledge of them." Likewise, J. A. Symonds in the *Academy* praised the author of "The Red Flag" for his "intense feeling for the terrible," his "realism," and his "passionate sympathy with the oppressed." Yet the poem merely presents juxtapositions of luxurious wealth and miserable poverty, overlaid with the contrast between a tenuous peace in London versus the terrible political chaos of the Paris Commune. The fragile refrain "And there is *Peace* in London!" is repeated throughout, but no coherent program for social or political reform in England is ever presented. Throughout the poem, Noel as narrator takes the part of political commentator, not active participant. The poem is divided into two nearly equal parts: an on-the-scene report of the conditions in Paris and London and a series of satirical

caricatures which expose—through the device of the eavesdropping narrator—the tenuous hypocrisy that upper- and middle-class Londoners display toward the future course of society in the two capital cities. In "The Red Flag" Noel's honest realism is far more effective than his harshly contrived satire. The poem ends on an apocalyptic note with a nightmare vision of the destruction of London. Thus, Noel urges his point on his readers: indifference or resistance to social change will only bring cataclysmic disaster to England. If urban suffering is not alleviated soon, only a divine miracle can save London.

Alfred, Lord Tennyson admired some of the other poems in the volume: he thought "Azrael: A Dream of Pleasure" was "very lovely" and ranked "A Vision of the Desert," which both yearns for and doubts the concept of individual immortality, and "The Dweller in Two Worlds" among "the finest things" he had ever read. However, the laureate thought that "The Water-Nymph and the Boy," a highly sensuous poem based on a legendary lake of enchantment in the Black Forest, was immoral. Although the water-nymph's descriptions of the nude boy bathing are as intense as her final drowning of him, such lines as "A locust leaps upon his loins!" are marred by excessive alliteration.

After addressing contemporary issues directly in the *Red Flag* volume, Noel turned to subjects that were remote in either space or time in the other two volumes that he wrote during the 1870s—*Livingstone in Africa* (1874) and *The House of Ravensburg: A Drama* (1877). In the preface to *Livingstone in Africa,* he takes pains to justify the validity of writing poetry about contemporary themes. Although he feels that his material is peculiarly "modern," "English," "poetical," and "always interesting," its uniqueness lies in the "advantage of *remoteness*—remoteness, if not in time, at least in place." David Livingstone is the romantic hero—explorer in a land that is "a long way off." In a wider sense, he is depicted in the poem as a seeker for truth and humane values.

The seven cantos of *Livingstone in Africa* are, for the most part, a solitary meditation in which Livingstone reflects upon the people, scenes, and events that filled his life: "Now in my far enchanted solitude,/My long life moves before me like a dream. . . ." He also speculates on his hopes for the social and religious future of the African natives of "the dark continent," a land of beauty and terror. As a Christian missionary and British philanthropist who was of lowly origins, Livingstone both sym-

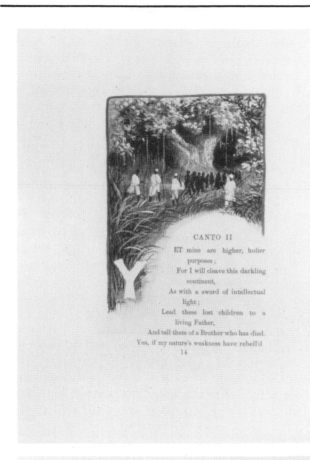

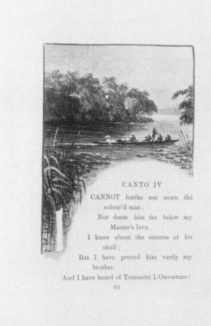

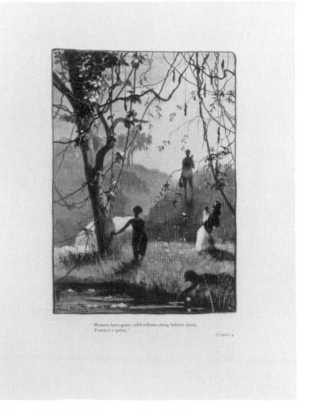

Illustrations by Hume Nisbet for the 1895 edition of Noel's Livingstone in Africa

pathized with and worked to improve the natives' conditions:

> I cannot loathe nor scorn the colour'd man;
> Nor deem him far below my Master's love.
> I know about the sutures of his skull;
> But I have proved him verily my brother.

While the explorer adamantly condemns the horrors associated with the slave trade, the poem itself is an interesting repository of nineteenth-century cultural attitudes. The African natives are depicted as mentally and spiritually backward, with some tribes still practicing human sacrifice in ceremonies replete with "frantic, half-lewd gestures." The poem fosters the doctrine of compassionate white supremacy—the "wise white friend"—and, in referring to the African natives, employs such diction as "the dwindling Dwarf," "naked savages," "feeble lowly-witted race," "poor dark savage brothers," "my blithe monkey-nimble negro boys," "rude nature's child," "these untutor'd children of the sun," "dark children," "lost children," "orphan'd sons," and "dusky children." In one memorable scene, the futility of cultural transference is depicted as a loyal native, "poor Sebwcku," superstitiously jumps overboard when he sees "fiery smoke" burst forth from a steamer and drowns symbolically in the port of civilization. Canto VII concludes the poem with an inspirational description of the explorer's death, the transport of his remains from the interior to the coast and over the sea to England, and the ceremony of his funeral in Westminster Abbey.

At least three contemporary reviewers hailed the poem as "an epic," and others were particularly attracted to its descriptions of the remote regions of Africa. The *Spectator* praised the poet's presentation of "the moral and physical nature of this great unknown world"; the *Scotsman* praised the "passages of tropical beauty, of tropical grandeur" drawn from "polymorphous African life"; and the *Weekly Review* concluded that the book was beautifully written, with descriptions that "glow with the sunshine of the tropics and the rich profusion of forest life." None of the reviewers objected to Noel's treatment of a contemporary figure as the subject of his long poem; in fact, Andrew Lang in the *Academy* specifically extolled the poet's "power of seeing the romance of contemporary history" as well as his "catholic sympathy with human life."

The House of Ravensburg: A Drama was Noel's sole attempt at writing extended poetic drama. Whereas *Livingstone in Africa* was remote in space,

The House of Ravensburg was remote in time, with the action taking place in England and Switzerland during the Peasants' War of the early fifteenth century. Although actual persons are referred to, the drama is not primarily historical. In fact, supernatural elements influence key actions in the work. Noel held his tragedy in high regard and conceived its characters in grand terms. In a letter to Havelock Ellis he wrote: "*Ravensburg* is the most human thing I have done, and expresses my pity for all tremendous problems of human destiny. *Ravensburg* expresses the idea of Nemesis or Heredity which so got hold of the Greeks and which I believe in as strongly—adapted to more modern ideas." Count Sigismund is the central figure in the tragedy; he is the troubled and tempted soul who suffers retribution and rebuke. After his death, the curse is passed on to his son, Ralph. The drama's action is fast-paced but often tends to melodrama. The scene set in a "dim-lit dungeon" with its "Iron Virgin," an instrument of torture and death, is perhaps the best example of the use of melodramatic and supernatural elements as the imprisoned Ralph discourses with the Phantom of Sigismund. The father on his return visit to earth suffers a double retribution as he witnesses and feels personal responsibility for the sins and sufferings of his son, who is now under the inherited curse. To add a dimension of comic relief, several prose speeches are given to commoners in the course of the high drama. In the end, a purgatorial climax sets the wheels of redemption in motion. Contemporary reception of the work was mixed: the *Spectator* found much of the volume to be "pale, indistinct, and blurred," but a few critics felt that it had considerable dramatic power and one even compared it favorably to Shakespeare's *Hamlet.*

From 1877 to 1881 was a period of intense personal grief and redirection for Noel. In January 1877, his youngest son, Eric, died at the age of five after a brief illness. Despair and doubt darkened the poet's outlook. As he reported: "For more than a year, I cared for nothing, not literature, not even Nature." He was able, however, to record his thoughts and feelings in a series of lyrics composed during the three years following the tragic event. In 1881 the forty-two poems were assembled for what became his best-known volume—*A Little Child's Monument.*

To read *A Little Child's Monument* is to experience Victorian sentimentality at its fullest indulgence. The poet's unrestrained outpouring of grief is immediate and largely unrefined by any controlling artistic unity or structure; his evocation of lingering memories of his young son and nostalgic haunts, from remote Alpine peaks to a London toy store, is continuous throughout the work. Although more than one contemporary reviewer compared Noel's tribute to Tennyson's *In Memoriam, A Little Child's Monument* clearly lacks the aesthetic distance, the disciplined sensibility, and the refined and subtle harmonies of the laureate's great elegiac tribute. There are no central or recurring images in the volume, and the only unifying artistic structure apparent in the *Monument* is the generalized movement of nineteenth-century spiritual autobiography from bleak doubt through passive resignation to assured faith. Noel suggests this general quality of loose sequence in a letter to his sister: "After Eric's death a complete revolution took place in my thoughts very gradually. My first book inspired by faith, gradually restored after his death, was the *Monument.* That is the record of doubt and despair at first, and of faith only towards the end." Noel's sorrow and anguish are, however, occasionally expressed with concise and poignant conviction:

> *"Measure him for his coffin,"*
> He heard a stranger say;
> And then he broke to laughing,
> *"God! measure my poor clay,*
> *And shut me in my coffin,*
> *A soul gone grey!*
> *For hope lies dead,*
> *Life is fled."*

Likewise, in the impressive poem *"De Profundis,"* the "Nay" section, with its surreal images of alienated terror and startling presentation of the dark night of the soul's despair, is far more powerful than the "Yea" section, with its bland depiction of assured Christian faith.

Other poems in *A Little Child's Monument* offer the idea of consolation: Eric's individual spirit is reflected in a universal admiration for the world's children. Poetically, this notion verges on triteness as in, for example, " 'That They All May Be One' ":

> Whene'er there comes a little child,
> My darling comes with him;
> Whene'er I hear a birdie wild
> Who sings his merry whim,
> Mine sings with him:
> . . . .
> And if one woundeth with harsh word,
> Or deed, a child, or beast, or bird,
> It seems to strike weak Innocence
> Through him. . . .

The sentiments expressed in these lines, however, had increasing significance for the direction of Noel's own life because he devoted more of his time to visiting children in hospitals, lecturing for fundraising drives for children's charities, and working directly for the newly founded Society for Prevention of Cruelty to Children. The volume itself performed its own work in Victorian society; it was a popular title which sold many copies and went through four editions. Contemporary readers and critics valued the collection's human sympathy and sincere conviction. Reviewers hailed it as "a poem of the affections," "a book of consolation for the bereaved," "an expression of utter grief," and a "wonderful variety of melodies" which displayed great pathos.

The experience of the death of his young son permanently altered Noel's philosophical and religious principles. A year after the success of *A Little Child's Monument,* he published a didactic prose treatise, *A Philosophy of Immortality* (1882), in which he argued for the spiritualist idea of "the permanent reality of human personality." He also worked for charitable causes in the 1880s. The most significant development in his verse during this period is a new tone of moderation and the increasing use of innocent children and idyllic country life to offset the misery of urban suffering. These tendencies are clearly evident in "A Lay of Civilization: Or London," the first poem in *Songs of the Heights and Deeps* (1885). In "The Red Flag" Noel employed a brash and vehement satire to condemn the rich and clerical authorities; however, in "A Lay of Civilization" he both presents the plight of the city and offers the hope of moderation and redeeming faith through nature and human goodness. Thus, the repeated refrain of the latter poem is the image of "Happy birds fluting in the leafy woods,/And children playing by the rivulet."

Cosmo Monkhouse in the *Academy* praised "A Lay of Civilization" for its balanced technique and ultimate faith in the defeat of evil. He was impressed both with the poet's "pictures of misery and wrong, of social and spiritual disease" and by the poet's strategy of contrasting "all this crime and ugliness with the beauty of nature and the purity of innocent children." Monkhouse preferred Noel's poem over James Thomson's "The City of Dreadful Night," first published in 1874, because Noel offered "lines of comfort" and the hope that evil need not triumph.

In "A Lay of Civilization" the poet continues to juxtapose the glaring contrasts of wealth and poverty in London, but he relents in his strident satiric attacks on the rich. Instead, he presents a grim picture of degradation and poverty that is caused more by the generalized forces of urbanization than by the rich specifically:

> Huge murmur from the throat of Babylon!
> Illimitable leagues of piles confused,
> ....
> Mean habitations, warrens of dun life,
> Tortuous, swarming; sullied, pale, cramped life
> ....
> This huge black whirlpool of the city sucks,
> And swallows, and encroaches evermore
> On vernal field, pure air, and wholesome heaven.

Besides praising the saving restoration of rural retreat, Noel offers several examples of pure and heroic children struggling to survive under urban oppression. At this point in his career, he views his poetry as a force for elevating, comforting, and inspiring the metropolitan masses: against the brutality of the city he sets instances of human compassion and love.

Several other poems in the volume are noteworthy. The meters of "Thalatta" and "Suspira" were meant to echo the rhythmic alternations of the sound of the sea. The scene of "Thalatta" is Land's End, England's westernmost point, and Noel's poem compares favorably with Swinburne's "On the Cliffs." "Melcha" is a somewhat didactic fairy tale concerning the impossibility of returning to an innocent land of enchantment.

A Modern Faust (1888) is the longest and the last of Noel's important volumes. It is not his best work because it mixes too many themes and issues in a loosely organized series of dream visions which contemplate the order and disorder of the human and natural realms. With its figure of the young quester whose soul is tempted to despair and doubt, the poem follows the tradition established by Marlowe and Goethe. Its Victorian predecessor is Arthur Hugh Clough's *Dipsychus,* first published in 1865. Indeed, the greatest similarities are to Clough's poem because Noel deals with social problems and mental outlooks peculiar to the nineteenth-century urban condition. One problem with the artistic movement of Noel's long poem is that books one to three are effective in their presentation of religious doubt and social indignation while books four through six are stereotypical, conventional, and sentimental in their presentation of the wealthy gentlemen's social indifference and the final resolution based on an assured Christian faith.

The most realistic and memorable section of *A Modern Faust* is "Earth's Torture-Chamber." Drawing on actual cases dealt with by the Society for the Prevention of Cruelty to Children, the poet describes with great sympathy incidents of child abuse and murder in London. Voices torment the sensitive humanist: "Whence cometh evil?"; "Do you believe in God, fool! after this?" Although the whole poem certainly draws on Noel's own experiences (many of which were previously treated in other works), the increasing reliance on the distancing device of visionary experience—"the whole in guise of dream"—throughout *A Modern Faust* weakens the poignancy of the social and religious dilemmas. These formless and fantastical tendencies make the allurements of the temple of fleshly pleasure, with its "undulating form voluptuous," the "Art-palace of the verbal epicure," and the library of "learned seclusion" seem unreal and anemic temptations from the start. The wanderer quickly puts these experiences behind and is driven to other visions as he seeks "the solution of problems that oppressed me" and "consolation for world-sorrow."

In his dreams, the youth must next endure an assembly of supercilious members of "good society" who ignorantly prescribe various nostrums for social ills. The dialogues of this entire section are given in prose. The confused Babel of these privileged voices fades into the equally bewildering din of the "mob-orators" and comic demagogues at Hyde Park Corner. In utter despair, the youth seeks refuge in the arms of Nature—on a remote rock by the sea. The comforts of nature, however, are short-lived: nightmare visions record violent storms and the carnage of shipwrecks. The "Demiurgic Powers" of nature are "indifferent to human joy or woe." In book six, "Order," the final section of *A Modern Faust,* the tormented hero's soul turns toward the light of Christian hope. A cast of courageous leaders is reviewed in an effort to prove that humanity is overcoming social oppression. However, many of these figures are far removed from the problems of London's East End: a "fair-flower-band" of innocent children sings around a heavenly fountain; Lord Gordon works as "England's Red-cross Knight" in China; Admiral Nelson rescues "shipwrecked souls"; and Father Damien cures lepers on a faraway Pacific island. The long poem which started as a tormented case history of a modern soul wracked by confusion and animated by indignation ends on a traditional note of social and religious resolution: Queen Victoria is praised in her jubilee year and Christ is lauded as the healer of "the human family."

The short poem *Poor People's Christmas* was

published as a separate volume in 1890; it deals primarily with the conventional figure of an exploited sempstress who sews luxurious gowns for wealthy ladies even on the cold and desolate anniversary of Christ's birth. *My Sea and Other Poems* (1896) is a posthumously published collection of poems about the sea's beauty and the spiritual meaning of nature. Several unpublished poems were printed for the first time in the collected works in 1902.

In enumerating some of the faults of Noel's poetry, Percy Addleshaw mentions the "full flood of words," the "often turgid eloquence," and the "involved meaning." He is also somewhat perturbed by the poet's outlook—"an almost Quixotic desire to destroy the world's evils." And yet, Addleshaw's overall estimation of the poet's work and life is very high. Addleshaw is one of a long line of critics who regrets the comparative neglect that Noel's verse has suffered. Perhaps Noel's earnest commitment to his own goals and his independent, often original voice are his most striking characteristics. Just after the poet's death, Henry Sidgwick, a noted reviewer, Cambridge don, and friend, wrote: "I have always felt that though he was keenly disappointed by the world's inadequate recognition of his genius, he did his work in life none the less resolutely, and brought out his great gifts, and remained nobly true to his ideal." For the modern reader there are more than a few poems in the large Noel canon that are more than quaint curiosities: his best poetry reflects a poignant and intelligent concern with the religious and social issues of Victorian society in general and with the urban condition in particular.

References:

Daniel C. Angus, "Mr. Roden Noel's Poems," *British Quarterly Review,* 78 (October 1883): 212-219;

Kenneth Walter Cameron, "Roden Noel, Poet and English Defender of Whitman," *American Transcendental Quarterly,* 12 (Fall 1971): 67-98;

Stewart Marsh Ellis, "Roden Noel," in his *Mainly Victorian* (London: Hutchinson, 1925), pp. 159-169;

Hoxie Neale Fairchild, "Buchanan and Noel," in his *Religious Trends in English Poetry,* volume 4 (New York: Columbia University Press, 1957), pp. 216-239;

Emily Hickey, "Roden Noel, Poet," *Nineteenth Century and After,* 91 (April 1922): 624-633;

J. Addington Symonds, "Hon. Roden Noel," in *The Poets and the Poetry of the Nineteenth Century: William Morris to Robert Buchanan,* edited by Alfred H. Miles (London: Routledge, 1905), pp. 81-88.

Papers:

There is an important collection of Noel's papers at Washington University, St. Louis, Missouri.

Arthur O'Shaughnessy
(14 March 1844-30 January 1881)

Jane C. Fredeman
University of British Columbia

BOOKS: *An Epic of Women and Other Poems* (London: Hotten, 1870);

Lays of France (Founded on the Lays of Marie.) (London: Ellis & Green, 1872);

Music and Moonlight: Poems and Songs (London: Chatto & Windus, 1874);

Toyland, by Arthur and Eleanor O'Shaughnessy (London: Daldy, Isbister, 1875);

Songs of a Worker (London: Chatto & Windus, 1881);

Poems of Arthur O'Shaughnessy, edited by William Alexander Percy (New Haven: Yale University Press, 1923).

Until 1964 when W. D. Paden published two corrective articles, it was commonly assumed that Arthur O'Shaughnessy was the illegitimate son of Edward Bulwer-Lytton and that he had become an expert herpetologist in the nearly twenty years he was employed in the Department of Natural History at the British Museum. The originator of the first notion was Edmund Gosse, who remained convinced of its truth; the second was upheld even by Richard Garnett, the keeper of printed books, who wrote the article on O'Shaughnessy for the *Dictionary of National Biography* and who must have known

Photographed by E. Forhead, Ventnor, Isle of Wight.

otherwise, since he came to the museum in the same year as O'Shaughnessy.

O'Shaughnessy did receive his first appointment to the museum in 1861, when he was seventeen, through Lord Lytton, who asked John Evelyn Denison, speaker of the House of Commons and one of the museum's trustees, to nominate the youth. Lytton's mistress, however, was O'Shaughnessy's aunt, Laura Deacon, with whom Lytton had four children, including a son who died in 1855; she was not O'Shaughnessy's mother, Louisa, who had married Oscar William O'Shaughnessy on 11 May 1843. Arthur William Edgar O'Shaughnessy was born less than a year later on 14 March 1844, and another son, Oscar Frederick, was born in 1846. Two years later Oscar died. Precisely how Louisa supported her sons is not known, but she came from a well-educated family and in the 1861 census she is listed as a schoolmistress.

His lack of formal education prevented

O'Shaughnessy from moving upward from his position as a transcriber in the Department of Printed Books, and this impediment, together with his knowledge that the museum preferred internal appointments, probably accounts for his decision to try for a post in the zoology department. On 2 November 1863 he was accepted for the position, but within a few months his ineptitude led to his transfer to the geology department, where his duties were essentially clerical. Both his lack of scientific knowledge and his indifference to acquiring it would undoubtedly have led to his dismissal by the standing committee of the museum when his case came to their attention in 1870 and 1872 were it not for the fortuitous feuding then going on among his superiors within the institution and for the intervention of Lord Lytton.

Much happier during the middle years of his short life were his literary and social friendships. With John Payne and John Nettleship, his closest friends in the late 1860s, he frequently attended the famous Sunday evening salons at the home of Dr. Westland Marston in Northumberland Terrace, Regent's Park, which R. E. Francillon describes so vividly in *Mid-Victorian Memories* (1914); and it was there that O'Shaughnessy first encountered his future wife. After Dr. Marston's death in 1870, the year in which Payne's and O'Shaughnessy's first volumes of verse were published, he was included in what Louise Chandler Moulton calls the "far famed evenings of Ford Madox Brown," where he met the members of London's literary elite, including Dante Gabriel Rossetti and the Pre-Raphaelites.

During this time, too, again with Payne and Nettleship, he was one of the triumvirate who became romantically involved with a married woman named Helen Snee, one of the reputed and, because of her six-month incarceration in 1876 for murder (actually attempted suicide), notorious beauties of the nineteenth century. In the three years before their relationship broke off in 1872, she served as his critic and amanuensis and discussed with him the works of twelfth-century chronicler Jean Froissart, the modern French poets, and their Pre-Raphaelite contemporaries. Their correspondence exposes Helen, a consumptive, as a kind of prototypical Camille, from whom O'Shaughnessy was probably fortunate to have escaped. Only a single letter survives from O'Shaughnessy to Helen against thirty-eight from her to him: written on 22 May 1870, it discusses the nature of "true love" and reveals the basis of thoughts which he never uttered with great profundity or originality in his poetry. He regards love "as the offer of heaven—as a hand held out to take our hand and lead us up to high stages of being that our desolate, solitary natures, full of undeveloped sympathies, and chilled and blighted aspirations, will never attain to."

The year after his break with Helen, and an apparent severance of his relationship with John Payne, he married Eleanor Marston, the daughter of Dr. Marston and sister of the blind poet Philip Bourke Marston, the close friend of Oliver Madox Brown. Though he declined an invitation to the wedding (26 June 1873), Rossetti sent "warmest wishes" for O'Shaughnessy's happiness, "personal and poetical." But he was to achieve neither. The O'Shaughnessys' first child, Westland Kyme, lived only from 31 July to 12 September 1874, and a second son was probably stillborn, since his birth was not registered. On 8 February 1879, Eleanor died, evidently of cirrhosis of the liver.

It would hardly be surprising after the loss of his family that, as Louise Chandler Moulton says, "there must have been a melancholy side to [his] sunny nature, for through his poetry there thrills forever a minor chord," but the theme of separation is present from his earliest works. The sonnet which concludes the title sequence of *An Epic of Women* is dated 1867 and repeats Antony's bitter thoughts on women in the poem "Cleopatra": "One woman bears and brings him up a man/Another woman slays him in the last." Whether all the poems in this section were written around the same date is not certain, but their themes are so similar that they may well be manifestations of the inspiration of false love that O'Shaughnessy mentions in his 1870 letter to Helen Snee. Although other poems in the volume also concern love, some hint at this particular type of musing on life in the grave—where death has no desire to cut short life, but digs the grave only as a place of rest and ease in case "life be vain/And love turn at the last to pain"; others portray an escapist world which he continually elaborated. But isolation in O'Shaughnessy is not simply the wages of love; alienation is also the lot of the poetic life itself, as "The Poet's Grave," the final poem in his first volume, makes painfully clear: "They buried the poet with thoughts of shame/And not as one who *believes*."

O'Shaughnessy has frequently been compared to A. C. Swinburne, and, while he is not as good a poet, similarities in intricate syntax, balanced phrasings, musical qualities, and alliteration are pronounced. Many of their shared characteristics may be explained by the fact that both were fluent in French. O'Shaughnessy's last volume, *Songs of a Worker* (1881), contains translations of several lesser

Decorated title page by John Nettleship for O'Shaughnessy's first poetry collection

known French poets, but the influence of Gautier and Baudelaire clearly had the greatest impact on his work.

"Bisclaveret" in his first volume, which Rossetti thought dominated "the whole series as regards dignity of execution" (as he wrote O'Shaughnessy in thanking him for his presentation copy on 15 October 1870), is certainly the best of O'Shaughnessy's adaptations of the lays of Marie de France, five more of which were published as *Lays of France* in 1872. Though B. Ifor Evans thought the genre "too tedious for adaptation," O'Shaughnessy was not trying to translate or even to adapt to English the twelfth-century verse novels of Marie based on Celtic legends. She was not concerned with courtly love or Platonic ideals but with physical passion, almost always outside of marriage. For her, true love was a mutual passion exacting equal obligations from the man and the woman, and it was this reciprocal aspect of her view of love that probably most appealed to O'Shaughnessy. "Bisclaveret" differs both from the whole of O'Shaughnessy's lyrical canon and from the rest of the lays, which at least maintain the essential outlines of Marie's stories. He goes beyond Marie's concerns in his abstract portrayal of the dominant emotions of the werewolf Bisclaveret as loneliness and fear.

In 1874, O'Shaughnessy published his third volume of poetry, *Music and Moonlight,* in which his poetic capacities and faults are most evident—his penchant for musical expression and his lack of self-criticism in revising his poems to avoid repetition and diffuseness. His best-known poem, which opens the volume, epitomizes both these traits. Entitled "Ode," its initial lines—"We are the music-makers/And we are the dreamers of dreams"— stand as an epithet on the poet as maker and compress the poem's content: that the world is remade continually in the prophet's or singer's words. Many of the poems in this volume treat love, dead or dying; others detail moments of remembered love sublime.

Helen Snee, who served as O'Shaughnessy's critic and amanuensis during the period of their romantic involvement in the late 1860s and early 1870s

The calm tone of these poems and their lyric resignation have led certain critics to see O'Shaughnessy as narrow. While it is true that his stanza forms are not novel, his diction is essentially monosyllabic, his vocabulary limited and repetitive, and his imagery undistinctive, notwithstanding these strictures, his simplicity and music do lend a charm and effectiveness to his verse. Like Swinburne, O'Shaughnessy was fascinated by the dimensions accessible in poetry through the manipulation of sound effects, and William Percy, editor of O'Shaughnessy's *Poems* (1923), was unquestionably correct in his assessment of the role of music in his poetry: "So perfect was his ear he was never unmusical even when he was saying nothing. His marvellous sense of the value of vowels and consonants, his flair for rhyme, the rise and fall of his own cadences, intoxicated him into diffuseness and lured him into using certain words again and again because just the sound of them was to him beautiful." His obsession with sound flaws his poetry certainly, but only because he was unable to control it; at his best, it is one of his singular distinctions as a poet.

O'Shaughnessy collaborated with his wife, Eleanor, on the volume of children's stories entitled *Toyland,* published in 1875, a volume distinguished as much by Arthur Boyd Houghton's frontispiece as by its literary contents. In the year of O'Shaughnessy's death, his cousin, the Reverend A. W. Deacon, who tried in vain to disabuse Gosse of the notion that Lord Lytton was the poet's father, prepared his final work, *Songs of a Worker,* for the press. That volume was not a climactic capstone to O'Shaughnessy's poetic career, and he remains today unfairly remembered as the author of the single pair of memorable lines quoted above from "Ode." But to view O'Shaughnessy merely as a "music maker" and "dreamer of dreams" is equally as simplistic as accepting the unfortunate label that has clung to William Morris from the prologue to his *The Earthly Paradise:* the "Idle singer of an empty day."

Biographies:

Louise Chandler Moulton, *Arthur O'Shaughnessy: His Life and His Work with Selections from his Poems* (London: Mathews & Lane, 1894);

Clement Shorter, *A Pathetic Love Episode in a Poet's Life. Being Letters to Arthur W. E. O'Shaughnessy. Also a Letter from him Containing a Dissertation on Love* (London: Privately printed, 1916);

Oskar Brönner, *Das Leben Arthur O'Shaughnessy's* (Heidelberg: Winters, 1933);

W. D. Paden, "Arthur O'Shaughnessy: The Ancestry of a Victorian Poet," *Bulletin of the John Rylands Library,* 46 (March 1964): 429-447.

References:

George K. Anderson, "Marie de France and Arthur O'Shaughnessy: A Study in Victorian Adaptation," *Studies in Philology,* 36 (July 1939): 529-549;

Bernarda C. Broers, "O'Shaughnessy," in her *Mysticism in the Neo-Romanticists* (Amsterdam: Paris, 1913);

B. Ifor Evans, "Minor Pre-Raphaelite Poets," in *English Poetry in the Later Nineteenth Century* (London: Methuen, 1933);

Hoxie Neale Fairchild, "Rima's Mother," *PMLA,* 68 (June 1953): 357-370;

H. Buxton Forman, "John Payne and Arthur O'Shaughnessy," in his *Our Living Poets: An Essay in Criticism* (London: Tinsley, 1871);

R. E. Francillon, *Mid-Victorian Memories* (London: Hodder & Stoughton, 1914);

William E. Fredeman, "Arthur W. E. O'Shaughnessy," in his *Pre-Raphaelitism: A Bibliocritical Study* (Cambridge: Harvard University Press, 1965);

Richard Garnett, "Arthur O'Shaughnessy," in *The Poets and the Poetry of the Century,* volume 8, edited by A. H. Miles (London: Hutchinson, 1892);

Sanford M. Goldstein, "The Poetry of Arthur O'Shaughnessy," Ph.D. dissertation, University of Wisconsin, 1953;

Edmund Gosse, "Arthur O'Shaughnessy," in *The English Poets: Selections with Critical Introductions by Various Writers,* volume 4, edited by T. H. Ward (London: Macmillan, 1880);

Gosse, "Arthur O'Shaughnessy," in his *Silhouettes* (London: Heinemann, 1925);

Walter Hamilton, "Arthur W. E. O'Shaughnessy," in his *The Aesthetic Movement in England* (London: Reeves & Turner, 1882);

Nancy Hauser, "Arthur O'Shaughnessy and the Doomed Circle," *Columbia Library Columns,* 18 (1969): 17-24;

Lafcadio Hearn, "Three Silences: Arthur O'Shaughnessy," *Complete Lectures on Art, Literature, and Philosophy,* volume 3 (Tokyo: Hokuseido Press, 1932);

Hans Klenk, *Nachwirkungen Dante Gabriel Rossetti* (Berlin: Erlangen, 1932);

Richard Le Gallienne, "Arthur O'Shaughnessy," in his *Retrospective Reviews,* volume 2 (London: Lane, 1896);

F. L. Lucas, "A Painted Lily," in his *Authors Dead and Living* (New York: Macmillan, 1926);

W. D. Paden, "Arthur O'Shaughnessy in the British Museum: or, the Case of the Misplaced Fusees and the Reluctant Zoologist," *Victorian Studies,* 8 (September 1964): 7-30.

Francis Turner Palgrave

(28 September 1824-24 October 1897)

Megan Nelson
University of British Columbia

SELECTED BOOKS: *Preciosa: A Tale,* anonymous (London: Chapman, 1852);

Idyls and Songs, 1848-1854 (London: Parker, 1854);

The Passionate Pilgrim, or Eros and Anteros, as Henry J. Thurston (London: Chapman & Hall, 1858);

Official Catalogue of the Fine Art Department of the International Exhibition of 1862 (London: Printed for H. M. Commissioners by Truscott, Son & Simmons, 1862); republished as *Handbook to the Fine Art Collections in the International Exhibition of 1862* (London: Macmillan, 1862);

Essays on Art (London & Cambridge: Macmillan, 1866; New York: Hurd & Houghton, 1867);

Hymns (London: Macmillan, 1867; enlarged, London: Macmillan, 1868; New York: Randolph, 1868);

The Five Days Entertainments at Wentworth Grange (London: Macmillan, 1868; Boston: Roberts Brothers, 1868);

Gems of English Art in This Century (London & New

York: Routledge, 1869);

Lyrical Poems (London & New York: Macmillan, 1871);

A Lyme Garland: Being Verses, Mainly Written at Lyme Regis, or Upon the Scenery of the Neighbourhood (Lyme: Privately printed, 1874);

The Visions of England (London: Privately printed, 1880; London: Macmillan, 1881);

The Life of Jesus Christ, Illustrated from the Italian Painters (London: National Society, 1885);

Ode for the Twentieth of June (London, 1887); republished as *Ode for the Twenty-first of June 1887* (Oxford: Clarendon Press, 1887);

Amenophis and Other Poems, Sacred and Secular (London: Macmillan, 1892);

Landscape in Poetry from Homer to Tennyson (London & New York: Macmillan, 1897).

OTHER: *The Golden Treasury of the Best Songs and Lyrical Poems in the English Language,* edited by Palgrave (Cambridge & London: Macmillan, 1861; revised and enlarged, London & New York: Macmillan, 1891);

Arthur Hugh Clough, *Poems,* memoir by Palgrave (Cambridge & London: Macmillan, 1862);

William Shakespeare, *Songs and Sonnets,* edited by Palgrave (London & Cambridge: Macmillan, 1865; New York: Crowell, 1898);

Alfred Tennyson, *Lyrical Poems,* edited by Palgrave (London: Macmillan, 1865; New York: Stokes & Allen, 1866);

William Wordsworth, *A Selection from the Works of William Wordsworth,* edited by Palgrave (London: Moxon, 1865);

Walter Scott, *Poetical Works,* edited by Palgrave (London: Macmillan, 1866; Philadelphia: Lippincott, 1866);

The Children's Treasury of English Song, edited by Palgrave (2 volumes, London: Macmillan, 1875; 1 volume, New York: Macmillan, 1875); republished as *The Children's Treasury of Lyric Poetry,* 1 volume (London: Macmillan, 1876);

Scott, *The Lay of the Last Minstrel and The Lady of the Lake,* edited by Palgrave (London: Macmillan, 1883);

Scott, *Marmion and The Lord of the Isles,* edited by Palgrave (London: Macmillan, 1883);

John Keats, *The Poetical Works of John Keats,* edited by Palgrave (London: Macmillan, 1884; New York: Macmillan, 1884);

Robert Herrick, *Chrysomela: A Selection from the Lyric Poems of Robert Herrick,* edited by Palgrave

(London: Macmillan, 1887; New York: Macmillan, 1888);

J. C. Shairp, *Glen Desseray,* edited by Palgrave (London & New York: Macmillan, 1888);

The Treasury of Sacred Song Selected from the English Lyrical Poetry of Four Centuries, edited by Palgrave (Oxford: Clarendon Press, 1889);

The Golden Treasury Selected from the Best Songs and Lyrical Poems in the English Language, second series, edited by Palgrave (London & New York: Macmillan, 1897).

SELECTED PERIODICAL PUBLICATIONS:
Poetry:

"The Reign of Law," *Macmillan's Magazine,* 17 (November 1867): 34-37;

"Elegy in Memory of Percy, Lord Strangford,"

Macmillan's Magazine, 19 (February 1869): 355, 356;

"Brecon Bridge," *Cornhill Magazine,* 22 (July 1870): 98;

"The Lost *Euridyce,* 24th March, 1878," *Contemporary Review,* 32 (May 1878): 257, 258;

"Pausanias and Cleonice; an Old-Hellenic Ballad," *Macmillan's Magazine,* 54 (August 1886): 280-286;

"A Halcyon Day in Summer," *Macmillan's Magazine,* 58 (October 1888): 471;

"At 29, de Vere Gardens," *Athenaeum,* no. 3248 (25 January 1890): 116;

"In pace," *Nineteenth Century,* 32 (November 1892): 837-839;

"Eutopia," *Spectator,* 78 (30 January 1897): 174.
Criticism:
"On Readers in 1760 and 1860," *Macmillan's Magazine,* 1 (April 1860): 487-489;

"The Growth of English Poetry," *Quarterly Review,* 110 (October 1861): 435-459;

"Arthur Hugh Clough," *Fraser's Magazine,* 65 (April 1862): 527-536;

"English Poetry from Dryden to Cowper," *Quarterly Review,* 112 (July 1862): 146-179;

"Descriptive Poetry in England from Anne to Victoria," *Fortnightly Review,* 5 (June 1866): 298-320;

"On the Scientific Study of Poetry," *Fortnightly Review,* 12 old series, 6 new series (August 1869): 163-178;

"The Province and Study of Poetry," *Macmillan's Magazine,* 53 (March 1886): 332-347;

"William Barnes and his poems of rural life in the Dorset dialect," *National Review,* 8 (February 1887): 818-839;

"On the direct influence over style in poetry, exercised by the other fine arts, sculpture and painting especially, with illustrations ancient and modern," *National Review,* part one, 9 (May 1887): 352-369; part two, 10 (October 1887): 202-218.

Francis Turner Palgrave is remembered today for his *Golden Treasury of the Best Songs and Lyrical Poems in the English Language* (1861), one of the best-known and loved anthologies in English. In his own time, however, he was known also as a controversial critic of art and literature; a close friend and follower of Alfred, Lord Tennyson; and a poet in his own right. The twentieth century has overlooked Palgrave's original work, preferring his presentation of the works of others, yet Palgrave's criticism was widely respected by his peers, and his

poetry shows his desire to experiment with many styles and forms of the lyric.

Born in Great Yarmouth, Palgrave was brought up in London, where his father, the medieval historian Sir Francis Palgrave, worked at setting up the Public Record Office. Although Sir Francis raised his four boys as Anglo-Catholics, he had been born Francis Cohen, becoming a Christian and changing his name upon marriage. The family tried to suppress his ancestry, but in later years, A. C. Swinburne and Dante Gabriel Rossetti referred maliciously to Francis Turner's middle-class Victorian attitudes as "Cohenisms," which they defined as the behavior of "fools and quacks of divers colours."

The Palgrave boys were given an intensive education in literature, religion, and the arts, which was followed in Palgrave's case by study at the Charterhouse School. In 1843 Palgrave went up to Balliol College, Oxford, where he joined a secret society called Decade whose members, including Matthew Arnold and Arthur Hugh Clough, dominated English letters for the next fifty years. At Oxford Palgrave was known as "Madonna Palgrave" because he had so many Italian religious engravings in his rooms, and he was, next to Clough and in Clough's own words, "accounted the wildest and most écervelé republican going." After he left Oxford, he spent part of 1848 in Paris observing the progress of the new French republic.

Although he took a first-class honors degree in 1847 and won a fellowship at Exeter College, Palgrave left the university at the beginning of 1849 to enter the newly formed Education Office of the Privy Council, where he remained until his retirement in 1884. During his years there he wrote almost all his poetry and criticism.

Palgrave's first meeting with Tennyson in March 1849 marked the beginning of a lifelong friendship between the two. Palgrave was devoted to Tennyson, to whom he dedicated *The Golden Treasury,* although his slavish attentions often irritated the reclusive laureate. On an 1860 holiday in Cornwall, Palgrave pursued Tennyson so unrelentingly that Tennyson finally secretly resolved to escape, explaining to their companions that "all day long I am trying to get a quiet moment for reflection . . . but before I have finished a couplet I hear Palgrave's voice like a bee in a bottle, making the neighbourhood resound with my name, and I have to give myself up to escape the consequences." Infuriated, Tennyson attempted to flee, but he was unable to escape. As Charles Tennyson relates in his 1944 biography of his grandfather, "the last scene

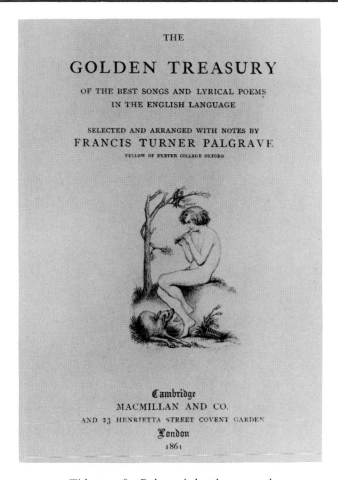

THE

GOLDEN TREASURY

OF THE BEST SONGS AND LYRICAL POEMS
IN THE ENGLISH LANGUAGE

SELECTED AND ARRANGED WITH NOTES BY
FRANCIS TURNER PALGRAVE
FELLOW OF EXETER COLLEGE OXFORD

Cambridge
MACMILLAN AND CO.
AND 23 HENRIETTA STREET COVENT GARDEN
London
1861

Title page for Palgrave's best-known work

of the comedy . . . shows Tennyson moving off in the dog-cart and Palgrave jumping up beside him to his evident surprise, and driving away with him amid protest and explanations."

Although Palgrave's contemporaries knew him as an editor, critic, and poet, his first published book was a novel, *Preciosa* (1852), a thinly disguised tale of his own youthful disappointment in love. His first book of verse, *Idyls and Songs, 1848-1854* (1854), showed an interest in the lyric that would endure throughout his career. The book deals with four kinds of lyric poetry: translation of Greek and Latin lyrics, elegies, love lyrics, and verse discussions of the morality of art, a recurrent theme in Palgrave's criticism. All of Palgrave's poetry is lyrical; his choice of the lyric form for *The Golden Treasury* reflects his own taste and experiments.

After *Idyls and Songs,* Palgrave produced no volumes of secular poetry until 1871, although he did produce a volume of original *Hymns* (1867) and contribute verse to magazines. From 1854 to 1871 he concentrated on his friendship with Tennyson,

his career in the Education Department, his criticism, and his work as an editor and anthologist. The appearance of his second novel, *The Passionate Pilgrim, or Eros and Anteros* (published pseudonymously in 1858), excited little critical attention, although reviewers commented on its psychological insight. About 1860, Palgrave went through a period of great depression in which he apparently contemplated suicide, perhaps over the loss of his early love, Georgina Alderson. He was, however, restored to health by his marriage to Cecil Greville Milnes in 1862.

Palgrave began collecting the lyrics for *The Golden Treasury* late in 1860, enlisting the aid of Tennyson, Thomas Woolner, and George Miller in making the final choices. Tennyson's contribution to *The Golden Treasury* has been greatly overemphasized by critics, who have generally assumed that Palgrave could not have produced such a high-quality book on his own. Tennyson, whose tastes were more catholic than Palgrave's, did influence the selection of lyrics in the volume, but Palgrave kept final editorial control firmly in his own hands. *The Golden Treasury* was an immediate success and has not been out of print in the more than one hundred years since its publication. This success is remarkable, particularly in view of the fact that Palgrave's editing principles are highly idiosyncratic, even by cavalier Victorian standards.

Palgrave's reputation as an art critic had a more variable course. In 1862 Palgrave was commissioned to write the *Official Catalogue of the Fine Art Department of the International Exhibition of 1862,* which included not only the fine arts but also stained glass and ironwork. When the guide appeared, however, it was bitterly attacked in the correspondence column of the *London Times* by "Jacob Omnium" (Matthew Higgins), a reformer and friend of William Makepeace Thackeray. He accused Palgrave, with justice, of bias in favor of the works of the Pre-Raphaelite sculptor Thomas Woolner, with whom Palgrave was living at the time. The authorities withdrew the catalogue three weeks after publication, but Palgrave arranged for publication of a very carefully censored, unofficial edition later that year.

Palgrave's critical reputation began to recover in 1863 with his appointment as art critic to the *Saturday Review,* where he stayed for three years. Some of the articles he wrote in this capacity were collected for publication in 1866 as *Essays on Art.* After leaving the *Saturday Review,* he wrote freelance articles for several magazines but turned down a permanent position at the *Times* on the grounds that he did not wish his personal dislike for the work of the younger artists to discourage them.

Between 1865 and 1888, Palgrave edited selections of poetry by Shakespeare, Wordsworth, Sir Walter Scott, and J. C. Shairp; produced a children's book, *The Five Days Entertainments at Wentworth Grange* (1868); and produced his volume of *Hymns.* The hymns were really sacred poems, varying from what his daughter Gwenllian F. Palgrave called "abstruse and complex" philosophical speculations to children's songs, which were much appreciated for the simple language which made them highly suitable for use in schools.

The year 1871 saw the appearance of his *Lyrical Poems,* which included some verses from *Idyls and Songs* and followed the earlier volume's format in devoting sections to different forms of the lyric. Palgrave's growing prosperity allowed him to buy a country house in Lyme Regis in 1872; two years later he published *A Lyme Garland: Being Verses, Mainly Written at Lyme Regis, or Upon the Scenery of the Neighbourhood* (1874) to aid a local charity.

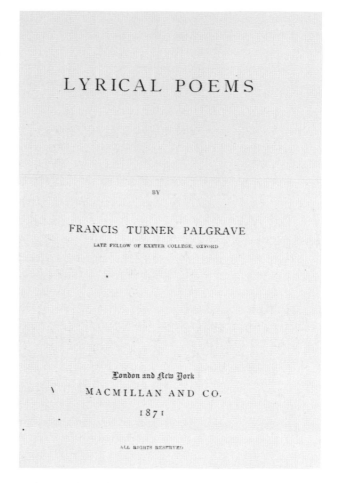

Title page for Palgrave's second poetry collection (courtesy of Thomas Cooper Library, University of South Carolina)

His next works were *The Children's Treasury of English Song* (1875) and a privately printed series of historical poems which appeared in 1880. *The Visions of England* is a cycle of poems about events in English history which reflects Palgrave's mature political views; as Gwenllian Palgrave writes in her 1899 biography: "As a young man my father had held Liberal opinions, but as time went on these views gradually changed, and his sympathies were subsequently altogether with the Conservative party; a fervent patriotic feeling and unqualified respect for the Royal Family especially dominated his views." *The Visions of England* was commercially published by Macmillan in 1881, and it became his most admired volume of poetry.

Palgrave retired from the civil service in 1884 but had only a brief holiday before he successfully contested the election to the chair of poetry at Oxford, which he held for two consecutive five-year terms from 1885 to 1895. His old Balliol friends,

The country home at Lyme Regis purchased by Palgrave in 1872

Matthew Arnold and J. C. Shairp, had held the position before him; Arnold had refused renomination to give Palgrave a better chance.

As professor of poetry, he gave lecture series that reflected his enduring poetic and critical interests, including one on neglected poets, such as the dialect poet William Barnes, and one on the relationship between art and poetry which was published as his final book, *Landscape in Poetry from Homer to Tennyson* (1897). As official representative of poetry at Oxford, he was also called upon to write public poetry, including an ode to commemorate Queen Victoria's jubilee visit to Oxford in 1887.

He still found time to pursue his interests as anthologist and poet. In 1889 he produced a new anthology, *The Treasury of Sacred Song,* which he followed with his last book of poems, *Amenophis and Other Poems, Sacred and Secular* (1892). This final volume added the long philosophical poem "Amenophis" to a collection of new and previously published lyrics. He gathered most of his final energies for a new *Golden Treasury,* the "second series," which appeared only a few days before his death in October 1897.

When Palgrave put together the first *Golden Treasury* in 1861, he excluded living poets because Tennyson did not want to be included. After Tennyson's death in 1892, Palgrave began to plan a selection of verse by poets who were alive in 1861, but the second-series volume was not a success, reflecting, as it did, the mid-Victorian taste of a man over seventy who ignored many brilliant young poets of the 1890s in favor of his often-mediocre contemporaries.

Any discussion of Palgrave's achievement focuses inevitably on his ability to present the work of others, rather than on his own talents. Although he produced nearly a dozen works of poetry and fiction, Palgrave's reputation has always rested on his abilities as an editor and critic. As a poet, he was an adequate but unoriginal craftsman; as a man, he was at the same time highly opinionated and deferential to those of greater ability, which made him a good editor but a somewhat obsequious friend. He prided himself on his friendships with the titled and influential of his time, including W. W. Gladstone, John Henry Newman, Robert Browning, Benjamin Jowett, Arnold, Clough, and Tennyson. His enduring achievement rests on his ability to turn the process of editing into a creative art. As J. W. Mackail wrote in his sketch of Palgrave for the *Dictionary of National Biography, The Golden Treasury* "remains one of those rare instances in which critical work has a substantive imaginative value, and entitles its author to rank among creative artists."

References:

Christopher Clausen, "The Palgrave Version," *Georgia Review,* 34 (1980): 277-289;

B. Ifor Evans, "Tennyson and the Origins of *The Golden Treasury,*" *Times Literary Supplement,* 8 December 1932, p. 941;

Colin J. Horne, "Palgrave's *Golden Treasury,*" in *English Association Studies Collected for the English Association,* new series, edited by Sir Philip Magnus (London: English Association, 1949);

Naomi Lewis, "Palgrave and his *Golden Treasury,*" Listener, 4 (January 1962): 23, 26;

Gwenllian F. Palgrave, *Francis Turner Palgrave: His Journals and Memories of His Life* (London: Longmans, Green, 1899).

Papers:

Most of Palgrave's papers are in Great Britain at the British Library and the Tennyson Research Centre. Lesser repositories include Bodleian Library and Balliol College, Oxford; Trinity College, Cambridge; and the East Sussex Record Office, Lewes. In North America, Palgrave's papers are in the Berg Collection at the New York Public Library and the University of British Columbia Library, Vancouver, Canada. Lesser repositories include the Humanities Research Center, University of Texas at Austin, and the Beinecke Rare Book and Manuscript Library at Yale University.

Coventry Patmore

A. W. Heidemann
Carleton University

BIRTH: Woodford, Essex, 23 July 1823, to Peter and Eliza Robertson Patmore.

MARRIAGES: 11 September 1847 to Emily Augusta Andrews; children: Milnes, Tennyson, Emily, Bertha, Gertrude, Henry. 18 July 1864 to Marianne Byles. 13 September 1881 to Harriet Robson; child: Epiphanius.

DEATH: Lymington, Hampshire, 26 November 1896.

SELECTED BOOKS: *Poems* (London: Moxon, 1844);

Tamerton Church-Tower and Other Poems (London: Pickering, 1853);

The Betrothal, anonymous (London: Parker, 1854; Boston: Ticknor & Fields, 1856);

The Espousals, anonymous (London: Parker, 1856; Boston: Ticknor & Fields, 1856);

The Angel in the House (London: Parker, 1858; New York: Dutton, 1876);

Faithful For Ever (London: Parker, 1860; Boston: Ticknor & Fields, 1861);

The Victories of Love (Boston: Burnham, 1862; London & Cambridge: Macmillan, 1863); revised and enlarged as *The Victories of Love and Other Poems* (New York: Cassell, 1888);

Odes, anonymous (London: Privately printed, 1868; Boston: Privately printed, 1936?);

The Unknown Eros and Other Odes I-XXI, anonymous (London: Bell, 1877); revised, enlarged, and signed by Patmore as *The Unknown Eros and Other Odes I-XLVI* (London: Bell, 1878);

Amelia (London: Privately printed, 1878); enlarged as *Amelia, Tamerton Church-Tower, etc.; with a Prefatory Study of English Metrical Law* (London: Bell, 1878);

How I Managed and Improved My Estate (London: Bell, 1886);

Hastings, Lewes, Rye and the Sussex Marshes (London: Bell, 1887);

Principle in Art (London: Bell, 1889; revised, London: Bell, 1898);

Religio Poetae (London: Bell, 1893; revised, London: Bell, 1898);

The Rod, the Root and the Flower (London: Bell, 1895);

Courage in Politics, and Other Essays, 1885-1896, edited by Frederick Page (London & New York: Oxford University Press, 1921);

because of a poet's subject or the manner in which he treats it, popularity can reveal something about a reading public and, thus, something about a period or an age. On that account alone Coventry Patmore is a significant figure in the history of nineteenth-century literature. For a brief time he was one of the most widely read poets in England and had a large following in the United States as well. By Victorian standards, even more by modern ones, sales of *The Angel in the House* (1858), the work which achieved for him his renown, were astonishing. By the time he died, over a quarter of a million copies of the poem had been sold.

Though he has enthusiastic defenders among the critics today Patmore is read by few, and of those who do read him as many go to him out of historical or sociological interest as out of an interest in his poetry. The particular way he understood and wrote about his chosen subjects, love and marriage, and the religious aura in which he surrounded them reflect a sensibility with which the modern, secular age has lost touch. This is unfortunate because, however removed from the present he may seem, he remains not only a genuine poet but also in some ways, a unique one.

Patmore was born on 23 July 1823, at Woodford in Essex, the eldest child of Peter and Eliza Patmore. His father was a nonbeliever, his mother a Scots Presbyterian. Like Robert Browning, Patmore was given little formal education. Rather, he simply read in his father's library. He was a precocious child, showing a talent for mathematics and painting and, later, an interest in science; but his passion was literature, and he read widely in the English classics from an early age. Patmore's fondness for literature was not surprising. His father was an editor, novelist, and critic and counted among his friends and acquaintances Charles Lamb, Leigh Hunt, William Hazlitt, Richard Monckton Milnes, and Bryan Waller Proctor (Barry Cornwall).

When Patmore was sixteen, his father sent him to a branch of the Collège de France in Paris, where he remained only six months. The sojourn there is significant not for the language he learned—more German than French, he was to say later on—but for his falling in love. Although today we might perceive that experience as no more than an adolescent infatuation, it was nothing of the sort for the passionate young Patmore, and if it was not reciprocated—the young Englishwoman with whom he had fallen in love found him at best amusing—it nevertheless made a profound impression on him. He had not yet decided on poetry as a career but, unknown to himself, he had found

Coventry Patmore, 1886 (photo by G. Bradshaw)

Seven Unpublished Poems by Coventry Patmore to Alice Meynell (London: Privately printed, 1922).

Collections: *Poems, by Coventry Patmore,* 4 volumes (London: Bell, 1879);

Poems, by Coventry Patmore, edited by Basil Champneys (London: Bell, 1906);

The Poems of Coventry Patmore, edited by Frederick Page (London & New York: Oxford University Press, 1949).

OTHER: *The Children's Garland from the Best Poets,* selected and edited by Patmore (London: Macmillan, 1862);

St. Bernard on the Love of God, translated by Patmore and Marianne Patmore (London: Kegan Paul, 1881).

In the literary world popularity is not a necessary criterion for importance. However, whether

his subject. By the time he was prepared to make his commitment to poetry at the age of nineteen he had decided that he would be the poet of love, reciprocated love, which for Patmore came to mean married love.

The first volume of his poetry, entitled simply *Poems,* was published in 1844 when Patmore was twenty-one. As one might expect, the subject of love figures fairly importantly in both narratives and lyrics, two of the longer poems apparently having been occasioned by his Paris infatuation. Though the volume was viciously attacked in *Blackwood's Edinburgh Magazine,* its reception was generally an enthusiastic one; and overnight Patmore found himself something of a sensation. The young poet's success was as much the result of his father's influence as it was of an objective assessment of the volume. Edmund Gosse, in his biography of Patmore written over a half century later, still speaks of the volume as having been written "not in borrowed tones, but in the voice of a new person"; yet it is not the voice of a new person that we hear in the *Poems* as much as it is—as one might expect in a poet publishing for the first time and at an early age—a collection of voices of poets Patmore had heard from his childhood.

The voice of Tennyson's early poems is in Patmore's volume. Just as pronounced, though, are the voices of an older generation, those of Wordsworth and Coleridge (voices which haunted the young Tennyson too). The diction, meters, and rhythms of their ballad imitations are much in evidence. Patmore also demonstrates Wordsworth's and Coleridge's penchant for natural description. The mainly derivative quality of the *Poems* makes their interest now mainly academic. Patmore himself was dissatisfied with them and claimed he was rushed into publication by his father. Although he continued to rework some of them over the years, his final judgment is suggested by his refusal to include them in the four-volume edition, his collected poems, published in 1879.

If 1844 brought exhilaration to Patmore it was short-lived. As a young man his father had been a dandy, and now, in his middle age, his extravagance had carried over into his financial affairs. Not long after the publication of the poems those affairs took a turn for the worse. Out of desperation the elder Patmore made a last attempt to right them and speculated heavily in railway stock. The gamble failed and, having lost everything, he was forced to flee the country. The young Patmore, who had just reached his majority and was anticipating with some confidence a future which would provide him the

leisure to continue his career as a poet, suddenly found himself destitute.

Desperate, Patmore turned to the only marketable skill he possessed besides his poetry, prose writing, and in so doing began his career as a critic, an occupation that would engage him until middle age and to which he would return in the last decade of his life. The early years were difficult ones. For the first fifteen months after his father left, the reviews he wrote were his only means of support, and a not altogether steady one: on at least one occasion he is reported to have spent his last few pence on ice cream. Although the bravura of such gestures was no doubt attractive to a young man on his own for the first time, Patmore realized that gestures were not the stuff on which to build a future, and in 1846, through the intercession of Monckton Milnes, he became an assistant librarian at the British Museum, a position he was to hold for the next twenty years.

Both his writing and his librarianship yielded results which Patmore could not have foreseen. Although he wrote on numerous subjects—there are, for example, over two dozen articles on architecture—his main interest, as one would expect, was literature, and through the review work he was forced to reread the standard English authors and to consider for the first time many English, Continental, and American contemporary ones as well. The reading and review writing broadened his literary interests. Equally important, they forced him to entertain questions he had not asked himself before, the purpose of art, for example, or the role of the poet. Finally, they made him one of the most prolific poet-critics of his century. Donne, Herbert, Shakespeare, Browne, Goldsmith, Coleridge, Keats, Shelley, Tennyson, Ruskin, and Carlyle—these are only some of the writers whose work he addressed.

Patmore's criticism is not systematic or theoretically coherent. He never approached criticism from a systematic or theoretical point of view. Nor is his criticism particularly original. Art has a moral function; the poet is a seer; poetry is organic; great literature is impersonal—ideas such as these easily find their slots under the majority or strong minority opinion of the time. Yet, though he was forced into criticism, Patmore never took his critical work cavalierly. He detested puffery and what he called "chat" and was prepared to take issue even with those he knew and respected, as he did with Tennyson, who was both a friend and a mentor in Patmore's early years. Because of the seriousness with which he approached it, therefore, his criticism throws a particularly illuminating light on his poetry. One example can serve to illustrate. There is a recurrent reference in his prose to what Patmore calls "masculine" and "feminine" powers, powers which he claimed all geniuses possess. The terms become a convenient framework for a multitude of contrasts—for example, in style, the energy of the masculine versus the grace of the feminine. The obvious fundamentalness of the concept and, moreover, the very number of occurrences of its use demonstrate how importantly the sexual principle figured in his vision of reality and thus how salient it is to the understanding of his poetry.

The amount and range of Patmore's reading grew also through his position at the British Museum. His work there left him with many idle hours, and he filled them with an even greater variety of books than that imposed upon him by his review work. It was in the British Museum that he began to study Roman Catholic theology, at first widely and then more narrowly as his interests focused. These studies were to have a profound influence on him. He read the mystics—St. John of the Cross, St. Theresa of Avila and, chiefly, St. Bernard of Clairvaux, whom he was to translate later; and he read St. Thomas Aquinas, about whom he came to know more than any English poet with the exception of Gerard Manley Hopkins. His writings, even to the end of his life, are sprinkled with references to Aquinas, as were, according to the poet Arthur Symons, his conversations. Patmore himself credited the *Summa Theologica* of Aquinas with showing him better than he knew before "that true poetry and true theological science had to do with one and the same ideal."

It is difficult, if not impossible, to uncover the exact sources of a man's thought. Though Patmore himself liked to say that, rather than providing him with new ideas, his reading clarified his own intuitions, there is ample evidence in his work of the legacy of his more influential reading. From Emerson he acquired strong idealism, from Wordsworth the purity of the child's vision, the sacramental qualities of nature, and the transformational powers of the poet, from Coleridge an interest in human psychology and the tendency toward a symbolic apprehension of the universe. Swedenborg's claim on Patmore is too profound to be reduced to summary, though his chief legacy is perhaps his idea of the sexual duality of being (the division of all being into male and female halves, which, opposed and apart, move toward unity). Yet there is no question that, built upon or mixed with these influences, the writings of the saints during the years at the British

Museum began to assume for Patmore a controlling and shaping power, and that out of it emerged several of his lifelong convictions.

One of these was the presence of order in the universe, an order which, both in its natural and human spheres, was a reflection of a divine order and of its fulfillment. Another was the existence of a "final cause," that is, that being exists and can be defined by the end toward which it moves. Both of these ideas are fundamental in Thomist thought. Even more pronounced in its influence perhaps is the view in the *Summa* of the human body. Aquinas saw it, not as Patmore's earlier readings of Platonism had shown it, as a trap from which the soul longed to escape, but as the perfect complement to the soul, the thing which gave the soul its completeness. Moreover, the *Summa* stressed that the dignity of the body was made manifest in the Incarnation, God's assumption of the human form, and that the motivation for the Incarnation was the divine love for man. St. Bernard had stressed this love as well, emphasizing its ardor and claiming the most apt symbol for the mutual love of God and the individual human soul to be the love of husband and wife. The measure of the influence of these ideas can be found in all of Patmore's writing but especially in the poetry, in its controlling theme of married love, which over the years Patmore perceived more and more clearly as the symbol of the marriage of God and man. "This," Patmore had scribbled in a note discovered in his papers after his death, "is the burning heart of the Universe."

No matter how powerful the sway of his reading, however, it remains in the end a moot question whether such a note and all the poetry embodying its zealous conviction would have been written at all had it not been for one other influence. Patmore was neither an intellectual nor a philosopher. What in the end defined his character was not his intelligence, though his contemporaries were all quick to acknowledge it, but his passions, and his profoundest beliefs, whatever their sources, rested finally on his affective life. In 1847 Patmore met and married Emily Augusta Andrews, and in her, miraculously as far as he was concerned, he found a living source and confirmation of his great theme's truth.

By all accounts she was beautiful—Browning's "A Face" was inspired by her—and she became the center of Patmore's life and the catalyst for his art, the woman, he wrote as an inscription to *The Angel in the House,* "by whom and for whom I became a poet." If Basil Champneys's account of Emily Patmore in his biography of the poet borders on hagiography, it is nevertheless certain that his

Emily Augusta Andrews Patmore, Patmore's first wife. Portrait by John Brett.

account of her was based on fact. She possessed a spiritual as well as a physical beauty, and it is a tribute to her that the lean years as librarian and critic were the happiest of Patmore's life. She entertained and enchanted his friends—Tennyson, Browning, Ruskin, Carlyle, Emerson, Hawthorne and others—was a reader of his poetry and an adviser to him, and gave him six children. In all respects she was an inspiration.

By 1849 Patmore had completed "Tamerton Church-Tower," though it was not published until several years later, in a volume called *Tamerton Church-Tower and Other Poems.* The title poem, a long narrative-descriptive piece, tells the story of a ride taken by a young man with his friend to meet his friend's fiancée. The young man himself meets a young woman, courts her, and marries her, only to have her drown at sea. The story is slight and is intended as a frame to contrast the emotional state of the young man before and after the woman's death, mainly through descriptions of nature, especially some vivid and exact meteorological conditions. Although the poem is more ambitious than one of his biographers, Derek Patmore, suggests—"a preliminary experiment and effort

prior to . . . *The Angel in the House*"—it and the entire volume still show Patmore struggling to free himself from his early influences. Some of the roughness of his *Poems* is smoothed over, but the importance of the volume lies in its inclusion of two short poems which were later to be incorporated in *The Angel in the House* and which name its two principal characters: "Felix: Love's Apology" and "Honoria: Ladies' Praise."

By 1853, when *Tamerton Church-Tower and Other Poems* was published, Patmore was composing rapidly. In 1854 *The Betrothal* appeared. This was book one of *The Angel in the House.* Book two, *The Espousals,* appeared two years later, and the combined books were published, for the first time under Patmore's name, in 1858. Each of the two books consists of a prelude and twelve cantos, which in turn are made up of from two to five short "preludes" followed by a narrative or "idyll." The entire poem is rounded off with an epilogue. Patmore thought of the poem as a kind of domestic epic, yet, though it is long, its story, very unlike that of an epic, is slight. Felix Vaughn is a young poet who falls in love with a beautiful young woman, Honoria. He receives permission from her father to court her. The body of the narrative portion of the poem recounts their courtship—walks taken together, church services attended, dances—and their accompanying feelings. At the end of book one Honoria accepts Felix's proposal of marriage and the two become engaged. The second book continues

Patmore in 1855, a year after publication of The Betrothal, *book one of* The Angel in the House. *Drawing by John Brett.*

the details of the courtship: attending a ball, for example, or writing love letters. At the end of book two they are married.

A summary of events of the poem does as much justice to *The Angel in the House* as it does to *Paradise Lost*. Patmore felt that the age of narrative poetry was over. He was not interested in external incident. Whether or not he was taking his cue again from Wordsworth—Wordsworth had said of his own poetry in *The Preface* (1800) that "the feeling therein developed gives importance to the action and the situation and not the action and situation to the feeling"—Patmore was clearly part of a nineteenth-century development in poetry which gave precedence to emotional or psychological exploration over plot and incident. As examples he already had the mood pieces of Tennyson's early work (which he always maintained were Tennyson's best) and, though he was not a great admirer of Browning, Browning's first monologues.

The initial public response to *The Angel in the House* was unenthusiastic. Not until a favorable review by Patmore's friend Aubrey de Vere in the powerful *Edinburgh Review* and news of the poem's popularity in the United States—Emerson and Hawthorne were both admirers of the poem—did *The Angel in the House* begin to attract large numbers of readers. The reluctance in England to accept the poem was in part an uncertainty about its form, which was new and unique for the time. The combination of two distinct modes, the narrative and the lyric, something that Patmore had settled on only after considerable deliberation and effort, seemed curious.

Once his readers overcame the difficulty of the form, however, they found a poem which embodied one of the sacred tenets of Victorian culture. Christian marriage, Patmore was saying, presented the possibility of perfect fulfillment for man and the source of the highest joy he could know. By following the characters of Felix and Honoria in the evolution of their romance—in their early acquaintance, their doubts and hesitations, their elation at being accepted by one another, the triumph of their marriage and the serenity of their married life—he was showing how love that exists before marriage and grows into greater maturity after, with its natural fruition of children, offers man in its range, intensity, and variableness the full complement of human experience. It was a theme that Victorian readers wanted to hear.

The Angel in the House has for many modern readers several failings. There are lapses into sentimentality and an absence of realism. The charac-

ters and their mostly rural setting seem pastoral, too far removed from urban, industrial society with its attendant evils to have any meaning. It can be argued just as well, however, that this is part of the poem's charm and that no matter how far removed from us they are, the young lovers are revealed with a freshness and a universality that transcend the boundaries of their Victorian setting.

That this latter view is in the end the more accurate and fair can be seen when one examines the poem's structure. At its best it functions beautifully, subtly, its parts working symbiotically. The preludes, exalting, choruslike, soft, or witty, seem to grow naturally into the idyll that follows. The idyll in its turn grows out of and yet turns back to the preludes, particularizing, illustrating, demonstrating in the characters' actions or thoughts emotional or psychological truth. The structure of the poem becomes a metaphor for its theme: the angel, or love, is incarnated and given shape in the house, the body, as the preludes are given flesh or form in the narrative. The test of the poem's formal success is to read the lyrical and narrative sections separately: the preludes alone, though sometimes forceful, wither without the narrative, while the narrative without the preludes appears trivial, banal, and bland. Together, however, they reveal Patmore's unusual talent for seeing the exceptional in the apparently quotidian and for transforming the events of daily life into the powerful and the moving.

Patmore's domestic epic did not stop with *The Angel in the House*. As he had conceived his poem, there were to be six parts: the two books of the *Angel;* two that were to end the poem on the hope which remains for individual love in death, books he never wrote; and the middle two, *Faithful For Ever,* published separately in 1860, and *The Victories of Love*, which appeared serially in *Macmillan's Magazine* and in book form in 1862.

In *The Victories of Love*, the title Patmore chose for these combined third and fourth books, the happy circumstances and outcome of the courtship and marriage of Felix and Honoria are contrasted to those of a pair of lovers who are less fortunate in their means and, so it seems in the beginning of their story at least, in the fate that brings them together. Frederick, the protagonist, is Honoria's rejected suitor, and he and Jane, his wife, must overcome an initial incompatibility if their marriage is to survive. Instead of the idyllic life of Felix and Honoria, we are given the wandering and near despair of Frederick, the homeliness and feelings of inadequacy in Jane. In *The Angel in the House* Felix and Honoria have their children gathered around

The Railway.   133

~5~

I found the Book she had used, and stay'd
   For Evening Prayers, in grief's despite
Felt grief assuaged, then homeward stray'd,
   Weary beforehand of the night.
The blackbird, in the shadowy wood,
   Talk'd to himself; and eastward grew
In heaven the symbol of my mood,
   Where one bright star engross'd the blue.

5.

I pass'd the home of my regret :
   The clock was chiming in the hall,
And one sad window open yet,
   Although the dews began to fall.
Her distance shew'd her worth's true scope!
   How airy of heart and innocent
That loveliness which sicken'd hope,
   And wore the world for ornament!
O, no one loved her half enough,
   Not ev'n her sisters and the Dean.
All tenderness save mine seem'd rough,
   Officious, ignorant, and mean.
I wonder'd, would her bird be fed,
   Her rose-plots water'd, she not by?
Loading my breast with angry dread
   Of light, unlikely injury.
So, fill'd with love and fond remorse,
   I paced this Goshen, every part,

Patmore's additions to section nine, book one of The Angel in the House *(collection of Gordon N. Ray, courtesy of The Pierpont Morgan Library)*

Endow'd with reliquary force
　To heal and raise from death my heart.
How tranquil and unsecular
　The precinct! Once, through yonder gate,
I saw her go, and knew from far
　Her noble form and gentle state;
Her dress had touch'd this door-post; here
　She turn'd her face and laugh'd, with looks
Like moonbeams on a wavering mere;
　This was her stall: these were her books;
Here had she knelt: here, now, I stay'd
　For Evening Prayers: in grief's despite
Felt grief assuaged; then homeward stray'd,
　Weary beforehand of the night.
The blackbird in the shadowy wood
　Talk'd to himself; and eastward grew
In heaven the symbol of my mood,
　Where one bright star engross'd the blue.

them. Frederick and Jane must watch two of their children die. In *The Victories of Love* Patmore shows married love being won but only with determination. The poem ends happily with an epithalamium celebrating the marriage of Frederick and Jane's child, but not before we have seen the death of Jane.

There are other differences. Patmore switches from the octosyllabic quatrain of *The Angel in the House* to the octosyllabic couplet. He offers a greater number of characters, and, most distinct of all, he moves from the format of the prelude-narrative to one of a series of letters. This has the effect of placing even less emphasis on narrative and, correspondingly, a greater one on characterization.

The Victories of Love has generally been considered less successful than *The Angel in the House*. Missing in the poem is a sense of finish, the quality the Pre-Raphaelites had admired in his 1844 *Poems* and which he had himself urged on them: never leave a poem "till the whole of it be brought to a pitch of excellence perfectly satisfactory," he had said; "it is the last rub that polishes the mirror." The sometimes clouded mirror in *The Victories of Love* has to do with the poem's structure and its inherent difficulties. It disallows the overview Patmore had sought and achieved by the preludes in *The Angel in the House* and thus precludes a firm narrative control. With the wholly dramatic structure—the letters are like monologues—transitions are not always smooth and there is difficulty in maintaining balance. Frederick, for example, disappears too abruptly in the poem. The couplet too is sometimes hard to control. Patmore is sometimes gnomic or epigrammatic when the situation demands the more informal or expansive style of the letter.

This is not to say that the poem is a failure. The keen psychological aperçus of *The Angel in the House* continue in *The Victories of Love,* and the multiple points of view allow for a greater concentration and development of the supporting characters, though the focus remains throughout on Frederick and Jane. By modern standards the later poem has a greater verisimilitude than *The Angel in the House,* focusing as it does on lovers who initially are as likely to part as they are to remain together. There is, on the whole, a greater range of feeling than in *The Angel,* and in some instances the feeling is more intense, particularly in the poignant last letters of Jane as she nears her death. The thematic core of the poem, in spite of its dramatic structure, is never lost sight of and is revealed either in single lines of letters—"Image and glory of the man,/As he of God, is woman," Jane writes to Frederick—or in whole utterance, as in the wedding sermon closing

the poem, which provides as complete a statement of Patmore's philosophy of love as can be found in his poetry.

If there are failures in *The Victories of Love,* one is more likely to find the explanation for them in the circumstances under which the poem was written rather than in faulty artistic conception. Even before the publication of the complete *Angel in the House* Emily Patmore's health had begun to suffer. At first the lapses were temporary, and she would quickly recover; but these recoveries themselves were short-lived, and by 1861 Patmore knew that she was dying. Throughout the composition of *The Victories of Love,* then, the threat of his wife's death hung over him. Though one cannot be sure, it is reasonable to expect that his distraction could have caused the greater looseness of control one senses in the poem. Certainly it helps to explain the pathos which pervades it. The inspiration for the realization of love and life fulfilled in *The Angel in the House,* Emily was now the source of the melancholy spirit which continually intruded in its sequel. Her death of consumption in the summer of 1862 left Patmore shattered. He was to marry again, but the exuberance and joy of the years with his first wife were never recaptured.

The years immediately following Emily Patmore's death were desolate ones for the poet. His meager means forced him to board his four youngest children with friends, and, with his two older boys already gone from home in pursuit of their careers, he lived alone. The effect of the death upon him and upon his poetry is suggested by the postscript he attached to *The Victories of Love* in 1863. Withdrawing his intention to write the projected fifth and sixth books, "It is well," he said, "for the interest in poetry in this great and hitherto unapproached theme, that my weak voice has been hushed. I no longer have, at every step, the needful encouragement of an approval which was all that my heart valued of fame." By 1864, Patmore, who himself had never enjoyed vigorous health, was obliged to ask sick leave from his position at the British Museum. It was granted, and he left for the warmer climate of Rome. Yet, like his sojourn in Paris at the age of sixteen, the seemingly innocent holiday had unexpected consequences. It was to mark the end of the first phase of Patmore's adult life.

Emily Patmore had known her husband well. She had predicted, and feared, Patmore's conversion to Catholicism, to which he had been attracted for years. "When I am gone," Patmore records her saying on her deathbed, "they (the Catholics) will

*Marianne Byles Patmore in an 1871 drawing by John Brett.
Patmore met Marianne Byles in Rome two years after the death of
his first wife. They married in the summer of 1864.*

get you." She had also recognized that the emphasis on marital love in his poetry had been born not only of intellectual conviction but also of passionate need and thus foresaw that he would marry again, and welcomed it. In her will she left her blessing and her wedding ring for his second wife. By the summer of 1864 both the event she feared and the one she welcomed had taken place. Patmore was received into the Church, and he and Marianne Byles, whom he had met in Rome, were married.

The years of Patmore's second marriage are something of a puzzle. Marianne Byles was an heiress and, because the marriage thus brought with it financial security, Patmore was able to resign his librarian's post. His health was still not strong, and, with his recovery in mind, he purchased and moved to a four-hundred-acre estate in Sussex, which he named Heron's Ghyll. Life in the country seemed to agree with him. His health improved. He threw himself into the improvement of the house and grounds and surrounded himself with the accoutrements of the country squire. His children were reunited with him, and his wife, though she knew she could never replace Emily, was nevertheless devoted to him and to her stepchildren. From all the accounts of his friends, the marriage, if not the ideal one that he had had with Emily, was comfortable, and Patmore a happy man.

Yet there is ample evidence to suggest that

Heron's Ghyll, the four-hundred-acre estate in Sussex purchased by Patmore in the mid-1860s

there were deeper currents running within him far less serene that his rustic life indicated. In a play on Richard Lovelace's lines from "To Lucasta, Going to the Wars" and in an allusion to Emily ("Honor" refers to Honoria, the heroine of *The Angel in the House* whom Patmore identifies with his first wife), he writes in a letter to Marianne, "I could not love thee, dear, so much/Loved I not 'Honor' more." The touch is light and the lines are a tribute to his affection for his wife, yet they recall as well his inability to forget Emily. The odes he began to write after Emily's death and during these years of his second marriage are not light, however. Later to become incorporated into his volume entitled *The Unknown Eros,* they reveal the deeper currents clearly and are disturbed, full of remorse, anxiety, and restlessness. Earthly compensation for his wife's death appears either to elude him or to remain with him only temporarily. In lieu of it there begins to emerge a search for divine love, one of the themes which predominates in *The Unknown Eros.* "Love makes the life to be/A fountain perpetual of virginity," he says in "Deliciae Sapientiae De Amore," a poem he wrote in these troubled years:

> For, lo, the Elect
> Of generous Love, how named soe'er, affect
> Nothing but God,
> Or mediate or direct,
> Nothing but God,
> The Husband of the Heavens:
> And who Him love, in potence great or small,
> Are, one and all,
> Heirs of the Palace glad,
> And inly clad
> With the bridal robes of ardour virginal.

We are left, then, with a dual picture of Patmore during the years at Heron Ghyll. On the one hand there was the public Patmore, the family patriarch and man of property, building aviaries and breeding fish, surrounded by his St. Bernards, marveling at the achievements of a new thrash machine, and threatening poachers with a pistol. And on the other there was the private Patmore, whose poetry became introspective, who, apparently in disillusion, took to burning secretly his published works—the copies he owned of the *Odes* he had privately printed in 1868 and unsold copies of *The Angel in the House* he had purchased from his publisher—and who in his letters spoke of a sense of uselessness and failure, of waiting to die.

Even as he burned his published works, however, Patmore continued to write through the early 1870s. In the meantime his estate prospered to the point that, because of the many improvements, it had become too expensive for Patmore to manage. In 1874, therefore, he sold it and moved back to London. His stay was brief, only a year, but it was exactly what he needed. It took him out of his seclusion and put him back into touch with old friends such as Ruskin and Carlyle. Though his health began to fail him again and he was forced once more to move from the city, he was renewed by the encouragement he had received. His new location, in Hastings, spurred his enthusiasm even higher. The house that became available there, Milward Mansion, was one he had known and, as a boy, resolved to live in one day. He had enjoyed childhood holidays in Hastings and had spent his honeymoon there with Emily. His return with his family to this place from his past was like a tonic. Rejuvenated after the years of uncertainty, his poetry began to come quickly again, and the first edition of *The Unknown Eros* was published, anonymously, in 1877. A second edition with fifteen new poems appeared a year later.

With *The Unknown Eros* Patmore moved to a form of poem quite different from anything he had published before. The tight metrical organization of both *The Angel in the House* and *The Victories of Love* are abandoned for a looser, freer form, one Patmore claimed was his own new discovery. There are no longer the quatrains and couplets of the two earlier poems, and rhyme, though it is retained, is used irregularly, though it is often balanced with assonance. The line length is also irregular; some lines are long, others as brief as two syllables, and there are no stanza units. The changes were carefully plotted: Patmore claimed that the forms of his previous poems did not meet the requirements for the sustained seriousness he was seeking in *The Unknown Eros.* At the same time he needed the flexibility that the range of these poems demanded, a form which could accommodate the meditative, the satiric, the ecstatic.

The Unknown Eros is his most ambitious work. In it Patmore addresses the subject he had proposed for the concluding, but later abandoned, two books of his earlier, abandoned domestic epic: the hope which remains for individual love in death. The work is divided into two books, the first focused mainly on that world explored in *The Angel in the House* and *The Victories of Love:* Patmore examines man in the three spheres of his earthly existence—in nature, in his individual relationships, illustrated in the poem by the love between man and woman and its loss by death, and in society. The most affecting of the poems are those dealing with love and death, no doubt because they recall, as some of the letters from *The Victories of Love* do, Patmore's still passionately felt memory of Emily. In them one finds a full, often surprising exploration of feeling in the contemplation of the death of the loved one—agony, fatigue, even petulance: "It was not like your great and gracious ways!," the lover says at the beginning of "Departure,"

> Do you, that have nought other to lament,
> Never, my Love, repent
> Of how, that July afternoon,
> You went,
> With sudden, unintelligible phrase,
> And frighten'd eye,
> Upon your journey of so many days,
> Without a single kiss, or a good-bye?

The book's pattern, however, is like that of a classical elegy, toward consolation, which for Patmore, the Christian poet, is the gain of the Divine Presence. In the last poem of book one, "Vesica Piscis," Patmore, speaking through the fisherman St. Peter, can say:

> "I have labour'd through the Night, nor yet
> Have taken aught;
> But at Thy word I will again cast forth the net!"
> And, lo, I caught
> (Oh, quite unlike and quite beyond my thought,)
> Not the quick, shining harvest of the Sea,
> For food, my wish,
> But Thee!

The second book leaves the earthly world to concentrate on Man's relationship with God, showing him aspiring to and eventually possessing and possessed by Divine Love. In these poems, especially the ones dealing with Eros and Psyche, Patmore's adapted symbols for God and the soul, we are given both the poet's clearest vision of the ardor that moves the Creator and the created toward each other and his most daring poetic expression of that vision. In the poems the mutual love of man and woman, which for Patmore had always had inherent in it and was in fact the paradigm of the mutual love of God and man, has been transformed, and we see unclothed something of the intensity that inspired Patmore to write the scenes of rural outings, ballroom dances, and drawing-room badinage which comprise *The Angel in the House:* " 'O, too much joy; O, touch of airy fire;/O, turmoil of content; O, unperturb'd desire,' " cries Psyche the soul as she is

infused by the fiery love of her Divine Lover.

The ambition of Patmore's odes was not matched by a corresponding enthusiasm in their public reception. The pendulum of public taste had swung away from the poet of *The Angel in the House,* and *The Unknown Eros* was virtually ignored. Patmore's disappointment was assuaged somewhat in the years that followed when he began to gain admirers from a new generation—the critic Edmund Gosse, who later wrote a biography of him, and, among others, the poets Francis Thompson, Lionel Johnson, Robert Bridges, and Gerard Manley Hopkins. But their number was small, and they tended to restrict their support, praising *The Unknown Eros* but retaining their reservations about his earlier work. It was now clear to Patmore that the heady reception he had won with *The Angel in the House* was never to be repeated.

In the meantime his personal life was struck with tragedy. In 1880 his second wife died. An even greater blow, however, was the death of his daugh-

Harriet Robson, who became Patmore's third wife on 13 September 1881

ter Emily, who was closer to him than any of his other children and knew him and understood him almost as well as her mother had. A nun, and a poet herself, she had read and criticized his odes and offered him encouragement when there was none to be found elsewhere. She died in 1882. Her death was not the last in the family, however. Only a year later, Henry, Patmore's youngest son, like his sister also a poet, died as well. Although the lack of sympathetic response to *The Unknown Eros* weighed heavily upon Patmore, it was more the death of his two children which ended his career as a poet. He continued revisions for a collected edition, but he wrote no more new poems.

The early 1880s began the third and last stage of Patmore's life. In the last years of his second marriage his wife had become a chronic invalid, and many of her duties had been assumed by Harriet Robson, who had already been serving the family as a governess to Patmore's daughters. In 1881 Robson became Patmore's third wife. Young and resil-

John Singer Sargent's 1894 portrait of Patmore (National Portrait Gallery)

ient, it was she who saw him through the series of family deaths. She gave him as well, late in his life, a son, a consolation for the loss of his two children. Unlike Marianne Byles, who had always been retiring and who had failed to understand his later poems, Harriet Robson was outgoing, vivacious, and interested in his poetry, and she enjoyed the role of a poet's wife. She was affectionate, a defender of his reputation, and, in his last years, his nurse.

Though Patmore began to age rapidly in his sixties, he did not stop working. The final decade of his life saw his return once again to prose. He wrote over a hundred articles and reviews, most of them appearing in the *St. James's Gazette*. He also produced several prose volumes during this period, including *Principle in Art* (1889) and *Religio Poetae* (1893), both selections of earlier essays, and *The Rod, the Root and the Flower* (1895), a collection of jottings and aphorisms.

In 1891 Patmore moved again, to Lymington, and it was there that he spent his final years. He lived in an isolated house at the seaside with his wife, his young son, and two unmarried daughters. Though these years were ones of growing seclusion he continued to maintain contact with the outside world. He entertained occasionally at his home— Francis Thompson was a frequent visitor and John Singer Sargent came to paint him—and visited in London with Wilfred Meynell and Meynell's poet wife Alice, with whom Patmore had formed a deep (some have suggested a passionate) friendship. Through the Meynells he met several of the new London literati, including W. E. Henley and Frank Harris. Patmore's health was failing, however, and by 1894 he had grown very weak. He died, following a cold, in November of 1896.

Assessment of Coventry Patmore's poetry has always been problematic for several reasons. In his own lifetime the decline of interest in *The Angel in the House* and *The Victories of Love* and the unenthusiastic reception of his later work had much to do with his conversion to Catholicism and remarriage after his first wife died. The Protestant public could not separate the poet from the proselyte. Nor could readers forgive him for forgetting Emily (he had not, of course). Patmore was also conservative, even reactionary in his later years, and he made no effort to disguise his opinion in his conversations, letters, essays, or poetry. In the poem "1867" he recalls the passing of the Second Reform Bill as "the year of the great crime,/When the false English Nobles and their Jew [Benjamin Disraeli],/By God demented, slew/The Trust they stood twice pledged to keep

The Lodge, Lymington, where Patmore spent his final years

from wrong." Attitudes such as this made him appear outmoded, to say the least, to the liberal and progressive reading public.

To many late-twentieth-century readers Patmore remains a man outdistanced by history because of his religious, political, and social views. Today it is not his Catholicism which would be suspect but the fact that it is theologically conservative and conforms so closely to nineteenth-century doctrine. His faith might be granted him, if begrudgingly, but its depth questioned because it was so unswerving and true. Modern faith, at least in literature, is legitimatized only when it is hard-won or threatened by doubt. Patmore's remarriages would be accepted easily enough, but his attitude to women—here he would appear to be most reactionary—would be rejected outright. In keeping with his doctrinaire conservatism and nineteenth-century Catholicism, Patmore saw women as legally and socially inferior. His view of marriage, with its necessity for the subjugation of a wife to her husband, hinged on this understanding of women. To a secular age it means little that on the spiritual level Patmore saw woman as man's equal or even his superior and that he saw the married state as sacramental and man's chief means of knowing

God. Taken out of the context of the religious, to which Patmore's perception of women and society is inextricably bound, his ideas appear passé.

There are other reasons, literary ones, which make assessing Patmore difficult. Among critics Patmore has had his enthusiasts and his detractors. These have ranged from Sir Herbert Read, who placed him in the company of Dante and Donne, and John Heath-Stubbs, who saw him as the great Victorian poet, to an array of others who find him sentimental, ridiculous, or at best amusingly eccentric. For most, however, the difficulty is to find a proper context for evaluating his work. Should he be seen in the line of the English mystic poets? Parts of *The Unknown Eros* would suggest that a comparison with, say, the seventeenth-century poet Richard Crashaw would be appropriate. And yet *The Angel in the House* with its country idylls and *The Victories of Love* with its psychological probing of characters immediately suggest the limitation of this category. Is he to be relegated to the relatively minor status of a Catholic poet? Because his poetry transcends his Catholicism, this label would be as unfair to him as it would be to Hopkins. His wit in some of the preludes in *The Angel in the House* aligns him with the metaphysical poets, but as often as he is inclined to

In theme and technique Paton's Hesperus *(1857), depicting Arthurian lovers, shows his affinity with the Pre-Raphaelites during the decade of the 1850s (Glasgow Museum and Art Gallery).*

but the poem fails to invest its subject with tragic grandeur. Given Paton's pronounced mythological tastes, it is curious that he failed to find resonance in the ship's classical name; one might expect a pun, for example, on Christoph Willibald Gluck's famous aria "Che faro senza Euridice?" ("Where are you now, Euridice?"). The curmudgeonly outburst on the "steam machine" is indicative of the poem's failure to find a proper tone or focus.

Archaisms are more appropriate to the medieval setting of "The Tomb in the Chancel," in which the alliteration and the heaviness of the verse ("his clangorous life-moil long since done,/Sir Everard Raby in his hauberk slept") help to distance the material from the reader. But it is a sign of ineptitude that Paton speaks of the knight's "craven mail," since the poem does not question Raby's courage elsewhere or treat him ironically. "With the

Sunshine and the Swallows" shows Paton's love of Miltonic exotic words; "Tyrrhenian" redeems the bland words preceding it. But otherwise it seems a trite exercise in nostalgia: "She is coming, my beloved, o'er the sea!"

Paton was also the author of *A Christmas Carol,* included in *The New Amphion,* "the book of the Edinburgh University fancy fair," in 1886 and published posthumously in pamphlet form in 1907. He provided illustrations for Shelley's *Prometheus Unbound* (1844), Coleridge's *Rime of the Ancient Mariner* (1863), and William Edmondstoune Aytoun's *Lays of the Scottish Cavaliers* (1863). Paton died in Edinburgh in December 1901. Margaret Bloomhill Paton, his wife of more than forty years and mother of their eleven children, had died the preceding year.

John Payne

(23 August 1842-11 February 1916)

C. W. Willerton
Abilene Christian University

BOOKS: *The Masque of Shadows and Other Poems* (London: Pickering, 1870);

Intaglios: Sonnets (London: Pickering, 1871);

Songs of Life and Death (London: King, 1872);

Lautrec: A Poem (London: Pickering, 1878);

New Poems (London: Newman, 1880);

The Descent of the Dove and Other Poems (London: Privately printed, 1902);

Vigil and Vision: New Sonnets (London: Villon Society, 1903);

Twelve Sonnets de Combat [supplement to *Vigil and Vision*] (London: Privately printed, 1903);

Songs of Consolation (London: Simkin, Marshall, Hamilton, Kent, 1904);

Sir Winfrith and Other Poems (Olney: Thomas Wright, 1905);

Verses for the Newton-Cowper Centenary (Olney: Cowper Press, 1907);

The Quatrains of Ibn et Tefrid (London?: Privately printed, 1908);

Carol and Cadence: New Poems, MDCCCCII-MDCCCCVII (London: Villon Society, 1908); republished in part as *Nature and Her Lover and Other Poems*

from *"Carol and Cadence"* (Olney: John Payne Society, 1922);

Flower o' the Thorn (London: Villon Society, 1909);

Humoristica, three series (London?: Privately printed, 1909-1910);

The Way of the Winepress (Olney: John Payne Society, 1920);

The Autobiography of John Payne, edited by Thomas Wright (Olney: Thomas Wright, 1926).

Collections: *The Poetical Works of John Payne,* 2 volumes (London: Villon Society, 1902);

Selections from the Poetry of John Payne, edited by Tracy and Lucy Robinson (New York: Lane/Bodley Head, 1906).

TRANSLATIONS: *The Poems of Master François Villon* (London: Villon Society, 1878);

The Book of the Thousand Nights and One Night, 9 volumes (London: Villon Society, 1882-1884); parts republished as *Book of the Thousand Nights and One Night* (London: Privately printed, 1906) and *Abou Mohammed the Lazy, and Other*

John Payne, 1904

Tales from the Arabian Nights (Olney: John Payne Society, 1906);

Tales from the Arabic (3 volumes, London: Privately printed, 1884; 4 volumes, London: Villon Society, 1884-1889);

Alaeddin and the Enchanted Lamp; Zein ul Asnam and the King of the Jinn (London: Privately printed, 1885?; London: Villon Society, 1889);

The Decameron of Boccaccio, 3 volumes (London: Villon Society, 1886);

The Novels of Matteo Bandello, 6 volumes (London: Villon Society, 1890);

The Quatrains of Omar Kheyyam (London: Villon Society, 1898);

The Poems of Shemseddin Mohammed Hafiz, 3 volumes (London: Villon Society, 1901);

Flowers of France: The Romantic Period, 2 volumes (London: Villon Society, 1906);

Flowers of France: The Renaissance Period (London: Villon Society, 1907);

The Poetical Works of Heinrich Heine, 3 volumes (London: Villon Society, 1911);

Flowers of France: The Latter Days, 2 volumes (London: Villon Society, 1913);

Flowers of France: The Classic Period (London: Villon Society, 1914).

Determined to be recognized as a great poet, John Payne left behind hundreds of pages of poems as well as a worshipful John Payne Society. Neither the poetry nor the Society has endured. His best legacy was his translations of Villon, *The Decameron, The Arabian Nights,* and other exotic poems and tales. Payne's own poems, most of them written in the 1870s, ranged from ballads to sonnets to bizarre dramatic monologues and showed impressive ingenuity in versification and imagery. His early poems were well received. Over the years, however, his poems failed to progress beyond their Pre-Raphaelite models in subject, mood, or language. The blast of originality never came that could have lifted Payne's work to a level with Dante Gabriel Rossetti's or A. C. Swinburne's. Despite his helping found the Villon Society and promoting Stéphane Mallarmé's work among his friends, Payne's contribution to English aestheticism was minor.

Payne's love of books, languages, and exotic stories, as well as his craving for recognition, began in his boyhood. Several of his ancestors had been wealthy and powerful, but members of Payne's own immediate family were neither. His father, John Edward Hawkins-Payne, was a linguist and an inventor but a poor businessman. Financial losses put an end to young John Payne's schooling, forcing him to work at the age of thirteen. But he had already begun to love languages and poetry. At the age of ten he had translated some of Horace's odes, and at twelve he had imitated Thomas Babington Macaulay's *Lays of Ancient Rome* by writing of the Roman conquest of Britain. Between the ages of thirteen and nineteen, Payne worked as a clerk, an assistant in a newspaper office, and an usher in two schools. He was morbidly shy. Even years later, writing his *Autobiography,* Payne attacked his father as a heartless Philistine for sending him "out into the world a mere mass of naked nerve, to fight a solitary battle at a frightful disadvantage." But young Payne had some compensations in living in romantic Bristol (the family having moved from London after the financial crisis) and in studying languages. French, Latin, and Greek he had learned at school, but on his own he acquired German, Spanish, Italian, Arabic, Persian, and other languages. Payne writes in his *Autobiography* that by the age of twenty-one he had translated Dante's *Divine Comedy,* major works by Goethe, Lessing, and Calderón, short poems by Heine, Schiller, and other German poets, and lyrics from Spanish, Ital-

Payne's parents, John Edward and Betsy Rogers Hawkins-Payne. According to his biographer Thomas Wright, "John, who had a particular detestation for conjoined names, would never use the hyphenated form [of his surname]."

ian, Portuguese, and French poets.

This strenuous, bookish adolescence readied Payne not only for translating and for writing poetry but also for breaking into London literary society. At age nineteen Payne began a five-year apprenticeship to a London solicitor (he eventually made a career in chancery and conveyancing). Young Payne roamed London, visited often the home of George Henry Lewes and George Eliot (Lewes's son had been Payne's schoolfellow), and read Ralph Waldo Emerson's essays, which stirred him to write original poetry. By 1866, near the end of his legal training, Payne became friends with two other energetic young men, the artist John Trivett Nettleship and the poet Arthur O'Shaughnessy. Nicknamed the Triumvirate, they were often guests of Richard Garnett and of Dr. Westland Marston, father of the poet Philip Bourke Marston. But before long, Payne and O'Shaughnessy had made their way into the Pre-Raphaelite coterie itself. By 1868 Payne had met Ford Madox Brown, Edward

Burne-Jones, William Bell Scott, Theodore Watts (later Watts-Dunton), and Simeon Solomon. At Brown's house they gathered with the Rossetti brothers and sister, William Morris's wife Jane Burden Morris, Mathilde Blind, and the American poet Joaquin Miller (who wore cowboy garb). At about this time Payne also met the young woman who would become his Beatrice—Mrs. Helen Snee.

Golden-haired, delicate, fluent in French, a great reader of Swinburne, Helen Snee won the devotion of both Payne and O'Shaughnessy. Born Helen Matthews, 15 June 1845, she married and was widowed early. Her second marriage, to Frederick Snee, a traveler for a brewery, came when she was twenty-two. O'Shaughnessy's first book of poems, *An Epic of Women* (1870), was mainly inspired by Helen Snee; the volume was illustrated by Nettleship and dedicated to Payne. Apparently Snee inspired some of the poems in Payne's *Songs of Life and Death* (1872) and *New Poems* (1880). But most of his poems about her appear decades later in

Carol and Cadence (1908). Her vivacity in literary company was displaced periodically by gloom and suffering from ill health. Years after her death Payne referred to her as "a beloved companion." Idealizing her, he saw a parallel between her inspiration of his poetry and Beatrice's inspiration of Dante's. All his life a temperamental bachelor and a solitary worker, Payne was mainly immune to romance; Helen Snee can be called his great love, but only in a spiritual sense.

The decade of their friendship saw Payne's rise as a poet. During 1868 and 1869, while the Triumvirate was meeting one writer or artist after another, Payne had worked at sonnets and ballads. *The Masque of Shadows,* appearing in September 1870, comprised "The Rime of Redemption," "The Building of the Dream," "The Romaunt of Sir Floris," and the title poem. Payne's volume of sonnets, *Intaglios,* written before the ballads, was delayed in publication until 1871. These volumes established his promise as a poet. Swinburne praised

The artist John Trivett Nettleship (photo by Elliott & Fry). The close friendship of Nettleship, Payne, and the poet Arthur O'Shaughnessy gave rise to their nickname, "The Triumvirate."

The Masque of Shadows; even thirty-five years later he recalled "The Rime of Redemption" as "a masterpiece." Matthew Arnold praised *Intaglios* in a letter to Payne. Rossetti acclaimed both books. *Intaglios* became Payne's passport to the French literary world. It won him not only the affection of the poet Théodore de Banville but also a visit from Mallarmé, who was to become a great friend. In 1872 Payne's third book, *Songs of Life and Death,* appeared to favorable reviews. A few months later he contributed, by invitation, to a collection of memorial poems for Théophile Gautier, who had died in October. The next year Payne visited Paris. He stayed with Mallarmé and was introduced to Victor Hugo, Anatole France, Villiers de L'Isle-Adam, Jules Laforgue, and other writers.

Payne flourished. By mid-1875 he was well along in translating Villon's poems. But in April 1876 came the shock of Helen Snee's arrest. Her physical suffering and her high-strung temperament had gradually led her to contemplate suicide. Though she had always denied actually resolving to kill herself, she had decided to procure the means in case her pain should become unbearable. Through a newspaper advertisement and under an alias, Snee had found a medical student who would advise her in the "experiment" of concocting an untraceable poison. But when letters between them accidentally reached the authorities, they were arrested for conspiracy to murder Snee. Payne, who had not seen her for a year, rushed to serve as her lawyer throughout the trial. Convicted in June, Snee was imprisoned for six months, her accomplice for eighteen. Payne was distressed at the outcome but had done all he could.

His work on Villon resumed. In 1877, after reading samples of his translation to a group of enthusiasts, he joined them in founding the Villon Society. The next year his translation became the first publication by the society. Payne's *The Poems of Master François Villon* was praised by de Banville, Mallarmé, Matthew Arnold, and others. The *Westminster Review* and other journals reviewed it favorably. His next translation project, a nine-volume version of *The Arabian Nights* (1882-1884), was already underway. In early 1879 he was publishing samples anonymously. But 1880 brought a double shock: the critical failure of his *New Poems* and the death of Helen Snee. Weak from phthisis, she sent for Payne but died before he could come. Payne was devastated. Losing Helen Snee, he also lost his desire to write original poetry. Payne's next two decades are given almost wholly to translation. The death of O'Shaughnessy in 1881 seemed to

Helen Snee, the inspiration for many poems in Payne's Carol
and Cadence *and for O'Shaughnessy's volume* An Epic
of Women

confirm that a chapter in Payne's life had ended.

Some observations about Payne's poems of the
1870s suffice to characterize virtually all his original
poetry. In his ballads he often follows Morris in
medievalism, vivid detail, and emphasis on high
passion. In both ballads and sonnets, Payne follows
Rossetti in obsessively combining love and death.
But Payne's imagery runs to opulence, often dragging down the action. In "The Romaunt of Sir
Floris" a quest for the Grail takes the knight
through deadly battles with monsters to a healing of
his wounds by Sir Galahad and finally a kiss and
exhortation from Christ. But the description of his
journey to Paradise is tedious; in making the journey gorgeous, Payne pores over dozens of
gemstones and names enough flowers to occupy a
botanist. "The Fountain of Youth" also has a quest
and a long journey through exotic scenery but gives
more emphasis to character. "Salvestra" is better; a
story of unrequited love, it has suspense, pathos,
and vigor—in short, the qualities of Boccaccio's
Decameron, from which Payne took the story. These
poems illustrate a constant in Payne's ballads: they
are best when they emphasize plot and worst when
they emphasize description. "The Rime of Redemption," "The Ballad of Shameful Death," and
"The Ballad of May Margaret" profit by avoiding
elaborate description and telling a brief, dramatic
story. But "The Building of the Dream" is dragged
down by sensuous description, telling of an old
knight who wins endless bliss then grows weary of it.

Like Payne's ballads, his more bizarre narratives are most effective when they emphasize plot
over description. *Lautrec* (separately published in
1878), a monologue by a female vampire, is no
match for Poe's work, and "Thorgerda," a
monologue by a Norse witch, is no match for Swinburne's. Still, their action and suspense, as well as
exotic description, hold the attention. In contrast,
"The Masque of Shadows," spoken by a dead soul
traveling through mystical states, is a bore. Trying
to imagine the unimaginable, Payne loses track of
human interest.

Of course, Payne's sonnets (in *Intaglios, New
Poems,* and elsewhere) are less prone to excessive
description than are the ballads, but they sometimes
share a lack of firm conception. Because many are
set in a Pre-Raphaelite dreamland, they are most
successful when the mood is powerful ("Haunted
Life," "Dream-Life") or the personification vivid
("Tropic Flower"). Although Payne's sonnets are
not so original and moving as Rossetti's, neither do
they suffer lapses into obscurity. Payne's sonnets are
weakest when they degenerate into mannerism
("The Garden of Adonis"). His occasional sonnets
(on Corot and on Rabelais, for example) are usually
interesting, though more for their imagery than for
their sentiment. The poems consisting of a series of
sonnets (such as "Winter Roses" and "On the Borders of the Night") keep the vigor and music of the
sonnet while allowing Payne extra space to ac-
cumulate images and build mood.

Payne's translations during the 1880s and
1890s are impressive in bulk and in range of languages. Translating *The Arabian Nights* occupied
Payne until mid-1882 and nearly brought him into
collaboration with the flamboyant traveler and
translator Richard Burton. When Burton announced that his own *Arabian Nights* was underway,
Payne suggested that they join forces. But Payne
had such a head start that Burton finally acted
merely as proofreader for Payne's second volume.
(Burton published his own version in 1885-1886.)
He also invited Payne to join the Kama Shastra
Society, which aimed at publishing Eastern erotica.
Payne refused with distaste. His next projects were
supplements to *The Arabian Nights*—the three-

volume *Tales from the Arabic* (1884) and a set of stories, "Alaeddin" and "Zein ul Asnam" (which formed one volume in the mid-1880s and later became the fourth volume of *Tales*). Payne's translation of *The Decameron* appeared in 1886. During the 1890s he translated the Renaissance novelist Matteo Bandello and the poetry of Omar Khayyám. His translation of the fourteenth-century poet Hafiz (Shemseddin Mohammed) appeared in 1901.

The next year, however, publication of Payne's *Poetical Works* signaled his return to writing original verse. He had broken the drought only once since Helen Snee's death, writing "The Grave of My Songs" in 1896. But at the end of January 1902 he had experienced, as he put it, "an attack of verse-production" and in six weeks had written 4,000 lines. In mid-1902 he collected his earlier poems into the two-volume *Poetical Works*. A few months later he produced a supplement made up of recent poems, *The Descent of the Dove and Other Poems;* he had only twenty-five copies printed, however, supposing that the title poem would offend orthodox Christians. In September 1902 Payne wrote the memoranda that comprise his *Autobiography*. (This monument to Payne's vanity was pub-lished in 1926 by his biographer Thomas Wright of Olney.) *Vigil and Vision* (1903) included 150 sonnets out of 224 he had written during a nine-week "attack." Its supplement, *Twelve Sonnets de Combat,* appeared the same year. In 1905 Payne cheerfully permitted Wright and others to form the John Payne Society, dedicated to appreciating and publishing his works. *Carol and Cadence* (1908) marked Payne's return to the ballad form with such poems as "The Rime of Melisande" and "The Death of Hafiz." It also included most of his lyrics on Helen Snee. He mourned her in "Alas!" and "The Grave of My Songs" and commemorated her beauty and sweetness in numerous other poems. Wright called the book "Payne's *Vita Nuova.*" In Payne's lifetime, *Flower o' the Thorn* was his last volume of serious original poems. (*The Way of the Winepress* appeared posthumously in 1920.) He produced it in 1909, complaining bitterly about how few subscribers it had found.

In addition to these works, Payne, now in his sixties, worked at translation, producing his last volumes of *Flowers of France* (1913, 1914) and his last volumes of *The Poetical Works of Heinrich Heine* (1911). He also produced two strange items, *The*

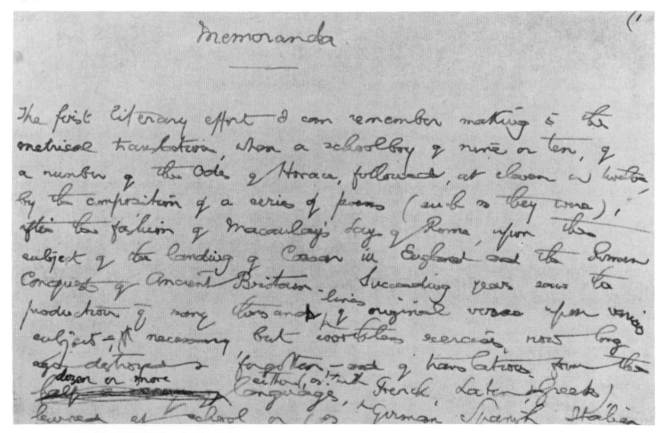

Excerpt from the first manuscript page of Payne's "Memoranda," which were published in 1926 as The Autobiography of John Payne *(Thomas Wright,* The Life of John Payne, *1919)*

Quatrains of Ibn et Tefrid (1908) and *Humoristica* (1909-1910), tokens of his irascibility in old age. The first is a practical joke, a fake translation of a fictitious poet; the second, in three series, is an attack in mock nursery rhymes on various public figures. After 1913 Payne's health weakened; within two years he was blind. He lived to finish a last translation, "The Marvelous History of Seif ben Dhi Yezn, King of Yemen," but it was never published. When he died at age seventy-three, he had outlived his friends and become more solitary and opinionated than ever.

Payne's poetry did not survive him for long, though his translations did. His friends Tracy and Lucy Robinson had tried to promote his work in America with their *Selections from the Poetry of John Payne* (1906). The Payne Society published two small collections after his death, and Wright prepared *The Life of John Payne* (1919) and edited Payne's *Autobiography*. But these were only ripples which faded quickly. An associate and translator of great writers, Payne thought himself their equal. Neither his poems nor Wright's adoring biography has persuaded modern readers to agree.

References:

C. R. McGregor Williams, *John Payne* (Paris: Presses Modernes, 1926);

Thomas Wright, *The Life of John Payne* (London: Unwin, 1919).

Christina Rossetti

H. B. de Groot
University of Toronto

BIRTH: London, 5 December 1830, to Gabriele and Frances Polidori Rossetti.

DEATH: London, 29 December 1894.

BOOKS: *Verses* (London: Privately printed at G. Polidori's, 1847);

Goblin Market and Other Poems (Cambridge & London: Macmillan, 1862);

The Prince's Progress and Other Poems (London: Macmillan, 1866);

Poems (Boston: Roberts Brothers, 1866);

Commonplace and Other Stories (London: Ellis, 1870; Boston: Roberts Brothers, 1870);

Sing-Song: A Nursery Rhyme Book (London: Routledge, 1872; Boston: Roberts Brothers, 1872; revised and enlarged, London: Macmillan, 1893);

Annus Domini: A Prayer for Each Day of the Year, founded on a Text of Holy Scripture (Oxford & London: Parker, 1874);

Speaking Likenesses, with Pictures thereof by Arthur Hughes (London: Macmillan, 1874; Boston: Roberts Brothers, 1875);

Goblin Market, The Prince's Progress, and Other Poems (London & New York: Macmillan, 1875); republished as *Poems* (Boston: Roberts Brothers, 1876);

Seek and Find: A Double Series of Short Studies on the Benedicite (London & Brighton: Society for Promoting Christian Knowledge/New York: Young, 1879);

A Pageant and Other Poems (London: Macmillan, 1881; Boston: Roberts Brothers, 1881);

Called to be Saints: The Minor Festivals Devotionally Studied (London & Brighton: Society for Promoting Christian Knowledge/New York: Young, 1881);

Poems (Boston: Roberts Brothers, 1882);

Letter and Spirit: Notes on the Commandments (London & Brighton: Society for Promoting Christian Knowledge/New York: Young, 1883);

Time Flies: A Reading Diary (London & Brighton: Society for Promoting Christian Knowledge, 1885; Boston: Roberts Brothers, 1886);

Poems, new and enlarged edition (London & New York: Macmillan, 1890);

The Face of the Deep: A Devotional Commentary on the Apocalypse (London & Brighton: Society for Promoting Christian Knowledge/New York: Young, 1892);

Verses: Reprinted from "Called to be Saints," "Time Flies," "The Face of the Deep" (London & Brighton: Society for Promoting Christian Knowledge/New York: Young, 1893);

New Poems, Hitherto Unpublished or Uncollected, edited

by William M. Rossetti (London & New York: Macmillan, 1896);

Maude: A Story for Girls (London: Bowden, 1897; enlarged, Chicago: Stone, 1897);

Poetical Works, edited by William M. Rossetti (London & New York: Macmillan, 1904);

The Complete Poems of Christina Rossetti, edited by R. W. Crump, volume 1- (Baton Rouge & London: Louisiana State University Press, 1979-).

The publication in 1862 of Christina Rossetti's *Goblin Market and Other Poems* marked the first literary success of the Pre-Raphaelites. Since then her poetry has never lacked readers, and it has stood the test of time better than the work of many of her contemporaries. In 1911 Ford Madox Hueffer (Ford Madox Ford) saw her as an essentially modern figure: "I consider Christina Rossetti to be the greatest master of words—at least of English words—that the nineteenth century gave us. . . . although the range of her subjects was limited— although it was limited very strictly within the bound of her personal emotions—yet within those limits she expressed herself consummately." Both sides of that view have been echoed many times.

Christina Rossetti was the daughter of an Italian father and a half-English, half-Italian mother. She was the sister of Maria Francesca Rossetti, who was to become the author of a study of Dante; of Dante Gabriel Rossetti, the painter and poet; and of William Michael Rossetti, critic, editor, translator, and custodian of family manuscripts. Although she felt affection toward her father, she was much closer to her mother, from whom she inherited a strong lifelong religious commitment. Initially this commitment was Evangelical in orientation, but it became Anglo-Catholic in the early 1840s. It was shared by Maria (who, unlike Christina, possessed a religious vocation and ended her life as a member of an Anglican Sisterhood) but not by her father or by her brothers. The split between the claims of worldly passion and otherworldly faith which was to become central to Christina Rossetti's life and to her poetry may well have found its origins in this tension between her Italian and her English ancestry.

Christina Rossetti was especially close to her maternal grandfather, Gaetano Polidori. When she was small, Polidori lived in the country, in Buckinghamshire. Christina stayed often at her grandfather's, and her early encounters with the countryside and its animal life profoundly affected her and left their mark on much of her poetry. In 1839 Polidori moved back to London and the visits to the

Christina Rossetti, 1863

countryside ceased. Considering Christina's love of nature, there is poignancy in the fact that she would spend most of the rest of her life in dark and gloomy London houses.

Christina was healthy as a child but often ill during adolescence. Her illnesses at this time were probably psychosomatic, and one of her doctors is reported to have diagnosed them as "a kind of religious mania." She read widely but not studiously or systematically: the *Arabian Nights,* medieval ballads, the works of Scott, the poetry of Keats and Tennyson, Gothic fiction (Mrs. Radcliffe, "Monk" Lewis, and especially Maturin), as well as Italian poetry (Metastasio in particular).

Most of these literary influences can be found in her first book, *Verses* (1847), which Polidori printed on his own press. The most substantial poem in this volume is "The Dead City." Based on material from the *Arabian Nights,* it recounts a dream-visit to a city in which the guests at a banquet have turned to stone. Its sixteen-year-old author did not as yet have the technique to sustain a narrative of 280 lines, but there are some passages which

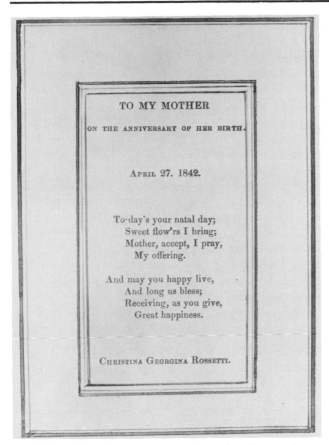

TO MY MOTHER

ON THE ANNIVERSARY OF HER BIRTH.

APRIL 27. 1842.

To-day's your natal day;
Sweet flow'rs I bring;
Mother, accept, I pray,
My offering.

And may you happy live,
And long us bless;
Receiving, as you give,
Great happiness.

CHRISTINA GEORGINA ROSSETTI.

Rossetti's earliest surviving poem, written when she was eleven years old and printed by her maternal grandfather, Gaetano Polidori

point forward to her mature work. Particularly interesting is the luscious enumeration of the fruits at the banquet, a careful detailing which anticipates much Pre-Raphaelite poetry and points forward to Rossetti's own "Goblin Market." The *Verses* also show some of the themes which are characteristic of her later poems and which, at this stage, cannot always have been based on her own experience: early death, the rejection by a loved one, the fleetingness of love and beauty, the need for resignation. Resignation is not always present, however: the ballad "Fair Margaret," never republished, shows a certain joy taken in the unhappiness of the faithless lover. That too is a note which would recur in Christina Rossetti's work.

In the fall of 1848 Rossetti became engaged to James Collinson, a young painter who had already exhibited at the Royal Academy and who was one of the members of the Pre-Raphaelite Brotherhood. Rossetti had initially refused him since he was a Roman Catholic, but she accepted him when he returned to the Church of England. When he once

again converted to Roman Catholicism in 1850, she broke off the engagement. Although great things had initially been expected from Collinson (by Dante Gabriel Rossetti, in particular), he later seemed to those who knew him a somewhat ridiculous figure of mediocre talent, likely to go to sleep at the slightest provocation. For that reason both contemporary observers and later commentators have often been unable to imagine what Christina Rossetti saw in him. Although the nature and intensity of Rossetti's feelings remain unclear, there is no reason to doubt that she considered herself in love with Collinson. Nor is it strange that a young woman of strict Anglican convictions would consider doctrinal and denominational differences a bar to marriage—which is not to say that other possibly unconscious motives did not play a part as well.

The Rossettis had never been affluent. When Christina was young, her father had eked out his salary as professor of Italian at King's College, London with more lucrative private tuition. After 1842, as ill health and deteriorating sight forced him to give up all his teaching, the family had to look for other sources of income. Maria Rossetti became a governess, and Frances opened, with Christina's help, a small day school in North London. In 1853 Christina and Frances moved, with Gabriele, to Frome in Somerset, where they attempted to run a school. (It was the only time in Christina's life that

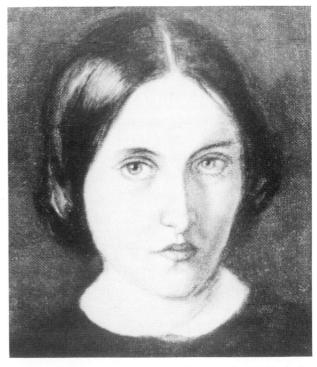

Christina Rossetti at age seventeen, the first oil painting by her brother Dante Gabriel (courtesy of Mrs. Lucy O'Conor)

Rossetti's sketches of her brothers: Dante Gabriel, drawn when Christina was seventeen (courtesy of Mrs. Imogen Dennis), and William Michael (University of British Columbia)

she resided outside London.) The attempt proved a failure, and early in 1854 the family moved back to London. After this date the family income was largely provided by William, who had been employed at the Excise (Inland Revenue) Office since 1845 and who, from 1850, began to earn some money through his literary journalism. Gabriele Rossetti died on 26 April 1854.

Beginning in 1848 Christina Rossetti had several poems published in periodicals: two were printed in the *Athenaeum* and seven in the *Germ,* the short-lived Pre-Raphaelite publication of 1850. For the latter group Rossetti used the pseudonym Ellen Alleyn, a name invented for her by Dante Gabriel. An attempt by him in January 1861 to interest the influential critic John Ruskin in his sister's poems failed, for Ruskin found in them too many "quaintnesses and offences," complaining in particular about the "wilfulness" of their metrical effects, a judgment which interestingly and ironically anticipates Christina Rossetti's own later verdict on Emily Dickinson's poetry ("a wonderfully Blakean gift, but therewithal a startling recklessness of poetic ways and means").

Dante Gabriel Rossetti was more successful in his approaches to the publisher Alexander Macmillan, who brought out three of Christina's poems in *Macmillan's Magazine* in 1861. Of these, "Uphill" was the first poem to receive fairly wide notice. It remains one of her finest achievements. Christina had from her childhood been drawn to the poetry of George Herbert, as the early "Charity," an acknowledged imitation of Herbert's "Virtue," shows. In "Uphill," the parable about the way to salvation, the steep ascent with the comfort of the inn at its end is in its clear outline and simple diction very much in the literary tradition of Herbert, but in this poem Christina Rossetti was able to give a personal voice to the traditional theme.

In 1862 Macmillan published *Goblin Market and Other Poems.* The poem "Goblin Market" (a title first suggested by Dante Gabriel) shows Christina Rossetti's work at its finest. It is a disturbing fairy tale about two sisters. One of them, Laura, cannot resist the call of the goblins and allows them to come to her in the evening in the glen; she buys their fruit with a lock of her hair and tastes the juice. The next night Laura again lingers but cannot hear the gob-

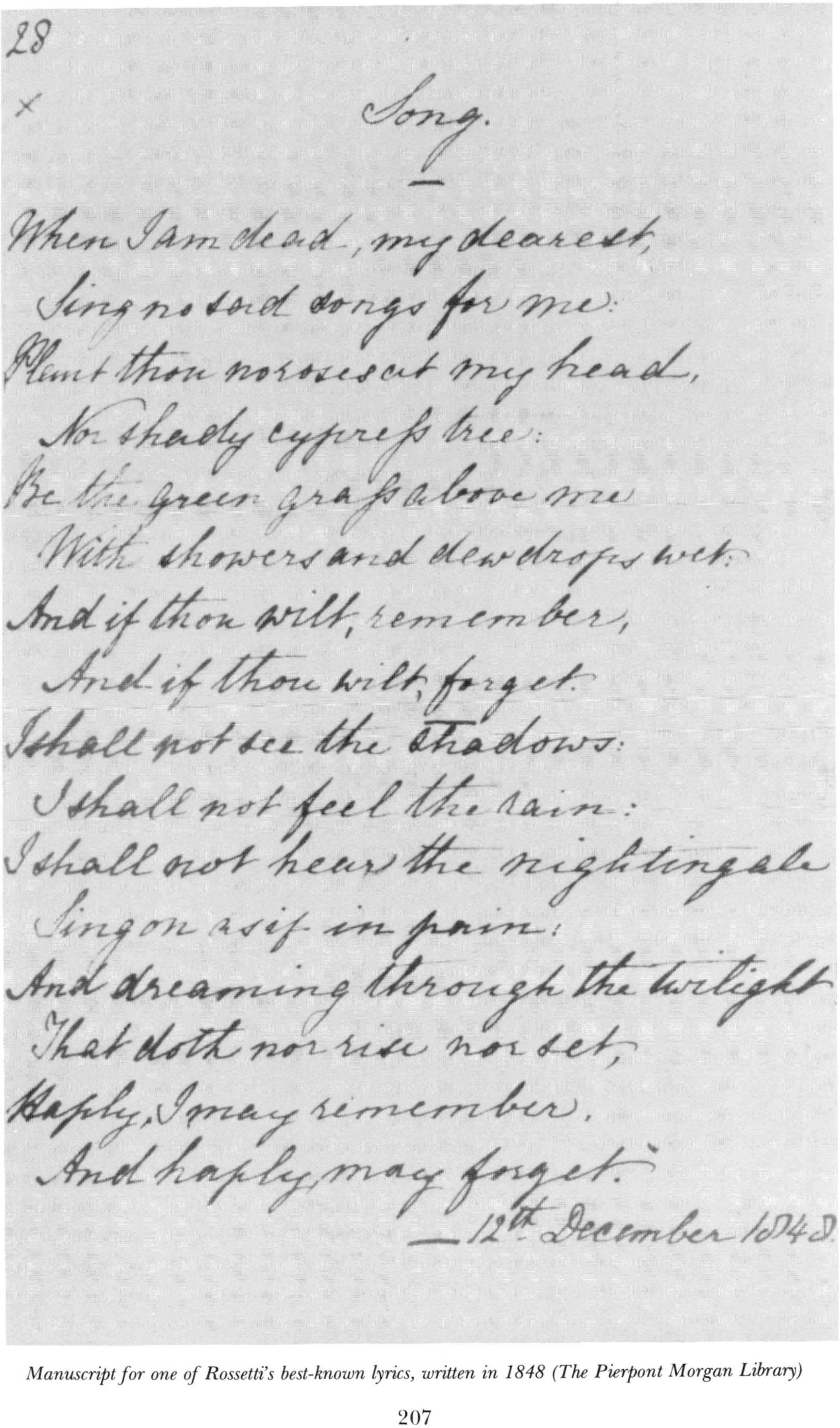

28

✕

Song.

—

When I am dead, my dearest,
  Sing no sad songs for me:
Plant thou no roses at my head,
  Nor shady cypress tree:
Be the green grass above me
  With showers and dewdrops wet:
And if thou wilt, remember,
  And if thou wilt, forget.

I shall not see the shadows,
  I shall not feel the rain:
I shall not hear the nightingale
  Sing on as if in pain:
And dreaming through the twilight
  That doth nor rise nor set,
Haply, I may remember,
  And haply may forget.
                — 12th December 1848.

Manuscript for one of Rossetti's best-known lyrics, written in 1848 (The Pierpont Morgan Library)

lins. She pines away. Her sister Lizzie, who can hear them, goes to confront them and makes them smear her face with the juices of their fruits. The goblins, however, cannot get her to open her mouth and taste. Lizzie rushes home and gets Laura to suck the juices from her face. The juices work as a painful antidote and Laura is brought back to health and contentment. Years later, both sisters have married and have children.

It is clear that the fairy tale is symbolic at least up to a point. The temptation which the goblins hold out has a sexual suggestiveness: at several points we are told of the dead Jeanie, perhaps their sister, "who should have been a bride" but who could not wait until marriage. Lizzie's action of vicarious suffering and her willingness to risk her own life and salvation in order to save Laura are perhaps suggestive of the Atonement. Yet the power of the poem depends on the fact that its details never harden into allegory. Rossetti's audacious use of rhyme ("luscious" rhymes with "blushes," for instance) and meter (the poem's "dedoggerelised Skeltonic" in George Saintsbury's phrase) which so shocked Ruskin are central to the poem's vitality, as is the presentation of the goblins as essentially comic creatures dangerous in their comicality.

"Goblin Market" ends with an affectionate tribute: "there is no friend like a sister . . . / To fetch one if one goes astray." "Sister Maude" presents a very different relationship between two sisters. Here it is Maude who, out of jealousy, has betrayed her sister's love affair and has caused the death of her sister's lover—or at least that is what the sister who speaks the poem asserts. Uncharitably, she ends the poem by saying that she might just get into Heaven but that Maude never will. The theme of the treacherous sister is a familiar one in traditional ballads, but it seems to have held an especially powerful attraction for Christina Rossetti. It recurs in "Noble Sisters," a dialogue between a married woman in love with "a young man tall and strong" and her sister who, out of prudence or jealousy, has sent the young man packing. The fact that the relationship between sisters is presented so very differently in these three poems may well reflect an ambivalence in Rossetti's own relationship with her elder sister Maria and may indeed have something to do with actual events. At any rate William Michael Rossetti told Mackenzie Bell, Christina's biographer, that the final lines of "Goblin Market" "indicate *something:* apparently [Christina] considered herself to be chargeable with some sort of spiritual backsliding, against which Maria's influence had

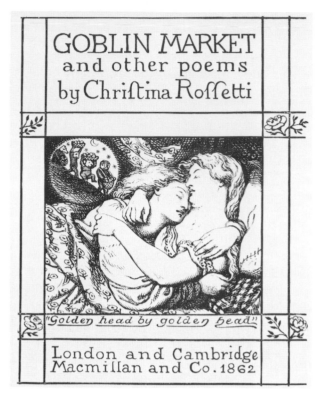

Decorated title page by Dante Gabriel Rossetti for his sister's first commercially published poem collection

been exercised beneficially." The contrast between the impulsive and the cautious sister indicates inner tension. Winston Weathers has offered a convincing reading of "Goblin Market" in which Laura, Lizzie, and Jeanie are seen as different aspects of the self and the marriages of Laura and Lizzie represent a regaining of wholeness.

Other poems in the 1862 volume explore similar tensions, but these are not so harmoniously resolved: in "Love from the North" the claims of the sensitive bridegroom prove less compelling than those of the strong lover; in "Cousin Kate" a seduced girl is set against her cousin who held out for a wedding ring; in the sonnet "A Triad" three women try to fulfill themselves through love but destroy themselves in different ways: one throws herself into a life of shame, the second becomes "a sluggish wife," the third "famished died for love."

Many of the poems in *Goblin Market and Other Poems* speak in a quiet melodious and elegiac way of lost love and happiness or express a longing for the forgetfulness of death. "Spring," a poem which opens by celebrating vitality and new beginnings, modulates in its last stanza to musing on mutability. Typical of such moods of resigned sadness is the

Original illustrations from Rossetti's Goblin Market *(1862)*

sonnet "Remember." Although the octave is an appeal to the lover to remember the speaker after her death, the sestet suggests that it is not the remembering which is all important: "Better by far you should forget and smile/Than that you should remember and be sad." Resignation, not just to death but to being forgotten as well, becomes a self-imposed duty which revokes the dramatic urgency of the first half of the poem. "After Death" takes a rather different line. Here the speaker finds that the man whom she loved and who did not love her sheds tears of pity for her now that she is dead. It is that knowledge which compensates her for having missed his love during her lifetime. She rejects any sense of scoring a triumph over him, though perhaps a more subtle triumph can be found in that very rejection: "very sweet it is/To know he still is warm tho' I am cold."

In these poems Rossetti's fascination with death is evident. Arthur Symons has well characterized this fascination as one "of interest, sad but scarcely unquiet interest in what the dead are doing underground, in their memories, if memories they have, of the world they have left." One wonders, however, whether "scarcely unquiet" really does justice to the tensions in these poems. The phrase is certainly not applicable to "The Hour and the Ghost," a disturbing dramatic ballad in which the dead lover jealously draws a woman away from her bridegroom into "the outcast weather." The basic theme occurs in many traditional ballads but the poem's most horrifying detail, reserved until the end, presents a new twist: the ghost confidently predicts that the bridegroom will have no difficulty in finding another woman, "one much more fair."

There are still other elements of interest in the poems of the 1862 volume. In his notes to the *Poetical Works* (1904) William Michael Rossetti commented on "the odd freakishness which flecked the extreme and almost obsessive seriousness" of Christina's thought. The poem on which he was specifically commenting is "My Dream," a poem with all the curious disturbing inconsequentiality of dreaming, although Christina later asserted that it was "not a real dream." That "odd freakishness" is also found in "Winter: My Secret," but here there is a complex tension between the poem's quizzical tone and its intense commitment to privacy. An altogether lighter poem is the catty "No, Thank You, John" (apparently based on Christina's attitude toward an admirer, the painter John Brett), in which a hopeless lover is firmly put in his place.

Other poems strike different notes. "A Birthday" is an ecstatic celebration of happiness, of being in love, and of being loved. "Shut Out," which in manuscript has the revealing title of "What happened to me," is a powerful poem about isolation: in the first half of the poem the speaker can only look through the iron bars of the gate at the garden which once was hers; in the second half even this glimpse is denied to her because a wall has been built. Of the explicitly religious poems, the sonnet "The World" is especially impressive: the octave shows the world's daytime blandishments, the sestet its loathsome reality.

In preparing *Goblin Market and Other Poems* for the press Christina Rossetti received considerable assistance from Dante Gabriel. He advised her on which poems to select, discussed possible revisions, helped with proofreading, made two illustrations, and suggested division of the poems into two groups with the second headed "Devotional Pieces." Unwisely, this division was adopted, but it fails to acknowledge the centrality of Christina's faith to her very being as a woman and as a poet. It would appear from a notation on the endpapers of some copies of *Goblin Market* that two thousand were printed. The volume was well received, and in 1865 a second edition was brought out. This time the sales were disappointing: of the one thousand copies printed, 450 remained unsold in 1870.

As early as 1863 both Dante Gabriel Rossetti and Macmillan put considerable pressure on Christina to bring out a new volume, but she was not ready to do so until 1865. The volume was published the following year under the title *The Prince's Progress and Other Poems.* Dante Gabriel designed the binding and the woodcuts for the title page and frontispiece. Many of the poems in the volume had been written in the few years preceding publication, but some went back much earlier; the volume included three poems which had already been printed in 1847 in *Verses,* as well as the evocative "Spring Quiet," which in its original form also dates from that year. Once again Dante Gabriel Rossetti made suggestions about which poems to select and about possible revisions. Christina welcomed these and often left the final decisions to her brother, but the

letters which William later included in *Rossetti Papers* (1903) show that in some cases, when she felt confident about her own judgment, she refused to be budged.

It was Dante Gabriel who first suggested that the dirge for a love which has come too late, written in 1861 (and first published in *Macmillan's Magazine* in 1863), should become the conclusion of a narrative poem. Christina turned this poem into a dark variation of the Sleeping Beauty motif, a half-serious, half-mocking narration about a prince who, on his way to his bride, is continually sidetracked—by a pretty milkmaid, an alchemist, sheer boredom, his own near-drowning. When he finally arrives at his destination, his bride has died. It has often been suggested that the poem deals figuratively with the long, drawn-out relationship and delayed marriage between Dante Gabriel Rossetti and Elizabeth Siddal. The suggestion is a plausible one, but it would be a mistake to read the poem exclusively as an allegory of that kind. The poem lacks the dramatic urgency of "Goblin Market," yet its metrical freedoms (which Dante Gabriel was uneasy about) and its mixture of tones is effective.

The pattern of "A Triad" reappears in

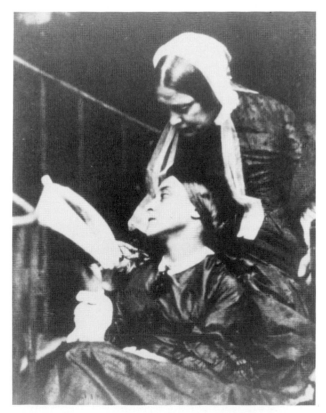

Rossetti and her mother, Frances Polidori Rossetti, photographed by Lewis Carroll (courtesy of Mrs. Imogen Dennis)

"Maiden-Song," but the conclusion of the latter poem is less bleak: two sisters, apprehensive about their other sister Margaret's greater beauty, make sure that they find lovers by leaving Margaret at home. They take up with handsome shepherds, but Margaret is courted and won by a king. This is another of Rossetti's adaptations of fairy-tale motifs. Other poems ("The Poor Ghost," "The Ghost's Petition," and, in a rather different way, "Jessie Cameron") show Christina Rossetti's continued interest in the adaptation of traditional ballad material. The cattiness of some of the earlier poems reappears in "Queen of Hearts" and "A Ring Posy."

Most of the poems in *The Prince's Progress and Other Poems* repeat moods and motifs which are found in Rossetti's first published volume. The end of "Autumn," for instance, movingly evokes the desolation so central to much of her poetry: "My trees are not in flower, / I have no bower, / And gusty creaks my tower, / And lonesome, very lonesome, is my strand." "On the Wing" is a very powerful sonnet: the octave dramatizes one kind of tragedy, courting pigeons devoured by a hawk, the sestet another—in her dream the watching woman finds her loved one gone and hears only thin and plaintive sounds coming from where he had appeared to be. Very fine too is "Eve," in which the use of the biblical situation universalizes and gives larger resonance to the familiar motif of lost happiness.

Two poems, however, represent an attempt by the poet to extend her range. One of these, originally titled "Under the Rose" but later given the ponderous title " 'The Iniquity of the Fathers upon the Children,' " is a dramatic monologue in which the poet imagines what it would be like to be illegitimate. Dante Gabriel Rossetti appears to have been unhappy about this poem, but Christina, although she agreed to revisions, refused to suppress it altogether for reasons she outlined in a letter to her brother: "whilst I endorse your opinion of the unavoidable and indeed much-to-be-desired unreality of women's work on social matters, I yet incline to include within female range such an attempt as this. . . ." Christina's concern with the subject of illegitimacy must be connected with the work she undertook in the 1860s at the House of Charity, an institution in Highgate devoted to the rescue of prostitutes and unmarried mothers. The words "House of Charity" also occur in a pencil notation on the manuscript "From Sunset to Star Rise," perhaps suggesting that the poem was intended as an imaginary utterance of such a woman. William Michael Rossetti was rather baffled by this sugges-

tion, and it is probable that Christina merely wished to distance personal concerns in this poem as she did elsewhere—in "L. E. L.," for instance.

The other poem in which we find a broadening of subject matter is "A Royal Princess," which had first appeared, fittingly, in an 1863 anthology published for the relief of victims of the Lancashire cotton famine. The poem deals with starvation, poverty, and social inequality. It is rather strident in tone and does not represent Christina Rossetti's poetry at its best, although passages have something of the power and the indignation of Keats's "Isabella," a resemblance which Dante Gabriel noted with some dismay.

Later in her career Rossetti avoided such overtly political subjects. "It is not in me, and therefore it will never come out of me," she wrote to Dante Gabriel in 1870, "to turn to politics or philanthropy with Mrs. Browning." When in 1871 she wrote two poems on the war between France and Germany, she emphasized in a headnote that it was "human sympathy, not political bias" which she tried to express. When she did voice opinions on political issues, they were often very conservative. "Does it not appear," she wrote to Augusta Webster, who had tried to interest her in the cause of female suffrage, "as if the Bible was based upon an understood unalterable distinction between men and women, their position, duties, privileges?" Yet at the same time she argued that the woman suffragists did not go far enough: "if female rights are sure to be overborne for lack of female voting influence, then I confess I feel disposed to shoot ahead of my instructresses, and to assert that female *M. P.'s* are only right and reasonable. Also I take exception at the exclusion of married women from the suffrage."

Some time in the 1860s Rossetti was again sought in marriage, this time by Charles Cayley, whom the Rossettis first met when he was a pupil of Gabriele. Cayley, who had developed into a distinguished linguist, as his *terza rima* translation of Dante shows, has been described by Virginia Woolf as an "abstract and erudite man who shuffled about the world in a state of absent-minded dishabille," but Christina's feelings toward him were clearly warm. Yet she refused him. In William Michael Rossetti's words, "she enquired into his creed and found he was not a Christian." Her relationship with Cayley appears to have gone much deeper than that with Collinson had, and she and Cayley remained friends. The relationship left its mark on much of her poetry, as is most clearly seen in the Italian sequence "Il Rosseggiar dell' Oriente." She

Rossetti's suitor Charles Cayley, circa 1866. According to William Michael Rossetti, his sister rejected Cayley because "she enquired into his creed and found he was not a Christian."

kept the sequence carefully locked away, and it was not published until after her death.

As in the case of her relationship with James Collinson, later commentators have reacted with surprise to Christina's involvement with Cayley. Indeed, one scholar, Lona Mosk Packer, constructed her 1963 biography on the hypothesis that the dominant love in Christina Rossetti's life was for the (married) painter and poet William Bell Scott. Such a relationship cannot be documented, however, and there is substantial evidence against it in the assertion by William Michael Rossetti, a scrupulously truthful witness, that Collinson and Cayley were the only men outside the immediate family with whom Christina had important relationships.

Packer's speculations derive in part from the mistaken assumption that there is a direct correspondence between the events of Christina Rossetti's life and the emotions expressed in her poetry. In October 1849, when she was still engaged to

Collinson, she wrote in "Seeking Rest": "My Spring will never come again;/My pretty flowers have blown/For the last time." In November 1857, on the other hand, at a time when there do not appear to have been any close relationships with anyone outside the immediate family, she wrote the ecstatic "My Birthday": ". . . the birthday of my life/Is come, my love is come to me." The tone of this poem is especially surprising in that in Rossetti's manuscript notebook it is flanked by two very different poems, the first part of "Memory," a very somber poem indeed ("My heart dies inch by inch"), and "An Apple Gathering," in which the heavily symbolic apple blossoms were plucked too early ("Then in due season when I went to see/I found no apples there"). It is possible to interpret "A Birthday," as Hoxie Neale Fairchild has done, as a religious poem which gives expression to a mystical apprehension of Christ. Such an apprehension, however, is as uncharacteristic of Christina Rossetti's poetry as is the sense of togetherness with a human lover. Moreover, if "A Birthday" is a religious poem, would it not have been included in the devotional section of *Goblin Market and Other Poems?*

Christina Rossetti traveled outside Great Britain on only two occasions. With Frances and William she visited northern France in 1862 and northern Italy in 1865. The latter journey had a profound impact on her, as is especially clear in two of her poems: in "En Route" she sees herself as an exile from her mother country; in "Enrica, 1865" "we Englishwomen, trim, correct," concealing warmheartedness under a cold exterior, "all-courteous out of self-respect," are contrasted with an Italian woman whose warmth is natural and spontaneous. "Doing all from self-respect" is a phrase that occurs as early as 1850 in the poem "Is and Was." William Michael Rossetti writes that it can be traced to a comment by a lady on Christina herself, who was accused of doing " 'all from self-respect,' not from fellow-feeling with others, or from kindly consideration for them." The remark clearly rankled and must have involved Christina in some painful self-scrutiny.

Since adolescence Christina's health had not been good. She was very ill in 1855, and her illness was then, as again in 1864, misdiagnosed as tuberculosis. In 1871 she contracted Graves' disease. She recovered, but the illness had affected her heart and also disfigured her, largely because of the protrusion of the eyes which it caused.

In 1870 Rossetti completed a series of poems for children which was published in 1872 as *Sing-Song: A Nursery Rhyme Book,* illustrated by Arthur

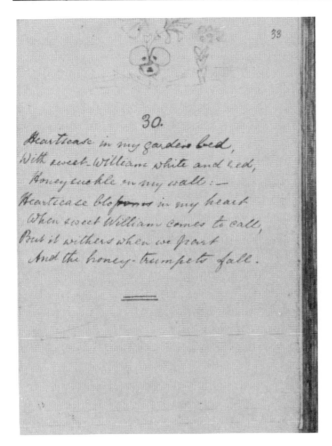
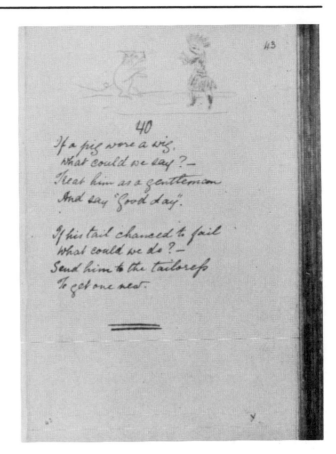

Pages from Rossetti's notebook for 1870 recording poems later published in her volume of children's verse, Sing-Song *(British Library)*

Hughes. There is considerable variation within the series: some poems are moralistic and pious, some show Christina's freakish sense of humor, others are highly imaginative. It was Dante Gabriel Rossetti who best characterized the poems when he called them "admirable things, alternating between the merest babyism and a sort of Blakish wisdom and tenderness." A second edition containing five new poems as well as other alterations was published in 1893.

In 1875 Macmillan brought out Christina's first collected edition, *Goblin Market, The Prince's Progress, and Other Poems.* Poems from the earlier volumes were carefully rearranged, and thirty-seven poems, most of which had been previously published in periodicals or anthologies, were added. Of these, "The Longest Room" (written as early as 1856 and published in *Macmillan's Magazine* in 1864) is the lengthiest and most ambitiously conceived. The poem deals with a contrast between two sisters: the elder is discontented with her humdrum life and longs for the heroic world of the Homeric poems; the younger is resigned and puts her faith in Christ. The epilogue shows how, twenty years later,

the younger one has married and found fulfillment as wife and mother, whereas her sister has had to resign herself to a life alone, to accept "the lowest place,/The place assigned [her] here" and to long for final deliverance at the Last Judgment. The dialogue between the sisters dramatizes not only the alternative possibilities but also the tension between conflicting choices.

The finest of the newly added poems, however, are the "Christmas Carol" ("In the bleak mid-winter"), now a familiar part of the Anglican liturgy most often sung in the setting by Gustav Holst; the powerful lament of the captive Jews "By the Waters of Babylon, B.C. 570"; and "Amor Mundi," the terrifying dialogue of a couple hastening toward eternal damnation. In the 1875 collection "Amor Mundi" was significantly printed immediately before "Uphill." W. H. Auden, who included the poem in the anthology *Poets of the English Language* (1952), may have been influenced by it in the epilogue to his *The Orators* (1932).

Five poems from the earlier volumes were dropped: "A Triad," "Sister Maude," "Cousin Kate," "Light Love," and "A Ring Posy." In the case of the last poem it would seem that Christina Rossetti feared that its savage irony might be interpreted as unchristian smugness; in the other cases she apparently (as William Michael wrote with regard to "A Triad") "with overstrained scrupulosity, considered [their] moral tone to be somewhat open to exception." This scrupulosity is reflected in other incidents: she decided to give up playing chess because she found she enjoyed winning; she insisted on pasting strips of paper over the antireligious passages in Swinburne's *Atalanta in Calydon* (a poem she otherwise much admired); she objected to nudity in paintings, especially when perpetrated by woman artists; she rejected Wagner's *Parsifal* unseen and unheard: "I should not dare witness such a treatment of such a subject."

A Pageant and Other Poems appeared in 1881. The volume takes its title from the subtitle of its opening poem, "The Months: A Pageant," a work which has been staged several times, usually in girls' schools but once in the vast space of London's Albert Hall. "The Months: A Pageant" does not represent Christina Rossetti's poetry at its best. Although she considered it "among the best and most wholesome things" she had written, to others the word "wholesome" is an indication of the work's limitations. Its most interesting passage is October's description of November: "Here comes my youngest sister, looking dim,/And grim,/With dismal ways"—lines which, in the family circle, Christina would apply to herself.

A much more substantial work is the sonnet sequence "Monna Innominata." William Michael Rossetti was convinced that the sonnets were very personal poems, largely inspired by Christina's feelings for Cayley; Christina, however, was at pains to distance the poems' subjectivity by presenting them as the supposed utterances of a woman beloved by a poet of the age preceding Dante and Petrarch. At the same time the note which she prefixed to the poems shows her wish to present them as minor-key variations on Elizabeth Barrett Browning's "Sonnets from the Portuguese"—the kind of poems the latter might have written "had [she] only been unhappy instead of happy."

A Pageant and Other Poems contains a second sonnet cycle, "Later Life," a series of twenty-eight poems of which the fourteenth, "When Adam and Eve left Paradise," is especially fine. Impressive too is "An Old-World Thicket," a poem about earthly suffering and about the end of suffering through the Redemption. Interestingly, it opens with a very deliberate allusion to the opening of Dante's *Divine Comedy*. When Rossetti was a child, her father was

obsessively preoccupied with his own esoteric and cryptogrammic interpretations of Dante. At the time the father's obsession made it difficult for the Rossetti children to find much interest in Dante, but Christina, like Maria, Dante Gabriel, and William Michael, was to rediscover his poetry later in life. She also wrote two articles on Dante.

In 1883 Rossetti was asked to write a life of Elizabeth Barrett Browning. She was attracted by this idea, but in the end she declined as Robert Browning appeared unwilling to lend active cooperation. She did, however, accept a commission to write on Anne Radcliffe. This project would have afforded her an opportunity to explore again the works of an author whom she had read enthusiastically in childhood, but she had to give up the plan when she was unable to assemble enough material.

Christina Rossetti's later years were somber and lonely. She accepted and even welcomed her life of devoted service; yet it is clear from her poetry how acute her sense of deprivation was. Dante Gabriel went through a severe mental and physical crisis in 1872 and only partially recovered. He died in 1882. Maria died of cancer in 1876. William Michael was married in 1874 to Lucy Madox Brown, daughter of the painter Ford Madox Brown. Initially William and his wife lived in the same house as Christina and Frances, but relations between the agnostic Lucy and the scrupulously devout Christina soon became strained. In 1876 Christina and Frances moved to a new house which they shared with two Polidori aunts. Charles Cayley died in 1883, Frances in 1886. Christina, herself in increasingly poor health, continued to look after her aunts, who lived on until 1890 and 1893. Only with the death of Aunt Charlotte in 1890 could Christina be said to be financially well off.

Goblin Market, The Prince's Progress, and Other Poems was republished several times, and in 1890 Macmillan brought out a new collected edition entitled *Poems*. Christina had hoped that she would be able to reorder all the poems, but the publisher insisted on reusing the stereotyped plates of the 1875 text. As a result she had to satisfy herself with adding to the 1875 poems the verses published in *A Pageant and Other Poems*, together with seventeen new poems.

In 1876 Rossetti had failed to interest Macmillan in a devotional work, a mixture of prose and verse with the unlikely title "Young Plants and Polished Corners." Five years later (retitled *Called to be Saints*) it was published by the Society for Promoting Christian Knowledge. Three other devotional volumes followed, of which two, *Time Flies: A*

Christina Rossetti's funeral, Highgate Cemetery, 2 January 1894

Reading Diary (1885) and *The Face of the Deep: A Devotional Commentary on the Apocalypse* (1892), included poetry. In 1893 the SPCK published the poems from these volumes, in a revised text and with one new poem added, under the title *Verses*. The volume sold well and was republished many times. Although some of the devotional poems are fine poetry and although the poems were carefully ordered in the 1893 edition, they are better read in their original settings than in the monotonous accumulations of the 1893 *Verses* or the 1904 *Poetical Works*.

Rossetti was much involved with the work of the SPCK. She returned the royalties on *The Face of the Deep* and, in order to save the Society money, she wrote out a completely new text for *Verses*. In the last year of her life, however, she broke with the Society over its refusal to take a stand against vivisection, an issue about which she had strong feelings. (The poem "A Poor Old Dog" had been composed for an antivivisection bazaar.)

In May 1892 Rossetti was diagnosed as suffering from cancer, and surgery failed to stop the disease. She died two years later after much physical suffering aggravated by feelings of guilt and doubts about salvation.

In 1896, two years after Christina Rossetti's death, William Michael Rossetti edited *New Poems*. The poems in this volume can be divided in three groups: those of Christina's last years, those published in periodicals or anthologies but not previously collected, and those which Christina had left unpublished either because she considered them too personal or because she thought them inferior to her best work. Preeminent among the first group are "Sleeping at last" and "Heaven overarches earth and sea." These moving poems can be thought of as complementary and as representative of two of the central concerns of Christina's poetry, the longing for the release of death and the desire for eternal life. Among poems previously published in periodicals "An Echo from Willowwood" is of special interest. This poem, which William Michael Rossetti dates "circa 1870" and which had been published in 1890 in the *Magazine of Art,* is a variation of Dante Gabriel's Willowwood sonnets in "The House of Life." Christina's poem is much less dramatic than his sonnets but in its muted way it achieves a moving tenderness. Among the very personal poems, "In an Artist's Studio," written in 1856, is especially fine. It deals with Dante Gabriel's obsessive use of Elizabeth Siddal as a model in his drawings and paintings and registers, sadly and sympathetically, the contrast between the hopeful beginnings of their relationship and the unhappiness which followed.

New Poems was carefully edited and annotated. Whenever possible for each poem the precise or approximate date of composition was given. When the volume was published William was criticized for including too much inferior work, and it is true that the volume contains poems of which the only distinction is that they were written by Christina Rossetti. On the whole, however, William's choices were judicious. As early as 1897 he proposed a complete edition of the poems to Macmillan, and the text for this edition was finished by the summer of 1899. Nothing happened for several years, in part because the publisher failed to act, and in part because the SPCK raised difficulties. Entitled *Poetical Works,* the edition was finally published in 1904; it has remained the standard edition of Christina's poetry (and will continue to be so, at least until all volumes of R. W. Crump's edition of the *Complete Poems* are published).

The *Poetical Works* of 1904 were carefully prepared. William Michael Rossetti took considerable trouble to hunt up earlier printings in periodicals and anthologies (assisted in this by J. P. Anderson's bibliography in Mackenzie Bell's 1898 biography), the quality of transcription and proofreading is high, and the memoir and annotations are invaluable. The arrangement of the edition is awkward, however, as it combines grouping according to length or subject matter with chronological ordering, thus destroying the sequences which Christina had carefully worked out. This reordering also means that poems which the poet had wished to retain are published side by side with those she considered unsuccessful. There is also inconsistency in the principle of selection. If William had wanted to include only those poems which show genuine artistic merit, he included far too many; if he was concerned with presenting a complete edition of an important poet, it is not clear why he chose to exclude sixty-nine mainly (but not exclusively) early poems, for which he simply listed titles in an appendix.

One of the most distinctive qualities of Christina Rossetti's poetry and a quality which her work shares with much of the best Pre-Raphaelite poetry and painting is the ability to register small visual detail with freshness and precision, as in "where

lizards lived / In strange metallic mail" ("From House to Home") or in "the pendulum spider / Swings from side to side" ("Summer"). Often natural images are given symbolic overtones in ways which, as Gisela Hönnighausen has demonstrated in a 1972 article, show a special awareness of and interest in traditional emblematic significations. With these concerns for both realistic and symbolic notation Christina Rossetti combined a very acute and delicate sense of melody and cadence, as in the ending of "May": "It passed away with sunny May, / With all sweet things it passed away, / And left me old, and cold, and grey."

It is often said that Rossetti restricted her subject matter too narrowly, or (perhaps a more damaging accusation) that the attitudes which she brought to bear on her subjects were too restricted. As early as 1869 Harry Buxton Forman compared her work with that of Elizabeth Barrett Browning, who was said to have greater scope and powers but pronounced inferior to Christina in sheer craftsmanship. Even earlier, in 1853, Dante Gabriel Rossetti had commented in a letter on his sister's "Sleep at Sea," complaining about a repetitiveness in her poetry and diagnosing a failure to meet the Pre-Raphaelite criterion of truth to nature: "The latter verses of this are most excellent; but some, which I remember vaguely, about 'dreaming of a lifelong ill' (etc., etc., *ad libitum*), smack rather of the old shop. I wish you would try any rendering either of narrative or sentiment from real abundant Nature, which presents much more variety, even in any one of its phases, than all such 'dreamings.'" (The "vaguely remembered" lines were in fact "Some dream, forgetful / Of a lifelong ache." Christina, who could be stubborn, left them unchanged.)

There are, however, many poems in which Christina Rossetti is able to break through such limitations. Undeniably, her strong lyric gifts are often held in check by her moral and theological scruples, but at times it is that very tension which gives her best poems their distinctive quality.

Letters:

Rossetti Papers 1862 to 1870, edited by William Michael Rossetti (London: Sands, 1903);

The Family Letters, edited by William Michael Rossetti (London: Brown, Langham, 1908);

Three Rossettis. Unpublished Letters to and from Dante Gabriel, Christina, William, edited by Janet Camp Troxell (Cambridge: Harvard University Press, 1937);

The Rossetti-Macmillan Letters, edited by Lona Mosk

Packer (Berkeley: University of California Press, 1963).

Bibliographies:

William E. Fredeman, *Pre-Raphaelitism: A Bibliocritical Study* (Cambridge: Harvard University Press, 1965);

Rebecca W. Crump, *Christina Rossetti: A Reference Guide* (Boston: G. K. Hall, 1976).

References:

John Adlard, "Christina Rossetti: Strategies of Loneliness," *Contemporary Review,* 221 (September 1972): 146-150;

Georgina Battiscombe, *Christina Rossetti: A Divided Life* (London: Constable, 1981);

Mackenzie Bell, *Christina Rossetti* (London: Burleigh, 1898);

C. M. Bowra, "Christina Rossetti," in his *The Romantic Imagination* (Cambridge: Harvard University Press, 1949), pp. 245-270;

R. W. Crump, "Eighteen Moments' Monuments: Christina Rossetti's *Bouts-Rimés* Sonnets in the Troxell Collection," *Princeton University Library Chronicle,* 33 (1972): 210-229;

Diane D'Amico, "Christina Rossetti: The Maturin Poems," *Victorian Poetry,* 19 (Summer 1981): 117-137;

H. B. de Groot, "Christina Rossetti's 'A Nightmare': A Fragment Completed," *Review of English Studies,* n. s. 24 (1973): 48-52;

Walter de la Mare, "Christina Rossetti," in *Essays by Divers Hands, 6, Transactions of the Royal Society of Literature,* edited by G. K. Chesterton (London: Oxford University Press, 1926), pp. 79-116;

Ifor B. Evans, *English Poetry of the Later Nineteenth Century* (London: Methuen, 1933), pp. 65-80;

Evans, "The Sources of Christina Rossetti's 'Goblin Market,' " *Modern Language Review,* 28 (April 1933): 156-163;

Hoxie Neale Fairchild, *Religious Trends in English Poetry IV: 1830-1880* (New York: Columbia University Press, 1957), pp. 302-316;

Barbara Fass, "Christina Rossetti and St. Agnes' Eve," *Victorian Poetry,* 14 (Spring 1976): 33-46;

Buxton H. Forman, "Criticism on Contemporaries: No. VI. The Rossettis, Part I," *Tinsley's Magazine,* 5 (August 1869): 59-67;

Edmund Gosse, "Christina Rossetti," *Century Magazine,* 46 (June 1893): 211-217;

Gisela Hönnighausen, "Emblematic Tendencies in the Works of Christina Rossetti," *Victorian Poetry,* 10 (Spring 1972): 1-15;

Ford Madox Hueffer, "Christina Rossetti," *Fortnightly Review,* n. s. 89 (March 1911): 422-429;

Cora Kaplan, "The Indefinite Disclosed: Christina Rossetti and Emily Dickinson," in *Women Writing and Women Writing About Women,* edited by Mary Jacobus (London: Croom Helm, 1979);

David A. Kent, "Sequence and Meaning in Christina Rossetti's *Verses* (1893)," *Victorian Poetry,* 17 (Autumn 1979): 259-264;

Alice Law, "The Poetry of Christina Rossetti," *Westminster Review,* 143 (April 1895): 444-453;

M. M. Mahood, "Two Anglican Poets," in her *Poetry and Humanism* (London: Cape, 1950);

Jerome McGann, "Christina Rossetti's Poems: A New Edition and a Revaluation," *Victorian Studies,* 23 (Winter 1980): 237-254;

Dorothy Mermin, "Heroic Sisterhood in *Goblin Market,*" *Victorian Poetry,* 21 (Summer 1983): 107-118;

Ellen Moers, *Literary Women* (Garden City: Doubleday, 1976);

Lona Mosk Packer, *Christina Rossetti* (Berkeley: University of California Press, 1963);

Christopher Ricks, " 'O where are you going?'. W. H. Auden and Christina Rossetti," *Notes and Queries,* 205 (December 1960): 472;

Dolores Rosenblum, "Christina Rossetti: The Inward Pulse," in *Shakespeare's Sisters: Feminist Essays on Women Poets,* edited by Sandra M. Gilbert and Susan Gubar (Bloomington: Indiana University Press, 1979);

Rosenblum, "Christina Rossetti's Religious Poetry: Watching, Looking, Keeping Vigil," *Victorian Poetry,* 20 (Spring 1982): 33-49;

Geoffrey W. Rossetti, "Christina Rossetti," *Criterion,* 10 (October 1930): 95-117;

William Michael Rossetti, *Some Reminiscences,* 2 volumes (London: Brown, Langham, 1906);

George Saintsbury, "The Pre-Raphaelite School," in his *A History of English Prosody from the Twelfth Century to the Present Day,* volume 3 (London: Macmillan, 1910);

Mary F. Sanders, *The Life of Christina Rossetti* (London: Hutchinson, 1930);

Dorothy Stuart, *Christina Rossetti* (London: Macmillan, 1930);

Thomas Burnett Swann, *Wonder and Whimsey: The Fantastic World of Christina Rossetti* (Francestown, N.H.: Marshall Jones, 1960);

Arthur Symons, "Miss Rossetti's Poetry," *London Quarterly Review,* 68 (1887): 338-350;

Symons, "The Rossettis," in his *Dramatis Personae*

(Indianapolis: Bobbs-Merrill, 1923), pp. 118-131;

Eleanor Walter Thomas, *Christina Georgina Rossetti* (New York: Columbia University Press, 1932);

John O. Waller, "Christ's Second Coming: Christina Rossetti and the Premilleniarist William Dodsworth," *Bulletin of the New York Public Library,* 73 (September 1969): 465-482;

R. D. Waller, "The Young Rossettis: Christina," in his *The Rossetti Family, 1824-1854* (Manchester: Manchester University Press, 1932), pp. 217-242;

Theodore Watts-Dunton, "Christina Rossetti," in his *Old Familiar Faces* (London: Jenkins, 1916), pp. 117-206;

Watts-Dunton, "Reminiscences of Christina Rossetti," *Nineteenth Century,* 37 (February 1895): 355-366;

Winston Weathers, "Christina Rossetti: The Sister-hood of Self," *Victorian Poetry,* 3 (Spring 1965): 81-89;

Virginia Woolf, "I am Christina Rossetti," *Nation and Athenaeum,* 48 (6 December 1930): 322-324;

Marya Zaturenska, *Christina Rossetti: A Portrait with a Background* (New York: Macmillan, 1949).

Papers:
Some of Christina Rossetti's notebooks are held by the British Library, London, and the Bodleian Library, Oxford. The printer's copy for most of *A Pageant and Other Poems* is at the Humanities Research Center, University of Texas at Austin; that for *Sing-Song* is in the British Library; and that for *Verses* (1893) is at the King's School, Canterbury. Other important manuscript collections are at Princeton University and the University of British Columbia.

Dante Gabriel Rossetti

Florence S. Boos
University of Iowa

BIRTH: London, 12 May 1828, to Gabriele and Frances Polidori Rossetti.

EDUCATION: Royal Academy, 1846-1848.

MARRIAGE: 23 May 1860 to Elizabeth Eleanor Siddal.

DEATH: Birchington, Kent, 9 April 1882.

BOOKS: *Sir Hugh the Heron: A Legendary Tale in Four Parts* (London: Privately printed, 1843);

Poems (London: Privately printed, 1869; enlarged, London: Privately printed, new edition with slightly different contents; London: Ellis, 1870; Boston: Roberts Brothers, 1870); republished with slightly different contents as *Poems. A New Edition* (London: Ellis, 1881);

Ballads and Sonnets (London: Ellis & White, 1881; Boston: Roberts Brothers, 1882);

Ballads and Narrative Poems (Hammersmith: Kelmscott Press, 1893);

Sonnets and Lyrical Poems (Hammersmith: Kelmscott Press, 1894);

Jan Van Hunks (London: Printed for T. Watts-Dunton, 1912); republished as *Dante Gabriel Rossetti: Jan Van Hunks,* edited by John Robert Wahl (New York: New York Public Library, 1952);

The Paintings and Drawings of Dante Gabriel Rossetti (1828-1882): A Catalogue Raisonné, edited by Virginia Surtees, 2 volumes (London: Oxford University Press, 1971).

Collections: *The Collected Works of Dante Gabriel Rossetti,* edited by William M. Rossetti, 2 volumes (London: Ellis, 1886); republished as *The Poetical Works of Dante Gabriel Rossetti,* 1 volume (London: Ellis, 1891); enlarged as *The Poems of Dante Gabriel Rossetti with Illustrations from His Own Pictures and Designs,* 2 volumes (London: Ellis, 1904); revised and enlarged as *The Works of Dante Gabriel Rossetti,* 1 volume (London: Ellis, 1911).

TRANSLATION: *The Early Italian Poets* (London: Smith, Elder, 1861; London: Simpkin, Marshall, Hamilton, Kent/New York: Scribners, 1861); republished as *Dante and His Circle*

Dante Gabriel Rossetti, 1867

(London: Ellis & White, 1874; Boston: Roberts Brothers, 1876).

Gabriel Charles Dante Rossetti, who assumed the professional name Dante Gabriel Rossetti, was born 12 May 1828 at No. 38 Charlotte Street, Portland Place, London, the second child and eldest son of Gabriele Rossetti (1783-1854) and Frances Polidori Rossetti (1800-1886). Gabriele Rossetti was a Dante scholar, who when younger had been exiled from Naples for writing poetry in support of the Neapolitan Constitution of 1819. He settled in London in 1824, where in 1826 he married the daughter of a fellow Italian expatriate and man of letters; Frances Polidori had trained as a governess and supervised her children's early education. Gabriele Rossetti supported the family as a professor of Italian at King's College, London, until his eyesight and general health deteriorated in the 1840s. Frances then attempted to support the family as a teacher of French and Italian and unsuccessful founder of two day schools. Few Victorian families were as gifted: Maria Rossetti (1827-1876) was described as talented, enthusiastic, and domineering as a child; in later life she published *A Shadow of Dante* (1871) and became an Anglican nun (1873); William Michael Rossetti (1829-1919) was along with his brother an active member of the Pre-Raphaelite Brotherhood and became an editor, man of letters, and memoirist; the youngest child, Christina Georgina Rossetti (1830-1894), became an introspective lyrical poet.

Dante Gabriel Rossetti was bilingual from early childhood and grew up in an atmosphere of émigré political and literary discussion. From childhood he intended to be a painter and illustrated literary subjects in his earliest drawings. He was tutored at home in German and read the Bible, Shakespeare, Goethe's *Faust, The Arabian Nights,* Dickens, and the poetry of Scott and Byron. At the age of eight he entered Mr. Paul's day school in Portland Place and a year later began studies at King's College School, which he attended for five years, from 1837 to 1842. From 1842 to 1846 he attended Cary's Academy of Art to prepare for the Royal Academy, which he entered in July 1846. After more than a year in the Academy Antique School, Rossetti left to apprentice himself to the historical painter Ford Madox Brown, who later became his closest lifelong friend. He also continued his extensive reading of poetry—Poe, Shelley, Coleridge, Blake, Keats, Browning, and Tennyson—and romantic and satiric fiction—Maturin, Thackeray, Meinhold, de la Motte-Fouqué, Charles Wells—and began in 1845 translations from the Italian (Dante's *Vita Nuova* and British Museum volumes of Dante's little-known predecessors) and German medieval poetry (Hartmann von Ave's twelfth-century *Der Arme Heinrich,* parts of the *Nibelungenlied*). The former were published as *The Early Italian Poets* in 1861. In 1847 and 1848 Rossetti began several important early poems—"My Sister's Sleep," "The Blessed Damozel," "The Bride's Prelude," "On Mary's Portrait," "Ave," "Jenny," "Dante at Verona," "A Last Confession," and several sonnets, including "Retro Me Sathana" and a trio, "The Choice." There is some evidence that Rossetti might have wished to take up poetry as a career but felt impelled to turn to painting to earn his living. In 1848 he wrote the poet and critic Leigh Hunt about the possibility of supporting himself by writing poetry, and his dual impulses toward art and poetry may have hindered his development as a painter.

In 1848 Rossetti joined with six other young men, mostly painters, who shared an interest in

Pencil and chalk self-portrait by Rossetti, March 1847 (National Portrait Gallery)

The Pre-Raphaelite Brothers provided each other with companionship, criticism, and encouragement early in their careers and defended each other against initial public hostility. Dante Gabriel Rossetti shaped the group's literary tastes, pressed for the founding of the *Germ,* and published in it several poems, including "My Sister's Sleep," an early version of "The Blessed Damozel," and six sonnets on paintings. He also contributed an allegorical prose tale, "Hand and Soul," in which a thirteenth-century Italian painter, Chiaro dell' Erma, is visited by a woman representing his soul, who tells him, "Paint me thus, as I am. . . . so shall thy soul stand before thee always. . . ."—an early suggestion of Rossetti's later artistic preoccupation with dreamlike, heavily stylized female figures. In 1849 Rossetti accompanied William Holman Hunt to France and exhibited his first oil painting, *The Girlhood of Mary Virgin,* at the Free Exhibition in London; in 1850 he exhibited his *Ecce Ancilla Domini* at the National Institution. P.R.B. meetings became sporadic by 1851, and the group had disbanded by 1853; it had served its purpose, which was to provide initial professional encouragement to its members.

In 1850, at the age of twenty-two Rossetti met

contemporary poetry and an opposition to certain stale conventions of contemporary academy art. Their name, Pre-Raphaelite Brotherhood, honored Lasinio's engravings of paintings by Gozzoli and others who decorated Pisa's Campo Santo. In a general way, the Pre-Raphaelite Brotherhood sought to introduce new forms of thematic seriousness, high coloration, and attention to detail into contemporary British art. Talented members of the group included John Everett Millais, its most skilled painter and future president of the Royal Academy, and William Holman Hunt, a painter inclined to religious themes and dedicated to accurate representation of natural phenomena. The painter James Collinson soon left the brotherhood on religious grounds and was unofficially succeeded by the painter Walter Howell Deverell. Other members were the sculptor Thomas Woolner; the future art critic Frederic Stephens; and William Michael Rossetti, who as P.R.B. secretary kept a journal of activities and edited the six issues of its periodical, the *Germ* (1850). Associates of the group included the older painter Ford Madox Brown, the painter and poet William Bell Scott, the poet Coventry Patmore, and Christina Rossetti, six of whose poems appeared in the *Germ.*

The Girlhood of Mary Virgin, Rossetti's first exhibited oil (The Tate Gallery, London). His models were his mother, Frances, sister Christina, and brother William Michael.

1307
No.

CYCLOGRAPHIC SOCIETY.
CRITICISM SHEET.

Subject of Picture or Quotation :—

Margaret, having abandoned virtue and caused the deaths of her mother and brother, is tormented by the Evil Spirit at Mass, during the chaunting of the "Dies Irae." — (Goethe's Faust.)

Evil Spirit.— How different, Margaret, it was, with thee when, full of innocence, thou camest before the altar, and did kneel thee at its foot lisping thy prayers out of the well-thumbed book, half in the playfulness of childhood, half as if a sense of God were in thy soul; how is it with thee now? Within thine heart what guilt and evil doing? &c.

Margaret.— Woe, woe, these fearful thoughts! they seem to hold me and come over me Spirit of myself.

choir (chaunting) — "Dies irae, dies illa" "Solvet saeclum in favilla"

Evil Spirit — The glorified their countenances turn away from thee; to stretch to thee the hand the pure & stainless shudder. Woe to thee!

Date   July 27, /48   Signature   Gabriel C. Rossetti

The Members of the C. S. are requested to write their remarks *in Ink*, concisely and legibly, avoiding SATIRE or RIDICULE, which ever defeat the true end of criticism, and are more likely to produce unkindly feeling and dissension.

A very clever & original design, beautifully executed. The figures which deserve the greatest attention are the four figures praying to the left: the young girl's face is very pretty but the head is too large; the other three are full of piety. The Devil is in my opinion a mistake; his head wants drawing & the horns through the cowl are common-place & therefore objectionable. The right arm of Margaret should have been shewn; for by hiding the Devil's right hand, (which is not sufficiently prominent) you are impressed with the idea that he is tearing her to pieces for a meal. The drawing & composition of Margaret are original & expressive of utter prostration. The greatest objection is the figure with his back towards you who is unaccountably short; the pleasing group of lovers should have occupied his place. The Girl & child in the foreground are well introduced & exquisite in feeling. The flaming sword highly emblematical of the subject which is well chosen & with a few alterations in its treatment should be painted. Chairs out of perspective.

J. E. Millais

This design is in such perfect feeling as to give me a far higher idea of Goethe than I have before obtained either from a translation, or the artificial illustrations of Retzsch, the Margaret here is wonderful, Margaret enduring the tauntings of the evil spirit who is forcing her weight of sin into her crouching and repenting self. The children are beautifully introduced, without in the slightest interfering with the principal figure, and the holy heads around are beautifully devotional through WP never having the evil over he has not got it sufficiently grand, or near so good as the other parts, excepting the elevated hand which most appropriately accords with the utter prostration of Margaret

W H Hunt

Criticism sheet with comments by John Everett Millais and William Holman Hunt on a drawing by Rossetti. The sketching and drawing club known as the Cyclographic Society was an immediate forerunner of the Pre-Raphaelite Brotherhood (courtesy of William E. Fredeman).

Present, at Hunt's, himself,
Millais, Stephens, & W. M.
Rossetti

P. R. B.

13 Jan.y 1851.   In consideration of the unsettled
& unwritten state of the rules guiding the
P. R. B., it is deemed necessary to determine &
adopt a recognized system.

The P. R. B. originally consisted of 7 members — Hunt, Millais, Dante & W.m Rossetti, Stephens, Woolner & another; & has been reduced
to 6 by the withdrawal of the last. It was
at first positively understood that the P.R.B.
is to consist of these persons & no others, — se-
cession of any original member not being
contemplated: & the principle that neither
this highly important rule, nor any other
affecting the P. R. B., can be ~~finally adopted,~~ repealed, or
or any finally adopted,
modified, unless on unanimous consent
of the members is hereby declared permanent.

First page of the rules drafted for the Pre-Raphaelite Brotherhood (courtesy of William E. Fredeman)

No. 2. *(Price One Shilling.)* FEBRUARY, 1850.

With an Etching by JAMES COLLINSON.

The Germ:

Thoughts towards Nature

In Poetry, Literature, and Art.

When whoso merely hath a little thought
Will plainly think the thought which is in him,—
Not imaging another's bright or dim,
Not mangling with new words what others taught;
When whoso speaks, from having either sought
Or only found,—will speak, not just to skim
A shallow surface with words made and trim,
But in that very speech the matter brought:
Be not too keen to cry—"So this is all!—
A thing I might myself have thought as well,
But would not say it, for it was not worth!"
Ask: "Is this truth?" For is it still to tell
That, be the theme a point or the whole earth,
Truth is a circle, perfect, great or small?

London:

AYLOTT & JONES, 8, PATERNOSTER ROW.

G. F. TUPPER, Printer, Clement's Lane, Lombard Street.

Cover for the second of six issues of the Pre-Raphaelite journal (George Price Boyce's copy from the Collection of William E. Fredeman)

Elizabeth Eleanor Siddal, "Lizzie," then sixteen or seventeen years old. According to William Michael Rossetti, she was the daughter of a Sheffield cutler and was working as a millinery shop assistant when Walter Deverell persuaded her to serve as an artist's model. After 1850, she became a model for many of Rossetti's drawings and paintings, including a series of informal sketches made in the early 1850s and a large watercolor exhibited in 1852 and 1853, *Beatrice at a Marriage Feast Denies Dante Her Salutation.* Lizzie Siddal and Rossetti became engaged about 1851 but did not marry for several years. Her recurrent respiratory illness, his financial difficulties, and some mutual ambivalence may have contributed to the delay. Lizzie Siddal shared Rossetti's poetic and artistic interests and under his tutelage produced a series of watercolors and melancholy verses (collected in *The Poems and Drawings of Elizabeth Siddal,* edited by Roger Lewis and Mark Samuels Lasner, 1978).

In 1856 several university undergraduates, including William Morris and Edward Burne-Jones, began a journal modeled after the *Germ.* Entitled the *Oxford and Cambridge Magazine,* it had a run of twelve issues to which Rossetti contributed three poems—an early version of "The Burden of Nineveh," "The Staff and the Scrip," and a revised version of "The Blessed Damozel." In 1857 Rossetti responded to an invitation to paint murals on the Oxford Union Debating Hall and was joined in this project by Morris, Burne-Jones, and the Oxford undergraduate Algernon Swinburne. While there, he also met Jane Burden and introduced her to her future husband William Morris.

In 1860 Rossetti and Lizzie Siddal were married; during twenty-odd months of married life, Rossetti painted steadily, saw publication of *The Early Italian Poets,* and cofounded the firm of designers Morris, Marshall, Faulkner, and Co. with Morris, Brown, Burne-Jones, Philip Webb, Charles Faulkner, and Peter Marshall. The firm did decorative work for churches and private houses, and Rossetti designed furniture and stained-glass windows. The birth of a dead child in May 1861 depressed Lizzie. On 10 February 1862 she and Rossetti dined with Swinburne at a hotel; afterward Rossetti left Lizzie alone, returning home later to find her nearly dead of an overdose of laudanum. She died the next day and left a final poem with a note requesting that he care for her brother. As a last tribute Rossetti placed a manuscript of his poems in his wife's grave, a decision he later regretted.

After the death of his wife, Rossetti moved to No. 16 Cheyne Walk, Chelsea, a large house on the Thames which contained a first-floor drawing room and, according to William Michael Rossetti, "hardly less than a dozen" bedrooms above. For a while, Rossetti and his brother shared these premises with Swinburne and George Meredith. Here he helped Alexander Gilchrist's widow, Anne, complete the two-volume *Life of William Blake. . . . With Selections from his Poems* (1863), which Gilchrist had left at his death; Rossetti edited and "regularized" many of the poems and prepared headnotes. He also continued to paint steadily, completing *Joan of Arc* (1863), *Beata Beatrix* (1864), *The Beloved* (1865-1866), *Monna Vanna* (1866), *Venus Verticordia* (1864), *The Blue Bower* (1865), and several watercolors and designs. Despite his reluctance to exhibit his paintings in public, he acquired several patrons and became relatively prosperous. One of his models, the blond and full-bodied Fanny Cornforth, became Rossetti's resident mistress, and later, housekeeper; she appears in several paintings of this period (*Bocca Baciata, The Blue Bower, Aurelia, The Loving Cup,* and *Found,* begun in 1854 but never finished). Though never publicly acknowledged, the liaison with Cornforth seems to have become the steadiest sexual relationship of Rossetti's life.

In 1868, Rossetti persuaded Jane Burden Morris, then in ill health, to begin sittings for a series of paintings, and his portraits of her, in crayon, pencil, and oil, are usually considered his most striking artistic work. William Michael Rossetti commented of Jane Morris's appearance: "in the extraordinarily *impressive*—the profound and abstract—type of beauty of Mrs. Morris, he found an ideal more entirely responsive than any other to his aspiration in art. . . . For idealizing there was but one process—to realize." In 1868 Rossetti painted *Mrs. William Morris* and *La Pia* in oil and drew *Aurea Catena* and *Reverie* in crayon; later he painted her in *Pandora, Mariana,* the large *Dante's Dream* (she was Beatrice), *Proserpine, Water Willow, Venus Astarte, Mnemosyne, La Donna della Finestra,* and *The Daydream.* Letters from Rossetti to Jane Morris reveal that by 1869 she had become the center of his emotional life: "All that concerns you is the all-absorbing question with me. . . . no absence can ever make me so far from you again as your presence did for years. For this long inconceivable change, you know now what my thanks must be." Jane Morris's health continued to trouble her throughout the 1870s; she seems to have suffered from the combined effects of a weak back, a pinched spinal nerve, and an

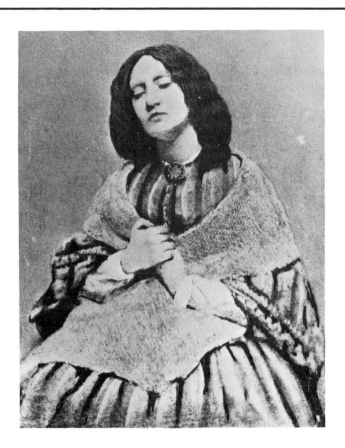

Photograph of Rossetti's wife, Elizabeth Siddal Rossetti, with explanatory note by William Michael Rossetti (courtesy of William E. Fredeman)

Jane Burden, about the time Rossetti introduced her to her future husband, William Morris. Detail of a portrait sketch by Rossetti made at Oxford, 1858 (National Gallery of Ireland, Dublin).

unidentified neurological disorder. In 1866 and 1867, Rossetti also had begun to suffer from physical and mental complaints which burdened him for the rest of his life: uncertain eyesight, headaches, insomnia, a hydrocele which made sitting difficult and required periodic drainage, and growing fear of, and distaste for, the outer world. Preoccupation with Jane Morris's health sometimes seemed to provide Rossetti with an external focus for his anxieties.

Early in the 1850s Rossetti had written several poems: ballads such as "The Staff and the Scrip" (1851-1852) and early versions of "Sister Helen" and "The Burden of Nineveh." In the mid-1850s, he wrote sonnets and short lyrics on themes of failed opportunity, wistful regret, or the recognition of an earlier love. Later in the decade several poems followed, on prostitution ("Jenny," completed in 1858), the failure of past love ("A New Year's Burden," 1859), and satisfied sexuality ("The Song of the Bower," 1860). In his *Family Letters with a Memoir* (1895), William Michael Rossetti does not record that any of the sonnets in his brother's major literary work, "The House of Life," were written between 1856 and 1861. Rossetti wrote "Lost Days" in 1862,

the year of Lizzie's death, then no more until 1867.

In startling contrast, the years of Rossetti's relationship with Jane Morris coincided with his most vigorous poetic activity since the early days of the P.R.B. In 1868, for example, he wrote seven "House of Life" sonnets: four comprising the "Willowwood" sequence, two paired as "Newborn Death," and the proudly possessive "The Portrait,"

> Let all men note
> That in all years (O Love, thy gift is this!)
> They that would look on her must come to me.

The year 1869 was an annus mirabilis: in addition to about seventeen "House of Life" sonnets (an exact number is difficult to determine; numbers 92 and 93, "The Sun's Shame," for example, are listed as written sometime from 1869 to 1873), Rossetti worked on revisions to "Dante at Verona," "Jenny," and "A Last Confession"; composed the highly erotic "Eden Bower" and "Troy Town"; wrote several more sonnets on pictures; and began "The Stream's Secret," which he completed the next year. In the March 1869 *Fortnightly Review,* he published the four Willowwood sonnets, whose presentation of erotic frustration and intensity exemplifies his best style, as in Love's song from sonnet three:

Beata Beatrix, Rossetti's portrait of his wife, Lizzie, painted two years after her suicide in 1862 (The Tate Gallery, London)

The Rossetti family photographed in 1863 by Lewis Carroll. Left to right: Dante Gabriel, Christina, Frances, William Michael.

"O Ye, all ye that walk in Willowwood,
 That walk with hollow faces burning white;
What fathom-depth of soul-struck widowhood,
 What long, what longer hours, one lifelong night,
Ere ye again, who so in vain have wooed
 Your last hope lost, who so in vain invite
Your lips to that their unforgotten food,
 Ere ye, ere ye again shall see the light!"

Rossetti decided in 1869 to publish a volume of his poems, and in October he employed Charles Augustus Howell and others to exhume the manuscript from his wife's grave. Rossetti's year of production was not without its shadows: in his 1892 *Autobiographical Notes,* William Bell Scott related that during a visit to Scotland, Rossetti showed fear at a chaffinch which he felt contained the spirit of his dead wife. In January 1870, Rossetti wrote Jane Morris: "For the last two years I have felt distinctly the clearing away of the chilling numbness that surrounds me in the utter want of you; but since then other obstacles have kept steadily on the increase, and it comes too late." The "obstacles" seem to be their ill health, not her lack of interest or William Morris's opposition. In the spring of 1870 Rossetti rested his eyesight at the estate of Barbara Bodichon in Scalands, Sussex, near Jane Morris, at Hastings for her health. The Morrises visited Ros-

setti together, and Jane Morris remained with him while her husband returned to work. The fifteen 1870 "House of Life" sonnets carry such tranquil titles as "Youth's Spring-tribute," "A Day of Love," and "Life-in-love."

At Scalands Rossetti also began to drink chloral with whiskey to counter his insomnia. According to William Michael Rossetti this remedy was suggested by a friend, the American journalist William Stillman, but Rossetti can hardly have been unaware of the dangers of his choice—Lizzie, after all, had died of an overdose of morphia. Chloral induces paranoia and depression, both latent traits of Rossetti's character. His suspiciousness, reclusiveness, and fear of strangers steadily worsened.

Morris seemed mildly pleased at Rossetti's fine portraits of his wife but obviously understood their titles' literary allusions to entrapped or mistreated wives (*La Donna della Finestra, La Pia, Persephone*), women pining for an absent love (*Mariana*), and a woman immortalized by a poet not her husband (*Beatrice*). In 1868 and 1870 Morris was also at work on his most ambitious poem, *The Earthly Paradise,* which he dedicated to his wife. It contains several lyrics and tales of acutely frustrated love, including the 1869 "The Lovers of Gudrun," in which Gudrun marries a man she does not love and incites her husband to murder her former lover. Gudrun

Rossetti's revisions and additions for the ballad "Sister Helen" written by him in a copy of Poems *(Leipzig: Tauchnitz, 1873). His note on the flyleaf reads: "This copy contains alterations to be adopted in reprinting. D. G. R. 1879" (Anderson Galleries, sale 1806, 11-13 February 1924).*

scorns her obedient husband, who dies worn by guilt, frustration, and grief, while she survives to a robust if reflective old age. Morris's letters of 1870 and 1871 and several private, grieving lyrics reveal that he blamed himself for his failure to hold his wife's love and strove to realize an ethic of unselfish friendship, respect for the sexual freedom of women as well as men, and suppression of self-pity.

Rossetti had two "trial books" of his *Poems* printed privately in late 1869 and early 1870 and revised them for publication by F. S. Ellis in April 1870. He was sufficiently worried about their re-

ception to accept offers by Swinburne, Morris, Colvin, and others who admired his poetry to prepare advance reviews (in his memoir William Michael Rossetti asserts that they volunteered to do this). Quite aware of the situation's ironies, Morris wrote in the *Academy* of his friend's work: "To conclude, I think these lyrics, with all their other merits, the most *complete* of their time; no difficulty is avoided in them: no subject is treated vaguely, languidly, or heartlessly; as there is no commonplace or second-hand thought left in them to be atoned for by beauty of execution, so no thought is allowed to overshadow that beauty of art which compels a real poet to speak in verse and not in prose. Nor do I know what lyrics of any time are to be called great if we are to deny that title to these."

In May 1871, Morris leased Kelmscott Manor in southern Oxfordshire, together with Rossetti and F. S. Ellis, his publisher and Rossetti's, who seldom visited it; in July Morris left his wife and daughters at Kelmscott and set out resolutely for Iceland, source of the Norse literature of which he had begun serious study and whose heroic exemplars may have suggested some solace. Later in July Rossetti arrived at Kelmscott. Morris returned to London in September and visited Kelmscott for short periods, and Rossetti remained until October.

During this period Rossetti wrote "Down Stream," "The Cloud Confines," "Sunset Wings," thirty new sonnets for "The House of Life," and began a romantic ballad, "Rose Mary," in which a dark-haired, gray-eyed heroine's purity in love leads to divine forgiveness for a lapse in chastity. At age forty-two Rossetti wrote his first ballad in which an "unchaste" woman is neither a witch ("Sister Helen"), a snake ("Eden Bower"), or trivial and thoughtless ("Jenny"). Even in "Rose Mary," though, exoneration requires her death. The "House of Life" sonnets of 1871 are threatened by a sense of the brevity of love, as in "Love and Hope":

Cling heart to heart; nor of this hour demand
    Whether in very truth, when we are dead,
    Our hearts shall wake to know Love's golden head
Sole sunshine of the imperishable land;
Or but discern, through night's unfeatured scope,
Scorn-fired at length the illusive eyes of Hope.

Despite such pervasive fears, these sonnets' calmest moments proclaim deep appreciation of love, as in "The Dark Glass":

Not I myself know all my love for thee:
    How should I reach so far, who cannot weigh
    To-morrow's dower by gage of yesterday?
Shall birth and death and all dark names that be
As doors and windows bared to some loud sea,
    Lash deaf mine ears and blind my face with spray;
    And shall my sense pierce love,—the last relay
And ultimate outpost of eternity?

Rossetti and Jane Morris's brief period of apparent happiness and (presumably) sexual liaison has attracted biographers by its supposed romantic unconventionality. It might be more sympathetic as well as realistic to keep in mind the situation's infirmities and constraints: Rossetti's obesity, addiction,

hydrocele, bad eyesight, and growing anxieties; and Jane Morris's ever-present children, neuralgia, and bad back.

In October 1871 the *Contemporary Review* published a pseudonymous article by Thomas Maitland (Robert Buchanan), who reacted against Sidney Colvin's praise of "The Blue Bower" for its "marvellous fleshliness of the flesh," and attacked Rossetti as a leader of a school of poets of sensual lust: "he is fleshly all over, from the roots of his hair to the tip of his toes." Buchanan was a penurious minor poet who had resented a slighting reference to him in a review by William Michael Rossetti. Rossetti replied with an article in the *Athenaeum,* "The Stealthy School of Criticism," and Buchanan then expanded his views for publication under his own name in the spring of 1872 as *The Fleshly School of Poetry and Other Phenomena of the Day.* In this lucubration, he added a lengthy attack on "The House of Life" as a "hotbed" of "nasty phrases," which virtually "wheel[ed]. . ." the poet's "nuptial couch into the public streets." Of his brother's response, William Michael Rossetti wrote in his memoir:

> His fancies now ran away with him, and he thought that the pamphlet was a first symptom in a widespread conspiracy for crushing his fair fame as an artist and a man, and for hounding him out of honest society. . . .
>
>   It is a simple fact that, from the time when the pamphlet had begun to work into the inner tissue of his feelings, Dante Rossetti was a changed man, and so continued till the close of his life.

In an atmosphere of Victorian prudery, it was not unreasonable to fear harm from such a pamphlet. Still, most of Rossetti's poetic predecessors and contemporaries, Tennyson, Robert Browning, Elizabeth Barrett Browning, Morris, and Swinburne, had survived worse reviews, and much of Buchanan's article in fact blasted Swinburne rather than Rossetti. Almost all the reviews of Rossetti's 1870 *Poems* were favorable, and the book had sold unusually well (four editions in 1870). Few in Rossetti's actual or potential audience were likely to share Buchanan's extreme prudery. Rossetti was deeply proud of the originality of his best work, which did, after all, idealize male heterosexual fantasies; yet he retained a good deal of social and sexual conservatism. His own ambivalence, heightened by the effects of his growing drug dependence, seemed to leave him unusually vulnerable to Buchanan's Philistine attack.

More directly, Rossetti may also have feared public exposure of his relationship with Jane Morris. In "Prelude to the Last Decade," published in the *Bulletin of the John Rylands Library* (1970-1971), William E. Fredeman notes that the printed version of Buchanan's pamphlet applies the accusations of sensuality at greater length to "The House of Life" and identifies its "house" with the brothel of "Jenny."

In any case, after leaving Kelmscott on 2 June 1872, Rossetti suffered a complete mental breakdown with auditory hallucinations of accusing voices. He was taken to the Roehampton home of his friend Dr. Thomas Gordon Hake, where he attempted to commit suicide (as had Lizzie) with an overdose of laudanum. He then spent the summer under the care of friends and associates, at Roehampton, then at F. M. Brown's house in Fitzroy Square, and at three residences in Scotland, two of which, Stobhall and Urrard House, were lent by one of his art patrons, the Liberal M.P. William Graham. During this period he was accompanied by George Hake, the son of his friend, who served as general assistant and secretary, and he was visited by Fanny Cornforth and the Morrises.

A portion of his fine collection of Oriental china was sold for income, and his paintings were removed from his home for safekeeping. Rossetti's earnings had been high for a painter of the 1870s—they fluctuated between somewhere above one and more than three thousand pounds—but he was anxious lest knowledge of his ill health would make his clients press for completion of commissions and more reluctant to provide advance payment. By September 1872 he was able to paint again, and in the same month he returned to Kelmscott, from which he wrote his brother that experience had taught him dependence on "the society of the one necessary person." He remained at Kelmscott until the summer of 1874, employed Charles Augustus Howell as agent to sell his pictures in London, and received frequent visits from Jane Morris.

William Morris's letters of October and November 1872 show muted strain ("I have had a fit of low spirits—for no particular reason that I could tell"; "I shall not be there [Kelmscott] much now I suppose"). Perhaps partly in response, Morris completed *Love Is Enough,* a masque on the sufficiency of ideal love; in 1873 he visited Italy, then made another strenuous summer trip to Iceland.

Rossetti's poetic productivity revived once

Fanny Cornforth, Rossetti's mistress and the model for several of his paintings, including Bocca Baciata, The Blue Bower, Aurelia, *and* Found

again in 1873, and he finished seven single sonnets and the double sonnet "The Sun's Shame." The sonnets of this period are melancholy and resonant, but the familiar themes of suffused passion have begun to merge with new ones—the creation of art and intimations of immortality, expressed in the following verses from "The Heart of the Night":

> Alas, the soul!—how soon must she
> Accept her primal immortality,—
> The flesh resume its dust whence it began?
>
> O Lord of work and peace! O Lord of life!
> O Lord, the awful Lord of will! though late,
> Even yet renew this soul with duteous breath:
> That when the peace is garnered in from strife,
> The work retrieved, the will regenerate,
> This soul may see thy face, O Lord of death!

In 1873 Rossetti continued to paint steadily, using Jane Morris as a model for *Proserpine* and Alexa Wilding for *La Ghirlandata*. Jane Morris seemed to absent herself more and more frequently, and during one such absence in 1874 Rossetti left Kelmscott for Chelsea. There his health continued to decline, and in 1874 he seems to have written no "House of Life" sonnets, and only one obituary sonnet on the death of Oliver Madox Brown. His volume of *Early Italian Poets* was republished that year, under the title *Dante and His Circle*. In 1875 he wrote three sonnets, in 1876 two short poems, and in 1877 one sonnet to accompany a picture, "Astarte Syriaca."

After Kelmscott, Rossetti rented several country residences in succession for privacy. Jane Morris visited him for an extended period at Bognor in 1875, but she became increasingly unavailable for sittings in ensuing years, and his loneliness and anxieties about his work seem to have grown. Jane's letters of the mid-1870s indicate a decline in her own health; she found it difficult to sit and suffered from faints. At one point in 1879, Rossetti chided her with reluctance to pose, since she would be no more uncomfortable with him than at home, and she assured him in response that she would be "but too happy to feel myself of use again."

In 1876, however, Jane Morris's daughter Jenny began to suffer from epileptic fits, and anxiety about Jenny's health as well as her own led to extended trips with the George Howard family to European spas. Rossetti's chief daily concern remained the production and sale of his paintings, doubtless necessary but scarcely absorbing. Rossetti's valetudinarian phobias and increasingly paranoid suspicions may also have contrasted more and more unfavorably with William Morris's energy, prosperity, affectionate goodwill, and attentive concern for the Morrises' children. In any case, Rossetti suffered further breakdowns in 1877 and 1879, and his letters of the period indicate that Jane disapproved of his most melancholy poems and his depressive statements.

In 1875 he completed the oil painting *La Bella Mano,* in 1877 *Venus Astarte* and *The Sea-Spell,* and in the next three years *La Donna della Finestra* (1879) and *The Day-Dream* (1880), modeled by Jane, and *A Vision of Fiametta* (1878), modeled by Marie Stillman. In 1878 he returned to ballads once again and began a historical ballad, "The White Ship," and in 1879 he completed a ballad begun in 1871, "Rose Mary."

A last surge of poetic energy in 1880 and 1881 anticipated the publication of his poems in 1881. In this edition, he added six sonnets to "The House of Life," completed seventeen more sonnets and short poems, revised "Sister Helen," finished "The White Ship," and wrote a carefully developed historical ballad, "The King's Tragedy." The final sonnets and short poems reflect in sometimes eschatological language on the nature and source of art, as in the famous introductory sonnet to "The House of Life":

> A Sonnet is a moment's monument,—
>   Memorial from the Soul's eternity
>   To one dead deathless hour.
> ....
> A Sonnet is a coin: its face reveals
>   The soul,—its converse, to what Power 'tis due:—
> Whether for tribute to the august appeals
>   Of Life, or dower in Love's high retinue,
> It serve; or, 'mid the dark wharf's cavernous breath,
> In Charon's palm it pay the toll to Death.

In "The King's Tragedy" Rossetti returned to the mingled political, literary, and romantic themes of his early "Dante at Verona," but unlike the obsessive passions of his ballads of the late 1860s and 1870s (such as "Eden Bower" and "Troy Town"), "The King's Tragedy" presents a love which, though frustated by death, is deep and sustained.

In 1881 Rossetti sold one of his largest and best paintings, *Dante's Dream,* to the Walker Art Gallery in Liverpool. Although his volumes of *Poems* and *Ballads and Sonnets* (1881) were quietly but favorably received, he had entered a final pattern of depressive ill health. A sudden decline in February 1882 caused him to move to Birchington, where he revised the comic poem *Jan Van Hunks,* was visited by his mother, William, and Christina, and died of blood poisoning from uric acid on 9 April 1882. At his death he left behind the almost completed "Joan of Arc" and "Salutation of Beatrice."

Rossetti's father, Gabriele, had died at seventy-one in 1854 and his mother, Frances, died soon after her son, in 1886 at age eighty-five. Christina lived until 1894 and William Rossetti until 1919. Brown died in 1893, Scott in 1896; the invalid Jane Morris survived until 1914. Rossetti was buried in Birchington churchyard, under a tombstone designed by his lifelong friend Ford Madox Brown and near a stained-glass memorial window designed by Frederick Shields. A fountain and bust by Brown were placed in Cheyne Walk.

If one moderates them somewhat, many of

Rossetti's tombstone at Birchington-on-Sea, designed by his lifelong friend Ford Madox Brown

quaintances formed a fresh audience, which seemed to soothe reminders of his former self.

Had Rossetti curbed his use of chloral and lived another decade, he might have doubled his oeuvre. Striking shifts in range and manner occur in the last poems, and reflections on old subjects of sexuality and failed ambition are graced by a new and mediating detachment. Even his paintings after 1870, such as the large oil *Dante's Dream,* show somewhat improved ability to arrange a complex canvas (his greatest weakness throughout his career). Some of his late designs for oil paintings, such as *The Boat of Love* and *The Death of Lady Macbeth,* were at least as good as any he had done earlier. Rossetti was haunted by a (perhaps partially accurate) private assessment of his weaknesses as a painter and obsessed with Jane Morris as a model. Yet he was perhaps right that his intense response to such private archetypes was the chief distinction of his work. Perhaps he might have found a new focus for this intensity had he lived a few more years. Likewise, of course, he might also have improved his technical ability, or finished more of the poetry which at some level he yearned to write, had he painted fewer lucrative replicas and painted more slowly.

It would be wrong, at any rate, to sentimentalize Rossetti as a victim of "tragic loves." It seemed to serve some inner purpose for Rossetti to idealize women who were withdrawn, invalid, and/or melancholic. Their genuine alienation (literal, in the case of Elizabeth Siddal and Jane Morris, from their families, potential friends, and class origins) seems to have provided some counterpart for an inner sense of inadequacy and isolation in him. In some way he seemed to need serious emotional attachments with women which were poised on the edge of abrogation and withdrawal. In any case, a sense of this equilibration heightened the effects both of his paintings and of his poetry.

Critics have differed in assessing the quality of Rossetti's poetic achievement and in their preferences for different periods of his work. Directly after his death, the later ballads and "The House of Life" were much admired. In the early twentieth century, "The House of Life" was still considered among his best works, but attention shifted to ballads, such as "The Blessed Damozel," to which William Michael Rossetti assigned an earlier date. In fact, it is difficult to date Rossetti's work or divide it into periods, since he continually revised poems begun as a young man. The texts to many early poems—"The Blessed Damozel," "Sister Helen," "The Burden of Nineveh," "The Portrait," "Jenny,"

Rossetti's self-estimates were accurate. Had he been able when young to choose a literary career, he would probably have been a better poet than painter; he was a more genuinely original and skillful writer than many who were more prolific. In part, his achievement was vicarious: he galvanized others in many ways not easily measured. In his youth, he was capable of infectious and gregarious enthusiasm for the work of others, however obscure, but resentment at his own lack of fame deepened gradually as he aged. Insecurity and self-reproach manifested themselves in all but his earliest poems. Behind his self-confident, even peremptory manner with artistic associates, he seemed to need a praise-filled, even sheltering environment for completion of work: first the P.R.B.; then his intimates of the "Jovial Campaign" to paint the Oxford Union Debating Hall and, later, the members of the Firm; and, finally, Jane Morris and a few faithfully supportive friends. His final surge of poetic effort, for example, benefited from the ministrations of Theodore Watts. He withdrew from former friends in his last years, but new ac-

"Dante at Verona," and several of the sonnets—gradually became near-palimpsests. His revisions often do add structure and plot to the ballads and cohesion and elegance to the sonnets. Even slight verbal changes may heighten a poem's cumulative effect. Compare, for example, the 1847 and 1881 versions of stanza seven of one of his most admired poems, "The Blessed Damozel":

> 1847: Heard hardly, some of her new friends,
>   Playing at holy games,
> Spake gentle-mouthed among themselves
>   Their virginal chaste names;
> And the souls mounting up to God
>   Went by her like thin flames.

> 1881: Around her, lovers, newly met
>   'Mid deathless love's acclaims
> Spoke evermore among themselves
>   Their heart-remembered names;
> And the souls mounting up to God
>   Went by her like thin flames.

When Rossetti was young, his bright pictorialism, concrete detail, archaisms, and sublimated sexuality reflected rather conventional aspects of contemporary poetic sensibility. His poems on grief, loss, and inadequacy in the 1850s, by contrast, were some of his best work. Consider "The Landmark" (1854):

>   . . . —I had thought
>   The stations of my course should rise unsought,
> As altar-stone or ensigned citadel.

> But lo! the path is missed, I must go back,
>   And thirst to drink when next I reach the spring
> Which once I stained, which since may have grown
>   black.
>   Yet though no light be left nor bird now sing
> As here I turn, I'll thank God, hastening,
> That the same goal is still on the same track.

By the late 1860s his sense of failure had evolved into an oppressive fear about identity, evident in "A Superscription":

> Look in my face; my name is Might-have-been;
>   I am also called No-more, Too-late, Farewell;
>   Unto thine ear I hold the dead sea-shell
> Cast up thy Life's foam-fretted feet between;

> Unto thine eyes the glass where that is seen
>   Which had Life's form and Love's, but by my
>   spell
>   Is now a shaken shadow intolerable,
> Of ultimate things unuttered the frail screen.

> Mark me, how still I am! But should there dart
>   One moment through thy soul the soft surprise
>   Of that winged Peace which lulls the breath of
>   sighs—
> Then shalt thou see me smile, and turn apart
> Thy visage to mine ambush at thy heart
>   Sleepless with cold commemorative eyes.

In Rossetti's middle and later poetry, sexual love became a near-desperate desire to transcend time. Passion's benefit is not pleasure or mutual relaxation but a poignant hope that one moment may endure. This shift brought radical changes in themes and style. In the opening sonnet of the early triplet "The Choice" (1848) sexual attraction is an enjoyable minor distraction:

> Now kiss, and think that there are really those,
>   My own high-bosomed beauty, who increase
>   Vain gold, vain lore, and yet might
>   choose our way!
>   Through many years they toil; then on a
>   day
>   They die not,—for their life was death,—but
>   cease;
> And round their narrow lips the mould falls close.

Still, the sequence ends with an admonition to aspire to "higher" ends and greater achievement: "And though thy soul sail leagues and leagues beyond,/Still, leagues beyond those leagues, there is more sea." In contrast, by 1869 love has become awesome and solemn, as in "Lovesight":

> O love, my love! if I no more should see
> Thyself, nor on the earth the shadow of thee,
>   Nor image of thine eyes in any spring,—
> How then should sound upon Life's darkening slope
> The ground-whirl of the perished leaves of Hope,
>   The wind of Death's imperishable wing?

Sexual frustration and resentment in this period have become diffused indictments of more general injustice, as in "The Sun's Shame":

> Beholding youth and hope in mockery caught
>   From life; and mocking pulses that remain
>   When the soul's death of bodily death is fain;
> Honour unknown, and honour known unsought;
> And penury's sedulous self-torturing thought
>   On gold, whose master therewith buys his bane;
>   And longed-for woman longing all in vain
> For lonely man with love's desire distraught;
> And wealth, and strength, and power, and pleasant-
>   ness,
>   Given unto bodies of whose souls men say,
>   None poor and weak, slavish and foul, as they:—

Fair copy of the poem published "The Blessed Damozel," probably made circa 1873 when Rossetti was beginning the painting of the same title (The Pierpont Morgan Library)

Beholding these things, I behold no less
The blushing morn and blushing eve confess
    The shame that loads the intolerable day.

By comparison, the final sonnets of Rossetti's life are tranquil, even celebratory. "The Song-Throe" (1880) offers assurance that real pain may eventuate in the perfection of great art:

By thine own tears thy song must tears beget,
    O Singer! Magic mirror thou hast none
    Except thy manifest heart; and save thine own
Anguish or ardour, else no amulet.
        . . . nay, more dry
    Than the Dead Sea for throats that thirst and sigh,
That song o'er which no singer's lids grew wet.

The Song-god—He the Sun-god—is no slave
    Of thine: thy Hunter he, who for thy soul
    Fledges his shaft: to no august control
Of thy skilled hand his quivered store he gave:
But if thy lips' loud cry leap to his smart,
The inspir'd recoil shall pierce thy brother's heart.

In several ways "The House of Life" sonnets make more sense in their roughly reconstructible chronological order than in the sequence of happiness-followed-by-loss in which Rossetti arranged them, but in any rearrangement all but the very earliest sonnets (such as the moralistic "Retro Me, Sathana") are among the finest examples of their genre in English. Some of his romantic ballads, "The Blessed Damozel," "Sister Helen," "Rose Mary," and "The King's Tragedy," are perhaps as good as any literary ballads of the period. Rossetti also possessed a gift for the grotesque, embodied in the comic "Jan Van Hunks" and perhaps to a degree in "Sister Helen" and "Eden Bower." "Jenny" was the first major Victorian poem to present a prostitute who is sexually attractive and not entirely responsible for her fate. If the poem now seems condescending and evasive, it took some stubbornness for Rossetti to address the issue at all, and "Jenny" remains one of the more interesting "contemporary subject" poems of its period.

It is difficult to compare Rossetti's achievement with that of the other Victorian poets. For its modest size, Rossetti's poetic work is wide in manner and subject. He was a talented experimenter, and his heightened rhythms and refrains influenced other mid-and late-century poetry. He was also an important popularizer of Italian poetry in England and a major practitioner of the sonnet. Certainly, he lacked the strong, confident range and impressively subtle lyricism of Tennyson and Browning, but his

erotic spirituality and gift for the dramatic were his own, and Swinburne, Meredith, Wilde, and Symons benefited from the liberating influence of his example. Rossetti was perhaps as significant for his effect on others as for his own work, a judgment that he himself came to make with growing bitterness. His critical remarks on Romantic and contemporary literature were often cogent and influenced all around him—the P.R.B. when he was young; later the Morris and Burne-Jones circle; and finally, Walter Pater and a later generation of poets who sought escape from moralistic art.

Rossetti's attempt to create a unified oeuvre of poetry and painting was also pioneering and extended conceptions of both arts. Through such painters as Burne-Jones, Sandys, and Waterhouse, Rossetti had a further indirect influence on the literature of the Decadence. He also conceived the idea of the *Germ*, the first little magazine of literature and art, and with Brown, Morris, Burne-Jones, and Webb helped cofound the movement to extend the range of decorative art and improve the quality of book design. Rossetti's poetry is not as important as that of Tennyson, Browning, or Hopkins, but it would be difficult to name others who clearly excelled him at his best and even more difficult to imagine later nineteenth-century Victorian poetry and art without his influence. His writings can perhaps best be viewed as an unusually acute expression of Victorian social uncertainty and loss of faith. Rossetti's poetry on the absence of love is as bleakly despairing as any of the century, and no poet of his period conveyed more profoundly certain central Victorian anxieties: metaphysical uncertainty, sexual anxiety, and fear of time.

Letters:
William Michael Rossetti, ed., *Dante Gabriel Rossetti: His Family Letters with a Memoir*, 2 volumes (London: Ellis, 1895);
Oswald Doughty and John Robert Wahl, eds., *The Letters of Dante Gabriel Rossetti*, 4 volumes (Oxford: Clarendon Press, 1965, 1967);
John Bryson, ed., *Dante Gabriel Rossetti and Jane Morris: Their Correspondence* (Oxford: Clarendon Press, 1976).

Bibliographies:
William E. Fredeman, "William Morris and His Circle: A Selective Bibliography of Publications, 1960-62," *William Morris Society Journal*, 1, no. 4 (1964): 23-33;
Fredeman, "Dante Gabriel Rossetti," in his *Pre-Raphaelitism: A Bibliocritical Study* (Cambridge:

Harvard University Press, 1965), pp. 90-105;

Fredeman, "William Morris and His Circle: A Selective Bibliography of Publications, 1962-63," *William Morris Society Journal,* 2, no. 1 (1966): 13-36;

Fredeman, "The Pre-Raphaelites," in *The Victorian Poets: A Guide to Research,* edited by Frederick Faverty (Cambridge: Harvard University Press, 1968), pp. 251-316;

Francis L. Fennell, *Dante Gabriel Rossetti: An Annotated Bibliography* (New York: Garland, 1982).

Biographies:

William Michael Rossetti, *Dante Gabriel Rossetti As Designer and Writer* (London: Ellis, 1895);

William Michael Rossetti, ed., *Dante Gabriel Rossetti: His Family Letters with a Memoir,* 2 volumes (London: Ellis, 1895);

William Michael Rossetti, *Some Reminiscences,* 2 volumes (New York: Scribners, 1906);

Oswald Doughty, *A Victorian Romantic: Dante Gabriel Rossetti* (London: Oxford University Press, 1949);

William E. Fredeman, *Prelude to the Last Decade: Dante Gabriel Rossetti in the Summer of 1872* (Manchester: John Rylands Library, 1971);

Brian and Judy Dobbs, *Dante Gabriel Rossetti: An Alien Victorian* (London: Macdonald & Jane's, 1977).

References:

Florence S. Boos, *The Poetry of Dante G. Rossetti: A Critical and Source Study* (The Hague: Mouton, 1976);

Ronnalie Howard, *The Dark Glass: Vision and Technique in the Poetry of Dante Gabriel Rossetti* (Athens: Ohio University Press, 1972);

Joan Rees, *The Poetry of Dante Gabriel Rossetti: Modes of Self-Expression* (Cambridge: Cambridge University Press, 1981);

David G. Riede, *Dante Gabriel Rossetti and the Limits of Victorian Vision* (Ithaca: Cornell University Press, 1983);

William Michael Rossetti, *P.R.B. Journal: William Michael Rossetti's Diary of the Pre-Raphaelite Brotherhood, 1849-1853,* edited by William E. Fredeman (Oxford: Clarendon Press, 1975);

David Sonstroem, *Rossetti and the Fair Lady* (Middleton, Conn.: Wesleyan University Press, 1971);

Richard L. Stein, *The Ritual of Interpretation: Literature and Art in Ruskin, Rossetti, and Pater* (Cambridge: Harvard University Press, 1975);

Lionel Stevenson, *The Pre-Raphaelite Poets* (Chapel Hill: University of North Carolina Press, 1972);

Victorian Poetry: An Issue Devoted to the Works of Dante Gabriel Rossetti, edited by William E. Fredeman, 20, nos. 3 and 4 (1982);

Joseph Vogel, *Dante Gabriel Rossetti's Versecraft* (Gainesville: University of Florida Press, 1971).

Papers:

Collections in the United States which include manuscripts and letters by Rossetti are at the Library of Congress; the library of the Wilmington [Delaware] Society of the Fine Arts; Princeton University Library; the Pierpont Morgan Library; and the Humanities Research Center at the University of Texas, Austin. In Great Britain Rossetti manuscripts may be found in the British Library; the library of the Victoria and Albert Museum; and the Fitzwilliam Museum, Cambridge.

George Augustus Simcox

(1841-1905)

Byron Nelson
West Virginia University

BOOKS: *Prometheus Unbound: A Tragedy* (London: Smith, Elder, 1867);

Poems and Romances (London: Strahan, 1869);

Recollections of a Rambler (London: Chapman & Hall, 1874);

A History of Latin Literature from Ennius to Boethius, 2 volumes (London: Longmans, Green, 1883; New York: Harper, 1883).

OTHER: *The Orations of Demosthenes and Aeschines on the Crown*, edited by Simcox and William Henry Simcox (Oxford: Clarendon Press, 1872).

Born in London in 1841, George Augustus Simcox received a scholarship to Corpus Christi College, Oxford, in 1858 and began his classical studies in earnest. In addition to his poetry and classical studies, Simcox contributed essays on such contemporary literary figures as Renan, Shelley, Charles Kingsley, and Harriet Martineau to several critical journals, including *North British Review, Fortnightly, Nineteenth Century,* and *Academy.* His massive edition of the orations of Demosthenes and Aeschines was a joint production with his brother, the Reverend William Henry Simcox.

Alfred H. Miles selected Simcox's long narrative poem "The Soldan's Daughter" and a wistful sonnet, "A Chill in Summer," for inclusion in *The Poets and Poetry of the Nineteenth Century* (1906) and detected the influence of A. C. Swinburne and William Morris on Simcox's verse.

"The Soldan's Daughter" (in twenty-five stanzas) appeared in Simcox's most original volume of verse, *Poems and Romances* (1869). A narrative of the abduction of a sultan's daughter by a crusader, the poem escapes conventionality by an ironic and rather cynical ending. Simcox's use of stock elements is not particularly convincing, and the three weakest elements in the poet's narrative style are his use of archaisms, his redundancies, and a tendency to bathos.

Indeed, the poem falls into bathos by the second line, since the promise of the opening phrase, "The Soldan's daughter of Babylon," requires a more colorful verb and object to catch the reader's attention than "Went out to pluck her roses." To achieve medieval color, the poem is sprinkled with such words and phrases as "sward," "caitiff," "knightly mail," "caitiff and craven," and "smote sore," which unfortunately alone cannot invoke the desired medieval atmosphere. The redundancies in the verse are all too obviously motivated by uninspired attempts to make lines scan, as in "blithe of cheer." Occasionally, the narrative focus suffers through inept compression of a complex series of events, as in

> The charger started, the dead man fell,
> He floated down the stream:
> The knight rose softly and spread a sail,
> And they floated on till the stars grew pale.

Sometimes the poetry suffers at the expense of a graphic passage designed to titillate: "He caught at the long white beard, and smote/with the gardening knife on the Soldan's throat."

Still, the narrative is rescued from trite moralizing on the superiority of Christianity to paganism by the deft ironic twists of the poem's conclusion, in which the Red Cross Knight marries not the princess but a flirtatious novice of the convent to which the princess had been sent for religious instruction. Conversely, the nuns to whom the princess had gone for Christian catechism overemphasize the attractions of convent life and persuade the princess to become a nun.

The bittersweet elements of "A Chill in Summer" turn an already acrid lyric into a confusingly cynical exercise with no clear focus. Unlike "The Soldan's Daughter," in which the ironic twists of the conclusion spare the poem from the anticipated sentimentality, "A Chill in Summer" remains sour throughout.

On 4 September 1905 the *London Times* reported that Simcox, then staying at Ballycastle, near Belfast, had mysteriously disappeared. "It is considered most probable," the *Times* concluded on 26 September, "that he fell over the cliffs into the sea. . . .The brilliant promise of youth was hardly confirmed by the output of subsequent years." Though Simcox could, on occasion, be a skillful narrative poet, his work as a classical scholar and editor outweighs his contributions to English verse. His classical tastes are best reflected in his first published volume, a version of *Prometheus Unbound* (1867); in his scholarly edition of *The Orations of Demosthenes and Aeschines on the Crown* (1872); and by his *A History of Latin Literature from Ennius to Boethius* (1883).

George R. Sims
(2 September 1847-4 September 1922)

Christopher D. Murray
University of Regina

SELECTED BOOKS: *The Dagonet Ballads* (London: Francis, 1879);

The Ballads of Babylon (London: Fuller, 1880);

Zeph, and Other Stories (London: Fuller, 1880);

The Theatre of Life (London: Fuller, 1881);

How the Poor Live (London: Chatto & Windus, 1883);

The Lifeboat, and Other Poems (London: Fuller, 1883);

Stories in Black and White (London: Fuller, 1885);

Rogues and Vagabonds (London: Chatto & Windus, 1885; New York: Munro, 1886);

The Ring o' Bells (London: Chatto & Windus, 1886);

Mary Jane's Memoirs (London: Chatto & Windus, 1887; New York: Ivers, 1887);

Mary Jane Married: Tales of a Village Inn (London: Chatto & Windus, 1888);

Land of Gold, and Other Poems (London: Fuller, 1888);

The Dagonet Reciter and Reader, in Prose and Verse (London: Chatto & Windus, 1888);

Tales of To-Day (London: Chatto & Windus, 1889; New York: Lovell, 1889);

The Case of George Candlemas (London: Chatto & Windus, 1890);

Dramas of Life (London: Chatto & Windus, 1890; New York: United States Book Company, 1890);

A Bunch of Primroses (London & New York: Tuck, 1890);

Nellie's Prayer (London & New York: Tuck, 1890);

Tinkletop's Crime (London: Chatto & Windus, 1891; New York: Webster, 1891);

Dagonet Ditties (London: Chatto & Windus, 1891);

Memoirs of a Mother-in-Law (London: Newnes, 1892; New York: Waverly, 1892);

My Two Wives, and Other Stories (London: Chatto & Windus, 1894);

Memoirs of a Landlady (London: Chatto & Windus, 1894);

Dagonet on Our Islands (London: Unwin, 1894);

Scenes from the Show (London: Chatto & Windus, 1894);

Dagonet Abroad (London: Chatto & Windus, 1895);

The Ten Commandments (London: Chatto & Windus, 1896);

As It Was in the Beginning: Life Stories of To-Day (London: White, 1896);

The Coachman's Club: or, Tales Told Out of School (London: White, 1897);

Dorcas Dene, Detective: Her Adventures (London: White, 1897);

Dorcas Dene, Detective: Her Adventures, second series (London: White, 1898);

Dagonet Dramas of the Day (London: Chatto & Windus, 1898);

Once Upon a Christmastime (London: Chatto & Windus, 1898);

In London's Heart (London: Chatto & Windus, 1900; New York: Buckles/London: Chatto & Windus, 1900);

Without the Limelight: Theatrical Life as it is (London: Chatto & Windus, 1900);

The Small-Part Lady and Other Stories (London: Chatto & Windus, 1900);

A Blind Marriage, and Other Stories (London: Chatto & Windus, 1901);

Nat Harlowe, Mountebank (London: Cassell, 1902);

Biographs of Babylon: Life-Pictures of London's Moving Scenes (London: Chatto & Windus, 1902);

Young Mrs. Caudle (London: Chatto & Windus, 1904);

Among My Autographs (London: Chatto & Windus, 1904);

The Life We Live (London: Chatto & Windus, 1904);

Li Ting of London, and Other Stories (London: Chatto & Windus, 1905);

The Mysteries of Modern London (London: Pearson, 1906);

Two London Fairies (London: Greening, 1906);

For Life—and After (London: Chatto & Windus, 1906);

London by Night (London: Greening, 1906);

His Wife's Revenge (London: Chatto & Windus, 1907);

Watches of the Night (London: Greening, 1907);

The Mystery of Mary Anne, and Other Stories (London: Chatto & Windus, 1907);

The Black Stain (London: Jarrolds, 1908);

Joyce Pleasantry, and Other Stories (London: Chatto & Windus, 1908);

The Devil in London (London: S. Paul, 1908; New York: Dodge, 1909);

The Death Gamble (London: S. Paul, 1909);

The Cabinet Minister's Wife (London: S. Paul, 1910);

Off the Track in London (London: Jarrolds, 1911);

Behind the Veil: True Stories of London Life (London: Greening, 1913);

The Bluebeard of the Bath (London: Pearson, 1915);

My Life: Sixty Years' Recollections of Bohemian London (London: Nash, 1917);

Glances Back (London: Jarrolds, 1917);

Prepare to Shed Them Now: The Ballads of George R. Sims, edited by Arthur Calder-Marshall (London: Hutchinson, 1968).

PLAYS: *The Lights o' London,* London, Princess's Theatre, 10 September 1881; New York, Union-Square Theatre, 5 December 1881;

The Romany Rye, London, Princess's Theatre, 10 June 1882; New York, Booth's Theatre, 18 September 1882;

In the Ranks, by Sims and Henry Pettitt, New York, Standard Theatre, 1 November 1883; London, Adelphi Theatre, 6 November 1883;

Harbour Lights, by Sims and Pettitt, London, Adelphi Theatre, 23 November 1885; New York, Wallack's Theatre, 26 January 1887;

The English Rose, by Sims and Robert Buchanan, London, Adelphi Theatre, 2 August 1890; New York, Proctor's Theatre, 9 March 1892;

The Trumpet Call, by Sims and Buchanan, London, Adelphi Theatre, 1 August 1891.

OTHER: *Balzac's Contes Dramatiques,* translated by Sims (London: Chatto & Windus, 1874);

Living London, edited by Sims, 3 volumes (London & New York: Cassell, 1901-1903).

No one would have been more surprised than George Sims himself that posterity should recognize him not as the immensely popular crusading journalist, not as the writer of several highly successful melodramas, not as a writer of melodramatic novels and short stories, nor as the bon vivant and man-about-town—the celebrity lending his name to the promotion of dog food and hair restorer—but as the writer of verse. "In the Workhouse: Christmas Day" is remembered yet, and in its time was rivaled only by Thomas Babington Macaulay's "Horatius" as a recitation piece. Sims with his ballads hit upon a successful formula and used it to draw attention to the appalling conditions of the London slums. But verse played a small role in his busy existence, and he wrote little after his dramatic successes in the 1880s.

Sims was born into a prosperous London family with Chartist sympathies on his mother's side. His life reflects such a background. Educated at

Hanwell Military College and the university at Bonn, he was sent down from the latter for his exuberant behavior. He entered the family business, an early assignment being to give Henry Mayhew, now remembered for his survey of *London Labor and the London Poor* (1864), a tour of it, but he aspired to write. For several years he enjoyed a bohemian existence by night while dutifully working in London by day. In 1874, however, he joined the staff of *Fun*, and three years later joined the *Referee* and contributed a weekly column, "Mustard and Cress," which appeared, under the pseudonym Dagonet, without fail until his death. In 1881 Gilbert Dalziel commissioned him and Frederick Barnard to prepare a series of illustrated articles entitled "How the Poor Live" for a new journal, the *Pictorial World*. Sims reached and caught an audience that more serious researchers did not. His work, as he put it in his autobiography, *My Life: Sixty Years' Recollections of Bohemian London* (1917), caused "something of a sensation." Questions were asked in Parliament, innumerable sermons preached, and eventually a Royal Commission on the Housing of

the Poor was instituted; the process of amelioration had begun.

Sims's journalism had its light side, principally a celebration of English middle-class amusements. He wrote of horse racing, of showing dogs, of boxing, of the resorts catering to Londoners' need for recreation (Brighton being his favorite), and of good living generally. A very hardworking man, he produced novels and short stories, also melodramas and burlesques, many of which enjoyed lucrative runs in London, the provinces, and abroad. At one time in the 1880s four of his plays were running concurrently in the West End, an achievement equaled once, apparently, but not surpassed in his lifetime.

Popular when first appearing in the daily press, Sims's ballads were praised by critics of note when published in book form. Robert Buchanan's enthusiastic review of an edition of *The Dagonet Ballads* for the February 1881 *Contemporary Review* led to friendship with Sims, with whom he collaborated on several melodramas; Bret Harte, on arriving in England, first wished to meet not Tenny-

Sims in an endorsement for silk hats from the Hatter's Gazette *(April 1885) and as the model of elegance in the* London Tailor and Record of Fashion *(1887)*

son, Browning, or Gladstone but Dagonet. His ballads reached and reach yet a wide audience, for Sims has been accorded an honor enjoyed by few minor Victorian poets: a modern edition, published in 1968. The title, however, *Prepare to Shed Them Now,* anticipates, even courts, the ballads' potential risibility. Overly sentimental they are, but better writers than Sims succumbed to the maudlin, the staple of much Victorian art, in an age when human suffering on a large scale was close at hand for the middle classes to observe. Arthur Calder-Marshall stresses the sociological importance of Sims's ballads, whose literary characteristics are "colloquial language and heavily accented verse," with a first-person narrator telling "a melodramatic story, expressing often opinions which appeared almost blasphemous but which in fact robustly restated

simple faith." Sims, himself in many ways the quintessential good-hearted, highly sociable Englishman, cleverly manipulated his readers into identifying with people whose experience was vastly different from their own. Profoundly aware of the best elements in the English character, he appealed across the chasms of class to the English passion for fair play. No revolutionary—he loved the good life too much to risk its overthrow—George Sims gently but firmly educated his readers. He was immensely gratified to discover that Charles Booth, credited with the implementation of state old-age pensions, began his career as a social reformer because of Sims's most famous ballad. Sims wrote not for posterity but for social improvement; in his day he was remarkably successful.

Joseph Skipsey
(17 March 1832-3 September 1903)

Peter Quartermain

BOOKS: *Poems* (Newcastle-upon-Tyne?: Privately printed, 1859);

Poems, Songs and Ballads (London & Newcastle-upon-Tyne: Privately printed, 1862);

The Collier Lad and other lyrics (Newcastle-upon-Tyne: Privately printed, 1864);

Poems (Newcastle-upon-Tyne: Privately printed, 1871);

A Book of Miscellaneous Lyrics (Bedlington: Privately printed, 1878); revised as *A Book of Lyrics, including songs, ballads and chants* (London: D. Bogue, 1881);

Carols from the Coal-Fields and other songs and ballads (London: Scott, 1886); republished as *Carols, Songs and Ballads* (London: Scott, 1888);

The Poet as Seer and Singer (Newcastle-upon-Tyne: Literary and Philosophical Society, 1890);

Songs and Lyrics, Collected and Revised (London: Scott, 1892);

Selected Poems, edited by Basil Bunting (Sunderland: Ceolfrith Press, 1976).

OTHER: *The Lyrics and Minor Poems of Percy Bysshe Shelley,* prefatory notice by Skipsey (London: Scott, 1884; New York: J. Pott, 1885);

The Poems of Samuel Taylor Coleridge, prefatory notice by Skipsey (London: Scott, 1884);

The Poems of William Blake, prefatory notice by Skipsey (London: Scott, 1885);

The Poems of Robert Burns, prefatory notice by Skipsey (London & New York: Scott, 1885);

The Songs of Robert Burns, prefatory notice by Skipsey (London: Scott, 1885);

The Poetical Works of Edgar Allan Poe, prefatory notice by Skipsey (London: Scott, 1885).

In 1839, when he was seven, Joseph Skipsey went to work as "trapper" in the coal mines at Percy Main, near North Shields, "when the sum total of his learning," as he later wrote in the preface to *A Book of Miscellaneous Lyrics* (1878), "consisted in his ability to read his A.B.C., or at most his A.B. ab card"—that is, the alphabet, upper and lowercase. His job was to regulate the ventilation by opening and shutting a trapdoor when the tubs of coal came through, for sixteen hours a day, in the dark. Except in midsummer and on Sundays, he only saw light when a passing putter or hewer gave him the end of his farthing candle. The child passed the time by making up little songs his mates picked up and sang, and it was here, by the light of the occasional candle, that he taught himself to read and

Joseph Skipsey

write by using his finger in the dust or a bit of chalk to imitate the print on playbills and notices. At the pit where he worked, the men and boys were raised and lowered on an endless chain with rope stirrups. He saw another seven-year-old whose hold slipped on the way up, and who called to his brother behind, "A'm gannen to faal, Jimmy." "Slide doon to me, hinney," his brother said, but could not hold him. Both were killed at the shaft bottom. Skipsey's best work records the life of the miner as it was lived, from within: he is one with the people he observes.

Joseph Skipsey, the eighth child of Cuthbert and Isabella Bell Skipsey, was born on 17 March 1832 at Percy Main, during a turbulent strike in which the miners were seeking to work twelve hours a day, eleven days a fortnight, at threepence an hour (less deductions). On 8 July Cuthbert Skipsey stepped between a special constable and a miner he was bullying, to make peace, and was shot dead by the constable. It is hardly surprising, then, to read in Robert Spence Watson's 1909 memoir of his old friend, *Joseph Skipsey: His Life and Work,* that Skipsey "was too serious. He scarcely possessed humour. All his stories were of actual life, and generally of serious episodes in his own life." And this is where

Skipsey's strengths as a writer lay, as he well knew; only one of his many poems ("The Reign of Gold") can be called a poem of protest or overtly political; the best of his work (such as "Get Up!," which Dante Gabriel Rossetti described as "equal to anything in the language for direct and quiet pathetic force," or "Mother Wept") springs from a direct and immediate perception of the miner's daily life, its customs, pains, and pleasures, portrayed with direct simplicity of feeling and sympathy. It should be better known than it is.

"Get Up!"

"Get up!" the caller calls, "Get up!"
    And in the dead of night,
To win the bairns their bite and sup,
    I rise a weary wight.

My flannel dudden donn'd, thrice o'er
    My birds are kiss'd, and then
I with a whistle shut the door
    I may not ope again.

When he was seventeen, Skipsey was promoted in the mine to be a putter at five shillings a week. For a week's wages he bought a complete Shakespeare; before then, his only reading had been the Bible (which for a while he tried to learn by heart), Pope's translation of the *Iliad,* and Milton's *Paradise Lost.* In the years immediately following, he was to read Burns, some Greek drama in translation, Goethe's *Faust,* and the poetry of Heine. In 1852, when he was twenty, Skipsey walked to London and found a job working for the railroad; after two years, married to his landlady, Sara Ann Hendley, he returned north and worked as a miner for six months at Coatbridge, Scotland. Then he went to the Pemberton collieries near Sunderland, and—after trying his hand for a brief spell as a schoolteacher in a colliery village—he worked at Choppington, Northumberland. At last, when he was twenty-seven, his efforts to get out of mining were rewarded when, after publishing his first book of *Poems* (1859; no known copies survive), he got a job (through the offices of James Clephan, editor of the *Gateshead Observer*) as under-storekeeper at the ironworks of Hawks, Crawshay and Sons in Gateshead. He stayed on until 1863, when one of his children was killed in the factory. He thereupon moved to Newcastle-upon-Tyne as assistant librarian to the Newcastle Literary and Philosophical Society (one of the major libraries in the north); as he somewhat ruefully admitted, he did not do the job "in an altogether satisfactory way," since he was too busy reading the books to look after the members' wants. On the advice of his friends, therefore, he returned to the mines in 1864 as a hewer and stayed in mining until 1882, when he was fifty. From 1882 to 1885 he and Sara Skipsey were caretakers of the Bentinck Board-Schools in Mill Lane, Newcastle, and in 1883, almost twenty years after his departure, he lectured the Literary and Philosophical Society on "The Poet as Seer and Singer." In 1888, largely through the efforts of his friend Robert Spence Watson, he became porter and janitor at Armstrong College (later Durham University College of Science), which opened that year. But here too Skipsey was a misfit: Lord Carlisle, walking with the principal, paused to talk to Skipsey, who put down two scuttles of coal in order to shake hands. "I saw from that time," says Spence Watson, "that it was quite impossible to have a College where the scientific men came to see the Principal and the artistic and literary men came to see the porter. It was not easy to find the proper place for Joseph Skipsey." Skipsey left the college in June 1889.

By this time several of Skipsey's works had

Skipsey in miner's attire

been published, and he had gained a considerable reputation in literary and artistic circles. His friend Thomas Dixon (the Sunderland cork cutter to whom John Ruskin addressed the letters in *Time and Tide*) had taken Skipsey to London in 1880 and introduced him to Edward Burne-Jones, at whose house he met Dante Gabriel and William Michael Rossetti, the Holman Hunts, and Theodore Watts (later Watts-Dunton). Watts had already reviewed Skipsey's *A Book of Miscellaneous Lyrics* favorably in the *Athenaeum,* and D. G. Rossetti had written Skipsey a long appreciative letter on the same book on 29 October 1878. In September 1880 Burne-Jones managed to get Skipsey a civil list pension of £10 a year (increased in 1886 to £25, with a gift of £50 from the Royal Bounty). It was as a result of his growing reputation that Walter Scott (of Newcastle) engaged Skipsey as the first general editor of the Canterbury Poets series, for which he edited six volumes. His prefaces, especially to Robert Burns's *Poems* and *Songs,* both published in 1885, are insightful.

On 24 June 1889, on the recommendation of Browning, Tennyson, Burne-Jones, the Rossettis, Andrew Lang, Bram Stoker, William Morris, Edmund Gosse, and other literary notables, Joseph and Sara Skipsey were appointed successors to the Chataways as custodians of Shakespeare's birthplace at Stratford-upon-Avon (and were nearly denied the post on the grounds of their "pronunciation"). Too many disputatious American tourists arguing that Bacon wrote Shakespeare, combined with the sheer boredom of repeatedly giving the same tours and same speeches and with Sara Skipsey's homesickness for the north led the Skipseys to resign the post on 31 October 1891. Henry James's story "The Birthplace" was suggested to him by what he heard of Skipsey's experiences at Stratford; Skipsey felt, says Spence Watson, that if he stayed on at Stratford "he would end by doubting the very existence of Shakespeare."

The Skipseys spent the rest of their lives living on his pension; they were helped by their children, with whom they lived in turns. Skipsey wrote little (much of it weak), recited much (especially Shakespeare), and visited such friends as Spence Watson in Newcastle and Thomas and Annie Bunting in Scotswood. Sara Skipsey died in August 1902, and on 3 September 1903 Skipsey, aged seventy-one, died in his son Cuthbert's house at Harraton. Two of his five sons and the eldest of three daughters survived him.

Skipsey is a very uneven poet whose best work was written before he achieved his modest fame in the late 1870s. His literary success drew him away from the world he knew, and there can be no doubt that "The Hartley Calamity" (1862), which tells the story of the 204 men and boys (most of the male population of the village) who suffocated in the colliery after a six-day struggle to dig them out, contributed to his reputation. It is a powerful poem indeed: Basil Bunting, reading the poem to an audience largely of miners in Sunderland in 1976, moved his listeners to tears. Skipsey's great strength as a poet lies in the direct simplicity of his language and feeling. When he read from his own works, his reading "was not at all like the reading or recitation of other men," says Spence Watson: "He waited quietly until he felt the spirit of that which he was about to do come upon him. Then he was as one possessed, everything but the poem was forgotten, but that he made live, or perhaps I should more truly say that he incarnated it; he actually became the poem himself. His features changed with every

expression of the verse, his hands, nay, even his fingers, expressed the meaning of the words, and that meaning thoroughly revealed itself. It was far beyond what you had thought of, but it stood out clear for you ever afterwards." In his later work there is, as Bunting says in his judicious and valuable preface to Skipsey's *Selected Poems* (1976), too much middle-class fashionableness, for Skipsey "abandons the life he knew for a life he saw only distorted and on paper. He 'tries to be clever.' A few such poems succeed, but most of them are . . . apt to seem arch or irritable when he probably meant to be witty."

References:

Robert Spence Watson, *Joseph Skipsey: His Life and Work* (London & Leipsic: Unwin, 1909);

Theodore Watts-Dunton, "Skipsey's Poems," *Athenaeum*, no. 2664 (16 November 1878): 618-619.

A. C. Swinburne

David G. Riede
University of Rochester

BIRTH: London, 5 April 1837, to Charles Henry and Jane Hamilton Swinburne.

EDUCATION: Balliol College, Oxford, 1856-1859.

DEATH: London, 10 April 1909.

SELECTED BOOKS: *The Queen-Mother. Rosamond. Two Plays* (London: Pickering, 1860; Boston: Ticknor & Fields, 1866);

Atalanta in Calydon (London: Moxon, 1865; Boston: Ticknor & Fields, 1866);

Chastelard (London: Moxon, 1865; New York: Hurd & Houghton/Boston: Dutton, 1866);

Poems and Ballads (London: Moxon, 1866); republished as *Laus Veneris, and Other Poems and Ballads* (New York: Carleton/London: Moxon, 1866);

A Song of Italy (London: Hotten, 1867; Boston: Ticknor & Fields, 1867);

William Blake: A Critical Essay (London: Hotten, 1868; New York: Dutton, 1906);

Notes on the Royal Academy Exhibition, 1868, by Swinburne and William Michael Rossetti (London: Hotten, 1868);

Songs before Sunrise (London: Ellis, 1871; Boston: Roberts Brothers, 1871);

Under the Microscope (London: White, 1872; Portland, Maine: Mosher, 1899);

Bothwell (London: Chatto & Windus, 1874);

George Chapman: A Critical Essay (London: Chatto & Windus, 1875);

Songs of Two Nations (London: Chatto & Windus, 1875);

Essays and Studies (London: Chatto & Windus, 1875);

Erechtheus (London: Chatto & Windus, 1876);

A Note on Charlotte Brontë (London: Chatto & Windus, 1877);

Poems and Ballads, Second Series (London: Chatto & Windus, 1878; New York: Crowell, 1885?);

A Study of Shakespeare (London: Chatto & Windus, 1880; New York: Worthington, 1880);

Songs of the Springtides (London: Chatto & Windus, 1880; New York: Worthington, 1882?);

Studies in Song (London: Chatto & Windus, 1880; New York: Worthington, 1880);

Specimens of Modern Poets: The Heptalogia or The Seven Against Sense (London: Chatto & Windus, 1880);

Mary Stuart (London: Chatto & Windus, 1881; New York: Worthington, 1881);

Tristram of Lyonesse and Other Poems (London: Chatto & Windus, 1882; Portland, Maine: Mosher, 1904);

A Century of Roundels (London: Chatto & Windus, 1883; New York: Worthington, 1883);

A Midsummer Holiday and Other Poems (London: Chatto & Windus, 1884);

Marino Faliero (London: Chatto & Windus, 1885);

Miscellanies (London: Chatto & Windus, 1886; New York: Worthington, 1886);

A Study of Victor Hugo (London: Chatto & Windus, 1886);

Locrine (London: Chatto & Windus, 1887; New York: Alden, 1887);

A Study of Ben Jonson (London: Chatto & Windus, 1889; New York: Worthington, 1889);

Poems and Ballads, Third Series (London: Chatto & Windus, 1889);

The Sisters (London: Chatto & Windus, 1892; New York: United States Book Company, 1892);

Astrophel and Other Poems (London: Chatto & Windus, 1894; London: Chatto & Windus/New York: Scribners, 1894);

Studies in Prose and Poetry (London: Chatto & Windus, 1894; London: Chatto & Windus/New York: Scribners, 1894);

Robert Burns. A Poem (Edinburgh: Printed for the Members of the Burns Centenary Club, 1896);

The Tale of Balen (London: Chatto & Windus, 1896; New York: Scribners, 1896);

Rosamund, Queen of the Lombards (London: Chatto & Windus, 1899; New York: Dodd, Mead, 1899);

Love's Cross-Currents: A Year's Letters (Portland, Maine: Mosher, 1901; London: Chatto & Windus, 1905);

Poems & Ballads, Second & Third Series (Portland, Maine: Mosher, 1902);

Percy Bysshe Shelley (Philadelphia: Lippincott, 1903);

A Channel Passage and Other Poems (London: Chatto & Windus, 1904);

The Poems of Algernon Charles Swinburne, 6 volumes (London: Chatto & Windus, 1904; New York & London: Harper, 1904);

The Tragedies of Algernon Charles Swinburne, 6 volumes (London: Chatto & Windus, 1905; New York: Harper, 1905);

Swinburne, by G. F. Watts (National Portrait Gallery)

The Duke of Gandia (London: Chatto & Windus, 1908; New York & London: Harper, 1908);

The Age of Shakespeare (New York & London: Harper, 1908; London: Chatto & Windus, 1908);

The Marriage of Monna Lisa (London: Privately printed, 1909);

In the Twilight (London: Privately printed, 1909);

The Portrait (London: Privately printed, 1909);

The Chronicle of Queen Fredegond (London: Privately printed, 1909);

Of Liberty and Loyalty (London: Privately printed, 1909);

Ode to Mazzini (London: Privately printed, 1909);

Shakespeare (London, New York, Toronto & Melbourne: Henry Frowde, 1909);

The Ballade of Truthful Charles and Other Poems (London: Privately printed, 1910);

A Criminal Case (London: Privately printed, 1910);

The Ballade of Villon and Fat Madge (London: Privately printed, 1910);

The Cannibal Catechism (London: Privately printed, 1913);

Les Fleurs du Mal and Other Studies (London: Privately printed, 1913);

Charles Dickens (London: Chatto & Windus, 1913);

A Study of Victor Hugo's "Les Misérables" (London: Privately printed, 1914);

Pericles and Other Studies (London: Privately printed, 1914);

Thomas Nabbes: A Critical Monograph (London: Privately printed, 1914);

Christopher Marlowe in relation to Greene, Peele and Lodge (London: Privately printed, 1914);

Lady Maisie's Bairn and Other Poems (London: Privately printed, 1915);

Félicien Cossu: A Burlesque (London: Privately printed, 1915);

Théophile (London: Privately printed, 1915);

Ernest Clouët (London: Privately printed, 1916);

A Vision of Bags (London: Privately printed, 1916);

The Death of Sir John Franklin (London: Privately printed, 1916);

Poems From "Villon" and Other Fragments (London: Privately printed, 1916);

Poetical Fragments (London: Privately printed, 1916);

Posthumous Poems, edited by Edmund Gosse and Thomas James Wise (London: Heinemann, 1917);

Rondeaux Parisiens (London: Privately printed, 1917);

The Italian Mother and Other Poems (London: Privately printed, 1918);

The Ride from Milan and Other Poems (London: Privately printed, 1918);

A Lay of Lilies and Other Poems (London: Privately printed, 1918);

Queen Yseult, A Poem in Six Cantos (London: Privately printed, 1918);

Lancelot, The Death of Rudel and Other Poems (London: Privately printed, 1918);

Undergraduate Sonnets (London: Privately printed, 1918);

The Character and Opinions of Dr. Johnson (London: Privately printed, 1918);

The Queen's Tragedy (London: Privately printed, 1919);

French Lyrics (London: Privately printed, 1919);

Contemporaries of Shakespeare (London: Heinemann, 1919);

Ballads of the English Border, edited by William A. MacInnes (London: Heinemann, 1925);

Lesbia Brandon, edited by Randolph Hughes (London: Falcon Press, 1952);

New Writings by Swinburne, edited by Cecil Y. Lang (Syracuse: Syracuse University Press, 1964).

Collection: *The Complete Works of Algernon Charles Swinburne,* edited by Edmund Gosse and Thomas J. Wise, 20 volumes (London: Heinemann/New York: Wells, 1925-1927).

Algernon Charles Swinburne is justly regarded as the major Victorian poet most profoundly at odds with his age and as one of the most daring, innovative, and brilliant lyricists to ever write in English. Less justly, his reputation still depends largely on the two early volumes, *Atalanta in Calydon* (1865) and *Poems and Ballads* (1866), with which he shocked and outraged Victorian sensibility, introducing into the pious, stolid age a world of fierce atheism, strange, powerful passions, fiery paganism, and a magnificent new lyrical voice the likes of which had never before been heard. But Swinburne must be remembered for other things as well. His radical republicanism, really a worship of the best instincts of man, pushed Victorian humanism well beyond the "respectable" limits of Matthew Arnold's writings, his critical writings on art and literature greatly influenced the aesthetic climate of his age, and his extraordinary imitative facility made him a brilliant, unrivaled parodist. Most important, the expression of his eroticism in many poems about nature, particularly about the sea, wind, and sun, make him the Victorian period's greatest heir of the Romantic poets, and it is in Swinburne's nature poetry that the unbroken Romantic tradition running through the nineteenth century is most clearly seen.

Many of Swinburne's lifelong passions, and particularly his fierce love of sea, wind, and sun, were fostered during his early childhood at East Dene, Bonchurch, on the Isle of Wight. A descendant of two ancient, aristocratic, and highly inbred families, Swinburne was born into the highest English nobility. His mother, Lady Jane Hamilton Swinburne, was a daughter of the third Earl of Ashburnham; his father, Lady Jane's second cousin, was Admiral Charles Henry Swinburne, who could trace his ancestry back to a Swinburne peerage that had been, in his son's phrase, "dormant or forfeit since the thirteenth or fourteenth century." Swinburne's aristocratic background contributed in later life to a high-handed disdain of the lower classes, but it also contributed, paradoxically, to his rabid republicanism. He was much influenced by his colorful grandfather who, as the poet never tired of saying, "had enjoyed the personal friendship of Mirabeau and Wilkes." In addition, both the Ashburnhams and the Swinburnes had a long history of political rebellion since, as

Swinburne put it, his family "in every Catholic rebellion from the days of my own Queen Mary to those of Charles Edward had given their blood like water and their lands like dust for the Stuarts." Swinburne himself attributed his own rebellious streak to his family background, commenting in 1875 that "when this race chose at last to produce a poet, it would have been at least remarkable if he had been content to write nothing but hymns and idylls for clergymen and young ladies to read out in chapels and drawing-rooms." His family, at least as he romanticized it, had left him certain standards to live up to. A still more important legacy of Swinburne's early childhood, however, was his love of nature. Though he was born, by his own questionable account, "all but dead and certainly not expected to live an hour," he was a vigorous and reckless lover of the outdoors. At East Dene, and at the nearby family seats of the Swinburnes at Capheaton and of the Ashburnhams at Ashburnham Place, he rode horses with reckless abandon, reveling in the sensations of speed, wind, and sun. Most of all, he loved the sea. Later in life he accounted for the "endless passionate returns to the sea" in his poetry by recalling one of his earliest memories: "As for the sea, its salt *must* have been in my blood before I was born. I can remember no earlier enjoyment than being held up naked in my father's arms and brandished between his hands then shot like a stone from a sling through the air, shouting and laughing with delight, head foremost into the coming wave." Swinburne's many later writings on the sea echo this childlike rapture of submission. In fact, the submission to great men that characterized his republicanism, the submission to primitive sensual passions and the masochism that characterize his erotic writings, and especially the submission to elemental forces of nature described throughout his poetry are all evoked in this illuminating comment. Indeed, the blend of masochism with incestuous love and strangely erotic descriptions of the pleasures of riding and sea-bathing in the quasiautobiographical novels *Love's Cross-Currents* and *Lesbia Brandon* reveals the fusion of Swinburne's most intense passions. His hopeless love for his cousin Mary Gordon evidently owed much to her companionship and shared joy in the wild pleasures of nature.

Swinburne knew milder pleasures as well. His histrionic bent found an outlet in amateur theatricals with his sisters and cousin, and at an early age he was reveling in the more solitary pleasures of literature. He began to enjoy Shakespeare at the age of six and other Renaissance dramatists soon after. By the time he entered Eton in 1849, he was also a fervent admirer of Dickens, to whose works he remained devoted all his life, frequently, in fact, falling into the idiom of such comic characters as Sairey Gamp. By this time, too, his mother had taught him French and Italian, and he was soon fluent in both languages. To this early training he was ultimately to owe the distinction of being one of the most widely read men of his age in Continental literature.

Swinburne's four years at Eton seem to have had an inordinate importance for him. In his later years he would constantly begin conversations with the prologue "When I was a kid at Eton," and indeed it was at Eton that most of his lifelong interests took root. He now read not only Shakespeare but also the other Elizabethan and Jacobean dramatists with extraordinary enthusiasm and thoroughness, and he now first developed his undying hero-worship of Victor Hugo and Walter Savage Landor. It must have been at Eton also that he developed the flagellation mania that was to remain with him to a greater or lesser degree for the rest of his life. He later wrote numerous letters recounting in gory detail the floggings that had left him bloody but unbowed. He no doubt was flogged, as was the custom, but his later accounts of a tutor preparing the flogging-room with "burnt scents" or choosing a "*sweet* place out of doors with smell of firwood" or allowing him to "saturate my face with eau-de-Cologne" before a beating have the ring of the fictional accounts of floggings that he enjoyed writing and reading.

Whatever Swinburne may have suffered at the hands of his tutors, he was at least, unlike Shelley, not bullied by his schoolfellows. Like Shelley, he had no interest in field sports, and in other respects impressed his companions as rather exotic, but he did show considerable physical courage in riding, in swimming, and perhaps even in enduring the customary floggings. Swinburne was evidently left sufficiently alone to follow his own pursuits, among which one of his favorites, as his schoolmate and cousin Lord Redesdale recalled, was reading: "I can see him now sitting perched up Turk-or-tailor wise in one of the windows looking out on the yard, with some huge old-world tome, almost as big as himself, upon his lap, the afternoon sun setting on fire the great mop of red hair. There it was that he emancipated himself, making acquaintance with Shakespeare (minus Bowdler), Marlowe, Spenser, Ben Jonson, Ford, Massinger, Beaumont and Fletcher, and other poets and playwrights of the sixteenth and seventeenth centuries. His tendency was great towards Drama, especially Tragic Drama. He had a great sense of humour in others. He would quote

Dickens, especially Mrs. Gamp, unwearyingly; but his own genius leaned to tragedy." His genius leaned so heavily to tragedy that he wrote several Jacobean tragedies before and during his stay at Eton. His juvenile tragedies were, of course, schoolboyish in many ways; Mary Gordon, later Mary Disney-Leith, recalled them as of a "bloodcurdling and highly tragic nature, in which a frequent stage direction—'stabs the king'—passed into a family joke." But one of these plays, *"The Unhappy Revenge,"* survives in manuscript to exhibit a precocious talent for imitative verse and a foretaste of Swinburne's later analysis of the coupling of pain with sensuality.

Possibly because he was becoming a disciplinary problem, Swinburne left Eton early, at the age of sixteen, to be privately tutored by the Reverend John Wilkinson at Cambo, Northumberland. He was evidently a difficult pupil, scanting his studies to ride on the moors and bathe in the sea. Wilkinson had trouble controlling him, but it was at this time that Swinburne met Lady Pauline Trevelyan, whom he came to regard as a second mother and who now and later had a calming influence on him. Nevertheless, Swinburne was not yet ready to settle down to a life of quiet study, for in 1854, motivated by the Balaklava charge in the Crimean War which, he said, "eclipsed all other visions," he declared his ambition to be a cavalry officer, a desire that his parents wisely thwarted. He would have made an unusual cavalry officer; in addition to his tiny physique, he was extremely excitable and given, from early childhood, to spastic twitching of his arms and hands. Also, though a courageous rider, he was reckless and frequently thrown. Throughout his life he was, like Byron, defensive about his physical defects and eager to defend himself from what he called "bitterly contemptuous remarks about my physical debility and puny proportions." He often defended himself by referring to an exploit that occurred shortly after his request to join the cavalry. In the winter of 1854 he found a "chance of testing my nerve in the face of death" by scaling the reputedly inaccessible Culver Cliff on the Isle of Wight, which he did, at genuinely great peril. Swinburne's accounts of the exploit reveal what has often been called his virility complex, but they reveal also the love of primitive encounters with nature that informs much of his best verse.

In January 1856, after a final year of preparation with the Reverend Russell Woodford at Kempsford, Gloucestershire, Swinburne matriculated at Balliol College, Oxford. At Oxford the Republican enthusiasm that he had more or less inherited from his grandfather became a passion. He was much influenced by a classmate, John Nichol. Nichol, the founder of the Old Mortality Society, a republican and freethinker, became a lifelong friend. Swinburne hung in his room a portrait of Orsini, the would-be assassin of Napoleon III, and began to write verse in praise of regicide. Nichol also contributed to Swinburne's emerging atheism. Swinburne had been raised as a devout Anglo-Catholic, and had kept his faith intact until he reached Oxford. His comments on a Catholic mass that he had seen during a visit to Cologne as recently as 1855 indicate how strong the will to worship had been in him: "I felt quite miserable, it was such a wretched feeling that while they all were praying, old men and tiny children kneeling together, I was not one of them, I was shut out as it were. I could have sat down and cried, I was so unhappy." This faith was soon shattered, but his need to worship remained: he became a worshipper of great Republicans, great poets, and, interestingly, of "old men and tiny children." Throughout his later life, he never lost his devotion to the great old republican Giuseppe Mazzini, or the great old poets Landor and Hugo, or tiny children.

During the fall of 1857, when the Pre-Raphaelites and others were at Oxford on their "jovial campaign" to decorate the Oxford Union, Swinburne came under an influence even stronger than Nichol's. Delighted by the high spirits of the artistic temperament in its wildest form, he was quickly drawn into close and enduring friendships with Dante Gabriel Rossetti, William Morris, and Ned Jones (later Sir Edward Burne-Jones). The immediate attraction was mutual: on meeting Swinburne, Jones instantly remarked, "Now we are four and not *three*." Under their influence Swinburne soon began to write what might be called Pre-Raphaelite verse. Most notably, *Queen Yseult,* published in the Old Mortality Society's monthly journal, *Undergraduate Papers,* is a close imitation of William Morris's early work, both in matter and manner. Though he did not long continue to write Pre-Raphaelite pastiche, the abiding influence of Morris and Rossetti shows up in much of *Poems and Ballads* (1866), particularly in such poems as "Laus Veneris" and "The Leper." More important, Swinburne developed a new aestheticism, which did not induce him to abandon his political poetry but did encourage him to write more for the sake of the beauty of verse itself.

After the departure of Rossetti, Jones, and Morris, Swinburne remained at Oxford, exhibiting rather more wild bohemian mannerisms but studying hard enough to earn some academic honors, riding hard enough to fall, splinter some teeth and sprain his jaw, and writing poetry. The poetry reflected Swinburne's varied interests. "The Death of Sir John Franklin"(published in pamphlet form in 1916 and collected a year later in *Posthumous Poems),* written on a set topic for a poetry competition in 1860, effectively expresses his love for courageous exploits and for the sea. The unpublished "Laugh and Lie Down," a drama, as Swinburne later said, "after (a long way after) the late manner of Fletcher," reflects his love of the early dramatists and also, as Philip Henderson has said in *Swinburne: Portrait of a Poet* (1974), gives "full expression to the sexual ambiguity of his nature" by providing two young boys who also masquerade as girls, one of whom is whipped to death by a tyrannical woman. Swinburne also remained politically conscious. When, in 1858, he and his parents encountered Napoleon III in passing, the poet disdained to remove his hat because, as he later told Edmund Gosse "in an ecstasy of ironic emphasis," he did not wish "to be obliged to cut off my hand at the wrist the moment I returned to the hotel." A year previously, in "A Song in Time of Order," he had written of Napoleon III the rather enthusiastic lines "We shall see Buonaparte the Bastard/Kick heels with his throat in a rope."

Swinburne studied fairly hard in his last two years at Oxford, even going so far as to "break my teeth more or less for months" over the "dead constitutional records" of a work by Henry Hallam. But in the end he failed to take his examinations. Though he left Oxford without a degree through his own fault, he liked to compare himself with Shelley and observe that "Oxford has turned out poets in more senses than one."

Shortly after leaving Oxford, Swinburne published his first plays, with financial backing from his father. *The Queen-Mother* and *Rosamond* (published together in 1860) are not entirely successful, but they anticipate the strengths and weaknesses of many of Swinburne's later plays. Certainly they were a great advance on his earlier efforts, though they remain too strongly reminiscent of the drama of an earlier age. The verse is often excellent, but like Keats, Shelley, Browning, and Tennyson, Swinburne remained enslaved to the nineteenth-century view of Elizabethan models: his emphasis was too much on long set speeches and characterization and too little on dramatic action, so the dramas, especially *The Queen-Mother,* move slowly, awkwardly, and sometimes too predictably. Both plays are concerned with the pleasures of sadistic

Caricature by Max Beerbohm: "Riverside Scene. *Algernon Swinburne taking his great new friend [Edmund] Gosse to see Gabriel Rossetti"* (© Eva Reichmann).

violence, the overwhelming power of passionate love, and the terrible, destructive power of passionate women.

The Queen-Mother is set in the court of Charles IX, at the time of the murder of the Huguenots in 1572. As the title suggests, the queen mother is the power behind the throne in a court in which, Swinburne later wrote, "debauchery of all kinds, and murder in all forms, were the daily matter of excitement or of jest." The setting provided a perfect opportunity for Swinburne to revel in Grand Guignol, and he made the most of it. *Rosamond,* shorter and less gruesome, is somewhat more successful than *The Queen-Mother.* Through the characters of King Henry's mistress, Rosamond, and his wife, Queen Eleanor, Swinburne more subtly explores the theme of the fatal woman and the destructive power of love. The play is best remembered for one speech, in which Rosamond projects her female fatality into mythic proportion: "Yea, I am found the woman in all tales/The face caught always in the story's face. . . ."

The publication of the plays did not make much of a stir despite two brief but hostile reviews, but by this time Swinburne, newly settled in London with a £400 annuity from his father, was already becoming known in artistic and literary circles. In 1860, after leaving Oxford, he had moved into rooms at 16 Grafton Street, Fitzroy Square, near

Faustine, *oil painting by Maxwell Armfield in which Swinburne is depicted with a woman who represents his ideal of malevolent beauty (Palais de Tokyo, Paris). When Swinburne's poem "Faustine," about a sadistic Roman empress, was first published in the* Spectator *(31 May 1862), John Ruskin wrote, "it made me all hot, like pies with the devil's fingers in them. It's glorious!"*

Rossetti, Morris, and Burne-Jones. Through them he met several other artists and writers, including George Meredith, Ford Madox Brown, John Ruskin, Simeon Solomon, and eventually James McNeill Whistler. In addition, through Richard Monckton Milnes (later Lord Houghton), he met a rich mix of people, including Browning, Tennyson, and the adventurer Richard Burton. He was especially intimate at this time with Burne-Jones and his wife Georgie, and still more with Rossetti and his wife Elizabeth ("Lizzie") Siddal Rossetti. He enjoyed a close and boisterous friendship with Lizzie in par-

ticular, and had in fact dined with Lizzie and Rossetti at the Sablonière Hotel on 10 February 1862, the night on which Lizzie killed herself with an overdose of laudanum. After her death, Rossetti, Swinburne, and on an occasional basis, George Meredith and Rossetti's brother William, took up communal living at Tudor House, Cheyne Walk, in Chelsea. Both Rossetti and Swinburne were creatures of flamboyant habits, so life at Tudor House was, to say the least, irregular. Swinburne contributed in no small degree. Even before reading Milnes's copy of Sade's *Justine* in 1862, he had declared his discipleship to the "divine" Marquis de Sade, and he delighted in shrilly declaiming the joys of Sadic eroticism. More seriously, he was beginning to drink excessively, perhaps through the influence of Richard Burton, who is credited with introducing him to brandy in 1862. By 1864 or 1865 Swinburne, in Edmund Gosse's words, was a drunkard. With increasing regularity, he was being deposited dead drunk on the doorstep of Tudor House. One incident of 1863 seems characteristic: at three in the morning by Gosse's account, Rossetti was "wakened by a tremendous knocking, and on looking out of the window, he saw Algernon being held up in the arms of a policeman, with a whole bevy of gutterboys accompanying; he had been out on a spree, and no one knew where. Rossetti went out and let him in, and had a fearful time with him, 'screaming and splashing about,'" before he got him to bed. Within the house his antics included sliding down bannisters and dashing naked around the house with Simeon Solomon. One less than sympathetic observer recalled that Swinburne was almost as strange when sober, since "his one idea of rational conversation was to dance and skip all over the room, reciting poetry at the top of his voice, and going on and on with it." Such a description is an exaggeration, of course, but he was extremely excitable, especially when reciting verse or talking politics. The impression that the "demoniac boy," as Ruskin called him, was making on literary London in the early 1860s can be seen in the impression he made on Henry Adams in 1862. Adams's famous description compares Swinburne to "a tropical bird, high-crested, long-beaked, quick-moving, with rapid utterances and screams of humor, quite unlike any English lark or nightingale. One could hardly call him a crimson macaw among owls, and yet no ordinary contrast availed." But this strange apparition, this exotic bird, Adams noted, was remarkably impressive in the prodigious range of his learning and memory, and was also "astonishingly gifted, and convulsingly droll."

Swinburne's convulsing drollery appears in several burlesques in French and English that were written in the early 1860s but not published until Cecil Lang's *New Writings by Swinburne* appeared in 1964. In both the French tale *La Fille du Policeman* and the French play, *La Soeur de la Reine,* Swinburne brilliantly parodied Victor Hugo's productions on English topics and brilliantly pilloried Queen Victoria. Swinburne's description, in a letter, of a now missing part of the play gives the flavor of both the play and the tale. He describes how the queen had been seduced by Wordsworth, "who had scandal-

Swinburne, Dante Gabriel Rossetti, Fanny Cornforth, and William Michael Rossetti at Tudor House, Cheyne Walk, Chelsea, circa 1863 (Collection of Mrs. Virginia Surtees)

ously abused his privileged position as Laureate to seduce her by means of recitations 'de cette poesié fiévreuse et palpitante de sensualité—cette excursion'" and of "sa chanson érotique de Betty-Foy!" *La Fille du Policeman,* described by Meredith as "the funniest rampingest satire on French novelists dealing with English themes that you can imagine," describes an attempt by Prince Albert, "le prince prolétaire," to supplant Victoria. Swinburne summed up the themes in a letter to William Bell Scott: "Rape, perjury, murder, opium, suicide, treason, Jesuitry, are the mildest ingredients." As the ingredients indicate, Swinburne's broad and bawdy humor in these immensely funny farces was not far dissociated from his more serious concerns, and it has occasionally been suggested that under cover of persiflage he was able to liberate his deepest feelings.

The impressive ability to mimic that made *La Fille du Policeman* and *La Soeur de la Reine* superb parodies of Hugo later surfaced in superb parodies of Tennyson, Browning, Rossetti, Swinburne himself, and others collected in *Specimens of Modern Poets: The Heptalogia or The Seven Against Sense* (1880), a volume that conclusively proves Swinburne, as Cecil Lang has said, "quite simply (to use his own kind of phrase), the greatest parodist who ever lived." In 1862 Swinburne's talent very nearly enabled him to perpetrate two brilliant hoaxes. In a series of critical articles on Victor Hugo in the *Spectator* he planted a number of references to two nonexistent French writers and then submitted critical essays on their recent works. The first of these, a review of *Les Amours Étiques* by Félicien Cossu, was actually set in type, but after receiving the second, on *Les Abîmes* by Ernest Clouët, the editor of the *Spectator,* perhaps suspecting a hoax or perhaps appalled by the obscene subject matter of Cossu and Clouët, declined to print either. And the subject matter assuredly was offensive, for Swinburne had used his unrivaled gift for parody to produce such remarkable "excerpts" from decadent French poetry as the appalling couplet in which Cossu admires his mistress's charms: "Sa crapule a l'odeur fraîche et chaste du lait;/Et son vomissement quelque chose qui plaît." Swinburne's tone in describing such works as "Une Nuit de Sodome" and "Spasme d'Amour" is one of controlled outrage as he ironically undermines the strict Victorian ideas of propriety: "Accusations are often put forward, at home and abroad, against the restrictions imposed by a possibly exaggerated sense of decency on the English literature of the present day. We have seen what are the results of a wholly unfettered license; base effeminacy of feeling, sordid degradation of intellect, loathsome impurity of expression, in a word every kind of filth and foolery which a shameless prurience can beget on a morbid imagination." These were, of course, precisely the charges that would soon be aimed in earnest at Swinburne's own work.

A much more important prose work of 1862 is the satiric epistolary novel *A Year's Letters* (pseudonymously serialized in the *Tatler* in 1877 and published as *Love's Cross-Currents* in 1901 by Mosher of Portland, Maine). Both *A Year's Letters* and *Lesbia Brandon* (not published until Randolph Hughes's edition in 1952), begun soon after but never finished, are masterful quasiautobiographical accounts of the aristocratic Victorian world that shaped Swinburne's character, "a world," wrote Edmund Wilson in *The Novels of A. C. Swinburne* (1962), "in which the eager enjoyment of a glorious out-of-door life of riding and swimming and boating is combined with adultery, incest, enthusiastic flagellation and quiet homosexuality." The subtle analysis of characters and relationships, the close portraits of an aristocratic way of life, the power of description, and the precise, beautifully cadenced prose of these works reveal Swinburne's genuine, but often unrecognized talents as a novelist.

Swinburne was, of course, primarily a poet, and during the prolific years from 1860 to 1862 he was a very busy one. In addition to a large body of lyrics, many of which were to appear in *Poems and Ballads,* Swinburne completed at this time his tragedy *Chastelard* (not published until 1865), the first play in the eventually massive trilogy about Mary Queen of Scots that would include *Bothwell* (1874) and *Mary Stuart* (1881). Swinburne was drawn to the history of Mary Stuart both by his family's historic attachment to the Stuart cause and by his attraction to the character of Mary, whom he saw as a strong and fatal woman. Chastelard's bitter expression of his love for the queen pithily expresses Swinburne's main concern: "men must love you in life's spite;/For you will always kill them, man by man/Your lips will bite them dead; yea, though you would,/You shall not spare one; all will die of you." Though weakened, as were *The Queen-Mother* and *Rosamond,* by Swinburne's penchant for sacrificing dramatic movement to long, lyric speeches, *Chastelard* is a considerable poetic achievement. Since Swinburne's deep emotional involvement with the theme of painful, fatal love infuses his verse with passionate lyricism, his faults as a dramatist are largely redeemed by his powers as a poet. *Bothwell* and *Mary Stuart* are far less successful. By the time they were written Swinburne had become immersed in historical scholarship aimed at vindicating the character of Mary Stuart by proving her "the most fearless, the most keen-sighted, the most ready-witted, the most high-gifted and high-spirited of women." Unfortunately the plays became clotted with historic detail as Swinburne, in his own words, became "choked and stifled with the excessive wealth of splendid subjects." In his effort to include all significant events he lost much of the inspired lyricism of *Chastelard. Bothwell* in particular swelled to colossal proportions. Though the two later plays were well received on publication, they are rarely read today.

In the summer of 1863 Swinburne left London for East Dene to be present at the death of his favorite sister, Edith. While there he began writing *Atalanta in Calydon,* which he continued to work on during a subsequent long visit to neighboring

Northcourt, the home of his cousin Mary Gordon. At Northcourt he was enraptured by Mary's piano performances of Handel, which he said influenced the impassioned cadences of *Atalanta,* and still more enraptured with reckless gallops across the moors with Mary, during which he recited the magnificent first chorus of *Atalanta,* beginning "When the hounds of spring are on winter's traces." In the winter of 1864 he left Northcourt to visit Italy, where he saw the paintings that he described in his splendid essay "Notes on Designs of the Old Masters at Florence" (published in the *Fortnightly Review* in July 1868 and collected in *Essays and Studies,* 1875), an essay that significantly influenced British art criticism by helping to mold the critical style of Walter Pater. After this prolonged absence, Swinburne finally returned to London, where he once again saw much of Mary Gordon. Though he never told his love, by this time his childhood affection for her had evidently deepened into intense passion. Mary's failure to reciprocate in kind was the major tragedy of his life.

Late in 1864 Mary Gordon announced her impending marriage to Colonel R. W. Disney-Leith, sending Swinburne into bitter agonies of despair and long darkening his outlook on life. Apparently alluding to this experience years later, he remarked that it had left his "young manhood a 'barren stock.' " His desolation is movingly recorded in one of his greatest lyrics, "The Triumph of Time": "I have put my days and dreams out of mind,/Days that are over, dreams that are done." The same stoical note is sounded in the beautiful companion poems, "Les Noyades" and "A Leave-Taking," but what is perhaps most interesting in all of these poems is a startling transference of passion from the woman to the sea. These poems, like all of Swinburne's great nature poems, express a kind of oceanic eroticism in which the poet's passion and despair are fused in a longing to merge utterly with oblivious elemental nature: "I will go back to the great sweet mother,/Mother and lover of men, the sea./I will go down to her, I and none other,/Close with her, kiss her and mix her with me."

He was, no doubt, stoical in his further relations with Mary Gordon, though he later described in "Notes on Poems and Reviews" another spiritual refuge for a man "foiled in love and weary of loving": "refuge in those 'violent delights' which have 'violent ends,' in fierce and frank sensualities which at least profess to be no more than they are." Swinburne resumed with a vengeance the dissolute London life he had previously led. He passed from heavy drinking to chronic alcoholism and became a more ardent and more serious devotee of flagellation and other "fierce and frank sensualities." The next fifteen years of Swinburne's life are full of incidents, some funny and all sad, in which he paid the price for debauchery. But in the first few years following 1864, before his alcoholism had physically debilitated him, Swinburne had more pleasure than pain from his antics. He became increasingly intimate with Richard Burton who, after long evenings of drinking, would carry him out, unconscious, under one arm, and send him home in a cab. Burton, like other intimates of this period, including Simeon Solomon, George Powell, Charles Augustus Howell, and Lord Houghton, shared and encouraged his mania for flagellation and other unorthodox sexual practices, though Swinburne's deviance remained confined to conversation, flagellation literature, and letters exchanging tales of whippings at Eton.

In 1865 and 1866 Swinburne became a literary lion and a literary scandal with the publication of *Atalanta in Calydon, Chastelard* and *Poems and Ballads*. *Atalanta in Calydon,* still justly regarded as one of Swinburne's supreme achievements, became a masterpiece partly because his choices of subject and form were perfectly adapted to his concerns and talents. The imitation of Aeschylean tragedy gave him an opportunity to exercise his superb lyrical gifts, the choice of the pagan Greek setting enabled him to express his virulent antitheism convincingly, and the Meleager myth provided a vehicle with which to express his obsession with the fatal power of passion and of women. The play centers on the conflict between Meleager and his mother Althaea over his passionate love for the chaste huntress Atalanta. During the hunt for the wild boar that is ravaging Calydon, Meleager kills both of Althaea's brothers, who had abused Atalanta. At Meleager's birth, the Fates had prophesied that he would die when the brand then burning the fire was fully burnt; Althaea, who had extinguished and saved it, burns it after the death of her brothers, slaying her own son in compliance with the ancient code of retribution for blood spilled.

Meleager's love for Atalanta, who has taken a vow of virginity and upholds the ideal of chastity, constitutes a denial of natural cycles of generation, of the fertility associated throughout the play with Althaea. His love, which forsakes, in effect, the natural and inevitable for the ideal and unattainable, epitomizes the bleakly pessimistic dictum of the gods that "Joy is not, but love of joy shall be." Perhaps the clearest expression of the play's nihilistic theme comes from Althaea:

The gods have wrought life, and desire of life,
Heart's love and heart's division; but for all
There shines one sun and one wind blows till night.
And when night comes the wind sinks and the sun,
And there is no light after, and no storm,
But sleep and much forgetfulness of things.

Man should recognize and accept the only certainties: elemental nature and death. Swinburne's play is clearly to be understood not merely as a refutation of the Greek gods and ideals but also as a refutation of any idealism or religion that endorsed chastity, a Blakean code-word for moral repression. Theism, as Swinburne saw it, represses man's primitive, pagan impulses, denies man's role in nature, and so the play couples erotic love with the poet's equally erotic, in a larger sense, love of elemental nature. Consequently *Atalanta in Calydon* is a forceful attack on traditional Christianity, which Swinburne, like Blake, saw as an instrument of moral repression that sets the ideals of the soul in conflict with the needs of the body. The message is summed up in the famous antitheistic chorus that denounces "The supreme evil, God," who "shapes the soul, and makes her a barren wife/To the earthly body and grievous growth of clay."

Atalanta in Calydon, however, is not merely a play with a message; it also represents a masterful rebirth of the powerful lyricism of Greek tragedy. Rejecting all belief in a beneficent scheme of things and even in the possibility of joy, it is Swinburne's most pessimistic major work, yet in its surging rhythms, in its fusion of the imagery of natural cycles, it achieves the intensity that Keats saw as the essential quality of tragic art, the intensity that is "capable of making all disagreeables evaporate, from their being in close relationship with Beauty & Truth."

Before the publication of *Atalanta in Calydon* in March 1865, Swinburne had been known only among the artistic circles of Rossetti and Lord Houghton. His critical articles in the *Spectator* had been published anonymously and *The Queen-Mother* and *Rosamond* had been virtually unnoticed. But the reviews of *Atalanta* saluted him as a major new poet, raising him instantly near to the status of Tennyson and Browning. The critics caviled about the extent to which the tragedy was truly Greek and about the lushness of imagery and obscurity of diction, but they recognized Swinburne's great lyrical power and mastery of language. Somewhat surprisingly, the moral tone, the savage antitheism, of the play went almost unnoticed. Swinburne's position as a ranking poet was further consolidated the following

autumn with the publication of *Chastelard,* which was considered by some reviewers superior to *Atalanta.* On the whole, however, the notices of *Chastelard* were somewhat less complimentary than those of *Atalanta.* Critics were disposed to admire the poetry but objected to what they saw as an ungenerous treatment of Mary Stuart. Worse, troubled by its sensuality and irreverence, the reviewers were becoming uneasy about Swinburne's moral tone. The *Spectator,* for example, complained that a "want of moral and intellectual relief for the coarseness of passion, and for the deep physical instincts of tenderness or cruelty on which he delights to employ his rich imagination, strikes us as a radical deformity of his poetry."

The stage, clearly, was being set for the outraged reception of *Poems and Ballads,* which Swinburne was then preparing for publication. Such friends as Rossetti, Ruskin (through Swinburne's "good angel," Lady Trevelyan), and Meredith, hearing " 'low mutterings' from the lion of British prudery," as Meredith put it, urged him to cut some of the more offensive verses for the sake of his reputation, but in vain. Contending that he had "written nothing to be ashamed of " (though he had himself described "Dolores" as "boiling and gushing infamy"), Swinburne determined to face the teeth of the British lion as the volume was published in August 1866. The result was one of the most savage critical barrages in literary history. Critics called the author of "Anactoria" and "Dolores" the "libidinous laureate of a pack of satyrs" and compared him to "Gito, seated in the tub of Diogenes, conscious of the filth and whining at the stars." His poems are "prurient trash," the product of "the spurious passion of a putrescent imagination." So great was the outrage that the publisher, Moxon, withdrew the book from circulation and Swinburne was able to have it republished only through the disreputable firm of J. C. Hotten, the publisher of a line of sordid flagellation literature.

Unfortunately, the howls of outraged Victorian propriety have too often distracted readers from the real merits of *Poems and Ballads.* For example, "Dolores," the most blatantly shocking of the poems, has received a disproportionate share of attention ever since the mid-Victorian students at Oxford used to walk arm in arm across the lawns, chanting its blasphemous litany to the sadistic antivirgin, "Our Lady of Pain." Yet even "Dolores" has a serious point, for Swinburne is singing the nihilistic theme of *Atalanta in Calydon* in a different key: "For the crown of our life as it closes/Is darkness, the fruit thereof dust/No thorns go as deep as a

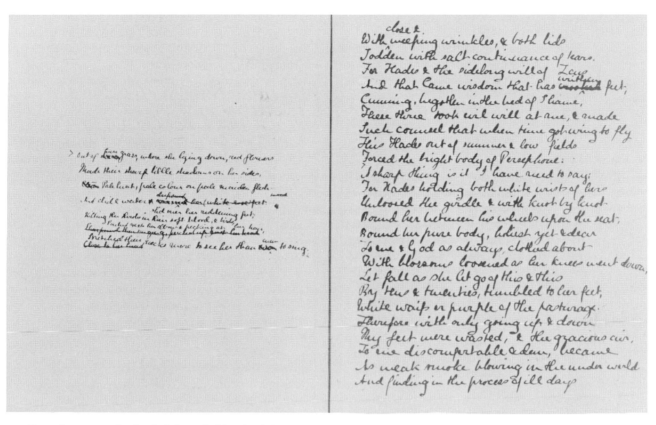

From the manuscript for Swinburne's "At Eleusis," written circa 1864-1865 and collected in Poems and Ballads, *1866*
(The Pierpont Morgan Library)

rose's,/And love is more cruel than lust." "Dolores" describes the phase that Swinburne himself evidently passed through, when a man "foiled in love and weary of loving" takes refuge in "fierce and frank sensualities which at least profess to be no more than they are."

In fact, none of the poems, written in the early and mid-1860s, were designed merely to shock. Even the perverse eroticism of "Dolores" and "Faustine," the necrophilia of "The Leper," and the sadistic lesbianism of the masterful "Anactoria" analyze and pay tribute to a part of human nature that may not be genteel but is at least genuine. The volume links frank and fierce eroticism, moreover, with Swinburne's violent but philosophically acute antitheism, for the pleasures of the flesh are consistently viewed as a response to the moral repression of Christianity, which chastens the flesh and denies the pleasures of mortal life for the hope of a dubious immortal reward and so enforces the maxim that "Joy is not, but love of joy shall be." Christianity, for Swinburne as for Blake and Nietzsche, had robbed modern life of its passionate energies, and so he attacked it in the famous couplet

of "The Hymn to Proserpine" in *Poems and Ballads*: "Thou hast conquered, O Pale Galilean; the world has grown grey from thy breath;/We have drunken of things Lethean, and fed on the fullness of death." For Swinburne, the one solace for the wretched human condition is that it ends, and so, as he beautifully expresses it in "The Garden of Proserpine,"

From too much love of living,
    From hope and fear set free,
We thank with brief thanksgiving
    Whatever gods may be
That no life lives for ever;
That dead men rise up never,
That even the weariest river
    Winds somewhere safe to sea.

In a few poems, most notably "Hesperia" and "Sapphics," Swinburne's pessimism is lightened as he begins to form the new faith that was to sustain him for the rest of his life. Annihilation of the old faiths, of the accepted verities, brought for Swinburne, as for Nietzsche, a belief in renewed scope for creation. After the fierce passions had been spent, they could be transmuted into compassion for the human condition and eternally memorialized in song. The savage lust of Sappho celebrated in "Anactoria," for example, could be preserved in her song, passed on down through the ages to Swinburne and transformed into the gentler compassion of his "Sapphics." Man could attain a measure of immortality by linking his consciousness in a communion of song with past and future generations; Swinburne could share the consciousness of Sappho, as future generations of poets could share the consciousness of Swinburne and of all who had contributed to the human spirit.

Not surprisingly, most of Swinburne's finest poetry after *Poems and Ballads* is elegiac, and also not surprisingly, his first full expression of his new faith was to come in his elegy for Baudelaire, the magnificent "Ave atque Vale," written in July 1867 after Swinburne had heard premature rumors of his French contemporary's death and published in the *Fortnightly Review* in January 1868 after Baudelaire obligingly died on 31 August 1867. The greatest consolation for Baudelaire was that the life of passion and pain, "Fierce loves, and lovely leaf-buds poisonous" in Swinburne's phrase, was over, that he had found the peace of oblivion, but the greatest consolation for Swinburne is that because the poet lived life intensely, he passed on works that reproduced the sound of his "sad soul." Clasping a book by Baudelaire (*Les Fleurs du Mal,* although the title is not mentioned), Swinburne is in communion with his spirit, "As though a hand were in my hand to hold." Baudelaire is able to reach out from oblivion to comfort the mourner: death is defeated not by the ascetic repression of the body by the soul but by energetic life and creation. The void left by Christianity is filled with a religion of art, and human life is given significance. As the metaphorical clasping of hands implies, the lonely isolation of the individual is overcome by communion in art.

Swinburne's life during these years reflects both the wildness of his erotic writings and the more chastened mood of his elegiac poems. His life in London was occasionally interrupted by visits to the Continent and to the sea, but when in the city he continued to drink, now so heavily that he was falling into a pattern of chronic illness. From the mid-1860s until 1879 his life fell into a depressing routine of alcoholic dissolution in London, collapse, rescue by his parents, and drying-out periods at his family's new home in Holmwood. The wildest anecdotes about Swinburne—those by which he is most often judged—all date from this period. In addition to the drinking, he was doing his best to live

a sexually dissolute life. Late in 1867, Rossetti and others, thinking it a shame that Swinburne should write so well of love and have so little experience of it, contrived to set him up with an American circus performer, Adah Menken. Menken did her best and inspired some genuine affection in Swinburne, who referred to her as his mistress, but she had no chance of real success, for as she remarked to Rossetti, "I can't make him understand that biting's no use!" According to Edmund Gosse the affair only lasted about six weeks. It was also in the late 1860s that Swinburne actually put his flagellation mania into practice with frequent visits to Verbena Lodge, a specialized brothel where, as Edmund Gosse put it, "two golden-haired and rouge-cheeked ladies received, in luxuriously furnished rooms, gentlemen whom they consented to chastise for large sums." The sums charged were evidently too large, for Swinburne quarreled over the money in 1869 and never returned. His obsession with flagellation, though certainly reflecting an important part of his psychic life, was mostly a lark for him and never brought him any real grief. His alcoholism was a different matter and was becoming an inconvenience in more ways than one. Though he vigorously denied it, his many illnesses during these years were almost certainly caused by the undermining of his constitution by alcohol. He preferred to blame his sickness on the flu, or indigestion, or even, as he put it in a letter, the "perfume of Indian lilies in a close bedroom." He was also becoming a public scandal, as the famous incident of his ejection from the Arts club, cited by Gosse, illustrates. In the spring of 1870, extremely drunk after dinner at the club, Swinburne had trouble finding his hat, "which, on account of the great size of his head, was of excessive capacity. He tried one hat after another, and as each pinched his brows he flung it to the floor; finally in a towering and ungovernable rage, he danced and stamped upon the hats." When sober, Swinburne was every inch a gentleman, forgot what he had done when drunk, and vehemently denied that he might ever have done anything unworthy of a gentleman. Swinburne's most bizarre tastes were vicariously indulged, but because he spoke of them indiscreetly he developed an international reputation for profligacy of all kinds. In response to the uproar over his immorality in *Poems and Ballads* and to continuing journalistic abuse of his writings and his character, Swinburne declared that he had an image to live up to, and he seems, like Baudelaire, to have encouraged rumors about his own vice. The strangest rumors had him engaging in pederasty and bestiality with a monkey, which he is said to have eaten later. But as Oscar Wilde said, Swinburne was "a braggart in matters of vice, who had done everything he could to convince his fellow citizens of his homosexuality and bestiality, without being in the slightest degree a homosexual or a bestializer." Even Swinburne's physical appearance and innocent mannerisms told against him. His diminutive size and an apparently innate tendency to tremble violently when excited looked like the result of debilitating alcoholism, and his voluble enthusiasm gave the impression that he was raving insanely. But despite all of his wildness, Swinburne's friends during this period remembered quieter moments, when his innate generosity of spirit and deeply affectionate nature more than made up for his flamboyance. In fact, the libidinous satyr of the press was actually something of a lost innocent: his friends seem to have particularly loved him for his childlike incapacity to cope with the world.

Even before the publication of *Poems and Ballads,* much of Swinburne's poetry was beginning to take a new direction. His aesthetic dogma in the early 1860s, best expressed in the critical masterpiece *William Blake* (begun in 1863 and published in 1868), had been an unqualified expression of art for art's sake, but he had never abandoned his ardent republicanism, and in 1866 he began to write rather shrill political lyrics. He repudiated his earlier aesthetic doctrines in a letter to William Michael Rossetti—"It was only Gabriel and his followers in art (l'art pour l'art) who for a time frightened me from speaking out"—and dedicated himself passionately to the cause of European republicanism. In this mood he wrote *A Song of Italy* (published in pamphlet form in 1867) and his "Ode on the Insurrection in Candia," which inspired the republican leader Mazzini's exhortation to Swinburne to abandon "songs of egotistical love" and write "a series of Lyrics for the Crusade." Swinburne's meeting with Mazzini, one of the major events in his life, was apparently brought about by his old master at Oxford, Benjamin Jowett, and other friends in an effort to bring his life under some control. On meeting Mazzini he dropped to his knees to kiss his hero's hands and felt that he would willingly die for him, and for the cause—but he did not reform.

He did, however, proudly write the series of "Lyrics for the Crusade," eventually publishing two volumes of republican lyrics, *Songs before Sunrise* (1871) and *Songs of Two Nations* (1875). Of all his works, Swinburne had the highest regard for *Songs before Sunrise,* the volume he most wanted to be remembered for, but with few exceptions the republican poems are too verbose, too dogmatic, too

mechanically allegorized, and too shrill for most readers. Swinburne was a master of invective, but calling the church a putrescent, leprous, "haggard harlot" and the Trinity a "triple-headed hound of hell" and instructing a dead king to "Go down to hell" does not make great lyric poetry. *Songs of Two Nations* has no saving moments, but *Songs before Sunrise* is partially redeemed by several fine lyrics in which the verse is more controlled and in which Swinburne is inspired by more than spleen or a vague adoration of an allegorical goddess of liberty. The occasional flashes of power and beauty most often result from Swinburne's central doctrine—a doctrine central also to *Atalanta in Calydon* and most of all to his best late poetry—that the eternal spirit of nature and the eternal spirit of humanity are one. Liberty is associated with the free forces of elemental nature, to which the human spirit must submit itself, rejecting the shackles of all inhibiting creeds. Significantly, however, the submission to elemental forces reflects the same psychic need as in the erotic poetry, a longing for merger with an identity greater than the poet's own. Even Swinburne's abstract abasement before the "Spirit of Man" and actual abasement before such heroes as Mazzini, Landor, and Hugo reflects a deep need to submit his identity to some greater force.

Songs before Sunrise received a very mixed reception when first published. Not surprisingly the reviewers who had been shocked by the blasphemy in Swinburne's earlier volumes were shocked once again. Delight in "the reddest of Red Republicanism" was now added to the list of Swinburne's other sins: blasphemy, atheism, sensualism, and vacuousness bordering on insanity. Further, the criticisms that were to be aimed at much of Swinburne's later work now began to be clearly heard: his mastery of verse disguised a paucity of thought in the endless, sonorously alliterated cadences, his verse was monotonous, and he did not know when to stop. *Songs before Sunrise* eventually found, and continues to find, enthusiastic admirers, and even when first published it found defenders. The liberal and radical journals praised Swinburne for submitting his lyrical genius to a higher cause than love and lust, and even many of the hostile reviewers conceded his poetic powers. All in all, the critical climate in the 1870s became far more congenial to Swinburne than it had been in the previous decade.

Bothwell, which Swinburne had labored on for many years and finally had published in 1874, finally convinced his contemporaries that he had reformed and left them free at last to praise his art without disparaging his character. A new respect for Swinburne's intelligence and learning was also emerging, perhaps partly because he was beginning to be recognized as an important critic by the mid-1870s; both his fine book on George Chapman and his splendid *Essays and Studies* appeared in 1875. Swinburne's literary criticism, like his art criticism, is too much neglected in our time, so it is perhaps worth noting that his studies of Elizabethan and Jacobean dramatists, ground-breaking in their own time, retain their usefulness and importance in ours, and that his estimates of the early dramatists and of his French and English contemporaries have stood the test of time better than, say, those of Matthew Arnold. Swinburne's fellow critics recognized the merit of his studies, but they also recognized the faults: a tendency to praise too extravagantly what he liked, to attack too vituperatively anyone who disagreed with him, and to overload his long and sometimes clogged and convoluted sentences with alliteration. Swinburne's vituperation is often amusing and his extravagant praise shows a real generosity of spirit, but his overloaded prose, still usually beautiful and effective in the 1870s, eventually became so marred by meretricious mannerisms as to become almost unreadable. Nevertheless, his studies of Blake, Chapman, Ford, Shakespeare, Byron, Keats, Rossetti, and Arnold remain not only readable, but also essential to serious students of those authors.

Swinburne's career was generally on the rise in the 1870s for several reasons, but it was the publication of *Erechtheus* in 1876 that brought him all but universal praise and established him firmly and unquestionably, in the eyes of his contemporaries, as a great living poet. The praise of *Erechtheus* was well merited, for Swinburne was at the height of his lyrical powers. It would be easy to neglect the play's depth of thought or its intensely focused construction but difficult in the extreme to deny the sonorous and majestic lyricism exemplified in the second chorus:

> Out of the north wind grief came forth,
>   And the shining of the sword out of the sea.
> Yea, of old, the first-blown blast blew the prelude of
>   this last,
> The blast of his trumpet upon Rhodope.

Reverting to the Aeschylean model that he exploited so brilliantly in *Atalanta in Calydon,* Swinburne chose as his subject the legend of the saving of Athens, the first republic, the seat of Greek culture, the perfect type of the eternal City of Man. The legend was perfectly designed to express both the noblest ideals of his republicanism and his faith in the holiness of undying art, the truest expression of the spirit of man. The central event, the sacrifice of the maiden Chthonia for the salvation of Athens, epitomizes Swinburne's newfound faith that the nobility of submission to a larger cause, the nobility of dying for freedom, enables mankind to overcome the tyranny of death, for Chthonia "dead, shalt live/Till Athens live not." And Athens, Swinburne knew, would live as long as the race of man in the hearts of all great republicans and all great poets.

As with *Atalanta in Calydon,* the triumph of *Erechtheus* is in its perfect fusion of form and content. The thematic concerns are not baldly stated, as they too often were in the dogmatism and facile allegories of the republican lyrics, but are implicit in the dramatic conflict and subtly drawn out by the deft synthesis of imagery. The images associated with Chthonia, for example, link her death with sexual consummation, birth, and, in general, acceptance of cyclical change and individual mortality. The complex of imagery associating Chthonia and Athens with suffering, wisdom, song, and the indomitable spirit of man, moreover, points to Swinburne's antitheistic belief that accepting the finality of individual mortality liberates the creative energies that enable Athens and all great civilizations to triumph over time and the annihilation of oblivion. The nihilism of *Atalanta in Calydon* is gone, as though Atalanta had surrendered her maidenhead to Meleager, accepting with Althaea the place of the individual in nature's cycles.

Erechtheus, published a turbulent decade after *Atalanta,* is a more mature and, in its more serene power, arguably a greater achievement, yet something is missing. The tone of clamorous insistence of the demoniac boy of 1866 has vanished. The positive outlook of Swinburne's republican and aesthetic faith is partly responsible, no doubt, but so too are the depressant qualities of aging and of alcohol. After repeated cycles of alcoholism and collapse, Swinburne was in fact aging rapidly, declining into serious ill health, melancholy, and loneliness. At times the demoniac boy continued to emerge in the old exuberant blasphemy and obscenity, and more important in declamations of poetry and of republican indignation, but fits of deep depression were becoming more and more common. Even with the praise of *Erechtheus* fresh in his ears, Swinburne was lamenting the "rather dull monotonous puppet-show of my life, which often strikes me as too barren

Theodore Watts-Dunton and Swinburne in the garden of Watts-Dunton's home, the Pines

of action or enjoyment to be much worth holding on to." Never one to parade a private grief, he softened the comment with a characteristic reference to the pleasures of the sea and of "verse in its higher moods," but Edmund Gosse recalled that throughout the late 1870s Swinburne would often lapse into melancholy silences, occasionally interrupted by tales "plaintive and rather vague, about his loneliness, the sadness of his life, the suffering he experiences from the slander of others." Swinburne was withdrawing more and more from the gay London life, huddling alone in his rooms with the alcoholic dysentery he preferred to call the flu. At one point in 1878, at a time when, in his own words, he had "hardly ever felt wearier and weaker," Swinburne seemed to have disappeared from the face of the earth as he moved from 3 Great James Street to new rooms in Russell Square, neglecting to inform his anxious family and friends.

Yet in the midst of this depression Swinburne was seeing through the press his *Poems and Ballads, Second Series* (1878). Generally regarded as his finest collection of lyrics, the volume includes such triumphs as "A Forsaken Garden," "At a Month's End," "Ave atque Vale," "A Vision of Spring in Winter," and a magnificent series of translations from Villon. Alcohol had evidently had a sedative effect on Swinburne's muse, for the lyrics, magnificent as they are, are quieter, more serene than their predecessors. A note of despair does, assuredly,

creep into the volume, most emphatically in the famous "A Forsaken Garden," which uses the image of the sea eroding the land to describe the death of the garden, of young lovers, and even of love itself. The only consolation is that once all earthly life and love is dead, death, with no more victims, turns upon itself: "As a god self-slain on his own strange altar,/Death lies dead." Yet as "Ave atque Vale" and the many other elegies in the volume express, comfort can be taken in the very fact of the inevitability of oblivion that frees every man from the painful vicissitudes of existence. Also throughout the volume the other comfort expressed in "Ave atque Vale" is set forth, revealing the theme that was to be Swinburne's most fruitful for the next thirty years: individual death is, thankfully, inevitable, but human passions, redeemed in song, endure: "Dust that covers/Long dead lovers/Song blows off with breath that brightens." As "The Last Oracle" makes clear, the faith in song is a genuine religion, a worship of Apollo, the "sun-god and the singing-god of the Greeks." But Swinburne remains as fiercely antitheistic as ever, since Apollo symbolizes the human creativity that can make and unmake gods—as the poet put it elsewhere, "the inner sunlight of human thought or imagination and the gift of speech and song."

Unfortunately, in 1878 and 1879 Swinburne seemed heading toward the oblivion of death that would cut off his speech and song. He was saved only by the timely intervention of Theodore Watts (later Watts-Dunton), the stolid lawyer, critic, and poet whom Rossetti once aptly called a hero of friendship. Watts interrupted the poet's rapid decline, whisking him off to Putney (at that time on the outskirts of London) and miraculously restoring his tiny but surprisingly strong constitution with a regimen of broths and outdoor walks. Soon after, as Swinburne was further recuperating at Holmwood under his mother's supervision, Watts and Lady Jane Swinburne, convinced that a return to his former life would soon prove fatal, made permanent plans for the wayward Dionysian: he would set up housekeeping with Watts in Putney. And so he did, spending the last thirty years of his life ensconced at No. 2, the Pines, safely isolated from the temptations of city life and of his former friends. The domestication of the demoniac youth, the wild pagan, the satyr, the scourge of Victorian respectability, has always impressed observers as both terribly sad and, in some ways, irresistibly comic. Watts's reputed method of coping with his new housemate's alcoholism epitomizes the tragicomedy. By Coulson Kernahan's account in *Swinburne as I Knew Him* (1919), the poet was weaned from brandy to port because port was "Tennyson's drink," from port to burgundy, the drink of "La Belle France" and of "Dumas' immortal Three Musketeers," from burgundy to claret, "the proper drink of gentlemen," and finally from claret to "Shakespeare's brown October, our own glorious and incomparable beer!" And so Watts firmly and consistently, but with exquisite tact, handled Swinburne's childlike incapacity to cope with life. He was always on hand to see that the poet changed his wet clothes after a walk in the rain, to get him on the right train to visit his mother, to shield him from dangerous guests, to soothe his occasionally ruffled dignity and praise his work. Under Watts's guidance (imperceptible to the poet, who firmly believed in his independence), Swinburne gradually fell into a monotonous but pleasant routine. Because Watts said it would be unbecoming, Swinburne had promised never to go into any of the pubs "in the village," but every morning at precisely eleven o'clock he would leave the Pines, walk briskly across Putney Heath to the neighboring village of Wimbledon, and drop into the Rose and Crown tavern. With the same regularity he would return for lunch and his ration of one glass of beer, ascend to his room for a nap, return at 6:30 to read aloud from Dickens and eat dinner, and at 10:00 retire to his books and work late into the night. At first the routine was broken by visits from old friends, but these gradually grew less frequent as Swinburne's advancing deafness made conversation more difficult and as his old friends began to die off. He did not usually like to meet new people, but as the years passed literary pilgrims occasionally were brought to lunch at the Pines, and some of them, most notably Max Beerbohm, have left bemused accounts of the comfortable domesticity of Watts fussing over Swinburne like a protective maiden aunt.

The routine sounds stultifying, but Swinburne was genuinely happy. His health was excellent, he had a deep affection for Watts, he immensely enjoyed his evening readings of Dickens, and he loved the neighboring heath which, with its glorious hawthorn, seemed to him an unrivaled landscape. The routine was broken by annual excursions with Watts to the sea, by visits to his mother and sisters, and by occasional visits to Jowett at Oxford. The most notable break in the routine occurred in 1882, when Watts and Swinburne went by invitation to a celebration in honor of Victor Hugo in Paris. Swinburne's first meeting with his idol should have been a great occasion, but both poets were by now so deaf that they could not quite understand one another. The visit was something of a fiasco, but Swinburne remembered it fondly.

Yet another alleviation came in the form of young Bertie Mason, Watts's nephew who had come with his parents to live at the Pines. Swinburne had always loved children, but at the Pines his love grew to a passion. He loved all babies, frequently peering into their prams as he passed them on his morning walks, but Bertie was special to Swinburne, who described him as "the sweetest thing going at any price." So great was Swinburne's devotion that Bertie's parents may have become a little unsettled about it, and perhaps in an attempt to curb it, they sent the child away on an extended holiday. Absence only made the heart grow fonder, and Swinburne wrote *A Dark Month,* a series of intolerably mawkish poems commemorating each day of loneliness.

A Dark Month (incongruously bound with *Tristram of Lyonesse,* 1882) and multitudes of other "baby poems" account in part for the widespread belief that though Watts saved Swinburne's life, he helped to kill his inspiration. There were other signs of Swinburne's artistic decline. His republicanism was gradually turning to jingoistic imperialism. Poems such as "The Commonweal," "The Armada," and "England: An Ode" make it all too clear that Mazzini's poet, the poet of regicide, had become Victoria's poet. Seemingly "born and baptized into the church of rebels," as he said Blake was, Swinburne was now the rankest of apostates. There is a certain consistency in his views, since a strain of intolerance and of cultural monism had always run through his republicanism. In 1886 he condemned the "anarchists and intriguers whose policy is to break up the state" with the observation that "the first principle of a Republican is and must be Unity." He consistently flattered himself with the strange observation that Mazzini would have agreed with him. He unabashedly supported the British effort in the Boer War, and he was among the most fervent celebrants of Victoria's jubilee. Part of his turnabout was probably due to sheer ignorance, since in his isolation at the Pines his only informants were the newspapers and the conversation of the patriotic Watts. He evidently believed that the British were the most benevolent of despots, and it is worth remembering that earlier, upon hearing of the savagely brutal, sadistic despotism of Governor Edward Eyre in Jamaica, he had allied himself against such defenders of Eyre as Carlyle, Ruskin, Dickens, Kingsley, and Tennyson.

The baby poems, the imperialism, and a steady stream of clumsily vituperative prose naturally enough disillusioned the admirers of the magnificent pagan of earlier days and led to a general disparagement of Swinburne's late work. The monotony of his life, it is said, is reflected in the tediousness of his verse; the diminished sphere of activity is apparent in a diminished range of thought and feeling in the poetry. To a great extent the charges are accurate. Much of the late poetry is uninspired, a haze of words, and Swinburne was becoming quite unnecessarily prolix: as his mother complained, he never knew when to stop. In addition, his late plays, *Mary Stuart* (1881), *Marino Faliero* (1885), *Locrine* (1887), *Rosamund, Queen of the Lombards* (1899), and *The Duke of Gandia* (1908), did not significantly add to his stature as a dramatist since, despite frequent fine passages of verse, they retained the structural weakness and artificiality of his earlier plays in the Elizabethan manner. Only the strange autobiographical play, *The Sisters* (1892), broke new ground by bringing verse drama into a modern setting, but the dialogue is awkwardly artificial and the melodramatic plot is only intriguing because it closely reflects what must have been a recurring fantasy for the aging poet. Young Reginald Clavering has become the cavalry officer that young Algernon Swinburne had dreamed of being, has been wounded at Waterloo, and has been too modest to declare his love to the beautiful cousin with whom, as a boy, he had enjoyed wild gallops. But in the fantasy world of the play the cousin, a surrogate Mary Gordon, declares her love for him, and after a short period of ecstatic bliss, the two are accidentally murdered and die with a kiss. The play, significantly dedicated to Mrs. Disney-Leith, is oddly touching in its transparent revelations of the poet's unfulfilled wish for happiness.

The Sisters is not a successful work, but in many ways it suggests that Swinburne was not, as is often said, cut off from his old sources of inspiration. The celebration of passionate love and the desire for death with the beloved recall the themes of "Anactoria," "The Leper," "The Triumph of Time," "Les Noyades," and many other early poems; the oceanic eroticism suggested in Reginald Clavering's splendid description of the sea is reminiscent of countless passages in earlier poems, letters, and especially in the novels. Even the conviction that the great literature of the past impinges constantly on the present is suggested by the inclusion of a Jacobean interlude that mirrors the main plot.

All of these sources of inspiration, so strangely expressed in *The Sisters,* are brilliantly fused in many great lyrical achievements written during the thirty years at the Pines, for the many volumes of poetry produced in this period contain, mixed in with the baby-worship and the imperialism, many more important poems than has generally been thought. Only a sampling of these poems can be mentioned, but they include "Thalassius" and "On the Cliffs" from *Songs of the Springtides* (1880); "Off Shore," "Evening on the Broads," and "By the North Sea" from *Studies in Song* (1880); the masterful title poem of *Tristram of Lyonesse and Other Poems* (1882); many of the lyrics in *A Century of Roundels* (1883); "A Ballad of Sark" and the title poem of *A Midsummer Holiday and Other Poems* (1884); "To a Seamew" and "Neap-Tide" from *Poems and Ballads, Third Series* (1889); "A Nympholept" and "Loch Torridon" from *Astrophel and Other Poems* (1894); the fine Arthurian narrative, *The Tale of Balen* (1896); and "The Lake of Gaube," "The Promise of the Hawthorn," "Hawthorn Tide," and "The Passing of the Hawthorn" from *A Channel Passage and Other Poems* (1904). These noteworthy poems, written over twenty-five years, form a unit because they all express, with consummate artistry, variations on themes from Swinburne's most enduring sources of inspiration—the sea, the wind, human passions, and the great poetic tradition from Sappho and Aeschylus to Shakespeare and Shelley. Swinburne

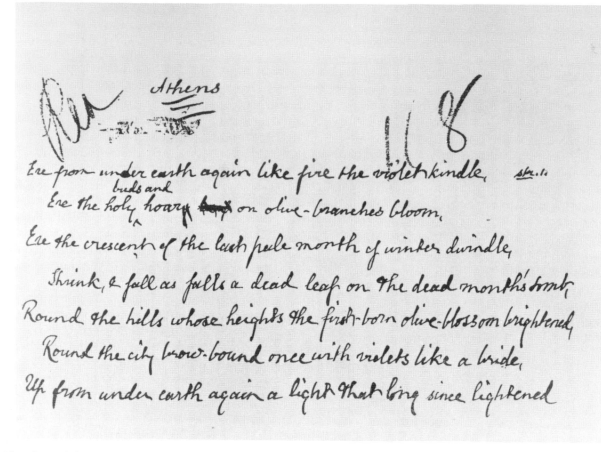

First lines of the manuscript for Swinburne's "Athens: An Ode," collected in Tristram of Lyonesse and Other Poems, *1882
(Anderson Galleries, sale 1820, 17-20 March 1924)*

had certainly never been inspired by London—he is the least urban of poets—so his rescue by Watts could not, and did not, remove him from his sources of inspiration. The years at Putney may not have been tragic after all.

One of Swinburne's finest poems, "On the Cliffs," was written at Holmwood in 1879, shortly after Watts had rescued Swinburne from his rooms on Guildford Street. It is a sort of spiritual autobiography which expresses the themes of *Poems and Ballads, Second Series* in the most richly complex and precise syntax that Swinburne ever achieved. The setting, as in "The Forsaken Garden" and later "By the North Sea," is a crumbling cliff that is being slowly eaten away by the sea—Swinburne's favorite image for his belief that all earthly life, even the earth itself, is destined for oblivion. But looking over the desolate scene, the poet recalls certain words of Sappho and in doing so realizes that she has not died wholly, that her words and therefore her very passions are alive as they influence his own perception of nature. Further, nature can no longer

be viewed as indifferent or hostile, for in the unchanging sea, the sea that inspired Sappho, the heart of Sappho is preserved. Nature and the divinity in man, incarnate in the Word—not Christ but the song of Sappho—are brought into harmony, and human existence is given meaning. Swinburne came to see a divinity in nature that could bring all things into harmonious unison, but he was no pantheist, for as he puts it in "On the Cliffs," the divinity Apollo was simply "man's live breath," the "ruling song" "wherein all earth and heaven and sea/Were molten in one music." Though he was embarking on the quiet, secluded life of the Pines, Swinburne's faith in the redemptive powers of song interestingly included a belief in the necessity of the hot passions of love expressed in his demoniac youth, for he insisted that redeeming song must be "kindled," as he said in "Thalassius," by the "love/That life and death are fashioned of."

His fierce antitheism had survived as virulently as ever. In "By the North Sea" he is more quietly and also more thoughtfully and thoroughly blasphemous than he had been in "Dolores." In "By the North Sea" the sea devours a church in which man, ironically, "Hailed a God more merciful than Time" and graves where the dead futilely "awaited/Long the archangel's re-creating word." He had not lost the desire to shock his prim contemporaries either, for as he worked on the erotic scenes of *Tristram of Lyonesse* he gleefully anticipated their likely effect on British matrons. Far from being designed merely to shock, however, *Tristram* expresses Swinburne's deepest artistic impulses and shows plainly how his early eroticism merged with his late love of nature. The poem perfectly exemplifies what John D. Rosenberg, in the 1968 Modern Library edition of Swinburne's *Selected Poetry and Prose,* calls the "erotic interpenetration of nature and man," a fusion of human love and song in "multitudinous unison" with nature. In a description that recalls the erotic death-wish of "Les Noyades" and the settings of "A Forsaken Garden," "On the Cliffs," and "By the North Sea," in *Tristram* Tristram and Iseult do not merely die but are fused together as "their four lips become one silent mouth," and, buried on a crumbling sea-cliff, they are ultimately made one in the peace and "The light and sound and darkness of the sea." The eroticism, the longing for oblivion, the love of nature are present, and so, too, is the faith in redemptive song: "And one deep chord throbs all the music through,/The chord of change unchanging." Like many of the late poems, *Tristram of Lyonesse* deepens Swinburne's affirmation of passionate life, his unblinking acceptance of death, his love for elemental nature, and his faith that the imaginative power of poetry can fuse nature and man in beauty in the undying song of man.

Unlike most of his contemporaries, Swinburne never lost the Romantic faith in the redemptive power of imagination; he never forsook the bardic role of the poet. It is true that he remained remarkably consistent in his chief sources of inspiration. Yet despite persistent criticisms that his art was consistent because stagnant, that his art ceased to develop, his ideas did deepen and mature, and at least occasionally he rose, in his later years, to heights of unsurpassed lyrical virtuosity. The first stanza of the very late "The Lake of Gaube" (published in *A Channel Passage and Other Poems,* 1904) reveals his undiminished lyrical skill and verbal precision, as well as his vision of the "erotic interpenetration" of man and nature:

> The sun is lord and god, sublime, serene,
>> And sovereign on the mountains: earth and air
>> Lie prone in passion, blind with bliss unseen
>> By force of sight and might of rapture, fair
>> As dreams that die and know not what they were.
> The lawns, the gorges, and the peaks are one
> Glad glory, thrilled with sense of unison
> In strong compulsive silence of the sun.

Though his major achievements over the last thirty years of his life went largely unrecognized, though his most perceptive critics were offended by his often fatuous effusions, and though the sales of his works declined, Swinburne was generally recognized toward the end of his life as England's greatest living poet. His jingoism had atoned for his earlier "Red Republicanism" and his baby poems had reconciled him to the British matron. In fact, after the death of Tennyson in 1892, Queen Victoria, considering the empty post of poet laureate, is reputed to have been told that Swinburne was the greatest poet in her realm. Perhaps in view of Swinburne's earlier regicidal principles, the honor went instead to Alfred Austin. Swinburne would have scorned it, as he scorned an honorary degree from Oxford in 1908 and as he was prepared to scorn a Nobel Prize that was falsely reported to be coming his way in the

A. C. Swinburne, 1895 (photo by Elliott & Fry, Bassano & Vandyck Studios, London)

Swinburne in 1900, by R. P. Staples (National Portrait Gallery)

read over his grave. As he was quietly interred in the churchyard on his native Isle of Wight, the rector of Bonchurch, in the interests of decorum, did let drop a few Christian sentiments, but his last words were more apt and more truly decorous, as he bade farewell to "a creative art-genius of the first order, one of the most lovable great men of the later Victorian age, and one of the sweetest and most musical English poets who ever lived."

Swinburne's death brought the eulogies generally attendant on the death of a great poet, but posterity has not been kind to his reputation. The reasons are not difficult to understand. In the first place, his very great influence on the late nineteenth and early twentieth centuries has not always been appreciated. He had many imitators, but no good ones, for his virtuosity was inimitable. Yet his bittersweet paganism had significantly altered the flavor of his age, and the sensibilities of authors as diverse as Hardy, D. H. Lawrence, Yeats, Eugene O'Neill, and Pound were saturated by Swinburne. In addition, he was among the last of the great Victorians, and in the reaction against Victorianism his early rebelliousness could not atone for his late conformity and political apostasy. But most serious, his verse, despite its undeniable virtuosity, impressed readers as diffuse and devoid of intellectual content. Swinburne was aware of such charges in his own lifetime and brilliantly parodied his own supposedly vacuous virtuosity in "Poeta Loquitur" (written in 1889 and published posthumously in *The Italian Mother and Other Poems,* 1918):

> My philosophy, politics, free-thought!
>   Are worth not three skips of a flea,
> And the emptiest of thoughts that can be thought
>   Are mine on the sea.

Thanks to his sense of irony and his gift of mimicry, Swinburne could make fun of himself with greater skill than any of his critics could show, but he always wanted to be remembered not only as a great poet, but as a great poetic thinker as well. He would be gratified that the most recent critical assessments of his poetry are beginning to recognize that in his best work a vigorous and courageous intellect shines through the complex imagery and majestic music of his song. He would also have been gratified by T. S. Eliot's recognition that at his best Swinburne's music and intellect cohere in a perfect aesthetic fusion of form and content, that even his diffuseness, as Eliot says, "requires what there is no reason to call anything but genius. . . . What he gives is not images and ideas and music, it is one thing with a curious

same year. Nevertheless, the consensus was clear that he was unsurpassed, and that opinion was not surprising since his rebelliousness and consummate artistry had contributed mightily to forming the cultural climate of the late Victorian age. He had, after all, greatly influenced the style and thought of Pater, Wilde, and a host of other writers of the yellow 1890s, and his work was greatly admired by such very different writers as W. B. Yeats, Thomas Hardy, and the young Ezra Pound.

Swinburne's death in 1909 was the result of the reckless childishness that Watts had tried to protect him from for thirty years. With the ever vigilant Watts seriously ill in bed and for once not at his post, Swinburne sallied out for his morning walk on a particularly cold and rainy day and caught a cold that quickly turned into double pneumonia. After a period of delirious declamations in Greek—probably recitations from his beloved Aeschylus—he died on the morning of 10 April shortly after his seventy-second birthday. "Up to his last moment," according to Watts-Dunton, "he cherished the deepest animosity against the Creed," and according to his wish the Burial Service was not

Letter written by George Meredith to Theodore Watts-Dunton three days after Swinburne's death (Maurice Buxton Forman, A Bibliography of the Writings in Prose and Verse of George Meredith, 1922) mixture of suggestion of all three." Eventually, perhaps, Swinburne's profundity of thought will gain full recognition, but in the meantime his stature as a major poet rests securely on his daring and skillful metrical innovations, his astonishing versatility in the use of lyric forms, and his frank and fierce paganism. Though it is sometimes taken as disparagement, Tennyson's famous remark that his contemporary was "a reed through which all things blow into music" expresses the enduring quality of Swinburne's achievement. The winds of primitive, savage, and joyous passions from love, from the elemental forces of nature, the sea and sky, and from the "ruling song" of man blew through Swinburne's remarkably open, responsive sensibility, and came forth in sophisticated yet joyous and primitive song. Tennyson's comment not only does justice to Swinburne's indubitable talent for lyrical beauty, but also, perhaps accidentally, to his less-recognized gift for translating the immediacy of experience into verse.

Letters:

The Swinburne Letters, edited by Cecil Y. Lang, 6 volumes (New Haven: Yale University Press, 1959-1962).

Bibliographies:

Thomas James Wise, *A Bibliography of the Writings of Swinburne,* 2 volumes (London: Privately printed, 1919, 1920); revised as *A Bibliography of the Writings in Prose and Verse of Algernon Charles Swinburne,* volume 20 of *The Complete Works of Algernon Charles Swinburne* (London: Heinemann/New York: Wells, 1927);

William E. Fredeman, "Algernon Charles Swinburne," in his *Pre-Raphaelitism: A Bibliocritical Study* (Cambridge: Harvard University Press, 1965), pp. 216-220;

Clyde K. Hyder, "Algernon Charles Swinburne," in *The Victorian Poets: A Review of Research,* revised edition, edited by F. E. Faverty (Cambridge: Harvard University Press, 1968), pp. 227-250;

Kirk H. Beetz, *Algernon Charles Swinburne: A Bibliography of Secondary Works, 1861-1980* (Metuchen, N.J. & London: Scarecrow Press, 1982).

Biographies:

Edmund Gosse, *The Life of Algernon Charles Swinburne* (New York: Macmillan, 1917);

Coulson Kernahan, *Swinburne as I Knew Him* (London: Lane, 1919);

Clara Watts-Dunton, *The Home Life of Swinburne* (London: Philpot, 1922);

Georges Lafourcade, *La Jeunesse de Swinburne, 1837-1867,* 2 volumes (London: Oxford University Press, 1928);

Lafourcade, *Swinburne: A Literary Biography* (London: Bell, 1932);

Mollie Panter-Downes, *At the Pines* (London: Hamilton, 1971);

Ian Fletcher, *Swinburne* (Harlow: Longman, 1973);

Philip Henderson, *Swinburne: Portrait of a Poet* (New York: Macmillan, 1974);

Donald Thomas, *Swinburne: The Poet in His World* (New York: Oxford University Press, 1979).

References:

Julian Baird, "Swinburne, Sade, and Blake: The Pleasure-Pain Paradox," *Victorian Poetry,* 9 (Spring-Summer 1971): 49-75;

Max Beerbohm, "No. 2, The Pines: Reminiscences of Swinburne," in his *And Even Now* (New York: Dutton, 1921), pp. 55-88;

C. M. Bowra, "*Atalanta in Calydon,*" in his *The Romantic Imagination* (Cambridge: Harvard University Press, 1949), pp. 221-244;

Leslie Brisman, "Swinburne's Semiotics," *Georgia Review,* 31 (Fall 1977): 578-597;

E. K. Brown, "Swinburne: A Centenary Estimate," *University of Toronto Quarterly,* 6 (January 1937): 215-235;

Samuel C. Chew, *Swinburne* (Boston: Little, Brown, 1929);

T. E. Connolly, *Swinburne's Theory of Poetry* (Albany: State University of New York Press, 1964);

David A. Cook, "The Content and Meaning of Swinburne's 'Anactoria,'" *Victorian Poetry,* 9 (Spring-Summer 1971): 77-93;

T. S. Eliot, "Swinburne as Critic" and "Swinburne as Poet," in his *The Sacred Wood* (London: Methuen, 1920), pp. 17-24, 144-150;

Leonard M. Findlay, "Swinburne and Tennyson," *Victorian Poetry,* 9 (Spring-Summer 1971): 217-236;

Robert A. Greenberg, "Swinburne and the Redefinition of Classical Myth," *Victorian Poetry,* 14 (Autumn 1976): 175-195;

H. J. C. Grierson, *Swinburne* (London: Longmans, 1953);

Anthony H. Harrison, "The Aesthetics of Androgyny in Swinburne's Early Poetry," *Tennessee Studies in Literature,* 23 (1978): 87-99;

Lafcadio Hearn, "Studies in Swinburne," in his *Pre-Raphaelite and Other Poets* (New York:

Dodd, Mead, 1922), pp. 122-179;

Clyde K. Hyder, *Swinburne's Literary Career and Fame* (Durham: Duke University Press, 1933);

Hyder, ed., *Swinburne: The Critical Heritage* (London: Routledge, Kegan Paul, 1970);

Cecil Y. Lang, "Swinburne's Lost Love," *PMLA*, 74 (March 1959): 123-130;

F. L. Lucas, "Swinburne," in his *Ten Victorian Poets* (Cambridge: University Press, 1948);

Richard Mathews, "Heart's Love and Heart's Division: The Quest for Unity in *Atalanta in Calydon*," *Victorian Poetry*, 9 (Spring-Summer 1971): 35-48;

Jerome J. McGann, *Swinburne: An Experiment in Criticism* (Chicago: University of Chicago Press, 1971);

Richard D. McGhee, " 'Thalassius': Swinburne's Poetic Myth," *Victorian Poetry*, 5 (Summer 1967): 127-136;

Kerry McSweeney, "Swinburne's *Poems and Ballads* (1866)," *Studies in English Literature*, 11 (Autumn 1971): 671-685;

McSweeney, *Tennyson and Swinburne as Romantic Naturalists* (Toronto: University of Toronto Press, 1980);

Ross C. Murfin, "Athens Unbound: A Study of Swinburne's *Erechtheus*," *Victorian Poetry*, 12 (Autumn 1974): 205-217;

Murfin, *Swinburne, Hardy, Lawrence and the Burden of Belief* (Chicago: University of Chicago Press, 1978);

Harold Nicolson, *Swinburne* (London: Macmillan, 1926);

Morse Peckham, *Victorian Revolutionaries: Speculations on Some Heroes of a Cultural Crisis* (New York: Braziller, 1970), pp. 250-305;

Robert L. Peters, *The Crowns of Apollo: Swinburne's Principles of Literature and Art* (Detroit: Wayne State University Press, 1965);

Ezra Pound, "Swinburne versus Biographers," *Poetry*, 11 (March 1918): 322-329;

Mario Praz, *The Romantic Agony*, translated by Angus Davidson (London: Oxford University Press, 1933), pp. 413-433;

Meredith B. Raymond, *Swinburne's Poetics: Theory and Practice* (The Hague: Mouton, 1971);

John R. Reed, "Swinburne's *Tristram of Lyonesse*: The Poet-Lover's Song of Love," *Victorian Poetry*, 4 (Spring 1966): 99-120;

Paul de Reul, *L'Oeuvre de Swinburne* (London: Oxford University Press, 1922);

George M. Ridenour, "Swinburne on 'The Problem to Solve in Expression,' " *Victorian Poetry*, 9 (Spring-Summer 1971): 129-144;

Ridenour, "Time and Eternity in Swinburne: Minute Particulars in Five Poems," *English Literary History*, 45 (Spring 1978): 107-130;

David G. Riede, *Swinburne: A Study of Romantic Mythmaking* (Charlottesville: University Press of Virginia, 1978);

John D. Rosenberg, "Swinburne," *Victorian Studies*, 11 (December 1967): 131-152;

William R. Rutland, *Swinburne: A Nineteenth-Century Hellene* (Oxford: Blackwell, 1931);

George Saintsbury, "Mr. Swinburne," in his *Corrected Impressions* (New York: Dodd, Mead, 1895), pp. 60-78;

Mark Siegchrist, "Artemis's Revenge: A Reading of Swinburne's *Atalanta in Calydon*," *Studies in English Literature*, 20 (Autumn 1980): 895-912;

Arthur Symons, "Swinburne," in his *Studies in Strange Souls* (London: Sawyer, 1929), pp. 50-83;

Geoffrey Tillotson, "Swinburne," in his *Mid-Victorian Studies* (London: Athlone Press, 1965), pp. 209-215;

T. Earle Welby, *A Study of Swinburne* (New York: Doran, 1926);

Welby, *The Victorian Romantics: 1850-1870* (London: Howe, 1929);

William Wilson, "Algernon Agonistes: 'Thalassius,' Visionary Strength, and Swinburne's Critique of Arnold's 'Sweetness and Light,' " *Victorian Poetry*, 19 (Winter 1981): 381-395;

Thomas L. Wymer, "Swinburne's Tragic Vision in *Atalanta in Calydon*," *Victorian Poetry*, 9 (Spring-Summer 1971): 1-16.

Papers:

The largest single collection of manuscripts and letters is at the British Library. Large collections of letters are at the Beinecke Rare Book and Manuscript Library, Yale University; Rutgers University Library; the National Library of Wales; and the Brotherton Library, Leeds University. Extensive collections of manuscripts are at the Humanities Research Center, University of Texas at Austin; the New York Public Library; the Mayfield Library, Syracuse University; the Brotherton Library, Leeds University; the Huntington Library, San Marino, California; the Public Library of New South Wales; the Pierpont Morgan Library; the Free Library of Philadelphia; Trinity College of Cambridge University; the Library of Congress; and the libraries of Rutgers, Harvard, Yale, Princeton, and the University of Michigan.

James Thomson
(B.V.)

William Lutz
Rutgers University

BIRTH: Port Glasgow, Scotland, 23 November 1834, to James and Sarah Kennedy Thomson.

EDUCATION: Royal Military Academy, Chelsea, 1850-1854.

DEATH: London, 3 June 1882.

SELECTED BOOKS: *A Commission of Inquiry on Royalty, Etc.* (London, 1876);

The Story of a Famous Old Jewish Firm (London, 1876);

The Devil in the Church of England and The One Thing Needful (London: Secularist, 1876);

The Pilgrimage to Saint Nicotine (Liverpool: Cope's Tobacco Plant, 1878);

The City of Dreadful Night and Other Poems (London: Reeves & Turner, 1880; Portland, Maine: Mosher, 1903);

Vane's Story, Weddah and Om-el-Bonain, and Other Poems (London: Reeves & Turner, 1880);

Address on the Opening of the New Hall of the Leicester Secular Society, Sunday, March 6, 1881 (Leicester, 1881?);

Essays and Phantasies (London: Reeves & Turner, 1881);

The Story of a Famous Old Jewish Firm and Other Pieces in Prose and Rime (London: Printed for B. E. and W. L. S., 1883);

Satires and Profanities, edited by G. W. Foote (London: Progressive Publishing, 1884);

A Voice from the Nile and Other Poems, edited by Bertram Dobell (London: Reeves & Turner, 1884);

Shelley: A Poem; with Other Writings Relating to Shelley, by the Late James Thomson (B.V.): to which is added an Essay on the Poetry of William Blake by the same author (London: Privately printed, 1884);

Selections from Original Contributions by James Thomson to "Cope's Tobacco Plant" (Liverpool: Cope's Tobacco Plant, 1889);

Poems, Essays and Fragments, edited by John M. Robertson (London: A. and H. B. Bonner, 1892);

Biographical and Critical Studies, edited by Dobell (London: Reeves & Turner and Bertram Dobell, 1896);

James Thomson ("B.V.") on George Meredith (London: Privately printed, 1909);

Walt Whitman: The Man and the Poet, edited by Dobell (London: Bertram Dobell, 1910);

Poems and Some Letters of James Thomson, edited by Anne Ridler (London: Centaur Press, 1963);

The Speedy Extinction of Evil and Misery, edited by William David Schaefer (Berkeley & Los Angeles: University of California Press, 1967).

Collection: *The Poetical Works of James Thomson (B.V.)*, edited by Bertram Dobell, 2 volumes (London: Reeves & Turner and Bertram Dobell, 1895).

Little noted during his lifetime, Thomson's work continues to draw scant attention from students and critics. As a writer of verse, Thomson is tucked away under the category of minor poets of his age. His prose, including his literary criticism, is rarely read or consulted today. Yet Thomson offers much for the student of Victorian literature. Noted for his major poem, "The City of Dreadful Night," he is almost completely ignored as a literary critic, essayist, and reviewer. While critics have paid due attention to his pessimism, atheism, and republicanism, little attention has been paid to the intellectual struggle which led him to these beliefs, a struggle which reflects an aspect of Victorian intellectual life too often neglected today. Because he went his solitary way with his unorthodox critical, political, and religious beliefs, Thomson is significant as a writer who gives a different view of his age. He was self-educated, middle-class, and very much the observer of the changing ideas and values of his time. Never a member of established literary circles, Thomson lived in a world foreign to such men as Thomas Carlyle, John Ruskin, and Matthew Arnold. His writings record the doubt, despair, hope, and frustration of the nonestablishment, unrecognized, but hardworking Victorian writer.

Born in Port Glasgow, Scotland, Thomson was the first of two children; his brother was born some eight years later. His father, James Thomson, was a captain in the merchant service, and from what sketchy information there is available he seems to have been a clever, cheerful man. Thomson's mother, Sarah Kennedy Thomson, was a deeply religious woman and follower of Edward Irving. In contrast to her husband, she had a pensive, melancholy nature. But these personalities, different though they may have been, did not produce an unhappy home life for the young Thomson. Whenever his father was home from the sea, he enjoyed singing, reading, and reciting poetry. The religious training of the children was strict, and Thomson was forced to memorize the Irvingite catechism, but from all evidence, Thomson's early home life was warm and loving.

In 1840, however, this pleasant existence was shattered when Thomson's father suffered a paralytic stroke while on a sea voyage and returned home seriously affected in both mind and body. Instead of the cheerful, singing parent he had once known, Thomson now confronted a stranger who was temperamental, disagreeable, and subject to mental instability. After about a year, the senior Thomson subsided into permanent weakness of mind and became a silent, brooding shell of the man Thomson once knew.

An immediate result of the father's illness was financial difficulty for the family. In 1842 the family moved to London's East End, where Thomson's brother, John, was born. By this time the situation was desperate. In November of that year, through the help of family friends, Thomson was placed in the Royal Caledonian Asylum in London, a school for the children of poor Scottish soldiers and sailors. Shortly after he entered this school, Thomson's mother died and his infant brother was placed in the care of an aunt in Glasgow. The family dissolved and Thomson's father died in 1853, but the news of his death had little if any effect on Thomson.

Although we have few details of his first eight years, we do know that Thomson's early life was greatly influenced by his mother's adherence to the strongly emotional Irvingite religion. Although not as rigorous as Calvinism, the Irvingite creed was strict, and Thomson's mother saw to it that her son was properly reared. Besides memorizing the assembly's *Shorter Catechism,* Thomson regularly attended services with his mother and knew the many hymns and tracts that were so integral a part of the religion. His church experience made a deep and lasting impression on the young Thomson. Later, when Thomson announced his atheism, he dem-

onstrated the intense bitterness toward religion peculiar to the man thoroughly versed in doctrine.

Although Thomson's placement in a state institution at the age of eight may evoke images of the lonely, suffering child, just the opposite was the case. The Asylum was not a Dickensian house of horrors but a school designed to prepare children for earning a living through a trade with due attention paid to their religious training. Thomson fitted nicely into the school. He was popular with his classmates, demonstrated that he had a good mind, especially in mathematics, and developed a love of music that he retained for the rest of his life. He also began to read widely, a habit which also stayed with him. For eight years Thomson was a student and resident of the Caledonian Asylum, a period he remembered as the happiest of his life.

But these happy years passed quickly, and it was soon time to leave the school and take up a career. Thomson wanted to become a clerk in a bank or some other business. But such positions demanded a training period of unpaid apprenticeship, and Thomson lacked the necessary funds. His teachers at the Asylum recommended the profession of army schoolmaster, and although it did not appeal to him, Thomson reluctantly agreed since he could think of no other solution to the problem of earning a living. In 1850 Thomson entered the Royal Military Asylum, Chelsea, to begin preparation as an army schoolmaster.

Thomson continued to be popular with his classmates. Although he did not particularly like the career he had chosen, he turned all his energies to it. He was a good student, with a remarkable memory and a natural aptitude for mathematics. In addition to his regular studies, he mastered several languages on his own. In his own reading he was pursuing with vigor a remarkably wide range of authors. Shelley had replaced Byron as his poetic idol and Swift and DeQuincy were his prose idols. In addition, he read Swift, Fielding, Smollett, Sterne, and Defoe, as well as Shakespeare, Jonson, Spenser, and Milton. Thus at an early age Thomson was busy laying the groundwork for his later intellectual life: mathematics provided him with the logical and analytical quality of mind which was to be characteristic of his writings in later years, and the love of reading and literature provided him with the background for his own literary career.

As part of his training to be a schoolmaster, Thomson had to serve as an assistant teacher at a regular post in order to gain practical experience. In 1851 he was sent to Ballincollig, Ireland, a post located amid beautiful country scenery. Joseph Barnes, the regular teacher, befriended Thomson and treated him with great kindness. Barnes and his wife readily took Thomson into their home, and it became for him the first real home he had known in some nine years. So close was the relationship that Thomson was given the pet name Co (for precocious) by Mrs. Barnes. Thomson never forgot the peace and contentment he found with his new friends, and some ten years later he wrote six sonnets addressed to Joseph and Alice Barnes.

At Ballincollig, Thomson also met Charles Bradlaugh, a soldier stationed at the post. Bradlaugh was only a year older than Thomson, and the two struck up a close friendship that would last for more than twenty years. It was a curious friendship for these two who were unlike in many ways. Bradlaugh was a proclaimed atheist and radical at a time when Thomson still believed in Christianity and the prevailing political system, but these very differences seemed to bring them together.

While stationed at Ballincollig, Thomson met Matilda Weller, the fourteen-year-old daughter of a sergeant at the post. He saw her, and indeed her whole family, often since he was a frequent visitor to their home. Shortly after his return to the Royal Military Asylum, Chelsea, Thomson was notified that Matilda Weller had suddenly taken sick and died. With no documentation or proof, several biographers have described Thomson's reaction to the news of Matilda's death in exceedingly dramatic terms. Charles Bradlaugh completely dismissed the idea of romance between Thomson and the girl. (Bradlaugh, in fact, says that she was younger than fourteen, more like twelve or thirteen.) Henry Salt, one of Thomson's biographers, interviewed Matilda Weller's younger brother, Henry, and discovered that he knew of no romance nor engagement between the teacher and his sister but chose to ignore this information in his biography. Thomson himself makes no direct reference to this supposed romance in any of his letters, diaries, journals, and notebooks. The romance seems to have existed only in the minds of Thomson's biographers. We may therefore discount those theories which hold that Thomson's later pessimism and alcoholism had their origins in his grief over the death of Matilda Weller.

Thomson returned to finish his studies at Chelsea in 1853. His intellectual abilities and efforts continued unabated, so that he completed his studies ahead of time and was allowed to leave the school before his scheduled term was up. In 1854 he finished at Chelsea and officially enlisted as a schoolmaster in the army, a position he was to hold for eight years.

As an army schoolmaster Thomson was considered a soldier not a civilian. He wore the uniform of the regiment to which he was assigned and was subject to the usual military discipline. His duties were simple; he taught children in the morning and soldiers in the evening, besides giving extra lessons to those who needed special help. The life was simple and dull. The posts where he served were drab and the soldiers not intellectually exciting. Dutifully, Thomson did what was expected of him. Outside of the classroom he was popular with his associates and the soldiers without being intimate with any of them, while inwardly he was going through a great spiritual struggle. The quietly assured Christian who had discussed theology with the atheist Bradlaugh was beginning the questioning and searching that would ultimately lead him into his own form of atheism. He was also serving his apprenticeship as a poet, writing late at night and then rewriting and discarding his verses the next day. For a man of Thomson's intellect and literary appetite there must have been many moments when he missed the long discussions he had enjoyed with Bradlaugh at Ballincollig. He filled some of his leisure hours with long walks in the countryside, while free time in the evenings was used for study. He gave up mathematics despite the great promise he had demonstrated at Chelsea and turned instead to languages. By hard work he taught himself German, French, Italian, and some Spanish, Latin, and Greek, and he continued to read widely in English literature. In about 1856 he became seriously interested in the works of Robert Browning and George Meredith. Thomson was transferred frequently. After serving at Aldershot, Dublin, and Curragh Camp, he returned to Aldershot, and finally, in 1862, he was stationed at Portsmouth.

While at Portsmouth Thomson went to visit a fellow teacher at Aldershot. During the course of the visit, on a dare or because of a wager, Thomson swam to a small boat moored in a pond where swimming was forbidden. Charges were brought and Thomson was discharged from the army on 30 October 1862. This punishment seems drastic for such a seemingly trifling offense, but it appears that the swimming incident was an excuse for the army to rid itself of Thomson, for already he had succumbed to the vice which was to haunt him for the rest of his life, alcoholism.

Thomson's early biographers have glossed over his discharge from the army despite the evidence that Thomson was drinking heavily as early as 1856. Bradlaugh claimed that there was no doubt that alcoholism, or at least chronic drunkenness, was the reason for Thomson's discharge. Indeed, Bradlaugh claimed frequently to have rescued Thomson from fits of drinking.

Thomson was, on the whole, a sociable man, popular with many people and a welcome guest in many homes. But at times bouts of drinking would come upon him like uncontrollable fits. Thomson's life is dotted with periods during which he would disappear for weeks on alcoholic binges. During such times he would become a completely different man. His was truly a Jekyll-Hyde existence, difficult, if not impossible, for his friends to adjust to.

Thomson was an alcoholic, an atheist, and a pessimist. His alcoholism has often been discussed in relation to his pessimism, and many have tried to trace the source of his compulsive drinking. Various reasons have been offered, from the death of Matilda Weller to a disease inherited from his father, but such explanations are speculative at best.

Thomson's career in the army was not entirely without literary effort. Before his discharge he did have a few prose works and some poetry published. The poetry appeared mainly in *Tait's Edinburgh Magazine* from 1852 to 1862, while most of the prose was published in the *National Reformer* and in the *London Investigator*, journals founded by his friend Charles Bradlaugh. Thomson signed his poems Crepusculus and in the *London Investigator* he signed his essays B.V., the pen name that he was to use for the rest of his life. The *National Reformer* pieces appeared under the pseudonyms X, Sigrat, J.S.T, T.J., J.T., and later, B.V. B.V. stood for Bysshe Vanolis. Bysshe was chosen out of Thomson's great admiration for Shelley, and Vanolis was an anagram of the name of another poet he admired, Novalis.

Thomson's earliest published work, a short, twenty-six line poem entitled "Love's Dawn," appeared in the October 1858 issue of *Tait's Edinburgh Review*. This was followed by other poems, most of them undistinguished and representative of a poet in the process of learning his craft and trying new techniques. Among the poems he wrote in the army is an unpublished work, "Suggested by Matthew Arnold's 'Stanzas from the Grand Chartreuse,'" which demonstrates his love for Browning. His long poem "A Festival of Life," published in *Tait's* in April 1859, demonstrates the influence of his beloved Shelley. During the period when he was contributing to *Tait's* Thomson wrote a poem which foreshadowed his major work, "The City of Dreadful Night," and which also demonstrated his emerging pessimistic philosophy. "The Doom of a City" was never published in a journal but appeared after his death in *A Voice from the Nile and Other Poems* (1884), edited by Bertram Dobell. Thomson had begun the journey of doubt and despair which was to take him to his major poem while at the same time robbing him of what little faith and hope he still possessed.

During his time in the military Thomson was also writing prose, though he preferred poetry, his first love. Among his early essays is "Notes on Emerson," which was published in the 1 December 1858 *Investigator*. The next year he published in the same journal an essay on Robert Burns, "A Few Words about Burns." Also, while stationed briefly on the isle of Jersey he wrote a review of Robert Browning's *Men and Women* for the local paper, the *Jersey Independent*. Before his discharge from the army in 1862, Thomson wrote eight published essays, most dealing with literary matters. During this same time he produced some thirty-four published poems and wrote ten poems which were published later in his life or after his death. Other poems written during this period that were never published are preserved only in manuscript at the Bodleian Library of Oxford University.

The essay on Emerson is representative of the work of a young man trying his hand at criticism. An unrestrained panegyric for Emerson which lacks substantial discussion of Emerson's works, the essay has value only in its revelation of Thomson's enthusiasm for Emerson. The essay on Burns is similarly enthusiastic and lacking in analysis. However, the essay on Browning is a solid piece of criticism. At a time when Elizabeth Barrett was considered the better poet of the two Brownings, Thomson finds Robert Browning worth attention. Robert Browning's poetry abounds in the richest materials of poetry: "profound and original thought, keen perceptions, knowledge both broad and deep, clear moral insight, wonderful dramatic ability, and passion of the true white heat." Those who would charge Browning with obscurity, Thomson remarks curtly, "have never *studied* him." For Thomson, Browning possesses a "bold, vigorous, healthy spirit," much like the "spirit of Chaucer and the great Elizabethan dramatists." Thomson concludes his review by declaring that "Tennyson is a rare 'literary luxury' for us all . . . but Robert Browning is indeed the poet of Men and Women."

Thomson was not quite twenty-eight years old when he was discharged from the army. Suddenly thrown upon his own means, he immediately went to London where Charles Bradlaugh, who had not seen him since they were both stationed at Ballincollig, welcomed him into his home. Thomson lived with Bradlaugh, his wife, and their two small daughters for four years. After years of living alone or in an institution, Thomson found the joys of family life pleasant.

Thomson joined the staff of Bradlaugh's *National Reformer,* the official publication of the Secular Society, but his relationship with the journal was never clear. His position cannot have been full-time because Bradlaugh obtained other positions for Thomson, such as secretary to the Polish Committee, a group organized to aid Poland's revolt against Russia. He also worked briefly in a solicitor's office and held other short-term, minor positions. Although the *National Reformer* paid Thomson, this income was not adequate and he was forced to seek supplementary funds.

The employment offered by Bradlaugh through the *National Reformer* helped Thomson in his time of need, but his association with the journal and the fact that almost all of his writing was published there were detrimental to Thomson's hopes of achieving success as a serious writer. The *National Reformer* was atheist and politically radical. Working for the *National Reformer* was to be associated with Bradlaugh and identified as one of his kind. And Bradlaugh was not the kind of man to endear himself to the British upper classes.

There were advantages to working for this type of publication. At least Thomson had a regular outlet for his writing, and just about anything he wrote appeared in the journal. He was free to choose his own subjects, even if he did not receive an objective hearing from critics or the public.

From 1862 to 1866, Thomson had more prose than poetry published, which is understandable considering the publication he was writing for. As Thomson himself said in an 1874 letter to William Michael Rossetti, "Of course the great bulk of the readers are poorly educated, and care little or nothing for poetry or any other art; care, in fact, nothing for literature, but only as a club to hit persons and lords on the head with." The intellectual level of the *National Reformer* was not as low as Thomson suggests. Although the journal was sensationalistic at times, it did present serious discussion on current, and sometimes controversial, topics. Thomson's essays during this time reflect his wide-ranging interests and include a piece on "The Athanasian Creed," one of religious satire, "The Story of a Famous Old Jewish Firm" (published in pamphlet form in 1876), and an essay on his theory of literature and the poet, "Per Contra: The Poet, High Art, Genius." This last essay signals a shift in Thomson's theory of poetic composition. In "Per Contra: The Poet, High Art, Genius" Thomson explains that poetry is a craft and not the product of a spontaneous and irresistible moment of inspiration visited upon the poet. The poet must carefully construct and refine a poem. At the same time, William Blake and Heinrich Heine, not Alexander Pope and John Dryden, became his new heroes, despite his conviction that poetry was a craft. Thomson was beginning to shed his Shelleyan view of poetry and start his journey to realism.

Thomson's poetry of this period is undistinguished. The *National Reformer* published Thomson's "Vane's Story," a long, serious poem dealing with his view of man and religion. His poem "Sunday up the River" was accepted for publication in *Fraser's Magazine.*

"Vane's Story" has many faults, especially its structural weaknesses. It is a long, episodic piece which has no sense of unity. However, the poem marks Thomson's shift from idealism to more pragmatic concerns:

> God exists, or not indeed,
> Quite irrespective of our creed;
> We live, or live not, after death,
> Alike whatever be our faith;
> And not a single truth, in brief,
> Is modified by our belief.

Thomson would approach life as a realist, seeing things as they really are. "Sunday up the River" is an impersonal and objective account of what Thomson saw, not of what he felt or thought.

In October 1866 Thomson moved out of the Bradlaugh home and took up lodgings by himself in London. During his stay with the Bradlaughs his alcoholism had grown steadily worse. For the next few years Thomson lived by himself and moved from one cheap, furnished, cheerless room to another. In December 1867 he wrote the poem "In the Room," which is a depressing picture of his new lodgings. The furniture of a room narrates the story of the unhappy occupant who, it is revealed at the end of the poem, has committed suicide. Thomson achieves a direct, personal effect on the reader by his use of few but provocative details to describe the room. The cupboard complains that it gets no sweets or cakes, only a "pinch of meal, a crust" all week long. The fireplace grumbles that the few dead cinders it holds have been "unburned for days and days." The table says that the lodger "wrote so long/That I grew weary of his weight." No matter, replies the fireplace, since all that he wrote he burned. Ultimately the reader shares Thomson's sense of being so cut off from human contact that only the furniture knows or cares that the occupant of the room is dead. It is the creation of this sense of loneliness that makes "In the Room" one of Thomson's masterpieces. In the late 1860s and early 1870s Thomson frequently visited the Bradlaughs and spent many days in the British Museum reading and writing in an attempt to avoid the loneliness of his room which heightened his sense of melancholy.

Thomson had great hopes for his long, Oriental narrative *Weddah and Om-el-Bonain,* which he completed in 1869. Taking the plot from Stendhal's *De l'Amour* (1822), Thomson expanded and elaborated on the basic material until he had a poem of one thousand lines. During a tribal war in Arabia, Om-el-Bonain marries the chief of another tribe to gain his support for her people. When her lover Weddah returns from the war she hides him in a chest only to have her husband learn that she and Weddah are having an affair and bury the unopened chest. Om-el-Bonain dies soon after on her lover's grave. Although the plot is fully developed with great detail, it moves quickly. However, the poem fails because the characters are so wooden and stiff that it is hard to feel sympathy for them. The poem does contain descriptive passages of real lyrical quality, and it drew favorable comments from William Michael Rossetti when Thomson sent him a copy. Later, when the poem was published in the collection *Vane's Story, Weddah and Om-el-Bonain, and Other Poems* (1880), both George Meredith and A. C. Swinburne praised it. Yet Thomson tried for almost a year to publish the poem in a journal he considered "respectable" and failed. Finally, he gave up and turned once again to the *National Reformer,* where the poem did appear from November 1871 through January 1872. The experience was typical of many in Thomson's life.

The year 1869 was a particularly unhappy one for Thomson. Perhaps loneliness, lack of literary success, or financial insecurity prompted Thomson's particularly deep depression that year, but whatever the cause, the effects are somewhat startling. The entry for Thomson's diary for Sunday, 4 November 1869, reads: "—Burned all my old papers, manuscripts, and letters save the book MSS, which have been already in great part printed. It took me five hours to burn them, guarding against chimney on fire, and keeping them thoroughly burning. I was sad and stupid—scarcely looked into any; had I begun reading them, I might never have finished their destruction. All the letters; those which I had kept for twenty years, those which I had kept for more than sixteen. I felt myself like one who, having climbed halfway up a long rope (35 on the 23rd inst.), cuts off all beneath his feet; he must climb on, and can never touch the old earth again without a fatal fall. The memories treasured in the letters can never, at least in great part, be revived in my life again, nor in the lives of the friends yet living who wrote them. But after this terrible year, I could do no less than consume the past. I can now better face the future, come in what guise it may." Thomson in November of 1869 was a man burning his bridges. What documents he destroyed in the fire we can only guess, but in that fire were consumed Thomson's dreams and many jottings from his apprenticeship as a writer.

Although Thomson attempted to start anew after that "terrible year," 1870 brought no change in his fortunes; indeed, they seemed to worsen. Bradlaugh had given up the editorship of the

National Reformer and turned the journal over to his assistants. Thomson still contributed as regularly as before, but now he felt unsure of a market for his writings. He began to seek other means of work to supplement his income from writing, but by this time his attacks of alcoholism were more and more frequent and his work habits were quite irregular. As a result, no reputable company would employ him, and he was forced to seek jobs with companies of questionable financial stability. Three times in a row the companies he worked for closed their doors without paying his wages. Life became increasingly difficult.

Thomson became a student of the Italian poet and pessimist Giacomo Leopardi and published twelve translations of Leopardi's works in the *National Reformer* during 1867 and 1868. Beginning with the 3 October 1869 issue of the *National Reformer,* Thomson's essay on the poet was published in eleven parts. Thomson's studies of Leopardi are significant in that they confirm his shift from theist to atheist, from optimist to pessimist. In January 1870 Thomson began his major work, "The City of Dreadful Night," working on the poem in bits and pieces and writing eleven of the twenty-one sections over the next two years before his dull life was rather pleasantly interrupted by a trip to America.

In 1872 Thomson was employed as secretary of the Champion Gold and Silver Company, whose main interests were located in Central City, Colorado. Thomson was instructed by the board of directors of the company to go to Central City to investigate the company's mine and act as the company's representative on the scene. Here was an opportunity to escape from the dreadful city and embark upon a stimulating new adventure.

Although his stay in the United States was brief, he enjoyed it immensely and delighted in his new surroundings. The scenery itself was an adventure for a man who for years had known only the dark, grimy streets of London. Never before had he seen anything to compare to the Rocky Mountains, "the big vertebrae of this longish backbone of America" as he referred to them in a letter to William Michael Rossetti. Thomson's recommendation to the directors that the company's speculations in Central City were unsound\ended his sojourn in America. After only seven months he left Central City and returned to London, arriving at the end of January 1873 to find that his luck was as bad as ever.

Thomson's traveling and living expenses had been paid by the company. However, he received only a small part of his salary since the contract was apparently only verbal and not officially authorized by the board of directors. In addition, the company ceased operation, and Thomson found himself once again in London financially destitute and without a job. Nothing had changed; he was exactly in the situation he had been in when he burned his papers some two years before. His trip had altered neither him nor his life, and he fell quickly back into his old pattern of living. He did not even write a poem about his experiences.

Bradlaugh managed to secure another job for Thomson and another chance for him to escape from London. Just six months after his return from America, Thomson took the position of special correspondent for the *New York World,* a job which took him to Spain to report on the Carlist rebellion. Thomson was sent in anticipation of the civil war that was expected to break out momentarily, but, as he soon found out, there was little to report because there was not much of a revolution. Life with the Carlist army proved agreeable. Since there was little fighting, Thomson was able to turn his attention to the beauty of the Spanish countryside and to enjoy the long siestas and elaborate entertainment provided for the troops by the peasants. Then, too, there were pleasant conversations in the evenings with other reporters. Thomson enjoyed the job of war correspondent.

This pleasant carefree life did not last long. Early in September 1873 Thomson suffered sunstroke, and for two weeks he was confined to bed. While recovering, he received a letter of recall from the *World* which was not entirely unexpected since he had sent only three reports to his employers during the month he had been in Spain. Thomson returned to London to experience financial difficulties once again. Because he had failed, in his employer's opinion, to fulfill his obligation, Thomson was paid only a portion of the promised salary. But this time there was an additional problem; the sunstroke he had suffered had weakened his health and the sudden return to the damp autumn of London precipitated an illness that left him in such a condition that he could not read or write for several weeks. Thomson was in a familiar situation: alone, jobless, and penniless in London. The year 1873 ended with Thomson more desperate than ever.

Although 1873 was a typically bad year for Thomson personally, as a poet he completed his finest work, "The City of Dreadful Night." After returning from Spain he set to work on the poem, and despite his illness, he had completed a rough

Page from the manuscript for Thomson's "The City of Dreadful Night" (The Pierpont Morgan Library)

draft by the end of the year. Thomson later told a friend that while he was recovering from the sunstroke in Spain he had worked out a portion of the poem in his mind. The first two months of 1874 were spent polishing and revising the poem for publication. Thomson was again working full-time at the only job he could find, writing for the *National Reformer*. And once again he turned to the *Reformer* as the journal he could find to publish his poetry.

"The City of Dreadful Night" is Thomson's masterpiece, which completes his journey to atheism and pessimism. No longer the Romantic nor even a realist, in this poem Thomson sees life stripped of all hope and illusion:

> I find no hint throughout the Universe
> Of good or ill, of blessing or of curse;
> I find alone Necessity Supreme.

The poem is an expression of Thomson's despair and weariness. It is his clearest statement that the laws of the universe are unconscious of man, supreme over him, and unchangeable:

The world rolls round for ever like a mill;
It grinds out death and life and good and ill;
It has no purpose, heart or mind or will.

Man, therefore, can only await the oblivion of death:

Nay, does it treat him harshly as he saith?
It grinds him some slow years of bitter breath,
Then grinds him back into eternal death.

The nameless narrator of the poem wanders the streets of the lonely city looking for but never finding hope or meaning. The wanderer discovers only that God does not exist, that man's spirit is not immortal, and that necessity alone is the supreme law of nature:

The sense that every struggle brings defeat
Because Fate holds no prize to crown success;
That all the oracles are dumb or cheat
Because they have no secret to express;
That none can pierce the vast black veil uncertain
Because there is no light beyond the curtain;
That all is vanity and nothingness.

The importance of "The City of Dreadful Night" to students of Victorian literature has not been fully appreciated. In an age of doubt, Thomson was the supreme doubter. New scientific discoveries were forcing many Victorian writers to question the importance of man in the universe and coincidentally their own faith. The answers at which they arrived left many of them disillusioned. Matthew Arnold, Alfred, Lord Tennyson, and Arthur Hugh Clough among others gave voice to their doubts in a large body of Victorian literature marked by disappointment, depression, and pessimism. No one, however, expressed the doubt and pessimism so clearly, so pointedly, so unfalteringly as Thomson in "The City of Dreadful Night." It is precisely because "The City of Dreadful Night" is such a clear and complete expression of this pessimism that it is such an important work. With this poem, Thomson joins the long line of writers and philosophers who had faith, lost that faith and with it their hope, and despaired.

The poem appeared in four installments from March and May of 1874; the length of each division was not determined by any logical division of the poem but by the need for copy to fill space. Even though it appeared in the *National Reformer*, Thomson's poem attracted some attention, and it is from this point that Thomson's recognition as a poet can be dated. The poem received notices in several

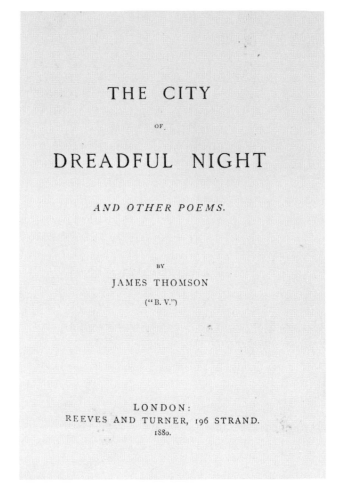

THE CITY

OF

DREADFUL NIGHT

AND OTHER POEMS.

BY

JAMES THOMSON

("B. V.")

LONDON:
REEVES AND TURNER, 196 STRAND.
1880.

Title page for Thomson's first book of poetry (courtesy of Thomas Cooper Library, University of South Carolina). Although the title poem received praise from a number of well-known poets when it was published in the National Reformer *in 1874, it was not until six years later that Bertram Dobell's efforts to interest a book publisher in Thomson's work proved successful.*

journals, none of them dealing with it at length. Yet the notices did prompt further attention and cause a spate of applications at the office of the *National Reformer* for numbers of the journal containing the poem by the unknown B.V. Thomson received praise for his work from William Michael Rossetti, Philip Bourke Marston, George Meredith, and George Eliot. Biographer Henry Salt mentions, without documentation, that Ralph Waldo Emerson and Henry Wadsworth Longfellow expressed desire to read the poem when its fame had reached America a few months later. But the most important person Thomson met through the publication of his poem was Bertram Dobell, who proposed that Thomson's poems be collected for publication in book form. Although Dobell's efforts to find a publisher were not successful until 1880, Thomson was cheered to discover someone who appreciated his poetry so much.

The physical decline which had started with Thomson's return from Spain continued. His general health was very poor, his nerves were in a bad state, and he suffered increasingly frequent attacks of insomnia and alcoholism. His only source of income continued to be the writing he did for the *National Reformer,* and this was barely enough to support his meager needs. But then this source of income ceased when for some unknown reason Thomson and Bradlaugh quarreled, and Thomson left the journal in July 1875. Neither Thomson nor Bradlaugh ever revealed the reason for the break. There is some indication that it was Thomson's alcoholism which prompted the argument, but whatever the cause, a close friendship of over twenty years came to a sudden end. So complete was the break, that, except for one or two meetings over business matters, the two men never met or spoke to each other again.

Thomson was desperate for money, and, fortunately he was able to find a regular outlet for his writing a few months later. *Cope's Tobacco Plant* was a monthly magazine published by the Liverpool tobacco firm of the same name. Although intended primarily as a means of advertising their firm and products, it was well written and counted many well-known writers among its contributors. Thomson was himself a keen lover of tobacco, so when he had to write essays in praise of smoking he did so with ease. Most important to Thomson was the steadiness of the income the periodical provided for five years. The rate of pay was liberal and payment was always made promptly. Thomson always spoke of his connection with the monthly with pleasure and gratitude.

In the mid-1870s Thomson turned his attention to writing prose. From 1874 to 1880 he wrote a series of long essays on eight authors for the *National Reformer* and *Cope's Tobacco Plant.* The eight authors he chose to discuss were Walt Whitman, Stendhal, Heinrich Heine, Saint-Amant, Rabelais, Ben Jonson, John Wilson, and James Hogg. While Thomson's pieces are not critical essays, they do reveal his tastes in literature. Of particular note is his vigorous defense of Whitman, a poet whom the literary establishment of the time considered an egomaniac, a charlatan, and a writer of obscenity whose verse lacked any sense of rhyme or meter. Thomson, however, found Whitman a supreme poet who stood beside Shelley.

Thomson was also connected with the *Secular-*

ist, a new journal established by G. W. Foote and G. H. Holyoake. The publication began in January 1876, and over the next year and a half Thomson contributed some seventy-one items, for which he was never paid. In June 1877, the *Secularist* merged with the *Secular Review* and Thomson was dropped from the staff. Thus Thomson continued his fragile existence, living as best he could on what his writing brought him. It was never enough, however, and his financial situation worsened no matter what he did.

Thomson's life had become a grim struggle for survival. His health was declining rapidly and his fits of alcoholism became more frequent and more severe. Financially he was in a worse position than ever, despite his regular contributions to *Cope's.* He continued to seek a publisher for a volume of his poetry, but the search was fruitless, and he sank even further into despondency. The only encouraging aspect of Thomson's life at this point was his acquaintance with some literary figures. In December 1876, he met Mathilde Blind, and through her he met Arthur O'Shaughnessy and Philip Bourke Marston. Although Thomson was a good conversationalist and entertaining in social gatherings, these contacts seem to have come too late to do him any good. Physically and mentally he was worn-out; spiritually he was too despondent and disheartened to become actively involved in life again.

In 1879 Thomson began a regular correspondence with George Meredith. How extensive the correspondence was is not known, but in June 1880 Thomson spent a day with Meredith at Meredith's home in Box Hill, and a year later he was again a guest for a day. But Thomson's acquaintance with Meredith failed to open any new literary doors for him.

In March 1880 Dobell arranged for publication of a volume of Thomson's poetry containing *The City of Dreadful Night and Other Poems.* After five years of searching Dobell had located a publisher willing to take the risk. Here at last was a ray of hope. Thomson believed that if a volume of his own writing were ever published, it would aid him in securing a regular position at a decent salary.

Almost to a man the reviewers condemned "The City of Dreadful Night" when it was published in Thomson's collection. Any praise they had was for the other poems, such as "Sunday at Hampstead," "Sunday up the River," and "In the Room." Thomson was not really surprised by the reaction of the critics since he knew his beliefs were unpopular. Some reviewers did attempt to be fair. George

Saintsbury recognized the merits of the collection's title poem, while George Augustus Simcox headed his article "A New Poet" and presented a careful, balanced review of the book which dealt fairly with the poet and his poetry. But the highest praise came from George Meredith, who wrote to Thomson, calling the volume an "admirable and priceless book of verse . . . of such rarely equalled good work."

In spite of the generally poor reviews the book turned out to be a modest financial success. The publishers asked for another volume, and Thomson immediately set to work gathering material for it. In October 1880 a second volume of Thomson's poetry, *Vane's Story, Weddah and Om-el-Bonain, and Other Poems,* was published. The book did not sell as well as its predecessor, but Thomson immediately prepared a third volume for publication, a collection of his prose. This third book, *Essays and Phantasies,* published in April 1881, was a complete failure.

Nine years after its publication only some three hundred copies had been sold and the rest sat in a warehouse, where most were eventually destroyed in a fire. The entire publishing venture was bittersweet for Thomson. One book could be counted a success, one was a failure, and the other met with a mediocre response. At least Thomson had achieved his primary goal: the publication in book form of some of his writings. But good fortune, in the form of a decent paying position, did not materialize, and Thomson found himself once more trying to subsist on his meager income from writing for *Cope's.* Like the trips to America and Spain, the publishing episode was merely a brief respite in the inevitable decline he saw in his life.

In March 1881 Thomson went to Leicester, where he had been invited to attend the opening of a new Secularist hall. There he met J. W. Barrs and his sister, and the three quickly became friends. In

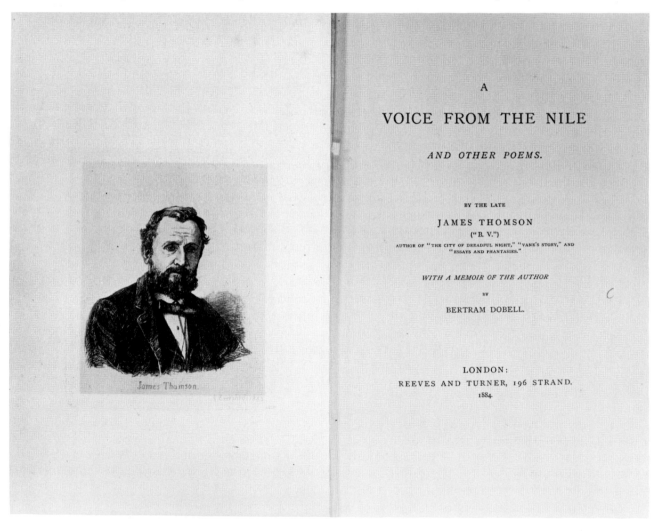

Frontispiece and title page for the posthumously published collection that includes Thomson's "The Doom of a City" (courtesy of Thomas Cooper Library, University of South Carolina)

July he returned to the Barrs' home in the country for a very pleasant five and one-half week stay. In January 1881 *Cope's* had ceased publication, and he was without a steady source of income; but, fortunately, the Barrs repeatedly asked Thomson to stay with them. Visits to the Barrs greatly helped his financial situation.

If his financial situation was precarious at least Thomson was writing, and, more important, he managed to have his essays published in more respectable journals. In the September, October, and November 1881 issues of *Athenaeum* his long essay "Notes on the Structure of Shelley's 'Prometheus Unbound' " appeared. In December 1881, his essay on Browning, "The Ring and the Book," was published in the *Gentlemen's Magazine.* He also completed another essay on Browning, "Notes on the Genius of Robert Browning," which was published in 1882 in the *Browning Society's Transactions.* He became a charter member of the Browning Society and was scheduled to give a paper at the January 1882 meeting. But Thomson still had no reliable source of income to replace the money he stopped receiving when *Cope's* ceased publication.

The Barrs encouraged him to write and attempted to build up his health. They also attempted to cure his alcoholism by keeping all liquor from the house. In April 1882 while visiting the Barrs he managed to slip away from their house and was found some hours later in a local pub quite drunk. The remaining month and a half of Thomson's life was spent in alcoholic binges, minor jail sentences, and at least one brief stay in the alcoholic ward of a hospital. After being thrown out of his London room by his landlord, he returned and attempted to set fire to the building. His physical appearance degenerated; the once well-groomed Thomson now shuffled down the street in worn carpet slippers that exposed his bare feet. His hair and beard were unkempt, and his clothes were dirty and ragged from sleeping in alleys. During this time his friends tried repeatedly to help him, but he refused all aid.

On 1 June Thomson went to Philip Bourke Marston's apartment, and after a scene he collapsed in the bedroom. A short while later William Sharp arrived for an unannounced visit and checked Thomson to discover that he was not sleeping but had suffered a severe hemorrhage. Herbert Clarke, also by chance, arrived and saw Thomson, "a man with a careworn face, a remarkably furrowed forehead, and a leadened complexion; a ghastly figure." The three men attempted to take Thomson to his rooms but the landlord refused them entry. Next they summoned a doctor to Marston's apartment.

Front cover for volume one of the collection edited by Bertram Dobell in 1895, thirteen years after Thomson's death

Upon the doctor's recommendation Thomson was taken immediately to a hospital. The next day, 2 June 1882, Sharp and Marston visited him and found he was conscious and quite confident that he would be out of the hospital in three days. Thomson was right; the following night he died. Recent evidence suggests that Thomson's death, and his behavior during the last weeks of his life, was the result of cancer of the colon, a disease from which he may have suffered as early as 1876. He was buried on 8 June in Highgate New Cemetery with the Secularist Burial Service read by Theodore Wright. Thomson's friends never revealed his final words, for his final comment on life was unprintable.

Thomson's reputation continues to be that of a minor poet with little if any attention paid to his prose. "The City of Dreadful Night" is treated more as a curiosity than as the important work that it is. Thomson is, however, one of the finest examples of a middle-class, self-educated Victorian author whose work gives a portrait of his struggle to come to terms with the new ideas and changing values of his age. It is unfortunate that he is not more often or more seriously studied by literary critics and historians, for he expresses in his works an important aspect of the Victorian era.

Biographies:

Henry S. Salt, *The Life of James Thomson ("B.V.")* (London: Reeves & Turner and Bertram Dobell, 1889; revised, London: Watts, 1914);

Bertram Dobell, *The Laureate of Pessimism* (London: Bertram Dobell, 1910);

James Edward Meeker, *The Life and Poetry of James Thomson (B.V.)* (New Haven: Yale University Press, 1917);

Imogene B. Walker, *James Thomson (B.V.)* (Ithaca: Cornell University Press, 1950);

Charles Vachot, *James Thomson (1834-1882)* (Paris: Didier, 1964).

References:

Kenneth Hugh Byron, *The Pessimism of James Thomson (B.V.) in Relation to His Times* (London, The Hague & Paris: Mouton, 1965);

William David Schaefer, *James Thomson (B.V.): Beyond "The City"* (Berkeley & Los Angeles: University of California Press, 1965).

Papers:

Manuscripts, diaries, and notebooks by James Thomson are at the Pierpont Morgan Library, New York; the Rationalist Press Association Library, London; the Bodleian Library, Oxford University; and the British Library, London.

Augusta Webster
(30 January 1837-5 September 1894)

Florence S. Boos
University of Iowa

BOOKS: *Blanche Lisle, and Other Poems,* as Cecil Home (Cambridge & London: Macmillan, 1860);

Lilian Gray, A Poem, as Cecil Home (London: Smith, 1864);

Lesley's Guardians, as Cecil Home (London: Macmillan, 1864);

Dramatic Studies (London & Cambridge: Macmillan, 1866);

A Woman Sold and Other Poems (London & Cambridge: Macmillan, 1867);

Portraits (London & Cambridge: Macmillan, 1870; enlarged, London & New York: Macmillan, 1893);

The Auspicious Day (London: Macmillan, 1872);

Yu-Pe-Ya's Lute. A Chinese Tale in English Verse (London: Macmillan, 1874);

Disguises; A Drama (London: Kegan Paul, 1879);

A Housewife's Opinions (London: Macmillan, 1879);

A Book of Rhyme (London: Macmillan, 1881);

In a Day; A Drama (London: Kegan Paul, Trench, 1882);

Daffodil and the Croäxaxicans: A Romance of History (London: Macmillan, 1884);

The Sentence; A Drama (London: Unwin, 1887);

Selections from the Verse of Augusta Webster (London: Macmillan, 1893);

Mother and Daughter. An Uncompleted Sonnet-Sequence, edited by William Michael Rossetti (London: Macmillan, 1895).

TRANSLATIONS: *The Prometheus Bound of Aeschylus,* edited by Thomas Webster (London & Cambridge: Macmillan, 1866);

The Medea of Euripides (London & Cambridge, 1868).

The poet Augusta Webster was distinctive for her forcefulness, psychological acuity, and reforming spirit. She evinced the first two in her narrative poetry, lyrics, sonnets, translations, dramatic monologues, novel, and plays and the last in her suffragism and work for the London School Board. Her literary work was well reviewed, and its sub-

Augusta Webster

sequent neglect has been unwarranted. She wrote several effective women's monologues (including "A Castaway," spoken by a prostitute) and created some complex and believable dramatic heroines.

Webster's forms and mannerisms were pioneered in works by others—Robert Browning's monologues, Elizabeth Barrett Browning's sarcastic declamations, and Alfred Tennyson's lyric interludes. Though derivative in form, her poetry often uses such patterns with great skill, and her plays at their best balance mild reformism with romance.

Webster was born Julia Augusta Davies in 1837. Her maternal grandfather was Joseph Hume (1767-1843), a close friend of Charles Lamb, William Hazlitt, and William Godwin; his daughter, Webster's mother, Julia Hume (1803-1897), married the naval officer George Davies (1806-1876). Webster's childhood was spent on the ship *Griper,* in various harbors in southern England (1837-1843), at Banff Castle in northern Scotland (1843-1848), at Penzance in Cornwall (1849-1851), and after 1851, in Cambridge, where her father was chief constable of Cambridgeshire. She attended classes at the Cambridge School of Art, studied Greek to help a younger brother, learned Italian and Spanish, and became fluent in French in Paris and Geneva. In

December 1863 she married Thomas Webster, a fellow and later law lecturer at Trinity College; the couple had one daughter and moved to London in 1870, where Thomas Webster practiced law.

Augusta Webster's earliest works include an article for *Macmillan's,* two volumes of poetry, and a three-volume novel, all published between 1860 and 1864 under the pseudonym Cecil Home. The article, "The Brissons" (*Macmillan's,* November 1861), recounts with great feeling the 1851 rescue of the survivors of a shipwreck off the coast of Cornwall; the two volumes of poetry, *Blanche Lisle, and Other Poems* (1860) and *Lilian Gray* (1864), rework the theme of a woman betrayed by her suitor. Both volumes show the influence of Tennyson's *Poems* (1842) and Elizabeth Barrett Browning's *Aurora Leigh* (1857), but the first volume contains some lively refrain ballads ("Cruel Agnes," "The Bitter Knight," "Edith"), and the verse narrative *Lilian Gray* is more carefully structured than its predecessor, *Blanche Lisle.* The novel *Lesley's Guardians* (1864) embeds the fickle-lover motif in a plot with some unconventional touches. The heroine endures a period of genteel poverty as a student-artist in France, and her visits to her British guardians and relatives provide the occasion for some sharp reflections on the socially enforced waste of women's time. Her eventual marital fortunes are contrasted with those of a wealthy but homely French romantic rival, Stephanie, and a more self-consciously independent English friend, Marion, and the author maintains some balance of sympathy for all three. On the title page of the copy of *Lesley's Guardians* which she gave to her fellow poet Jean Ingelow, Webster wrote, "One of my early failures." With the partial exception of a long fairy-tale romance for children, *Daffodil and the Croäxaxicans: A Romance of History* (1884), she never returned to the novel form. This seems unfortunate, for Webster's genuine gift for description of women's reflections and social relationships never found full expression in her essays or dramas.

In 1866 she began to publish under her own name—a translation of Aeschylus's *Prometheus Bound,* and, when this was well reviewed, of Euripides' *Medea* in 1868. In 1866 at age twenty-nine, she also produced *Dramatic Studies*, eight dramatic monologues of remorse, renunciation, and compromise; three are spoken by women. Webster's debt to Robert Browning in *Dramatic Studies* is most apparent in the first two monologues, "A Preacher" and "A Painter." In the first, a Victorian preacher contrasts his lack of religious intensity with the powerful emotions he can evoke in his hearers and reflects on the inconsistency of his private tolerance for the foibles he denounces from the pulpit. Unlike most of Browning's casuists, however, the preacher is fundamentally decent, self-aware, and troubled by his imperfections. In "A Painter," the Victorian protagonist regrets that the financial constraints of marriage have hindered his best work (compare Browning's "Andrea del Sarto"), but loves his wife Ruth, who—unlike Andrea's Lucrezia—tries to encourage his art. "The Snow Waste" was the poem most admired by contemporary reviewers and the sole poem from this volume chosen by Webster for inclusion in her 1893 *Selections.* Like a condemned sinner in Dante's *Inferno,* the poem's speaker, trapped in snow, recounts his jealousy and macabre murder of his wife and brother-in-law.

Two of the women in *Dramatic Studies,* Jeanne d'Arc and Sister Annunciata, are spiritual, self-sacrificing heroines who suffer much irresolution and inner turmoil. Jeanne d'Arc, in prison, is alternately frightened and enraptured by memories of her angelic visitations, and Sister Annunciata celebrates the anniversary of her entrance into the convent, but her attempts to pray yield to poignant memories of her lover. In the second part of "Sister Annunciata," the Abbess Ursula praises the now-dead Annunciata, whose tranquil death has followed spiritual visions. But Ursula's simplistic comments on Annunciata's struggle only widen the incongruous distance between inner experiences and their outer interpretations.

Reviewers praised *Dramatic Studies.* The *Saturday Review* for 9 February 1867 declared it "marked by many signs of remarkable power," and the *Westminster Review* for October 1866 remarked that "Mrs. Webster shows not only originality, but what is nearly as rare, trained intellect and self-command."

Webster's next work, *A Woman Sold and Other Poems,* was published in 1867. It is considerably longer than *Dramatic Studies* (288 pages to *Dramatic Studies'* 165) and shows more variety in poem length, tone, viewpoint, and stanzaic form. The volume's five long narrative poems and forty-two lyrics again recall Tennyson's *Poems* (1842) as well as Elizabeth Barrett Browning's *Poems* (1844) and Robert Browning's *Dramatic Romances & Lyrics* (1845); there are lesser debts to Christina Rossetti and perhaps to William Morris. The volume's final long narrative, eighty-nine pages of blank verse entitled "Lota," evokes themes and devices of Elizabeth Barrett Browning's *Aurora Leigh.* Some of

"Lota" 's reminiscences, social descriptions, and intermittent pathos reflect Webster's genuine talent for third-person narrative.

The volume's forty-two shorter lyrics exhibit a variety of verse patterns, situations, and emotions; Webster's ballads, short narrative lyrics, and dialogue poems—for example, "The River," "Two Maidens," "The Heiress' Wooer," and "The Hidden Wound"—are the most successful. Her Tennysonian poems tend toward greater optimism, as in the close of "Shadow":

> Dark, dark, as when dull autumn yields his breath;
>   Strange days when will ye change and let me see
> A little sunshine ere I pass in death?
> . . . .
> Oh! dark all night—but, if the morning come,
>   I shall awaken, in whichever world,
> With opening eyes, and know myself at home.

The *Saturday Review* complimented Webster's "admirably subtle analytic power" in *A Woman Sold,* and the *Leader* commented on her "masculine" set of mind.

Webster's next poetic work, *Portraits,* a volume of thirteen dramatic monologues, appeared in 1870, the same year as the first trade edition of Dante Gabriel Rossetti's *Poems.* Two editions were published in February and August and a third, with an additional poem, in 1893. One of the best of the five monologues spoken by women is "Medea in Athens," Webster's partial defense of Euripides' heroine. Medea fantasizes about Jason's image of her as he dies:

> She tossed her head back, while her brown hair
>   streamed
> Gold in the wind and sun, and her face glowed
> With daring beauty; "What of woes," she cried,
> "If only they leave time for love enough?"

One of the monologues by women in *Portraits* is the striking sketch of a prostitute, "A Castaway." Webster's poem is less conventional and censorious than Rossetti's "Jenny," included in *Poems:* her middle-class heroine, who has had to sacrifice her education for that of her brother, compares her behavior with the respectable hypocrisies of her clients and criticizes the double standards of kept married women who look down on her. She admits, however, that she does not respect the role she is paid to play.

Webster's cautious feminism also emerges in two of the other monologues. In "Faded," an aging, unmarried woman reflects on the social conditions which limit "respectable" women to roles of passivity and negation, and a male Victorian intellectual in "Tired" examines the limitations of his "unconventional" marriage to a lower-class woman, who has eagerly embraced the dreariest conventions of middle-class matronhood. The *English Independent* praised the author of *Portraits* as "a daring genius" whose work was distinguished for its "air of reality and . . . deep sense of seriousness," and the April 1870 *Westminster Review* remarked, "if she only remains true to herself she will most assuredly take a higher rank as a poet than any woman has yet done." Unfortunately, Webster wrote very little poetry after 1870.

In 1872, she published her first play, *The Auspicious Day,* a complex melodrama whose principal themes are the evils of superstition and the need for constancy in love. Many individual scenes are excellent, but the final marriage between discredited lovers seems arbitary and inconclusive.

Her next work, *Yu-Pe-Ya's Lute* (1874), based on a French version of a Chinese tale, hovers somewhere between translation and original poem. Its combination of pathos and exotic elements creates a delicate and moving allegory. A prince, Yu-Pe-Ya, plays his lute in a forest and is amazed to find a peasant, Tse-Ky, who understands his music. After testing Tse-Ky's musical ability, the prince confesses deep loneliness and pledges Tse-Ky to eternal friendship. When the latter insists he must return to support his aged parents, the prince gives him two gold ingots, and the two promise to meet in the forest a year hence. A year later the woods are empty, and the prince learns that Tse-Ky bought books with the gift but died from exhaustion of work and study. The prince adopts Tse-Ky's father as his own, plays a final elegy to his friend, and shatters the lute over the grave. The tale's egalitarian message tempers its pervasive sense of death and loss, and its lyrical descriptions and songs are effective. A good Victorian poet, the lute is deeply troubled by beauty's transience:

> "And the sweet pain
> Of present ecstasy, knowing it must wane,
> Thrilled in my heart; and then the long regret
> Of one who going ere nightfall gazes yet
> On home or mother or the friend he had.
> Delight was all, and all delight was sad."

In 1879, Webster produced *A Housewife's Opinions,* a collection of essays which had originally appeared in the *London Examiner*. The title is pre-sumably mock deprecation, for Webster's topics range widely. The early essays are undercut by forced jocularity, but the later style improves in force. In "Vocations and Avocations" she criticizes the elaborate social role imposed on the upper-middle-class Victorian woman: "So that, on the whole, if she has at all the central business in life which can be called a vocation, it is to let her acquaintances make tatters of her time and to make tatters of theirs in return."

In 1879 Webster also produced her second drama. *Disguises* is a romantic comedy whose disguised identities in a rural setting vaguely suggest the pastoral world of *As You Like It* or *A Winter's Tale*. The play's protagonists embody two contrasting value systems: on the one hand, love of dominance and court intrigue, and on the other, respect for honesty, political freedom, and simplicity of life. Reviewers found *Disguises* a major work: "Mrs. Webster," wrote the critic for the *Scotsman,* "has produced an original drama which is by far the most important contribution made to this department of English literature in recent years."

Webster turned her attention to municipal politics in the 1870s and in 1879 was elected a member of the London School Board from Chelsea by a margin of 4,000 votes. In a summary of Webster's life for the *Dictionary of National Biography,* Elizabeth Lee describes her advocacy of state-supported and improved education for the poor: "She threw herself heart and soul into the work. Mrs. Webster was a working member of the board. She was anxious to popularize education . . . and she anticipated the demand that, as education is a national necessity, it should also be a national charge. . . . Her leanings were frankly democratic. . . ." In the early 1880s her health forced trips to Italy, and she did not seek reelection in 1882, but she ran again successfully in 1885.

Webster's 1881 *A Book of Rhyme* contains a graceful seasonal sequence of thirty poems which she called "English stornelli" (Theodore Watts-Dunton believed the proper term for the eight-line stanza form she used was *risputti*) and sixty other lyrics, most of them brief. The *stornelli/risputti* have something of the effect of a sonnet sequence but lack the conclusive force of the sonnet form's sestets. As usual, the *Westminster Review* was enthusiastic: "The *Stornelli* are a series of wonderful picture verses, *huitains,* containing each a little study, carved like a gem by a skillful master-hand."

Webster's 1882 tragedy *In a Day* was the only one of her plays to be produced, at Terry Theatre in London in 1890; according to Elizabeth Lee, the

Websters' daughter played the heroine. The play offers a version of the classic stoic dilemma of the sage on the rack. Myron, unjustly accused of treason, refuses to permit his two slaves, Klydone, his betrothed, and Olymnios, his former teacher, to give testimony on his behalf under torture. When they volunteer without his knowledge, Olymnios holds fast but Klydone breaks, and all three then commit suicide. Unfortunately, *In a Day*'s good set pieces are too static to sustain strong dramatic interest.

Perhaps Webster's best play was *The Sentence* (1887), a domestic tragedy based on incidents recorded by the Roman biographer and historian Suetonius. The play's evil characters are plausibly complex and show enough attractive qualities to maintain irony and suspense. *The Sentence*'s baroque intrigues and unexpected complications eventuate in a certain ironic justice, as one utterly corrupt character (Caligula) outmaneuvers two others (Stellio and Aeonia).

The Sentence was very favorably reviewed and strongly admired by Christina and William Michael Rossetti. The latter praised the play as "the one supreme thing amid the work of *all* British poetesses . . . one of the masterpieces of European drama."

Only one more book by Webster was published in her lifetime, an 1893 volume of *Selections,* which included nine miscellaneous poems that had earlier appeared in magazines. At her death in September 1894, she left behind a few short lyrics and an uncompleted sonnet sequence on her daughter. William Michael Rossetti included these in the posthumously published *Mother and Daughter* (1895) and remarked that the sonnets formed the first poetic sequence on the title's subject. In fact, they represent one of the few sustained sequences about parental love of any kind. In them Webster transfers several familiar conventions of romantic love to the maternal—for example, its exclusivity:

> You know not. You love yours with various stress;
> This with a graver trust, this with more pride;

> This maybe with more needed tenderness:
> I by each uttermost passion of my soul
> Am turned to mine; she is one, she has the whole:
> How should you know who appraise love and
> divide?

After Webster's death critical enthusiasm for her work waned. She seems to have lacked the network of literary connections which helped other poets—Coventry Patmore, Thomas Woolner, William Allingham, Arthur O'Shaughnessy, or Edmund Gosse—find their places in standard literary histories. Much of her work was in little-read genres—the lyric fable, the long verse narrative, and the closet drama. She shifted genres too frequently and her best mode of expression—the dramatic monologue—was almost completely associated with Robert Browning. Apart from a few reviews, after her death only William Michael Rossetti, Theodore Watts-Dunton, Elizabeth Lee (who wrote the two-page memoir for the *Dictionary of National Biography*), and Mackenzie Bell (author of an appreciative introductory essay to Webster's verse for volume seven of A. H. Miles's *Poets and Poetry of the Century*) wrote significant responses to her work.

This neglect is unjust. Webster filled a significant gap between the work of Elizabeth Barrett Browning's and Christina Rossetti's maturity and the early poems of Alice Meynell. She had a sharp sense of humor and was skilled at portraying themes of revenge, romantic love, and religious self-renunciation. More interesting, she provided a realistic, sympathetic, and analytic view of the experience of middle-class women in several of her works. One would not speak of a Websterian style of poetry, but one might speak of a Websterian view of female character and achievement. Her best dramatic monologues and plays, the poetic tale *Yu-Pe-Ya's Lute,* and several of her ballads, essays, and lyrics can still be read with the respect once accorded them by the *Westminster Review.*

Thomas Woolner
(17 December 1825-7 October 1892)

Craig Turner
Texas A & M University

BOOKS: *My Beautiful Lady* (London: Macmillan, 1863);
Pygmalion (London: Macmillan, 1881);
Silenus (London: Macmillan, 1884);
Tiresias (London: Bell, 1886);
Poems: Nelly Dale. Children (London: Bell, 1887).

Thomas Woolner, R.A., remains most noteworthy as one of the seven founding members of the Pre-Raphaelite Brotherhood in 1848. In his own lifetime he was far better known as a sculptor than as a poet, but in the true Pre-Raphaelite spirit he sought to be the universal artist in pursuing both the visual and the verbal arts.

Thomas Woolner, son of Thomas and Rebecca Leeks Woolner, was born at Hadleigh in Suffolk. His early life was notable for his great love and close observation of nature and for his fastidiousness as a promising scholar—two traits that would characterize his artistic career in later life. His education began near Ipswich and was continued after age ten at boarding school in Brixton until the family moved to London. Though his father was not sympathetic to his son's artistic ambitions, Woolner's stepmother paid for him to begin studying painting with Henry Behnes at age thirteen. After his teacher's sudden death, young Woolner was allowed to further develop his artistic talents under the guidance of the painter's brother, the sculptor William Behnes. A great favorite of the master's, Woolner continued to carve for Behnes until he entered the Royal Academy Schools on Behnes's advice and encouragement the day before his seventeenth birthday. The following year, 1843, his model group entitled *Eleanor sucking the poison from Prince Edward's wound* was exhibited at the Royal Academy, and in 1844 his ambitious life-sized group *Death of Boadicea* was exhibited in Westminster Hall and favorably mentioned in the *Athenaeum*. The Society of Arts awarded Woolner its silver medal for his original-design bas-relief entitled *Affection* in 1845 when he was but twenty years of age.

While he continued modeling, exhibiting, and studying at the Academy, Woolner struck up an acquaintance with a dynamic young personality

Thomas Woolner (National Portrait Gallery)

from the Royal Academy Antique School, Dante Gabriel Rossetti. Rossetti had already conceived the idea of a secret artistic coterie with two other Academy students from the Life School, William Holman Hunt and the precocious John Everett Millais; these three invited James Collinson, William Michael Rossetti, Frederic George Stephens, and Woolner to join them in forming the Pre-Raphaelite Brotherhood in August of 1848. The P.R.B.—as they preferred to refer to their clandestine revolutionary organization—dedicated themselves to promoting artistic principles in contrast with those of the conventional art of the day. Woolner's Stanhope Street studio soon became a favorite place for the members of the Brotherhood to smoke, drink tea, and discuss topics such as Robert Browning's poetry and John Ruskin's theories of art.

Chief among Dante Gabriel Rossetti's early ambitions was the establishment of a monthly magazine in which to publish the writings and etchings of the P.R.B. On 14 July 1849 they met at Woolner's to discuss and to decide on the fate of the contemplated journal: Rossetti prevailed over the objections of most of the Brotherhood regarding the high cost of such a project, and *Monthly Thoughts in Literature and Art* — a title which was to evolve into the *Germ* before its publication — was officially initiated. While William Michael Rossetti was chosen as editor of the projected publication by his brother and Woolner, the Brotherhood's only sculptor played an important role in the *Germ*'s short life. For example, it was Woolner who proposed that all contributions to the magazine be published anonymously, and it was Woolner who introduced to the P.R.B. the aspiring young poet Coventry Patmore, a contributor to the first three issues of the *Germ*. On 1 January 1850 when the first issue appeared, Woolner's two poems "My Beautiful Lady" and "Of My Lady in Death" were the first and second items in the journal and the longest poems in the number; these two poems were also the subjects of William Holman Hunt's cover etchings for the initial issue. Woolner's short lyric "O When and Where" appeared in the second *Germ,* while his longer "Emblems" was included in the third issue.

In reference to "My Beautiful Lady" and "Of My Lady in Death," William Michael Rossetti, the P.R.B.'s secretary and journal keeper, recorded that Coventry Patmore "praised Woolner's poems immensely, saying however that they were sometimes slightly over-passionate and 'sculpturesque' in character." Both poems are self-consciously unpoetical in diction, though they are equally self-conscious in their reliance on catalogues of metaphors and similes to propagate the pathetic fallacy. At their worst, the simplicity of these poems today seems awkward and forced as in these lines from "My Beautiful Lady":

> This is why I thought weeds were
>   beautiful;—
> Because one day I saw my lady pull
>   Some weeds up near a little brook,

>   Which home most carefully she took,
>   Then shut them in a book.

At their best, however, they are naively ornamental, even charming:

> My lady's voice, altho' so very mild,
> Maketh me feel as strong wine would a child;
>   My lady's touch, however slight,
>   Moves all my senses with its might,
>   Like to a sudden fright.

Poet William Allingham, an early admirer of Pre-Raphaelite verse, was so enamored of Woolner's "My Beautiful Lady" that he memorized the poem when it first appeared in the *Germ*. "Emblems" is a more labored attempt to adhere to the advertisement in the second and subsequent issues which explains that the critical posture of the *Germ* is "to encourage and enforce an entire adherence to the simplicity of nature":

> The sun seemed like my sense of life,
>   Now weak, that was so strong;
> The fountain—that continual pulse
>   Which throbbed with human song:
> The bird lay dead as that wild hope
>   Which nerved my thoughts when young.
> These symbols had a tongue.

From 1849 to 1851 Woolner supported himself by modeling portrait medallions as he continued to sculpt with little success. His inability to sell the statues exhibited or to receive commissions to pursue new ones led him in 1852 to strike out with two friends for the Australian gold fields in quest of his fortune. The event of their sailing inspired his friend Ford Madox Brown's picture *The Last of England*. In Australia Woolner found a harsh climate, much hard work, and very little gold. Thus, after several months of prospecting with little reward, he again turned to modeling medallion likenesses in Melbourne and later in Sydney. In 1854 Woolner left for England in hopes of receiving the commission for a proposed statue of Australian Statesman William Charles Wentworth which was to be awarded in London. He did not receive the commission — it was never awarded and the money was used for a scholarship in Australia — but Woolner seems to have by this time found a niche for himself: his portrait medallions of literary acquaintances such as Alfred, Lord Tennyson, Thomas Carlyle, and Coventry Patmore had come

Woolner's portrait medallion of Thomas Carlyle

to be quite popular and had won for him a growing reputation. For the remainder of his life Woolner pursued an increasingly successful career as a popular sculptor in England and Australia, and he became friend or acquaintance to many leading Englishmen of the period.

In 1848 he had begun to develop a long, constant relationship with the Tennysons which was to prove especially important. Woolner, for instance, furnished Tennyson with basic stories for two of his 1864 poems. Woolner was particularly proud of the sea story which he had heard just prior to leaving Australia and which the poet laureate turned into "Enoch Arden," but he also provided Tennyson with the sermon story which became "Alymer's Field." Tennyson in turn was to influence greatly Woolner's own poetic style and choice of subject matter.

An event of more importance to Woolner than the publication of Tennyson's poems was the sculptor's marriage in 1864 to Alice Gertrude Waugh, younger sister of Fanny, the first wife of William Holman Hunt. The Woolners had two sons and four daughters and a seemingly successful marriage.

In 1863 Woolner had published a volume entitled *My Beautiful Lady* which, three years later, went into a third edition. It included both "Lady" poems from the *Germ* as well as a dozen other pieces in the same vein. His next volume, *Pygmalion,* was not published until 1881. It marks a departure from Woolner's earlier P.R.B. verse and reveals the influence of his long relationship with Tennyson. The theme—typical of the poetry of Woolner's later period—is classical and is developed in blank verse. In a letter to William Gladstone, Woolner explains the choice of Pygmalion as his subject by noting that the story "has not been understood as an artist understands it, and I hope I have succeeded in making the story intelligible." The main faults of Woolner's poem are that, first, as with his own sculpture, the characters never come to life, as the opening line of "Of My Lady in Death" intimates, "All seems a painted show." Second, as with much of his statuary, Woolner seeks to accomplish too much.

Pygmalion is a sculptor of great genius who models the Olympian gods in all their greatness; he extracts from Athena the promise of life for his statue of Hebe and falls in love and marries Ianthe, the model for Hebe. Having lost the favor of his

*Top: drawing of Woolner in 1852 by Dante Gabriel Rossetti;
bottom: caricature by Rossetti, 1850, now at the City Museum
and Art Gallery, Birmingham*

neighbors because of malicious false rumors, Pygmalion defeats three treacherous villains who have spread the rumors and who ambush him, thus winning back the good will of the people. He uses his dead father's battle plan to defeat the invading Egyptians and—finally—he becomes King of Cyprus and presumably lives happily ever after.

Woolner retains for Pygmalion and for his other mythological poems of the 1880s, *Silenus* (1884) and *Tiresias* (1886), his earlier penchant for simple, sometimes awkward syntax and diction and heavy reliance on nature imagery:

> Look not so dolorous, Pygmalion.
> The loves of maidens are like scents of
>   flowers,
> In giving forth their sweetness each
>   complete.
> If the tall lily scorn to gathered be,
> The drooping jessamine perchance may
>   shower
> Her stars upon me bright and odorous.

Indeed, Aglaia's assessment of the statue Hebe in *Pygmalion* might well describe all three of Woolner's classical poems of the 1880s:

> The features wanted rarer loveliness;
> An easier grace to sway throughout the form;
> A closer fineness in the lengths and joints.

Woolner's last book, *Poems* (1887), includes *Nelly Dale,* a pastoral subject treated in ballad style, and *Children,* a piece composed on the text of William Wordsworth's "Heaven lies about us in our Infancy." Cardinal John Henry Newman's remarkably frank comments regarding *Silenus* in an 1884 letter to Woolner seem typical of readers of the sculptor's poetry: "In some respects I am little fitted to be your critic: for (tho' I am not sure) you seem to me to have some deeper meaning than the smooth and calm tenor of your versification makes necessary, but what this is I cannot determine."

Woolner's last score of years was characterized by great financial success and public recognition for his sculpture. In 1871 he became an associate of the Royal Academy, and in 1874 he was accorded full membership. He was appointed professor of sculpture in 1877 but resigned in 1879 having never lectured. He was appointed or selected for membership in clubs and societies throughout the 1860s and the 1870s, and many of the wealthy or famous in England during the period became subjects for his medallions, busts, or statues. He continued to work and was busy casting a bronze statue titled *The Housemaid* in the final months of his life. He underwent an operation in the fall of 1892 and was thought to be recuperating when he died of a heart seizure on 7 October of that year.

Woolner will continue to occupy a noteworthy place in English literary history as a charter member of the Pre-Raphaelite Brotherhood and as friend to such writers as Tennyson, Carlyle, Patmore, and Allingham. He will also be remembered as a sculptor of some talent. But as a poet Woolner himself recognized and confessed his deficiencies to William Bell Scott: "poetry is not my proper work in this world . . . I must sculpture it, not write it."

Bibliography:

William E. Fredeman, "Thomas Woolner," in his *Pre-Raphaelitism: A Biocritical Study* (Cambridge: Harvard University Press, 1965), pp. 149-150.

Biographies:

Amy Woolner, *Thomas Woolner, R.A., Sculptor and Poet: His Life in Letters* (London: Chapman & Hall, 1917);

Timothy Hilton, *The Pre-Raphaelites* (New York: Abrams, 1970), p. 32.

References:

William Michael Rossetti, *The P.R.B. Journal,* edited by William E. Fredeman (London: Oxford University Press, 1975);

Rossetti, ed., *Pre-Raphaelite Diaries and Letters* (London: Hurst & Blackett, 1900);

William Bell Scott, *Autobiographical Notes of the Life of William Bell Scott and Notices of His Artistic and Poetic Circle of Friends, 1830-1882,* edited by William Minto, volume 1 (London: Osgood, 1892), p. 271;

Lionel Stevenson, *The Pre-Raphaelite Poets* (Chapel Hill: University of North Carolina Press, 1972).

Appendix I

Victorian Poetry: Five Critical Views

Editors' Note

The essays included in this appendix deal with three topics: the conflict between aesthetic and moral art, the place of poetry in the age of the novel, and the debate over the social versus formal qualities of poetry. Although no single methodology characterizes the five essays, published from 1868 to 1882, they all recognize the need for the artistic integrity of poetry and echo the belief in what Matthew Arnold in "The Study of Poetry" announces as the new power of verse: "more and more," he explains, "mankind will discover that we have to turn to poetry to interpret life for us, to console us, to sustain us." The poets and critics who wrote these essays understand the paradox that art can be independent and at the same time a part of society. They all participate in the late-Victorian effort to transform poetry into a form expressing both thought and feeling. In these essays they succeeded in transmitting to their readers something of the energy, pleasure, and stimulation of poetry they experienced themselves.

Aesthetic Poetry

Walter Pater

Pater's essay was originally published as "Poems by William Morris," Westminster Review, *90 (Old Series), 34 (New Series) (October 1868): 300-309. The slightly shortened version reprinted here is from Pater's* Appreciations *(London & New York: Macmillan, 1873), pp. 213-227.*

THE "aesthetic" poetry is neither a mere reproduction of Greek or medieval poetry, nor only an idealisation of modern life and sentiment. The atmosphere on which its effect depends belongs to no simple form of poetry, no actual form of life. Greek poetry, medieval or modern poetry, projects, above the realities of its time, a world in which the forms of things are transfigured. Of that transfigured world this new poetry takes possession, and sublimates beyond it another still fainter and more spectral, which is literally an artificial or "earthly paradise." It is a finer ideal, extracted from what in relation to any actual world is already an ideal. Like some strange second flowering after date, it renews on a more delicate type the poetry of a past age, but must not be confounded with it. The secret of the enjoyment of it is that inversion of home-sickness known to some, that incurable thirst for the sense of escape, which no actual form of life satisfies, no poetry even, if it be merely simple and spontaneous.

The writings of the "romantic school," of which the aesthetic poetry is an afterthought, mark a transition not so much from the pagan to the medieval ideal, as from a lower to a higher degree of passion in literature. The end of the eighteenth century, swept by vast disturbing currents, experienced an excitement of spirit of which one note was a reaction against an outworn classicism severed not more from nature than from the genuine motives of ancient art; and a return to true Hellenism was as much a part of this reaction as the sudden preoccupation with things medieval. The medieval tendency is in Goethe's *Goetz von Berlichingen,* the Hellenic in his *Iphigenie.* At first this medievalism was superficial, or at least external. Adventure, romance in the frankest sense, grotesque individualism—that is one element in medieval poetry, and with it alone Scott and Goethe dealt. Beyond them were the two other elements of the medieval spirit: its mystic religion at its apex in Dante and Saint Louis, and its mystic passion, passing here and there into the great romantic loves of rebellious flesh, of Lancelot and Abelard. That stricter, imaginative medievalism which re-creates the mind of the Middle Age, so that the form, the presentment grows outward from within, came later with Victor Hugo in France, with Heine in Germany.

In the *Defence of Guenevere: and Other Poems,* published by Mr. William Morris now many years ago, the first typical specimen of aesthetic poetry, we have a refinement upon this later, profounder medievalism. The poem which gives its name to the volume is a thing tormented and awry with passion, like the body of Guenevere defending herself from the charge of adultery, and the accent falls in strange, unwonted places with the effect of a great cry. In truth these Arthurian legends, in their origin prior to Christianity, yield all their sweetness only in a Christian atmosphere. What is characteristic in them is the strange suggestion of a deliberate choice between Christ and a rival lover. That religion, monastic religion at any rate, has its sensuous side, a dangerously sensuous side, has been often seen: it is the experience of Rousseau as well as of the Christian mystics. The Christianity of the Middle Age made way among a people whose loss was in the life of the senses partly by its aesthetic beauty, a thing so profoundly felt by the Latin hymn-writers, who for one moral or spiritual sentiment have a hundred sensuous images. And so in those imaginative loves, in their highest expression, the Provençal poetry, it is a rival religion with a new rival *cultus* that we see. Coloured through and through with Christian sentiment, they are rebels against it. The rejection of one worship for another is never lost sight of. The jealousy of that other lover, for whom these words and images and refined ways of sentiment were first devised, is the secret here of a borrowed, perhaps factitious colour and heat. It is the mood of the cloister taking a new direction, and winning so a later space of life it never anticipated.

Hereon, as before in the cloister, so now in the *château,* the reign of reverie set in. The devotion of the cloister knew that mood thoroughly, and had sounded all its stops. For the object of this devotion was absent or veiled, not limited to one supreme plastic form like Zeus at Olympia or Athena in the

Acropolis, but distracted, as in a fever dream, into a thousand symbols and reflections. But then, the Church, that new Sibyl, had a thousand secrets to make the absent near. Into this kingdom of reverie, and with it into a paradise of ambitious refinements, the earthly love enters, and becomes a prolonged somnambulism. Of religion it learns the art of directing towards an unseen object sentiments whose natural direction is towards objects of sense. Hence a love defined by the absence of the beloved, choosing to be without hope, protesting against all lower uses of love, barren, extravagant, antinomian. It is the love which is incompatible with marriage, for the chevalier who never comes, of the serf for the *châtelaine,* of the rose for the nightingale, of Rudel for the Lady of Tripoli. Another element of extravagance came in with the feudal spirit: Provençal love is full of the very forms of vassalage. To be the servant of love, to have offended, to taste the subtle luxury of chastisement, of reconciliation—the religious spirit, too, knows that, and meets just there, as in Rousseau, the delicacies of the earthly love. Here, under this strange complex of conditions, as in some medicated air, exotic flowers of sentiment expand, among people of a remote and unaccustomed beauty, somnambulistic, frail, androgynous, the light almost shining through them. Surely, such loves were too fragile and adventurous to last more than for a moment.

That monastic religion of the Middle Age was, in fact, in many of its bearings, like a beautiful disease or disorder of the senses: and a religion which is a disorder of the senses must always be subject to illusions. Reverie, illusion, delirium: they are the three stages of a fatal descent both in the religion and the loves of the Middle Age. Nowhere has the impression of this delirium been conveyed as by Victor Hugo in *Notre Dame de Paris.* The strangest creations of sleep seem here, by some appalling licence, to cross the limit of the dawn. The English poet too has learned the secret. He has diffused through *King Arthur's Tomb* the maddening white glare of the sun, and tyranny of the moon, not tender and far-off, but close down—the sorcerer's moon, large and feverish. The colouring is intricate and delirious, as of "scarlet lilies." The influence of summer is like a poison in one's blood, with a sudden bewildered sickening of life and all things. In *Galahad: a Mystery,* the frost of Christmas night on the chapel stones acts as a strong narcotic: a sudden shrill ringing pierces through the numbness: a voice proclaims that the Grail has gone forth through the great forest. It is in the *Blue Closet* that this delirium

reaches its height with a singular beauty, reserved perhaps for the enjoyment of the few.

A passion of which the outlets are sealed, begets a tension of nerve, in which the sensible world comes to one with a reinforced brilliancy and relief—all redness is turned into blood, all water into tears. Hence a wild, convulsed sensuousness in the poetry of the Middle Age, in which the things of nature begin to play a strange delirious part. Of the things of nature the medieval mind had a deep sense; but its sense of them was not objective, no real escape to the world without us. The aspects and motions of nature only reinforced its prevailing mood, and were in conspiracy with one's own brain against one. A single sentiment invaded the world: everything was infused with a motive drawn from the soul. The amorous poetry of Provence, making the starling and the swallow its messengers, illustrates the whole attitude of nature in this electric atmosphere, bent as by miracle or magic to the service of human passion.

The most popular and gracious form of Provençal poetry was the *nocturn,* sung by the lover at night at the door or under the window of his mistress. These songs were of different kinds, according to the hour at which they were intended to be sung. Some were to be sung at midnight—songs inviting to sleep, the *serena,* or *serenade;* others at break of day—waking songs, the *aube,* or *aubade.* This waking-song is put sometimes into the mouth of a comrade of the lover, who plays sentinel during the night, to watch for and announce the dawn: sometimes into the mouth of one of the lovers, who are about to separate. A modification of it is familiar to us all in *Romeo and Juliet,* where the lovers debate whether the song they hear is of the nightingale or the lark; the aubade, with the two other great forms of love-poetry then floating in the world, the sonnet and the epithalamium, being here refined, heightened, and inwoven into the structure of the play. Those, in whom what Rousseau calls *les frayeurs nocturnes* are constitutional, know what splendour they give to the things of the morning; and how there comes something of relief from physical pain with the first white film in the sky. The Middle Age knew those terrors in all their forms; and these songs of the morning win hence a strange tenderness and effect. The crown of the English poet's book is one of these appreciations of the dawn:—

"Pray but one prayer for me 'twixt thy closed lips,
    Think but one thought of me up in the stars.

The summer-night waneth, the morning light slips,
    Faint and gray 'twixt the leaves of the aspen,
        betwixt the cloud-bars,
That are patiently waiting there for the dawn:
    Patient and colourless, though Heaven's gold
Waits to float through them along with the sun.
Far out in the meadows, above the young corn,
    The heavy elms wait, and restless and cold
The uneasy wind rises; the roses are dun;
Through the long twilight they pray for the dawn,
Round the lone house in the midst of the corn.
    Speak but one word to me over the corn,
    Over the tender, bow'd locks of the corn."

It is the very soul of the bridegroom which goes forth to the bride: inanimate things are longing with him: all the sweetness of the imaginative loves of the Middle Age, with a superadded spirituality of touch all its own, is in that!

The Defence of Guenevere was published in 1858; *The Life and Death of Jason* in 1867; to be followed by *The Earthly Paradise;* and the change of manner wrought in the interval, entire, almost a revolt, is characteristic of the aesthetic poetry. Here there is no delirium or illusion, no experiences of mere soul while the body and the bodily senses sleep, or wake with convulsed intensity at the prompting of imaginative love; but rather the great primary passions under broad daylight as of the pagan Veronese. This simplification interests us, not merely for the sake of an individual poet—-full of charm as he is—but chiefly because it explains through him a transition which, under many forms, is one law of the life of the human spirit, and of which what we call the Renaissance is only a supreme instance. Just so the monk in his cloister, through the "open vision," open only to the spirit, divined, aspired to, and at last apprehended, a better daylight, but earthly, open only to the senses. Complex and subtle interests, which the mind spins for itself may occupy art and poetry or our own spirits for a time; but sooner or later they come back with a sharp rebound to the simple elementary passions—anger, desire, regret, pity, and fear: and what corresponds to them in the sensuous world—bare, abstract fire, water, air, tears, sleep, silence, and what De Quincey has called the "glory of motion."

This reaction from dreamlight to daylight gives, as always happens, a strange power in dealing with morning and the things of the morning. Not less is this Hellenist of the Middle Age master of dreams, of sleep and the desire of sleep—sleep in which no one walks, restorer of childhood to men—dreams, not like Galahad's or Guenevere's, but full of happy, childish wonder as in the earlier world. It is a world in which the centaur and the ram with the fleece of gold are conceivable. The song sung always claims to be sung for the first time. There are hints at a language common to birds and beasts and men. Everywhere there is an impression of surprise, as of people first waking from the golden age, at fire, snow, wine, the touch of water as one swims, the salt taste of the sea. And this simplicity at first hand is a strange contrast to the sought-out simplicity of Wordsworth. Desire here is towards the body of nature for its own sake, not because a soul is divined through it.

And yet it is one of the charming anachronisms of a poet, who, while he handles an ancient subject, never becomes an antiquarian, but animates his subject by keeping it always close to himself, that betweenwhiles we have a sense of English scenery as from an eye well practised under Wordsworth's influence, as from "the casement half opened on summer-nights," with the song of the brown bird among the willows, the "Noise of bells, such as in moonlit lanes / Rings from the grey team on the market night." Nowhere but in England is there such a "paradise of birds," the fern-owl, the water-hen, the thrush in a hundred sweet variations, the ger-falcon, the kestrel, the starling, the pea-fowl; birds heard from the field by the townsman down in the streets at dawn; doves everywhere, pink-footed, grey-winged, flitting about the temple, troubled by the temple incense, trapped in the snow. The sea-touches are not less sharp and firm, surest of effect in places where river and sea, salt and fresh waves, conflict.

In handling a subject of Greek legend, anything in the way of an actual revival must always be impossible. Such vain antiquarianism is a waste of the poet's power. The composite experience of all the ages is part of each one of us: to deduct from that experience, to obliterate any part of it, to come face to face with the people of a past age, as if the Middle Age, the Renaissance, the eighteenth century had not been, is as impossible as to become a little child, or enter again into the womb and be born. But though it is not possible to repress a single phase of that humanity, which, because we live and move and have our being in the life of humanity, makes us what we are, it is possible to isolate such a phase, to throw it into relief, to be divided against ourselves in zeal for it; as we may hark back to some choice space of our own individual life. We cannot truly conceive the age: we can conceive the element it has contributed to our culture: we can treat the subjects of the age bringing that into relief. Such an attitude towards Greece, aspiring to but never actually reaching its way of conceiving life, is what is possible for art.

The modern poet or artist who treats in this way a classical story comes very near, if not to the Hellenism of Homer, yet to the Hellenism of Chaucer, the Hellenism of the Middle Age, or rather of that exquisite first period of the Renaissance within it. Afterwards the Renaissance takes its side, becomes, perhaps, exaggerated or facile. But the choice life of the human spirit is always under mixed lights, and in mixed situations, when it is not too sure of itself, is still expectant, girt up to leap forward to the promise. Such a situation there was in that earliest return from the overwrought spiritualities of the Middle Age to the earlier, more ancient life of the senses; and for us the most attractive form of classical story is the monk's conception of it, when he escapes from the sombre atmosphere of his cloister to natural light. The fruits of this mood, which, divining more than it understands, infuses into the scenery and figures of Christian history some subtle reminiscence of older gods, or into the story of Cupid and Psyche that passionate stress of spirit which the world owes to Christianity, constitute a peculiar vein of interest in the art of the fifteenth century.

And so, before we leave *Jason* and *The Earthly Paradise,* a word must be said about their medievalisms, delicate inconsistencies, which, coming in a poem of Greek subject, bring into this white dawn thoughts of the delirious night just over and make one's sense of relief deeper. The opening of the fourth book of *Jason* describes the embarkation of the Argonauts: as in a dream, the scene shifts and we go down from Iolchos to the sea through a pageant of the Middle Age in some French or Italian town. The gilded vanes on the spires, the bells ringing in the towers, the trellis of roses at the window, the close planted with apple-trees, the grotesque undercroft with its close-set pillars, change by a single touch the air of these Greek cities and we are at Glastonbury by the tomb of Arthur. The nymph in furred raiment who seduces Hylas is conceived frankly in the spirit of Teutonic romance; her song is of a garden enclosed, such as that with which the old church glass-stainer surrounds the mystic bride of the song of songs. Medea herself has a hundred touches of the medieval sorceress, the sorceress of the Streckelberg or the Blocksberg: her mystic changes are Christabel's. It is precisely this effect, this grace of Hellenism relieved against the sorrow of the Middle Age, which forms the chief motive of *The Earthly Paradise:* with an exquisite dexterity the two threads of sentiment are here interwoven and contrasted. A band of adventurers sets out from Norway, most northerly of northern lands, where the plague is raging—the bell continually ringing as they carry the Sacrament to the sick. Even in Mr. Morris's earliest poems snatches of the sweet French tongue had always come with something of Hellenic blitheness and grace. And now it is below the very coast of France, through the fleet of Edward the Third, among the gaily painted medieval sails, that we pass to a reserved fragment of Greece, which by some divine good fortune lingers on in the western sea into the Middle Age. There the stories of *The Earthly Paradise* are told, Greek story and romantic alternating; and for the crew of the *Rose Garland,* coming across the sins of the earlier world with the sign of the cross, and drinking Rhine-wine in Greece, the two worlds of sentiment are confronted.

One characteristic of the pagan spirit the aesthetic poetry has, which is on its surface—the continual suggestion, pensive or passionate, of the shortness of life. This is contrasted with the bloom of the world, and gives new seduction to it—-the sense of death and the desire of beauty: the desire of beauty quickened by the sense of death. But that complexion of sentiment is at its height in another "aesthetic" poet of whom I have to speak next, Dante Gabriel Rossetti.

Every Man His Own Poet;
or, The Inspired Singer's Recipe Book

W. H. Mallock

Signed "A Newdigate Prizeman," Mallock's "Recipe Book" was originally published in pamphlet form (Oxford: Shrimpton, 1872). The version reprinted here is from the enlarged edition (London: Simkin, Marshall, 1877).

INTRODUCTION

To have attempted in former times a work of this description, would have seemed, we cannot deny, to savour either of presumption or of idiotcy, or more probably of both. And rightly. But we live in times of progress. The mystery of yesterday is the common-place of to-day; the Bible, which was Newton's oracle, is Professor Huxley's jest-book; and students at the University now lose a class for not being familiar with opinions which but twenty years ago they would have been expelled for dreaming of. Everything is moving onward swiftly and satisfactorily; and if, when we have made all faiths fail, we can only contrive to silence the British Association, and so make all knowledge vanish away, there will lack nothing but the presence of a perfect charity to turn the nineteenth century into a complete kingdom of heaven. Amongst changes, then, so great and so hopeful—amongst the discoveries of the rights of women, the infallibility of the Pope, and the physical basis of life, it may well be doubted if the great fathers of ancient song would find, if they could come back to us, anything out of the way or ludicrous in a recipe-book for concocting poetry.

Some, indeed, object that poetry is not progressive. But on what grounds this assertion is based, it is not possible to conjecture. Poetry is as much progressive as anything else in these days of progress. Free-thought itself shews scarcely more strikingly those three great stages which mark advance and movement. For poetry, like Free-thought, was first a work of inspiration, secondly of science, and lastly now of trick. At its first stage it was open to only here and there a genius; at its next to all intelligent men; and at its third to all the human race. Thus, just as there is no boy now, but can throw stones at the windows which Bishop Colenso has broken, so there is scarcely even a young lady but can raise flowers from the seed stolen out of Mr. T*nn*s*n's garden.

And surely, whatever, in this its course of change, poetry may have lost in quality, is more than made up for by what it has gained in quantity. For, in the first place, it is far pleasanter to the tastes of a scientific generation, to understand how to make bad poetry than to wonder at good; and secondly, as the end of poetry is pleasure, that we should make it each for ourselves is the very utmost that we can desire, since it is a fact in which we all agree, that nobody's verses can please a man so much as his own.

OF THE NATURE OF POETRY

Poetry as practised by the latest masters, is the art of expressing what is too foolish, too profane, or too indecent to be expressed in any other way. And thus, just as a consummate cook will prepare a most delicate repast out of the most poor materials, so will the modern poet concoct us a most popular poem from the weakest emotions, and the most tiresome platitudes. The only difference is, that the cook would prefer good materials if he could get them, whilst the modern poet will take the bad from choice. As far, however, as the nature of materials goes, those which the two artists work with are the same—*viz.*, animals, vegetables, and spirits. It was the practice of Shakespeare and other earlier masters to make use of all these together, mixing them in various proportions. But the moderns have found that it is better and far easier to employ each separately. Thus Mr. Sw*nb*rne uses very little else but animal matter in the composition of his dishes, which it must be confessed are somewhat unwholesome in consequence; whilst the late Mr. Wordsworth, on the contrary, confined himself almost exclusively to the confection of primrose pudding, and flint soup, flavoured with the lesser celandine, and only now and then a beggar-boy boiled down in it to give it a colour. The robins and drowned lambs which he was wont to use, when an additional piquancy was needed, were employed so sparingly that they did not destroy in the least the general vegetable tone of his productions; and these form in consequence an unimpeachable Lenten diet. It is difficult to know what to say of Mr. T*nn*s*n, as the milk and water of which his books are composed chiefly, make it almost impossible to discover what was the original nature of the materials he has boiled down in it. Mr. Shelley, too, is perhaps somewhat embarrassing to classify; as, though spirits are what he affected most, he made use of a large amount of vegetable matter also. We shall be probably not far wrong in describing his material as a kind of methyllated spirits, or pure psychic alcohol, strongly tinctured with the barks of trees, and rendered below proof by a quantity of sea-water. In this division of the poets, however, into animalists, spiritualists, and vegetarians, we must not be discouraged by any such difficulties as these; but must bear in mind that in whatever manner we may neatly classify anything, the exceptions and special cases will always far outnumber those to which our rule applies.

But in fact, at present, mere theory may be set entirely aside; for although in case of action, the making and adhering to a theory may be the surest guide to inconsistency and absurdity, in poetry these results can be obtained without such aid.

The following recipes, compiled from a careful analysis of the best authors, will be found, we trust, efficient guides for the composition of genuine poems. But the tyro must bear always in mind that there is no royal road to anything, and that not even the most explicit directions will make a poet all at once of even the most fatuous, the most sentimental, or the most profane.

RECIPES

The following are arranged somewhat in the order in which the student is recommended to begin his efforts. About the more elaborate ones, which come later, he may use his own discretion as to which he will try first; but he must previously have had some training in the simpler compositions, with which we deal before all others. These form as it were a kind of palaestra of folly, a very short training in which will suffice to break down that stiffness and self-respect in the soul, which is so incompatible with modern poetry. Taking, therefore, the silliest and commonest of all kinds of verse, and the one whose sentiments come most readily to hand in vulgar minds, we begin with directions,

HOW TO MAKE AN ORDINARY LOVE POEM

Take two large and tender human hearts, which match one another perfectly. Arrange these close together, but preserve them from actual contact by placing between them some cruel barrier. Wound them both in several places, and insert through the openings thus made a fine stuffing of wild yearnings, hopeless tenderness, and a general admiration for stars. Then completely cover up one heart with a sufficient quantity of chill churchyard mould, which may be garnished according to taste with dank waving weeds or tender violets: and promptly break over it the other heart.

HOW TO MAKE A PATHETIC MARINE POEM

This kind of poem has the advantage of being easily produced, yet being at the same time pleasing, and not unwholesome. As, too, it admits of no variety, the chance of going wrong in it is very small. Take one midnight storm, and one fisherman's family, which, if the poem is to be a real success, should be as large and as hungry as possible, and must contain at least one innocent infant. Place this last in a cradle, with the mother singing over it, being careful that the babe be dreaming of angels, or else smiling sweetly. Stir the father well up in the storm until he disappears. Then get ready immediately a quantity of cruel crawling foam, in which serve up the father directly on his reappearance, which is sure to take place in an hour or two, in the dull red morning. This done, a charming saline effervescence will take place amongst the remainder of the family. Pile up the agony to suit the palate, and the poem will be ready for perusal.

HOW TO MAKE AN EPIC POEM LIKE MR. T*NN*S*N

(The following, apart from its intrinsic utility, forms in itself a great literary curiosity, being the original directions from which the Poet Laureate composed the Arthurian Idylls.)

To compose an epic, some writers instruct us first to catch our hero. As, however, Mr. Carlyle is the only person on record who has ever performed this feat, it will be best for the rest of mankind to be content with the nearest approach to a hero available, namely a prig. These animals are very plentiful, and easy to catch, as they delight in being run after. There are however many different kinds, not all equally fit for the present purpose, and amongst which it is very necessary to select the right one. Thus, for instance, there is the scientific and atheistical prig, who may be frequently observed eluding notice between the covers of the "Westminster Review;" the Anglican prig, who is often caught exposing himself in the "Guardian;" the Ultramontane prig, who abounds in the "Dublin Review;" the scholarly prig, who twitters among the leaves of the "Academy;" and the Evangelical prig, who converts the heathen, and drinks port wine. None of these, and least of all the last, will serve for the central figure, in the present class of poem. The only one entirely suitable is the blameless variety. Take, then, one blameless prig. Set him upright in the middle of a round table, and place beside him a beautiful wife, who cannot abide prigs. Add to these one marred goodly man; and tie the three together in a bundle with a link or two of Destiny. Proceed, next, to surround this group with a large number of men and women of the nineteenth century, in fancy-ball costume, flavoured with a great many very possible vices, and a few impossible virtues. Stir these briskly about for two volumes, to the great annoyance of the blameless prig, who is, however, to be kept carefully below swearing-point, for the whole time. If he once boils over into any natural action or exclamation, he is forthwith worthless, and you must get another. Next break the wife's reputation into small pieces; and dust them well over the blameless prig. Then take a few vials of tribulation and wrath, and empty these generally over the whole ingredients of your poem: and, taking the sword of the heathen, cut into small pieces the greater part of your minor characters. Then wound slightly the head of the blameless prig; remove him suddenly from the table, and keep in a cool barge for future use.

HOW TO MAKE A POEM LIKE MR. M*TTH*W A*N*LD

Take one soulful of involuntary unbelief, which has been previously well flavoured with self-satisfied despair. Add to this one beautiful text of Scripture. Mix these well together; and as soon as ebullition commences, grate in finely a few regretful allusions to the New Testament and the Lake of Tiberias, one constellation of stars, half-a-dozen allusions to the nineteenth century, one to Goethe, one to Mont Blanc, or the Lake of Geneva; and one also, if possible, to some personal bereavement. Flavour the whole with a mouthful of "faiths" and "infinites," and a mixed mouthful of "passions," "finites," and "yearnings." This class of poem is concluded usually with some question, about which we have to observe only that it shall be impossible to answer.

HOW TO MAKE AN IMITATION OF MR. BR*WN*NG

Take rather a coarse view of things in general. In the midst of this, place a man and a woman, her and her ankles, tastefully arranged on a slice of Italy, or the country about Pornic. Cut an opening across the breast of each, until the soul becomes visible, but be very careful that none of the body be lost during the operation. Pour into each breast as much as it will hold of the new strong wine of love: and, for fear they should take cold by exposure, cover them quickly up with a quantity of obscure classical quotations, a few familiar allusions to an unknown period of history, and a half-destroyed fresco by an early master, varied every now and then with a reference to the fugues or toccatas of a quite-forgotten composer.

If the poem be still intelligible, take a pen and remove carefully all the necessary particles.

HOW TO MAKE A MODERN PRE-RAPHAELITE POEM

Take a packet of fine selected early English, containing no words but such as are obsolete and unintelligible. Pour this into about double the quantity of entirely new English, which must have never been used before, and which you must compose yourself, fresh as it is wanted. Mix these together thoroughly till they assume a colour quite different from any tongue that was ever spoken, and the material will be ready for use.

Determine the number of stanzas of which your poem shall consist, and select a corresponding number of the most archaic or most peculiar words in your vocabulary, allotting one of these to each stanza; and pour in the other words round them, until the entire poem is filled in.

This kind of composition is usually cast in shapes. These, though not numerous—amounting in all to something under a dozen—it would take too long to describe minutely here: and a short visit to Mr. ——'s shop in King street, where they are kept in stock, would explain the whole of them. A favourite one, however, is the following, which is of very easy construction. Take three damozels, dressed in straight night-gowns. Pull their hair-pins out, and let their hair tumble all about their shoulders. A few stars may be sprinkled into this with advantage. Place an aureole about the head of each, and give each a lily in her hand, about half the size of herself. Bend their necks all different ways, and set them in a row before a stone wall, with an apple-tree between each, and some large flowers at their feet. Trees and flowers of the right sort are very plentiful in church windows. When you have arranged all these objects rightly, take a cast of them in the softest part of your brain, and pour in your word-composition as above described.

This kind of poem is much improved by what is called a burden. This consists of a few jingling words, generally of an archaic character, about which we have only to be careful that they have no reference to the subject of the poem they are to ornament. They are inserted without variation between the stanzas.

In conclusion we would remark to beginners that this sort of composition must be attempted only in a perfectly vacant atmosphere; so that no grains of common-sense may injure the work whilst in progress.

HOW TO MAKE A NARRATIVE POEM LIKE MR. M*RR*S

Take about sixty pages-full of the same word-mixture as that described in the preceding; and dilute it with a double quantity of mild modern Anglo-Saxon. Pour this composition into two vessels of equal size, and into one of these empty a small mythological story. If this does not put your readers to sleep soon enough, add to it the rest of the language in the remaining vessel.

HOW TO MAKE A SPASMODIC POEM LIKE
MR. R*B*RT B*CH*N*N

This is a very troublesome kind of poem to make, as it requires more effort and straining than any other. You are yourself also one of the principal ingredients; and it is well, therefore, to warn you, before you use yourself for this purpose, that you will be good for nothing else after you have done so. The other ingredients, which, like those of a quack medicine, are mostly gathered under the moon, or in a planetary hour, must be first prepared as follows.

For a poem of a hundred lines (enough to satisfy one person) take ten verses-full of stardew, twenty-five verses-full of the tides of night, fifteen of passion-pale proud women, well idealized, five of starry ice-crystals, ten of dank grass and night-shade, fifteen of aching solitude, and twenty of frost-silvered mountain peaks, bubbling runnels, and the sea. Into these put the moon, with stars *ad libitum;* and sprinkle the whole over with broken panes of a Grub-street garret window. This done, your next step is to prepare *yourself.* The simplest way is to proceed as follows.

Take yourself, and make eyes at it in the glass

until you think it looks like Keats, or the "Boy Chatterton." Then take an infinite yearning to be a poet, and a profound conviction that you never can be one, and try to stifle the latter. This you will not be able to do. The aim of the endeavour is to make the conviction restive. Then put the two together into yourself; and the conviction will immediately begin to splutter, and disturb you. This you will mistake for the struggles of genius, and you will shortly after be thrown into the most violent convulsions. As soon as you feel these beginning, jump into the middle of your other ingredients; your movements will before long whip them up into an opaque froth, which as soon as you are tired out and become quiet, will settle, and leave your head protruding from the centre. Sprinkle the whole with imitation heart's-blood, and serve.

HOW TO MAKE A SATANIC POEM, LIKE THE LATE
LORD BYRON

(This recipe is inserted for the benefit of those poets who desire to attain what is called originality. This is only to be got by following some model of a past generation, which has ceased to be made use of by the public at large. We do not however recommend this course, feeling sure that all writers in the end will derive far more real satisfaction from producing fashionable, than original verses; which two things it is impossible to do at the same time.)

Take a couple of fine deadly sins; and let them hang before your eyes until they become racy. Then take them down, dissect them, and stew them for some time in a solution of weak remorse; after which they are to be devilled with mock-despair.

HOW TO MAKE A PATRIOTIC POEM LIKE
MR. SW*NB*RNE

Take one blaspheming patriot, who has been hung or buried for some time, together with the oppressed country belonging to him. Soak these in a quantity of rotten sentiment, till they are completely sodden; and in the mean while get ready an indefinite number of Christian kings and priests. Kick these till they are nearly dead; add copiously broken fragments of the Catholic church, and mix all together. Place them in a heap upon the oppressed country; season plentifully with very coarse expressions; and on the top carefully arrange your patriot, garnished with laurel or with parsley: surround with artificial hopes for the future, which are never meant to be tasted. This kind of poem is cooked in verbiage, flavoured with Liberty, the taste of which is much heightened by the introduction of a few high gods, and the game of Fortune. The amount of verbiage which Liberty is capable of flavouring, is practically infinite.

CONCLUSION

We regret to have to offer this work to the public in its present incomplete state, the whole of that part treating in detail of the most recent section of modern English poetry, *viz.,* the blasphemous and the obscene, being completely wanting. It was found necessary to issue this from an eminent publishing firm in Holywell street, Strand, where, by an unforeseen casualty, the entire first edition was seized by the police, and is at present in the hands of the Society for the Suppression of Vice. We incline however to trust that this loss will have but little effect; as indecency and profanity are things in which, even to the dullest, external instruction is a luxury, rather than a necessity. Those of our readers, who, either from sense, self-respect, or other circumstances, are in need of a special training in these subjects, will find excellent professors of them in any public-house, during the late hours of the evening; where the whole sum and substance of the fieriest school of modern poetry is delivered nightly; needing only a little dressing and flavouring with artificial English to turn it into very excellent verse.

The Study of Poetry

Matthew Arnold

Originally published as the "general introduction" to Thomas Humphrey Ward's four-volume anthology The English Poets *(London & New York: Macmillan, 1880).*

"The future of poetry is immense, because in poetry, where it is worthy of its high destinies, our race, as time goes on, will find an ever surer and surer stay. There is not a creed which is not shaken, not an accredited dogma which is not shown to be questionable, not a received tradition which does not threaten to dissolve. Our religion has materialised itself in the fact, in the supposed fact; it has attached its emotion to the fact, and now the fact is failing it. But for poetry the idea is everything; the rest is a world of illusion, of divine illusion. Poetry attaches its emotion to the idea; the idea *is* the fact. The strongest part of our religion to-day is its unconscious poetry."

Let me be permitted to quote these words of my own, as uttering the thought which should, in my opinion, go with us and govern us in all our study of poetry. In the present work it is the course of one great contributory stream to the world-river of poetry that we are invited to follow. We are here invited to trace the stream of English poetry. But whether we set ourselves, as here, to follow only one of the several streams that make the mighty river of poetry, or whether we seek to know them all, our governing thought should be the same. We should conceive of poetry worthily, and more highly than it has been the custom to conceive of it. We should conceive of it as capable of higher uses, and called to higher destinies, than those which in general men have assigned to it hitherto. More and more mankind will discover that we have to turn to poetry to interpret life for us, to console us, to sustain us. Without poetry, our science will appear incomplete; and most of what now passes with us for religion and philosophy will be replaced by poetry. Science, I say, will appear incomplete without it. For finely and truly does Wordsworth call poetry "the impassioned expression which is in the countenance of all science"; and what is a countenance without its expression? Again, Wordsworth finely and truly calls poetry "the breath and finer spirit of all knowledge": our religion, parading evidences such as those on which the popular mind relies now; our philosophy, pluming itself on its reasonings about causation and finite and infinite being; what are they but the shadows and dreams and false shows of knowledge? The day will come when we shall wonder at ourselves for having trusted to them, for having taken them seriously; and the more we perceive their hollowness, the more we shall prize "the breath and finer spirit of knowledge" offered to us by poetry.

But if we conceive thus highly of the destinies

of poetry, we must also set our standard for poetry high, since poetry, to be capable of fulfilling such high destinies, must be poetry of a high order of excellence. We must accustom ourselves to a high standard and to a strict judgment. Sainte-Beuve relates that Napoleon one day said, when somebody was spoken of in his presence as a charlatan: "Charlatan as much as you please; but where is there *not* charlatanism?"—"Yes," answers Sainte-Beuve, "in politics, in the art of governing mankind, that is perhaps true. But in the order of thought, the art, the glory, the eternal honour is that charlatanism shall find no entrance; herein lies the inviolableness of that noble portion of man's being." It is admirably said, and let us hold fast to it. In poetry, which is thought and art in one, it is the glory, the eternal honour that charlatanism shall find no entrance; that the noble sphere be kept inviolate and inviolable Charlatanism is for confusing or obliterating the distinctions between excellent and inferior, sound and unsound or only half-sound, true and untrue or only half-true. It is charlatanism, conscious or unconscious, whenever we confuse or obliterate these. And in poetry, more than anywhere else, it is unpermissible to confuse or obliterate them. For in poetry the distinction between excellent and inferior, sound and unsound or only half-sound, true and untrue or only half-true, is of paramount importance. It is of paramount importance because of the high destinies of poetry. In poetry, as a criticism of life under the conditions fixed for such a criticism by the laws of poetic truth and poetic beauty, the spirit of our race will find, we have said, as time goes on and as other helps fail, its consolation and stay. But the consolation and stay will be of power in proportion to the power of the criticism of life. And the criticism of life will be of power in proportion as the poetry conveying it is excellent rather than inferior, sound rather than unsound or half-sound, true rather than untrue or half-true.

The best poetry is what we want; the best poetry will be found to have a power of forming, sustaining, and delighting us, as nothing else can. A clearer, deeper sense of the best in poetry, and of the strength and joy to be drawn from it, is the most precious benefit which we can gather from a poetical collection such as the present. And yet in the very nature and conduct of such a collection there is inevitably something which tends to obscure in us the consciousness of what our benefits should be, and to distract us from the pursuit of it. We should therefore steadily set it before our minds at the outset, and should compel ourselves to revert constantly to the thought of it as we proceed.

Yes; constantly in reading poetry, a sense for the best, the really excellent, and of the strength and joy to be drawn from it, should be present in our minds and should govern our estimate of what we read. But this real estimate, the only true one, is liable to be superseded, if we are not watchful, by two other kinds of estimate, the historic estimate and the personal estimate, both of which are fallacious. A poet or a poem may count to us historically, they may count to us on grounds personal to ourselves, and they may count to us really. They may count to us historically. The course of development of a nation's language, thought, and poetry, is profoundly interesting; and by regarding a poet's work as a stage in this course of development we may easily bring ourselves to make it of more importance as poetry than in itself it really is, we may come to use a language of quite exaggerated praise in criticising it; in short, to over-rate it. So arises in our poetic judgments the fallacy caused by the estimate which we may call historic. Then, again, a poet or a poem may count to us on grounds personal to ourselves. Our personal affinities, likings, and circumstances, have great power to sway our estimate of this or that poet's work, and to make us attach more importance to it as poetry than in itself it really possesses, because to us it is, or has been, of high importance. Here also we over-rate the object of our interest, and apply to it a language of praise which is quite exaggerated. And thus we get the source of a second fallacy in our poetic judgments—the fallacy caused by an estimate which we may call personal.

Both fallacies are natural. It is evident how naturally the study of the history and development of a poetry may incline a man to pause over reputations and works once conspicuous but now obscure, and to quarrel with a careless public for skipping, in obedience to mere tradition and habit, from one famous name or work in its national poetry to another, ignorant of what it misses, and of the reason for keeping what it keeps, and of the whole process of growth in its poetry. The French have become diligent students of their own early poetry, which they long neglected; the study makes many of them dissatisfied with their so-called classical poetry, the court-tragedy of the seventeenth century, a poetry which Pellisson long ago reproached with its want of the true poetic stamp, with its *politesse stérile et rampante,* but which nevertheless has reigned in France as absolutely as if it had been the perfection of classical poetry indeed. The dissatisfaction is natural; yet a lively and accomplished critic, M. Charles d'Héricault, the editor of Clément Marot, goes too far when he says that "the cloud of glory playing round a classic is a mist as dangerous to the future of a literature as it is intolerable for the purposes of history." "It hinders," he goes on, "it hinders us from seeing more than one single point, the culminating and exceptional point; the summary, fictitious and arbitrary, of a thought and of a work. It substitutes a halo for a physiognomy, it puts a statue where there was once a man, and hiding from us all trace of the labour, the attempts, the weaknesses, the failures, it claims not study but veneration; it does not show us how the thing is done, it imposes upon us a model. Above all, for the historian this creation of classic personages is inadmissible; for it withdraws the poet from his time, from his proper life, it breaks historical relationships, it blinds criticism by conventional admiration, and renders the investigation of literary origins unacceptable. It gives us a human personage no longer, but a God seated immovable amidst His perfect work, like Jupiter on Olympus; and hardly will it be possible for the young student, to whom such work is exhibited at such a distance from him, to believe that it did not issue ready made from that divine head."

All this is brilliantly and tellingly said, but we must plead for a distinction. Everything depends on the reality of a poet's classic character. If he is a dubious classic, let us sift him; if he is a false classic, let us explode him. But if he is a real classic, if his work belongs to the class of the very best (for this is the true and right meaning of the word *classic, classical*), then the great thing for us is to feel and enjoy his work as deeply as ever we can, and to appreciate the wide difference between it and all work which has not the same high character. This is what is salutary, this is what is formative; this is the great benefit to be got from the study of poetry. Everything which interferes with it, which hinders it, is injurious. True, we must read our classic with open eyes, and not with eyes blinded with superstition; we must perceive when his work comes short, when it drops out of the class of the very best, and we must rate it, in such cases, at its proper value. But the use of this negative criticism is not in itself, it is entirely in its enabling us to have a clearer sense and a deeper enjoyment of what is truly excellent. To trace the labour, the attempts, the weaknesses, the failures of a genuine classic, to acquaint oneself with his time and his life and his historical relationships, is mere literary dilettantism unless it has that clear

sense and deeper enjoyment for its end. It may be said that the more we know about a classic the better we shall enjoy him; and, if we lived as long as Methuselah and had all of us heads of perfect clearness and wills of perfect steadfastness, this might be true in fact as it is plausible in theory. But the case here is much the same as the case with the Greek and Latin studies of our schoolboys. The elaborate philological groundwork which we require them to lay is in theory an admirable preparation for appreciating the Greek and Latin authors worthily. The more thoroughly we lay the groundwork, the better we shall be able, it may be said, to enjoy the authors. True, if time were not so short, and schoolboys' wits not so soon tired and their power of attention exhausted; only, as it is, the elaborate philological preparation goes on, but the authors are little known and less enjoyed. So with the investigator of "historic origins" in poetry. He ought to enjoy the true classic all the better for his investigations; he often is distracted from the enjoyment of the best, and with the less good he overbusies himself, and is prone to over-rate it in proportion to the trouble which it has cost him.

The idea of tracing historic origins and historical relationships cannot be absent from a compilation like the present. And naturally the poets to be exhibited in it will be assigned to those persons for exhibition who are known to prize them highly, rather than to those who have no special inclination towards them. Moreover the very occupation with an author, and the business of exhibiting him, disposes us to affirm and amplify his importance. In the present work, therefore, we are sure of frequent temptation to adopt the historic estimate, or the personal estimate, and to forget the real estimate; which latter, nevertheless, we must employ if we are to make poetry yield us its full benefit. So high is that benefit, the benefit of clearly feeling and of deeply enjoying the really excellent, the truly classic in poetry, that we do well, I say, to set it fixedly before our minds as our object in studying poets and poetry, and to make the desire of attaining it the one principle to which, as the *Imitation* says, whatever we may read or come to know, we always return. *Cum multa legeris et cognoveris, ad unum semper oportet redire principium.*

The historic estimate is likely in especial to affect our judgment and our language when we are dealing with ancient poets; the personal estimate when we are dealing with poets our contemporaries, or at any rate modern. The exaggerations due to the historic estimate are not in themselves, perhaps, of very much gravity. Their report hardly enters the general ear; probably they do not always impose even on the literary men who adopt them. But they lead to a dangerous abuse of language. So we hear Caedmon, amongst our own poets, compared to Milton. I have already noticed the enthusiasm of one accomplished French critic for "historic origins." Another eminent French critic, M. Vitet, comments upon that famous document of the early poetry of his nation, the *Chanson de Roland*. It is indeed a most interesting document. The *joculator* or *jongleur* Taillefer, who was with William the Conqueror's army at Hastings, marched before the Norman troops, so said the tradition, singing "of Charlemagne and of Roland and of Oliver, and of the vassals who died at Roncevaux"; and it is suggested that in the *Chanson de Roland* by one Turoldus or Théroulde, a poem preserved in a manuscript of the twelfth century in the Bodleian Library at Oxford, we have certainly the matter, perhaps even some of the words, of the chant which Taillefer sang. The poem has vigour and freshness; it is not without pathos. But M. Vitet is not satisfied with seeing in it a document of some poetic value, and of very high historic and linguistic value; he sees in it a grand and beautiful work, a monument of epic genius. In its general design he finds the grandiose conception, in its details he finds the constant union of simplicity with greatness, which are the marks, he truly says, of the genuine epic, and distinguish it from the artificial epic of literary ages. One thinks of Homer; this is the sort of praise which is given to Homer, and justly given. Higher praise there cannot well be, and it is the praise due to epic poetry of the highest order only, and to no other. Let us try, then, the *Chanson de Roland* at its best. Roland, mortally wounded, lays himself down under a pine-tree, with his face turned towards Spain and the enemy—

> De plusurs choses à remembrer li prist,
> De tantes teres cume li bers cunquist,
> De dulce France, des humes de sun lign,
> De Charlemagne sun seignor ki l'nurrit.

That is primitive work, I repeat, with an undeniable poetic quality of its own. It deserves such praise, and such praise is sufficient for it. But now turn to Homer—

> ["Hōs phato tous d'ēdē katechen phusidzoos aia
> en Lakedaimoni auphi philē en patridi gaiē"]

We are here in another world, another order of poetry altogether; here is rightly due such supreme praise as that which M. Vitet gives to the *Chanson de Roland*. If our words are to have any meaning, if our judgments are to have any solidity, we must not heap that supreme praise upon poetry of an order immeasurably inferior.

Indeed there can be no more useful help for discovering what poetry belongs to the class of the truly excellent, and can therefore do us most good, than to have always in one's mind lines and expressions of the great masters, and to apply them as a touchstone to other poetry. Of course we are not to require this other poetry to resemble them; it may be very dissimilar. But if we have any tact we shall find them, when we have lodged them well in our minds, an infallible touchstone for detecting the presence or absence of high poetic quality, and also the degree of this quality, in all other poetry which we may place beside them. Short passages, even single lines, will serve our turn quite sufficiently. Take the two lines which I have just quoted from Homer, the poet's comment on Helen's mention of her brothers;—or take his

> [A deilō, ti sphōi domen Pēlēi anakti
> Thneta? humeis d'eston agērō t' athanatō te.
> hēhina dustēnoisi met' andrasin alge echēton?]

the address of Zeus to the horses of Peleus;—or take finally his

> [Kai se, geron, to prin men akouomen olbion einai.]

the words of Achilles to Priam, a suppliant before him. Take that incomparable line and a half of Dante, Ugolino's tremendous words—

> Io no piangeva; sì dentro impietrai.
> Piangevan elli . . .

take the lovely words of Beatrice to Virgil—

> Io son fatta da Dio, sau mercè, tale,
> Che la vostra miseria non mi tange,
> Nè fiamma d'esto incendio non m'assale . . .

take the simple, but perfect, single line—

> In la sua volontade è nostra pace.

Take of Shakespeare a line or two of Henry the Fourth's expostulation with sleep—

> Wilt thou upon the high and giddy mast

Seal up the ship-boy's eyes, and rock his brains
In cradle of the rude imperious surge . . .

and take, as well, Hamlet's dying request to
Horatio —

If thou didst ever hold me in thy heart,
Absent thee from felicity awhile,
And in this harsh world draw thy breath in pain
To tell my story . . .

Take of Milton that Miltonic passage —

Darken'd so, yet shone
Above them all the archangel; but his face
Deep scars of thunder had intrench'd, and care
Sat on his faded cheek . . .

add two such lines as —

And courage never to submit or yield
And what is else not to be overcome . . .

and finish with the exquisite close to the loss of
Proserpine, the loss

. . . which cost Ceres all that pain
To seek her through the world.

These few lines, if we have tact and can use them,
are enough even of themselves to keep clear and
sound our judgments about poetry, to save us from
fallacious estimates of it, to conduct us to a real
estimate.

The specimens I have quoted differ widely
from one another, but they have in common this:
the possession of the very highest poetical quality. If
we are thoroughly penetrated by their power, we
shall find that we have acquired a sense enabling us,
whatever poetry may be laid before us, to feel the
degree in which a high poetical quality is present or
wanting there. Critics give themselves great labour
to draw out what in the abstract constitutes the
characters of a high quality of poetry. It is much
better simply to have recourse to concrete
examples; — to take specimens of poetry of the
high, the very highest quality, and to say: The
characters of a high quality of poetry are what is
expressed *there*. They are far better recognised by
being felt in the verse of the master, than by being
perused in the prose of the critic. Nevertheless if we
are urgently pressed to give some critical account of
them we may safely, perhaps, venture on laying
down, not indeed how and why the characters arise,
but where and in what they arise. They are in the
matter and substance of the poetry, and they are in
its manner and style. Both of these, the substance
and matter on the one hand, the style and manner
on the other, have a mark, an accent, of high beauty,
worth, and power. But if we are asked to define this
mark and accent in the abstract, our answer must
be: No, for we should thereby be darkening the
question, not clearing it. The mark and accent are as
given by the substance and matter of that poetry, by
the style and manner of that poetry, and of all other
poetry which is akin to it in quality.

Only one thing we may add as to the substance
and matter of poetry, guiding ourselves by Aristotle's profound observation that the superiority of
poetry over history consists in its possessing a higher
truth and a higher seriousness ([philosophōteron
kai spoudaio teron]). Let us add, therefore, to what
we have said, this: that the substance and matter of
the best poetry acquire their special character from
possessing, in an eminent degree, truth and seriousness. We may add yet further, what is in itself
evident, that to the style and manner of the best
poetry their special character, their accent, is given
by their diction, and, even yet more, by their movement. And though we distinguish between the two
characters, the two accents, of superiority, yet they
are nevertheless vitally connected one with the
other. The superior character of truth and seriousness, in the matter and substance of the best poetry,
is inseparable from the superiority of diction and
movement marking its style and manner. The two
superiorities are closely related, and are in steadfast
proportion one to the other. So far as high poetic
truth and seriousness are wanting to a poet's matter
and substance, so far also, we may be sure, will a
high poetic stamp of diction and movement be
wanting to his style and manner. In proportion as
this high stamp of diction and movement, again, is
absent from a poet's style and manner, we shall find,
also, that high poetic truth and seriousness are absent from his substance and matter.

So stated, these are but dry generalities; their
whole force lies in their application. And I could
wish every student of poetry to make the application
of them for himself. Made by himself, the application would impress itself upon his mind far more
deeply than made by me. Neither will my limits
allow me to make any full application of the
generalities above propounded; but in the hope of
bringing out, at any rate, some significance in them,
and of establishing an important principle more
firmly by their means, I will, in the space which
remains to me, follow rapidly from the commence-

ment the course of our English poetry with them in my view.

Once more I return to the early poetry of France, with which our own poetry, in its origins, is indissolubly connected. In the twelfth and thirteenth centuries, that seed-time of all modern language and literature, the poetry of France had a clear predominance in Europe. Of the two divisions of that poetry, its production in the *langue d'oil* and its productions in the *langue d'oc,* the poetry of the *langue d'oc,* of southern France, of the troubadours, is of importance because of its effect on Italian literature;— the first literature of modern Europe to strike the true and grand note, and to bring forth, as in Dante and Petrarch it brought forth, classics. But the predominance of French poetry in Europe, during the twelfth and thirteenth centuries, is due to its poetry of the *langue d'oil,* the poetry of northern France and of the tongue which is now the French language. In the twelfth century the bloom of this romance-poetry was earlier and stronger in England, at the court of our Anglo-Norman kings, than in France itself. But it was a bloom of French poetry; and as our native poetry formed itself, it formed itself out of this. The romance-poems which took possession of the heart and imagination of Europe in the twelfth and thirteenth centuries are French; "they are," as Southey justly says, "the pride of French literature, nor have we anything which can be placed in competition with them." Themes were supplied from all quarters; but the romance-setting which was common to them all, and which gained the ear of Europe, was French. This constituted for the French poetry, literature, and language, at the height of the Middle Age, an unchallenged predominance. The Italian Brunetto Latini, the master of Dante, wrote his *Treasure* in French because, he says, *"la parleure en est plus délitable et plus commune à toute gens."* In the same century, the thirteenth, the French romance-writer, Christian of Troyes, formulates the claims, in chivalry and letters, of France, his native country, as follows:—

Or vous ert par ce livre apris,
Que Gresse ot de chevalerie
Le premier los et de clergie;
Puis vint chevalerie à Rome
Et de la clergie la some,
Qui ore est en France venue.
Diex doinst qu'ele i soit retenue,
Et que li lius li abelisse
Tant que de France n'isse
L'onor qui s'i est arestée!

"Now by this book you will learn that first Greece had the renown for chivalry and letters; then chivalry and the primacy in letters passed to Rome, and now it is come to France. God grant it may be kept there; and that the place may please it so well, that the honour which has come to make stay in France may never depart thence!"

Yet it is now all gone, this French romance-poetry, of which the weight of substance and the power of style are not unfairly represented by this extract from Christian of Troyes. Only by means of the historic estimate can we persuade ourselves now to think that any of it is of poetical importance.

But in the fourteenth century there comes an Englishman nourished on this poetry, taught his trade by this poetry, getting words, rhyme, metre from this poetry; for even of that stanza which the Italians used, and which Chaucer derived immediately from the Italians, the basis and suggestion was probably given in France. Chaucer (I have already named him) fascinated his contemporaries, but so too did Christian of Troyes and Wolfram of Eschenbach. Chaucer's power of fascination, however, is enduring; his poetical importance does not need the assistance of the historic estimate; it is real. He is a genuine source of joy and strength, which is flowing still for us and will flow always. He will be read, as time goes on, far more generally than he is read now. His language is a cause of difficulty for us; but so also, and I think in quite as great a degree, is the language of Burns. In Chaucer's case, as in that of Burns, it is a difficulty to be unhesitatingly accepted and overcome.

If we ask ourselves wherein consists the immense superiority of Chaucer's poetry over the romance-poetry—why it is that in passing from this to Chaucer we suddenly feel ourselves to be in another world, we shall find that his superiority is both in the substance of his poetry and in the style of his poetry. His superiority in substance is given by his large, free, simple, clear yet kindly view of human life,—so unlike the total want, in the romance-poets, of all intelligent command of it. Chaucer has not their helplessness; he has gained the power to survey the world from a central, a truly human point of view. We have only to call to mind the Prologue to *The Canterbury Tales.* The right comment upon it is Dryden's: "It is sufficient to say, according to the proverb, that *here is God's plenty.*" And again: "He is a perpetual fountain of good sense." It is by a large, free, sound representation of things, that poetry, this high criticism of life, has truth of substance; and Chaucer's poetry has truth of substance.

Of his style and manner, if we think first of the romance-poetry and then of Chaucer's divine liquidness of diction, his divine fluidity of movement, it is difficult to speak temperately. They are irresistible, and justify all the rapture with which his successors speak of his "gold dew-drops of speech." Johnson misses the point entirely when he finds fault with Dryden for ascribing to Chaucer the first refinement of our numbers, and says that Gower also can show smooth numbers and easy rhymes. The refinement of our numbers means something far more than this. A nation may have versifiers with smooth numbers and easy rhymes, and yet may have no real poetry at all. Chaucer is the father of our splendid English poetry; he is our "well of English undefiled," because by the lovely charm of his diction, the lovely charm of his movement, he makes an epoch and founds a tradition. In Spenser, Shakespeare, Milton, Keats, we can follow the tradition of the liquid diction, the fluid movement, of Chaucer; at one time it is his liquid diction of which in these poets we feel the virtue, and at another time it is his fluid movement. And the virtue is irresistible.

Bounded as is my space, I must yet find room for an example of Chaucer's virtue, as I have given examples to show the virtue of the great classics. I feel disposed to say that a single line is enough to show the charm of Chaucer's verse; that merely one line like this—

O martyr souded in virginitee!

has a virtue of manner and movement such as we shall not find in all the verse of romance-poetry;—but this is saying nothing. The virtue is such as we shall not find, perhaps, in all English poetry, outside the poets whom I have named as the special inheritors of Chaucer's tradition. A single line, however, is too little if we have not the strain of Chaucer's verse well in our memory; let us take a stanza. It is from *The Prioress's Tale,* the story of the Christian child murdered in a Jewry—

My throte is cut unto my nekke-bone
Saidè this child, and as by way of kinde
I should have deyd, yea, longè time agone;
But Jesu Christ, as ye in bookès finde,
Will that his glory last and be in minde,
And for the worship of his mother dere
Yet may I sing *O Alma* loud and clere.

Wordsworth has modernised this Tale, and to feel how delicate and evanescent is the charm of verse,

we have only to read Wordsworth's first three lines of this stanza after Chaucer's—

My throat is cut unto the bone, I trow,
Said this young child, and by the law of kind
I should have died, yea, many hours ago.

The charm is departed. It is often said that the power of liquidness and fluidity in Chaucer's verse was dependent upon a free, a licentious dealing with language, such as is now impossible; upon a liberty, such as Burns too enjoyed, of making words like *neck, bird,* into a dissyllable by adding to them, and words like *cause, rhyme,* into a dissyllable by sounding the *e* mute. It is true that Chaucer's fluidity is conjoined with this liberty, and is admirably served by it; but we ought not to say that it was dependent upon it. It was dependent upon his talent. Other poets with a like liberty do not attain to the fluidity of Chaucer; Burns himself does not attain to it. Poets, again, who have a talent akin to Chaucer's, such as Shakespeare or Keats, have known how to attain to his fluidity without the like liberty.

And yet Chaucer is not one of the great classics. His poetry transcends and effaces, easily and without effort, all the romance-poetry of Catholic Christendom; it transcends and effaces all the English poetry contemporary with it, it transcends and effaces all the English poetry subsequent to it down to the age of Elizabeth. Of such avail is poetic truth of substance, in its natural and necessary union with poetic truth of style. And yet, I say, Chaucer is not one of the great classics. He has not their accent. What is wanting to him is suggested by the mere mention of the name of the first great classic of Christendom, the immortal poet who died eighty years before Chaucer,—Dante. The accent of such verse as

In la sua volontade è nostra pace . . .

is altogether beyond Chaucer's reach; we praise him, but we feel that this accent is out of the question for him. It may be said that it was necessarily out of the reach of any poet in the England of that stage of growth. Possibly; but we are to adopt a real, not a historic, estimate of poetry. However we may account for its absence, something is wanting, then, to the poetry of Chaucer, which poetry must have before it can be placed in the glorious class of the best. And there is no doubt what that something is. It is the [spoudaiotēs], the high and excellent seriousness, which Aristotle assigns as one of the grand virtues of poetry. The substance of Chaucer's poetry, his view of things and his criticism of life, has largeness, freedom, shrewdness, benignity; but it has not this high seriousness. Homer's criticism of life has it, Dante's has it, Shakespeare's has it. It is this chiefly which gives to our spirits what they can rest upon; and with the increasing demands of our modern ages upon poetry, this virtue of giving us what we can rest upon will be more and more highly esteemed. A voice from the slums of Paris, fifty or sixty years after Chaucer, the voice of poor Villon out of his life of riot and crime, has at its happy moments (as, for instance, in the last stanza of *La Belle Heaulmière*) more of this important poetic virtue of seriousness than all the productions of Chaucer. But its apparition in Villon, and in men like Villon, is fitful; the greatness of the great poets, the power of their criticism of life, is that their virtue is sustained.

To our praise, therefore, of Chaucer as a poet there must be this limitation; he lacks the high seriousness of the great classics, and therewith an important part of their virtue. Still, the main fact for us to bear in mind about Chaucer is his sterling value according to that real estimate which we firmly adopt for all poets. He has poetic truth of substance, though he has not high poetic seriousness, and corresponding to his truth of substance he has an exquisite virtue of style and manner. With him is born our real poetry.

For my present purpose I need not dwell on our Elizabethan poetry, or on the continuation and close of this poetry in Milton. We all of us profess to be agreed in the estimate of this poetry; we all of us recognise it as great poetry, our greatest, and Shakespeare and Milton as our poetical classics. The real estimate, here, has universal currency. With the next age of our poetry divergency and difficulty begin. An historic estimate of that poetry has established itself; and the question is, whether it will be found to coincide with the real estimate.

The age of Dryden, together with our whole eighteenth century which followed it, sincerely believed itself to have produced poetical classics of its own, and even to have made advance, in poetry, beyond all its predecessors. Dryden regards as not seriously disputable the opinion "that the sweetness of English verse was never understood or practised by our fathers." Cowley could see nothing at all in Chaucer's poetry. Dryden heartily admired it, and, as we have seen, praised its matter admirably; but of its exquisite manner and movement all he can find to say is that "there is the rude sweetness of a Scotch tune in it, which is natural and pleasing, though not

perfect." Addison, wishing to praise Chaucer's numbers, compares them with Dryden's own. And all through the eighteenth century, and down even into our own times, the stereotyped phrase of approbation for good verse found in our early poetry has been, that it even approached the verse of Dryden, Addison, Pope, and Johnson.

Are Dryden and Pope poetical classics? Is the historic estimate, which represents them as such, and which has been so long established that it cannot easily give way, the real estimate? Wordsworth and Coleridge, as is well known, denied it; but the authority of Wordsworth and Coleridge does not weigh much with the young generation, and there are many signs to show that the eighteenth century and its judgments are coming into favour again. Are the favourite poets of the eighteenth century classics?

It is impossible within my present limits to discuss the question fully. And what man of letters would not shrink from seeming to dispose dictatorially of the claims of two men who are, at any rate, such masters in letters as Dryden and Pope; two men of such admirable talent, both of them, and one of them, Dryden, a man, on all sides, of such energetic and genial power? And yet, if we are to gain the full benefit from poetry, we must have the real estimate of it. I cast about for some mode of arriving, in the present case, at such an estimate without offence. And perhaps the best way is to begin, as it is easy to begin, with cordial praise.

When we find Chapman, the Elizabethan translator of Homer, expressing himself in his preface thus: "Though truth in her very nakedness sits in so deep a pit, that from Gades to Aurora and Ganges few eyes can sound her, I hope yet those few here will so discover and confirm that, the date being out of her darkness in this morning of our poet, he shall now gird his temples with the sun,"—we pronounce that such a prose is intolerable. When we find Milton writing: "And long it was not after, when I was confirmed in this opinion, that he, who would not be frustrate of his hope to write well hereafter in laudable things, ought himself to be a true poem,"—we pronounce that such a prose has its own grandeur, but that it is obsolete and inconvenient. But when we find Dryden telling us: "What Virgil wrote in the vigour of his age, in plenty and at ease, I have undertaken to translate in my declining years; struggling with wants, oppressed with sickness, curbed in my genius, liable to be misconstrued in all I write,"—then we exclaim that here at last we have the true English prose, a prose such as we would all gladly use if we only knew how.

Yet Dryden was Milton's contemporary.

But after the Restoration the time had come when our nation felt the imperious need of a fit prose. So, too, the time had likewise come when our nation felt the imperious need of freeing itself from the absorbing preoccupation which religion in the Puritan age had exercised. It was impossible that this freedom should be brought about without some negative excess, without some neglect and impairment of the religious life of the soul; and the spiritual history of the eighteenth century shows us that the freedom was not achieved without them. Still, the freedom was achieved; the preoccupation, an undoubtedly baneful and retarding one if it had continued, was got rid of. And as with religion amongst us at that period, so it was also with letters. A fit prose was a necessity; but it was impossible that a fit prose should establish itself amongst us without some touch of frost to the imaginative life of the soul. The needful qualities for a fit prose are regularity, uniformity, precision, balance. The men of letters, whose destiny it may be to bring their nation to the attainment of a fit prose, must of necessity, whether they work in prose or in verse, give a predominating, an almost exclusive attention to the qualities of regularity, uniformity, precision, balance. But an almost exclusive attention to these qualities involves some repression and silencing of poetry.

We are to regard Dryden as the puissant and glorious founder, Pope as the splendid high priest, of our age of prose and reason, of our excellent and indispensable eighteenth century. For the purposes of their mission and destiny their poetry, like their prose, is admirable. Do you ask me whether Dryden's verse, take it almost where you will, is not good?

> A milk-white Hind, immortal and unchanged,
> Fed on the lawns and in the forest ranged.

I answer: Admirable for the purposes of the inaugurator of an age of prose and reason. Do you ask me whether Pope's verse, take it almost where you will, is not good?

> To Hounslow Heath I point, and Banstead Down;
> Thence comes your mutton, and these chicks my
>   own.

I answer: Admirable for the purposes of the high priest of an age of prose and reason. But do you ask me whether such verse proceeds from men with an adequate poetic criticism of life, from men whose criticism of life has a high seriousness, or even, without that high seriousness, has poetic largeness, freedom, insight, benignity? Do you ask me whether the application of ideas to life in the verse of these men, often a powerful application, no doubt, is a powerful *poetic* application? Do you ask me whether the poetry of these men has either the matter or the inseparable manner of such an adequate poetic criticism; whether it has the accent of

> Absent thee from felicity awhile . . .

or of

> And what is else not to be overcome . . .

or of

> O martyr souded in virginitee!

I answer: It has not and cannot have them; it is the poetry of the builders of an age of prose and reason. Though they may write in verse, though they may in a certain sense be masters of the art of versification, Dryden and Pope are not classics of our poetry, they are classics of our prose.

Gray is our poetical classic of that literature and age; the position of Gray is singular, and demands a word of notice here. He has not the volume or the power of poets who, coming in times more favourable, have attained to an independent criticism of life. But he lived with the great poets, he lived, above all, with the Greeks, through perpetually studying and enjoying them; and he caught their poetic point of view for regarding life, caught their poetic manner. The point of view and the manner are not self-sprung in him, he caught them of others; and he had not the free and abundant use of them. But whereas Addison and Pope never had the use of them, Gray had the use of them at times. He is the scantiest and frailest of classics in our poetry, but he is a classic.

And now, after Gray, we are met, as we draw towards the end of the eighteenth century, we are met by the great name of Burns. We enter now on times where the personal estimate of poets begins to be rife, and where the real estimate of them is not reached without difficulty. But in spite of the disturbing pressures of personal partiality, of national partiality, let us try to reach a real estimate of the poetry of Burns.

By his English poetry Burns in general belongs to the eighteenth century, and has little importance for us.

> Mark ruffian Violence, distain'd with crimes,
> Rousing elate in these degenerate times;
> View unsuspecting Innocence a prey,
> As guileful Fraud points out the erring way;
> While subtle Litigation's pliant tongue
> The life-blood equal sucks of Right and Wrong!

Evidently this is not the real Burns, or his name and fame would have disappeared long ago. Nor is Clarinda's love-poet, Sylvander, the real Burns either. But he tells us himself: "These English songs gravel me to death. I have not the command of the language that I have of my native tongue. In fact, I think that my ideas are more barren in English than in Scotch. I have been at *Duncan Gray* to dress it in English, but all I can do is desperately stupid." We English turn naturally, in Burns, to the poems in our own language, because we can read them easily; but in those poems we have not the real Burns.

The real Burns is of course in his Scotch poems. Let us boldly say that of much of this poetry, a poetry dealing perpetually with Scotch drink, Scotch religion, and Scotch manners, a Scotchman's estimate is apt to be personal. A Scotchman is used to this world of Scotch drink, Scotch religion, and Scotch manners; he has a tenderness for it; he meets its poet half way. In this tender mood he reads pieces like the *Holy Fair* or *Halloween*. But this world of Scotch drink, Scotch religion, and Scotch manners is against a poet, not for him, when it is not a partial countryman who reads him; for in itself it is not a beautiful world, and no one can deny that it is of advantage to a poet to deal with a beautiful world. Burns's world of Scotch drink, Scotch religion, and Scotch manners, is often a harsh, a sordid, a repulsive world; even the world of his *Cotter's Saturday Night* is not a beautiful world. No doubt a poet's criticism of life may have such truth and power that it triumphs over its world and delights us. Burns may triumph over his world, often he does triumph over his world, but let us observe how and where. Burns is the first case we have had where the bias of the personal estimate tends to mislead; let us look at him closely, he can bear it.

Many of his admirers will tell us that we have Burns, convivial, genuine, delightful, here—

> Leeze me on drink! it gies us mair
> Than either school or college;
> It kindles wit, it waukens lair,
> It pangs us fou o' knowledge.

> Be't whisky gill or penny wheep
> Or ony stronger potion,
> It never fails, on drinking deep,
> To kittle up our notion
>   By night or day.

There is a great deal of that sort of thing in Burns, and it is unsatisfactory, not because it is bacchanalian poetry, but because it has not that accent of sincerity which bacchanalian poetry, to do it justice, very often has. There is something in it of bravado, something which makes us feel that we have not the man speaking to us with his real voice; something, therefore, poetically unsound.

With still more confidence will his admirers tell us that we have the genuine Burns, the great poet, when his strain asserts the independence, equality, dignity, of men, as in the famous song *For a' that and a' that*—

> A prince can mak' a belted knight,
>   A marquis, duke, and a' that;
> But an honest man's aboon his might,
>   Guid faith he mauna fa' that!
> For a' that, and a' that,
>   Their dignities, and a' that,
> The pith o' sense, and pride o' worth,
>   Are higher rank than a' that.

Here they find his grand, genuine touches; and still more, when this puissant genius, who so often set morality at defiance, falls moralising—

> The sacred lowe o' weel-placed love
>   Luxuriantly indulge it;
> But never tempt th' illicit rove
>   Tho' naething should divulge it.
> I waive the quantum o' the sin,
>   The hazard o' concealing,
> But och! it hardens a' within,
>   And petrifies the feeling.

Or in a higher strain—

> Who made the heart, 'tis He alone
>   Decidedly can try us;
> He knows each chord, its various tone;
>   Each spring, its various bias.
> Then at the balance let's be mute,
>   We never can adjust it;
> What's *done* we partly may compute,
>   But know not what's resisted.

Or in a better strain yet, a strain, his admirers will say, unsurpassable—

To make a happy fire-side clime
        To weans and wife,
That's the true pathos and sublime
        Of human life.

There is criticism of life for you, the admirers of Burns will say to us; there is the application of ideas to life! There is, undoubtedly. The doctrine of the last quoted lines coincides almost exactly with what was the aim and end, Xenophon tells us, of all the teaching of Socrates. And the application is a powerful one; made by a man of vigorous understanding, and (need I say?) a master of language.

But for supreme poetical success more is required than the powerful application of ideas to life; it must be an application under the conditions fixed by the laws of poetic truth and poetic beauty. Those laws fix as an essential condition, in the poet's treatment of such matters as are here in question, high seriousness;—the high seriousness which comes from absolute sincerity. The accent of high seriousness, born of absolute sincerity, is what gives to such verse as

     In la sua volontade è nostra pace . . .

to such criticism of life as Dante's, its power. Is this accent felt in the passages which I have been quoting from Burns? Surely not; surely, if our sense is quick, we must perceive that we have not in those passages a voice from the very inmost soul of the genuine Burns; he is not speaking to us from these depths, he is more or less preaching. And the compensation for admiring such passages less, from missing the perfect poetic accent in them, will be that we shall admire more the poetry where that accent is found.

No; Burns, like Chaucer, comes short of the high seriousness of the great classics, and the virtue of matter and manner which goes with that high seriousness is wanting to his work. At moments he touches it in a profound and passionate melancholy, as in those four immortal lines taken by Byron as a motto for *The Bride of Abydos,* but which have in them a depth of poetic quality such as resides in no verse of Byron's own—

      Had we never loved sae kindly,
      Had we never loved sae blindly,
      Never met, or never parted,
      We had ne'er been broken-hearted.

But a whole poem of that quality Burns cannot make; the rest, in the *Farewell to Nancy,* is verbiage.

We arrive best at the real estimate of Burns, I think, by conceiving his work as having truth of matter and truth of manner, but not the accent or the poetic virtue of the highest masters. His genuine criticism of life, when the sheer poet in him speaks, is ironic; it is not—

     Thou Power Supreme, whose mighty scheme
       These woes of mine fulfil,
     Here firm I rest, they must be best
       Because they are Thy will!

It is far rather: *Whistle owre the lave o't!* Yet we may say of him as of Chaucer, that of life and the world, as they come before him, his view is large, free, shrewd, benignant,—truly poetic, therefore; and his manner of rendering what he sees is to match. But we must note, at the same time, his great difference from Chaucer. The freedom of Chaucer is heightened, in Burns, by a fiery, reckless energy; the benignity of Chaucer deepens, in Burns, into an overwhelming sense of the pathos of things;—of the pathos of human nature, the pathos, also, of non-human nature. Instead of the fluidity of Chaucer's manner, the manner of Burns has spring, bounding swiftness. Burns is by far the greater force, though he has perhaps less charm. The world of Chaucer is fairer, richer, more significant than that of Burns; but when the largeness and freedom of Burns get full sweep, as in *Tam o'Shanter,* or still more in that puissant and splendid production, *The Jolly Beggars,* his world may be what it will, his poetic genius triumphs over it. In the world of *The Jolly Beggars* there is more than hideousness and squalor, there is bestiality; yet the piece is a superb poetic success. It has a breadth, truth, and power which make the famous scene in Auerbach's Cellar, of Goethe's *Faust,* seem artificial and tame beside it, and which are only matched by Shakespeare and Aristophanes.

Here, where his largeness and freedom serve him so admirably, and also in those poems and songs where to shrewdness he adds infinite archness and wit, and to benignity infinite pathos, where his manner is flawless, and a perfect poetic whole is the result,—in things like the address to the mouse whose home he had ruined, in things like *Duncan Gray, Tam Glen, Whistle and I'll come to you my Lad, Auld Lang Syne* (this list might be made much longer),—here we have the genuine Burns, of whom the real estimate must be high indeed. Not a classic, nor with the excellent [spoudaiotēs] of the great classics, nor with a verse rising to a criticism of life and a virtue like theirs; but a poet with thorough truth of substance and an answering truth of style, giving us a poetry sound to the core. We all of us have a leaning towards the pathetic, and may be inclined perhaps to prize Burns most for his touches of piercing, sometimes almost intolerable, pathos; for verse like—

> We twa hae paidl't i' the burn
>   From mornin' sun till dine;
> But seas between us braid hae roar'd
>   Sin auld lang syne . . .

where he is as lovely as he is sound. But perhaps it is by the perfection of soundness of his lighter and archer masterpieces that he is poetically most wholesome for us. For the votary misled by a personal estimate of Shelley, as so many of us have been, are, and will be,—of that beautiful spirit building his many-coloured haze of words and images

> Pinnacled dim in the intense inane—

no contact can be wholesomer than the contact with Burns at his archest and soundest. Side by side with the

> On the brink of the night and the morning
>   My coursers are wont to respire,
> But the Earth has just whispered a warning
>   That their flight must be swifter than fire . . .

of *Prometheus Unbound,* how salutary, how very salutary, to place this from *Tam Glen*—

> My minnie does constantly deave me
>   And bids me beware o' young men;
> They flatter, she says, to deceive me;
>   But wha can think sae o' Tam Glen?

But we enter on burning ground as we approach the poetry of times so near to us—poetry like that of Byron, Shelley, and Wordsworth—of which the estimates are so often not only personal, but personal with passion. For my purpose, it is enough to have taken the single case of Burns, the first poet we come to of whose work the estimate formed is evidently apt to be personal, and to have suggested how we may proceed, using the poetry of the great classics as a sort of touchstone, to correct this estimate, as we had previously corrected by the same means the historic estimate where we met with it. A collection like the present, with its succession of celebrated names and celebrated poems, offers a good opportunity to us for resolutely endeavouring to make our estimates of poetry real. I have sought to point out a method which will help us in making them so, and to exhibit it in use so far as to put any one who likes in a way of applying it for himself.

At any rate the end to which the method and the estimate are designed to lead, and from leading to which, if they do lead to it, they get their whole value,—the benefit of being able clearly to feel and deeply to enjoy the best, the truly classic, in poetry,—is an end, let me say it once more at parting, of supreme importance. We are often told that an era is opening in which we are to see multitudes of a common sort of readers, and masses of a common sort of literature; that such readers do not want and could not relish anything better than such literature, and that to provide it is becoming a vast and profitable industry. Even if good literature entirely lost currency with the world, it would still be abundantly worth while to continue to enjoy it by oneself. But it never willl lose currency with the world, in spite of momentary appearances; it never will lose supremacy. Currency and supremacy are insured to it, not indeed by the world's deliberate and conscious choice, but by something far deeper,—by the instinct of self-preservation in humanity.

The English Renaissance of Art

Oscar Wilde

"The English Renaissance of Art" was originally a lecture delivered at Chickering Hall, New York, on 9 January 1882. On 10 January part of the lecture was published in the New York Tribune. *The version reprinted here, a collation of four of Wilde's drafts, first appeared in* Miscellanies, *volume 14 of* The First Collected Edition of the Works of Oscar Wilde *(London: Methuen, 1908), pp. 243-247.*

Among the many debts which we owe to the supreme aesthetic faculty of Goethe is that he was the first to teach us to define beauty in terms the most concrete possible, to realise it, I mean, always in its special manifestations. So, in the lecture which I have the honour to deliver before you, I will not try to give you any abstract definition of beauty—any such universal formula for it as was sought for by the philosophy of the eighteenth century—still less to communicate to you that which in its essence is incommunicable, the virtue by which a particular picture or poem affects us with a unique and special joy; but rather to point out to you the general ideas which characterise the great English Renaissance of Art in this century, to discover their source, as far as that is possible, and to estimate their future as far as that is possible.

I call it our English Renaissance because it is indeed a sort of new birth of the spirit of man, like the great Italian Renaissance of the fifteenth century, in its desire for a more gracious and comely way of life, its passion for physical beauty, its exclusive attention to form, its seeking for new subjects for poetry, new forms of art, new intellectual and imaginative enjoyments: and I call it our romantic movement because it is our most recent expression of beauty.

It has been described as a mere revival of Greek modes of thought, and again as a mere revival of mediaeval feeling. Rather I would say that to these forms of the human spirit it has added whatever of artistic value the intricacy and complexity and experience of modern life can give: taking from the one its clearness of vision and its sustained calm, from the other its variety of expression and the mystery of its vision. For what, as Goethe said, is the study of the ancients but a return to the real world (for that is what they did); and what, said Mazzini, is mediaevalism but individuality?

It is really from the union of Hellenism, in its breadth, its sanity of purpose, its calm possession of beauty, with the adventive, the intensified individualism, the passionate colour of the romantic spirit, that springs the art of the nineteenth century in England, as from the marriage of Faust and Helen of Troy sprang the beautiful boy Euphorion.

Such expressions as "classical" and "romantic" are, it is true, often apt to become the mere catchwords of schools. We must always remember that art has only one sentence to utter: there is for her only one high law, the law of form or harmony—yet between the classical and romantic spirit we may say that there lies this difference at least, that the one deals with the type and the other with the exception. In the work produced under the modern romantic spirit it is no longer the permanent, the essential truths of life that are treated of; it is the momentary situation of the one, the momentary aspect of the other that art seeks to render. In sculpture, which is the type of one spirit, the subject predominates over the situation; in painting, which is the type of the other, the situation predominates over the subject.

There are two spirits, then: the Hellenic spirit and the spirit of romance may be taken as forming the essential elements of our conscious intellectual tradition, of our permanent standard of taste. As regards their origin, in art as in politics there is but one origin for all revolutions, a desire on the part of man for a nobler form of life, for a freer method and opportunity of expression. Yet, I think that in estimating the sensuous and intellectual spirit which presides over our English Renaissance, any attempt to isolate it in any way from the progress and movement and social life of the age that has produced it would be to rob it of its true vitality, possibly to mistake its true meaning. And in disengaging from the pursuits and passions of this crowded modern world those passions and pursuits which have to do with art and the love of art, we must take into account many great events of history which seem to be the most opposed to any such artistic feeling.

Alien then from any wild, political passion, or from the harsh voice of a rude people in revolt, as our English Renaissance must seem, in its passionate cult of pure beauty, its flawless devotion to form, its exclusive and sensitive nature, it is to the French

Revolution that we must look for the most primary factor of its production, the first condition of its birth: that great Revolution of which we are all the children though the voices of some of us be often loud against it; that Revolution to which at a time when even such spirits as Coleridge and Wordsworth lost heart in England, noble messages of love blown across seas came from your young Republic.

It is true that our modern sense of the continuity of history has shown us that neither in politics nor in nature are there revolutions ever but evolutions only, and that the prelude to that wild storm which swept over France in 1789 and made every king in Europe tremble for his throne, was first sounded in literature years before the Bastille fell and the Palace was taken. The way for those red scenes by Seine and Loire was paved by that critical spirit of Germany and England which accustomed men to bring all things to the test of reason or utility or both, while the discontent of the people in the streets of Paris was the echo that followed the life of Émile and of Werther. For Rousseau, by silent lake and mountain, had called humanity back to the golden age that still lies before us and preached a return to nature, in passionate eloquence whose music still lingers about our keen northern air. And Goethe and Scott had brought romance back again from the prison she had lain in for so many centuries—and what is romance but humanity?

Yet in the womb of the Revolution itself, and in the storm and terror of that wild time, tendencies were hidden away that the artistic Renaissance bent to her own service when the time came—a scientific tendency first, which has borne in our own day a brood of somewhat noisy Titans, yet in the sphere of poetry has not been unproductive of good. I do not mean merely in its adding to enthusiasm that intellectual basis which is its strength, or that more obvious influence about which Wordsworth was thinking when he said very nobly that poetry was merely the impassioned expression in the face of science, and that when science would put on a form of flesh and blood the poet would lend his divine spirit to aid the transfiguration. Nor do I dwell much on the great cosmical emotion and deep pantheism of science to which Shelley has given its first and Swinburne its latest glory of song, but rather on its influence on the artistic spirit in preserving that close observation and the sense of limitation as well as of clearness of vision which are the characteristics of the real artist.

The great and golden rule of art as well as of life, wrote William Blake, is that the more distinct, sharp and defined the boundary line, the more perfect is the work of art; and the less keen and sharp the greater is the evidence of weak imitation, plagiarism and bungling. 'Great inventors in all ages knew this—Michael Angelo and Albert Dürer are known by this and by this alone'; and another time he wrote, with all the simple directness of nineteenth-century prose, 'to generalise is to be an idiot.'

And this love of definite conception, this clearness of vision, this artistic sense of limit, is the characteristic of all great work and poetry; of the vision of Homer as of the vision of Dante, of Keats and William Morris as of Chaucer and Theocritus. It lies at the base of all noble, realistic and romantic work as opposed to the colourless and empty abstractions of our own eighteenth-century poets and of the classical dramatists of France, or of the vague spiritualities of the German sentimental school: opposed, too, to that spirit of transcendentalism which also was root and flower itself of the great Revolution, underlying the impassioned contemplation of Wordsworth and giving wings and fire to the eagle-like flight of Shelley, and which in the sphere of philosophy, though displaced by the materialism and positiveness of our day, bequeathed two great schools of thought, the school of Newman to Oxford, the school of Emerson to America. Yet is this spirit of transcendentalism alien to the spirit of art. For the artist can accept no sphere of life in exchange for life itself. For him there is no escape from the bondage of the earth: there is not even the desire of escape.

He is indeed the only true realist: symbolism, which is the essence of the transcendental spirit, is alien to him. The metaphysical mind of Asia will create for itself the monstrous, many-breasted idol of Ephesus, but to the Greek, pure artist, that work is most instinct with spiritual life which conforms most clearly to the perfect facts of physical life.

'The storm of revolution,' as André Chenier said, 'blows out the torch of poetry.' It is not for some little time that the real influence of such a wild cataclysm of things is felt: at first the desire for equality seems to have produced personalities of more giant and Titan stature than the world had ever known before. Men heard the lyre of Byron and the legions of Napoleon; it was a period of measureless passions and of measureless despair; ambition, discontent, were the chords of life and art; the age was an age of revolt: a phase through which the human spirit must pass, but one in which it cannot rest. For the aim of culture is not rebellion but peace, the valley perilous where ignorant armies clash by night being no dwelling-place meet for her to whom the gods have assigned the fresh uplands and sunny heights and clear, untroubled air.

And soon that desire for perfection, which lay at the base of the Revolution, found in a young English poet its most complete and flawless realisation.

Phidias and the achievements of Greek art are foreshadowed in Homer: Dante prefigures for us the passion and colour and intensity of Italian painting: the modern love of landscape dates from Rousseau, and it is in Keats that one discerns the beginning of the artistic renaissance of England.

Byron was a rebel and Shelley a dreamer; but in the calmness and clearness of his vision, his perfect self-control, his unerring sense of beauty and his recognition of a separate realm for the imagination, Keats was the pure and serene artist, the forerunner of the pre-Raphaelite school, and so of the great romantic movement of which I am to speak.

Blake had indeed, before him, claimed for art a lofty, spiritual mission, and had striven to raise design to the ideal level of poetry and music, but the remoteness of his vision both in painting and poetry and the incompleteness of his technical powers had been adverse to any real influence. It is in Keats that the artistic spirit of this century first found its absolute incarnation.

And these pre-Raphaelites, what were they? If you ask nine-tenths of the British public what is the meaning of the word aesthetics, they will tell you it is the French for affectation or the German for a dado; and if you inquire about the pre-Raphaelites you will hear something about an eccentric lot of young men to whom a sort of divine crookedness and holy awkwardness in drawing were the chief objects of art. To know nothing about their great men is one of the necessary elements of English education.

As regards the pre-Raphaelites the story is simple enough. In the year 1847 a number of young men in London, poets and painters, passionate admirers of Keats all of them, formed the habit of meeting together for discussions on art, the result of such discussions being that the English Philistine public was roused suddenly from its ordinary apathy by hearing that there was in its midst a body of young men who had determined to revolutionise English painting and poetry. They called themselves the pre-Raphaelite Brotherhood.

In England, then as now, it was enough for a man to try and produce any serious beautiful work to lose all his rights as a citizen; and besides this, the pre-Raphaelite Brotherhood—among whom the names of Dante Rossetti, Holman Hunt and Millais will be familiar to you—had on their side three things that the English public never forgives: youth, power and enthusiasm.

Satire, always as sterile as it is shameful and as impotent as it is insolent, paid them that usual homage which mediocrity pays to genius—doing, here as always, infinite harm to the public, blinding them to what is beautiful, teaching them that irreverence which is the source of all vileness and narrowness of life, but harming the artist not at all, rather confirming him in the perfect rightness of his work and ambition. For to disagree with three-fourths of the British public on all points is one of the first elements of sanity, one of the deepest consolations in all moments of spiritual doubt.

As regards the ideas these young men brought to the regeneration of English art, we may see at the base of their artistic creations a desire for a deeper spiritual value to be given to art as well as a more decorative value.

Pre-Raphaelites they called themselves; not that they imitated the early Italian masters at all, but that in their work, as opposed to the facile abstractions of Raphael, they found a stronger realism of imagination, a more careful realism of technique, a vision at once more fervent and more vivid, an individuality more intimate and more intense.

For it is not enough that a work of art should conform to the aesthetic demands of its age: there must be also about it, if it is to affect us with any permanent delight, the impress of a distinct individuality, an individuality remote from that of ordinary men, and coming near to us only by virtue of a certain newness and wonder in the work, and through channels whose very strangeness makes us more ready to give them welcome.

La personnalité, said one of the greatest of modern French critics, *voilà ce qui nous sauvera.*

But above all things was it a return to Nature—that formula which seems to suit so many and such diverse movements: they would draw and paint nothing but what they saw, they would try and imagine things as they really happened. Later there came to the old house by Blackfriars Bridge, where this young brotherhood used to meet and work, two young men from Oxford, Edward Burne-Jones and William Morris—the latter substituting for the simpler realism of the early days a more exquisite spirit of choice, a more faultless devotion to beauty, a more intense seeking for perfection: a master of all exquisite design and of all spiritual vision. It is of the school of Florence rather than of that of Venice that he is kinsman, feeling that the close imitation of Nature is a disturbing element in imaginative art. The visible aspect of modern life disturbs him not; rather is it for him to render eternal all that is beautiful in Greek, Italian, and Celtic legend. To Morris we owe poetry whose perfect precision and clearness of word and vision has not been excelled in the literature of our country, and by the revival of the decorative arts he has given to our individualised romantic movement the social idea and the social factor also.

But the revolution accomplished by this clique of young men, with Ruskin's faultless and fervent eloquence to help them, was not one of ideas merely but of execution, not one of conceptions but of creations.

For the great eras in the history of the development of all the arts have been eras not of increased feeling or enthusiasm in feeling for art, but of new technical improvements primarily and specially. The discovery of marble quarries in the purple ravines of Pentelicus and on the little low-lying hills of the island of Paros gave to the Greeks the opportunity for that intensified vitality of action, that more sensuous and simple humanism, to which the Egyptian sculptor working laboriously in the hard porphyry and rose-coloured granite of the desert could not attain. The splendour of the Venetian school began with the introduction of the new oil medium for painting. The progress in modern music has been due to the invention of new instruments entirely, and in no way to an increased consciousness on the part of the musician of any wider social aim. The critic may try and trace the deferred resolutions of Beethoven to some sense of the incompleteness of the modern intellectual spirit, but the artist would have answered, as one of them did afterwards, 'Let them pick out the fifths and leave us at peace.'

And so it is in poetry also: all this love of curious French metres like the Ballade, the Villanelle, the Rondel; all this increased value laid on elaborate alliterations, and on curious words and refrains, such as you will find in Dante Rossetti and Swinburne, is merely the attempt to perfect flute and viol and trumpet through which the spirit of the age and the lips of the poet may blow the music of their many messages.

And so it has been with this romantic movement of ours: it is a reaction against the empty conventional workmanship, the lax execution of previous poetry and painting, showing itself in the work of such men as Rossetti and Burne-Jones by a far greater splendour of colour, a far more intricate wonder of design than English imaginative art has shown before. In Rossetti's poetry and the poetry of Morris, Swinburne and Tennyson a perfect precision and choice of language, a style flawless and fearless, a seeking for all sweet and precious melodies and a sustaining consciousness of the musical value of each word are opposed to that value which is merely intellectual. In this respect they are one with the romantic movement of France of which not the least characteristic note was struck by Théophile Gautier's advice to the young poet to read his dictionary every day, as being the only book worth a poet's reading.

While, then, the material of workmanship is being thus elaborated and discovered to have in itself incommunicable and eternal qualities of its own, qualities entirely satisfying to the poetic sense and not needing for their aesthetic effect any lofty intellectual vision, any deep criticism of life or even any passionate human emotion at all, the spirit and the method of the poet's working—what people call his inspiration—have not escaped the controlling influence of the artistic spirit. Not that the imagination has lost its wings, but we have accustomed ourselves to count their innumerable pulsations, to estimate their limitless strength, to govern their ungovernable freedom.

To the Greeks this problem of the conditions of poetic production, and the places occupied by either spontaneity or self-consciousness in any artistic work, had a peculiar fascination. We find it in the mysticism of Plato and in the rationalism of Aristotle. We find it later in the Italian Renaissance agitating the minds of such men as Leonardo da Vinci. Schiller tried to adjust the balance between form and feeling, and Goethe to estimate the position of self-consciousness in art. Wordsworth's definition of poetry as 'emotion remembered in tranquillity' may be taken as an analysis of one of the stages through which all imaginative work has to pass; and in Keats's longing to be 'able to compose without this fever' (I quote from one of his letters), his desire to substitute for poetic ardour 'a more thoughtful and quiet power,' we may discern the most important moment in the evolution of that artistic life. The question made an early and strange appearance in your literature too; and I need not remind you how deeply the young poets of the French romantic movement were excited and stirred by Edgar Allan Poe's analysis of the workings of his own imagination in the creating of that supreme imaginative work which we know by the name of *The Raven*.

In the last century, when the intellectual and

didactic element had intruded to such an extent into the kingdom which belongs to poetry, it was against the claims of the understanding that an artist like Goethe had to protest. 'The more incomprehensible to the understanding a poem is the better for it,' he said once, asserting the complete supremacy of the imagination in poetry as of reason in prose. But in this century it is rather against the claims of the emotional faculties, the claims of mere sentiment and feeling, that the artist must react. The simple utterance of joy is not poetry any more than a mere personal cry of pain, and the real experiences of the artist are always those which do not find their direct expression but are gathered up and absorbed into some artistic form which seems, from such real experiences, to be the farthest removed and the most alien.

'The heart contains passion but the imagination alone contains poetry,' says Charles Baudelaire. This too was the lesson that Théophile Gautier, most subtle of all modern critics, most fascinating of all modern poets, was never tired of teaching — 'Everybody is affected by a sunrise or a sunset.' The absolute distinction of the artist is not his capacity to feel nature so much as his power of rendering it. The entire subordination of all intellectual and emotional faculties to the vital and informing poetic principle is the surest sign of the strength of our Renaissance.

We have seen the artistic spirit working, first in the delightful and technical sphere of language, the sphere of expression as opposed to subject, then controlling the imagination of the poet in dealing with his subject. And now I would point out to you its operation in the choice of subject. The recognition of a separate realm for the artist, a consciousness of the absolute difference between the world of art and the world of real fact, between classic grace and absolute reality, forms not merely the essential element of any aesthetic charm but is the characteristic of all great imaginative work and of all great eras of artistic creation — of the age of Phidias as of the age of Michael Angelo, of the age of Sophocles as of the age of Goethe.

Art never harms itself by keeping aloof from the social problems of the day: rather, by so doing, it more completely realises for us that which we desire. For to most of us the real life is the life we do not lead, and thus, remaining more true to the essence of its own perfection, more jealous of its own unattainable beauty, is less likely to forget form in feeling or to accept the passion of creation as any substitute for the beauty of the created thing.

The artist is indeed the child of his own age,

but the present will not be to him a whit more real than the past; for, like the philosopher of the Platonic vision, the poet is the spectator of all time and of all existence. For him no form is obsolete, no subject out of date; rather, whatever of life and passion the world has known, in desert of Judaea or in Arcadian valley, by the rivers of Troy or the rivers of Damascus, in the crowded and hideous streets of a modern city or by the pleasant ways of Camelot — all lies before him like an open scroll, all is still instinct with beautiful life. He will take of it what is salutary for his own spirit, no more; choosing some facts and rejecting others with the calm artistic control of one who is in possession of the secret of beauty.

There is indeed a poetical attitude to be adopted towards all things, but all things are not fit subjects for poetry. Into the secure and sacred house of Beauty the true artist will admit nothing that is harsh or disturbing, nothing that gives pain, nothing that is debatable, nothing about which men argue. He can steep himself, if he wishes, in the discussion of all the social problems of his day, poor-laws and local taxation, free trade and bimetallic currency, and the like; but when he writes on these subjects it will be, as Milton nobly expressed it, with his left hand, in prose and not in verse, in a pamphlet and not in a lyric. This exquisite spirit of artistic choice was not in Byron: Wordsworth had it not. In the work of both these men there is much that we have to reject, much that does not give us that sense of calm and perfect repose which should be the effect of all fine, imaginative work. But in Keats it seemed to have been incarnate, and in his lovely *Ode on a Grecian Urn* it found its most secure and faultless expression; in the pageant of the *Earthly Paradise* and the knights and ladies of Burne-Jones it is the one dominant note.

It is to no avail that the Muse of Poetry be called, even by such a clarion note as Whitman's, to migrate from Greece and Ionia and to placard REMOVED and TO LET on the rocks of the snowy Parnassus. Calliope's call is not yet closed, nor are the epics of Asia ended; the Sphinx is not yet silent, nor the fountain of Castaly dry. For art is very life itself and knows nothing of death; she is absolute truth and takes no care of fact; she see (as I remember Mr. Swinburne insisting on at dinner) that Achilles is even now more actual and real than Wellington, not merely more noble and interesting as a type and figure but more positive and real.

Literature must rest always on a principle, and temporal considerations are no principle at all. For to the poet all times and places are one; the stuff he deals with is eternal and eternally the same: no theme is inept, no past or present preferable. The steam whistle will not affright him nor the flutes of Arcadia weary him: for him there is but one time, the artistic moment; but one law, the law of form; but one land, the land of Beauty—a land removed indeed from the real world and yet more sensuous because more enduring; calm, yet with that calm which dwells in the faces of the Greek statues, the calm which comes not from the rejection but from the absorption of passion, the calm which despair and sorrow cannot disturb but intensify only. And so it comes that he who seems to stand most remote from his age is he who mirrors it best, because he has stripped life of what is accidental and transitory, stripped it of that 'mist of familiarity which makes life obscure to us.'

Those strange, wild-eyed sibyls fixed eternally in the whirlwind of ecstasy, those mighty-limbed and Titan prophets, labouring with the secret of the earth and the burden of mystery, that guard and glorify the chapel of Pope Sixtus at Rome—do they not tell us more of the real spirit of the Italian Renaissance, of the dream of Savonarola and of the sin of Borgia, than all the brawling boors and cooking women of Dutch art can teach us of the real spirit of the history of Holland?

And so in our day, also, the two most vital tendencies of the nineteenth century—the democratic and pantheistic tendency and the tendency to value life for the sake of art—found their most complete and perfect utterance in the poetry of Shelley and Keats who, to the blind eyes of their own time, seemed to be as wanderers in the wilderness, preachers of vague or unreal things. And I remember once, in talking to Mr. Burne-Jones about modern science, his saying to me, 'the more materialistic science becomes, the more angels shall I paint: their wings are my protest in favour of the immortality of the soul.'

But these are the intellectual speculations that underlie art. Where in the arts themselves are we to find that breadth of human sympathy which is the condition of all noble work; where in the arts are we to look for what Mazzini would call the social ideas as opposed to the merely personal ideas? By virtue of what claim do I demand for the artist the love and loyalty of the men and women of the world? I think I can answer that.

Whatever spiritual message an artist brings to his aid is a matter for his own soul. He may bring judgment like Michael Angelo or peace like Angelico; he may come with mourning like the great Athenian or with mirth like the singer of Sicily; nor is it for us to do aught but accept his teaching, knowing that we cannot smite the bitter lips of Leopardi into laughter or burden with our discontent Goethe's serene calm. But for warrant of its truth such message must have the flame of eloquence in the lips that speak it, splendour and glory in the vision that is its witness, being justified by one thing only—the flawless beauty and perfect form of its expression: this indeed being the social idea, being the meaning of joy in art.

Not laughter where none should laugh, nor the calling of peace where there is no peace; not in painting the subject ever, but the pictorial charm only, the wonder of its colour, the satisfying beauty of its design.

You have most of you seen, probably, that great masterpiece of Rubens which hangs in the gallery of Brussels, that swift and wonderful pageant of horse and rider arrested in its most exquisite and fiery moment when the winds are caught in crimson banner and the air lit by the gleam of armour and the flash of plume. Well, that is joy in art, though that golden hillside be trodden by the wounded feet of Christ and it is for the death of the Son of Man that that gorgeous cavalcade is passing.

But this restless modern intellectual spirit of ours is not receptive enough of the sensuous element of art; and so the real influence of the arts is hidden from many of us: only a few, escaping from the tyranny of the soul, have learned the secret of those high hours when thought is not.

And this indeed is the reason of the influence which Eastern art is having on us in Europe, and of the fascination of all Japanese work. While the Western world has been laying on art the intolerable burden of its own intellectual doubts and the spiritual tragedy of its own sorrows, the East has always kept true to art's primary and pictorial conditions.

In judging of a beautiful statue the aesthetic faculty is absolutely and completely gratified by the splendid curves of those marble lips that are dumb to our complaint, the noble modelling of those limbs that are powerless to help us. In its primary aspect a painting has no more spiritual message or meaning than an exquisite fragment of Venetian glass or a blue tile from the wall of Damascus: it is a beautifully coloured surface, nothing more. The channels by which all noble imaginative work in painting should touch, and do touch the soul, are not those of the truths of life, nor metaphysical truths. But that pictorial charm which does not depend on any literary reminiscence for its effect on the one hand, nor is yet a mere result of communicable technical skill on the other, comes of a certain inventive and creative handling of colour. Nearly always in Dutch painting and often in the works of Giorgione or Titian, it is entirely independent of anything definitely poetical in the subject, a kind of form and choice in workmanship which is itself entirely satisfying, and is (as the Greeks would say) an end in itself.

And so in poetry too, the real poetical quality, the joy of poetry, comes never from the subject but from an inventive handling of rhythmical language, from what Keats called the 'sensuous life of verse.' The element of song in the singing accompanied by the profound joy of motion, is so sweet that, while the incomplete lives of ordinary men bring no healing power with them, the thorn-crown of the poet will blossom into roses for our pleasure; for our delight his despair will gild its own thorns, and his pain, like Adonis, be beautiful in its agony; and when the poet's heart breaks it will break in music.

And health in art—what is that? It has nothing to do with a sane criticism of life. There is more health in Baudelaire than there is in [Kingsley]. Health is the artist's recognition of the limitations of the form in which he works. It is the honour and the homage which he gives to the material he uses— whether it be language with its glories, or marble or pigment with their glories—knowing that the true brotherhood of the arts consists not in their borrowing one another's method, but in their producing, each of them by its own individual means, each of them by keeping its objective limits, the same unique artistic delight. The delight is like that given to us by music—for music is the art in which form and matter are always one, the art whose subject cannot be separated from the method of its expression, the art which most completely realises the artistic ideal, and is the condition to which all the other arts are constantly aspiring.

And criticism—what place is that to have in our culture? Well, I think that the first duty of an art critic is to hold his tongue at all times, and upon all subjects: *C'est un grand avantage de n'avoir rien fait, mais il ne faut pas en abuser.*

It is only through the mystery of creation that one can gain any knowledge of the quality of created things. You have listened to *Patience* for a hundred nights and you have heard me for one only. It will make, no doubt, that satire more piquant by knowing something about the subject of it, but you must not judge of aestheticism by the satire of Mr. Gilbert. As little should you judge of

the strength and splendour of sun or sea by the dust that dances in the beam, or the bubble that breaks on the wave, as take your critic for any sane test of art. For the artists, like the Greek gods, are revealed only to one another, as Emerson says somewhere; their real value and place time only can show. In this respect also omnipotence is with the ages. The true critic addresses not the artist ever but the public only. His work lies with them. Art can never have any other claim but her own perfection: it is for the critic to create for art the social aim, too, by teaching the people the spirit in which they are to approach all artistic work, the love they are to give it, the lesson they are to draw from it.

All these appeals to art to set herself more in harmony with modern progress and civilisation, and to make herself the mouthpiece for the voice humanity, these appeals to art 'to have a mission,' are appeals which should be made to the public. The art which has fulfilled the conditions of beauty has fulfilled all conditions: it is for the critic to teach the people how to find in the calm of such art the highest expression of their own most stormy passions. 'I have no reverence,' said Keats, 'for the public, nor for anything in existence but the Eternal Being, the memory of great men and the principle of Beauty.'

Such then is the principle which I believe to be guiding and underlying our English Renaissance, a Renaissance many-sided and wonderful, productive of strong ambitions and lofty personalities, yet for all its splendid achievements in poetry and in the decorative arts and in painting, for all the increased comeliness and grace of dress, and the furniture of houses and the like, not complete. For there can be no great sculpture without a beautiful national life, and the commercial spirit of England has killed that; no great drama without a noble national life, and the commercial spirit of England has killed that too.

It is not that the flawless serenity of marble cannot bear the burden of the modern intellectual spirit, or become instinct with the fire of romantic passion—the tomb of Duke Lorenzo and the chapel of the Medici show us that—but it is that, as Théophile Gautier used to say, the visible world is dead, *le monde visible a disparu.*

Nor is it again that the novel has killed the play, as some critics would persuade us—the romantic movement of France shows us that. The work of Balzac and of Hugo grew up side by side together; nay, more, were complementary to each other, though neither of them saw it. While all other forms of poetry may flourish in an ignoble age, the splendid individualism of the lyrist, fed by its own passion, and lit by its own power, may pass as a pillar of fire as well across the desert as across places that are pleasant. It is none the less glorious though no man follow it—nay, by the greater sublimity of its loneliness it may be quickened into loftier utterance and intensified into clearer song. From the mean squalor of the sordid life that limits him, the dreamer or the idyllist may soar on poesy's viewless wings, may traverse with fawn-skin and spear the moonlit heights of Cithaeron though Faun and Bassarid dance there no more. Like Keats he may wander through the old-world forests of Latmos, or stand like Morris on the galley's deck with the Viking when king and galley have long since passed away. But the drama is the meeting-place of art and life; it deals, as Mazzini said, not merely with man, but with social man, with man in his relation to God and to Humanity. It is the product of a period of great national united energy; it is impossible without a noble public, and belongs to such ages as the age of Elizabeth in London and of Pericles at Athens; it is part of such lofty moral and spiritual ardour as came to Greek after the defeat of the Persian fleet, and to Englishman after the wreck of the Armada of Spain.

Shelley felt how incomplete our movement was in this respect, and has shown in one great tragedy by what terror and pity he would have purified our age; but in spite of *The Cenci* the drama is one of the artistic forms through which the genius of the England of this century seeks in vain to find outlet and expression. He has had no worthy imitators.

It is rather, perhaps, to you that we should turn to complete and perfect this great movement of ours, for there is something Hellenic in your air and world, something that has a quicker breath of the joy and power of Elizabeth's England about it than our ancient civilisation can give us. For you, at least, are young; 'no hungry generations tread you down,' and the past does not weary you with the intolerable burden of its memories nor mock you with the ruins of a beauty, the secret of whose creation you have lost. That very absence of tradition, which Mr. Ruskin thought would rob your rivers of their laughter and your flowers of their light, may be rather the source of your freedom and your strength.

To speak in literature with the perfect rectitude and insouciance of the movements of animals, and the unimpeachableness of the sentiment of trees in the woods and grass by the roadside, has been defined by one of your poets as a flawless triumph of art. It is a triumph which you above all nations may be destined to achieve. For the voices that have their dwelling in sea and mountain are not the chosen music of Liberty only; other messages are there in the wonder of wind-swept height and the majesty of silent deep—messages that, if you will but listen to them, may yield you the splendour of some new imagination, the marvel of some new beauty.

'I foresee,' said Goethe, 'the dawn of a new literature which all people may claim as their own, for all have contributed to its foundation.' If, then, this is so, and if the materials for a civilisation as great as that of Europe lie all around you, what profit, you will ask me, will all this study of our poets and painters be to you? I might answer that the intellect can be engaged without direct didactic object on an artistic and historical problem; that the demand of the intellect is merely to feel itself alive; that nothing which has ever interested men or women can cease to be a fit subject for culture.

I might remind you of what all Europe owes to the sorrow of a single Florentine in exile at Verona, or to the love of Petrarch by that little well in Southern France; nay, more, how even in this dull, materialistic age the simple expression of an old man's simple life, passed away from the clamour of great cities amid the lakes and misty hills of Cumberland, has opened out for England treasures of new joy compared with which the treasures of her luxury are as barren as the sea which she has made her highway, and as bitter as the fire which she would make her slave.

But I think it will bring you something besides this, something that is the knowledge of real strength in art: not that you should imitate the works of these men; but their artistic spirit, their artistic attitude, I think you should absorb that.

For in nations, as in individuals, if the passion for creation be not accompanied by the critical, the aesthetic faculty also, it will be sure to waste its strength aimlessly, failing perhaps in the artistic spirit of choice, or in the mistaking of feeling for form, or in the following of false ideals.

For the various spiritual forms of the imagination have a natural affinity with certain sensuous forms of art—and to discern the qualities of each art, to intensify as well its limitations as its powers of expression, is one of the aims that culture sets before us. It is not an increased moral sense, an increased moral supervision that your literature needs. Indeed, one should never talk of a moral or an immoral poem—poems are either well written or badly written, that is all. And, indeed, any element of morals or implied reference to a standard of good or evil in art is often a sign of a certain incompleteness of vision, often a note of discord in the harmony of an imaginative creation; for all good work aims at a purely artistic effect. 'We must be careful,' said Goethe, 'not to be always looking for culture merely in what is obviously moral. Everything that is great promotes civilisation as soon as we are aware of it.'

But, as in your cities so in your literature, it is a permanent canon and standard of taste, an increased sensibility to beauty (if I may say so) that is lacking. All noble work is not national merely, but universal. The political independence of a nation must not be confused with any intellectual isolation. The spiritual freedom, indeed, your own generous lives and liberal air will give you. From us you will learn the classical restraint of form.

For all great art is delicate art, roughness having very little to do with strength, and harshness very little to do with power. 'The artist,' as Mr. Swinburne says, 'must be perfectly articulate.'

This limitation is for the artist perfect freedom: it is at once the origin and the sign of his strength. So that all the supreme masters of style—Dante, Sophocles, Shakespeare—are the supreme masters of spiritual and intellectual vision also.

Love art for its own sake, and then all things that you need will be added to you.

This devotion to beauty and to the creation of beautiful things is the test of all great civilised nations. Philosophy may teach us to bear with equanimity the misfortunes of our neighbours, and science resolve the moral sense into a secretion of sugar, but art is what makes the life of each citizen a sacrament and not a speculation, art is what makes the life of the whole race immortal.

For beauty is the only thing that time cannot harm. Philosophies fall away like sand, and creeds follow one another like the withered leaves of autumn; but what is beautiful is a joy for all seasons and a possession for all eternity.

Wars and the clash of armies and the meeting of men in battle by trampled field or leaguered city, and the rising of nations there must always be. But I think that art, by creating a common intellectual atmosphere between all countries, might—if it could not overshadow the world with the silver wings of peace—at least make men such brothers that they would not go out to slay one another for the whim or folly of some king or minister, as they do in Europe. Fraternity would come no more with the hands of Cain, nor Liberty betray freedom with the kiss of Anarchy; for national hatreds are always strongest where culture is lowest.

'How could I?' said Goethe, when reproached for not writing like Körner against the French. 'How could I, to whom barbarism and culture alone are of importance, hate a nation which is among the most cultivated of the earth, a nation to which I owe a great part of my own cultivation?'

Mighty empires, too, there must always be as long as personal ambition and the spirit of the age are one, but art at least is the only empire which a nation's enemies cannot take from her by conquest, but which is taken by submission only. The sovereignty of Greece and Rome is not yet passed away, though the gods of the one be dead and the eagles of the other tired.

And we in our Renaissance are seeking to create a sovereignty that will still be England's when her yellow leopards have grown weary of wars and the rose of her shield is crimsoned no more with the blood of battle; and you, too, absorbing into the generous heart of a great people this pervading artistic spirit, will create for yourselves such riches as you have never yet created, though your land be a network of railways and your cities the harbours for the galleys of the world.

I know, indeed, that the divine natural prescience of beauty which is the inalienable inheritance of Greek and Italian is not our inheritance. For such an informing and presiding spirit of art to shield us from all harsh and alien influences, we of the Northern races must turn rather to that strained self-consciousness of our age which, as it is the keynote of all our romantic art, must be the source of all or nearly all our culture. I mean that intellectual curiosity of the nineteenth century which is always looking for the secret of the life that still lingers round old and bygone forms of culture. It takes from each what is serviceable for the modern spirit—from Athens its wonder without its worship, from Venice its splendour without its sin. The same spirit is always analysing its own strength and its own weakness, counting what it owes to East and to West, to the olive-trees of Colonus and to the palm-trees of Lebanon, to Gethsemane and to the garden of Proserpine.

And yet the truths of art cannot be taught: they are revealed only, revealed to natures which have made themselves receptive of all beautiful impressions by the study and worship of all beautiful things. And hence the enormous importance given to the decorative arts in our English Renaissance; hence all that marvel of design that comes from the hand of Edward Burne-Jones, all that weaving of tapestry and staining of glass, that beautiful working in clay and metal and wood which we owe to William Morris, the greatest handicraftsman we have had in England since the fourteenth century.

So, in years to come there will be nothing in any man's house which has not given delight to its maker and does not give delight to its user. The children, like the children of Plato's perfect city, will grow up 'in a simple atmosphere of all fair things'—I quote from the passage in the *Republic*—'a simple atmosphere of all fair things, where beauty, which is the spirit of art, will come on eye and ear like a fresh breath of wind that brings health from a clear upland, and insensibly and gradually draw the child's soul into harmony with all knowledge and all wisdom, so that he will love what is beautiful and good, and hate what is evil and ugly (for they always go together) long before he knows the reason why; and then when reason comes will kiss her on the cheek as a friend.'

That is what Plato thought decorative art could do for a nation, feeling that the secret not of philosophy merely but of all gracious existence might be externally hidden from any one whose youth had been passed in uncomely and vulgar surroundings, and that the beauty of form and colour even, as he says, in the meanest vessels of the house, will find its way into the inmost places of the soul and lead the boy naturally to look for that divine harmony of spiritual life of which art was to him the material symbol and warrant.

Prelude indeed to all knowledge and all wisdom will this love of beautiful things be for us; yet there are times when wisdom becomes a burden and knowledge is one with sorrow: for as every body has its shadow so every soul has its scepticism. In such dread moments of discord and despair where should we, of this torn and troubled age, turn our steps if not to that secure house of beauty where there is always a little forgetfulness, always a great joy; to that *città divina,* as the old Italian heresy called it, the divine city where one can stand, though only for a brief moment, apart from the division and terror of the world and the choice of the world too?

This is that *consolation des arts* which is the key-note of Gautier's poetry, the secret of modern life foreshadowed—as indeed what in our century is not?—by Goethe. You remember what he said to the German people: 'Only have the courage,' he said, 'to give yourselves up to your impressions, allow yourselves to be delighted, moved, elevated, nay instructed, inspired for something great.' The courage to give yourselves up to your impressions:

yes, that is the secret of the artistic life—for while art has been defined as an escape from the tyranny of the senses, it is an escape rather from the tyranny of the soul. But only to those who worship her above all things does she ever reveal her true treasure: else will she be as powerless to aid you as the mutilated Venus of the Louvre was before the romantic but sceptical nature of Heine.

And indeed I think it would be impossible to overrate the gain that might follow if we had about us only what gave pleasure to the maker of it and gives pleasure to its user, that being the simplest of all rules about decoration. One thing, at least, I think it would do for us: there is no surer test of a great country than how near it stands to its own poets; but between the singers of our day and the workers to whom they would sing there seems to be an ever-widening and dividing chasm, a chasm which slander and mockery cannot traverse, but which is spanned by the luminous wings of love.

And of such love I think that the abiding presence in our houses of noble imaginative work would be the surest seed and preparation. I do not mean merely as regards that direct literary expression of art by which, from the little red-and-black cruse of oil or wine, a Greek boy could learn of the lionlike splendour of Achilles, of the strength of Hector and the beauty of Paris and the wonder of Helen, long before he stood and listened in crowded marketplace or in theatre of marble; or by which an Italian child of the fifteenth century could know of the chastity of Lucrece and the death of Camilla from carven doorway and from painted chest. For the good we get from art is not what we learn from it; it is what we become through it. Its real influence will be in giving the mind that enthusiasm which is the secret of Hellenism, accustoming it to demand from art all that art can do in rearranging the facts of common life for us—whether it be by giving the most spiritual interpretation of one's own moments of highest passion or the most sensuous expression of those thoughts that are the farthest removed from sense; in accustoming it to love the things of the imagination for their own sake, and to desire beauty and grace in all things. For he who does not love art in all things does not love it at all, and he who does not need art in all things does not need it at all.

I will not dwell here on what I am sure has delighted you all in our great Gothic cathedrals. I mean how the artist of that time, handicraftsman himself in stone or glass, found the best motives for his art, always ready for his hand and always beautiful, in the daily work of the artificers he saw around him—as in those lovely windows of Chartres—where the dyer dips in the vat and the potter sits at the wheel, and the weaver stands at the loom: real manufacturers these, workers with the hand, and entirely delightful to look at, not like the smug and vapid shopman of our time, who knows nothing of the web or vase he sells, except that he is charging you double its value and thinking you a fool for buying it. Nor can I but just note, in passing, the immense influence the decorative work of Greece and Italy had on its artists, the one teaching the sculptor that restraining influence of design which is the glory of the Parthenon, the other keeping painting always true to its primary, pictorial condition of noble colour which is the secret of the school of Venice; for I wish rather, in this lecture at least, to dwell on the effect that decorative art has on human life—on its social not its purely artistic effect.

There are two kinds of men in the world, two great creeds, two different forms of natures: men to whom the end of life is action, and men to whom the end of life is thought. As regards the latter, who seek for experience itself and not for the fruits of experience, who must burn always with one of the passions of this fiery-coloured world, who find life interesting not for its secret but for its situations, for its pulsations and not for its purpose; the passion for beauty engendered by the decorative arts will be to them more satisfying than any political or religious enthusiasm, any enthusiasm for humanity, any ecstasy or sorrow for love. For art comes to one professing primarily to give nothing but the highest quality to one's moments, and for those moments' sake. So far for those to whom the end of life is thought. As regards the others, who hold that life is inseparable from labour, to them should this movement be specially dear: for, if our days are barren without industry, industry without art is barbarism.

Hewers of wood and drawers of water there must be always indeed among us. Our modern machinery has not much lightened the labour of man after all: but at least let the pitcher that stands by the well be beautiful and surely the labour of the day will be lightened: let the wood be made receptive of some lovely form, some gracious design, and there will come no longer discontent but joy to the toiler. For what is decoration but the worker's expression of joy in his work? And not joy merely—that is a great thing yet not enough—but that opportunity of expressing his own individuality which, as it is the essence of all life, is the source of all art. 'I have tried,' I remember William Morris saying to me once, 'I have tried to make each of my workers an

artist, and when I say an artist I mean a man.' For the worker then, handicraftsman of whatever kind he is, art is no longer to be a purple robe woven by a slave and thrown over the whitened body of a leprous king to hide and to adorn the sin of his luxury, but rather the beautiful and noble expression of a life that has in it something beautiful and noble.

And so you must seek out your workman and give him, as far as possible, the right surroundings, for remember that the real test and virtue of a workman is not his earnestness nor his industry even, but his power of design merely; and that 'design is not the offspring of idle fancy: it is the studied result of accumulative observation and delightful habit.' All the teaching in the world is of no avail if you do not surround your workman with happy influences and with beautiful things. It is impossible for him to have right ideas about colour unless he sees the lovely colours of Nature unspoiled; impossible for him to supply beautiful incident and action unless he sees beautiful incident and action in the world about him.

For to cultivate sympathy you must be among living things and thinking about them, and to cultivate admiration you must be among beautiful things and looking at them. 'The steel of Toledo and the silk of Genoa did but give strength to oppression and lustre to pride,' as Mr. Ruskin says; let it be for you to create an art that is made by the hands of the people for the joy of the people, to please the hearts of the people, too; an art that will be your expression of your delight in life. There is nothing 'in common life too mean, in common things too trivial to be ennobled by your touch'; nothing in life that art cannot sanctify.

You have heard, I think, a few of you, of two flowers connected with the aesthetic movement in England, and said (I assure you, erroneously) to be the food of some aesthetic young men. Well, let me tell you that the reason we love the lily and the sunflower, in spite of what Mr. Gilbert may tell you, is not for any vegetable fashion at all. It is because these two lovely flowers are in England the two most perfect models of design, the most naturally adapted for decorative art—the gaudy leonine beauty of the one and the precious loveliness of the other giving to the artist the most entire and perfect joy. And so with you: let there be no flower in your meadows that does not wreathe its tendrils around your pillows, no little leaf in your Titan forests that does not lend its form to design, no curving spray of wild rose or brier that does not live for ever in carven arch or window or marble, no bird in your air that is not giving the iridescent wonder of its colour, the exquisite curves of its wings in flight, to make more precious the preciousness of simple adornment. For the voices that have their dwelling in sea and mountain are not the chosen music of liberty only. Other messages are there in the wonder of wind-swept heights and the majesty of silent deep—messages that, if you will listen to them, will give you the wonder of all new imagination, the treasure of all new beauty.

We spend our days, each one of us, in looking for the secret of life. Well, the secret of life is in art.

L'Envoi

Oscar Wilde

Originally published as the introduction to Rennell Rodd's Rose Leaf and Apple Leaf *(Philadelphia: Stoddart, 1882).*

Amongst the many young men in England who are seeking along with me to continue and to perfect the English Renaissance—*jeunes guerriers du drapeau romantique,* as Gautier would have called us—there is none whose love of art is more flawless and fervent, whose artistic sense of beauty is more subtle and more delicate—none, indeed, who is dearer to myself—than the young poet whose verses I have brought with me to America; verses full of sweet sadness, and yet full of joy; for the most joyous poet is not he who sows the desolate highways of this world with the barren seed of laughter, but he who makes his sorrow most musical, this indeed being the meaning of joy in art—that incommunicable element of artistic delight which, in poetry, for instance, comes from what Keats called 'sensuous life of verse,' the element of song in the singing, made so pleasurable to us by that wonder of motion which often has its origin in mere musical impulse, and in painting is to be sought for, from the subject never, but from the pictorial charm only—the scheme and symphony of the colour, the satisfying beauty of the design: so that the ultimate expression of our artistic movement in painting has been, not in the spiritual vision of the Pre-Raphaelites, for all their marvel of Greek legend and their mystery of Italian song, but in the work of such men as Whistler and Albert Moore, who have raised design and colour to the ideal level of poetry and music. For the quality of their exquisite painting comes from the mere inventive and creative handling of line and colour, from a certain form and choice of beautiful workmanship, which, rejecting all literary reminiscence and all metaphysical idea, is in itself entirely satisfying to the aesthetic sense—is, as the Greeks would say, an end in itself; the effect of their work being like the effect given to us by music; for music is the art in which form and matter are always one—the art whose subject cannot be separated from the method of its expression; the art which most completely realizes for us the artistic ideal, and is the condition to which all the other arts are constantly aspiring.

Now, this increased sense of the absolutely satisfying value of beautiful workmanship, this recognition of the primary importance of the sensuous element in art, this love of art for art's sake, is the point in which we of the younger school have made a departure from the teaching of Mr. Ruskin,—a departure definite and different and decisive.

Master indeed of the knowledge of all noble living and of the wisdom of all spiritual things will he be to us ever, seeing that it was he who by the magic of his presence and the music of his lips taught us at Oxford that enthusiasm for beauty which is the secret of Hellenism, and that desire for creation which is the secret of life, and filled some of us, at least, with the lofty and passionate ambition to go forth into far and fair lands with some message for the nations and some mission for the world, and yet in his art criticism, his estimate of the joyous element of art, his whole method of approaching art, we are no longer with him; for the keystone to his aesthetic system is ethical always. He would judge of a picture by the amount of noble moral ideas it expresses; but to us the channels by which all noble work in painting can touch, and does touch, the soul are not those of truths of life or metaphysical truths. To him perfection of workmanship seems but the symbol of pride, and incompleteness of technical resource the image of an imagination too limitless to find within the limits of form its complete expression, or of love too simple not to stammer in its tale. But to us the rule of art is not the rule of morals. In an ethical system, indeed, of any gentle mercy good intentions will, one is fain to fancy, have their recognition; but of those that would enter the serene House of Beauty the question that we ask is not what they had ever meant to do, but what they have done. Their pathetic intentions are of no value to us, but their realized creations only. *Pour moi je préfère les poètes qui font des vers, les médecins qui sachent guérir, les peintres qui sachent peindre.*

Nor, in looking at a work of art, should we be dreaming of what it symbolises, but rather loving it for what it is. Indeed, the transcendental spirit is alien to the spirit of art. The metaphysical mind of Asia may create for itself the monstrous and many-breasted idol, but to the Greek, pure artist, that work is most instinct with spiritual life which conforms most closely to the perfect facts of physical life also. Nor, in its primary aspect, has a painting, for instance, any more spiritual message or meaning for us than a blue tile from the wall of Damascus, or a Hitzen vase. It is a beautifully coloured surface, nothing more, and affects us by no suggestion stolen from philosophy, no pathos pilfered from literature, no feeling filched from a poet, but by its own incommunicable artistic essence—by that selection of truth which we call style, and that relation of values which is the draughtsmanship of painting, by the whole quality of the workmanship, the arabesque of the design, the splendour of the colour, for these things are enough to stir the most divine and remote of the chords which make music in our soul, and colour, indeed, is of itself a mystical presence on things, and tone a kind of sentiment . . . all these poems aim, as I said, at producing a purely artistic effect, and have the rare and exquisite quality that belongs to work of that kind; and I feel that the entire subordination in our aesthetic movement of all merely emotional and intellectual motives to the vital informing poetic principle is the surest sign of our strength.

But it is not enough that a work of art should conform to the aesthetic demands of the age: there should be also about it, if it is to give us any permanent delight, the impress of a distinct individuality. Whatever work we have in the nineteenth century must rest on the two poles of personality and perfection. And so in this little volume, by separating the earlier and more simple work from the work that is later and stronger and possesses increased technical power and more artistic vision, one might weave these disconnected poems, these stray and scattered threads, into one fiery-coloured strand of life, noting first a boy's mere gladness of being young, with all its simple joy in field and flower, in sunlight and in song, and then the bitterness of sudden sorrow at the ending by Death of one of the brief and beautiful frendships of one's youth, with all those unanswered longings and questionings unsatisfied by which we vex, so uselessly, the marble face of death; the artistic contrast between the discontented incompleteness of the spirit and the complete perfection of the style that expresses it forming the chief element of the aesthetic charm of these particular poems;—and then the birth of Love, and all the wonder and the fear and the perilous delight of one on whose boyish brows the little wings of love have beaten for the first time; and the love-songs, so dainty and delicate, little swallow-flights of music, and full of such fragrance and freedom that they might all be sung in the open air and across moving water; and then autumn, coming with its choirless woods and odorous decay and ruined loveliness, Love lying dead; and the sense of the mere pity of it.

One might stop there, for from a young poet one should ask for no deeper chords of life than those that love and friendship make eternal for us; and the best poems in the volume belong clearly to a later time, a time when these real experiences become absorbed and gathered up into a form which seems from such real experiences to be the most alien and the most remote; when the simple expression of joy or sorrow suffices no longer, and lives rather in the stateliness of the cadenced metre, in the music and colour of the linked words, than in any direct utterance; lives, one might say, in the perfection of the form more than in the pathos of the feeling. And yet, after the broken music of love and the burial of love in the autumn woods, we can trace that wandering among strange people, and in lands unknown to us, by which we try so pathetically to heal the hurts of the life we know, and that pure and passionate devotion to Art which one gets when the harsh reality of life has too suddenly wounded one, and is with discontent or sorrow marring one's youth, just as often, I think, as one gets it from any natural joy of living; and that curious intensity of vision by which, in moments of overmastering sadness and despair ungovernable, artistic things will live in one's memory with a vivid realism caught from the life which they help one to forget—an old grey tomb in Flanders with a strange legend on it, making one think how, perhaps, passion does live on after death; a necklace of blue and amber beads and a broken mirror found in a girl's grave at Rome, a marble image of a boy habited like Erôs, and with the pathetic tradition of a great king's sorrow lingering about it like a purple shadow,—over all these the tired spirit broods with that calm and certain joy that one gets when one has found something that the ages never dull and the world cannot harm; and with it comes that desire of Greek things which is often an artistic method of expressing one's desire for perfection; and that longing for the old dead days which is so modern, so incomplete, so touching, being, in a way, the inverted torch of Hope, which burns the hand it should guide; and for many things a little sadness, and for all things a great love; and lastly, in the pinewood by the sea, once more the quick and vital pulse of joyous youth leaping and laughing in every line, the frank and fearless freedom of wave and wind waking into fire life's burnt-out ashes and into song the silent lips of pain,—how clearly one seems to see it all, the long colonnade of pines with sea and sky peeping in here and there like a flitting of silver; the open place in the green, deep heart of the wood with the little moss-grown altar to the old Italian god in it; and the flowers all about, cyclamen in the shadowy places, and the stars of the white narcissus lying like snow-flakes over the grass, where the quick, bright-eyed lizard starts by the stone, and the snake lies coiled lazily in the sun on the hot sand, and overhead the gossamer floats from the branches like thin, tremulous threads of gold,—the scene is so perfect for its motive, for surely here, if anywhere, the real gladness of life might be revealed to one's youth—the gladness that comes, not from the rejection, but from the absorption, of all passion, and is like that serene calm that dwells in the faces of the Greek statues, and which despair and sorrow cannot touch, but intensify only.

In some such way as this we could gather up these strewn and scattered petals of song into one perfect rose of life, and yet, perhaps, in so doing, we might be missing the true quality of the poems; one's real life is so often the life that one does not lead; and beautiful poems, like threads of beautiful silks, may be woven into many patterns and to suit many designs, all wonderful and all different: and romantic poetry, too, is essentially the poetry of impressions, being like that latest school of painting, the school of Whistler and Albert Moore, in its choice of situation as opposed to subject; in its dealing with the exceptions rather than with the types of life; in its brief intensity; in what one might call its fiery-coloured momentariness, it being indeed the momentary situations of life, the momentary aspects of nature, which poetry and painting

now seek to render for us. Sincerity and constancy will the artist, indeed, have always; but sincerity in art is merely that plastic perfection of execution without which a poem or a painting, however noble its sentiment or human its origin, is but wasted and unreal work, and the constancy of the artist cannot be to any definite rule or system of living, but to that principle of beauty only through which the inconstant shadows of his life are in their most fleeting moment arrested and made permanent. He will not, for instance, in intellectual matters acquiesce in that facile orthodoxy of our day which is so reasonable and so artistically uninteresting, nor yet will he desire that fiery faith of the antique time which, while it intensified, yet limited the vision; still less will he allow the calm of his culture to be marred by the discordant despair of doubt or the sadness of a sterile scepticism; for the Valley Perilous, where ignorant armies clash by night, is no resting-place meet for her to whom the gods have assigned the clear upland, the serene height, and the sunlit air,—rather will he be always curiously testing new forms of belief, tinging his nature with the sentiment that still lingers about some beautiful creeds, and searching for experience itself, and not for the fruits of experience; when he has got its secret, he will leave without regret much that was once very precious to him. 'I am always insincere,' says Emerson somewhere, 'as knowing that there are other moods': 'Les émotions,' wrote Théophile Gautier once in a review of Arsène Houssaye, 'Les émotions, ne se ressemblent pas, mais être ému –voilà l'important.'

Now, this is the secret of the art of the modern romantic school, and gives one the right keynote for its apprehension; but the real quality of all work which, like Mr. Rodd's, aims, as I said, at a purely artistic effect, cannot be described in terms of intellectual criticism; it is too intangible for that. One can perhaps convey it best in terms of the other arts, and by reference to them; and, indeed, some of these poems are as iridescent and as exquisite as a lovely fragment of Venetian glass; others as delicate in perfect workmanship and as single in natural motive as an etching by Whistler is, or one of those beautiful little Greek figures which in the olive woods round Tanagra men can still find, with the faint gilding and the fading crimson not yet fled from hair and lips and raiment; and many of them seem like one of Corot's twilights just passing into music; for not merely in visible colour, but in sentiment also—which is the colour of poetry—may there be a kind of tone.

But I think that the best likeness to the quality of this young poet's work I ever saw was in the landscape by the Loire. We were staying once, he and I, at Amboise, that little village with its grey slate roofs and steep streets and gaunt, grim gateway, where the quiet cottages nestle like white pigeons into the sombre clefts of the great bastioned rock, and the stately Renaissance houses stand silent and apart—very desolate now, but with some memory of the old days still lingering about the delicately-twisted pillars, and the carved doorways, with their grotesque animals, and laughing masks, and quaint heraldic devices, all reminding one of a people who could not think life real till they had made it fantastic. And above the village, and beyond the bend of the river, we used to go in the afternoon, and sketch from one of the big barges that bring the wine in autumn and the wood in winter down to the sea, or lie in the long grass and make plans *pour la gloire, et pour ennuyer les Philistins,* or wander along the low, sedgy banks, 'matching our reeds in sportive rivalry,' as comrades used in the old Sicilian days; and the land was an ordinary land enough, and bare, too, when one thought of Italy, and how the oleanders were robing the hillsides by Genoa in scarlet, and the cyclamen filling with its purple every valley from Florence to Rome; for there was not much real beauty, perhaps, in it, only long, white dusty roads and straight rows of formal poplars; but, now and then, some little breaking gleam of broken light would lend to the grey field and the silent barn a secret and a mystery that were hardly their own, would transfigure for one exquisite moment the peasants passing down through the vineyard, or the shepherd watching on the hill, would tip the willows with silver and touch the river into gold; and the wonder of the effect, with the strange simplicity of the material, always seemed to me to be a little like the quality of these the verses of my friend.

Appendix II

The Pre-Raphaelite Controversy

Editors' Note

The following essays by Robert Buchanan, Dante Gabriel Rossetti, and A. C. Swinburne are key documents in one of the nineteenth century's most highly charged literary controversies. It began in October 1871 with the Scottish novelist and poet Robert Buchanan's pseudonymous attack on Rossetti and the Pre-Raphaelites, ostensibly published as a review of Rossetti's *Poems* (1870) entitled "The Fleshly School of Poetry." Rossetti responded in December 1871 with "The Stealthy School of Criticism," defending his poetry and contradicting the charge that he favored "fleshliness as the . . . supreme end of poetic and fictional art." Buchanan reacted by expanding his initial attack into a ninety-seven-page pamphlet entitled *The Fleshly School of Poetry and Other Phenomena of the Day,* which was published under his own name. In the pamphlet Buchanan extended his attack to include the "vile poet" Swinburne as his final target. Swinburne replied with the virulent satire *Under the Microscope,* published in July 1872. Swinburne's style is vigorous and excessive, with one paragraph extending some twenty-seven pages. Calling Buchanan "the tadpole poet" who "will never grow into anything bigger than a frog," Swinburne uses inflammatory rhetoric to annihilate the critic. The controversy did not end with publication of Swinburne's pamphlet, although it is the last of the important writings reprinted here.

Buchanan produced a weak retort, "The Monkey and the Microscope," published in *St. Paul's Magazine* (August 1872), while in "The Devil's Due," published in the *London Examiner* (11 December 1875), Swinburne accused Buchanan of writing the anonymous poem *Jonas Fisher,* satirizing Swinburne and others (the poem was actually written by James Carnegie, Earl of Southesk). But Buchanan took the offensive, making libel charges which resulted in a sensational three-day trial (29 June-1 July 1876). He won a pyrrhic victory with a judgment in his favor of £150. Swinburne, who testified, was upset at the unwelcomed and unfriendly publicity; the trial marked a pause, if not a conclusion, to the public feuding. The controversy, however, had a devastating effect on Buchanan's career, and he finally retracted his attacks in the dedicatory poems to Rossetti in his novel *God and The Man* (1881). The two poems, reprinted below, were published together in the new edition of 1883:

TO AN OLD ENEMY

I would have snatch'd a bay leaf from thy brow,
    Wronging the chaplet on an honoured head;
In peace and tenderness I bring thee *now*
    A lily-flower instead.

Pure as thy purpose, blameless as thy song,
    Sweet as thy spirit, may this offering be:
Forget the bitter blame that did thee wrong,
    And take the gift from me!

                                        R. B.

October 1881.

TO DANTE GABRIEL ROSSETTI

Calmly, thy royal robe of Death around thee,
    Thou sleepest, and weeping Brethren round thee
        stand—
Gently they placed, ere yet God's angel crown'd thee,
    My lily in thy hand!

I never knew thee living, O my brother!
    But on thy breast my lily of love now lies;
And by that token, we *shall* know each other,
    When God's voice saith 'Arise!'

                                        R. B.

August 1882.

The Fleshly School of Poetry:
Mr. D. G. Rossetti

Thomas Maitland
(Robert Buchanan)

Originally published in Contemporary Review, *18 (October 1871): 334-350.*

If, on the occasion of any public performance of Shakespeare's great tragedy, the actors who perform the parts of Rosencranz and Guildenstern were, by a preconcerted arrangement and by means of what is technically known as "gagging," to make themselves fully as prominent as the leading character, and to indulge in soliloquies and business strictly belonging to Hamlet himself, the result would be, to say the least of it, astonishing; yet a very similar effect is produced on the unprejudiced mind when the "walking gentlemen" of the fleshly school of poetry, who bear precisely the same relation to Mr. Tennyson as Rosencranz and Guildenstern do to the Prince of Denmark in the play, obtrude their lesser identities and parade their smaller idiosyncrasies in the front rank of leading performers. In their own place, the gentlemen are interesting and useful. Pursuing still the theatrical analogy, the present drama of poetry might be cast as follows: Mr. Tennyson supporting the part of Hamlet, Mr. Matthew Arnold that of Horatio, Mr. Bailey that of Voltimand, Mr. Buchanan that of Cornelius, Messrs. Swinburne and Morris the parts of Rosencranz and Guildenstern, Mr. Rossetti that of Osric, and Mr. Robert Lytton that of "A Gentleman." It will be seen that we have left no place for Mr. Browning, who may be said, however, to play the leading character in his own peculiar fashion on alternate nights.

This may seem a frivolous and inadequate way of opening our remarks on a school of verse-writers which some people regard as possessing great merits; but in truth, it is scarcely possible to discuss with any seriousness the pretensions with which foolish friends and small critics have surrounded the fleshly school, which, in spite of its spasmodic ramifications in the erotic direction, is merely one of the many sub-Tennysonian schools expanded to supernatural dimensions, and endeavouring by affectations all its own to overshadow its connection with the great original. In the sweep of one single poem, the weird and doubtful "Vivien," Mr. Tennyson has concentrated all the epicene force which, wearisomely expanded, constitutes the characteristic of the writers at present under consideration; and if in "Vivien" he has indicated for them the bounds of sensualism in art, he has in "Maud," in the dramatic person of the hero, afforded distinct precedent for the hysteric tone and overloaded style which is now so familiar to readers of Mr. Swinburne. The fleshliness of "Vivien" may indeed be described as the distinct quality held in common by all the members of the last sub-Tennysonian school, and it is a quality which becomes unwholesome when there is no moral or intellectual quality to temper and control it. Fully conscious of this themselves, the fleshly gentlemen have bound themselves by solemn league and covenant to extol fleshliness as the distinct and supreme end of poetic and pictorial art; to aver that poetic expression is greater than poetic thought, and by inference that the body is greater than the soul, and sound superior to sense; and that the poet, properly to develop his poetic faculty, must be an intellectual hermaphrodite, to whom the very facts of day and night are lost in a whirl of aesthetic terminology. After Mr. Tennyson has probed the depths of modern speculation in a series of commanding moods, all right and interesting in him as the reigning personage, the walking gentlemen, knowing that something of the sort is expected from all leading performers, bare their roseate bosoms and aver that *they* are creedless; the only possible question here being, if any disinterested person cares twopence whether Rosencranz, Guildenstern, and Osric are creedless or not—their self-revelation on that score being so perfectly gratuitous? But having gone so far, it was and is too late to retreat. Rosencranz, Guildenstern, and Osric, finding it impossible to risk an individual bid for the leading business, have arranged all to play leading business together, and mutually to praise, extol, and imitate each other; and although by these measures they have fairly earned for themselves the title of the Mutual Admiration School, they have in a great measure succeeded in their object—to the general stupefaction of a British audience. It is time, therefore, to ascertain whether any of these gentlemen has actually in himself the making of a leading performer. It would be scarcely worth while, however, to inquire into the pretensions of the writers on merely literary grounds, because sooner or later all literature finds its own level, whatever criticism may say or do in the matter; but it unfortunately happens in the present case that the fleshly school of verse-writers are, so to speak, public offenders, because they are diligently spreading the seeds of disease broadcast wherever they are read and understood. Their complaint too is catching, and carries off many young persons. What the complaint is, and how it works, may be seen on a very slight examination of the works of Mr. Dante Gabriel Rossetti, to whom we shall confine our attention in the present article.

Mr. Rossetti has been known for many years as a painter of exceptional powers, who, for reasons best known to himself, has shrunk from publicly exhibiting his pictures, and from allowing anything like a popular estimate to be formed of their qualities. He belongs, or is said to belong, to the so-called Pre-Raphaelite school, a school which is generally considered to exhibit much genius for colour, and great indifference to perspective. It would be unfair to judge the painter by the glimpses we have had of his works, or by the photographs which are sold of the principal paintings. Judged by the photographs, he is an artist who conceives unpleasantly, and draws ill. He is distinctively a colourist, and of his capabilities in colour we cannot speak, though we should guess that they are great; for if there is any good quality by which his poems are specially marked, it is a great sensitiveness to hues and tints as conveyed in poetic epithet. These qualities, which impress the casual spectator of the photographs from his pictures, are to be found abundantly among his verses. There is the same thinness and transparence of design, the same combination of the simple and the grotesque, the same morbid deviation from healthy forms of life, the same sense of weary, wasting, yet exquisite sensuality; nothing virile, nothing tender, nothing completely sane; a superfluity of extreme sensibility, of delight in beautiful forms, hues, and tints, and a deep-seated indifference to all agitating forces and agencies, all tumultuous griefs and sorrows, all the thunderous stress of life, and all the straining storm of speculation. Mr. Morris is often pure, fresh, and wholesome as his own great model; Mr. Swinburne startles us more than once by some fine flash of insight;

but the mind of Mr. Rossetti is like a glassy mere, broken only by the dive of some water-bird or the hum of winged insects, and brooded over by an atmosphere of insufferable closeness, with a light blue sky above it, sultry depths mirrored within it, and a surface so thickly sown with water-lilies that it retains its glassy smoothness even in the strongest wind. Judged relatively to his poetic associates, Mr. Rossetti must be pronounced inferior to either. He cannot tell a pleasant story like Mr. Morris, nor forge alliterative thunderbolts like Mr. Swinburne. It must be conceded, nevertheless, that he is neither so glibly imitative as the one, nor so transcendently superficial as the other.

Although he has been known for many years as a poet as well as a painter—as a painter and poet idolised by his own family and personal associates—and although he has once or twice appeared in print as a contributor to magazines, Mr. Rossetti did not formally appeal to the public until rather more than a year ago, when he published a copious volume of poems, with the announcement that the book, although it contained pieces composed at intervals during a period of many years, "included nothing which the author believes to be immature." This work was inscribed to his brother, Mr. William Rossetti, who, having written much both in poetry and criticism, will perhaps be known to bibliographers as the editor of the worst edition of Shelley which has yet seen the light. No sooner had the work appeared than the chorus of eulogy began. Strange to say, moreover, no one accused Mr. Rossetti of naughtiness. What had been heinous in Mr. Swinburne was majestic exquisiteness in Mr. Rossetti. Yet we question if there is anything in the unfortunate "Poems and Ballads" quite so questionable on the score of thorough nastiness as many pieces in Mr. Rossetti's collection. Mr. Swinburne was wilder, more outrageous, more blasphemous, and his subjects were more atrocious in themselves; yet the hysterical tone slew the animalism, the furiousness of epithet lowered the sensation; and the first feeling of disgust at such themes as "Laus Veneris" and "Anactoria," faded away into comic amazement. It was only a little mad by letting off squibs; not a great strong man, who might be really dangerous to society. "I *will* be naughty!" screamed the little boy; but, after all, what did it matter? It is quite different, however, when a grown man, with the self-control and easy audacity of actual experience, comes forward to chronicle his amorous sensations, and, first proclaiming in a loud voice his literary maturity, and consequent responsibility, shamelessly prints and publishes such a piece of writing as this sonnet on "Nuptial Sleep":—

At length their long kiss severed, with sweet smart:
And as the last slow sudden drops are shed
From sparkling eaves when all the storm has fled,
So singly flagged the pulses of each heart.
Their bosoms sundered, with the opening start
Of married flowers to either side outspread
From the knit stem; yet still their mouths, burnt red,
Fawned on each other where they lay apart.
Sleep sank them lower than the tide of dreams,
  And their dreams watched them sink, and slid away.
Slowly their souls swam up again, through gleams
  Of watered light and dull drowned waifs of day;
Till from some wonder of new woods and streams
  He woke, and wondered more: for there she lay.

Here is a full-grown man, presumably intelligent and cultivated, putting on record for other full-grown men to read, the most secret mysteries of sexual connection, and that with so sickening a desire to reproduce the sensual mood, so careful a choice of epithet to convey mere animal sensations, that we merely shudder at the shameless nakedness. We are no purists in such matters. We hold the sensual part of our nature to be as holy as the spiritual or intellectual part, and we believe that such things must find their equivalent in all; but it is neither poetic, nor manly, nor even human, to obtrude such things as the themes of whole poems. It is simply nasty. Nasty as it is, we are very mistaken if many readers do not think it nice.

It must not be supposed that all Mr. Rossetti's poems are made up of trash like this. Some of them are as noteworthy for delicacy of touch as others are for shamelessness of expositon. They contain some exquisite pictures of nature, occasional passages of real meaning, much beautiful phraseology, lines of peculiar sweetness, and epithets chosen with true literary cunning. But the fleshly feeling is everywhere. Sometimes, as in "The Stream's Secret," it is deliciously modulated, and adds greatly to our emotion of pleasure at perusing a finely-wrought poem; at other times, as in the "Last Confession," it is fiercely held in check by the exigencies of a powerful situation and the strength of a dramatic speaker; but it is generally in the foreground, flushing the whole poem with unhealthy rose-colour, stifling the senses with overpowering sickliness, as of too much civet. Mr. Rossetti is never dramatic, never impersonal—always attitudinising, posturing, and describing his own exquisite emotions. He is the "Blessed Damozel," leaning over the "gold bar of heaven," and seeing

"Time like a pulse shake fierce
  Thro' all the worlds";

he is "heaven-born Helen, Sparta's queen," whose "each twin breast is an apple sweet"; he is Lilith the first wife of Adam; he is the rosy Virgin of the poem called "Ave," and the Queen in the "Staff and Scrip"; he is "Sister Helen" melting her waxen man; he is all these, just as surely as he is Mr. Rossetti soliloquising over Jenny in her London lodging, or the very nuptial person writing erotic sonnets to his wife. In petticoats or pantaloons, in modern times or in the middle ages, he is just Mr. Rossetti, a fleshly person, with nothing particular to tell us or teach us, with extreme self-control, a strong sense of colour, and a careful choice of diction. Amid all his "affluence of jewel-coloured words," he has not given us one rounded and noteworthy piece of art, though his verses are all art; not one poem which is memorable for its own sake, and quite separable from the displeasing identity of the composer. The nearest approach to a perfect whole is the "Blessed Damozel," a peculiar poem, placed first in the book, perhaps by accident, perhaps because it is a key to the poems which follow. This poem appeared in a rough shape many years ago in the *Germ*, an unwholesome periodical started by the Pre-Raphaelites, and suffered, after gasping through a few feeble numbers, to die the death of all such publications. In spite of its affected title, and of numberless affectations throughout the text, the "Blessed Damozel" has great merits of its own, and a few lines of real genius. We have heard it described as the record of actual grief and love, or, in simple words, the apotheosis of one actually lost by the writer; but, without having any private knowledge of the circumstance of its composition, we feel that such an account of the poem is inadmissible. It does not contain one single note of sorrow. It is a "composition," and a clever one. Read the opening stanzas:—

"The blessed damozel leaned out
  From the gold bar of Heaven;
Her eyes were deeper than the depth
  Of water stilled at even;
She had three lilies in her hand,
  And the stars in her hair were seven.
"Her robe, ungirt from clasp to hem,
  No wrought flowers did adorn,
But a white rose of Mary's gift,
  For service meetly worn;
Her hair that lay along her back
  Was yellow like ripe corn."

This is a careful sketch for a picture, which, worked into actual colour by a master, might have been worth seeing. The steadiness of hand lessens as the poem proceeds, and although there are several passages of considerable power,—such as that where, far down the void,

> "this earth
> Spins like a fretful midge,"

or that other, describing how

> "the curled moon
> Was like a little feather
> Fluttering far down the gulf,"—

the general effect is that of a queer old painting in a missal, very affected and very odd. What moved the British critic to ecstasy in this poem seems to us very sad nonsense indeed, or, if not sad nonsense, very meretricious affectation.

In a short notice from a well-known pen, giving the best estimate we have seen of Mr. Rossetti's powers as a poet, the *North American Review* offers a certain explanation for affectation such as that of Mr. Rossetti. The writer suggests that "it may probably be the expression of genuine moods of mind in natures too little comprehensive." We would rather believe that Mr. Rossetti lacks comprehension than that he is deficient in sincerity; yet really, to paraphrase the words which Johnson applied to Thomas Sheridan, Mr. Rossetti is affected, naturally affected, but it must have taken him a great deal of trouble to become what we now see him—such an excess of affectation is not in nature.[1] There is very little writing in the volume spontaneous in the sense that some of Swinburne's verses are spontaneous; the poems all look as if they had taken a great deal of trouble. The grotesque mediaevalism of "Stratton Water" and "Sister Helen," the mediaeval classicism of "Troy Town," the false and shallow mysticism of "Eden Bower," are one and all essentially imitative, and must have cost the writer much pains. It is time, indeed, to point out that Mr. Rossetti is a poet possessing great powers of assimilation and some faculty for concealing the nutriment on which he feeds. Setting aside the "Vita Nuova" and the early Italian poems, which are familiar to many readers by his own excellent translations, Mr. Rossetti may be described as a writer who has yielded to an unusual extent to the complex influences of the literature surrounding him at the present moment. He has the painter's imitative power developed in proportion to his lack of the poet's conceiving imag-

ination. He reproduces to a nicety the manner of an old ballad, a trick in which Mr. Swinburne is also an adept. Cultivated readers, moreover, will recognise in every one of these poems the tone of Mr. Tennyson broken up by the style of Mr. and Mrs. Browning, and disguised here and there by the eccentricities of the Pre-Raphaelites. The "Burden of Nineveh" is a philosophical edition of "Recollections of the Arabian Nights"; "A Last Confession" and "Dante at Verona" are, in the minutest trick and form of thought, suggestive of Mr. Browning; and that the sonnets have been largely moulded and inspired by Mrs. Browning can be ascertained by any critic who will compare them with the "Sonnets from the Portuguese." Much remains, nevertheless, that is Mr. Rossetti's own. We at once recognise as his own property such passages as this:—

> "I looked up
> And saw where a brown-shouldered harlot leaned
> Half through a tavern window thick with vine.
> Some man had come behind her in the room
> And caught her by her arms, and she had turned
> With that coarse empty laugh on him, as now
> He *munched her neck with kisses, while the vine
> Crawled in her back.*

Or this:—

> "As I stooped, her own lips rising there
> *Bubbled with brimming kisses* at my mouth."

Or this:—

> "Have seen your lifted silken skirt
> Advertise dainties through the dirt!"

Or this:—

> "What more prize than love to impel thee,
> *Grip* and *lip* my limbs as I tell thee!"

Passages like these are the common stock of the walking gentlemen of the fleshly school. We cannot forbear expressing our wonder, by the way, at the kind of women whom it seems the unhappy lot of these gentlemen to encounter. We have lived as long in the world as they have, but never yet came across persons of the other sex who conduct themselves in the manner described. Females who bite, scratch, scream, bubble, munch, sweat, writhe, twist, wriggle, foam, and in a general way slaver over their lovers, must surely possess some extraordinary qualities to counteract their otherwise most offensive mode of conducting themselves. It appears, however, on examination, that their poet-lovers conduct themselves in a similar manner. They, too, bite, scratch, scream, bubble, munch, sweat, writhe, twist, wriggle, foam, and slaver, in a style frightful to hear of. Let us hope that it is only their fun, and that they don't mean half they say. At times, in reading such books as this, one cannot help wishing that things had remained for ever in the asexual state described in Mr. Darwin's great chapter on Palingenesis. We get very weary of this protracted hankering after a person of the other sex; it seems meat, drink, thought, sinew, religion for the fleshly school. There is no limit to the fleshliness, and Mr. Rossetti finds in it its own religious justification much in the same way as Holy Willie:—

> "Maybe thou let'st this fleshly thorn
> Perplex thy servant night and morn,
>   'Cause he's so gifted.
> If so, thy hand must e'en be borne,
>   Until thou lift it."

Whether he is writing of the holy Damozel, or of the Virgin herself, or of Lilith, or Helen, or of Dante, or of Jenny the street-walker, he is fleshly all over, from the roots of his hair to the tip of his toes; never a true lover merging his identity into that of the beloved one; never spiritual, never tender; always self-conscious and aesthetic. "Nothing," says a modern writer, "in human life is so utterly remorseless—not love, not hate, not ambition, not vanity—as the artistic or aesthetic instinct morbidly developed to the suppression of conscience and feeling"; and at no time do we feel more fully impressed with this truth than after the perusal of "Jenny," in some respects the finest poem in the volume, and in all respects the poem best indicative of the true quality of the writer's humanity. It is a production which bears signs of having been suggested by Mr. Buchanan's quasi-lyrical poems, which it copies in the style of title, and particularly by "Artist and Model"; but certainly Mr. Rossetti cannot be accused, as the Scottish writer has been accused, of maudlin sentiment and affected tenderness. The two first lines are perfect:—

> "Lazy laughing languid Jenny,
> Fond of a kiss and fond of a guinea;"

And the poem is a soliloquy of the poet—who has been spending the evening in dancing at a casino—over his partner, whom he has accompanied home to the usual style of lodgings occupied by such ladies, and who has fallen asleep with her head upon his knee, while he wonders, in a wretched pun—

> "Whose person or whose purse may be
> The lodestar of your reverie?"

The soliloquy is long, and in some parts beautiful, despite a very constant suspicion that we are listening to an emasculated Mr. Browning, whose whole tone and gesture, so to speak, is occasionally introduced with startling fidelity; and there are here and there glimpses of actual thought and insight, over and above the picturesque touches which belong to the writer's true profession, such as that where, at daybreak—

> "lights creep in
> Past the gauze curtains half drawn-to,
> And *the lamp's doubled shade grows blue.*"

What we object to in this poem is not the subject, which any writer may be fairly left to choose for himself; nor anything particularly vicious in the poetic treatment of it; nor any bad blood bursting through in special passages. But the whole tone, without being more than usually coarse, seems heartless. There is not a drop of piteousness in Mr. Rossetti. He is just to the outcast, even generous; severe to the seducer; sad even at the spectacle of lust in dimity and fine ribbons. Notwithstanding all this, and a certain delicacy and refinement of treatment unusual with this poet, the poem repels and revolts us, and we like Mr. Rossetti least after its perusal. We are angry with the fleshly person at last. The "Blessed Damozel" puzzled us, the "Song of the Bower" amused us, the love-sonnet depressed and sickened us, but "Jenny," though distinguished by less special viciousness of thought and style than any of these, fairly makes us lose patience. We detect its fleshliness at a glance; we perceive that the scene was fascinating less through its human tenderness than because it, like all the others, possessed an inherent quality of animalism.

It is time that we permitted Mr. Rossetti to speak for himself, which we will do by quoting a fairly representative poem entire:—

LOVE-LILY

> "Between the hands, between the brows,
> Between the lips of Love-Lily,
> *A spirit is born whose birth endows*
> *My blood with fire to burn through me;*

Who breathes upon my gazing eyes,
   Who laughs and murmurs in mine ear,
At whose least touch my colour flies,
   And whom my life grows faint to hear.
"Within the voice, within the heart,
   Within the mind of Love-Lily,
A spirit is born who lifts apart
   His tremulous wings and looks at me;
Who on my mouth his finger lays,
   And shows, while whispering lutes confer,
That Eden of Love's watered ways
   Whose winds and spirits worship her.
"Brows, hands, and lips, heart, mind, and voice,
   Kisses and words of Love-Lily,—
Oh! bid me with your joy rejoice
   Till *riotous longing rest in me!*
Ah! let not hope be still distraught,
   But find in her its gracious goal,
Whose speech Truth knows not from her thought,
   Nor Love her body from her soul."

With the exception of the usual "riotous longing," which seems to make Mr. Rossetti a burthen to himself, there is nothing to find fault with in the extreme fleshliness of these verses, and to many people who live in the country they may even appear beautiful. Without pausing to criticise a thing so trifling—as well might we dissect a cobweb or anatomise a medusa—let us ask the reader's attention to a peculiarity to which all the students of the fleshly school must sooner or later give their attention—we mean the habit of accenting the last syllable in words which in ordinary speech are accented on the penultimate:—

   "Between the hands, between the brows,
    Between the lips of Love-Lil*ee!*"

which may be said to give to the speaker's voice a sort of cooing tenderness just bordering on a loving whistle.

    It is unnecessary to multiply examples of an affection which disfigures all these writers—Guildenstern, Rosencranz, and Osric; who, in the same spirit which prompts the ambitious nobodies that rent London theatres in the "empty" season to make up for their dullness by fearfully original "new readings," distinguish their attempt at leading business by affecting the construction of their grandfathers and great-grandfathers, and the accentuation of the poets of the court of James I. It is in all respects a sign of remarkable genius, from this point of view, to rhyme "was" with "grass," "death" with "lièth," "love" with "of," "once" with "suns," and so on *ad nauseam*. We are far from disputing the value of bad rhymes used occasionally to break up the monotony of verse, but the case is hard when such blunders become the rule and not the exception, when writers deliberately lay themselves out to be as archaic and affected as possible. Poetry is perfect human speech, and these archaisms are the mere fiddle-dedeeing of empty heads and hollow hearts. Bad as they are, they are the true indication of falser tricks and affectations which lie far deeper. They are trifles, light as air, showing how the wind blows. The soul's speech and the heart's speech are clear, simple, natural, and beautiful, and reject the meretricious tricks to which we have drawn attention.

    It is on the score that these tricks and affectations have procured the professors a number of imitators, that the fleshly school deliver their formula that great poets are always to be known because their manner is immediately reproduced by small poets, and that a poet who finds few imitators is probably of inferior rank—by which they mean to infer that they themselves are very great poets indeed. It is quite true that they are imitated. On the stage, twenty provincial "stars" copy Charles Kean, while not one copies his father; there are dozens of actors who reproduce Mr. Charles Dillon, and not one who attempts to reproduce Macready. When we take up the poems of Mr. O'Shaughnessy,[2] we are face to face with a second-hand Mr. Swinburne; when we read Mr. Payne's queer allegories,[3] we remember Mr. Morris's early stage; and every poem of Mr. Marston's reminds us of Mr. Rossetti. But what is really most droll and puzzling in the matter is, that these imitators seem to have no difficulty whatever in writing nearly, if not quite, as well as their masters. It is not bad imitations they offer us, but poems which read just like the originals; the fact being that it is easy to reproduce sound when it has no strict connection with sense, and simple enough to cull phraseology not hopelessly interwoven with thought and spirit. The fact that these gentlemen are so easily imitated is the most damning proof of their inferiority. What merits they have lie with their faults on the surface, and can be caught by any young gentleman as easily as the measles, only they are rather more difficult to get rid of. All young gentlemen have animal faculties, though few have brains; and if animal faculties without brains will make poems, nothing is easier in the world. A great and good poet, however, is great and good irrespective of manner, and often in spite of manner; he is great because he brings great ideas and new light, because his thought is a revelation; and, although it is true that a great manner generally accompanies great matter, the manner of great matter is almost inimitable. The great poet is not Cowley, imitated and idolised and reproduced by every scribbler of his time; nor Pope, whose trick of style was so easily copied that to this day we cannot trace his own hand with any certainty in the *Iliad;* nor Donne, nor Sylvester, nor the Della Cruscans. Shakespeare's blank verse is the most difficult and Jonson's the most easy to imitate, of all the Elizabethan stock; and Shakespeare's verse is the best verse, because it combines the great qualities of all contemporary verse, with no individual affectations; and so perfectly does this verse, with all its splendour, intersect with the style of contemporaries *at their best,* that we would undertake to select passage after passage which would puzzle a good judge to tell which of the Elizabethans was the author—Marlowe, Beaumont, Dekkar, Marston, Webster, or Shakespeare himself.

The great strong current of English poetry rolls on, ever mirroring in its bosom new prospects of fair and wholesome thought. Morbid deviations are endless and inevitable; there must be marsh and stagnant mere as well as mountain and wood. Glancing backward into the shady places of the obscure, we see the once prosperous nonsense-writers each now consigned to his own little limbo—Skelton and Gower still playing fantastic tricks with the mother-tongue; Gascoigne outlasting the applause of all, and living to see his own works buried before him; Silvester doomed to oblivion by his own fame as a translator; Carew the idol of courts, and Donne the beloved of schoolmen, both buried in the same oblivion; the fantastic Fletchers winning the wonder of collegians, and fading out through sheer poetic impotence; Cowley shaking all En-gland with his pindarics, and perishing with them; Waller, the famous, saved from oblivion by the natural note of one single song—and so on, through league after league of a flat and desolate country which once was prosperous, till we come again to these fantastic figures of the fleshly school, with their droll mediaeval garments, their funny archaic speech, and the fatal marks of literary consumption in every pale and delicate visage. Our judgment on Mr. Rossetti, to whom we in the meantime confine our judgment, is substantially that of the *North American Reviewer,* who believes that "we have in him another poetical man, and a man markedly poetical, and of a kind apparently, though not radically, different from any of our secondary writers of poetry, but that we have not in him a new poet of any weight"; and that he is "so affected, sentimental, and painfully self-conscious, that the best to be done in his case is to hope that this book of his, having unpacked his bosom of so much that is unhealthy, may have done him more good than it has given others pleasure." Such, we say, is our opinion, which might very well be wrong, and have to undergo modification, if Mr. Rossetti was younger and less self-possessed. His "maturity" is fatal.

1. "Why, sir, Sherry is dull, *naturally* dull; but it must have taken him a *great deal of trouble* to become what we now see him—such an excess of stupidity is not in nature."—*Boswell's Life.*

2. "An Epic of Women." By Arthur W. E. O'Shaughnessy. (Hotten.)

3. "The Masque of Shadows." By John Payne. (Pickering.)

The Stealthy School of Criticism

Dante Gabriel Rossetti

Originally published in Athenaeum, *2303 (16 December 1871): 792-794.*

Your paragraph, a fortnight ago, relating to the pseudonymous authorship of an article, violently assailing myself and other writers of poetry, in the *Contemporary Review* for October last, reveals a species of critical masquerade which I have expressed in the heading given to this letter. Since then, Mr. Sidney Colvin's note, qualifying the report that he intends to "answer" that article, has appeared in your pages; and my own view as to the absolute forfeit, under such conditions, of all claim to honourable reply, is precisely the same as Mr. Colvin's. For here a critical organ, professedly adopting the principle of open signature, would seem, in reality, to assert (by silent practice, however, not by enunciation,) that if the anonymous in criticism was—as itself originally inculcated—but an early caterpillar stage, the nominate too is found to be no better than a homely transitional chrysalis, and that the ultimate butterfly form for a critic who likes to sport in sunlight and yet to elude the grasp, is after all the pseudonymous. But, indeed, what I may call the "Siamese" aspect of the entertainment provided by the *Review* will elicit but one verdict. Yet I may, perhaps, as the individual chiefly attacked, be excused for asking your assistance now in giving a specific denial to specific charges which, if unrefuted, may still continue, in spite of their author's strategic *fiasco,* to serve his purpose against me to some extent.

The primary accusation, on which this writer grounds all the rest, seems to be that others and myself "extol fleshliness as the distinct and supreme end of poetic and pictorial art; aver that poetic expression is greater than poetic thought; and, by inference, that the body is greater than the soul, and sound superior to sense."

As my own writings are alone formally dealt with in the article, I shall confine my answer to myself; and this must first take unavoidably the form of a challenge to prove so broad a statement. It is true, some fragmentary pretence at proof is put in here and there throughout the attack, and thus far an opportunity is given of contesting the assertion.

A Sonnet entitled *Nuptial Sleep* is quoted and abused at page 338 of the *Review,* and is there dwelt upon as a "whole poem," describing "merely animal sensations." It is no more a whole poem, in reality, than is any single stanza of any poem throughout the book. The poem, written chiefly in sonnets, and of which this is one sonnet-stanza, is entitled *The House of Life;* and even in my first published instalment of the whole work (as contained in the volume under notice) ample evidence is included that no such passing phase of description as the one headed *Nuptial Sleep* could possibly be put forward by the author of *The House of Life* as his own representative view of the subject of love. In proof of this, I will direct attention (among the love-sonnets of this poem) to Nos. 2, 8, 11, 17, 28, and more especially 13, which, indeed, I had better print here.

LOVE-SWEETNESS

"Sweet dimness of her loosened hair's downfall
   About thy face; her sweet hands round thy head
   In gracious fostering union garlanded;
Her tremulous smiles; her glances' sweet recall
Of love; her murmuring sighs memorial;
   Her mouth's culled sweetness by thy kisses shed
   On cheeks and neck and eyelids, and so led
Back to her mouth which answers there for all:—

"What sweeter than these things, except the thing
   In lacking which all these would lose their sweet:—
   The confident heart's still fervour; the swift beat
And soft subsidence of the spirit's wing
Then when it feels, in cloud-girt wayfaring,
   The breath of kindred plumes against its feet?"

Any reader may bring any artistic charge he pleases against the above sonnet; but one charge it would be impossible to maintain against the writer of the series in which it occurs, and that is, the wish on his part to assert that the body is greater than the soul. For here all the passionate and just delights of the body are declared—somewhat figuratively, it is true, but unmistakably—to be as naught if not ennobled by the concurrence of the soul at all times. Moreover, nearly one half of this series of sonnets has nothing to do with love, but treats of quite other life-influences. I would defy any one to couple with fair quotation of Sonnets 29, 30, 31, 39, 40, 41, 43,

338

or others, the slander that their author was not impressed, like all other thinking men, with the responsibilities and higher mysteries of life; while Sonnets 35, 36, and 37, entitled *The Choice,* sum up the general view taken in a manner only to be evaded by conscious insincerity. Thus much for *The House of Life,* of which the sonnet *Nuptial Sleep* is one stanza, embodying, for its small constituent share, a beauty of natural universal function, only to be reprobated in art if dwelt on (as I have shown that it is not here) to the exclusion of those other highest things of which it is the harmonious concomitant.

At page 342, an attempt is made to stigmatize four short quotations as being specially "my own property," that is, (for the context shows the meaning,) as being grossly sensual; though all guiding reference to any precise page or poem in my book is avoided here. The first of these unspecified quotations is from the *Last Confession;* and is the description referring to the harlot's laugh, the hideous character of which, together with its real or imagined resemblance to the laugh heard soon afterwards from the lips of one long cherished as an ideal, is the immediate cause which makes the maddened hero of the poem a murderer. Assailants may say what they please; but no poet or poetic reader will blame me for making the incident recorded in these seven lines as repulsive to the reader as it was to the hearer and beholder. Without this, the chain of motive and result would remain obviously incomplete. Observe also that these are but seven lines in a poem of some five hundred, not one other of which could be classed with them.

A second quotation gives the last two lines *only* of the following sonnet, which is the first of four sonnets in *The House of Life* jointly entitled *Willowwood:* —

"I sat with Love upon a woodside well,
  Leaning across the water, I and he;
  Nor ever did he speak nor looked at me,
But touched his lute wherein was audible
The certain secret thing he had to tell;
  Only our mirrored eyes met silently
  In the low wave; and that sound seemed to be
The passionate voice I knew; and my tears fell.

"And at their fall, his eyes beneath grew hers;
And with his foot and with his wing-feathers
  He swept the spring that watered my heart's drouth.
Then the dark ripples spread to waving hair,
And as I stooped, her own lips rising there
  Bubbled with brimming kisses at my mouth."

The critic has quoted (as I said) only the last two

lines, and he has italicized the second as something unbearable and ridiculous. Of course the inference would be that this was really my own absurd bubble-and-squeak notion of an actual kiss. The reader will perceive at once, from the whole sonnet transcribed above, how untrue such an inference would be. The sonnet describes a dream or trance of divided love momentarily re-united by the longing fancy; and in the imagery of the dream, the face of the beloved rises through deep dark waters to kiss the lover. Thus the phrase, "Bubbled with brimming kisses," etc., bears purely on the special symbolism employed, and from that point of view will be found, I believe, perfectly simple and just.

A third quotation is from *Eden Bower,* and says,

"What more prize than love to impel thee?
Grip and lip my limbs as I tell thee!"

Here again no reference is given, and naturally the reader would suppose that a human embrace is described. The embrace, on the contrary, is that of a fabled snake-woman and a snake. It would be possible still, no doubt, to object on other grounds to this conception; but the ground inferred and relied on for full effect by the critic is none the less an absolute misrepresentation. These three extracts, it will be admitted, are virtually, though not verbally, garbled with malicious intention; and the same is the case as I have shown, with the sonnet called *Nuptial Sleep* when purposely treated as a "whole poem."

The last of the four quotations grouped by the critic as conclusive examples consists of two lines from *Jenny.* Neither some thirteen years ago, when I wrote this poem, nor last year when I published it, did I fail to foresee impending charges of recklessness and aggressiveness, or to perceive that even some among those who could really *read* the poem, and acquit me on these grounds, might still hold that the thought in it had better have dispensed with the situation which serves it for framework. Nor did I omit to consider how far a treatment from without might here be possible. But the motive powers of art reverse the requirement of science, and demand first of all an *inner* standing-point. The heart of such a mystery as this must be plucked from the very world in which it beats or bleeds; and the beauty and pity, the self-questionings and all-questionings which it brings with it, can come with full force only from the mouth of one alive to its whole appeal, such as the speaker put forward in the poem, —that is, of a young and thoughtful man of the world. To such a speaker, many half-cynical revulsions of feeling and reverie, and a recurrent presence of the impressions of beauty (however artificial) which first brought him within such a circle of influence, would be inevitable features of the dramatic relations portrayed. Here again I can give the lie, in hearing of honest readers, to the base or trivial ideas which my critic labours to connect with the poem. There is another little charge, however, which this minstrel in mufti brings against *Jenny,* namely, one of plagiarism from that very poetic self of his which the tutelary prose does but enshroud for the moment. This question can, fortunately, be settled with ease by others who have read my critic's poems; and thus I need the less regret that, not happening myself to be in that position, I must be content to rank with those who cannot pretend to an opinion on the subject.

It would be humiliating, need one come to serious detail, to have to refute such an accusation as that of "binding oneself by solemn league and covenant to extol fleshliness as the distinct and supreme end of poetic and pictorial art"; and one cannot but feel that here every one will think it allowable merely to pass by with a smile the foolish fellow who has brought a charge thus framed against any reasonable man. Indeed, what I have said already is substantially enough to refute it, even did I not feel sure that a fair balance of my poetry must, of itself, do so in the eyes of every candid reader, I say nothing of my pictures; but those who know them will laugh at the idea. That I may, nevertheless, take a wider view than some poets or critics, of how much, in the material conditions absolutely given to man to deal with as distinct from his spiritual aspirations, is admissible within the limits of Art,—this, I say, is possible enough; nor do I wish to shrink from such responsibility. But to state that I do so to the ignoring or overshadowing of spiritual beauty, is an absolute falsehood, impossible to be put forward except in the indulgence of prejudice or rancour.

I have selected, amid much railing on my critic's part, what seemed the most representative indictment against me, and have, so far, answered it. Its remaining clauses set forth how others and myself "aver that poetic expression is greater than poetic thought ... and sound superior to sense"—an accusation elsewhere, I observe, expressed by saying that we "wish to create form for its own sake." If writers of verse are to be listened to in such arraignment of each other, it might be quite competent to me to prove, from the works of my friends in question, that no such thing is the case with them; but my present function is to confine myself to my own defence. This, again, it is difficult

to do quite seriously. It is no part of my undertaking to dispute the verdict of any "contemporary," however contemptuous or contemptible, on my own measure of executive success; but the accusation cited above is not against the poetic value of certain work, but against its primary and (by assumption) its admitted aim. And to this I must reply that so far, assuredly, not even Shakespeare himself could desire more arduous human tragedy for development in Art than belongs to the themes I venture to embody, however incalculably higher might be his power of dealing with them. What more inspiring for poetic effort than the terrible Love turned to Hate,—perhaps the deadliest of all passion-woven complexities,—which is the theme of *Sister Helen,* and, in a more fantastic form, of *Eden Bower*—the surroundings of both poems being the mere machinery of a central universal meaning? What, again, more so than the savage penalty exacted for a lost ideal, as expressed in the *Last Confession;*—than the outraged love for man and burning compensations in art and memory of *Dante at Verona;*—than the baffling problems which the face of *Jenny* conjures up;—or than the analysis of passion and feeling attempted in *The House of Life,* and others among the more purely lyrical poems? I speak here, as does my critic in the clause adduced, of *aim,* not of *achievement;* and so far, the mere summary is instantly subversive of the preposterous imputation. To assert that the poet whose matter is such as this aims chiefly at "creating form for its own sake," is, in fact, almost an ingenuous kind of dishonesty; for surely it delivers up the asserter at once, bound hand and foot, to the tender mercies of contradictory proof. Yet this may fairly be taken as an example of the spirit in which a constant effort is here made against me to appeal to those who either are ignorant of what I write, or else belong to the large class too easily influenced by an assumption of authority in addressing them. The false name appended to the article must, as is evident, aid this position vastly; for who, after all, would not be apt to laugh at seeing one poet confessedly come forward as aggressor against another in the field of criticism?

It would not be worth while to lose time and patience in noticing minutely how the system of misrepresentation is carried into points of artistic detail,—giving us, for example, such statements as that the burthen employed in the ballad of *Sister Helen* "is repeated with little or no alteration through thirty-four verses," whereas the fact is, that the alteration of it in every verse is the very scheme of the poem. But these are minor matters quite thrown into the shade by the critic's more daring sallies. In addition to the class of attack I have answered above, the article contains, of course, an immense amount of personal paltriness; as, for instance, attributions of my work to this, that, or the other absurd derivative source; or again, pure nonsense (which can have no real meaning even to the writer) about "one art getting hold of another, and imposing on it its conditions and limitations"; or, indeed, what not besides? However, to such antics as this, no more attention is possible than that which Virgil enjoined Dante to bestow on the meaner phenomena of his pilgrimage.

Thus far, then, let me thank you for the opportunity afforded me to join issue with the Stealthy School of Criticism. As for any literary justice to be done on this particular Mr. Robert-Thomas, I will merely ask the reader whether, once identified, he does not become manifestly his own best "sworn tormentor"? For who will then fail to discern all the palpitations which preceded his final resolve in the great question whether to be or not to be his acknowledged self when he became an assailant?

And yet this is he who, from behind his mask, ventures to charge another with "bad blood," with "insincerity," and the rest of it (and that where poetic fancies are alone in question); while every word on his own tongue is covert rancour, and every stroke from his pen perversion of truth. Yet, after all, there is nothing wonderful in the lengths to which a fretful poet-critic will carry such grudges as he may bear, while publisher and editor can both be found who are willing to consider such means admissible, even to the clear subversion of first professed tenets in the *Review* which they conduct.

In many phases of outward nature, the principle of chaff and grain holds good,—the base enveloping the precious continually; but an untruth was never yet the husk of a truth. Thresh and riddle and winnow it as you may,—let it fly in shreds to the four winds,—falsehood only will be that which flies and that which stays. And thus the sheath of deceit which this pseudonymous undertaking presents at the outset insures in fact what will be found to be its real character to the core.

The Fleshly School of Poetry and Other Phenomena of the Day

Robert Buchanan

Originally published in pamphlet form (London: Strahan, 1872).

PREFACE

The nucleus of the following Essay was published last October in the *Contemporary Review,* with the signature "Thomas Maitland" affixed to it (without my knowledge), *in order that the criticism might rest upon its own merits, and gain nothing from the name of the real writer.* At the time of the publication I myself was yachting among the Scottish Hebrides. As the obscure "Thomas Maitland," however, happened to have uttered an unpleasant and startling truth, the fleshly gentlemen moved heaven, earth, and Jupiter Pluvius in order to create a storm, and (carefully eschewing the real literary question) they have used all the means in their hands to demonstrate that the criticism was the malicious and cowardly work of a rival poet, afraid to strike in broad day or under his real name, and adopting a pseudonym to conceal his real identity. For the correspondence on this subject—for Mr. Rossetti's own defence and the opinion of Mr. Rossetti's friends, as well as for my own simple explanation of the facts of the case—the reader is referred to the *Athenaeum* newspaper for December 16th and December 30th, 1871.

I have only one word to use concerning the attacks upon myself. They are the inventions of cowards, too spoilt with flattery to bear criticism, and too querulous and humorsome to perceive the real issues of the case.

My imputed crime is as follows: that I did not sign my own name to the article, and that I spoke in high terms of my own poems.

The first account has been disposed of by the simple statement that I did not sign the article at all. If it be retorted that the rule of the *Contemporary Review* is never to admit pseudonyms or unsigned articles, I answer that at least three of the regular contributors to that *Review* have habitually used pseudonyms, and that, in an early number of the same publication, Dean Mansell sharply criticized Mr. Mill in an unsigned article in which he spoke of himself in the third person, afterwards reprinting the article, with his own name, as "The Philosophy of the Conditioned."

The second count, which charges me with secret self-praise, is so absurd an attempt to distract judgment that it is almost unworthy of mention. In an opening paragraph (now suppressed for its weakness) I drew out a sort of sketch of *Hamlet* as "cast" by the contemporary poets, Mr. Tennyson of course assuming the leading character; and among the list of smaller parts I humorously spoke of myself as playing the part of—what? Horatio? The King? Polonius? Rosencranz? Guildenstern? Osric? Of none of these, small or great, but simply that of "Cornelius!" I imagined then that I was writing for readers who had read their Shakspere, or who had at any rate seen his great tragedy murdered on the stage, and never dreamt I should have to explain (as I am now forced to explain) that "Cornelius" is one of those two gentlemen who appear in Scene II. in the usual way of what are technically known as "utility" people, and after uttering together this one memorable line—

"In this and all things will we show our duty!"—

exeunt in all humility. In a subsequent scene they return, and Voltimand, the *other* gentleman, makes a speech, while "Cornelius" stands in the usual "utility" attitude, with one leg bent and one hand laid gracefully on his hips. This is the proud character I am accused of arrogating to myself in the grand list of contemporary performances! Surely, if I had been ambitious of obtruding my own merits, I might at least have gone in for Fortinbras or the First Gravedigger!

The other allusion to "my own poems" will be found on page 46 of this pamphlet. It simply chronicles a fact, and is neither complimentary nor the reverse.

The truth is, all this hubbub about the authorship is a vulgar farce, got up to distract public attention. My article was altered and my name suppressed with the best of all motives—that of letting the charges contained in it stand on their own merits, and that of saving me from the persecution of a clique of literary Mohawks; but it is a pity any alteration was made at all.

Be that as it may, let me entreat my readers not to let their attention be distracted by any consideration of me personally. Let them carefully accept and weigh the evidence brought forward in these pages, and judge the case on its own merits. The clatter that is being made about the authorship is only meant to excite the public against a patient examination of this "most damning" indictment against the Fleshly School of Poetry.

The most curious part of the whole affair remains to be told. It is delightful as showing the ratio of public intelligence. It appears that these poems of Mr. Rossetti have actually become favourites with that prude of prudes, the British matron; and several gentlemen tell me that their aunts and grandmothers see no harm in them! My own grandmother is not poetical, so I have not sought her opinion. But here I am front to front with the amazing fact that a large section of cultured people read poetry, and enjoy it, without the faintest perception of what it is all about—without the slightest wish to realise the images or the situations—without any more intellectual effort than they use when having their hair brushed! Conceive the mental state of the aunt or grandmother who could read such verses as this—

"I was a child beneath her touch—a man
When *breast to breast we clung*, even I and she,
A spirit when her spirit looked thro' me,—
A god when *all our life-breath met to fan
Our life's-blood, till love's emulous ardours ran,
Fire within fire, desire in deity!*"—

and merely think them sweetly pretty. It is hard to think ill of one's relations; but the mature females in question must be either very obtuse, or—very, very naughty!

The truth appears to be, that writing, however nasty, will be perfectly sanctified to English readers if it be moral in the legal sense; and thus a poet who describes sensual details may do so with impunity if he labels his poems—"Take notice! These sensations are strictly *nuptial;* these delights have been sanctioned by English law, and registered at Doctors' Commons!" We have here the reason that Mr. Rossetti has almost escaped censure, while Mr. Swinburne has been punished so severely; for Mr. Rossetti, in his worst poems, explains that he is speaking dramatically in the character of a *husband* addressing his *wife*. Animalism is animalism, nevertheless, whether licensed or not; and, indeed, one might tolerate the language of lust more readily on the lips of a lover addressing a mistress than on the lips of a husband virtually (in these so-called

"Nuptial" Sonnets) wheeling his nuptial couch out into the public streets.

ROBERT BUCHANAN

I

"Shakspere's an infernal humbug, Pip! I never read him. What the devil is it all about, Pip? There's a lot of feet in Shakspere's verse, but there ain't any legs worth mentioning in Shakspere's plays, are there, Pip?... Let us have plenty of leg pieces, Pip, and I'll stand by you!" — DICKENS'S *Martin Chuzzlewit*

Though this is a generation of great poets and teachers; though Tennyson, Browning, Victor Hugo, Carlyle, Emerson, and Walt Whitman are still amongst us, while Dickens (essentially a poet) and Landor have not long left us; though much of our public teaching (and notably that of the public press) is lofty and clean, there are not wanting signs that Sensualism, which from time immemorial has been the cancer of all society, is shooting its ulcerous roots deeper and deeper, and blotching more and more the fair surface of things. Coming this winter from a remote retreat in the Highlands to this great centre of life which men have named London, moving from street to street and from house to house, seeing all that a man with eyes can see, what are the objects which most impress themselves upon me? Not the old immemorial squalor of the slums, the hideous famine of the by-streets and lanes, the gaudy misery in numberless human faces (that is no novelty); nor the fatuous imbecility and superficiality of the moneyed vulgar, and the shapeless ugliness of women who feed high and take no exercise (that, too, is familiar, though not perhaps on so large a scale); nor the dark blotches of life where disease squats for ever, nor the follies of the last new fashion, nor the hideousness of the last new public building. All these things are passed on one side, as I approach a phenomenon so strange and striking that to a superstitious mind it might seem a portent, and so hideous that it converts this great city of civilisation into a great Sodom or Gomorrah waiting for doom. Look which way I will, the horrid thing threatens and paralyzes me. It lies on the drawing-room table, shamelessly naked and dangerously fair. It is part of the pretty poem which the belle of the season reads, and it breathes away the pureness of her soul like the poisoned breath of the girl in Hawthorne's tale. It covers the shelves of the great Oxford-Street librarian, lurking in the covers of three-volume novels. It is on the French booksellers'

counters, authenticated by the signature of the author of the "Visite de Noces." It is here, there, and everywhere, in art, literature, life, just as surely as it is in the "Fleurs de Mal," the Marquis de Sade's "Justine," or the "Monk" of Lewis. It appeals to all tastes, to all dispositions, to all ages. If the querulous man of letters has his "Baudelaire," the pimpled clerk has his *Day's Doings,* [1] and the dissipated artisan his *Day and Night.* The streets are full of it. Photographs of nude, indecent, and hideous harlots, in every possible attitude that vice can devise, flaunt from the shop-windows, gloated over by the fatuous glint of the libertine and the greedy open-mouthed stare of the day-labourer. Never was this Snake, which not all the naturalists of the world have been able to scotch, so vital and poisonous as now. It has penetrated into the very sweetshops; and there, among the commoner sorts of confectionery, may be seen this year models of the female Leg, the whole definite and elegant article as far as the thigh, with a fringe of paper cut in imitation of the female drawers and embroidered in the female fashion!

When things have come to such a pass as this, it is difficult to be quite serious in dealing with them. The foot-and-mouth disease is dreadful, but the Leg-disease, though generally fatal, is egregiously absurd into the bargain. Now, to begin with, there is nothing indecent in the human Leg itself; on the contrary, it is a most beautiful and useful member. Nor is it necessarily indecent to show the Leg, as some ladies do upon the stage, without in the least shocking our propriety. But the Leg, an excellent thing in itself, becomes insufferable if obtruded into every concern of life, so that instead of humanity we see a demon resembling the Manx coat-of-arms, cutting capers without a body or a head. The Leg, as a disease, is subtle, secret, diabolical. It relies not merely on its own intrinsic attractions, but on its atrocious suggestions. It becomes a spectre, a portent, a mania. Turn your eyes to the English stage. Shakspere is demolished and lies buried under hecatombs of Leg! Open the last new poem. Its title will possibly be this, or similar to this—"Leg is enough." Walk along the streets. The shop-windows teem with Leg. Enter a music-hall—Leg again, and (O tempora! O mores!) the Can-Can. Jack enjoys it down Wapping way just as Jones does in the Canterbury Hall. It is only in fashionable rooms and in the stalls of the theatre that Leg is at a discount; but that is not because life there is more innocent and modest, but because Leg is in the higher circles altogether eclipsed by its two most formidable rivals—Bosom and Back.

If popular writers are to be credited, there is

running rampant in English society a certain atrocious form of vice, a monster with two heads—one of which is called Adultery, the other Dipsomania—and these two heads, blind to all else in the world, leer and ogle at each other. I have not sufficient knowledge of English polite society to say whether or not the terrible impeachment is based on a careful study of facts; but I do know that the writings in which these facts have been chronicled, the prurient pictures given of vice masking in the garb of virtue, become in their turn, and for the very sake of the imputations they contain, the delight of vulgar debauches and heartless libertines. No form of animal is more common than he who, when charged with folly and immorality, retorts with a smile—"All very well, but I am no worse than my neighbours; virtue—fudge! there is no such thing, at least in English society; everything is bought and sold;"—and this enlightened person, hearing on the best authority that love of the best sort procurable and lust of the gaudiest sort possible are equally in the market for the highest bidder, prefers purchasing his indulgence as the humour seizes him to making a bargain for a life-luxury of which he may get thoroughly tired. Nothing, meantime, gratifies the free lover more than to be told that marriage is a farce and continence a sham, that all forms of life are equally heartless, and that his betters in the social scale only commit in secret the follies in which he indulges openly. Is it true, then, that English society is honeycombed and rotten? More than one form of literature says so. The smart journal says so. So does the novel of the period. So does the artistic Bohemian. For my own part I am inclined to believe (though, as I have said, on very insufficient knowledge) that true English life is infinitely purer and better than our smart writers and lady novelists imagine it to be; that the pure rose of English maidenhood still blows as brightly as ever; that, in a word, the canker lies on the surface and has not *yet* eaten down into the body social. How then account for the portentous symptoms which are everywhere appalling us? Thus. There is on the fringe of real English society, and chiefly, if not altogether, in London here, a sort of demi-monde, not composed, like that other in France, of simple courtesans, but of men and women of indolent habits and aesthetic tastes, artists, literary persons, novel writers, actors, men of genius and men of talent, butterflies and gadflies of the human kind, leading a lazy existence from hand to mouth. These persons "write for the papers." They publish books, often at their own expense. They, some of them, have titles. They belong to

clubs and they go to dinner parties. They paint pictures, sometimes good ones. They compose music, generally bad music. They lecture on art and literature to young ladies' schools. They read Balzac, Dumas *fils,* and the "cerebellic" autobiographies of Goethe. They are clever, refined, interesting, able, querulous. Nothing delights them more than to tear a reputation to pieces or to diagnose the seeds of moral disease in the healthiest subjects. Their religion is called culture, their narrow-mindedness is called insight. Their portraits are sold, along with those of nude harlots and lascivious courtesans, at a shilling per head in the public streets. Two peculiarities distinguish this class of persons to a careful eye—they are as oblivious to the fact that life has a past as that the soul has a future, and they are never by any chance seen in that English society which they profess to understand so thoroughly.

Now, if we carefully consider the question we are discussing, we shall in all possibility find that all the gross and vulgar conceptions of life which are formulated into certain products of art, literature, and criticism, emanate from this Bohemian class. Its members do not, we believe, penetrate far into life of any kind, but where they do penetrate they create the vices they perceive, and reflect phenomena in the distorted mirrors of their own moral consciousness. Possessing no religion, they imagine that English life is irreligious. Having no faith, they perceive no faith anywhere. Ingenious almost to diablerie, they will prove to you by critical theory that art is simply the method of getting most sweets out of one's living sensations—the knack, to put it metaphorically, of sucking your lollipop so as to extract out of it the best possible flavour. If a man speaks to them earnestly, they will smile and style him "didactic." If a man writes for them religiously, they will inwardly congratulate themselves on having passed quite beyond "that sort of thing." These men—and alas! these women—compose some of our poetry, paint some of our pictures, write a good deal of our formal criticism. Is it any wonder, therefore, that the poor bewildered public shakes its head over the terrible accounts put before it, and begins slowly but surely to share the scepticism and flippancy it at first considered so shocking? Is it any wonder that Leg-literature flourishes? Is it any wonder that wise men like Mr. Ruskin rail, and philosophers like Mr. Carlyle despair? There lies the seat of the cancer—there, in the Bohemian fringe of society. Will no courageous hand essay to cut it out? Will no physician come to put his finger in the true seat of the sore? There it is, spreading daily like all cancerous diseases, foul in itself and creating foulness. If we cannot destroy it altogether with some terrible caustic, let us at least take precautions to prevent it from spreading. The disease is worth the remedy, the remedy is worth a prayer.

It is my business in the present pages to deal only with one form of the moral phenomenon, to regard Sensualism only in so far as it affects contemporary poetry. My plan was at first broader, but I find it beyond my present materials. To deal with the question completely, to pass in review the effects of Sensualism on art, on music, on the drama, and above all to trace its physiological causes and consequences as expressed in all these different directions, would occupy far more time than I am able to bestow on the subject. Let me hope, however, that others may speak, now I have spoken, adding to mine their testimony and their protest.

II

"Whilom the sisters nine were vestal maids . . .
But since, I saw it painted on Fame's wings,
The Muses to be woxen wantonings.
Ye bastard poets, see your progeny!"
BISHOP HALL

The true history of European poetry is the history of European progress, from the narrow microscopic pedantry of mediaeval culture to the large telescopic sweep of modern thought and science. It is no part of my present plan to attempt the historical subject, except in so far as it affects the phenomena of the present day; and I need only indicate, therefore, how the ever-broadening poetry of humanity has flowed to us in one varying stream of increase since the day when, as Denham sings—

"Old Chaucer, like the morning star,
To us discovered day from far."

Chaucer and his contemporaries were, as all readers know, under deep obligations to the poets and romancists of mediaeval Italy; and it is a most significant token of Chaucer's pre-eminent originality that, while Gower and the rest had only been inspired to imitate what was bad in the great models, he, on the contrary, merely derived inspiration and solace from their music, assimilated what was noble in it, and carefully prepared a breezier and healthier poetic form of his own. What is grandest and best in Chaucer is Chaucer's exclusively. No better proof

can be had of his merit as the morning star of the modern school than a careful comparison of him, first with Boccaccio, then with Dante. All the limpid flow of narrative, the concentration and pomp of subject, all the lighter humour and sparkle, are to be found in the "Decameron." All the dramatic intensity, the quaint but tender realism, are (with mighty qualities superadded) to be discovered in Dante. But the quaint saline humour, the universality of sympathy, the childlike love of nature, and the supreme piteousness of modern poetry, dawned with the divine author of the "Canterbury Tales." Chaucer was emphatically the poet of the bourgeoisie, just as Shakspere and his brethren were the poets of the feudal idea; but with all these writers alike, with the author of the "Wife of Bath" as well as with the creator of Falstaff, humanity was beginning to get such a hearing for itself, and notably on the humorous side of the question, as would be certain in the long-run to blend both ideas, that of feudalism and that of the bourgeoisie, into the great modern sentiment of popular rights, duties, and affections. The great dramatists of the reign of Elizabeth, following in Chaucer's footsteps, appear, under some awful demoniac influence (for individually these men were destitute of beneficence), to have prepared for modern contemplation an unequalled gallery of human faces and souls—a gallery all-embracing in its range, photographing the meanest as well as the highest, and revealing to us, under all the dazzle and glitter of a sumptuous feudal style, the instincts which all men have in common, the compensations which each owes to the other, and the fair world in which each has an equal and indisputable share. Simply to picture men "in their habits as they live," no matter under what motive, was the highest possible beneficence; and this, in the golden dawn of our poetry, was done inimitably, with a beauty of thought and a wealth of resource unknown to any poet that has appeared since.

Such was the dawn of our poetry; and did ever dawn bid promise of a more glorious day?

But, alas! to the reddening of this fair promise succeeded no fulfilment. Just when light seemed fullest, time and season were miraculously altered, and a period arrived, an overclouding of the sun, a portentous darkess, wherein few could tell whether it was night or day. This darkness was of a vaporous nature, miasmic. It was a fever-cloud generated first in Italy and then blown westward; finally, after sucking up all that was most unwholesome from the soil of France, to fix itself on England, and breed in its direful shadow a race of monsters whose long line has not ceased from that to the present day.

Just previously to and contemporaneously with the rise of Dante, there had flourished a legion of poets of greater or less ability, but all more or less characterized by affectation, foolishness, and moral blindness: singers of the falsetto school, with ballads to their mistress's eyebrow, sonnets to their lady's lute, and general songs of a fiddlestick; peevish men for the most part, as is the way of all fleshly and affected beings; men so ignorant of human subjects and materials as to be driven, in their sheer bankruptcy of mind, to raise Hope, Love, Fear, Rage (everything but Charity) into human entities, and to treat the body and upholstery of a dollish woman as if, in itself, it constituted a whole Universe. In the ways of these poor devils Dante walked a little; and he has left us, in his "Vita Nuova," a book which carries the system of individual fantasy about as near perfection as possible, and (of course) invests a radically absurd line of thought with a fictitious and tremendous interest. The "Vita Nuova" is enormously fine in its way, as the self-revelation of a man in whom the world is interested, and to whom many conceits may be freely pardoned. It is quaint, fine, subtle, suggestive; but its chief value is this, that it was composed, in a tender moment, by the tremendous creature who wrote the story of Roman Catholicism in unfaltering and colossal cipher for the study of all forthcoming ages.

What was great and potent in Dante remained in the "Divine Comedy" and bore no seed. What was absurd and unnatural in Dante, mingling with foul exhalations from the brains of his brother poets, formed the miasmic cloud which obscured all English culture, generated madness even as far north as Hawthornden and Edinburgh, obscured Chaucer for centuries, darkened the way to the vast spaces of the Elizabethan drama, and generally bred in the very bones and marrow of English literature the veriest ague of absurdity ever known to keep human creature crazy. Surrey, a naturally strong man, sickened and died in the fever; his limpid English just preserving his foolish subjects from total oblivion; while Wyatt, affected in form as well as in substance, lingered through a long life of literary disease. Spenser and Drayton caught the complaint early, but, being men of robust genius, survived it. Shakspere had it, but his mighty spirit almost beautified disease itself, till he cast it off altogether, and clomb to the heaven-kissing hill where he wrote his plays. Poor old John Donne had the strangest possible attacks; he made a hard fight to recover his natural English health, but the reiterated relapses were too much for him; and there he

lies, with his books on his breast, quaint as a carven figure on a tomb—and as unreal. How name over all the other victims who died literary death in those days? How call up before the reader the sad shades of Davies, Carew, William Drummond, the two Fletchers, Habington, and all those once famous British bards? Gliding onward through the spectral host, we pass Crashaw, a Rossetti of the period, with twice the genius and half the advantages; and Suckling, immortal by virtue of his one true note—the "Ballad on a Wedding;" and Browne, the Elizabethan Keats, with his falsetto voice and occasional tones of really delicious cunning; till latterly, in a languid and depressed state of mind, we arrive before the prone figure of Cowley, who essayed to drive the very horses of the sun, and came to the cruel earth with a smash so prodigious. Poor ghosts! To think of it! All these persons were admired in their generation. Frankincense of praise and myrrh of flattery had been theirs to the full. They flattered each other, and they tickled the age. What pleased the public mind in Shakspere was the "quaint conceits" of his "wonderful" sonnets; his plays were nowhere for the time being. The Italian disease raged and devastated art, literature, and society. Now it was the simple sentimental form, light and dainty, symptomised by such verses as "To Roses in the Bosom of Castara," "Upon Cupid's Death and Burial in Cynthia's Cheeke," or "On a Mole in Celia's Bosom." Again it was the dull metaphysical type, deep-seated and incurable, with its "Negative Love," its "Answer to the Platonics," and "Love's Visibility." At one time the disease was scrofulous and foul-mouthed, sending forth addresses "To His Mistress's going to Bed," and "On the Happiness of a Flea on Celia's Body." At another the religious mania supervened, and all the language of passion was applied to divine things, startling us with coquettish addresses to the Magdalen, to "Mary's Tear," "On the Blessed Virgin's Bashfulness," and so on. But in all these cases, however extraordinary, however fatal, two results could be noted. The performances of the diseased persons afforded intense delight to a certain section of the public, and the amount of contemporary eulogy was almost always in proportion to the fatal nature of the disease.

With Cowley, the epidemic seemed to culminate. This prodigy of success overdid his character, and it seemed impossible for the lover's vein to be carried further by any other ambitious Bottom. Milton corrected his system with the strong tonics of the ancients; and Dryden, when he rose, fortified himself with the disinfectant of Roman satire. Nevertheless the disease lingered in the land, cooperating with new diseases from the corrupt court of France. It would be tiresome indeed to name all the poor creatures, from Cowley to Spratt, who suffered and died, more or less under the fatal influence. It was in positive despair, to resist the epidemic, that English literature hardened into the formal cleanliness of the Addisonian period. Classicism was used as an antidote, while Ambrose Phillips was delighting "society" with pieces like that "On the Little Lady Charlotte Pulteney drest to go to a Ball." [2] False love, false heroics, false pastoral pictures, false life, false thought, all more or less consequent on the foul corruptions from Italy and France, had shaken the whole fabric of English literature when Jonathan Swift composed his mock-erotic verses "On a beautiful Young Nymph going to Bed," and Pope & Co. their "Martinus Scriblerus on the Art of Sinking in Poetry;" but neither Pope nor Swift was strong enough to inaugurate a new and nobler art. English poetry was virtually dead.

A tranquil gleam of honest English light came with Cowper, whose patient and gentle services have scarcely yet been rated at their true worth. But the true seeds of a new life had been scattered abroad when Bishop Percy published his "Reliques." These seeds were slow to spring, the slower because they sank so deep. At last, however, Wordsworth came, and English literature was saved. Then, with one loud trumpet-note, Byron amazed matrons and disarmed critics. Then, with a shining face, Coleridge uttered stately syllables of mightiest thought. Then, too, Southey gave his help, now unjustly forgotten. Then Lamb and Hazlitt began to criticize, directing men's eyes back to the true fount of English thought and diction—the tales of Chaucer and the Elizabethan drama. Then Scott arose, simple and deep as the sea—freighted with golden argosies of history and lighted with the innumerable laughter of the waves. Then indeed poor England shook off her taint, and felt her heart beat with a truer, freer pulse,—

"For a sweet wind from heaven had come
    To blow her cares away."

Hope had come at last—more than a gleam,—a glorious azure burst. It was sad to think how many centuries had been wasted; but the invalid-literature of this country was not quite dead.

Strange to say, just at that very moment, when things looked brightest, honest Gifford had to demolish the Della Cruscan school, and Canning and Frere found it necessary to destroy Dr. Darwin. In both of these maniacal manifestations, but particu-

larly in the former, society and the small critics of the day delighted. The Della Cruscan poems were sung to guitars, and warbled by young ladies at their embroidery frames. They had one recommendation—they were harmless. They were neither demoralising nor dirty. They died a very speedy death, when once Gifford took the trouble to exterminate them; but perhaps they hardly needed so severe an operation. In our own day we have had, besides the Fleshly School under notice, the Spasmodic School, headed by Bailey, Smith, and Dobell; but these poets possessed great purity, and were unfairly treated. The worst argument against them was their comparative poetic silence after the date of Aytoun's attacks. All these so-called Schools over-exert themselves and end in phthisis. A great poet is a law to himself, and does not work in groups.

After this last futile development, the Italian disease would possibly have died out altogether. That it has not died, has been due to a fresh importation of the obnoxious matter from France. The Scrofulous School of Literature had been distinguishing itself for many a long year in Paris, but it reached its final and most tremendous development in Charles Baudelaire,—a writer to whom I must now direct the reader's attention.

III

CHARLES BAUDELAIRE

"Je cherche le vide, et le noir, et le nu!"
"I seek the Black, the Empty, and the Nude!"
                                        Fleurs de Mal

I have before me, as I write, the portrait of Baudelaire, the memoir by Gautier, the original edition of the "Fleurs de Mal," and the collected edition of Baudelaire's works, published since his death.

Gautier's memoir is a miracle of cunning writing, containing hardly a syllable with which one disagrees, and yet skilfully and secretly poisoning the mind of any unsuspicious reader. The best antidote I can recommend against such clever trash is the tiniest pinch of humour, the least sense of the absurd; for directly the whole thing is put in the proper light, contempt yields to laughter, and laughter dies away in pity for the poor "aestheticized" figures to whom we are being introduced. It may also be as well, at the same time, to call to mind how even the mighty genius of George

Sand, at first so promising and so commanding (in those days when even Mazzini's pure soul did it homage), slowly decomposed under the inner action of the artistic and self-critical instinct, until it falsified all hopes, and ended in utter demoralisation. This literary finessing, this intellectual fingering, constitutes a tithe of the genius of Hugo, a half of the genius of George Sand, the whole of the genius of Charles Baudelaire and his biographer. A little Shaksperian sense of quiddity would soon show us what a poor, attenuated, miserable scarecrow of humanity Baudelaire was in reality, and what a mere serving-man, self-deluded and self-deluding, is this poor old Gautier-Malvolio, who holds forth, "cross-garter'd," over his grave.

Gautier first met Baudelaire in "that grand salon in the most pure style of Louis XIV.," where the hasheesh-eaters of Paris were wont to hold their meetings; and his description of the furniture of this chamber is very great, quite in the spirit of a French upholsterer. Here is his vignette portrait of Baudelaire as he appeared on that occasion:—

> "Son aspect nous frappa: il avait les cheveux coupés très ras et du plus beau noir; ces cheveux, faisant des pointes régulières sur le front d'une éclatante blancheur, le coiffaient comme une espèce de casque sarrasin; les yeux, couleur de tabac d'Espagne, avaient un regard spirituel, profond, et d'une pénétration peut-être un peu trop insistante; quant à la bouche, meublée de dents très-blanches, elle abritait, sous une légère et soyeuse moustache ombrageant son contour, des sinuosités mobiles, voluptueuses et ironiques comme les lèvres des figures peintes par Léonard de Vinci; le nez, fin et délicat, un peu arrondi, aux narines palpitantes, semblait subodorer de vagues parfums lointains; une fossette vigoureuse accentuait le menton comme le coup de pouce final du statuaire; les joues, soigneusement rasées, contrastaient, par leur fleur bleuâtre que veloutait la poudre de riz, avec les nuances vermeilles des pommettes; le cou, d'une élégance et d'une blancheur féminines, apparaissait dégagé, partant d'un col de chemise rabattu et d'une étroite cravate en madras des Indes et à carreaux. Son vêtement consistait en un paletôt d'une étoffe noire lustrée et brillante, un pantalon noisette, des bas blancs et des escarpins vernis, le tout méticuleusement propre et correct, avec un cachet voulu de simplicité anglaise et comme l'intention de se séparer du genre artiste, à chapeaux de feutre mou, à vestes de velours, à vareuses rouges, a barbe prolixe et à crinière échevelée. Rien de trop frais ni de trop voyant dans cette tenue rigoureuse. Charles Baudelaire appartenait à ce dandysme sobre qui râpe ses habits avec du papier de verre pour leur ôter l'éclat endimanché et tout battant neuf si cher au philistin et si désagréable pour le vrai gentleman. Plus tard même, il rasa sa moustache, trouvant que c'était un reste de vieux chic pittoresque qu'il était puéril et bourgeois de conserver."—*Oeuvres de Baudelaire, précédées d'une notice par Théophile Gautier, Paris,* 1869.

This interesting creature, with his nose sniffing "distant perfumes," his carefully-shaven cheeks, and his general air of man-millinery, was in earnest conversation with the "model" Maryx, who, with the immobility acquired in the studio, was reclining on a couch, resting her superb head on a cushion, and attired "in a white robe, quaintly starred with red spots resembling drops of blood!" Hard by, at the window, sat another superb female, known as "La Femme au Serpent," from having sat to Clevinger when he painted his picture of that name. The latter, having thrown on a fauteuil "her mantle of black lace and the most delicious little green hood that ever covered Lucy Hocquet or Madame Baudraud, shook her yellow lioness-locks, still humid, for she came from the swimming school (L'Ecole de Natation), and from all her body, clad in muslin, exhaled like a naiad the fresh perfume of the bath!" In the same company were Jean Fenchères, the sculptor, and Jean Boissard, the latter with "his red mouth, teeth of pearl, and brilliant complexion." One scarcely knows which to admire most in this description,—the writer's fine apotheosis of the *lupanar* into an "artistic decameron," or the avidity with which he seizes on personal traits and on male and female millinery. He is "up" in both under and over-clothing, as worn by both sexes. He is, moreover, candour itself. He makes no secret of Baudelaire's little weaknesses and his own. "With an air quite simple, natural, and perfectly disengaged, he advanced some axiom satanically monstrous, or sustained with an icy *sang-froid* some theory of a mathematical exactness; for there was a vigorous method in the development of his absurdities." In a word, it is not denied that Baudelaire was that most unsympathetic of all beings, a cold sensualist, and that he carried into all his pleasures (until they slew him) the dandyism and the self-possession of a true child of Mephistopheles.

After a youth spent in wanderings in the East, and in acquiring, as Gautier naïvely says, "that love of the black Venus, for whom he had always a taste," Baudelaire returned to Paris, rented a little *chambre de garçon,* and assumed all the privileges of a literary life in the most debauched city of the world. His reading, which seems to have been of a very limited nature, developed his already singular disposition into true literary monstrosity, and the morbid nature of his tastes may be gathered from the fact that his first public effort was a translation of the American Tales of Edgar Poe. To Poe he seems to have borne an extraordinary resemblance, both in genius and in character. Equally clever, affected, and cold-blooded; equally incredulous of goodness and angry at philanthropy; equally self-indulgent and sensual, he lived as useless a life, died as wretched a death, and left for his legacy books even more worthless—the very dregs of his unhappy and sunless moral nature. Like Poe and Swinburne, he affected innovations in verse, and sought out the most morbid themes for poetical treatment. Encouraged by Poe, he tried to surpass him on his own ground—to triumph over him in the diablerie of horror. Encouraged in his turn, Mr. Swinburne has attempted to surpass Baudelaire, and to excel even that frightful artist in the representation of abnormal types of diseased lust and lustful disease.

"Art," said Baudelaire in effect, "has but one object, like life—that of exciting in the reader's soul the sensation of enjoyment. What poetry is to life, the drug hasheesh is to me personally, enabling me to extract supreme enjoyment out of the sheerly diabolical ideas of my own mind. I despise humanity, and I approve the devil." Animated by these noble sentiments, he killed himself by self-indulgence, and virtually exclaimed to the youth of France, with his dying breath, "Go ye and do likewise!"

I know well how much may be said in defence of a man like this by a wise and beneficent criticism; but I know, too, that defence has been overwrought, till mercy for the sinner has enlarged into sympathy with the sin. I am well aware, moreover—no man can be better aware—of the *charm* of writers like Baudelaire, and even of a certain service they may do to literature by careful attention to aesthetic form. Having few ideas, they endeavour to express them neatly, and with novelty. But no good can come to life or literature from the atrocious system of painting such figures in the light voluptuous colours of art; of exalting such contemptible persons into first-rate literary positions, and of evading the moral of their lives for the sake of pointing an epigram and delighting the fool. Charles Baudelaire lived and died a slave to his own devil;

every line he wrote was slave's work; every picture he ever painted was in one hue—the dark blood-tint of his own shame. And yet it is this man, this dandy of the brothel, this Brummel of the stews, this fifth-rate *littérateur,* who, adopting to a certain extent the self-explanatory and querulous system of the Italian school of poets, and carefully avoiding the higher issues of that noble school of which Hugo is the living head, has been chosen (by no angel certainly) to be the godfather as it were of the modern Fleshly School, and thus to fill the select salon of English literature with a perfume to which the smell of Mrs. Aphra Behn's books is savoury, and that of Catullus' "lepidum novum libellum" absolutely delicious.

This is our double misfortune—to have a nuisance, and to have it at second hand. We might have been more tolerant to an unclean thing, if it had been in some sense a product of the soil. We have never been foolish purists, here in England. We freely forgave Byron many a wicked turn, because we knew he loved much, because we saw how much he was the product of national forces darkly working to the light. We welcomed Goethe, even when he sent the "Elective Affinities" and the cerebellic autobiographies. But to be overrun with the brood of an inferior French sonnetteer, whose only originality was his hideousness of subject, whose only merit was in his nasal appreciation of foul odours, surely that is far too much: it would have been a little too much twenty years ago, when the Empire began creating its viper's nest in the heart of France; it is a hundred times too much *now,* when the unclean place has been burnt with avenging fire.

A few years before his death, Baudelaire published his chief work—"Fleurs de Mal." This book was a little too strong even for Paris under the Empire; so the censor came down, and some of the vilest poems were ruthlessly expunged. But Baudelaire gained his end, and secured a spurious notoriety. Some years later Mr. Swinburne thought the French poet's success worthy of emulation, and he therefore published his "Poems and Ballads," which was so very hot that his publishers dropped it like a blazing cinder in the very month of publication, and only one publisher, who shall be nameless, had the courage to lift it up.

All that is worst in Mr. Swinburne belongs to Baudelaire. The offensive choice of subject, the obtrusion of unnatural passion, the blasphemy, the wretched animalism, are all taken intact out of the "Fleurs de Mal." Pitiful! that any sane man, least of all any English poet, should think this dunghill worthy of importation! In the centre of his collection Baudelaire placed the most horrid poem ever written by man, a poem unmatched for simple hideousness even in Rome during the decadence—a piece worthy to be spoken by Ascyltos in Petronius Arbiter—and entitled "Femmes Damnées." The interlocutors in this piece are two women, who have just been guilty of the vilest act conceivable in human debauchery, but the theme and the treatment are too loathsome for description. Encouraged by the hideousness of "Femmes Damnées," Mr. Swinburne attempted to beat it in "Anactoria," a poem the subject of which is again that branch of crime which is generally known as the Sapphic passion. It would be tedious, apart from the unsavouriness of the subject, to pursue the analogy much further through individual poems. Perhaps the best plan is to give a few specimens of Baudelaire's quality, and leave the reader to compare them with Mr. Swinburne's book at leisure.

In the very first poem of his collection Baudelaire avows his true character, and accuses the reader of being not a whit better:—

"Hypocrite lecteur,—mon semblable,—mon frère!"

He purposes, he says, on his way (the way of all humanity) down to absolute Hell, to pass in review a few of the horrors he sees on his path. His way lies—

"Parmi les chacals, les panthères, les lices,
Les singes, les scorpions, les vautours, les serpents,
*Les monstres glapissants, hurlants, grognants, rampants
Dans la ménagerie infâme de nos vices!*"

And of all these monsters the most infernal is— L'Ennui! The very next poem sweetly chronicles the birth of the Poet, whose mother, affrighted and blaspheming, stretches her hands to God, crying: "Cursed be that night of fleeting pleasure, when my womb conceived my punishment!" In the next poem the poet is compared to the albatross, splendid on the wing, but almost unable to walk; and the comparison strikes me as very applicable to this poet himself, only that his whole book is a waddling, unwieldy, and unsuccessful attempt to begin a flight. In a number of short lyrics, he talks of poetry, music, and life, without affording us much edification (save in a really powerful picture called "Don Juan in Hell") till he begins to sing, not the delights of the flesh, but the morbid feelings of satiety. Accustomed to the Swinburnian female, we at once recognise her here in the original, as the serpent that dances, the cat that scratches and cries, and the large-limbed sterile creature who never conceives. She "bites," of course:—

"Pour exercer les dents à ce jeu singulier,
Il se faut chaque jour un coeur au râtelier!"

She has "cold eyelids that shut like a jewel:"—

"Tes yeux, où rien ne se révèle
De doux ni d'amer,
Sont *deux bijoux froids!*"

She is cold and "sterile:"—

"La froide majesté de la femme stérile!"

She is, necessarily, like "a snake:"—

. . ."un serpent qui danse," &c., &c.

She is, in fact, Faustine, Mary Stuart, Our Lady of Pain, Sappho, and all the rest,—quite as nasty, and to all intents and purposes, in spite of her attraction for young poets, seemingly as undesirable.

It is quite impossible for me, without long quotation, to fully represent the unpleasantness of Baudelaire, with his "vampires," his "cats," and "cat-like women," his poisons, his fiends, his phantoms, his long menagerie of horrors, his long catalogue of debaucheries. At one time we are in a brothel, and the poet is lying by the side of a dreadful Jewess with "cold eyelids:"—

"Une nuit que j'étais près d'une affreuse Juive,
Comme au long d'un cadavre un cadavre étendu!"

At another time we hear the poet saying to a fair companion—"Seek not my heart; the beasts have eaten it." Grim and wearied as he is, our poet is not above the favourite conceits of his school:—

"Tes hanches sont amoureuses
De ton dos et de ses seins,
Et tu ravis les coussins
Par tes poses langoureuses!"

And this is quite in the symbolizing style of the Italian school, of which I shall give many examples when treating of Mr. Rossetti:—

"*La Haine est un ivrogne* au fond d'une taverne,
Qui sent toujours la soif naître de la liqueur
Et se multiplier comme l'hydre de Lerne.

"—Mais les buveurs heureux connaissent leur vain-
    queur,
Et *la Haine est vouée à ce sort lamentable
De ne pouvoir jamais s'endormir sous la table!*"

At one time we have a poem on "her hair," in
the course of which we learn (what indeed we
should have guessed) that, as other persons delight
in love's "music," he (Baudelaire) revels in its "perfume." He is still insatiable, and yet uncomplimen-
tary, actually comparing his attack on her "cold
beauty" to the attack of a swarm of worms on a
corpse ("comme après un cadavre un choeur de
vermisseaux!") and yet crying fiercely:—

"Je chéris, O bête implacable et cruelle!
Jusqu' à cette froideur par où tu m'es plus belle!"

He finds delight in tracing resemblances between
this marble person and his cat:—

"Viens, mon beau chat, sur mon coeur amoureux;
    Retiens griffes de ta patte,
Et laisse-moi plonger dans tes beaux yeux
    Mêlés de métal et d'agate."

But it would be tedious indeed to trace all the morbid sensations of such a lover as this; at Paris or in
the East, he is equally used up and yet insatiable;
and after having tried all sorts of complexions, from
the pale wax-like Jewess of the Parisian brothel to
the black and lissom beauty of Malabar, he finds
himself still wretched and disgusted with human
nature. It is soon quite obvious that he is possessed
by the demon of Hasheesh. Thoughts horrible and
foul surge through his brain as the filth drives
through a sewer. At least half of all the "Fleurs de
Mal" read as if they had been written by a man in
one of the worst stages of delirium tremens. No one
certainly can accuse him of making crime look
beautiful. To him, in his own words,

"La Débauche et la Mort sont deux aimables filles!"

His crime is, that he sees *only* these two shapes on all
the solid earth, and avers that there is nothing left
for men but to sin and die. His dreams and thoughts
are wretched. The sun rises, and immediately he
pictures it shining, not into happy homes, but into
dens of crime and ghastly hospitals. Night comes,
but sleep comes not; and he only cries:—

"Voici le soir charmant, ami du criminel;
Il vient comme un complice, à pas de loup; le ciel

Se ferme lentement comme une grande alcôve,
Et l'homme impatient se change en bête fauve."

The gas-jets of prostitution are lit, and flare on the
doomed faces of pale women and jaded men. Some
few men sit at happy hearths, but the majority "have
never lived." On such a night, doubtless, he composed such poems as this, which I quote entire in all
its morbid pain and horror:—

"HORREUR SYMPATHIQUE"

" 'De ce ciel bizarre et livide,
Tourmenté comme ton destin,
Quels pensers dans ton âme vide
Descendent?—Réponds, libertin.'

"—Insatiablement avide
De l'obscur et de l'incertain,
Je ne geindrai pas comme Ovide
Chassé du paradis latin.

"Cieux déchirés comme des grèves
En vous se mire mon orgueil!
Vos vastes nuages en deuil
Sont les corbillards de mes rêves,
Et vos lueurs sont le reflet
De l'Enfer où mon coeur se plaît!"

Truly enough did Edward Thierry say, in
writing of this poetry, that "it is sorrow which ab-
solves and justifies it. The poet does not delight in
the spectacle of evil." Still, Baudelaire broods over
evil things with a tremendous persistency, a morbid
satisfaction, which shows a mind radically diseased
and a nature utterly heartless. In and out of season,
he invoked the spirit of Horror. Jaded with self-
indulgence he had a mad pleasure in considering
the world a charnel-house, and in posing the figures
of Love and Beauty in the agonies of disease and the
ghastly stillness of death. As a necessary pendant to
his pictures of human ugliness, he delighted to add
a few glimpses of divine malignity. Looking to the
section of his book called "Révolte," we find where
Mr. Swinburne got his first lesson in blasphemy. In
"The Denial of St. Peter" we have the following
picture of the Deity, quite in the fleshly manner:—

"Comme un tyran gorgé de viande et de vins,
Il s'endort au doux bruit de nos affreux blasphèmes!"

And after passing in review the horrible sufferings
of Christ, he concludes bitterly:—

"Saint Pierre a renié Jésus. . . . *Il a bien fait!*"

In another poem he draws a series of contrasts between the race of Cain and the race of Abel,—in other words, between the domestic type of humanity and the outcast type,—concluding in these memorable words:—

> "Race de Caïn, au ciel monte
> Et sur la terre jette Dieu!"

—words which bear a sort of resemblance, in their foolish and reckless no-meaning, to that passage in Mr. Swinburne's writings wherein the Devil is described as "*playing dice with God*" for the soul of Faustine. Next comes a piece entitled "Les Litanies de Satan," a prayer to the evil one:—

> "Père adoptif de ceux *qu'en sa noire colère*
> Du paradis terrestre a chassés Dieu le Père!"

and in conclusion a few lines called "Prayer:"—

> "Gloire et louange à toi, Satan, dans les hauteurs
> Du Ciel, où tu régnas, et dans les profondeurs
> De l'Enfer, où, vaincu, tu rêves en silence!
> Fais que mon âme un jour, sous l'Arbre de Science,
> Près de toi se repose, à l'heure ou sur ton front
> Comme un Temple nouveau ses rameaux s'épandront."

It will hardly be contended that Mr. Swinburne has surpassed this, although his effusions are wilder and more distorted; and we may well rejoice, meanwhile, that our contemporary blasphemy, as well as so much of our comtemporary bestiality, is no home-product, but an importation transplanted from the French Scrofulous School, and conveyed, with no explanation of its origin, at second hand.

Of a similar character to Baudelaire's "Fleurs de Mal" are his "Petites Poèmes en Prose," in which this cynic of the shambles touches on many themes besides lust and ennui, and touches none that he does not darken. There is here, as in the "Fleurs," an occasional delicacy of touch, a frequent delicacy of perfume, which deepens the prevalent horror and despair of the surrounding chapters. In one piece he compares the public to a dog, which flies in horror when offered some delicate scent, but greedily devours human ordure; and although he wishes us to infer that his own wares are too fine for so coarse a monster, the reader cannot help feeling that there is something in the nature of excrement

in his very choice of a foul metaphor to express his meaning. Indeed, throughout all his writings there is a parade of the olfactory faculty, which awakens the suspicion that Baudelaire, like Fabullus, had one day, after smelling some choice unguent, prayed God to "make him all nose"—

> "Quod tu cum olfacies, Deos rogabis,
> Totum ut te faciant, Fabulle, nasum!"

CAT., lib. xiii.

—and that the prayer had been actually granted. There is plenty of sensitiveness to smell, to touch, even to colour; there is even a kind of perception, neither very acute nor very exquisite, of the beauties of external form; but of that higher sensibility which perceives the subtle *nuances* of spiritual life and trembles to the beating of a tender human heart, there is not one solitary sign. This poetry is like absinthe, comparatively harmless perhaps if sipped in small quantities well diluted, but fatal if taken (as by Mr. Swinburne) in all its native strength and abomination.

Here I must leave the writings of Charles Baudelaire, only observing in conclusion that, in spite of their seeming originality, they belong really to the Italian school, in so far as they are the posings of an affected person before a mirror, the self-anatomy of a morbid nature, the satiated love-sonnets of a sensualist who is out of tune with the world and out of harmony with the life of men. They are, from another point of view, the *reductio ad horribilem* of that intellectual sensualism which Goethe (in one of a giant's weak moments) founded, and which Heine repeated with a shriller and more mocking tone in his "Buch der Lieder." But Baudelaire, not content with playing with wickedness occasionally, as Goethe did, not strong enough to gibe and jeer at it, as Heine did, and too morally weak ever to soar beyond it into the clear region inhabited by both these masters in their best moments, formed the monstrous *disjecta membra* of vice into the poetic Vampire we have been examining. There are flashes of beauty in the creature's eyes at times, but they scarcely charm us, and we willingly pass away from the moral dungeon in which it lurks.

A few years ago Baudelaire died. Mr. Swinburne immediately commemorated his death in some verses quite worthy of the deceased himself. Since that period, I am happy to say, Mr. Swinburne seems to have partly shaken off the horrible influence of the "Fleurs de Mal." Although, in his political effusions, the same sterile woman of the amours is seen sitting (as Mater Dolorosa) by the wild wayside,

"In a rent stained raiment, the robe of a cast-off bride,"

and as France,

"Spat upon, trod upon, whored!"

and although the blasphemy is repeated tenfold in a series of aimless attacks on a Deity who is assumed to be a shadow, there are not wanting signs that the poet is waking up from an evil dream. The Sapphic vein of Baudelaire has been abandoned to begin with. Next, let the same writer's blasphemous vein be abandoned too. Then, let Mr. Swinburne burn all his French books, go forth into the world, look men and women in the face, try to seek some nobler inspiration than the smile of harlotry and the shriek of atheism—and there will be hope for him. Thus far, he has given us nothing but borrowed rubbish, but even in his manner of giving there has been something of genius. His own voice may be worth hearing, when he chooses, once and for ever, to abandon the falsetto.

In the discussion which follows I have scarcely included Mr. Swinburne, because he is obviously capable of rising out of the fleshly stage altogether; and I have said little of Mr. Morris, because he has done some noble work quite outside his ordinary performances as a tale-telling poet. I have chosen rather to confine my attention to the gentleman who is formally recognised as the head of the school, who avows his poems to be perfectly "mature," and who has taken many years of reflection before formally appealing to public judgment. Far too self-possessed to indulge in the riotous follies of the author of "Chastelard," and infinitely too self-conscious to busy himself with the dainty tale-telling of the author of the "Earthly Paradise," the writer whose works I am about to examine has carefully elaborated a series of lyrical and semi-dramatic poems in the mediaeval manner, with certain qualities superadded which I shall have to criticize severely, and with the faults and insincerities so cunningly *disguised* that they seldom lurk on the surface in such a way as to awaken immediate suspicion.

Before turning to the writer in question, let me add a few words on the Fleshly School in general. What a great master has touched at one point of his poetic genius, has been expanded by the erotic school into a whole system of poetry in itself.

In the sweep of one single poem, the weird and doubtful "Vivien," Mr. Tennyson has concentrated all the epicene force which, wearisomely expanded, constitutes the characteristic of the writers at present under consideration; and if in "Vivien" he has indicated for them the bounds of sensualism in art, he has in "Maud," in the dramatic person of the hero, afforded distinct precedent for the hysteric tone and overloaded style which is now so familiar to readers of Mr. Swinburne. The fleshliness of "Vivien" may indeed be described as the distinct quality held in common by all the members of the last sub-Tennysonian school,[3] and it is a quality which becomes unwholesome when there is no moral or intellectual quality to temper and control it. Fully conscious of this themselves, the fleshly gentlemen have bound themselves by solemn league and covenant to extol fleshliness as the distinct and supreme end of poetic and pictorial art; to aver that poetic expression is greater than poetic thought, and by inference that the body is greater than the soul, and sound superior to sense; and that the poet, properly to develop his poetic faculty, must be an intellectual hermaphrodite, to whom the very facts of day and night are lost in a whirl of aesthetic terminology. After Mr. Tennyson has probed the depths of modern speculation in a series of commanding moods, all right and interesting in him as the reigning personage, the "walking gentlemen," knowing that something of the sort is expected from all leading performers, bare their bosoms and aver that *they* are creedless; the only possible question here being, if any disinterested person cares whether they are creedless or not— their self-revelation on that score being so perfectly uncalled for. It is time, nevertheless, to ascertain whether any of these gentlemen has actually in himself the making of a leading performer. It would be scarcely worth while to inquire into their pretensions on merely literary grounds, because sooner or later all literature finds its own level, whatever criticism may say or do in the matter; but it unfortunately happens in the present case that the Fleshly School of verse-writers are, so to speak, public offenders, because they are diligently spreading the seeds of disease broadcast wherever they are read and understood. Their complaint too is catching, and carries off many young persons. What the complaint is, and how it works, may now be seen on a very slight examination of the works of Mr. Dante Gabriel Rossetti.

IV

MR. DANTE GABRIEL ROSSETTI

"Who put bayes into blind Cupid's fist,
That *he* should crown what laureates him list?"
BISHOP HALL

Mr. Rossetti has been known for many years as a painter of exceptional powers, who, for reasons satisfactory to himself, has shrunk from publicly exhibiting his pictures, and from allowing anything like a popular estimate to be formed of their qualities. He belongs, or is said to belong, to the so-called Pre-Raphaelite school, a school which is generally considered to exhibit much genius for colour, and great indifference to perspective. It would be unfair to judge the painter by the glimpses I have had of his works, or by the photographs which are sold of the principal paintings. Judged by the photographs, he is an artist who conceives unpleasantly, and draws ill. Like Mr. Simeon Solomon, however, with whom he seems to have many points in common, he is distinctively a colourist, and of his capabilities in colour I cannot speak, though I should guess that they are good; for if there is any quality by which his poems are specially marked, it is a great sensitiveness to hues and tints as conveyed in poetic epithet. On the other hand, those qualities which impress the casual spectator of the photographs from his pictures are to be found abundantly among his verses. There is the same thinness and transparence of design, the same combination of the simple and the grotesque, the same morbid deviation from healthy forms of life, the same sense of weary, wasting, yet exquisite sensuality; nothing virile, nothing tender, nothing completely sane; a superfluity of extreme sensibility, of delight in affected forms, hues, and tints, and a deep-seated indifference to all agitating forces and agencies, all tumultuous griefs and sorrows, all the thunderous stress of life, and all the straining storm of speculation. Mr. Morris is often pure, fresh, and wholesome as his own great model; Mr. Swinburne startles us more than once by some fine flash of insight; but the mind of Mr. Rossetti is like a glassy mere, broken only by the dive of some water-bird or the motion of floating insects, and brooded over by an atmosphere of insufferable closeness, with a light blue sky above it, sultry depths mirrored within it, and a surface so thickly sown with water-lilies that it retains its glassy smoothness even in the strongest wind. Judged relatively to his poetic associates, Mr. Rossetti must be pronounced inferior to either. He

cannot tell a pleasant story like Mr. Morris, nor forge alliterative thunderbolts like Mr. Swinburne. It must be conceded, nevertheless, that he is neither so glibly imitative as the one, nor so transcendently superficial as the other.

Although he has been known for many years as a poet as well as a painter—as a painter and poet idolized by his own family and personal associates—and although he has often appeared in print as a contributor to magazines, Mr. Rossetti did not formally appeal to the public until rather more than a year ago, when he published a copious volume of poems, with the announcement that the book, although it contained pieces composed at intervals during a period of many years, "included nothing which the author believed to be immature." This work was inscribed to his brother, Mr. William Rossetti, who, having written much both in poetry and criticism, will perhaps be known to bibliographers as the editor of the worst edition of Shelley which has ever seen the light. No sooner had the work appeared than the chorus of eulogy began. "The book is satisfactory from end to end," wrote Mr. Morris in the *Academy;* "I think these lyrics, with all their other merits, the most complete of their time; nor do I know what lyrics of any time are to be called *great,* if we are to deny the title to these." On the same subject Mr. Swinburne went into a hysteria of admiration: "golden affluence," "jewel-coloured words," "chastity of form," "harmonious nakedness," "consummate fleshly sculpture;" and so on in Mr. Swinburne's well-known manner when reviewing his friends. Other critics, with a singular similarity of phrase, followed suit. Strange to say, moreover, no one accused Mr. Rossetti of naughtiness. What had been heinous in Mr. Swinburne was majestic exquisiteness in Mr. Rossetti. Yet I question if there is anything in the unfortunate "Poems and Ballads" more questionable on the score of thorough nastiness than many pieces in Mr. Rossetti's collection. Mr. Swinburne was wilder, more outrageous, more blasphemous, and his subjects were more atrocious in themselves; yet the hysterical tone slew the animalism, the furiousness of epithet lowered the sensation; and the first feeling of disgust at such themes as "Laus Veneris" and "Anactoria" faded away into comic amazement. It was only a little mad boy letting off squibs; not a great strong man, who might be really dangerous to society. "I *will* be naughty!" screamed the little boy; but, after all, what did it matter? It is quite different, however, when a grown person, with the self-control and easy audacity of actual experience, comes forward to chronicle his amorous sensations, and, first proclaiming in a loud voice his literary maturity, and consequent responsibility, shamelessly prints and publishes such a piece of writing as this sonnet on "Nuptial Sleep:"—

> *"At length their long kiss severed, with sweet smart:*
>   *And as the last slow sudden drops are shed*
>   *From sparkling eaves when all the storm has fled,*
> *So singly flagged the pulses of each heart.*
> *Their bosoms sundered, with the opening start*
>   *Of married flowers to either side outspread*
>   *From the knit stem; yet still their mouths, burnt red,*
> *Fawned on each other where they lay apart.*
>
> "Sleep sank them lower than the tide of dreams,
>   And their dreams watched them sink, and slid
>   away.
> Slowly their souls swam up again, through gleams
>   Of watered light and dull drowned waifs of day;
> Till from some wonder of new woods and streams
>   He woke, and wondered more: for there she
>   lay."

This, then, is "the golden affluence of words, the firm outline, the justice and chastity of form." Here is a full-grown man, presumably intelligent and cultivated, putting on record, for other full-grown men to read, the most secret mysteries of sexual connection, and that with so sickening a desire to reproduce the sensual mood, so careful a choice of epithet to convey mere animal sensations, that we merely shudder at the shameless nakedness. I am no purist in such matters. I hold the sensual part of our nature to be as holy as the spiritual or intellectual part, and I believe that such things must find their equivalent in art; but it is neither poetic, nor manly, nor even human, to obtrude such things as the themes of whole poems. It is simply nasty. Nasty as it is, we are very mistaken if many readers do not think it nice. What says the author of "A Scourge for Paper Persecutors," in 1625, of similar literature?—

> "Fine wit is shown therein, but finer 'twere
> If not attired in such bawdy geare;
> But be it as it will, the coyest dames
> In private read it for their closet games!"

English society of one kind purchases the *Day's Doings.* English society of another kind goes into ecstasy over Mr. Solomon's pictures—pretty pieces of morality, such as "Love dying by the breath of Lust." There is not much to choose between the two objects of admiration, except that painters like Mr. Solomon lend actual genius to worthless subjects,

and thereby produce veritable monsters—like the lovely devils that danced round St. Anthony. Mr. Rossetti owes his so-called success with our "aunts" and "grandmothers" to the same causes. In poems like "Nuptial Sleep," the man who is too sensitive to exhibit his pictures, and so modest that it takes him years to make up his mind to publish his poems, parades his private sensations before a coarse public, and is gratified by their idiotic applause.

It must not be supposed that all Mr. Rossetti's poems are made up of trash like this. They contain some fine pictures of nature, occasional passages of real meaning, much clever phraseology, lines of peculiar sweetness, and epithets chosen with true literary cunning. But the fleshly feeling is everywhere. Sometimes, as in "The Stream's Secret," it adds greatly to our emotion of pleasure at perusing a finely wrought poem; at other times, as in the "Last Confession," it is somewhat held in check by the exigencies of a powerful situation and the strength of a dramatic speaker; but it is generally in the foreground, flushing the whole poem with unhealthy rose-colour, stifling the senses with overpowering sickliness, as of too much civet. Mr. Rossetti is never dramatic, never impersonal—always attitudinising, posturing, and describing his own exquisite emotions. He is the "Blessed Damozel," leaning over the "gold bar of heaven," and seeing

> "Time like a pulse shake fierce
> Thro' all the worlds;"

he is "heaven-born Helen, Sparta's queen," whose "each twin breast is an apple sweet;" he is Lilith, the first wife of Adam; he is the rosy Virgin of the poem called "Ave," and the Queen in the "Staff and Scrip;" he is "Sister Helen" melting her waxen man; he is all these, just as surely as he is Mr. Rossetti soliloquising over Jenny in her London lodging, or the very nuptial person writing erotic sonnets to his wife. In petticoats or pantaloons, in modern times or in the middle ages, he is just Mr. Rossetti, a fleshly person, with nothing particular to tell us or teach us, with extreme self-control, a strong sense of colour, and a most affected choice of Latin diction. Amid all his "affluence of jewel-coloured words," he has not given us one rounded and noteworthy piece of art, though his verses are all art; not one poem which is memorable for its own sake, and quite separable from the displeasing identity of the composer. The nearest approach to a perfect whole is the "Blessed Damozel," a peculiar poem, placed first in the book, perhaps by accident, perhaps because it is a key to the poems which follow. This poem appeared in a rough shape many years ago in the *Germ,* an unwholesome periodical started by the Pre-Raphaelites, and suffered, after gasping through a few feeble numbers, to die the death of all such publications. In spite of its affected title, and of numberless affectations throughout the text, the "Blessed Damozel" has merits of its own, and a few lines of real genius. I have heard it described as the record of actual grief and love, or, in simple words, the apotheosis of one actually lost by the writer; but, without having any private knowledge of the circumstance of its composition, I feel that such an account of the poem is inadmissible. It does not contain one single note of sorrow. It is a "composition," and a clever one. Read the opening stanzas: —

> "The blessed damozel leaned out
>   From the gold bar of Heaven;
> Her eyes were deeper than the depth
>   Of water stilled at even;
> She had three lilies in her hand,
>   And the stars in her hair were seven.

> "Her robe, ungirt from clasp to hem,
>   No wrought flowers did adorn,
> But a white rose of Mary's gift
>   For service meetly worn;
> Her hair that lay along her back
>   Was yellow like ripe corn."

This is a careful sketch for a picture, which, worked into actual colour by a master, might have been worth seeing. The steadiness of hand lessens as the poem proceeds, and although there are several passages of considerable power,—such as that where, far down the void,

>   "this earth
> Spins like a fretful midge,"

or that other, describing how

>   "the curled moon
> Was like a little feather
> Fluttering far down the gulf,"—

the general effect is that of a queer old painting on a missal, very affected and very odd. What moved the British criticaster to ecstasy in this poem seems to me very sad nonsense indeed, or, if not sad nonsense, very meretricious affectation. Thus, I have seen the following verses quoted with enthusiasm, as italicised—

> "And still she bowed herself and stooped
>   Out of the circling charm;
> *Until her bosom must have made*
>   *The bar she leaned on warm,*
> And the lilies lay as if asleep
>   Along her bended arm.

> "From the fixed place of Heaven she saw
>   *Time like a pulse shake fierce*
> *Thro' all the worlds.* Her gaze still strove
>   Within the gulf to pierce
> Its path; and now she spoke as when
>   The stars sang in their spheres."

It seems to me that all these lines are very bad, with the exception of the two admirable lines ending the first verse, and that the italicised portions are quite without merit, and almost without meaning. On the whole, one feels disheartened and amazed at the poet who, in the nineteenth century, talks about "damozels," "citherns," and "citoles," and addresses the mother of Christ as the "Lady Mary,"—

> "With her five handmaidens, whose names
>   Are five sweet symphonies,
> Cecily, Gertrude, Magdalen,
>   Margaret, and Rosalys."

A suspicion is awakened that the writer is laughing at us. We hover uncertainly between picturesqueness and namby-pamby, and the effect, as Artemus Ward would express it, is "weakening to the intellect." The thing would have been almost too much in the shape of a picture, though the workmanship might have made amends. The truth is, that literature, and more particularly poetry, is in a very bad way when one art gets hold of another, and imposes upon it its conditions and limitations. In the first few verses of the "Damozel" we have the subject, or part of the subject, of a picture, and the inventor should either have painted it or left it alone altogether; and, had he done the latter, the world would have lost nothing. Poetry is something more than painting; and an idea will not become a poem because it is too smudgy for a picture.

In a short notice from a well-known pen, giving the best estimate we have seen of Mr. Rossetti's power as a poet, the *North American Review* offers a certain explanation for affectation such as that of Mr. Rossetti. The writer suggests that "it may probably be the expression of genuine moods of mind in natures too little comprehensive." We would rather believe that Mr. Rossetti lacks comprehension than that he is deficient in sincerity; yet really, to paraphrase the words which Johnson applied to Thomas

Sheridan, Mr. Rossetti is affected, naturally affected, but it must have taken him a great deal of trouble to become what we now see him—such an excess of affectation is not in nature.[4] There is very little writing in the volume spontaneous in the sense that some of Swinburne's verses are spontaneous; the poems all look as if they had taken a great deal of trouble. The grotesque mediaevalism of "Stratton Water" and "Sister Helen," the mediaeval classicism of "Troy Town," the false and shallow mysticism of "Eden Bower," are one and all essentially imitative, and must have caused the writer much pains. It is time, indeed, to point out that Mr. Rossetti is a poet possessing great powers of assimilation and some faculty for concealing the nutriment on which he feeds. Setting aside the "Vita Nuova" and the early Italian poems, which are familiar to many readers by his own excellent translations, Mr. Rossetti may be described as a writer who has yielded, to an unusual extent, to the complex influences of the literature surrounding him at the present moment. He has the painter's imitative power developed in proportion to his lack of the poet's conceiving imagination. He reproduces to a nicety the manner of an old ballad, a trick in which Mr. Swinburne is also an adept. Cultivated readers, moreover, will recognise in every one of these poems the tone of Mr. Tennyson broken up by the style of Mr. and Mrs. Browning, and disguised here and there by the eccentricities of the Pre-Raphaelites. The "Burden of Nineveh" is a philosophical edition of "Recollections of the Arabian Nights;" "A Last Confession" and "Dante at Verona" are, in the minutest trick and form of thought, suggestive of Mr. Browning; and that the sonnets have been largely moulded and inspired by Mrs. Browning, especially in points of phraseology, can be ascertained by any critic who will compare them with the "Sonnets from the Portuguese." Much remains, nevertheless, that is Mr. Rossetti's own. I at once recognise as his own property such passages as this:—

"I looked up
And saw where a brown-shouldered harlot leaned
Half through a tavern window thick with vine.
Some man had come behind her in the room
And caught her by her arms, and she had turned
With that coarse empty laugh on him, as now
He *munched her neck with kisses, while the vine
Crawled in her back.*"

Or this:—

"As I stooped, her own lips rising there
Bubbled with brimming kisses at my mouth."

Or this:—

"Have seen your lifted silken skirt
Advertise dainties through the dirt!"

Or this:—

"What more prize than love to impel thee,
Grip and *lip* my limbs as I tell thee!"[5]

Passages like these are the common stock of the walking gentlemen of the Fleshly School. I cannot forbear expressing my wonder, by the way, at the kind of women whom it seems the unhappy lot of these gentlemen to encounter. I have lived nearly as long in the world as they have, but never yet came across persons of the other sex who conduct themselves in the manner described. Females who bite, scratch, scream, bubble, munch, sweat, writhe, twist, wriggle, foam, and in a general way slaver over their lovers, must surely possess some extraordinary qualities to counteract their otherwise most offensive mode of conducting themselves. It appears, however, on examination, that their poet-lovers conduct themselves in a similar manner. They, too, bite, scratch, scream, bubble, munch, sweat, writhe, twist, wriggle, foam, and slaver, in a style frightful to hear of. At times, in reading such books as this, one cannot help wishing that things had remained for ever in the asexual state described in Mr. Darwin's great chapter on Palingenesis. We get very weary of this protracted hankering after a person of the other sex; it seems meat, drink, thought, sinew, religion, for the Fleshly School. There is no limit to the fleshliness, and Mr. Rossetti finds in it its own religious justification much in the same way as Holy Willie:—

"Maybe thou let'st this fleshly thorn
Perplex thy servant night and morn,
'Cause he's so gifted.
If so, thy hand must e'en be borne,
Until thou lift it."

Whether he is writing of the holy Damozel, or of the Virgin herself, or of Lilith, or of Helen, or of Dante, or of Jenny the street-walker, he is fleshly all over, from the roots of his hair to the tip of his toes; never a true lover merging his identity into that of the beloved one; never spiritual, never tender; always self-conscious and aesthetic. "Nothing in human life," says a modern writer, "is so utterly remorseless—not love, not hate, not ambition, not vanity—as the artistic or aesthetic instinct morbidly developed to the suppression of conscience and feeling;" and at no time do we feel more fully impressed with this truth than after the perusal of "Jenny," in some respects the cleverest poem in the volume, and in all respects the poem best indicative of the true quality of the writer's humanity. It is a production which bears signs of having been suggested by my own quasi-lyrical poems, which it copies in the style of title, and particularly by "Artist and Model;"[6] but certainly Mr. Rossetti cannot be accused, as I have been accused, of maudlin sentiment and affected tenderness. The first two lines are perfect:—

> "Lazy laughing languid Jenny,
> Fond of a kiss and fond of a guinea;"

and the poem is a soliloquy of the poet—who has been spending the evening in dancing at a casino—over his partner, whom he has accompanied home to the usual style of lodgings occupied by such ladies, and who has fallen asleep with her head upon his knee, while he wonders, in a wretched pun—

> "Whose person or whose purse may be
> The lodestar of your reverie?"

The soliloquy is long, and in some parts beautiful, despite a very constant suspicion that we are listening to an emasculated Mr. Browning, whose whole tone and gesture, so to speak, is occasionally introduced with startling fidelity; and there are here and there glimpses of actual thought and insight, over and above the picturesque touches which belong to the writer true profession, such as that where, at daybreak—

> "lights creep in
> Past the gauze curtains half drawn-to
> And *the lamp's doubled shade grows blue.*"

What I object to in this poem is not the subject, which any writer may be fairly left to choose for himself; nor anything particularly vicious in the poetic treatment of it; nor any bad blood bursting through in special passages. But the whole tone, without being more than usually coarse, seems heartless. There is not a drop of piteousness in Mr. Rossetti. He is just to the outcast, even generous; severe to the seducer; sad even at the spectacle of lust in dimity and fine ribbons. Notwithstanding all this, and a certain delicacy and refinement of treat-

ment unusual with this poet, the poem is repelling, and one likes Mr. Rossetti least after its perusal. The "Blessed Damozel" is puzzling, the "Song of the Bower" is amusing, the love-sonnet is depressing and sickening, but "Jenny," though distinguished by less special viciousness of thought and style than any of these, fairly makes the reader lose patience. Its fleshliness is apparent at a glance; one perceives that the scene was fascinating less through its human tenderness than because it, like all the others, possessed an *inherent* quality of Animalism. "The whole work," ("Jenny,") writes Mr. Swinburne, "is worthy to fill its place for ever as one of the most perfect poems of an age or generation. There is just the same life-blood and breadth of poetic interest in this episode of a London street and lodging as in the song of 'Troy Town' and the song of 'Eden Bower;' just as much, and no jot more,"—to which last statement I cordially assent; for there is bad blood in all, and breadth of poetic interest in none. "Vengeance of Jenny's case," indeed!—when such a poet as this comes fawning over her, with tender compassion in one eye and aesthetic enjoyment in the other![7]

It is time that I permitted Mr. Rossetti to speak for himself, which I will do by quoting a fairly representative poem entire:—

LOVE-LILY

"Between the hands, between the brows,
    Between the lips of Love-Lily,
A spirit is born whose birth endows
    My blood with fire to burn through me;
Who breathes upon my gazing eyes,
    Who laughs and murmurs in mine ear,
At whose least touch my colour flies,
    And whom my life grows faint to hear.

"Within the voice, within the heart,
    Within the mind of Love-Lily,
A spirit is born who lifts apart
    His tremulous wings and looks at me;
Who on my mouth his finger lays,
    And shows, while whispering lutes confer,
That Eden of Love's watered ways
    Whose winds and spirits worship her.

"Brows, hands, and lips, heart, mind, and voice,
    Kisses and words of Love-Lily,—
Oh! bid me with your joy rejoice
    Till *riotous longing rest in me!*
Ah! let not hope be still distraught,
    But find in her its gracious goal,
Whose speech Truth knows not from her thought,
    Nor Love her body from her soul."

With the exception of the usual "riotous longing," which seems to make Mr. Rossetti a burden to himself, there is nothing to find fault with in the extreme fleshliness of these verses, and to many people they may even appear beautiful. Without pausing to criticize a thing so trifling—as well might we dissect a cobweb or anatomize a medusa—let me ask the reader's attention to a peculiarity to which all the students of the Fleshly School must sooner or later give their attention—I mean the habit of accenting the last syllable in words which in ordinary speech are accepted on the penultimate:—

> "Between the hands, between the brows,
> Between the lips of Love-Lil*ee*!"

which may be said to give to the speaker's voice a sort of cooing tenderness just bordering on a loving whistle. Still better as an illustration are the lines:—

> "Saturday night is market night
> Everywhere, be it dry or wet,
> And market night in the Haymar-*ket*!"

which the reader may advantageously compare with Mr. Morris's

> "Then said the king,
> Thanked be thou; *neither for nothing*
> Shalt thou this good deed do to me;"

Or Mr. Swinburne's

> "In either of the twain
> Red roses full of rain;
> She hath for bondwo*men*
> All kinds of flowers."

It is unnecessary to multiply examples of an affectation which disfigures all these writers; who, in the same spirit which prompts the ambitious nobodies that rent London theatres in the "empty" season to make up for their dulness by fearfully original "new readings," distinguish their attempt at leading business by affecting the construction of their grandfathers and great-grandfathers, and the accentuation of the poets of the court of James I. It is in all respects a sign of remarkable genius, from this point of view, to rhyme "was" with "grass," "death" with "lieth," "gain" with "fountain," "love" with "of," "once" with "suns," and so on *ad nauseam*. I am far from disputing the value of bad rhymes used occasionally to break up the monotony of verse, but the case is hard when such blunders become the rule and not the exception, when writers deliberately lay themselves out to be as archaic and affected as possible. Poetry is perfect human speech, and these archaisms are the mere fiddlededeeing of empty heads and hollow hearts. Bad as they are, they are the true indication of falser tricks and affectations which lie far deeper. They are trifles light as air, showing how the wind blows. The soul's speech and the heart's speech are clear, simple, natural, and beautiful, and reject the meretricious tricks to which we have drawn attention.

It is on the score that these tricks and affectations have procured the professors a number of imitators, that the small writers of the Fleshly School deliver their formula that great poets are always to be known, because their manner is immediately reproduced by small poets, and that a poet who finds few imitators is probably of inferior rank—by which they mean to infer that they themselves are very great poets indeed. It is quite true that they are imitated. On the stage, twenty provincial "stars" copy Charles Kean, while not one copies his father; there are dozens of actors who reproduce Mr. Charles Dillon, and not one who attempts to reproduce Macready.

But what is really most droll and puzzling in the matter is, that these imitators seem to have no difficulty whatever in writing nearly, if not quite, as well as their masters. It is not bad imitation they offer us, but poems which read just like the originals; the fact being that it is easy to reproduce sound when it has no strict connection with sense, and simple enough to cull phraseology not hopelessly interwoven with thought and spirit. The fact that these gentlemen are so easily imitated is the most damning proof of their inferiority. What merits they have lie with their faults on the surface, and can be caught by any young gentleman as easily as the measles, only they are rather more difficult to get rid of. All young gentlemen have animal faculties, though few have brains; and if animal faculties without brains will make poems, nothing is easier in the world. A great and good poet, however, is great and good irrespective of manner, and often in spite of manner; he is great because he brings great ideas and new light, because his thought is a revelation; and, although it is true that a great manner generally accompanies great matter, the manner of great matter is almost inimitable. The great poet is not Cowley, imitated and idolized and reproduced by every scribbler of his time; nor Pope, whose trick of style was so easily copied that to this day we cannot trace his own hand with any certainty in the *Iliad;* nor Donne, nor Sylvester, nor the Della Cruscans. Shakspere's blank verse is the most difficult and

Jonson's the most easy to imitate of all the Elizabethan stock; and Shakspere's verse is the best verse, because it combines the great qualities of all contemporary verse, with no individual affectations: and so perfectly does this verse, with all its splendour, intersect with the style of contemporaries *at their best,* that we would undertake to select passage after passage which would puzzle a good judge to tell which of the Elizabethans was the author—Marlowe, Beaumont, Dekker, Marston, Webster, or Shakspere himself. The great poet is Dante, full of the thunder of a great Idea; and Milton, unapproachable in the serene white light of thought and sumptuous wealth of style; and Shakspere, all poets by turns, and all men in succession; and Goethe, always innovating, and ever indifferent to innovation for its own sake; and Wordsworth, clear as crystal and deep as the sea; and Tennyson, with his vivid range, far-piercing sight, and perfect speech; and Browning, great, not by virtue of his eccentricities, but because of his close intellectual grasp. Tell "Paradise Lost," the "Divine Comedy," in naked prose; do the same by *Hamlet, Macbeth,* and *Lear;* read Mr. Hayward's translation of "Faust;" take up the "Excursion," a great poem, though its speech is nearly prose already; turn the "Guinevere" into a mere story; reproduce Pompilia's last dying speech without a line of rhythm. Reduced to bald English, all these poems, and all great poems, lose much; but how much do they not retain? They are poems to the very roots and depths of being, poems born in and delivered from the soul, and treat them as cruelly as you may, poems they will remain. So it is with all good and thorough creations, however low in their rank; so it is with the "Ballad on a Wedding" and "Clever Tom Clinch," just as much as with the "Epistle of Karsheesh," or Goethe's torso of "Prometheus;" with Shelley's "Skylark," or Alfred de Musset's "A la Lune," as well as Racine's *Athalie,* Victor Hugo's "Parricide," or Hood's "Last Man." A poem is a poem, first as to the soul, next as to the form. The fleshly persons who wish to create form for its own sake are merely pronouncing their own doom. But *such* form! If the Pre-Raphaelite fervour gains ground, we shall soon have popular songs like this:—

"When winds do roar, and rains do pour,
  Hard is the life of the sail*or;*
He scarcely as he reels can tell
  The side-lights from the binn*acle;*
He looketh on the wild w*ater,*" &c.;

and so on, till the English speech seems the speech of raving madmen. Of a piece with other affectations is the device of a burden, of which the fleshly persons are very fond for its own sake, quite apart from its relevancy. Thus Mr. Rossetti sings:—

"Why did you melt your waxen man,
      Sister Helen?
To-day is the third since you began.
The time was long, yet the time ran,
      Little brother.
  (O mother, Mary mother,
Three days to-day between Heaven and Hell.)"

This burden is repeated, with little or no alteration, through thirty-four verses. About as much to the point is a burden of Mr. Swinburne's, something to the following effect:—

"We were three maidens in the green corn,
  Small red leaves in the mill-water;
Fairer maidens were never born,
  Apples of gold for the king's daughter."

Productions of this sort are "silly sooth" in good earnest, though they delight some newspaper critics of the day, and are copied by young gentlemen with animal faculties morbidly developed by too much tobacco and too little exercise. Such indulgence, however, would ruin the strongest poetical constitution; and it unfortunately happens that neither masters nor pupils were naturally very healthy. In such a poem as "Eden Bower" there is not one scrap of imagination, properly so called. It is a clever grotesque in the worst manner of Callot, unredeemed by a gleam of true poetry or humour. No good poet would have wrought into a poem the absurd tradition about Lilith; Goethe was content to glance at it merely, with a grim smile, in the great scene in the Brocken. I may remark here that productions of this unnatural and morbid kind are only tolerable when they embody a profound meaning, as do Coleridge's "Ancient Mariner" and "Cristabel." Not that we would insult the memory of Coleridge by comparing his exquisitely conscientious work with this affected rubbish about "Eden Bower" and "Sister Helen," although his influence in their composition is unmistakable. Still more unmistakable is the influence of that unwholesome poet, Beddoes, who, with all his great powers (unmistakably superior to those of any of the present Fleshly School), treated his subjects in a thoroughly insincere manner, and is now justly forgotten.

The great strong current of English poetry rolls on, ever mirroring in its bosom new prospects of fair and wholesome thought. Morbid deviations are endless and inevitable; there must be marsh and stagnant mere as well as mountain and wood. Glancing backward into the shady places of the obscure, we have seen the once prosperous nonsense-writers each now consigned to his own little limbo—Skelton and Gower still playing fantastic tricks with the mother-tongue; Gascoigne outlasting the applause of all, and living to see his own works buried before him;[8] Sylvester doomed to oblivion by his own fame as a translator; Carew the idol of courts, and Donne the beloved of schoolmen, both buried in the same oblivion; the fantastic Fletchers winning the wonder of collegians, and fading out through sheer poetic impotence; Cowley shaking all England with his pindarics, and perishing with them; Waller, the famous, saved from oblivion by the natural note of one single song[9]—and so on, through league after league of a flat and desolate country which once was prosperous, till we come again to these fantastic figures of the Fleshly School, with their droll mediaeval garments, their funny archaic speech, and the fatal marks of literary consumption on every pale and delicate visage. My judgment on Mr. Rossetti, to whom I in the meantime confine my judgment, is substantially that of the *North American Reviewer,* who believes that "we have in him another poetical man, and a man markedly poetical, and of a kind apparently, though not radically, different from any of our secondary writers of poetry, but that we have not in him a new poet of any weight;" and that he is "so affected, sentimental, and painfully self-conscious, that the best to be done in his case is to hope that this book of his, having unpacked his bosom of so much that is unhealthy, may have done him more good than it has given others pleasure."[10] Such, I say, is my opinion, which might very well be wrong, and have to undergo modification, if Mr. Rossetti were younger and less self-possessed. His "maturity" is fatal.

V

"THE HOUSE OF LIFE," &c., RE-EXAMINED

I had written thus far of Mr. Rossetti's poems, just after reading them for the first time when cruising among the Western Isles of Scotland in the summer of 1871, and I had published my criticism in the *Contemporary Review* for October (under cir-

cumstances explained in my preface), when Mr. Rossetti, goaded into a sense of grievance by the ill-advised sympathy of his friend the editor of the *Athenaeum,* "replied" to the audacious critic who, not being honoured by his personal acquaintance, dared to accuse him of poetic incompetence and literary immorality. Mr. Rossetti's letter, forming a whole page and a quarter of his favourite weekly print, now lies before me; and I am bound in honour to consider it in some detail.

After a preamble somewhat personal to myself,[11] Mr. Rossetti arrives at his first point, which amounts to this—that he is going to write a long article of self-defence to show he is indifferent. He then formally opens his case, and (that he may not hereafter accuse me of "garbling" his letter) I will quote his very words, only italicising them in certain places:—

> "The primary accusation, on which this writer grounds all the rest, seems to be that others and myself 'extol fleshliness as the distinct and supreme end of poetic and pictorial art; aver that poetic expression is greater than poetic thought; and, by inference, that the body is greater than the soul, and sound superior to sense.' As my own writings are alone formally dealt with in the article, I shall confine my answer to myself; and this must first take unavoidably *the form of a challenge to prove* so broad a statement. It is true, some fragmentary pretence at proof is put in here and there throughout the attack, and thus far an opportunity is given of contesting the assertion.
>
> "A Sonnet, entitled 'Nuptial Sleep,' is quoted and abused at page 338 of the *Review,* and is there dwelt upon as a 'whole poem,' describing 'merely animal sensations.' It is no more a whole poem in reality, than is any single stanza of any poem throughout the book. The poem, written chiefly in sonnets, and of which this is one sonnet-stanza, is entitled 'The House of Life;' and even in my first published installment of the whole work (as contained in the volume under notice) ample evidence is included that no such passing phase of description as the one headed 'Nuptial Sleep' could possibly be put forward by the author of 'The House of Life,' as his own representative view of the subject of love. In proof of this, I will direct attention (among the love-sonnets of this poem) to Nos. 2, 8, 11, 17, 28, and more especially 13, which, indeed, I had better print here.

LOVE-SWEETNESS

Sweet dimness of her loosened hair's downfall
     About thy face; her *sweet* hands round thy head
     In gracious fostering union garlanded;
Her tremulous smiles; her glances' *sweet* recall

Of love; her murmuring sighs memorial;
   Her mouth's culled sweetness by thy kisses shed
   On cheeks and neck and eyelids, and so led
Back to her mouth which answers there for all:—
What *sweeter* than these things, except the thing
   In lacking which all these would lose their *sweet:—*
   The confident heart's still fervour; the swift beat
And soft subsidence of the spirit's wing,
Then when it feels, in cloud-girt wayfaring,
   The breath of kindred plumes against its feet!

     "Any reader may bring any artistic charge he pleases against the above sonnet; but one charge it would be impossible to maintain against the writer of the series in which it occurs, and that is, the wish on his part to assert that the body is greater than the soul. For here *all the passionate and just delights of the body are declared—somewhat figuratively, it is true, but unmistakably—to be as naught if not ennobled by the concurrence of the soul at all times.(!)*[12] Moreover, nearly one half of this series of sonnets has nothing to do with love, but treats of quite other life-influences. I would defy any one to couple with fair quotation of Sonnets 29, 30, 31, 39, 40, 41, 43, or others, the slander that their author was not impressed, like all other thinking men, with the responsibilities and higher mysteries of life; while Sonnets 35, 36, and 37, entitled 'The Choice,' sum up the general view taken in a manner only to be evaded by conscious insincerity. Thus much for 'The House of Life,' of which the Sonnet 'Nuptial Sleep' is one stanza, *embodying, for its small constituent share, a beauty of natural universal function, only to be reprobated in art if dwelt on (as I have shown that it is not here) to the exclusion of those other highest things of which it is the harmonious concomitant.*"[13]

     Thus far Mr. Rossetti; and although it is rather hard to have to refer again to poems so unsavoury, I have no option but to accept the challenge, and judge Mr. Rossetti by "The House of Life" as an uncompleted whole. A reference to this poem, so far from changing my opinion, makes me wonder at the writer's misconception of its true character. It is flooded with sensualism from the first line to the last; it is a very hotbed of nasty phrases; but its nastiness—or its unwholesomeness—goes far deeper than any phraseology. It opens with a sonnet entitled "Bridal Love," wherein we are told that "Love,"

"Born with her life, creature of poignant thirst
And exquisite hunger,"

is preparing "with his warm hands our couch;" and so intense grows the poet's enthusiasm at this information that he exclaims, wildly addressing his lady in Sonnet II.,—

"O thou who at Love's hour ecstatically
   Unto my lips dost evermore present
   The body and blood of Love in Sacrament!"

—which is a pretty good beginning, quite apart from the blasphemy, for a writer in whose eyes a "beauty of natural universal function" is merely a "harmonious concomitant" of higher things. Sonnet III., entitled "Love's Light," describes harmlessly enough how,

"—in the dark hours (we two alone)
Close kissed and eloquent of still replies
Thy twilight-hidden glimmering visage lies;"

but in Sonnet IV. another and higher stage is reached, for the lady gives her lover a "consonant interlude" (which is the Fleshly for "kiss"), and—"somewhat figuratively, it is true, but unmistakably"—proceeds, as a mother suckles a baby, to afford him full fruition:—

"I was a child beneath her touch (!),—a man
   When *breast to breast we clung,* even I and she,—
   A spirit when her spirit lookt thro' me,—
A god when *all our life-breath met to fan*
Our life-blood, till love's emulous ardours ran,
   Fire within fire, desire in deity."

O malignant critic, who has dared to attaint the author of these sweet lines of "fleshliness!" Let the reader examine this passage phrase by phrase and word by word, dwelling particularly on the descriptive animalism of the last three lines. Why, much the same charge might be brought against that delicious effort of Thomas Carew, entitled "The Rapture," wherein (quite after the modern fleshly style) the whole business of love is chronicled in sublime and daring metaphor:—

"Then will I visit with a wandering kiss
The bower of roses and the grove of bliss,
Thence, passing o'er thy snowy Appenine,
Retire into thy grove of eglantine."[14]

Sonnet V. is our favourite already quoted, "Nuptial Sleep," and Sonnet VI., or "Supreme Surrender," tells us how—

"To all the spirits of love that wander by,
   Along *the love-sown fallow field of sleep*
   My lady lies apparent; and the deep
Calls to the deep; *and no one sees but I.*"

There is also this dainty touch about her hand:—

"First touched, the hand now warm around my neck
Taught memory long to mock desire."

Sonnet VII., "Love's Lovers," is meaningless, but in the best manner of Carew and Dr. Donne; and the same may be said of Sonnet VIII., "Passion and Worship." Sonnet IX., "The Portrait," is a good sonnet and good poetry, despite the epithets of "mouth's mould" and "long lithe throat." Sonnet X., the "Love Letter," is fleshly and affected, but stops short of nastiness. Sonnet XI. is also innocuous. Sonnets XII. to XX. are one profuse sweat of animalism, containing, amongst other gems, this euphuistic description of a kissing match:—

"Her mouth's culled sweetness by thy kisses shed
On cheeks, and neck, and eyelids, and so led
Back to her mouth which answers there for all;"

and scores of the author's pet phrases, the veriest pimples on the surface of style, like "wanton flowers," "murmuring sighs memorial," "sweet confederate music favourable," "hours eventual," "Love's philtred euphrasy," "culminant changes"—all familiar enough to us from the Della Cruscans; but culminating, in Sonnet XX., with an image in which the Euphuist would have rejoiced:—

"Her set gaze gathered, thirstier than of late, (!)
And as she kissed, her *Mouth became her Soul!*"

In Sonnet XXI., called "Parted Love," the lady has retired to get breath and arrange her clothes, and the lover is despairingly waiting from "the stark noon-height" to the "sunset's desolate disarray." Sonnets XXII. and XXIII. are too vague for description, but Landor would have stared to see his famous sea-shell image (which he accused Wordsworth of stealing) turned by the euphuistic-fleshly person into

"The speech-bound sea-shell's low *importunate strain.*"

The next four sonnets, called by the affected title of "Willow-wood," contain, besides the gem about "bubbling of brimming kisses," some fresh variations of a kiss:—

"Fast together, alive from the abyss,
Clung the *soul-wrung implacable close kiss.*"

An "implacable" kiss! Also:—

"So when the song died *did the kiss unclose,
And her face fell back drown'd.*"

The supreme silliness and worthlessness of "Willow-wood," however, could only be shown by quoting the four sonnets entire. Sonnet XXVIII., or "Still-born Love," will doubtless suggest to Mr. Rossetti's admirers other similar themes, and we shall speedily have poetry on "Love's Cross-birth" and "Love's Anaesthetics." Sonnets XXIX., XXX., and XXXI., Mr. Rossetti particularly challenges me to impeach; and I may at once admit that they are not nasty, though very, very silly. In Sonnet XXXII., however, we get back to the old imagery:—

"Even as the thistledown from pathsides dead
Glean'd by a girl in autumns of her youth,
Which one new year makes soft her marriage bed."

Mr. Rossetti is never so great as on "kisses" and "beds." In spite of euphuisms without end, we get nothing very spicy till we come to Sonnet XXXIX., one of those which Mr. Rossetti calls immaculate. Here, not content with picturing "Vain Virtues" as Virgins writhing in Hell, he describes the Fire as the Bridegroom, and pursues the metaphor to the very pit of beastliness:—

"Virgins. . . . whom the fiends compel
Together now, in snake-bound shuddering sheaves
Of anguish, while *the scorching Bridegroom leaves
Their refuse maidenhood (!) abominable!*"

There are ten sonnets to come, but *must* I quote from them? Surely I have quoted already *ad nauseam.* After the sonnets comes "Love-Lily," which I have already given in full; then "First Love Remembered;" then "Plighted Promise," a lyric which I am bound to copy, as it has never been equalled since the famous

"Fluttering fold thy feeble pinions"

of the "Rejected Addresses:"—

PLIGHTED PROMISE

"In a *soft-complexioned sky*
Fleeting rose and kindling grey,
Have you seen *Aurora* fly
At the break of day?
So my maiden, so my plighted may
Blushing cheek and gleaming eye
Lifts to look my way.

"Where the inmost leaf is stirred
With *the heart-beat of the grove,*

Have you heard a hidden bird
        Cast her note above?
So my lady, so my lovely love
        Echoing *Cupid's* prompted word,
        Makes a tune thereof.

"Have you seen, at heaven's mid-height,
        In the moon-rack's ebb and tide,
Venus leap forth burning white
        Pearl-pale and hide?
So *my bright breast-jewel, so my bride*
One sweet night when fear takes flight
        Shall leap against my side."

A "soft-complexioned sky!" the "heart-beat of the grove!" "Aurora, Cupid, Dian!" I rub my eyes, wondering if this can be the nineteenth century, till the last lines, with their "bright breast-jewel," recall me to my subject. But really quotations of this sort become the merest iteration. "The House of Life" contains eight songs more. Four of them, though sensuous in the extreme, have no direct reference to nasty subjects. The other four are sickly love-poems, swarming with affectations. My extracts however, must close with this verse from the "Song of the Bower" (Mr. Rossetti is great in "bowers"):—

"What were my prize, could I enter thy bower,
        This day, to-morrow, at eve or at morn?
Large lovely arms and a neck like a tower,[15]
        Bosom then heaving that now lies forlorn,
Kindled with love-breath, (the sun's kiss is colder!)
        Thy sweetness all near me, so distant to-day;
My hand round thy neck and thy hand on my shoulder,
        My mouth to thy mouth as the world melts away."

In this and a thousand other passages one thing is apparent: either Mr. Rossetti is stealing wholesale from Mr. Swinburne, or Mr. Swinburne has been all his life robbing Mr. Rossetti.

Having so far complied with Mr. Rossetti's request, and re-examined "The House of Life," I retain unchanged my impression that the sort of house meant should be nameless, but is probably the identical one where the writer found "Jenny." Once more, I should like to quote Mr. Rossetti, in the further passages of his high argument; but he is so very abusive that I am bound to condense his statement. After vindicating "The House of Life," he proceeds to say that the four extracts given [earlier and referred to in note 5], are grossly garbled, and printed "without reference to any precise page or poem," and that the poems themselves, if read wisely, would be found perfectly beautiful and

artistic. Turn, then, to the four poems in question. The first is "A Last Confession," which describes, in Mr. Browning's favourite manner, how an Italian, maddened by jealousy, murdered his mistress. This Italian, it may be remarked, is very like our author, for, besides being disagreeably affected, he had a morbid habit of *brooding* over unclean ideas and suspicions; insomuch that, as Mr. Rossetti truly observes, he is driven to frenzy by the real or fancied resemblance between the laugh of the harlot and that of his mistress. "Observe also," continues the bard, "that these are but seven lines in a poem of five hundred, not one other of which could be classed with them." Observe, I say in turn, that the whole poem is morbid and unwholesome, and must be drunk in as a whole to leave its full bad flavour. It positively reeks of murder, madness, and morbid lust, and whatever merit it possesses lies in the intensity of its ugly thoughts, from the first moment when the Italian began his courtship in this extraordinary fashion—

"What I knew I told
Of Venus and of Cupid,—strange old tales!"

—till, blinded with lustful rage, he confesses having murdered her, and tells his dreams:—

"She wrung her hair out in my dream
To-night, till all the darkness *reeked* of it.
I heard the blood between her fingers *hiss!*"

In justice we should observe that a madman is speaking; but this madman has Mr. Rossetti's gift, for here is the sort of conceit with which he delights the priest:—

"She had a mouth
Made to bring death to life,—*the underlip*
Suck'd in, as if it strove to kiss itself."

With the Della Cruscan, the attempt to seem subtle and striking becomes a positive mania. What would be said of a poet who wrote thus?—

Her nose inclined to heaven,
As if it tried to turn up at itself!

Yet the one metaphor is every whit as sensible and brilliant as the other.

The second of the four poems is the "bubble" poem from "The House of Life." The third is from "Eden Bower," a production which I would gladly quote entire. "Here again," it is observed, "no reference is given, and naturally the reader would suppose that a *human* embrace is described. The embrace, on the contrary, is that of a fabled snake-woman and a snake." Exactly; but will Mr. Rossetti describe a single passage in his poems where a human embrace *is* described? The lovers of the Fleshly School are invariably snake-like in their eternal wriggling, lipping, munching, slavering, and biting; and indeed, on reflection, "Eden Bower" may be fairly considered as a complete epitome of the art of love as practised by the coterie poets. Since Mr. Rossetti is dissatisfied, let us try again. His book is a lottery-bag—we draw blindfold—but are always sure of a prize:—

> "Bring thou close thine head *till it glisten*
> *Along my breast,* and *lip me,* and listen!"

Once more,—conjugal bliss of Adam and Lilith:—

> "What great joys had Adam and Lilith!
> *Sweet close rings of the serpent's twining,*
> *As heart in heart lay sighing and pining.*"[16]

The result (next verse):—

> "What *bright babes* had Lilith and Adam?
> Shapes that coiled in the woods and waters," &c.

All this is savoury, and the whole poem is still more so; so that the reader feels a horrible sense of sliminess, as if he were handling a yellow serpent or a conger eel. Let me try blindfold once more for another "draw." This time my prize is from "Troy Town;" but, before I quote, let me once more premise that the poem as a whole is fleshlier and sillier than any extract. Helen's breasts, described by herself:—

> "Each twin breast is an apple sweet!
> . . . .
> Mine are apples grown to the south
> (*O Troy Town!*)
> Grown to taste in the days of drouth,
> Taste and waste to the heart's desire;
> Mine are apples *meet for his mouth!*"

So that Paris, poor fellow, has a fair prospect of being *suckled* by Helen, and is likely, after "tasting" her "apples" or "breasts meet for his mouth," to "waste" them (whatever that means) "to his heart's desire."

But already I hear the amazed reader cry, with Macbeth, "Hold, enough!" I have thus piled example upon example, all out of one small volume of verse; and I might readily go on quoting for pages more. I reject altogether the insinuation that my criticism was based on private grounds. I do not know Mr. Rossetti, have no grievance against him, and I can quite believe that in private life he is a most exemplary person; but in his poetry—to go no further at present than that very small phase of a portentous phenomenon—there is a veritably stupendous preponderance of sensuality and sickly animalism. I base that belief, not merely on stray expressions such as I quoted, not merely on lines about the "lipping of limbs," bubbling of kisses, "fawning of lips" in bed, munching of mouths, and all the inordinate coarseness of the fleshly vocabulary, but on the persistent choice of subjects repulsive in themselves, and capable of fleshly treatment, such as the lyric about Jenny the street-walker, who "advertises dainties through the dirt," and is serenaded by the poet in a brothel; the poem about Lilith the Snake, and her gripping and lipping, and general arts of fornication; and the nuptial sonnet which Mr. Rossetti studiously refrains from quoting, knowing that it would condemn him fatally in all decent eyes. I said, and I say, that the very choice of these subjects is deplorable, and that their treatment is offensive; and I said, and say, that the morbid habit penetrates into the writer's treatment even when, as very seldom happens, he chooses a subject by no means morbid in itself: all this without going beyond Mr. Rossetti; but if I go a little further, and look at that phenomenon of which he is a phase, I find decency outraged, history falsified, purity sacrificed, art prostituted, language perverted, religion outraged, in one gibbering attempt to apotheosize vice and demolish art with the implements of blasphemy and passion; I find that Mary of Scotland is a biting and scratching harlot, Sappho a lustful wild beast, Christ and Christianity scandals and abortions; and pursuing further my inquiry into this phenomenon, finding religion distorted into lust, and lust raving in the very language of religion, I take occasion to say—on public grounds only, with no grudge, with no personal animosity whatever—that a number of men of real though very limited ability are, blinded by their own little knowledge, the praise of vile minds, and the applause of a heartless clique, rushing headlong to literary ruin, and dragging many of the young generation with them. What Mr. Rossetti says in explanation is only to the point in so far as it is deplorably convincing that he himself is utterly unconscious of his own offences; does not, in fact, discriminate between passion and sensuality; and endeavours, writhing under what he thinks an unmerited imputation, to save himself on the plea of personal purity and dramatic motive. No one can rejoice more than I do to hear that Mr. Rossetti attaches a certain importance to the soul as distinguished from the body, only I should like very much to know what he means by the soul; for I fear, from the sonnet he quotes, that he regards the feeling for a young woman's person, face, heart, and mind, as in itself quite a spiritual sentiment. In the poem entitled "Love-Lily" he expressly observes that Love cannot tell Lily's "body from her soul"—they are so inextricably blended. It is precisely this confusion of the two which, filling Mr. Rossetti as it eternally does with what he calls "riotous longing," becomes so intolerable to readers with a less mystic sense of animal function.

VI

PEARLS FROM THE AMATORY POETS

"Belial came last, than whom a spirit more lewd
Fell not from heaven, or more gross to love
Vice for itself."

Paradise Lost

I have thus carefully gone through Mr. Rossetti's poetry, not because it is by any means the best or worst verse of its kind, but because, being avowedly "mature," and having had the benefit of many years' revision, it is perhaps more truly representative of its class than the grosser verse of Mr. Swinburne, or the more careless and fluent verse of Mr. Morris. The main charge I bring against poetry of this kind is its sickliness and effeminacy; but if there be any truth in my own Theory of Literary Morality, as enunciated some years ago in the *Fortnightly Review,* the charge of indecency need not be pressed at all, as it is settled by the fact of artistic and poetic incompetence. The morality of any book is determinable by its value as literature—immoral writing proceeding primarily from insincerity of vision, and therefore being betokened by all those signs which enable us to ascertain the value of art as art. In the present case the matter is ludicrously simple; for we perceive that the silliness and the insincerity come, not by nature, but at second hand; Mr. Rossetti and Mr. Swinburne being the merest echoes—strikingly original in this—that they merely echo what is vile, while other imitators reproduce what is admirable. I am loath in this connection to incriminate Mr. Morris. That gentleman is so prolific, so fertile in resources, and is generally so innocent (despite the

ever-present *undertone* of fleshliness), that he may fairly be left to his laurels. He is open to the same *literary* criticism as the others, but, while often ingenuous, is never altogether unclean.

It may be interesting for the reader to compare, in a brief glance, the various poets of the Italian-English school with each other. To do so thoroughly would involve the serious task of perusing three-fourths of the forgotten English poets; for, since weeds ever grew quicker than flowers, the bulk of the poetic trash left behind by successive generations of verse-writers, from Surrey to Spratt, far outweighs the little collection of true poetry which may justly be esteemed classic and unimpeachable. But it may be observed here that all the poets of this school, though their name be legion, write very much alike. They are generally affected, and often nasty. "All that regards design, form, fable (which is the soul of poetry), all that concerns exactness or consent of parts (which is the body), will probably be wanting: only pretty conceptions, fine metaphors, glittering expressions, and something of a neat cast of verse (which are properly the dress, gems, or loose ornaments of poetry), may be found in their verses. Their colouring entertains the sight, but the lines and life are not to be inspected too narrowly." Such is Pope's criticism on Crashaw, and it will apply to any one of the school, certainly to Mr. Swinburne or Mr. Rossetti.

It need cause no wonder that verse-writers of this sort find admirers in proportion to their shallowness and affectation. This has been the case from the beginning, and it is the case now. The poems and plays of the egregious Cartwright, published in 1651, are preceded by panegyrics from all the wits of the time, no less than fifty in number, quite in the style of the Fleshly School and its Critics. Donne was the pride of collegians. Cowley was actually considered the glory and the wonder of his generation. Nowadays the anonymous press is a tremendous check on this sort of humbug, but there still linger old-fashioned journals with strings in the hands of a clique.[17] It is the *interest* of educated persons and schoolmen to exalt all artificial products, for they themselves can fairly hope to rival the stuff they praise and to get some sort of a position. If hothouse plants are in favour, any clever young fellow from a university can force them. And it thus happens that the Fleshly School, without ever reaching the general public, is in favour with the literary amateurs who yearly swarm from college, and ruin the profession of literature by writing anywhere and everywhere free of charge.

From time immemorial, poets of the Artificial School have written in the same way, and been admired for the same tricks; and indeed our modern poets can stand no comparison, even in subtle grossness, with their progenitors. Here are Cowley's lines on a paper written in juice of lemon, and read by the fire:—

"Nothing yet in thee is seen;
But when a genial heat warms thee within,
A new-born wood of various lines there grows,
      Here buds an L, and there a B,
      Here spouts a V, and there a T,
And all the flourishing letters stand in rows;"

which the reader may advantageously compare with Mr. Rossetti's description of a love-letter in p. 198 of his volume. The master above quoted, in his "Davideis," has the following awful passage:—

"The sun himself started with sudden fright,
To see his beams return so dismal light!"

This is performing a miracle certainly, but Mr. Rossetti performs a greater—he makes the "Silence" *speak*:—

"But therewithal the tremulous Silence said:
   'Lo, Love yet bids thy lady,' " &c. (Page 206.)

Thus sings, or screams, Mr. Swinburne:—

"Ah, that my lips were tuneless lips, but pressed
To the bruised blossom of thy scourged white breast!
Ah, that my mouth, for Muses' milk, were fed
On the sweet blood thy sweet small wounds had bled!
That with my tongue I felt them and could taste
The faint flakes from thy bosom to the waist!
That I could drink thy veins as wine, and eat
Thy breasts like honey."

Dr. Donne, however, had anticipated him in the same vein:—

"As the sweet sweat of roses in a still,
As that, which from chaf'd muskats' pores doth trill,
As the almighty balm of the early east,
Such are the sweat drops of my mistress' breast;
And on her neck her skin such lustre sets,
They seem no sweat drops, but pearl coronets."

These poets ever delight in the strangest and most far-fetched comparisons. Cleveland has a magnificent comparison of the sun to a *coal-pit;* but Rossetti, twenty times more cunning and subtle, sees that "vows" are the merest *bricks:*—

"We strove
To *build* with *fire-tried vows* the piteous home
Which memory haunts." (Page 208.)

Cowley compares his heart to a hand-grenado; in a similar spirit, Rossetti compares the Soul to a town, and (bent to hunt the simile to death) tells us that there are by-streets there, and that Hopes go about hunting for adventures at the public-houses!—

"So through that soul in restless brotherhood,
   They roam together now, and *wind among
      It's bye-streets, knocking at the dusty inns!*" (Page 231.)

Dr. John Donne is great on Tears: they are at one time "globes, nay worlds," containing their "Europe, Asia, and Africa;" and at another they are "wine," bottled "in crystal vials" for the tipple of lovers. Mr. Rossetti, in a semi-military spirit, thus describes a Moan:—

"A moan, the sighing wind's *auxiliary!*"

Quite in the spirit of Mr. Rossetti's fleshlier and commoner manner, in which he talks about his lady's hand teaching "memory to mock desire," is Cowley's exquisite meditation, addressed to his mistress:—

"Though in thy thoughts scarce any tracts have been
So much as of original sin,
Such charms thy beauty wears, as might
Desires in dying saints excite!"

This is the way Dr. John Donne writes in the beginning of the seventeenth century:—

"Are not thy kisses, then, as filthy, and more,
As a worm sucking an envenom'd sore?
Doth not thy fearful hand in feeling quake,
As one which gathering flowers still fears a snake?"

Could anything more closely resemble the horrible manner of Mr. Swinburne's "Anactoria?"
It is difficult to believe that our present school of poets have not drunk deep at the muddy Aganippe of their predecessors here in England, as well as at the poetic fountain polluted by the influx of the Parisian sewers. There is a coincidence of affectation in the following parallel passages:—

THE TROJAN HORSE

"A *mother,* I was without *mother* born,
In end, all arm'd, my *father* I brought forth!"
—DRUMMOND

"That horse, within whose populous womb
The *birth* was *death*."—ROSSETTI (p. 229).

Again, Mr. Rossetti, in Sonnet XXIX., compares LIFE to "a LADY" with whom he wandered from the "haunts of men," finding "all bowers amiss"(!) till he came to a place "where only woods and waves could hear our kiss," and who, as an awful result, bare him three children, Love, Song—

> "Whose hair
> Blew like a flame and blossomed like a wreath,
> And Art, *whose eyes were worlds by God found fair*."[18]

Nearly as absurd, but less subtle and harassing, is the passage in Drummond's "Hymn to the Fairest Fair," wherein we have the following incarnate metaphor of no less shadowy a shape than "Providence!"—

> "With faces two, like sisters, sweetly fair,
> Whose blossoms no rough autumn can impair,
> Stands Providence, and doth her looks disperse
> Thro' every corner of the universe."

Nor must it be hastily concluded that Mr. Rossetti's "apples meet for the mouth" simile is quite original. Drummond in one passage calls his mistresses' hearts

> "Fruits of Paradise,
> Celestial cherries that so sweetly smell;"

and in another—the following sonnet—comes tremendously close upon the *best* modern manner, minus the "lipping" and the "munching:"—

> "Who hath not seen into her saffron bed
> The morning's goddess mildly her repose,
> Or her of whose pure blood first sprang the rose
> Lull'd in a slumber by a myrtle shade?
> Who hath not seen that sleeping white and red
> Makes Phoebe look so pale, which she did close
> In that Ionian hall to ease her woes,
> Which only lives by her dear kisses fed?
> Come but and see my lady sweetly sleep,
> The sighing rubies of those heavenly lips,
> *The Cupids which breasts' golden apples keep*,
> Those eyes which shine in midst of their eclipse;
> And he them all shall see, perhaps and prove
> She waking but persuadeth, now forceth love."

I have quoted this poem entire, because it is quite in the modern spirit, and would certainly, if printed in either Mr. Swinburne's or Mr. Rossetti's poems, have been considered beautiful; and partly because I should like the reader to compare it with the Swinburnian conception of "Love and Sleep, as known to the moderns:"—

> "Lying asleep between the strokes of night
>   I saw my love lean over my sad bed,
>   Pale as the duskiest lily's leaf or head,
> Smooth-skinned and dark with bare *throat made to bite!*
> Too wan for blushing and too warm for white,
>   But perfect coloured without white or red;
>   And her lips opened amorously, and said—
> I wist not what, saving one word—Delight!
> And all her face was honey to my mouth,
>   And all her body pasture to mine eyes;
>   The long lithe arms and hotter hands than fire,
> The *quivering flanks*, hair smelling of the south,
>   The bright light feet, the *splendid supple thighs*,
>   *And glittering eyelids of my soul's desire*."
> SWINBURNE'S *Poems and Ballads*, p. 316.

The reader whom this fascinates had better turn to Dr. Donne's eighteenth elegy, every line of which might have been written in our generation, wherein the nude female is compared to a Globe for the lover's exploration, and the whole Voyage is described with a terrific realism of detail and daring strength of metaphor which would fill even Mr. Rossetti with envy and despair. It is, unfortunately, rather too strong to quote, though not a grain more filthy than the above sonnet. Let me turn, by way of disinfectant, to a conceit in the true Della Cruscan style, from Mr. Rossetti's works. A very shadowy Entity is speaking, in a poem affectedly called "A Superscription:"—

> "Look in my face: my name is *Might-have-been*;
> I am also called *No-more, Too-late, Farewell*;
> Unto thine ear I hold the dead sea-shell," &c.
> (Page 234.)

This passage, although quite in the ancient manner, was perhaps composed on one of those days when Mr. Rossetti goes poaching in Mr. Swinburne's French "Slough of Uncleanness," for we find Baudelaire making use of very similar language:—

> "Trois mille six cents fois par heure, la Seconde
> Chuchote: *Souviens-toi!* Rapide avec sa voix
> D'insecte, *Maintenant* dit: Je suis *Autrefois!*"
> *Fleurs de Mal*, p. 245.

Truly, this sort of reading is wearing to the brain!

I have already alluded more than once to the foolish fleshliness which permeates the contemporary treatment of even avowedly *religious* themes.

For example, when Mr. Rossetti writes about the Virgin Mary, he begins in the true fantastic spirit of those older writers who spiritualised sensualism in their addresses to the Bridegroom and the Magdalen.

"Mother of the Fair Delight!"

he exclaims; and then proceeds with the following jargon:—

"Handmaid perfect in God's sight,
Now sitting fourth beside the Three,
Thyself a woman-Trinity,—
Being a daughter born to God,
Mother of Christ from stall to rood,
And Wife unto the Holy Ghost!!"

The poem improves as it proceeds, but it is fleshly to the last fibre,—quite, in fact, in the spirit of Richard Crashaw's poem on "The Weeper:"—

"What bright soft thing is this?
    Sweet Mary, thy fair eyes' expence?
        A moist spark it is,
        A watery diamond; from whence
The very term, I think, was found,
The water of a diamond.

"O 'tis not a tear,
    'Tis a star about to drop
        From thine eye its sphere;
    The sun will stoop and take it up,
Proud will his sister be to wear
This thine eye's jewel in her ear.

"O 'tis a tear,
    Too true a tear! for no sad eyne,
        How sad so e'er,
    Rain so true a tear as thine;
Each drop leaving a place so dear
Weeps for itself, is its own tear.

"Such a pearl as this is
    (Slipt from Aurora's dewy breast)
        The rose-bud's sweet lip kisses,
    And such the rose itself when vext
With ungentle flames, does shed,
Sweating in too warm a bed."

This is *meant* reverently, but what shall we say of Mr. Rossetti's "Love's *Redemption*," in which the act of sexual connection is outrageously and vilely compared to the administering of the sacramental bread and wine?—

"O thou, who at Love's hour ecstatically," &c.[19]

Compare, also, with Mr. Rossetti's pseudo-religious poems generally, those passages of Crashaw in which all the language of passion and lust is used to describe purely spiritual and religious sensations:—

"Amorous languishments, luminous trances,
    Sights which are not seen with eyes,
Spiritual and soul-piercing glances;
    Whose pure and subtle lightning flies
Home to the heart, and sets the house on fire;
And melts it down in sweet desire:
    Yet doth not stay
To ask the windows leave to pass that way.

"Delicious deaths, soft exhalations
Of soul! dear and divine annihilations!
    A thousand unknown rites
Of joys and rarified delights!"
                    On a Prayer Book sent to Mrs. M. R.

This might have been pardonable in a Roman Catholic of Selden's time, but the echo of it in a "mature" person of the nineteenth century is positively dreadful.[20]

I close this book of the "mature" person. I close Mr. Swinburne's volumes. I try to gather some definite impression, some thought, some light, from what I have been reading. I find my mind jaded, my whole body sick and distressed, a dull pain lurking in the region of the *medulla oblongata.* I try to picture up Mr. Rossetti's poetry, and I am dazzled by conceits in sixteenth-century costume,—"rosy hours," "Loves" with "gonfalons," damsels with "citherns," "soft-complexioned" skies; flowers, fruits, jewels, vases, apple-blossoms, lutes: I see no gleam of nature, not a sign of humanity; I hear only the heated ravings of an affected lover, indecent for the most part, and often blasphemous. I attempt to describe Mr. Swinburne; and lo! the Bacchanal screams, the sterile Dolores sweats, serpents dance, men and women wrench, wriggle, and foam in an endless alliteration (quite in Gascoigne's manner) of heated and meaningless words, the veriest garbage of Baudelaire flowered over with the epithets of the Della Cruscans.

"One moment!" observes a candid person as I write; "the emptiness and grossness of these may be admitted; but are not these writers quite unimpeachable on the ground of poetic *form,* and is that not a certain merit?" Something on this head has been said already. Let it be further said that no unsound soul is clad in a sound form; and that what holds true of matter and thought holds equally true of manner and style: both may seem rapid and strong, but neither will bear five minutes' criticism. Imagine an English writer pluming himself on his careful choice of diction, and publishing such a verse as the following:—

> "Nothing is better, I *well* think,
>   Than love; the hidden *well-water*
> Is not so delicate to drink:
>   This was *well* seen of me and her."
>   SWINBURNE'S *Poems and Ballads.*

Or this other of Mr. Rossetti:—

> "In painting her I shrined her face
>   'Mid mystic trees, where light falls in
> Hardly at all; a covert place
>   *Where you might think to find a din*
> *Of doubtful talk,* and a live flame
> Wandering, and many a shape *whose name*
>   *Not itself knoweth,* and old dew,
>   And your own footsteps meeting you,
> And all things going as they came." (Page 128.)

Apart altogether from the meaninglessness, was ever writing so formally slovenly and laboriously limp? I have no time to pile example on example; I leave that task to the reader, who will not have to hunt far or long for some of the worst writing in our language. Of a piece are such expressions as, "O their glance is loftiest *dole!*" "in grove the *gracile* Spring trembles;" "her soft body, dainty thin;" "handsome Jenny mine;" "smouldering senses;" "the rustling covert of my soul;" "a little *spray* of tears;" "culminant changes;" "wasteful warmth of tears;" "the sunset's desolate disarray;" "watered my heart's drouth;" "the wind's wellaway;" "a shaken shadow intolerable;" "that swallow's *soar*" (a swallow, by the way, does not soar); "my eyes, wide open, *had the run* of some ten weeds to rest upon;" and a thousand others, as bad or worse, all to be found in Mr. Rossetti's small volume; besides the thousands upon thousands to be found in the works of his more fruitful brethren.

It would be wasting time to criticize details so worthless, save for the purpose of showing that insincerity in one respect argues insincerity in all, and that where we find a man choosing worthless subjects and affecting trashy models, we may rely on finding his treatment, down to the tiniest detail, frivolous, absurd, and reckless. The affectation of carefulness in composition is in proportion to the affectation of subtlety of theme; and the result is a lamentable amount, not of valuable poetic form, but of sound and fury, signifying absolutely next to

nothing, and as shapeless and undigested as chaos itself.

VII

> "Away with love verses, sugared in rhyme—the intrigues, amours of idlers,
> Fitted for only banquets of the night, where dancers to late music slide;
> The unhealthy pleasures, extravagant dissipations of the few."
>
>   WALT WHITMAN

Is this London? Is this the year 1872? That peep of blue up yonder resembles the sky, and these figures that pass seem men and women. What evil dream, then, what malignant influence is upon me? Weary of surveying the poetry of the past, and listening to the amatory wails of generations, I walk down the streets, and lo! again harlots stare from the shop-windows, and the great Alhambra posters cover the dead-walls. I go to the theatre which is crowded nightly, and I listen in absolute amaze to the bestialities of *Geneviève de Brabant.* I walk in the broad day, and a dozen hands offer me indecent prints. I step into a bookseller's shop, and behold! I am recommended to purchase a reprint of the plays and novels of Mrs. Aphra Behn. I buy a cheap republican newspaper, thinking that there, at least, I shall find some relief, if only in the wildest stump oratory, and I am saluted instead in these words:—

> "FANNY HILL. Genuine edition, illustrated. Two volumes, 2s. 6d. each. Lovers' Festival, plates, 3s. 6d. Adventures of a Lady's Maid, 2s 6d. Intrigues of a Ballet Girl, 2s. 6d. Aristotle, illustrated, 2s. French Transparent Cards, 1s. the set. Cartes de Visite from life, 1s. List two stamps. London: H. D—, 15, St. M—— R——d, C——ll.
>
> "FANNY HILL, coloured plates, 2 vols. 4s.; Aristotle's Masterpiece, plates, 2s. 6d.; Life of the celebrated Moll Flanders, 5s. 6d.; Mysteries of a Convent, 1s. List sent on receipt of two stamps. E. B—, 9, R—n S—t, B— S—, E.
>
> "THE BACHELOR'S SCARF PIN, containing secret photos of pretty women, 24 stamps; French Cards, 1s. the set; Life of a Ballet Girl, 2s. 6d.; Bang-up Reciter, 2s.; Maria Monk, 1s. 6d.; Fanny Hill, with plates, 3s. 6d. Lists two stamps. C. N——, 4, K——'s S—— Avenue, B——."

Step where I may, the snake Sensualism spits its venom upon me. The deeper I probe the public sore, the more terrible I find its nature. I ask my physician for his experience; he only shakes his head, and dares not utter all he knows. I consult the police; they give me such details of unapproachable crime as fill my soul with horror. Returning home, I meet a friend, who tells me that the Society for the Suppression of Vice has at last stirred itself, and that the Lord Chamberlain, moreover, has interdicted the last foul importation from France.[21] O for a scourge to whip these money-changers of Vice for ever out of the Temple!

Now, God forbid that I should charge any living English poet with desiring to encourage debauchery and to demoralise the public. I believe that both Mr. Swinburne and Mr. Rossetti are honest men, pure according to their lights, loving what is beautiful, conscientiously following what inspiration lies within them. They do not quite realise that they are merely supplementing the literature of Holywell Street, and writing books well worthy of being sold under "sealed covers." Much of Mr. Swinburne's grossness has come of the mad aggressiveness of youth, fostered by reading the worst French poets. Nearly all Mr. Rossetti's effeminacy comes of eternal self-contemplation, of trashy models, of want of response to the needs and the duties of his time. What stuff is this they are putting forward, or suffering their coterie to put forward for them? It is time, they say, that the simple and natural delights of the Body should be sung as holy; it is unbearable, they echo, that purists should object to the record of sane pleasures of sense; it is just, they reiterate, that Passion should have its poetry and the Flesh its vindication.[22] As if the "simple and natural delights of the body" had not been occupying our poetry ever since the days of the "Confessio Amantis!" As if sane (and for that matter, insane) pleasures of sense had not been the stock-in-trade of nine-tenths of all our poets and poetasters, from Wyatt to Swinburne! As if Passion had been silent until this year of the Lord 1872, and as if, till the advent of a Rossetti, the world had entirely lost sight of the Flesh! The Flesh and the Body have been sung till the Muses are hoarse again. Two-thirds of our poetry is all Body; nine-tenths of our poets are all Flesh. One would think, from this outcry, that the amative faculty was a new organ discovered by some phrenological bard of the period, and never before traced as having any influence on the human race. One would fancy, from some of our modern criticisms, that the only English poets up to this

period had been Milton, holy Mr. Herbert, and the author of the "Christian Year!" One would swear, to hear these Cupids of the new Fleshly Epoch, that English literature had been veritably getting bluemouldy with too much virtue, and that the Spirit of Imagination had lived in a nunnery, fed on pulse and cold water, since Chaucer's time, instead of rioting in a lupanar, fed on hot meat and spiced wine, for hundreds upon hundreds of years!

Perhaps, if the truth were told, we have had a little too much of the Body. Perhaps, if we push the matter home, it is no more rational to rave of the "just delights of the flesh" than it would be to talk of the "glorious liberty" of "sweating" and the "sane celebration" of the right to "spit." Perhaps, after all, since so many centuries of Sexuality have done so little for poetry, it might be advantageous to give Spirituality a trial, and to see if *her* efforts to create a literature are equally unsuccessful.

In answer to all this, it may be retorted — in the easiest form of retort known to mankind — that *I* am a Philistine, that I would emasculate our poets altogether, and that I would substitute for passion the merest humanitarian and other "sentiment." Well, although I fear that I am a Puritan in a certain sense, I trust I am not a purist in the worst sense. My favourite ancient poet is the author of "Atys." I prefer Shakspere to Milton, and I would not obliterate a line, however coarse, of Chaucer. I love Rabelais, and hold (with Coleridge) that he is deep and pure as the sea. I know no pleasanter reading for an idle hour than La Fontaine, no richer reading for a thoughtful hour than certain (by no means unimpeachable) novels of Balzac. I see the strangest erotic forces in the loves of Wilhelm Meister, but I admit their beauty and their worth. I welcome Heine, and could listen to his mad laughter for a summer day. I love Byron better than Tupper, and of all Byron's books I best love "Don Juan." I reverence Hugo, and I see nothing in him that is shocking, save, perhaps, certain abominable eccentricities in "L'Homme qui Rit." I still beguile many an hour, when snug at anchor in some lovely Highland loch, with the inimitable, yet questionable, pictures of Parisian life left by Paul de Kock; and I know no sweeter poet in some respects than the egregious Alfred de Musset. To my thinking, there is no grander passage in literature than that tremendous scene between Ottilia and her paramour, in "Pippa Passes:" no one accuses the author of that, and of the "Ring and the Book," of neglecting love or overlooking the body; and yet I do daily homage to the genius of Robert Browning. I deem "Vivien" an essential pendant to that wonderful apotheosis of Masculine Chastity, which is the heart of that Arthurian epic on which the laureate has poured all his orient poetic wealth. I have praised Whitman,[23] and hope to praise him over and over again. I know no fresher, finer work of this generation than certain novels by Mr. Charles Reade, who is not generally considered an ascetic author. In one word, I have no earthly objection to the Body and the Flesh in their rightful time and place, as part of great work and noble art; I do not see any great wickedness in the old-fashioned use of the gaudriole; and I am ready (as any sane man must be ready) to regard with kindness, and even sympathy, all work of a really good and honest author, even if it here and there, as I may think, exceeds the just limits of reserve, and becomes indecent, as sometimes happens, by sheer force of power. But Flesh, merely as the Flesh, is too much for me. I find it foolish, querulous, affected, uninteresting. I do not admire its absurd manner of considering itself the Soul. I grudge it none of its just delights, even in the way of "lipping" and "munching;" only, let it enjoy them without making such a coil about them. The world never tires of *real* passion; it will listen to Burns's love-songs for ever; but fleshliness is not necessarily passion, and may abound in natures utterly passionless. There are many other functions of the flesh which it is not the custom to perform in public, but which are quite as interesting to third parties as what Shakspere calls "the deed." Really, if we set no limit to the flesh, it is certain to disgrace us in the long-run. It has already created a literature in Holywell Street. Shall we suffer it to found a poetry in St. John's Wood?

English Verse-poetry has been, up to the present moment, almost exclusively the property of querulous persons, engaged in contemplating their own images—either in an ordinary looking-glass or in the eyes of a fantastic female. We have had a certain number of great poets who have chosen to use rhymed and metrical speech—our very greatest, indeed, have spoken in this way; but many of our noblest—such as Bacon, Bunyan, and Thomas Carlyle—have chosen to use simple prose as their means of expression; and the last of these prose-poets has very recently, in a remarkable letter to a gentleman who had sent him some verses, protested energetically that he would infinitely have preferred a good bit of solid simple prose—that, in fact, Verse is an artificial sort of thing, by no means to be encouraged at this time of day. Rough and sweeping as this condemnation of Verse appears to be, there is a certain homely truth about it. It has been the unfortunate habit of most of our poets,

and especially of those we have been specially criticizing in this article, to use Verse as the vehicle of whatever thoughts are too thin or too fantastic, too much of the sweet-pea order of products, to stand without the aid of rhythmical props. Ideas too bald for prose, too trivial to stand unadorned, appear unique enough when subjected to the euphuistic process, and robed in all the wordy glitter of rhyme. If any English author, in good round prose, were to call Death "a seizure of malign vicissitude," and compare Life to a Lady with whom he ranged the world till he found a fit "bower" for nuptial performances; or if any author were to narrate for us, still in good round prose, such a savoury narrative as that of "The Leper" in Mr. Swinburne's poems, surely he would very soon receive his just deserts. Yet simply because such ideas and such stories are told in lines cut into certain lengths and jingling at the ends; solely because, by one-half the public, verse is *recognised* as an unnatural and altogether artificial form of speech, the trash of windy men is christened Art, and writers without one ray of imagination are accredited with the genius of song. It thus happens that, in the opinion of many people, the word "poet" is synonymous with "madman;" and we are told again and again not to judge such and such compositions too severely, as "they are *only* poetry." It thus happens that we every day behold the melancholy spectacle of inferior men giving themselves the airs of great men merely because they can write meretricious verses. Why, I will venture to say that there is more real genius and more true literary brilliance in any one of Mr. G. A. Sala's "Dutch Pictures" than in all the fleshly products heaped together, and yet Mr. Sala only calls himself a "special correspondent," and is far, very far, from being a "poetical" person.

If poetry—Verse-poetry—is to be anything else than an impediment to progress, if it is to become something better than the resource of feeble talents unable to stand without artificial aid, it must be more and more approximated to the natural language of men; it must be weeded of the hideous phraseology of the schools, and sown with the fresh and beautiful idioms of daily speech; and it must deal with great issues in which all men are interested, not with the "damnable face-making" of Narcissus in a mirror. Elsewhere, notably in Germany, such experiments are encouraged as tend to broaden and strengthen the resources of poetry, and to multiply its facilities; but here in England every fresh experiment in language is ridiculed and disliked, unless it be a retrograde experiment, trebling the limitations and quadrupling the affectations of ancient rhyme. Mr. Swinburne's eternal jingle, and Mr. Rossetti's affected harpsichord-melody, are admired, though they throw us back hundreds of years; but not one grain of sympathy has been shown for the metrical importations, often exquisite, of Mr. Matthew Arnold, the never-ending experiments of the late Arthur Hugh Clough (a giant who died young, and alas! has left no one who fills his place in the van of thought), and the wonderful poetic prose, or prose-poetry, of Walt Whitman. The public appears to be willing that verse-poetry should remain the property of men of talent, anxious to increase its already almost insuperable limitations; and it thus happens that our men and women of genius—such as Carlyle, Hugo, Reade, Emerson, Hawthorne—have written some of the best poetry of this generation in simple prose.[24]

The name of Poet was once a title of honour; it bids fair soon to be a title of ridicule. The form of Verse was at one period held to be the noblest possible kind of human utterance; but that form, remaining as it does in the swaddling-clothes of infant speech, will possibly be more or less abandoned as time rolls on by the thinkers and dreamers of the world. The word poetry may one day be identical with absurdity; and no one will jingle the cap and bells of rhyme but a fool. Is there no hope? Yes, a gleam. All the blundering and all the time-wasting in our literature have been caused by eternal posturing before the mirror. Each feeble talent has been so fascinated by his own image as to dwindle into an intellectual daisy or pine into a poetical primrose. Our literary shame has sprung from want of knowledge of how the world wags, of how men and women live and love, of what mighty forces are sweeping across the earth their angels' wings. Let the Sultan of Literature, if there be such a person (and if not, we might do worse than elect the functionary), issue forth an edict ordering the destruction of all *looking-glasses,* and the immediate silencing of all persons who introduce the subject of *their own emotions.* This would at least have the effect of driving our poets, if they *must* see themselves, to see themselves in flowing Rivers or the mighty Sea, and to wail aloud, if wail they must, to the four Winds of Heaven; and thus they might come in time to find how little account they themselves are in the great scheme of nature, and how much is to be done on earth besides making night and day hideous with sensual shadows and dreams. Yet, after all, I fear there would be evasion even then; for ten to one you would find some Simple Simon of the amatory type, driven to despair by the universal destruction of looking-glasses, filling the family washing-tub with water from the pump, and pining away into a shadow for love of his own image hovering therein!

1. Publications of this sort are at last being taken seriously in hand by the Society for the Suppression of Vice. As I write, the following appears in the weekly journals:—"THE 'DAY'S DOINGS' AGAIN.—At Bow-street police-court on Thursday, Frederick Shove, the publisher of the *Day's Doings,* an illustrated paper, appeared to a fresh summons, granted by Sir Thomas Henry, charged with publishing indecent prints and printed matter. Mr. Besley (instructed by Mr. Collette, of the Society for the Suppression of the Vice) prosecuted; Mr. Laxton, as before, defended. Mr. Besley said that a promise was made when the defendant was last summoned at this court that all matter or prints suggestive of indecency should be withdrawn for the future. He produced five copies of the *Day's Doings,* from which he read different articles of an obscene and vulgar nature, and pointed out a print of a nude woman, which was, in his opinion, even more objectionable. Mr. Laxton contended that the nude figure referred to was a copy of the work of a well-known artist, and to decrease its nudity drapery had been added to the figure. Sir Thomas Henry said the drapery was suggestive of even greater indecency. Sir Thomas Henry decided upon committing the case for trial, but said he would accept bail for the appearance of the defendant at the sessions, two sureties in £80 each, and the defendant's recognizances in £150."

2. These verses are worth studying, as showing how the only effect produced on the "poet of the period" by the sight of a little female child was the regret that the infant was not yet old enough "to be made love to."

3. I say sub-Tennysonian because these gentlemen, with all their affinities to the Italian and French race of sonnetteers, follow Tennyson in the historical sense, and touch nothing in their poetry which he has not lightly touched in some way. The ways of a great poet lead him in all directions, into all moods, while the way of a small poet is narrow and without variety. The gain of *good* in the Pre-Raphaelite style comes from the laureate; what is *bad* in it comes from Italy and France.

4. "Why, sir, Sherry is dull, *naturally* dull; but it must have taken him a *great deal of trouble* to become what we now see him—such an excess of stupidity is not in nature."—*Boswell's Life.*

5. Mr. Rossetti accuses me of garbling these four extracts, and alleges that they have a totally different effect when read with their context. In reply to this, let me observe that the four poems which supply these four extracts are full of coarseness from the first line to the last, and that no extract can fitly convey their unwholesomeness and indecency.

6. Commenting on this remark, Mr. Rossetti avers that he has "never read" my poems, and that, moreover, "Jenny" was written thirteen years ago.

7. Since the above was written, the *Quarterly Review* has spoken in very similar language to my own; and I agree with its strictures in every passage, save those which are levelled against Mr. Tennyson. The poet laureate is open to judgment, and is strong enough to bear it; but I hold it to be in all respects lamentable that he has been censured in the same breath as the men who owe to him what little in their writings is good and worthy. The *Review* speaks thus of "Jenny:"—

"We purpose to close our remarks on Mr. Rossetti's verse with some reflections on a poem which, we think, reveals characteristically the incapacity of the literary poet to deal with contemporary themes in an effective and straightforward manner. 'Jenny' is a poem on the subject of unfortunate women. A man is supposed to have followed a girl of this description to her house, where she falls asleep with her head on his knee, while he moralises on her condition. The majority of poets have, as we think wisely, avoided subjects of this sort. But assuming that success might justify its treatment, one of the first elements of success is that a piece should be brief and forcible. 'Jenny' is nearly four hundred lines long. The metre at the opening reminds us of one which Mr. Browning uses with characteristic force, but which in Mr. Rossetti's hands soon degenerates into feeble octosyllabic verse. The thought throughout is pretentious but commonplace. The moralist, beginning with something like a rhapsody on the appearance of the girl as she lies asleep, wonders what she is thinking about; he then reflects that her sleep exactly resembles the sleep of a pure woman; her face he feels might serve a painter as the model of a Madonna. We are thus imperceptibly edged on into the author's favourite regions of abstraction:—

'Yet, Jenny, looking long at you
The woman almost fades from view.
A cipher of man's changeless sum
Of lust past, present, and to come
Is left. A riddle that one shrinks
To challenge from the scornful sphinx.'

Exactly. So this profound philosopher, whose somewhat particular reflections on the charms of the sleeper have brought him at last face to face with the mystery of evil, coolly remarks:—

'Come, come, what good in thoughts like this?'

packs some gold in the girl's hair, and takes his leave. What good indeed? But why in that case, and if Mr. Rossetti had no power to deal otherwise with so painful a theme, could he not have spared us an useless display of affected sentiment and impotent philosophy?

"The style of the poem is as bad as the matter. Descriptions repulsively realistic are mixed up with imagery like that in Solomon's Song; the most familiar objects are described by the most unusual paraphrases; a London schoolboy, for instance, being called 'a wise unchildish elf,' while the similes are painfully farfetched. The heart of the woman is said to be—

'Like a rose shut in a book
In which pure women may not look,

For its base pages claim control
To crush the flower within the soul;
Where through each dead rose-leaf that clings,
Pale as transparent Psyche wings,
To the vile text, are traced such things
As might make lady's cheeks indeed
More than a living rose to read;
So nought save foolish foulness may
Watch with hard eyes the sure decay;
And so the life-blood of this rose,
Puddled with shameful knowledge, flows
Through leaves no chaste hand may unclose.'

Affectation and obscurity make the application of this difficult enough. It will not, however, escape notice that the simile is radically false, for whereas the point is that the woman's heart is alive in the midst of corruption, the rose in the book, to which the heart is compared, is dried and dead."

8. Gascoigne's verse is noticeable, like Mr. Swinburne's, for its laboured and wearisome alliteration; but the "Good Morrow" and "Good Night" are simple and graceful enough to save his fame from utter shipwreck.

9. "Go, lovely Rose."

10. It is only fair to add that the Reviewer merely gives this as the judgment he was "inclined" to pronounce, only that to say so in as many words might lead to the misconception that Mr. Rossetti had no literary merit whatever.

11. "Here a critical organ, professedly adopting the principle of open signature, would seem, in reality, to assert (by silent practice, however, not by enunciation,) that if the anonymous in criticism was—as itself originally inculcated—but an early caterpillar stage, the nominate too is found to be no better than a homely transitional chrysalis, and that the ultimate butterfly form for a critic who likes to sport in sunlight and yet to elude the grasp, is after all the pseudonymous." Surely human ingenuity never so tortured itself to clothe a simple meaning in cumbrous and affected words! The only parallel is the author's poetry, where a simple kiss becomes a "consonant interlude," and the ink in a love-letter is called "the smooth black stream that makes thy (the letter's) whiteness fair!"

12. My complaint precisely is, that Mr. Rossetti's "soul" *concurs* a vast deal too easily.

13. The italics are mine.—R. B.

14. For a production quite in our modern manner, the reader had better refer to this extraordinary poem. I dare not quote another word.

15. Compare Greene's "Menaphon's Eclogue:"—
"Her neck like to an ivory shining tower," &c.

16. Compare Carew:—

"Now in more subtle wreaths I will entwine
My sturdy limbs, my legs and thighs, with thine!"

17. That the system by which the school of verse-writers under criticism has made itself notorious is at last defeating itself, is evident from a recent article, entitled "Coterie Glory," in the *Saturday Review*—a journal which, I believe, has been more than once made use of by the friends of the gentlemen in question. The author of "Coterie Glory," in a number of decisive and perfectly well-tempered remarks, surveys the whole question, and on coming to the Fleshly School, openly admits, as if on certain knowledge, that the personal friends of the poets *write all the reviews*. This also, observes the reviewer, was the case with the once famous "Della Cruscan School," surviving now only, if it can be called survival, in Gifford's ponderous but effective satire.

"A little circle of mutual admiration contrived, by ingenious devices of criticism, to create in the outer world what for awhile looked like real fame. Afterwards we had the 'mystic' school, to which the authors of *Festus*, the *Roman*, and other kindred spirits, chronicled in full by Mr. Gilfillan, belonged."

After glancing at the kind of poetry produced by the Fleshly School, the writer continues:—

"It is clear that poetry of this order can appeal only to a limited class. It claims to be tried by a special jury of cultivated persons. This, however, is a very dangerous position for the jurors. They who have been at the pains of mastering such special qualifications, by a natural law, soon regard them as the only canons of taste; nothing which does not conform to them has the true ring. Having conquered caviare, they find all that pleases 'the general' tasteless. Philistinism itself is not more adverse to discrimination than this Pharisaic isolation. Once in this frame of mind, men rapidly unlearn judging in favour of believing; they feel that they do right to be partisans in such a cause; they taste the keen delights of initiation into a creed hidden from the vulgar; they reject all moderating or hostile criticism from the laity without, as proceeding from men not specially qualified; they tend to pass from faith into fanaticism. Hence also, the general attitude of criticism being of the tolerant or sceptical order already described, *the believers at first write all the reviews, and man every bastion of what Goethe somewhere calls the 'critical Zion.' That it has been so in the case of our later 'Pre-Raffaelites' is denied nowhere.* Crowns thus decreed may certainly and uninvidiously be described as 'Coterie Glory.'

"A curious sign, lastly, confirms the position which we have here advanced. It is the very essence of faith to be uncritical; to regard the day for criticism as passed. It seems to be simply impossible for the artist and his circle of believers to regard a criticism on his art as anything but a criticism on himself. Many of our readers who may have watched with amusement the recent squabble between Mr. Buchanan and Mr. Rossetti will recognise a proof of our statement. Into the merits of the case we decline to go; we do not ask whether Mr. Buchanan's attacks were well founded, whether he was entitled to use a pseudonym, or whether his article exhibited that good taste which is nowhere more called for than when a question of taste is the matter in discussion. Our point is, that the *'Fleshly School of Poetry' did, in the main, attempt to try Mr. Rossetti's verses, and not Mr. Rossetti himself as* distinct from Mr. Rossetti the author, by critical rules. That the poet, rudely roused from the security of fame, generated by the too friendly voices of disciples, should have regarded his reviewer as actuated by base personal motives was natural. But it is characteristic that the followers should be under the same impression. One of the latest of them has just published a further reply to Mr. Buchanan, which rivals what we had too fondly believed was the tone of discussion and the form of argument peculiar to the 'odium theologicum.' Mr. Forman, the writer, is so hurried away by zeal for his faith that, though known only as a critic, he prefixes to his paper a cruel (and in this case, we are sure, an inapplicable) motto, describing critics as the offspring of jealousy and literary failure. To re-state Mr. Buchanan's arguments in his own vocabulary appears to Mr. Forman, and we do not doubt appears in perfect good faith, equivalent to their refutation. To quote in full Mr. Rossetti's sonnet on 'Nuptial Sleep' is proof of its maiden modesty of phrase so absolute that a man must be, we cannot venture to say what, who denies it. The gist of the whole is, that every criticism made against the book is in fact levelled against the author. What reads like a remark that a rhyme is weak is really an ungentlemanly libel on the rhymester. It is obvious that this is the canon, not of criticism, but of fanatic faith; nay, that it implicitly treats criticism as sin. For what judgment is possible if critical blame is treated as personal malignity, and if to ascribe affectation to a song is the same as to insult an artist? Yet such is the impassioned spirit of coterie that this appears to be the underlying, though no doubt the wholly unconscious, postulate of the poet and his followers. We altogether disclaim such an inference; and give notice that when we say that Mr. Buchanan's attack is less damaging than Mr. Forman's defence, we do not thereby imply that Mr. Forman has a base or wilful intention to injure Mr. Rossetti. He is only what some writer calls 'that worst of enemies, your worshipper.'"—*Saturday Review*, Feb. 24th, 1872.

These remarks are worth attention, firstly, for their inherent truth; and secondly, because they come from a quarter which can certainly not be accused of friendliness to myself.

18. It is perhaps needless to remark the utter confusion of metaphor which makes a *love-act* with Life as Lady precede the *birth* of Love, &c. The language of this school will not bear a moment's serious investigation.

19. See [discussion of the sonnet "Bridal Love" in Section V above].

20. Hall, in the ninth satire of Book I., took occasion to attack this blending of incongruous ideas and symbols into affected religious verse. "Hence, ye profane!" he cried,

"—mell not with holy things,
That Sion's Muse from Palestina brings.
Parnassus is transformed to Sion Hill,
And iv'ry-palms her steep ascents done fill,
Now good St. Peter weeps pure Helicon,
And both the Maries make a music moan;
Yea, even the prophet of the heav'nly lyre,
Great Solomon, sings in the English quire,
And is become a new-found sonnetist,

Singing his love, the holy spouse of Christ,
Like as she were some light-skirts of the rest," &c.

21. An interdiction which, says the *Athenaeum*, "is the most wanton violation of liberty, and the unwarrantable interference with Art, that modern times' have witnessed!" It is to be hoped, however, that the Lord Chamberlain will not be dispirited by the indignation of Sir Charles Dilke's journal, which, as the leading organ of the Fleshly School, is as peculiar in its notions of literary decency as Sir Charles himself in his notions of political propriety.

22. See, for example, "A Woman's Estimate of Walt Whitman," addressed by an English Lady to W. M. Rossetti (1870).

23. There is at the present moment living in America a great ideal prophet, who is imagined by many men on both sides of the Atlantic to be one of the sanest and grandest figures to be found in literature, and whose books, it is believed, though now despised, may one day be esteemed as an especial glory of this generation. It is no part of my present business to eulogize Walt Whitman, or to protest against the popular misconceptions concerning him; but it just happens that I have been asked, honestly enough, how it is that I despise so much the Fleshly School of Poetry in England and admire so much the poetry which is widely considered unclean and animal in America? It is urged, moreover, that Mr. Rossetti and Mr. Swinburne merely repeat the immodesties of the author of "Leaves of Grass," and that to be quite consistent I must condemn all alike. Very true, if Whitman be a poet of *this* complexion, if his poetry be shot through and through with animalism as certain stuffs are shot through and through with silk. But it requires no great subtlety of sight to perceive the difference between these men. To begin with, there are Singers, imitative and shallow; while that other is a Bard, outrageously original and creative in the form and substance of his so-called verse. In the next place, Whitman is in the highest sense a spiritual person; every word he utters is symbolic: he is a colossal mystic; but in all his great work, the theme of which is spiritual purity and health, there are not more than fifty lines of a thoroughly indecent kind, and these fifty lines are embedded in passages in the noblest sense antagonistic to mere lust and indulgence. No one regrets the writing and printing of these fifty lines more than I do. They are totally unnecessary, and silly in the highest degree—silly as some of Shakspere's dirt is silly—silly in the way of Aristophanes, Rabelais, Victor Hugo—from sheer excess of aggressive life. Fifty lines, observe, out of a book nearly as big as the Bible; lines utterly stupid, and unpardonable in themselves; but to be forgiven, doubtless, for the sake of the spotless love and chastity surrounding them. It is Whitman's business to chronicle *all* human sensations in the person of the "Cosmical Man," or typical Ego; and when he comes to the sexual instincts, he tries to blend emotion and physiology together, to the utter destruction of all natural effect. Judging from the internal evidence of these passages, I should say that Whitman was by no means a man of strong animal passions. There is a frightful violence in his expressions, which an epicure in lust would have avoided. This part of his book, I guess, cost him a good deal of trouble; it is not written *con amore;* and, apart from its double or mystic meaning, is just what an old philosopher might write if he were trying to represent passion by the dim light of memory. At all events, here Whitman is talking nonsense, as is the way of all wise men at some unfortunate moment or other. Elsewhere, he is perhaps the most mystic and least fleshly person that ever wrote.

It is in a thousand ways unfortunate for Walt Whitman that he has been introduced to the English public by Mr. William Rossetti, and been loudly praised by Mr. Swinburne. Doubtless these gentlemen admire the American poet for all that is best in him; but the British public, having heard that Whitman is immoral, and having already a dim guess that Messrs. Swinburne and Rossetti are not over-refined, has come to the conclusion that his nastiness alone has been his recommendation. All this despite the fact that Mr. William Rossetti has expurgated the fifty lines or so in his edition.

I should like to disclaim, in this place, all sympathy with Whitman's pantheistic ideas. My admiration for this writer is based on the wealth of his knowledge, the vast roll of his conceptions (however monstrous), the nobility of his *practical* teaching, and (most of all perhaps) on his close approach to a solution of the true relationship between prose cadence and metrical verse. Whitman's style, extraordinary as it is, is his greatest contribution to knowledge. It is not impossible to foresee a day when Coleridge's feeling of the "wonderfulness of prose" may become universal, and our poetry (still, swathe-bound in the form of early infant speech, or rhyme) may expand into a literature blending together all that is musical in verse, and all that is facile and powerful in ordinary language. I do not think Whitman has *solved* the difficulty, but he sometimes comes tremendously close upon the arcana of perfect speech.

24. "The French Revolution," "Les Misérables," "The Cloister and the Hearth," Emerson's first set of Essays, and "The Scarlet Letter"—all these works are "poems" in the noblest sense.

Under the Microscope

A. C. Swinburne

Originally published in pamphlet form (London: White, 1872).

We live in an age when not to be scientific is to be nothing; the man untrained in science, though he should speak with the tongues of men and of angels, though he should know all that man may know of the history of men and their works in time past, though he should have nourished on the study of their noblest examples in art and literature whatever he may have of natural intelligence, is but a pitiable and worthless pretender in the sight of professors to whom natural science is not a mean but an end; not an instrument of priceless worth for the mental workman, but a result in itself satisfying and final, a substitute in place of an auxiliary, a sovereign in lieu of an ally, a goal instead of a chariot. It is not enough in their eyes to admit that all study of details is precious or necessary to help us to a larger and surer knowledge of the whole; that without the invaluable support and illumination of practical research and physical science, the human intellect must still as of old go limping and blinking on its way nowhither, lame of one foot at best and blind of one eye; the knowledge of bones and stones is good not merely as a part of that general knowledge of nature inward as well as outward, human as well as other, towards which the mind would fain make its way yet a little and again a little further through all obstruction of error and suffusion of mystery; it is in the bones and stones themselves, not in man at all or the works of man, that we are to find the ultimate satisfaction and the crowning interest of our studies. Not because the study of such things will rid us of traditional obstacles that lay in the way of free and fruitful thought, will clear the air of mythologic malaria, will purge the spiritual city from religious pestilence; not because each one new certitude attained must involve the overthrow of more illusions than one, and every fact we can gather brings us by so much nearer to the truth we seek, serves as it were for a single brick or beam in the great house of knowledge that all students and thinkers who have served the world or are to serve it have borne or will bear their part in helping to construct. The facts are not of value simply because they serve the truth; nor are there so many mansions as once we may have thought in this house of truth, nor so many ministers in its service. It is vain to reply, while admitting that truth cannot be reached by men who take no due account of facts, that each fact is not all the truth, each limb is not all the body, each thought is not all the mind; and that even men (if such there be) ignorant of everything but what other men have written may possibly not be ignorant of everything worth knowledge, destitute of every capacity worth exercise. One study alone, and one form of study, is worthy the time and the respect of men who would escape the contempt of their kind. Impressed by this consideration— impelled by late regret and tardy ambition to atone if possible for lost time and thought misspent—I have determined to devote at least a spare hour to the science of comparative entomology; and propose here to set down in a few loose notes the modest outcome of my morning's researches.

Every beginner must be content to start from the lowest point—to begin at the bottom if he ever hopes to reach the top, or indeed to gain any trustworthy foothold at all. Our studies should therefore in this case also be founded on a preliminary examination of things belonging to the class of the infinitely little; and of these we shall do well to take up first such samples for inspection as may happen to lie nearest at hand. As the traveller who may desire to put to profit in the interest of this science his enforced night's lodging "in the worst inn's worst room" must take for his subjects of study the special or generic properties of such parasites as may leap or creep about his place of rest or unrest; so the lodger in the house of art or literature who for once may wish in like manner to utilize his waste moments must not scorn to pay some passing attention to the varieties of the critical tribe. But if the traveller be a man of truly scientific mind, he will be careful to let no sense of irritation impair the value and accuracy of his research. Such evidence of sensitiveness or suffering would not indeed imply that he thought otherwise or more highly of these than of other parasites; it is but a nameless thing after all, unmentionable as well as anonymous, that has pierced his skin if it be really pierced, or inflamed his blood if it be indeed inflamed; but those are the best travellers whose natures are not made of such penetrable or inflammable stuff. A critic is, at worst, but what Blake once painted—the ghost of a flea; and the man must be very tough of skin or very tender of spirit who would not rather have to do with the shadow than the substance. The phantom confessed to the painter that he would destroy the world if his power were commensurate with his will; but then it was not. Exactly as much power as was given to Blake's sitter (if that term be in his case allowable) to destroy the world is given to the critic to destroy the creator; exactly so much of that enviable power has a Pontmartin (for example) on Hugo and Balzac, or an Austin (for example) on Tennyson and Browning, or a Buchanan (for example) on any living thing. Considering which fact, all men of sense and self-respect will assuredly be of one mind with the greatest Englishman left among us to represent the mighty breed of our elders since Landor went to find his equals and rejoin his kin among the Grecian shades "where Orpheus and where Homer are." It is long since Mr. Carlyle expressed his opinion that if any poet or other literary creature could really be "killed off by one critique" or many, the sooner he was so despatched the better; a sentiment in which I for one humbly but heartily concur.

There is one large and interesting class of the critical race which unfortunately has hitherto in great measure defied the researches of science. Any collector who by any fair means has secured a sample of this species may naturally be prone to exhibit it with pride among the choicer spoils of his museum; not indeed for its beauty, and certainly not for its rarity; it may be seen in every hedge and every morass, but the difficulty is to determine and distinguish any single specimen by its proper and recognizable name. This species is composed of the critics known only as anonyms. Being anonymous, how can its members be classified by any scientific system of nomenclature? A mere dabbler in the science like myself must not hope at his first start to secure a prize of this kind; such trophies are not for the hand of a beginner. The sciolist who thinks to affix its label and assign its place to any one specimen of the tribe will be liable to grave error. In the grand pantomime of anonymous criticism the actors shift their parts and change their faces so suddenly that no one whose life has not been spent behind the scenes can hope to verify his guess at the wearer of such or such a mask. We see Harlequin Virtue make love to the goddess Grundy, and watch if we can without yawning the raddled old columbine Cant perform her usual pirouettes in the ballet of morality; we have hardly heart to sit out, though revived on so rotten a stage by express desire, the

screaming farce of religion; and after all we are never sure whether it was Clown or Pantaloon whom we heard snuffling and wheezing in the side-scenes. We go for instance to the old Quarterly Theatre, confident that we shall see and hear the old actors in their old parts, or at least some worthy successor and heir to the sound stage traditions of the house; and indeed we find much the same show of decoration and much the same style of declamation as ever; but we had a tender and pardonable weakness for the old faces and the old voices; and now we cannot even tell if they are here or no; whether the part taken in the first act by an old familiar friend is not continued in the second by a new performer of much promise and ability, remarkable for his more than apish or parrot-like dexterity in picking up and reproducing the tricks and phrases, tones and gestures, of the stage-struck veteran in whose place he stands; but not the man we came to see. We cannot hang upon the actor's lips with the same breathless attention when we know not whether it be master or pupil who speaks behind the mask. What in the elder actor was a natural gift of personation is but an empirical knack of imitation in his copyist. At least we would fain know for certain whether the moral gambols performed before us are those of the old showman or his ape. Or say that we come thither as to church or lecture; it cannot tend to edification that we should not know whom we sit under. We are distracted throughout sermon-time by doubts whether the veiled preacher be indeed as we thought a man of gravity from his youth upwards, a holy and austere minister of the altar, a Nazarite of lifelong sanctity, a venerable athlete of the Church, about whose past there can be no more question than about his right to speak as one ordained to apostolic office and succession by laying on of hands; or haply a neophyte from the outer court, a deacon but newly made reverend, an interloper even it may be or a schismatic: the doubt is nothing short of agony. Imagine, gathered about the pulpit, a little flock of penitents who come gladly to be admonished, who ask nothing better than to be convinced of sin, who listen humbly to the pastoral rebuke, accept meekly the paternal chastisement, of the preacher who summons them before him to judgment; what will be their consternation if they have cause to suspect that it is not an orthodox shepherd of souls whose voice of warning is in their ears, but an intruder who has climbed into the sheepfold! Clown masquerading in the guise of Pantaloon; and in place of the man of God at whose admonition the sinner was wont to tremble with Felix, perhaps a comic singer, a rhymester of boyish burlesque; there is no saying who may not usurp the pulpit when once the priestly office and the priestly vesture have passed into other than consecrated hands. For instance, we hear in October, say, a discourse on Byron and Tennyson; we are struck by the fervour and unction of the preacher; we feel, like Satan, how awful goodness is, and see virtue in her shape how lovely; see, and pine our loss, if haply we too have fallen; we stand abashed at the reflection that never till this man came to show us did we perceive the impurity of a poet who can make his heroine "so familiar with male objects of desire" as to allude to such a person as an odalisque "in good society"; we are ashamed to remember that never till now did we duly appreciate the chastity of Dudù and her comrades, as contrasted with the depravity of the Princess Ida and her collegians; we blush, if a blush be left in us, to hear on such authority "that exception might be taken without excess of prudery to 'The Sisters,' " and to think that we should ever have got by heart, without a thought of evil to alloy the delight of admiration, a poem "in which sensual passion is coarsely blended with the sense of injured honour and revenge." We read, and regret that ever the fascination of verse should have so effectually closed our eyes and ears against all perception of these deplorable qualities in a poet whose name we have cherished from our childhood; and as we read there rises before us the august and austere vision of a man well stricken in years, but of life unspotted from the world, pure as a child in word and thought, stern as an apostle in his rebuke of youthful wantonness or maturer levity; we feel that in his presence no one would venture on a loose jest or equivocal allusion, no one dream of indulgence in foolish talking and jesting, which (as he would assuredly remind the offender), we know on the highest authority, is not convenient; and we call reverently to mind the words of a poet, in which the beauty of a virtuous old age is affectingly set forth.

> How sweet is chastity in hoary hairs!
>   How venerable the speech of an old man
> Pure as a maiden's, and a cheek that wears
>   In age the blush it wore when youth
>   began!
> The lip still saintly with a sense of prayers
>   Angelical, with power to bless or ban,
> Stern to rebuke tongues heedless of
>   control,—
> A virgin elder with a vestal soul.

Or perchance there may rise to our own lips the equally impressive tribute of a French writer at the same venerable shrine.

> Vieillard, ton âme austère est une âme d'élite:
> Et quand la conscience humaine a fait faillite,
> Ta voix sévère est comme un rappel qu'on
>   entend
> Sonner du fond de l'ombre ou le sort nous
>   attend.
> L'appétit nu, la chair affamée et rieuse,
> Source âpre et basse où boit la jeunesse
>   oublieuse,
> La luxure cynique au regard fauve et vil,
> Rentre, à ton aspect, comme un chien dans
>   son chenil.
> Jamais le rire impur ne vint souiller de fange
> Ta lèvre où luit le feu de l apôtre et de l'ange.
> Le satyre au chant rauque a peur devant tes
>   yeux;
> Le vice à ton abord frémit silencieux;
> Et la neige qui pleut sur ta tête qui penche,
> ·Quand on a vu ton coeur, ne semble plus si
>   blanche.

I know not whether the rebuke of venerable virtue had power to affect the callous conscience of the "hoarse-voiced satyr" thus convicted of "the depth of ill-breeding and bad taste"; but I cannot doubt that when in January a like parable was taken up in the same quarter against certain younger offenders, the thought that the same voice with the same weight of judgment in its tones was raised to denounce them must have struck cold to their hearts while it brought the blood to their cheeks. The likeness in turn of phrase and inflexion of voice was perfect; the air of age and authority, if indeed it was but assumed, was assumed with faultless and exquisite fidelity; the choice of points for attack and words to attack with was as nearly as might be identical. "No terms of condemnation could be too strong," so rang that "terrible voice of most just judgment," "for the revolting picturesqueness of A's description of the sexual relation"; it was illustrated by sacramental symbols of "gross profanity"; it gave evidence of "emasculate obscenity,"[1] and a deliberate addiction to "the worship of Priapus." The virtuous journalist, I have observed, is remarkably fond of Priapus; his frequent and forcible allusions to "the honest garden-god" recur with a devout iteration to be found in no other worshipper; for one such reference in graver or lighter verse you may find a score in prose of the moral and critical sort. Long since, in that incomparable satiric essay which won for its young author the deathless applause of Balzac—"magnifique préface d'un livre magnifique"—Théophile Gautier had occasion to remark on the intimate familiarity of the virtuous journalist with all the occult obscenities of literature, the depth and width of range which his studies in that line would seem to have taken, if we might judge by his numerous and ready citations of the titles of indecent books with which he would associate the title of the book reviewed. This problematic intimacy the French poet finds no plausible way to explain; and with it we must leave the other problem on which I have touched above, in the hope that some day a more advanced stage of scientific inquiry will produce men competent to resolve it. Meantime we may remark again the very twang of the former preacher in the voice which now denounces to our ridicule B's "want of sense," while it invokes our disgust as fire from heaven on his "want of decency," in the use of a type borrowed from the Christian mythology and applied to actual doings and sufferings; and once more we surely seem to "know the sweet Roman hand" that sets down our errors in its register, when the critic remarks on the absurd inconsequence of a poet who addresses by name and denounces in person a god in whose personal existence he does not believe. In the name of all divine persons that ever did or did not exist, what on earth or in heaven would the critic in such a case expect? Is it from the believers in a particular god or gods that he would look for exposure and denunciation of their especial creed? Would it be natural and rational for a man to attack and denounce a name he believes in or a person he adores, unnatural and irrational to attack and denounce by name a godhead or a gospel he finds incredible and abominable to him? When a great poetess apostrophized the gods of Hellas as dead, was the form of apostrophe made inconsequent and absurd by the fact that she did not believe them to be alive? For a choicer specimen of preacher's logic than this we might seek long without finding it. But we must not be led away into argument or answer addressed to the subjects of our research, while as yet the work before us remains unaccomplished. The self-imposed task is simple and severe; we would merely submit to the analysis of scientific examination the examiners of other men, bring under our microscope, as it were, the telescopic apparatus which they on their side bring to investigate from below things otherwise invisible to them, as they would be imperceptible from above but for the microscopic lens which science enables us in turn to apply to themselves and their appliances. As to answer, if any workman who has done any work of his own should be asked why he does not come forward to take up any challenge flung down to him, or sweep out of his way any litter of lies and insults that may chance to encumber it for a moment, his reply for his fellows and himself to those who suggest that they should engage in such a warfare might perhaps run somewhat thus: Are we cranes or mice, that we should give battle to the frogs or the pigmies? Examine them we may at our leisure, in the pursuit of natural history, if our studies should chance to have taken that turn; but as we cannot, when they speak out of the darkness, tell frog from frog by his croak, or pigmy from pigmy by his features, and are thus liable at every moment to the most unscientific errors in definition, it seems best to seek no further for quaint or notable examples of a kind which we cannot profitably attempt to classify. Not without regret, therefore, we resign to more adventurous explorers the whole range of the anonymous wilderness, and confine our own modest researches to the limits within which we may trust ourselves to make no grave mistakes of kind. But within these limits, too, there is a race which defies even scientific handling, and for a reason yet graver and more final. Among writers who publish and sign such things as they have to say about or against their contemporaries, there is still, as of old, a class which is protected against response or remark, as (to use an apt example of Macaulay's) "the skunk is protected against the hunters. It is safe, because it is too filthy to handle, and too noisome even to approach." To this class belong the creatures known to naturalists by the generic term of coprophagi; a generation which derives its sustenance from the unclean matter which produced it, and lives on the very stuff of which it was born:

> They are no vipers, yet they feed
> On mother-dung which did them breed:

and under this head we find ranked, for example, the workers and dealers in false and foul ware for minor magazines and newspapers, to whom now that they know their ears to be safe from the pillory and their shoulders from the scourge there is no restraint and no reply applicable but the restraint and the reply of the law which imposes on their kind the brand of a shameful penalty; and it is not every day that an honest man will care to come forward and procure its infliction on some representative rascal of the tribe at the price of having to swear that the spittle aimed at his face came from the lips of a liar; that he has not lived on such terms of intimacy with the honest gentleman at the bar that the confidential and circumstantial report given of his life and opinions, habits and theories, person and conversation, is absolutely to be taken for gospel by the curious in such matters. The age of Pope is past, and we no longer expect a man of note to dive into the common sink of letters for the purpose of unearthing from its native place and nailing up by the throat in sight of day any chance vermin that may slink out in foul weather to assail him. The celebrity of Oldmixon and Curll is no longer attainable by dint of scurrilous persistency in provocation; in vain may the sons of the sewer look up with longing eyes after the hope of such peculiar immortality as that bestowed by Swift on the names of Whiston and Ditton: upon their upturned faces there will fall no drop or flake of such unfragrant fame. When some one told Dr. Johnson that a noted libeller had been publicly kicked in the streets of Dublin, his answer was to the effect that he was glad to hear of so clever a man rising so rapidly in the world; when he was in London, no one at whom his personalities might be launched ever thought it worth while to kick him. There are writers apparently consumed by a vain ambition to emulate the rise in life thus achieved by one of their precursors; and it takes them some time to discover, and despond as they admit, that such luck is not always to be looked for. Some, as in fond hope of such notice, assume the gay patrician in their style, while others in preference affect the honest plebeian; but in neither case do they succeed in attracting the touch which might confer celebrity; the very means they take to draw it down on themselves suffice to keep it off; at each fresh emanation or exhalation of their malodorous souls it becomes more clearly impossible for man to approach them even "with stopped nostril and glove-guarded hand." When the dirtier lackeys of literature come forward in cast clothes to revile or to represent their betters, to caricature by personation or by defamation the masters of the house, men do not now look at them and pass by; they pass without looking, and have neither eye for the pretentions nor cudgel for the backs of the Marquis de Mascarille and the Vicomte de Jodelet.

Of such creatures, then, even though they be nothing if not critical, we do not propose to treat; but only of such examples of the critical kind as may be shown in public without apology by the collector, not retained (if retained at all) for necessary purposes of science on the most private shelves of his cabinet. Among these more presentable classes there is considerable diversity of kind to be traced by the discerning eye, though many signs and symptoms be in almost all cases identical. There is the critic who believes that no good thing can come

out of such a Nazarene generation as the men of his own time; and there is the critic who believes first in himself alone, and through himself in the gods or godlings of his worship and the eggs or nestlings hatched or addled under the incubation of his patronage. Between these two kinds there rages a natural warfare as worthy of a burlesque poets as any batrachomyomachy that ever was fought out. It is no bad sport to watch through a magnifying glass the reciprocal attack and defence of their little lines of battle and posts of vantage—

> Et, dans la goutte d'eau, les guerres du volvoce
>   Avec le vibrion.

In all times there have been men in plenty convinced of the decadence of their own age; of which they have not usually been classed among the more distinguished children. We are happy in having among us a critic of some culture and of much noisy pertinacity who will serve well enough to represent the tribe. I distinguish his book on "The Poetry of the Period," supplemented as I take it to be by further essays in criticism thrown out in the same line, not for any controversial purpose, and assuredly with no view of attempting to answer or to confute the verdicts therein issued, to prove by force of reasoning or proclaim by force of rhetoric that the gulf between past and present is less deep and distinct than this author believes and alleges it to be; that the dead were not so far above the average type of men, that the living are not so far below it, as writers of this type have always been equally prone to maintain. I have little taste for such controversy and little belief in its value; but even if the diversion of arguing as to what sort of work should be done or is being done or has been were in my mind preferable to the business of doing as seems to me best whatever work my hand finds to do, I should not enter into a debate in which my own name was mixed up. Whether the men of this time be men of a great age or a small is not a matter to be decided by their own assertion or denial; but in any case a man of any generation can keep his hand and foot out of the perpetual wrangle and jangle of "the petty fools of rhyme who shriek and sweat in pigmy jars," which recur in every age of literature with a pitiful repetition of the same cries and catchwords. I could never understand, and certainly I could never admire, the habit of mind or the form of energy which finds work and vent in demonstration or proclamation of the incompetence for all good of other men; but much less can I admire or understand the impulse which would thrust a man for-

must be sought out to revive its drooping credit and refresh its withered honours? *Quis vituperavit?* Has any one attacked his noble memory as a poet or a man, except here and there a journalist of the tribe of Levi or Tartuffe, or a blatant Bassarid of Boston, a rampant Maenad of Massachusetts? To wipe off the froth of falsehood from the foaming lips of inebriated virtue, when fresh from the sexless orgies of morality and reeling from the delirious riot of religion, may doubtless be a charitable office; but it is no proof of critical sense or judgment to set about the vindication of a great man as though his repute could by any chance be widely or durably affected by the confidences exchanged in the most secret place and hour of their sacred rites, far from the clamour of public halls and platforms made hoarse with holiness,

> Ubi sacra sancta acutis ululatibus agitant,

between two whispering priestesses of whatever god presides over the most vicious parts of virtue, the most shameless rites of modesty, the most rancorous forms of forgiveness—the very Floralia of evangelical faith and love. That two such spirits, naked and not ashamed, should so have met and mingled in the communion of calumny, have taken each with devout avidity her part in the obscene sacrament of hate, her share in the graceless eucharist of evil-speaking, is not more wonderful or more important than that the elder devotee should have duped the younger into a belief that she alone had been admitted to partake of a fouler feast than that eaten in mockery at a witch's sabbath, a wafer more impure from a table more unspeakably polluted—the bread of slander from the altar of madness or malignity, the bitter poison of a shrine on which the cloven tongue of hell-fire might ever be expected to reappear with the return of some infernal Pentecost. All this is as natural and as insignificant as that the younger priestess on her part should since have trafficked in the unhallowed elements of their common and unclean mystery, have revealed for hire the unsacred secrets of no Eleusinian initiation. To whom can it matter that such a plume-plucked Celaeno as this should come with all the filth and flutter of her kind to defile a grave which is safe and high enough above the abomination of her approach? Not, I should have thought, to those who hold most in honour all that was worthiest of men's honour in Byron. Surely he needs no defence against this posthumous conjugal effusion at second hand of such a venomous and virulent charity as might shame the veriest Christian to have

shown. And who else speaks evil of him but now and then some priest or pedagogue, frocked or unfrocked, in lecture or review? It should be remembered that a warfare carried into such quarters can bring honour or profit to no man. We are not accustomed to give back railing for railing that is flung at us from the pulpit or the street-corner. In the church as in the highway, the skirt significant of sex, be it surpliced or draggle-tailed, should suffice to protect the wearer from any reciprocity of vituperation. If it should ever be a clerical writer, whether of the regular or the secular order—an amateur who officiates by choice or by chance, or a registered official whose services are duly salaried—that may happen to review a book in which you may happen to have touched unawares on some naked nerve of his religious feeling or professional faith, you are not moved to any surprise or anger that he should liken you to a boy rolling in a puddle, or laugh at you in pity as he throws aside in disgust the proof of your fatuous ignorance; you know that this is the rhetoric or the reasoning of his kind, and that he means by it no more than a street-walker means by her curse as you pass by without response to her addresses; you remember that both alike may claim the freedom of the trade, and would as soon turn back to notice the one salutation as the other. Priests and prostitutes are a privileged class. Half of that axiom was long since laid down by Shelley; and it is not from any such quarter that he probably would have thought the fame of his friend in any such danger as to require much demonstration of championship. The worst enemies of Byron, as of all his kind, are not to be sought among such as these. They are his enemies who extol him for gifts which he had not and work which he could not do; who by dint of praising him for such qualities as were wanting to his genius call the attention of all men to his want of them; who are not content to pay all homage to his unsurpassed energy, his fiery eloquence, his fitful but gigantic force of spirit, his troubled but triumphant strength of soul; to his passionate courage, his noble wrath and pity and scorn, his bright and burning wit, the invincible vitality and sleepless vigour of action and motion which informs and imbues for us all his better part of work as with a sense of living and personal power; who are dissatisfied for him with this his just and natural part of praise, and by way of doing him right must needs rise up to glorify him for imagination, of which he had little, and harmony, of which he had none. Even when supporting himself as in "Manfred" on the wings of other poets, he cannot fly as straight or sing as true as they. It is not the mere fluid melody of dulcet and facile verse that is wanting to him; that he might want and be none the worse for want of it; it is the inner sense of harmony which cannot but speak in music, the innate and spiritual instinct of sweetness and fitness and exaltation which cannot but express itself in height and perfection of song. This divine concord is never infringed or violated in the stormiest symphonies of passion or imagination by any one of the supreme and sovereign poets: by Aeschylus or Shakespeare, in the tempest and agony of Prometheus or of Lear, it is no less surely and naturally preserved than by Sophocles or by Milton in the serener departure of Oedipus or the more temperate lament of Samson. In a free country Mr. Austin or any other citizen may of course take leave to set Byron beside Shelley or above him, as Byron himself had leave to set Pope beside or above Shakespeare and Milton; there is no harm done in either case even to Pope or Byron, and assuredly there is no harm done to the greater poets. The one thing memorable in the matter is the confidence with which men who have absolutely no sense whatever of verbal music will pronounce judgment on the subtlest questions relating to that form of art. A man whose ear is conscious of no difference between Offenbach and Beethoven does not usually stand up as a judge of instrumental music; but there is no ear so hirsute or so hard, so pointed or so long, that its wearer will not feel himself qualified to pass sentence on the musical rank of any poet's verse, the relative range and value of his metrical power or skill. If one man says for instance that Shelley outsang all rivals while Byron could not properly sing at all, and another man in reply is good enough to inform him what he meant to say and should have said was that Byron could not shriek in falsetto like Shelley and himself, the one betweenwhiles and the other at all times, what answer or appeal is possible? The decision must be left to each man's own sense of hearing, or to his estimate of the respective worth of the two opinions given. I have always thought it somewhat hasty on the part of Sir Hugh Evans to condemn as "affectations" that phrase of Pistol's — "He hears with ears"; to hear with ears is a gift by no means given to every man that wears them. Our own meanwhile are still plagued with the cackle of such judges on all points of art as those to whom Molière addressed himself in vain — "qui blâment et louent tout à contre-sens, prennent par où ils peuvent les termes de l'art qu'ils attrapent, et ne manquent jamais de les estropier et de les mettre hors de place. Hé! morbleu! messieurs, taisez-vous. *Quand Dieu ne vous a pas donné la connaissance d'une chose, n'apprêtez point à rire à ceux qui vous entendent parler;* et songez qu'en ne disant mot on croira peut-être que vous êtes d'habiles gens." Such another critic as Mr. Austin is Herr Elze, the German biographer who has been sent among us after many days to inform our native ignorance that Byron was the greatest lyric poet of England. A few more such examples should have been vouchsafed us of "things not generally known"; such as these for instance: that our greatest dramatic poet was Dr. Johnson, our greatest comic poet was Sir Isaac Newton, our best amatory poet was Lord Bacon, our best religious poet was Lord Rochester, our best narrative poet was Joseph Addison, and our greatest epic poet was Tom Moore. Add to these facts that Shakespeare's fame rests on his invention of gunpowder and Milton's on his discovery of vaccination, and the student thus prepared and primed with useful knowledge will in time be qualified to match our instructor himself for accurate science of English literature, biographical or critical. It is a truth neither more nor less disputable than these that Byron was a great lyric poet; if the statements proposed above be true, then that also is true; if they be not, it also is not. He could no more have written a thoroughly good and perfect lyric, great or small, after the fashion of Hugo or after the fashion of Tennyson, than he could have written a page of Hamlet or of Paradise Lost. Even in the "Isles of Greece," excellent as the poem is throughout for eloquence and force, he stumbles into epigram or subsides into reflection with untimely lapse of rhetoric and unseemly change of note. The stanza on Miltiades is an almost vulgar instance of oratorical trick — "a very palpable hit" it might be on a platform, but it is a very palpable flaw in a lyric. Will it again be objected that such dissection as this of a poem is but a paltry and injurious form of criticism? Doubtless it is; but the test of true and great poetry is just this, that it will endure, if need be, such a process of analysis or anatomy; that thus tried as in the fire and decomposed as in a crucible it comes out after all renewed and reattested in perfection of all its parts, in solid and flawless unity, whole and indissoluble. Scarcely one or two of all Byron's poems will stand any such test for a moment; and his enemies, it must again be explained, are those eyeless and earless panegyrists who will not let us overlook this infirmity. It is to Byron and not to Tennyson that Mr. Austin has proved himself an enemy; the enemies of Tennyson are critics of another class: they are those of his own household. They are not the men who bring against the sweetest and the noblest examples of his lyric work their charges of pettiness or tameness, contraction or inadequacy; who taste a savour of corruption in "The Sisters" or a savour of effeminacy in "Boadicea." They are the men who couple "In Memoriam" with the Psalms of David as a work akin to these in scope and in effect; who compare the dramatic skill and subtle power to sound the depths of the human spirit displayed in "Maud" with the like display of these gifts in Hamlet and Othello. They are the men who would set his ode on the death of Wellington above Shelley's lines on the death of Napoleon, his "Charge of the Light Brigade" beside Campbell's "Battle of the Baltic" or Drayton's "Battle of Agincourt," the very poem whose model it follows afar off with such halting and unequal steps. They are the men who find in his collection of Arthurian idyls,—the Morte d'Albert as it might perhaps be more properly called, after the princely type to which (as he tells us with just pride) the poet has been fortunate enough to make his central figure so successfully conform,—an epic poem of profound and exalted morality. Upon this moral question I shall take leave to intercalate a few words. It does not appear to me that on the whole I need stand in fear of misapprehension or misrepresentation on one charge at least—that of envious or grudging reluctance to applaud the giver of any good gift for which all receivers should be glad to return thanks. I am not aware—but it is possible that this too may be an instance of a man's blindness to his own defects—of having by any overt or covert demonstration of so vile a spirit exposed my name to be classed with the names, whether forged or genuine, of the rancorous and reptile crew of poeticules who decompose into criticasters; I do not remember to have ever as yet been driven by despair or hunger or malevolence to take up the trade of throwing dirt in the dark; nor am I conscious, at sight of my superiors, of an instant impulse to revile them. My first instinct, in such a case, is not the instinct of backbiting; I have even felt at such times some moderate sense of delight and admiration, and some slight pleasure in the attempt to express it loyally by such modest thanksgiving as I might. I hold myself therefore free to say what I think on this matter without fear of being taxed with the motives of a currish malignant. It seems to me that the moral tone of the Arthurian story has been on the whole lowered and degraded by Mr. Tennyson's mode of treatment. Wishing to make his central figure the noble and perfect symbol of an ideal man, he has removed not merely the excuse but the explanation of the fatal and tragic loves of Launcelot and Guenevere. The hinge of the whole legend of the Round Table, from its first glory to its final fall, is

the incestuous birth of Mordred from the connexion of Arthur with his half-sister, unknowing and unknown; as surely as the hinge of the Oresteia from first to last is the sacrifice at Aulis. From the immolation of Iphigenia springs the wrath of Clytaemnestra, with all its train of evils ensuing; from the sin of Arthur's youth proceeds the ruin of his reign and realm through the falsehood of his wife, a wife unloving and unloved. Remove in either case the plea which leaves the heroine less sinned against indeed than sinning, but yet not too base for tragic compassion and interest, and there remains merely the presentation of a vulgar adulteress. From the background of the one story the ignoble figure of Aegisthus starts into the foreground, and we see in place of the terrible and patient mother, perilous and piteous as a lioness bereaved, the congenial harlot of a coward and traitor. A poet undertaking to rewrite the Agamemnon who should open his poem with some scene of dalliance or conspiracy between Aegisthus and Clytaemnestra and proceed to make of their common household intrigue the mainspring of his plan, would not more deform the design and lower the keynote of the Aeschylean drama than Mr. Tennyson has lowered the note and deformed the outline of the Arthurian story by reducing Arthur to the level of a wittol, Guenevere to the level of a woman of intrigue, and Launcelot to the level of a "co-respondent." Treated as he has treated it, the story is rather a case for the divorce-court than for poetry. At the utmost it might serve the recent censor of his countrymen, the champion of morals so dear to President Thiers and the virtuous journalist who draws a contrast in favour of his chastity between him and other French or English authors, for a new study of the worn and wearisome old topic of domestic intrigue; but such "camelias" should be left to blow in the common hotbeds of the lower kind of novelist. Adultery must be tragic and exceptional to afford stuff for art to work upon; and the debased preference of Mr. Tennyson's heroine for a lover so much beneath her noble and faithful husband is as mean an instance as any day can show in its newspaper reports of a common woman's common sin. In the old story, the king, with the doom denounced in the beginning by Merlin hanging over all his toils and truimphs as a tragic shadow, stands apart in no undignified patience to await the end in its own good time of all his work and glory, with no eye for the pain and passion of the woman who sits beside him as queen rather than as wife. Such a figure is not unfit for the centre of a tragic action; it is neither ignoble nor inconceivable; but the besotted blindness of Mr. Tennyson's "blameless king" to the treason of a woman who has had the first and last of his love and the whole devotion of his blameless life is nothing more or less than pitiful and ridiculous. All the studious care and exquisite eloquence of the poet can throw no genuine halo round the sprouting brows of a royal husband who remains to the very last the one man in his kingdom insensible of his disgrace. The unclean taunt of the hateful Vivien is simply the expression in vile language of an undeniable truth; such a man as this king is indeed hardly "man at all"; either fool or coward he must surely be. Thus it is that by the very excision of what may have seemed in his eyes a moral blemish Mr. Tennyson has blemished the whole story; by the very exaltation of his hero as something more than man he has left him in the end something less. The keystone of the whole building is removed, and in place of a tragic house of song where even sin had all the dignity and beauty that sin can retain, and without which it can afford no fit material for tragedy, we find an incongruous edifice of tradition and invention where even virtue is made to seem either imbecile or vile. The story as it stood of old had in it something almost of Hellenic dignity and significance; in it as in the great Greek legends we could trace from a seemingly small root of evil the birth and growth of a calamitous fate, not sent by mere malevolence of heaven, yet in its awful weight and mystery of darkness apparently out of all due retributive proportion to the careless sin or folly of presumptuous weakness which first incurred its infliction; so that by mere hasty resistance and return of violence for violence a noble man may unwittingly bring on himself and all his house the curse denounced on parricide, by mere casual indulgence of light love and passing wantoness a hero king may unknowingly bring on himself and all his kingdom the doom imposed on incest. This presence and imminence of Ate inevitable as invisible throughout the tragic course of action can alone confer on such a story the proper significance and the necessary dignity: without it the action would want meaning and the passion would want nobility; with it, we may hear in the high funereal homily which concludes as with dirge-music the great old book of Sir Thomas Mallory some echo not utterly unworthy of that supreme lament of wondering and wailing spirits—

[poi dēta kranei, poi katalēxei
metakoimisthen menos atēs;]

The fatal consequence or corollary of this original flaw in his scheme is that the modern poet has been obliged to degrade all the other figures of the legend in order to bring them into due harmony with the degraded figures of Arthur and Guenevere. The courteous and loyal Gawain of the old romancers, already deformed and maligned in the version of Mallory himself, is here a vulgar traitor; the benignant Lady of the Lake, foster-mother of Launcelot, redeemer and comforter of Pelleas, becomes the very vilest figure in all that cycle of more or less symbolic agents and patients which Mr. Tennyson has set revolving round the figure of his central wittol. I certainly do not share the objection of the virtuous journalist to the presentation in art of an unchaste woman; but I certainly desire that the creature presented should retain some trace of human or if need be of devilish dignity. The Vivien of Mr. Tennyson's idyl seems to me, to speak frankly, about the most base and repulsive person ever set forth in serious literature. Her impurity is actually eclipsed by her incredible and incomparable vulgarity—("O ay," said Vivien, *that were likely too*"). She is such a sordid creature as plucks men passing by the sleeve. I am of course aware that this figure appears the very type and model of a beautiful and fearful temptress of the flesh, the very embodied and ennobled ideal of danger and desire, in the chaster eyes of the virtuous journalist who grows sick with horror and disgust at the license of other French and English writers; but I have yet to find the French or English contemporary poem containing a passage that can be matched against the loathsome dialogue in which Merlin and Vivien discuss the nightly transgressions against chastity, within doors and without, of the various knights of Arthur's court. I do not remember that any modern poet whose fame has been assailed on the score of sensual immorality—say for instance the author of "Mademoiselle de Maupin" or the author of the "Fleurs du Mal"—has ever devoted an elaborate poem to describing the erotic fluctuations and vacillations of a dotard under the moral and physical manipulation of a prostitute. The conversation of Vivien is exactly described in the poet's own phrase—it is "as the poached filth that floods the middle street." Nothing like it can be cited from the verse which embodies other poetic personations of unchaste women. From the Cleopatra of Shakespeare and the Dalilah of Milton to the Phraxanor of Wells, a figure worthy to be ranked not far in design below the highest of theirs, we may pass without fear of finding any such pollution. Those heroines of sin are evil, but noble in their evil way; it is the utterly ignoble quality of Vivien which makes her so unspeakably repulsive and unfit for artistic treatment. "Smiling saucily," she is simply a subject for the police-court. The "Femmes Damnées" of Baudelaire may be worthier of hell-fire than a common harlot like this, but that side of their passion which would render them amenable to the notice of the nearest station is not what is kept before us throughout that condemned poem; it is an infinite perverse refinement, an infinite reverse aspiration, "the end of which things is death"; and from the barren places of unsexed desire the tragic lyrist points them at last along their downward way to the land of sleepless winds and scourging storms, where the shadows of things perverted shall toss and turn for ever in a Dantesque cycle and agony of changeless change: a lyric close of bitter tempest and deep wide music of lost souls, not inaptly described by M. Asselineau as a "fulgurant" harmony after the fashion of Beethoven. The slight sketch in eight lines of Matha in "Ratbert" resumes all the imaginable horror and loveliness of a wicked and beautiful woman; but Hugo does not make her open her lips to let out the foul talk or the "saucy" smile of the common street. "La blonde fauve," all but naked among the piled-up roses, with feet dabbled in blood, and the laughter of hell itself on her rose-red mouth, is as horrible as any proper object of art can be; but she is not vile and intolerable as Vivien. I do not fear or hesitate to say on this occasion what I think and have always thought on this matter; for I trust to have shown before now that the poet in the sunshine of whose noble genius the men of my generation grew up and took delight has no more ardent or more loyal admirer than myself among the herd of imitative parasites and thievish satellites who grovel at his heels; that I need feel no apprehension of being placed "in the rank of verminous fellows" who let themselves out to lie for hatred or for hire—"qui quaestum non corporis sed animi sui faciunt," as Major Dalgetty might have defined them. Among these obscene vermin I do not hold myself liable to be classed; though I may be unworthy to express, however capable of feeling, the same abhorrence as the Quarterly reviewer of "Vivien" for the exhibition of the libidinous infirmity of unvenerable age. But these are not the grounds on which Mr. Austin objects to the ethical tendency of Mr. Tennyson's poetry. His complaint against all those of his countrymen who spend their time in writing verse is that their verse is devoted to the worship of "woman, woman, woman, woman." He "hardly likes to own sex with" a man who devotes his life to the love of a woman and is ready to lay down his life and to sacrifice his soul for the chance of preserving her reputation. It is probable that the reluctance would be cordially reciprocated. A writer about as much beneath Mr. Austin as Mr. Austin is beneath the main objects of his attack has charged certain poetry of the present day with constant and distasteful recurrence of devotion to "some person of the other sex." It is at least significant that this person should have come forward, for once under his own name, to vindicate the moral worth of Petronius Arbiter; a writer, I believe, whose especial weakness (as exhibited in the characters of his book) was not a "hankering" after persons "of the other sex." It is as well to remember where we may be when we find ourselves in the company of these anti-sexual moralists.

Effeminate therefore I suppose the modern poetry of England must be content to remain; but there is a poet alive of now acknowledged eminence, not hitherto assailed on this hand, about whom the masked or barefaced critics of the minute are not by any means of one mind—if mind we are to call the organ which forms and produces their opinions. To me it seems that the truth for good and evil has never yet been spoken about Walt Whitman. There are in him two distinct men of most inharmonious kinds; a poet and a formalist. Of the poet I have before now done the best I could to express, whether in verse or prose, my ardent and sympathetic admiration. Of the formalist I shall here say what I think; showing why (for example) I cannot for my own part share in full the fiery partisanship of such thoughtful and eloquent disciples as Mr. Rossetti and Dr. Burroughs. It is from no love of foolish paradox that I have chosen the word "formalist" to express my sense of the radical fault in the noble genius of Whitman. For truly no scholar and servant of the past, reared on academic tradition under the wing of old-world culture, was ever more closely bound in with his own theories, more rigidly regulated by his own formularies, than this poet of new life and limitless democracy. Not Pope, not Boileau, was more fatally a formalist than Whitman; only Whitman is a poet of a greater nature than they. It is simply that these undigested formulas which choke by fits the free passage of his genius are to us less familiar than theirs; less real or less evident they are not. Throughout his great book, now of late so nobly completed, you can always tell at first hearing whether it be the poet who speaks or the formalist. Sometimes in the course of two lines the note is changed, either by the collapse of the poet's voice into the tuneless twang of the formalist, or by the sudden break and rise of released music from the formalist's droning note into the clear sincere harmonies of the poet. Sometimes for one whole division of the work either the formalist intones throughout as to order, or the poet sings high and true and strong without default from end to end. It is of no matter whatever, though both disciples and detractors appear to assume that it must be at least in each other's eyes, whether the subject treated be conventionally high or low, pleasant or unpleasant. At once and without fail you can hear whether the utterance of the subject be right or wrong; this is the one thing needful, but then this one thing is needful indeed. Disciples and detractors alike seem to assume that if you object to certain work of Whitman's it must be because you object to his choice of topic and would object equally to any man's choice or treatment of it; if you approve, it must be that you approve of the choice of topic and would approve equally of any poem that should start for the same end and run on the same lines. It is not so in the least. Let a man come forward as does Whitman with prelude of promise that he is about to sing and celebrate certain things, fair or foul, great or small, these being as good stuff for song and celebration as other things, we wait, admitting that, to hear if he will indeed celebrate and sing them. If he does, and does it well and duly, there is an end; *solvitur ambulando;* the matter is settled once for all by the invaluable and indispensable proof of the pudding.

Now whenever the pure poet in Whitman speaks, it is settled by that proof in his favour; whenever the mere theorist in him speaks, it is settled by the same proof against him. What comes forth out of the abundance of his heart rises at once from that high heart to the lips on which its thoughts take fire, and the music which rolls from them rings true as fine gold and perfect; what comes forth by the dictation of doctrinal theory serves only to twist aside his hand and make the written notes run foolishly awry. What he says is well said when he speaks as of himself and because he cannot choose but speak; whether he speak of a small bird's loss or a great man's death, of a nation rising for battle or a child going forth in the morning. What he says is not well said when he speaks not as though he must but as though he ought; as though it behoved one who would be the poet of American democracy to do this thing or to be that thing if the duties of that office were to be properly fulfilled, the tenets of that religion worthily delivered. Never before was high poetry so puddled and adulterated with mere doctrine in its crudest form. Never was there less assimilation of the lower dogmatic with the higher prophetic element. It so happens that the present writer (*si quid id est*) is, as far as he knows, entirely at

one with Whitman on general matters not less than on political; if there be in Whitman's works any opinion expressed on outward and social or inward and spiritual subjects which would clash or contend with his own, or with which he would feel his own to be incapable of concord or sympathy, he has yet to find the passage in which that opinion is embodied. To him the views of life and of death set forth by Whitman appear thoroughly acceptable and noble, perfectly credible and sane. It is certainly therefore from no prejudice against the doctrines delivered that he objects in any case to the delivery of them. What he objects—to take two small instances—is that it is one thing to sing the song of all trades, and quite another thing to tumble down together the names of all possible crafts and implements in one unsorted heap; to sing the song of all countries is not simply to fling out on the page at random in one howling mass the titles of all divisions of the earth, and so leave them. At this rate, to sing the song of the language it should suffice to bellow out backwards and forwards the twenty-four letters of the alphabet. And this folly is deliberately done by a great writer, and ingeniously defended by able writers, alike in good faith, and alike in blind bondage to mere dogmatic theory, to the mere formation of foregone opinion. They cannot see that formalism need not by any means be identical with tradition: they cannot see that because theories of the present are not inherited they do not on that account become more proper than were theories of the past to suffice of themselves for poetic or prophetic speech. Whether you have to deliver an old or a brand-new creed, alike in either case you must first insure that it be delivered well; for in neither will it suffice you to deliver it simply in good faith and good intent. The poet of democracy must sing all things alike? let him sing them then, whether in rhyme or not is no matter,[2] but in rhythm he must needs sing them. What is true of all poets is among them all most markedly true of Whitman, that his manner and his matter grow together; that where you catch a note of discord there you will find something wrong inly, the natural source of that outer wrongdoing; wherever you catch a note of good music you will surely find that it came whence only it could come, from some true root of music in the thought or thing spoken. There never was and will never be a poet who had verbal harmony and nothing else; if there was in him no inner depth or strength or truth, then that which men took for music in his mere speech was no such thing as music.

By far the finest and truest thing yet said of Walt Whitman has been said by himself, and said worthily of a great man. "I perceive in clear moments," he said to his friend Dr. Burroughs, "that my work is not the accomplishment of perfections, but destined, I hope, always to arouse an unquenchable feeling and ardour for them." A hope, surely, as well grounded as it is noble. But it is in those parts of his work which most arouse this feeling and this ardour that we find him nearest that accomplishment. At such times his speech has a majestic harmony which hurts us by no imperfection; his music then is absolutely great and good. It is when he is thinking of his part, of the duties and properties of a representative poet, an official democrat, that the strength forsakes his hand and the music ceases at his lips. It is then that he sets himself to define what books, and to what purpose, the scriptural code of democracy must accept and reject; to determine, Pope himself and council in one, what shall be the canons and articles of the church, which except a democrat do keep whole and undefiled, without doubt he shall perish everlastingly. With more than Athanasian assurance, with more than Calvinistic rigour, it is then that he pronounces what things are democratic and of good report, what things are feudal and of evil report, in all past literature of the world. There is much in these canonical decrees that is consonant with truth and reason; there is not a little that is simply the babbling of a preacher made drunk with his own doctrine. For instance, we find that "the Democratic requirements" substantially and curiously fulfilled in the best Spanish literature are not only not fulfilled in the best English literature, but are insulted in every page. After this it appears to us that in common consistency the best remaining type of actual democracy in Europe here must be sought among French or Austrian Legitimists, if not on some imperial Russian or German throne. But Shakespeare is not only "the tally of Feudalism," he is "incarnated, uncompromising Feudaliam, in literature." Now Shakespeare has doubtless done work which is purely aristocratic in tone. The supreme embodiment in poetic form of the aristocratic idea is "Coriolanus." I cannot at all accept the very good special pleading of M. François-Victor Hugo against this the natural view of that great tragedy. Whether we like it or not, the fact seems to me undeniable that Shakespeare has here used all his art and might to subdue the many to the one, to degrade the figure of the people, to enhance and exalt the figure of the people's enemy. Even here, though, he has not done as in Whitman's view he does always; he has not left without shades the radiant figure, he has not left the sombre figure

without lights; there are blemishes here and there on the towering glory of Coriolanus, redeeming points now and then in the grovelling ignominy of the commons. But what if there were none? Is this play the keynote of Shakespeare's mind, the keystone of his work? If the word Democracy mean anything — and to Whitman it means much — beyond the mere profession of a certain creed, the mere iteration of a certain shibboleth; if it signify first the cyclic life and truth of equal and various humanity, and secondly the form of principles and relations, the code of duties and of rights, by which alone adult society can walk straight; surely in the first and greatest sense there has never been and never can be a book so infinitely democratic as the Plays of Shakespeare.

These among others are reasons why I think it foolish to talk of Whitman as the probable founder of a future school of poetry unlike any other in matter as in style. He has many of the qualities of a reformer; he has perhaps none of the qualities of a founder. For one thing, he is far too didactic to be typical; the prophet in him too frequently subsides into the lecturer. He is not one of the everlasting models; but as an original and individual poet, it is at his best hardly possible to overrate him; as an informing and reforming element, it is absolutely impossible. Never did a country need more than America such an influence as his. We may understand and even approve his reproachful and scornful fear of the overweening "British element" when we see what it has hitherto signified in the literature of his country. Once as yet, and once only, has there sounded out of it all one pure note of original song — worth singing, and echoed from the singing of no other man; a note of song neither wide nor deep, but utterly true, rich, clear, and native to the singer; the short exquisite music, subtle and simple and sombre and sweet, of Edgar Poe. All the rest that is not of mocking-birds is of corncrakes, varied but at best for an instant by some scant-winded twitter of linnet or of wren.

We have been looking up too long from the microscope; it is time to look in again and take note of the subject. We find indeed one American name on which our weekly critics cluster in swarms of praise; one poet whom they who agree in nothing else but hate agree to love and laud as king of American verse; who has sung, they tell us, a song at last truly national and truly noble. The singer is Mr. Lowell; but the song is none of the Biglow Papers, where the humours could not but tickle while the discords made us wince; we laughed, with ears yet flayed and teeth still on edge. The song so preferable to any "Drum-Tap" of Whitman's was a Thanksgiving Ode of wooden verse sawn into unequal planks and tagged incongruously with tuneless bells of rhyme torn from the author's late professional cap. It was modelled on the chaotic songs of ceremony done to order on state occasions by our laureates of the Restoration and Revolution; preferable in this alone, that the modern author had the grace not to call it Pindaric: which in the sense of Whitehall, not of Thebes, it was; being cut into verses uneven, misshapen, irregular, and irresponsive. As a speech it might have passed muster on the platform; as a song it gave out no sound but such as of the platform's wood. Nor indeed could it; for while it had something of thought and more of eloquence, there was within it no breath or pulse of the thing called poetry. This gracious chant among others has been much belauded—incomparably beyond any praise given in any such quarter to Whitman's deathless hymn of death—by a writer on poetry whom Mr. Austin has reviled with as much acrimony as if he were instead a poet; calling his poor fellow-critic "an ignorant and presumptuous scribbler, wholly unentitled to give an opinion on poetry at all." Far be it from me this time to dispute the perfect justice of the verdict; but I had some hope till now that there might be truth in the proverb, "Hawks do not pyke out hawks' een." It is painful for the naturalist to be compelled to register in his note-book the fact that there is none. It is sad that the hymnologist, to whom this fact may be yet unknown, should be obliged, after citing the peaceful example of the aviary, to reiterate the lesson that 'tis a shameful sight when critics of one progeny fall out and chide and fight.[3] Really they should remember that their office is to instruct; and if so, surely not by precept alone. If the monitors of the poetic school go together by the ears in this way in sight of all forms at once, what can be expected of those whom they were appointed (though God only knows by whom) to direct and correct at need? The dirtiest little sneak on the dunce's seat may be encouraged to play some blackguard's trick on better boys behind their backs, and so oblige some one who had no thought of bullying or of noticing such a cur to kick him out into the yard and cleanse the old school of scandalous rubbish. And what may not one of the headmasters (there are more than one in this school), at their next quarterly visitation, say to such a couple of monitors as this?

> Their little hands were never made
> To tear each other's eyes

Their little hands—can it be necessary to remind them?—were made to throw dirt and stones with impunity at passers-by of a different kind. This is their usual business, and they do it with a will; though (to drop metaphor for a while) we may concede that English reviewers—and among them the reviewer of the "Spectator"—have not always been unready to do accurate justice to the genuine worth of new American writers; among much poor patchwork of comic and serious stuff, which shared their welcome and diminished its worth, they have yet found some fit word of praise for the true pathos of Bret Harte, the true passion of Joaquin Miller. But the men really and naturally dear to them are the literators of Boston; truly, and in no good sense, the school of New England—Britannia pejor: a land of dissonant reverberations and distorted reflections from our own.[4] This preference for the province of reflex poets and echoing philosophers came to a climax of expression in the transcendant remark that Mr. Lowell had in one critical essay so taken Mr. Carlyle to pieces that it would seem impossible ever to put him together again. Under the stroke of that recollected sentence, the staggered spirit of a sane man who desires to retain his sanity can but pause and reflect on what Mr. Ruskin, if I rightly remember, has somewhere said, that ever since Mr. Carlyle began to write you can tell by the reflex action of his genius the nobler from the ignobler of his contemporaries; as ever having won the most of reverence and praise from the most honourable among these, and (what is perhaps as sure a warrant of sovereign worth) from the most despicable among them the most of abhorrence and abuse.

A notable example of this latter sort was not long since (in his "Fors Clavigera") selected and chastised by Mr. Ruskin himself with a few strokes of such a lash as might thenceforward, one would think, have secured silence at least, if neither penitence nor shame, on the part of the offender. This person, whose abuse of Mr. Carlyle he justly described as matchless "in its platitudinous obliquity," was cited by the name of one Buchanan—

> [hostis pot' estin, ei tod' au-
> tō philon keklēmenō—]

but whether by his right name or another, who shall say? for the god of song himself had not more names or addresses. Now yachting among the Scottish (not English) Hebrides; now wrestling with fleshly sin (like his countryman Holy Willie) in "a great city of civilization"; now absorbed in studious emulation of the Persae of Aeschylus or the "enormously fine" work of "the tremendous creature" Dante;[5] now descending from the familiar heights of men whose praise he knows so well how to sing, for the not less noble purpose of crushing a school of poetic sensualists whose works are "wearing to the brain"; now "walking down the streets" and watching "harlots stare from the shop-windows," while "in the broad day a dozen hands offer him indecent prints"; now "beguiling many an hour, when snug at anchor in some lovely Highland loch, with the inimitable, yet questionable, pictures of Parisian life left by Paul de Kock"; landsman and seaman, Londoner and Scotchman, Delian and Patarene Buchanan. How should one address him?

Matutine pater, seu Jane libentiùs audis?

As Janus rather, one would think, being so in all men's sight a natural son of the double-faced divinity. Yet it might be well for the son of Janus if he had read and remembered in time the inscription on the statue of another divine person, before taking his name in vain as a word wherewith to revile men born in the ordinary way of the flesh:—

> Youngsters! who write false names, and slink
> behind
> The honest garden-god to hide yourselves,
> Beware!

In vain would I try to play the part of a prologuizer before this latest rival of the Hellenic dramatists, who sings from the height of "mystic realism," not with notes echoed from a Grecian strain, but as a Greek poet himself might have sung, in "massive grandeur of style," of a great contemporary event. He alone is fit, in Euripidean fashion, to prologuize for himself.

> [Polus men en graphaisi kouk anōnumos
> pseustēs keklēmai Skotios,[6] asteōs t' esō,
> hosoi te pontou termonōn t' Atlantikōn
> naiousin exō skaphesi nēsiōtikois,
> tous men trephontas thōps apo glōsses
> sebō
> hosoi d' apoptuousi m' empiptō lathōn][7]

He has often written, it seems, under false or assumed names; always doubtless "with the best of all motives," that which induced his friends in his absence to alter an article abusive of his betters and suppress the name which would otherwise have signed it, that of saving the writer from persecution and letting his charges stand on their own merits; and this simple and very natural precaution has singularly enough exposed his fair fame to "the inventions of cowards"—a form of attack naturally intolerable though contemptible to this polyonymous moralist. He was not used to it; in the cradle where his genius had been hatched he could remember no taint of such nastiness. Other friends than such had fostered into maturity the genius that now lightens far and wide the fields of poetry and criticism. All things must have their beginnings; and there were those who watched with prophetic hope the beginnings of Mr. Buchanan; who tended the rosy and lisping infancy of his genius with a care for its comfort and cleanliness not unworthy the nurse of Orestes; and took indeed much the same pains to keep it sweet and neat under the eye and nose of the public as those on which the good woman dwelt with such pathetic minuteness of recollection in after years. The babe may not always have been discreet;

[nea de nēdus autarkes teknōn]

and there were others who found its swaddling clothes not invariably in such condition as to dispense with the services of the "fuller";

[gnapheus tropheus te tauton eichetēn telos.]

In effect there were those who found the woes and devotions of Doll Tearsheet or Nell Nameless as set forth in the lyric verse of Mr. Buchanan calculated rather to turn the stomach than to melt the heart. But in spite of these exceptional tastes the nursing journals, it should seem, abated no jot of heart or hope for their nursling.

> Petit poisson deviendra grand
> Pourvu que Dieu lui prête vie.

Petit bonhomme will not, it appears. The tadpole poet will never grow into anything bigger than a frog; not though in that stage of development he should puff and blow himself till he bursts with windy adulation at the heels of the laurelled ox.

When some time since a passing notice was bestowed by writers of another sort on Mr. Buchanan's dramatic performance in the part of Thomas Maitland, it was observed with very just indignation by a literary ally that Mr. Rossetti was not ashamed to avow in the face of heaven and the press his utter ignorance of the writings of that poet—or perhaps we should say of those poets. The loss was too certainly his own. It is no light thing for a man who has any interest in the poetic production of his time to be ignorant of works which have won from the critic who of all others must be most competent to speak on the subject with the authority of the most intimate acquaintance, such eloquence of praise as has deservedly been lavished on Mr. Buchanan. A living critic of no less note in the world of letters than himself has drawn public attention to the deep and delicate beauties of his work; to "the intense loving tenderness of the coarse woman Nell towards her brutal paramour, the exquisite delicacy and fine spiritual vision of the old village schoolmaster," &c. &c. This pathetic tribute to the poet Buchanan was paid by no less a person than Buchanan the critic. Its effect is heightened by comparison with the just but rigid severity of that writer's verdict on other men—on the "gross" work of Shakespeare, the "brutal" work of Carlyle, the "sickening and peculiar" work of Thackeray, the "wooden-headed," "hectic," and "hysterical" qualities which are severally notable and condemnable in the work of Landor, of Keats, and of Shelley. In like manner his condemnation of contemporary impurities is thrown into fuller relief by his tribute to the moral sincerity of Petronius and the "singular purity" of Ben Jonson. For once I have the honour and pleasure to agree with him; I find the "purity" of the author of "Bartholomew Fair" a very "singular" sort of purity indeed. There is however another play of that great writer's, which, though it might be commended by his well-wishers to the special study of Mr. Buchanan, I can hardly suppose to be the favourite work which has raised the old poet so high in his esteem. In this play Jonson has traced with his bitterest fidelity the career of a "gentleman parcel-poet," one Laberius Crispinus, whose life is spent in the struggle to make his way among his betters by a happy alternation and admixture of calumny with servility; one who will fasten himself uninvited on the acquaintance of a superior with fulsome and obtrusive ostentation of good-will; inflict upon his passive and reluctant victim the recitation of his verses in a public place; offer him friendship and alliance against all other poets, so as "to lift the best of them out of favour"; protest to him, "Do but taste me once, if I do know myself and my own virtues truly, thou wilt not make that esteem of Varius, or Virgil, or Tibullus, or any of 'em indeed, as now in thy ignorance thou dost; which I am content to forgive; I would fain see which of these could pen more verses in a day or with more facility than I." After this, it need hardly be added that the dog returns to his vomit, and has in the end to be restrained by authority from venting "divers and sundry calumnies" against the victim aforesaid "or any other eminent man transcending him in merit,

whom his envy shall find cause to work upon, either for that, or for keeping himself in better acquaintance, or enjoying better friends"; and the play is aptly wound up by his public exposure and ignominious punishment. The title of this admirable comedy is "The Poetaster; or, His Arraignment"; and the prologue is spoken by Envy.

It is really to be regretted that the new fashion of self-criticism should never have been set till now. How much petty trouble, how many paltry wrangles and provocations, what endless warfare of the cranes and pigmies might have been prevented— and by how simple a remedy! How valuable would the applauding comments of other great poets on their own work have been to us for all time! All students of poetry must lament that it did not occur to Milton for example to express in public his admiration of "Paradise Lost." It might have helped to support the reputation of that poem against the severe sentence passed by Mr. Buchanan on its frequently flat and prosaic quality. And, like all truly great discoveries, this one looks so easy now we have it before us, that we cannot but wonder it was reserved for Mr. Buchanan to make: we cannot but feel it singular that Mr. Tennyson should never have thought fit to call our attention in person to the beauties of "Maud"; that Mr. Browning should never have come forward, "motley on back and pointing-pole in hand," to bid us remark the value of "The Ring and the Book"; that Mr. Arnold should have left to others the task of praising his "Thyrsis" and "Empedocles." The last-named poet might otherwise have held his own even against the imputation of writing "mere prose" which now he shares with Milton: so sharp is the critical judgment, so high the critical standard, of the author of "The Book of Orm."

However, even in the face of the rebuke so deservedly incurred by the avowal of Mr. Rossetti's gross and deplorable ignorance of that and other great works from the same hand, I am bound in honesty to admit that my own studies in that line are hardly much less limited. I cannot profess to have read any book of Mr. Buchanan's; for aught I know, they may deserve all his praises; it is neither my business nor my desire to decide. But sundry of his contributions in verse and prose to various magazines and newspapers I have looked through or glanced over—not, I trust, without profit; not, I know, without amusement. From these casual sources I have gathered—as he who runs may gather—not a little information on no unimportant matters of critical and autobiographical interest. With the kindliest forethought, the most judicious care to anticipate the anxious researches of a late posterity, Mr. Buchanan has once and again poured out his personal confidences into the sympathetic bosom of the nursing journals. He is resolved that his country shall not always have cause to complain how little she knows of her greatest sons. Time may have hidden from the eye of biography the facts of Shakespeare's life, as time has revealed to the eye of criticism the grossness of his works and the purity of his rival's; but none need fear that the next age will have to lament the absence of materials for a life of Buchanan. Not once or twice has he told in simple prose of his sorrows and aspirations, his struggles and his aims. He has told us what good man gave him in his need a cup of cold water, and what bad man accused him of sycophancy in the expression of his thanks. He has told us what advantage was taken of his tender age by heartless publishers, what construction was put upon his gushing gratitude by heartless reviewers. He has told us that he never can forget his first friends; he has shown us that he never can forget himself. He has told us that the versicles of one David Gray, a poor young poeticule of the same breed as his panegyrist (who however, it should in fairness be said, died without giving any sign of future distinction in the field of pseudonymous libel), will be read when the works of other contemporaries "have gone to the limbo of affettuosos." (May I suggest that the library edition of Mr. Buchanan's collected works should be furnished with a glossary for the use of students unskilled in the varieties of the Buchananese dialect? Justly contemptuous as he has shown himself of all foreign affectations of speech or style in an English writer, such a remarkable word in its apparent defiance of analogy as the one last quoted is not a little perplexing to their ignorance. I hardly think it can be Scotch; at least to a southern eye it bears no recognizable affinity to the language of Burns.) In like manner, if we may trust the evidence of Byron, did Porson prophesy of Southey that his epics would be read when Homer and Virgil were forgotten; and in like manner may the humblest of his contemporaries prophesy that Mr. Buchanan's idyls will be read by generations which have forgotten the idyls of Theocritus and of Landor, of Tennyson and of Chénier.

In that singularly interesting essay on "his own tentatives" from which we have already taken occasion to glean certain flowers of comparative criticism Mr. Buchanan remarks of this contemporary that he seems rather fond of throwing stones in his (Mr. Buchanan's) direction. This contemporary, however, is not in the habit of throwing stones; it is a

pastime which he leaves to the smaller fry of the literary gutter. These it is sometimes not unamusing to watch as they dodge and shirk round the street-corner after the discharge of their popgun pellet, with the ready plea on their lips that it was not this boy but that—not the good boy Robert, for instance, but the rude boy Thomas. But there is probably only one man living who could imagine it worth his contemporary's while to launch the smallest stone from his sling in such a direction as that—who could conceive the very idlest of marksmen to be capable of taking aim unprovoked at so pitiful a target. Mr. Buchanan and his nursing journals have informed us that to his other laurels he is entitled to add those of an accomplished sportsman. Surely he must know that there are animals which no one counts as game—which are classed under quite another head than that. Their proper designation it is needless here to repeat; it is one that suffices to exempt them from the honour and the danger common to creatures of a higher kind. Of their natural history I did not know enough till now to remark without surprise that specimens of the race may be found which are ambitious to be ranked among objects of sport. For my part, as long as I am not suspected of any inclination to join in the chase, such as one should be welcome to lay that flattering unction to his soul, and believe himself in secret one of the nobler beasts of game: even though it were but a weasel that would fain pass muster as a hart of grice. It must no doubt be "very soothing" to Mr. Buchanan's modesty to imagine himself the object of such notice as he claims to have received; but we may observe from how small a seed so large a growth of self-esteem may shoot up:—

[smikrou genoit' an spermatos megas paphmēn.]

From a slight passing mention of "idyls of the gutter and the gibbet," in a passage referring to the idyllic schools of our day, Mr. Buchanan has built up this fabric of induction; he is led by even so much notice as this to infer that his work must be to the writer an object of especial attention, and even (God save the mark!) of especial attack. He is welcome to hug himself in that fond belief, and fool himself to the top of his bent; but he will hardly persuade any one else that to find his "neck-verse" merely repulsive—to feel no responsive vibration to "the intense loving tenderness" of his street-walker as she neighs and brays over her "gallows-carrion"—is the same thing as to deny the infinite value, the incalculable significance, to a great poet, of such matters as this luckless poeticule has here taken into his "hangman's hands." Neither the work nor the workman is to be judged by the casual preferences of social convention. It is not more praiseworthy or more pardonable to write bad verse about costermongers and gaol-birds than to write bad verse about kings and knights; nor (as would otherwise naturally be the case) is it to be expected that because some among the greatest of poets have been born among the poorest of men, therefore the literature of a nation is to suffer joyfully an inundation or eruption of rubbish from all threshers, cobblers, and milkwomen who now, as in the age of Pope, of Johnson, or of Byron, may be stung to madness by the gadfly of poetic ambition. As in one rank we find for a single Byron a score of Roscommons, Mulgraves, and Winchilseas, so in another rank we find for a single Burns a score of Ducks, Bloomfields, and Yearsleys. And if it does not follow that a poet must be great if he be but of low birth, neither does it follow that a poem must be good if it be but written on a subject of low life. The sins and sorrows of all that suffer wrong, the oppressions that are done under the sun, the dark days and shining deeds of the poor whom society casts out and crushes down, are assuredly material for poetry of a most high order; for the heroic passion of Victor Hugo's, for the angelic passion of Mrs. Browning's. Let another such arise to do such work as "Les Pauvres Gens" or the "Cry of the Children," and there will be no lack of response to that singing. But they who can only "grate on their scrannel-pipes of wretched straw" some pitiful "idyl" to milk the maudlin eyes of the nursing journals must be content with such applause as their own; for in higher latitudes they will find none.

It is not my purpose in this little scientific excursion to remark further than may be necessary on the symptoms of a poetical sort which the skilful eye may discern in the immediate objects of examination. To play the critic of their idyllic or satirical verse is not an office to which my ambition can aspire. Nevertheless, in the process of research, it may be useful to take note of the casual secretions observable in a fine live specimen of the breed in which we are interested, as well as of its general properties; for thus we may be the better able to determine, if we find that worth while, its special and differential attributes. I have therefore given a first and last glance to the poetic excretions of the present subject. Even from such things as these there might be something to learn, if men would bring to a task so unpromising and uninviting the patient eye and humble spirit of investigation by experiment. Such investigation would secure them

against the common critical fallacy of assuming that a poem must be good because written on a subject, and it may be written with an aim, not unworthy of a better man than the writer; that a bad poem, for instance, on the life of our own day and the sorrows of our own people can only be condemned by those who would equally condemn a good poem on the same subject; who would admit nothing as fit matter for artistic handling which was not of a more remote and ideal kind than this: a theory invaluable to all worthless and ambitious journeymen of verse, who, were it once admitted as a law, would have only the trouble left them of selecting the subject whereon to emit their superfluity of metrical matter. Akin to this is a fallacy more amiable if not less absurd; the exact converse of the old superstition that anything written "by a person of quality" must be precious and praiseworthy. The same unreasoning and valueless admiration is now poured out at the feet of almost any one who comes forward under the contrary plea, as a poet of the people; and men forget that by this promiscuous effusion of praise they betray as complete a disbelief in any real equality of natural rank as did those who fell down before their idols of the other class. Such critics seem bent on verifying the worn old jest of the Irish reformer: "Is not one man as good as another; ay, and a deal better too?" No one now writes or speaks as if he supposed that every man born in what is called the aristocratic class must needs and naturally, if he should make verses, take his place beside Shelley or Byron; the assumption would be felt on all hands as an impertinence rather than a compliment offered to that class; and how can it be other than an impertinence offered to a larger class to assume, or pretend to assume, that any one born in the opposite rank who may be put forward as a poet must naturally be the equal of Béranger or of Burns? Such an assumption is simply an inverted form of tuft-hunting; it implies at once the arrogant condescension of the patron to his parasite, and the lurking contempt of the parasite for his patron: not a beautiful or profitable combination of qualities.

A critic in the *Contemporary Review,* but neither Robert Maitland nor Thomas Buchanan, once took occasion to inquire with emphatic sarcasm, what did Shelley care, or what does another writer whom he did the honour to call the second Shelley—how undeservedly no one can be more conscious than the person so unduly exalted—care for the people, for the sufferings and the cause of the poor? To be accused of caring no more for the people than Shelley did may seem to some men much the same thing as to be accused of caring no more for France than Victor Hugo does, or for Italy than did one whose name I will not now bring into such a paper as this. But to some men, on the other hand, it may appear that this cruel charge will serve to explain the jealous acrimony with which the writer thus condemned and dismissed in such evil company "seems" incessantly and secretly to have assailed the fame of Mr. Buchanan—the rancorous malignity with which he must have long looked up from the hiding-place of a furtive obscurity towards the unapproachable heights, the unattainable honours, of the mountains climbed and the prizes grasped by the Poet of the Poor. It mattered little that his disguise was impenetrable to every other eye; that those nearest him had no suspicion of the villainous design which must ever have been at work in his brain, even when itself unconscious of itself; that his left hand knew not what his right hand was doing (as it most certainly did not) when it cast stones at the sweet lyrist of the slums; masked and cloaked, under the thickest muffler of anonymous or pseudonymous counterfeit, the stealthy and cowering felon stood revealed to the naked eye of honesty—stood detected, convicted, exposed to the frank and fearless gaze of Mr. Buchanan. Can a figure more pitiful or more shameful be conceived? The only atonement that can ever be made for such a rascally form of malevolence is that which is here offered in the way of confession and penance; the only excuse that can be advanced for such a viperous method of attack is that envy and hatred of his betters have ever been the natural signs and the inevitable appanages of a bad poet, whether he had studied in the fleshly or the skinny school. Remembering this, we can but too easily understand how Mr. Buchanan may have excited the general ill-will of his inferiors; we may deplore, but we cannot wonder, that the author of "Liz" and "Nell" should have aroused a sense of impotent envy in the author of "Jenny" and "Sister Helen"; it would not surprise though it could not but grieve us to hear that the author of "The Earthly Paradise" was inwardly consumed by the canker of jealousy when he thought of the "Legends of Inverburn"; while with burning cheeks and downcast eyes it must be confessed that the author of "Atalanta in Calydon" may well be the prey of rancour yet more keen than theirs when he looks on the laurels that naturally prevent him from sleeping—the classic chaplets that crown the author of "Undertones."

It is but too well known that the three minor minstrels above named, who may perhaps be taken as collectively equivalent in station and intelligence to the single Buchanan, have long been banded together in a dark and unscrupulous league to decry all works and all reputations but their own. In the first and third persons of this unholy trinity the reptile passions of selfishness and envy have constantly broken out in every variety of ugliness; in the leprous eruption of naked insult, in the cancerous process of that rank and rotten malevolence which works its infectious way by hints and indications, in the nervous spasm of epileptic agony which convulses the whole frame of the soul at another's praise, and ends in a sort of moral tetanus at sight of another's triumph. That thus, and thus only, have their wretched spirits been affected by the spectacle of good and great things done by other men, the whole course of their artistic life and the whole tenor of their critical or illustrative work may be cited against them to bear witness. The least reference to the latter will suffice to show the narrow range and the insincere assumption of their hollow and self-centered sympathies, the poisonous bitterness and the rancorous meanness of their furtive and virulent antipathies. Thomas Maitland, in his character of the loyal detective, has also done the state of letters some service by exposing the shameless reciprocity of systematic applause kept up on all hands by this "mutual admiration society." Especial attention should be given to the candid and clear-sighted remarks of the critic on the "puffing" reviews of his accomplices by the senior member of the gang, and of the third party to this plot by both his colleagues in corruption and conspiracy. If anyone outside their obscure and restricted circle of reciprocal intrigue and malignant secrecy has ever won from any of them the slightest dole of reluctant and grudging commendation, it has been easily traceable to the muddy source of self-interest or of sycophancy. To men of such long-established eminence and influence that it must evidently bring more of immediate profit to applaud them than to revile, there are writers who will ever be at hand to pour the nauseous libations of a parasite. Envy itself in such natures will change places on alternate days with self-interest; and a hand which the poor cur's tooth would otherwise be fain to bite, his tongue will then be fain to beslaver. More especially when there is a chance of discharging its natural venom in the very act of that servile caress; when the obsequious lip finds a way to insinuate by flattery of one superior some stealthy calumny of another. "Ah, my lord and master," says the jackal to the lion (or for that matter to any other animal from whose charity or contempt it may hope for toleration and a stray bone or so now and then), "observe how all other living creatures belong but to some sub-leonine class,[8] some school of dependents and sub-ordinates such as the poor slave who has now the honour to lick your foot!" This is a somewhat ignoble attitude on the poor slave's part, though excusable perhaps in a hungry four-footed brute; but if any such biped as a minor poet were to play such a game as this of the jackal's, what word could we properly apply to him? and what inference should we be justified in drawing as to the origin of his vicious antipathy to other names not less eminent than his chosen patron's? Might we not imagine that some of the men at whose heels he now snaps instead of cringing have found it necessary before now to "spurn him like a cur out of their way"? It is of course possible that a man may honestly admire Mr. Tennyson who feels nothing but scorn and distaste for Mr. Carlyle or Mr. Thackery; but if the latter feeling, expressed as it may be with barefaced and open-mouthed insolence, be as genuine and natural to him as the former, sprung from no petty grudge or privy spite, but reared in the normal soil or manured with the native compost of his mind,—the admiration of such an one is hardly a thing to be desired.

If however any one of that envious and currish triumvirate whom the open voice of honest criticism has already stigmatized should think in future of setting a trap for the illustrious object of their common malice, he will, it is to be hoped, take heed that his feet be not caught in his own snare. He will remember that the judgment of men now or hereafter on the work of an artist in any kind does not wholly depend on the evidence or the opinions of any Jack Alias or Tom Alibi who may sneak into court and out again when detected. He will not think to protect himself from the degradation of public exposure by the assumption of some such pseudonym as Joseph Surface or Seth Pecksniff. He will not feel that all is safe when he has assured the public that a review article alternating between covert praise of himself and overt abuse of his superiors was only through the merest "inadvertence" not issued in his own name; that it never would have appeared under the signature of Mr. Alias but that Mr. Alibi happened by the most untoward of accidents to be just then away "in his yacht" on a cruise among "the western Hebrides"; otherwise, and but for the blundering oversight of some unhappy publisher or editor, the passages which refer with more or less stealthy and suggestive insinuation of preference or of praise to the avowed publications of Mr. Alibi would have come before us with the warrant of that gentleman's honoured name. Credat Judaeus Apella! but even the

foolishest of our furtive triumvirate will hardly, I should imagine, expect that any son of circumcision or uncircumcision would believe such a "legend" or give ear to such an "idyl" as that. Rather will he be inclined to meditate somewhat thus, after the fashion of the American poetess at Elijah Pogram's levee: "To be presented to a Maitland," he will reflect, "by a Buchanan, indeed, an impressive moment is it on what we call our feelings. But why we call them so, or why impressed they are, or if impressed they are at all, or if at all we are, or if there really is, oh gasping one! a Maitland or a Buchanan, or any active principle to which we give those titles, is a topic spirit-searching, light-abandoned, much too vast to enter on at this unlooked-for crisis." Or it may be he will call to mind an old couplet of some such fashion as this:—

> A man of letters would Crispinus be;
> He is a man of letters; yes, of three.

How many names he may have on hand it might not be so easy to resolve: nor which of these, if any, may be genuine; but for the three letters he need look no further than his Latin dictionary; if such a reference be not something more than superfluous for a writer of "epiludes" who renders "domus exilis Plutonia" by "a Plutonian house of exiles": a version not properly to be criticized in any "school" by simple application of goose-quill to paper.[9] The disciple on whom "the deep delicious stream of the Latinity" of Petronius has made such an impression that he finds also a deep delicious morality in the pure and sincere pages of a book from which less pure-minded readers and writers less sincere than himself are compelled to turn away sick and silent with disgust after a second vain attempt to look it over—this loving student and satellite so ready to shift a trencher at the banquet of Trimalchio—has less of tolerance, we are scarcely surprised to find, for Aeschylean Greece than for Neronian Rome. Among the imperfect and obsolete productions of the Greek stage he does indeed assign a marked pre-eminence over all others to the Persae. To the famous epitaph of Aeschylus which tells only in four terse lines of his service as a soldier against the Persians, there should now be added a couplet in commemoration of the precedence granted to his play by a poet who would not stoop to imitate and a student who need not hesitate to pass sentence. Against this good opinion, however, we are bound to set on record the memorable expression of that deep and thoughtful contempt which a mind so enlightened and a soul so exalted must naturally feel for "the shallow and barbarous myth of Prometheus." Well may this incomparable critic, this unique and sovereign arbiter of thought and letters ancient and modern, remark with compassion and condemnation how inevitably a training in Grecian literature must tend to "emasculate" the student so trained: and well may we congratulate ourselves that no such process as robbed of all strength and manhood the intelligence of Milton has had power to impair the virility of Mr. Buchanan's robust and masculine genius. To that strong and severe figure we turn from the sexless and nerveless company of shrill-voiced singers who share with Milton the curse of enforced effeminacy; from the pitiful soprano notes of such dubious creatures as Marlowe, Jonson, Chapman, Gray, Coleridge, Shelley, Landor, "cum semiviro comitatu," we avert our ears to catch the higher and manlier harmonies of a poet with all his natural parts andpowers complete. For truly, if love or knowledge of ancient art and wisdom be the sure mark of "emasculation," and the absence of any taint of such love or any tincture of such knowledge (as then in consistency it must be) the supreme sign of perfect manhood, Mr. Robert Buchanan should be amply competent to renew the thirteenth labour of Hercules.

> One would not be a young maid in his way
> For more than blushing comes to.

Nevertheless, in a country where (as Mr. Carlyle says in his essay on Diderot) indecent exposure is an offence cognizable at police-offices, it might have been as well for him to uncover with less immodest publicity the gigantic nakedness of his ignorance. Any sense of shame must probably be as alien to the Heracleidan blood as any sense of fear; but the spectators of such an exhibition may be excused if they could wish that at least the shirt of Nessus or another were happily at hand to fling over the more than human display of that massive and muscular impudence, in all the abnormal development of its monstrous proportions. It is possible that our Scottish demigod of song has made too long a sojourn in "the land of Lorne," and learnt from his Highland comrades to dispense in public with what is not usually discarded in any British latitude far south of "the western Hebrides."

At this point, and even after this incomparable windfall in the way of entomology, I begin to doubt whether after all I shall ever make any way as a scientific student. The savours, the forms, the sounds, the contortions, of the singular living things which this science commands us to submit to examination, need a stouter stomach to cope with them than mine. No doubt they have their reasons for being; they were probably meant for some momentary action and passion of their own, harmful or harmless; and how can the naturalist suppose that merely by accurate analysis of their phenomena he has gauged the secret of their mysterious existence? It is so hard to see the reason why they should be, that we are compelled to think the reason must be very grave.

And if once we cease to regard such things scientifically, there is assuredly no reason why we should regard them at all. Historically considered, they have no interest whatever; the historian discerns no perceptible variation in their tribe for centuries on centuries. It is only because this age is not unlike other ages that the children of Zoilus whet their teeth against your epic, the children of Rymer against your play; the children—no, not the children; let us at least be accurate—the successors of Fréron and Desfontaines lift up their throats against your worship of women:

Monsieur Veuillot t'appelle avec esprit citrouille;

Mr. Buchanan indicates to all Hebridean eyes the flaws and affectations in your style, as in that of an amatory foreigner; Mr. Lowell assures his market that the best coin you have to offer is brass, and more than hints that it is stolen brass—whether from his own or another forehead, he scorns to specify; and the Montrouge Jesuit, the Grubstreet poet, the Mayflower Puritan, finds each his perfect echo in his natural child; in the first voice you catch the twang of Garasse and Nonotte, in the second of Flecknoe and Dennis, in the third of Tribulation Wholesome and Zeal-of-the-Land Busy. Perhaps then after all their use is to show that the age is not a bastard, but the legitimate heir and representative of other centuries; degenerate, if so it please you to say—all ages have been degenerate in their turn—as to its poets and workers, but surely not degenerate as to these. Poor then as it may be in other things, the very lapse of years which has left it weak may help it more surely to determine than stronger ages could the nature of the critical animal. Has not popular opinion passed through wellnigh the same stages with regard to the critic and to the toad? What was thought in the time of Shakespeare by dukes as well as peasants, we may all find written in his verse; but we know now on taking up a Buchanan that, though very ugly, it is not in the least venomous, and assuredly wears no precious jewel in its head. Yet is it rather like a newt or blindworm than a toad; there is a mendacious air of the old serpent about it at first sight; and the thing is not even viperous: its sting is as false as its tongue is; its very venom is a lie. But when once we have seen the fang, though innocuous, protrude from a mouth which would fain distil poison and can only distil froth, we need no revelation to assure us that the doom of the creature is to go upon its belly and eat dust all the days of its life.

1. *"Climène.* Il a une obscénité qui n'est pas supportable.
Elise. Comment dites-vous ce mot-là, madame?
Climène. Obscénité, madame.
Elise. Ah! mon Dieu! obscénité. Je ne sais ce que ce mot veut dire; mais je le trouve le plus joli di monde."
MOLIERE, La Critique de l'Ecole des Femmes, sc. 3.

2. In Dr. Burroughs' excellent little book there is a fault common to almost all champions of his great friend; they will treat Whitman as "Athanasius contra mundum:" they will assume that if he be right all other poets must be wrong; and if this intimation were confined to America there might be some plausible reason to admit it; but if we pass beyond and have to choose between Whitman and the world, we must regretfully drop the "Leaves of Grass" and retain at least for example the "Légende des Siècles." As to this matter of rhythm and rhyme, prose and verse, I find in this little essay some things which out of pure regard and sympathy I could wish away, and consigned to the more congenial page of some tenth-rate poeticule worn out with failure after failure, and now squat in his hole like the tailless fox he is, curled up to snarl and whimper beneath the inaccessible vine of song. Let me suggest that it may *not* be observed in the grand literary relics of nations that their best poetry has always, or has ever, adopted essentially the prose form, preserving interior rhythm only. I do not "ask dulcet rhymes from" Whitman; I far prefer his rhythms to any merely "dulcet metres"; I would have him in nowise other than he is; but I certainly do not wish to see his form or style reproduced at second hand by a school of disciples with less deep and exalted sense of rhythm. As to rhyme, there is some rhymed verse that holds more music, carries more weight, flies higher and wider in equal scope of sense and sound, than all but the highest human speech has ever done, and would have done no more, as no verse has done more, had it been unrhymed; witness the song of the Earth from Shelley's "Prometheus Unbound." Do as well without rhyme if you can, or do as well with rhyme, it is of no moment whatever; a thing not noticeable or perceptible except by pedants and sciolists; in either case your triumph will be equal. In a precious and memorable excerpt given by Dr. Burroughs from some article in the *North American Review,* the writer, a German by his name, after much gabble against prosody, observes with triumph as a final instance of the progress of language that *"the spiritualizing and enfranchising influence* of Christianity transformed Greek into an accentuated language." The present poets of Greece, I presume, know better than to waste their genius on the same ridiculous elaborations of corresponsive metre which occupied the pagan and benighted intellects of Aeschylus and Pindar. I have heard before now of many deliverances wrought by Christianity; but I had never yet perceived that among the most remarkable of these—"an outward and visible sign of an inward and spiritual grace"—was to be reckoned the transformation of the language spoken under Pericles into the language spoken under King Otho and King George.

3. I cannot help calling just now to mind an epigram—very rude, after the fashion of the time, but here certainly not impertinent but pertinent—cited by Boswell on a quarrel between two "beaux"; the second stanza runs thus, with one word altered of necessity, as that quarrel was not on poetry but on religion:—

"Peace, coxcombs, peace! and both agree;
    A., kiss thy empty brother;
The Muses love a foe like thee,
    But dread a friend like t'other."

4. Not that the British worshipper gets much tolerance for his countrymen in return. In an eloquent essay on the insolence of Englishmen towards Americans, for which doubtless there are but too good grounds, Mr. Lowell shows himself as sore as a whipped cutpurse of the days "ere carts had lost their tails" under the vulgar imputation of vulgarity. It is doubtless a very gross charge, and one often flung at Americans by English lackeys and bullies of the vulgarest order. Is there ever any ground for it discernible in the dainty culture of overbred letters which, as we hear, distinguishes New England? I remember to have read a passage from certain notes of travel in Italy published by an eminent and eloquent writer—that I could but remember his name and grace my page with it!—who after some just remarks on Byron's absurd and famous description of a waterfall, proceeds to observe that Milton was the only poet who ever made real poetry out of a cataract—"AND THAT WAS IN HIS EYE."

5. Lest it should seem impossible that these and the like could be the actual expressions of any articulate creature, I have invariably in such a context marked as quotations only the exact words of this unutterable author, either as I find them cited by others or as they fall under my own eye in glancing among his essays. More trouble than this I am not disposed to take with him.

6. For the occasions on which the word [Skotios] is to be spelt with a capital S, the student should consult the last-century glossaries of Lauder and Macpherson.

7. There are other readings of the last two lines:

[tous despotas men doulia sainō phreni,
hosoi de m'agnoousin (Cod Var. hosoisi d' eiṁ'agnotos) k.t.l.]

8. If we could imagine about 1820 some parasitic poeticule of the order of Kirke White classifying together Coleridge and Keats, Byron and Shelley, as members of "the sub-Wordsworthian school," we might hope to find an intellectual ancestor for Mr. Robert Buchanan; but that hope is denied us: we are reduced to believe that Mr. Buchanan must be autochthonous, or sprung

perhaps from a cairngorm pebble cast behind him by the hand of some Scotch Deucalion.

9. I am reminded here of another "contemporary" somewhat more notorious than this classic namesake and successor of George Buchanan, but like him a man of many and questionable names, who lately had occasion, while figuring on a more public stage than that of literature, to translate the words "Laus Deo semper" by "The laws of God for ever." It must evidently be from the same source that Mr. Buchanan and the Tichborne claimant have drawn their first and last draught of "the humanities." Fellow-students, whether at Stonyhurst or elsewhere, they ought certainly to have been. Can it be the rankling recollection of some boyish quarrel in which he came by the worst of it that keeps alive in the noble soul of Mr. Buchanan a dislike of "fleshly persons?" The result would be worthy of such a "fons et origo mali"—a phrase, I may add for the benefit of such scholars, which is not adequately or exactly rendered by "the fount of original sin." Perhaps some day we may be gratified—but let us hope without any necessary intervention of lawyers—by some further discovery of the early associations which may have clustered around the promising boyhood of Thomas Maitland. Meantime it is a comfort to reflect that the assumption of a forged name for a dirty purpose does not always involve the theft of thousands, or the ruin of any reputation more valuable than that of a literary underling. May we not now also hope that Mr. Buchanan's fellow-scholar will be the next (in old-world phrase) to "oblige the reading public" with his views on ancient and modern literature? For such a work, whether undertaken in the calm of Newgate or the seclusion of the Hebrides, or any other haunt of lettered ease and leisure, he surely could not fail to find a publisher who in his turn would not fail to find him an *alibi* whenever necessary—whether eastward or westward of St. Kilda.

Books for Further Reading

Altholz, Joseph L., ed. *The Mind and Art of Victorian England.* Minneapolis: University of Minnesota Press, 1976.

Altick, Richard. *The English Common Reader: A Social History of the Mass Reading Public, 1800-1900.* Chicago: University of Chicago Press, 1957.

Altick. *Victorian People and Ideas.* New York: Norton, 1973.

Appleman, Philip, William A. Madden, and Michael Wolff, eds. *1859: Entering An Age of Crisis.* Bloomington: Indiana University Press, 1959.

Armstrong, Isobel. *Language as Living Form in Nineteenth Century Poetry.* Totowa, N.J.: Barnes & Noble, 1982.

Armstrong, cd. *The Major Victorian Poets: Reconsiderations.* Lincoln: University of Nebraska Press, 1969.

Armstrong, ed. *Victorian Scrutinies: Reviews of Poetry, 1830-1870.* London: Athlone, 1972.

Ball, Patricia M. *The Heart's Events: The Victorian Poetry of Relationships.* London: Athlone, 1976.

Batho, Edith and Bonamy Dobree. *The Victorians and After, 1830-1914,* second revised edition. London: Cresset, 1950.

Beach, Joseph Warren. *The Concept of Nature in Nineteenth Century Poetry.* New York: Macmillan, 1936.

Briggs, Asa. *The Age of Improvement.* London & New York: Longmans, Green, 1959.

Buckler, William E. *The Victorian Imagination: Essays in Aesthetic Exploration.* New York: New York University Press, 1980.

Buckley, Jerome. *The Triumph of Time: A Study of the Victorian Concepts of Time, History, Progress and Decadence.* Cambridge: Harvard University Press, 1966.

Buckley. *The Victorian Temper: A Study in Literary Culture.* Cambridge: Harvard University Press, 1951.

Burn, W. L. *The Age of Equipoise: A Study of the Mid-Victorian Generation.* New York: Norton, 1965.

Bush, Douglas. *Science and English Poetry: A Historical Sketch, 1590-1950.* New York: Oxford University Press, 1950.

Charlesworth, Barbara. *Dark Passages: The Decadent Consciousness in Victorian Literature.* Madison: University of Wisconsin Press, 1965.

Chesterton, G. K. *The Victorian Age in Literature.* London: Williams & Norgate, 1913; New York: Holt, 1913.

Christ, Carol. *The Finer Optic: The Aesthetic of Particularity in Victorian Poetry.* New Haven: Yale University Press, 1975.

Conrad, Peter. *The Victorian Treasure-House.* London: Collins, 1973.

Cosslett, Tess. *The Scientific Movement and Victorian Literature*. New York: St Martin's, 1983.

Cruse, Amy. *The Victorians and Their Reading*. Boston & New York: Houghton Mifflin, 1935. Republished as *The Victorians and Their Books*. London: Allen & Unwin, 1935.

Dawson, Carl. *Victorian Noon: English Literature in 1850*. Baltimore & London: Johns Hopkins University Press, 1979.

Drinkwater, John. *Victorian Poetry*. London: Hodder & Stoughton, 1923; New York: Doran, 1924.

Ensor, R. C. K. *England, 1870-1914*. Oxford: Clarendon Press, 1936.

Fairchild, Hoxie N. *Religious Trends in English Poetry*. IV: *Christianity and Romanticism in the Victorian Era: 1830-1880;* V: *Gods of a Changing Poetry: 1880-1920*. New York: Columbia University Press, 1957, 1962.

Faverty, Frederic, ed. *The Victorian Poets: A Guide to Research*, second edition. Cambridge: Harvard University Press, 1968.

Fletcher, Pauline. *Gardens and Grim Ravines: The Language of Landscape in Victorian Poetry*. Princeton: Princeton University Press, 1983.

Foakes, R. A. *The Romantic Assertion: A Study in the Language of Nineteenth Century Poetry*. New Haven: Yale University Press, 1958.

Ford, George. *Keats and the Victorians: A Study of His Influence and Rise to Fame, 1821-1895*. New Haven: Yale University Press, 1944; London: Oxford University Press, 1944.

Fredeman, W. E. *Pre-Raphaelitism: A Bibliocritical Study*. Cambridge: Harvard University Press, 1965.

Gaunt, William. *The Pre-Raphaelite Tragedy*. London: Cape, 1942.

Gilbert, Sandra M. and Susan Gubar. *The Madwoman in the Attic: The Woman Writer and The Nineteenth Century Literary Imagination*. New Haven: Yale University Press, 1979.

Heyck, T. W. *The Transformation of Intellectual Life in Victorian England*. New York: St. Martin's, 1982.

Holloway, John. *The Proud Knowledge: Poetry, Insight and the Self, 1620-1920*. London: Routledge & Kegan Paul, 1977.

Hough, Graham. *The Last Romantics*. London: Duckworth, 1949; Totowa, N.J.: Barnes & Noble, 1961.

Houghton, Walter E. *The Victorian Frame of Mind, 1830-1870*. New Haven: Yale University Press, 1957.

Hunt, John Dixon. *The Pre-Raphaelite Imagination, 1848-1900*. Lincoln: University of Nebraska Press, 1977.

Jenkyns, Richard. *The Victorians and Ancient Greece*. Cambridge: Harvard University Press, 1981.

Johnson, E. D. H. *The Alien Vision of Victorian Poetry: Sources of the Poetic Imagination in Tennyson, Browning, and Arnold*. Princeton: Princeton University Press, 1952.

Johnson, Wendell Stacey. *Sex and Marriage in Victorian Poetry*. Ithaca, N.Y.: Cornell University Press, 1975.

Kermode, Frank. *Romantic Image*. London: Routledge & Kegan Paul, 1957; New York: Macmillan, 1957.

Kitson Clark, G. *The Making of Victorian England*. Cambridge: Harvard University Press, 1962.

Knoepflmacher, U. C. and G. B. Tennyson, eds. *Nature and the Victorian Imagination*. Berkeley: University of California Press, 1978.

Langbaum, Robert. *The Poetry of Experience: The Dramatic Monologue in Modern Literary Tradition*. New York: Random House, 1957; London: Chatto & Windus, 1957.

Levine, Richard A., ed. *Backgrounds to Victorian Literature*. San Francisco: Chandler, 1967.

Levine, ed. *The Victorian Experience: The Poets*. Athens: Ohio University Press, 1982.

Lucas, F. L. *Ten Victorian Poets*, third edition. Cambridge: Cambridge University Press, 1948.

McGhee, Richard D. *Marriage, Duty and Desire in Victorian Poetry and Drama*. Lawrence: Regents Press of Kansas, 1980.

Mermin, Dorothy. *The Audience in The Poem: Five Victorian Poets*. New Brunswick, N.J.: Rutgers University Press, 1983.

Miyoshi, Masao. *The Divided Self: A Perspective on the Literature of the Victorians*. New York: New York University Press, 1969.

Nelson, James G. *The Sublime Puritan: Milton and The Victorians*. Madison: University of Wisconsin Press, 1963.

Peckham, Morse. *Beyond the Tragic Vision: The Quest for Identity in the Nineteenth Century*. New York: Braziller, 1962.

Reed, John R. *Victorian Conventions*. Athens: Ohio University Press, 1975.

Roppen, Georg. *Evolution and Poetic Belief: A Study in Some Victorian and Modern Writers*. Oslo: Oslo University Press, 1956.

Schneewind, J. B. *Backgrounds of English Victorian Literature*. New York: Random House, 1970.

Stevenson, Lionel. *The Pre-Raphaelite Poets*. Chapel Hill: University of North Carolina Press, 1972.

Sussman, Herbert. *Victorians and The Machine: Literary Response to Technology*. Cambridge: Harvard University Press, 1968.

Tennyson, G. B. *Victorian Devotional Poetry: The Tractarian Mode*. Cambridge: Harvard University Press, 1980.

Thesing, William B. *The London Muse: Victorian Poetic Responses to the City*. Athens: University of Georgia Press, 1982.

Thomson, David. *England in the Nineteenth Century, 1815-1914*. Harmondsworth, U.K.: Penguin, 1950.

Tillotson, Geoffrey. *A View of Victorian Literature*. Oxford: Oxford University Press, 1978.

Tillotson, Kathleen and Geoffrey Tillotson. *Mid-Victorian Studies*. London: Athlone, 1965.

Vicinus, Martha. *The Industrial Muse: A Study of Nineteenth-Century British Working Class Literature*. New York: Barnes & Noble, 1974.

Vicinus, ed. *Suffer and Be Still: Women in the Victorian Age.* Bloomington: Indiana University Press, 1972.

Victorian Poetry. Stratford-upon-Avon Studies No. 15. London: Edward Arnold, 1972.

Warren, Alba H., Jr. *English Poetic Theory, 1825-1865.* Princeton: Princeton University Press, 1950.

Williams, Raymond. *Culture and Society, 1780-1950.* New York: Columbia University Press, 1958; London: Chatto & Windus, 1958.

Wright, Austin, ed. *Victorian Literature: Modern Essays in Criticism.* New York: Oxford University Press, 1961.

Young, G. M. *Victorian England: Portrait of An Age.* London: Oxford University Press, 1936.

Contributors

Carol L. Bernstein..*Bryn Mawr College*
Florence S. Boos.. *University of Iowa*
Tirthankar Bose ....*University of British Columbia*
Jerome Bump...*University of Texas at Austin*
Bruce A. Castner... *University of South Carolina*
Mabel L. Colbeck...*University of British Columbia*
Rowland L. Collins... *University of Rochester*
Cheryl S. Conover.. *West Virginia University*
Michael Darling...*Vanier College*
H. B. de Groot .... *University of Toronto*
Richard Eaton .... *West Virginia University*
Jane C. Fredeman ....*University of British Columbia*
K. L. Goodwin..*University of Queensland*
A. W. Heidemann .... *Carleton University*
Alan Hertz...*Jesus College, Cambridge*
Lori Duin Kelly .... *Carroll College*
Bernard R. Kogan..*University of Illinois at Chicago*
William Lutz... *Rutgers University*
Christopher D. Murray .... *University of Regina*
Byron Nelson .... *West Virginia University*
Megan Nelson ....*University of British Columbia*
Norman Page .... *University of Alberta*
Lawrence Poston ....*University of Illinois at Chicago*
Peter Quartermain ....*Vancouver, British Columbia*
David G. Riede ....*University of Rochester*
Patrick Scott...*University of South Carolina*
John F. Stasny .... *West Virginia University*
William B. Thesing .... *University of South Carolina*
Dorothea Mosley Thompson .... *Carnegie-Mellon University*
Richard Tobias ....*University of Pittsburgh*
Craig Turner..*Texas A & M University*
C. W. Willerton .... *Abilene Christian University*

Cumulative Index

Dictionary of Literary Biography, Volumes 1-35
Dictionary of Literary Biography Yearbook, 1980-1983
Dictionary of Literary Biography Documentary Series, Volumes 1-4

Cumulative Index

DLB before number: *Dictionary of Literary Biography*, Volumes 1-35
Y before number: *Dictionary of Literary Biography Yearbook*, 1980-1983
DS before number: *Dictionary of Literary Biography Documentary Series*, Volumes 1-4

A

Abbot, Willis J. 1863-1934 ....DLB29

Abbott, Jacob 1803-1879 ....DLB1

Abbott, Robert S. 1868-1940 ....DLB29

Abercrombie, Lascelles 1881-1938 ....DLB19

Abse, Dannie 1923- DLB27

Adair, James 1709?-1783? DLB30

Adamic, Louis 1898-1951 ....DLB9

Adams, Douglas 1952- Y83

Adams, Franklin P. 1881-1960 ....DLB29

Adams, Henry 1838-1918 ....DLB12

Adams, James Truslow 1878-1949 ....DLB17

Adams, John 1734-1826 ....DLB31

Adams, Samuel 1722-1803 ....DLB31

Ade, George 1866-1944 ....DLB11, 25

Adeler, Max (see Clark, Charles Heber)

AE 1867-1935 ....DLB19

Agassiz, Jean Louis Rodolphe 1807-1873 ....DLB1

Agee, James 1909-1955 ....DLB2, 26

Aiken, Conrad 1889-1973 ....DLB9

Ainsworth, William Harrison 1805-1882 ....DLB21

Akins, Zoë 1886-1958 ....DLB26

Albee, Edward 1928- DLB7

Alcott, Amos Bronson 1799-1888 ....DLB1

Alcott, Louisa May 1832-1888 ....DLB1

Alcott, William Andrus 1798-1859 ....DLB1

Aldington, Richard 1892-1962 ....DLB20

Aldis, Dorothy 1896-1966 ....DLB22

Aldiss, Brian W. 1925- DLB14

Alexander, James 1691-1756 ....DLB24

Algren, Nelson 1909-1981 ....DLB9; Y81, 82

Alldritt, Keith 1935- DLB14

Allen, Ethan 1738-1789 ....DLB31

Allen, Hervey 1889-1949 ....DLB9

Allen, James 1739-1808 ....DLB31

Allen, Jay Presson 1922- DLB26

Josiah Allen's Wife (see Holly, Marietta)

Allingham, William 1824-1889 ....DLB35

Allott, Kenneth 1912-1973 ....DLB20

Allston, Washington 1779-1843 ....DLB1

Alsop, George 1636-post 1673 ....DLB24

Alvarez, A. 1929- DLB14

Ames, Mary Clemmer 1831-1884 ....DLB23

Amis, Kingsley 1922- DLB15, 27

Amis, Martin 1949- DLB14

Ammons, A. R. 1926- DLB5

Anderson, Margaret 1886-1973 ....DLB4

Anderson, Maxwell 1888-1959 ....DLB7

Anderson, Paul Y. 1893-1938 ....DLB29

Anderson, Poul 1926- DLB8

Anderson, Robert 1917- DLB7

Anderson, Sherwood 1876-1941 ....DLB4, 9, DS1

Andrews, Charles M. 1863-1943 ....DLB17

Anhalt, Edward 1914- DLB26

Anthony, Piers 1934- DLB8

Archer, William 1856-1924 ....DLB10

Arden, John 1930- DLB13

Arensberg, Ann 1937- Y82

Arnold, Edwin 1832-1904 ....DLB35

Arnold, Matthew 1822-1888 ....DLB32

Arnow, Harriette Simpson 1908- DLB6

Arp, Bill (see Smith, Charles Henry)

Arthur, Timothy Shay 1809-1885 ....DLB3

Asch, Nathan 1902-1964 ....DLB4, 28

Ashbery, John 1927- DLB5; Y81

Asher, Sandy 1942- Y83

Ashton, Winifred (see Dane, Clemence)

Asimov, Isaac 1920- DLB8

Atherton, Gertrude 1857-1948 ....DLB9

E

G

I

J

N

O

P

Y

Z